NORTH CAROLINA
STATE BOARD OF COMMUNITY COLLEGES
LIBRARIES
WAKE TECHNICAL COMMUNITY COLLEGE

GREAT LIVES
FROM
HISTORY

GREAT LIVES FROM HISTORY

Ancient and Medieval Series

Volume 4
Niz-Sno

Edited by
FRANK N. MAGILL

SALEM PRESS

Pasadena, California   Englewood Cliffs, New Jersey

Copyright © 1988, by FRANK N. MAGILL
All rights in this book are reserved. No part of this work may be used or reproduced in any manner whatsoever or transmitted in any form or by any means, electronic or mechanical, including photocopy, recording, or any information storage and retrieval system, without written permission from the copyright owner except in the case of brief quotations embodied in critical articles and reviews. For information address the publisher, Salem Press, Inc., P.O. Box 50062, Pasadena, California 91105.

Library of Congress Cataloging-in-Publication Data
Great lives from history. Ancient and medieval series / edited by Frank N. Magill.
   p. cm.
   Includes bibliographies and index.
   Summary: A five-volume set of biographical sketches, arranged alphabetically, of 459 individuals whose contributions influenced world culture and the social development of societies flourishing in earlier centuries.
   Biography—To 500. 2. Biography—Middle Ages, 500-1500. [1. Biography—To 500. 2. Biography—Middle Ages, 500-1500. 3. World history.]
I. Magill, Frank Northen, 1907-
CT113.G74   1988   920'.009'01—dc19   88-18514
[B]
[920]
ISBN 0-89356-545-8 (set)
ISBN 0-89356-549-0 (volume 4)

LIST OF BIOGRAPHIES IN VOLUME FOUR

	page
Nizam al-Mulk	1477
Olaf, Saint	1484
Omar Khayyám	1490
Orcagna, Andrea	1495
Origen	1499
Osman	1504
Otto the Great	1510
Ou-yang Hsiu	1515
Ovid	1520
Pachacuti	1525
Pan Ku	1530
Pappus	1536
Parmenides	1541
Paul, Saint	1547
Paul of Aegina	1553
Peisistratus	1557
Peregrinus de Maricourt, Petrus	1563
Pericles	1569
Pérotin	1575
Peter, Saint	1580
Petrarch	1585
Phidias	1592
Philip II	1598
Philip II of Macedonia	1603
Philip IV the Fair	1609
Philip the Good	1614
Philo of Alexandria	1619
Piankhi	1624
Pindar	1630
Pisano, Andrea	1635
Pisano, Nicola, and Giovanni Pisano	1639
Pittacus of Mytilene	1644

GREAT LIVES FROM HISTORY

	page
Plato	1650
Plautus	1656
Pliny the Elder	1660
Plotinus	1665
Plutarch	1670
Polo, Marco	1675
Polybius	1681
Polygnotus	1685
Pompey the Great	1689
Porphyry	1695
Posidonius	1700
Praxiteles	1706
Priscian	1712
Priscillian	1717
Proclus	1722
Propertius, Sextus	1727
Protagoras	1732
Psamtik I	1737
Psellus, Michael	1741
Ptolemy	1747
Ptolemy Philadelphus	1752
Ptolemy Soter	1757
Pucelle, Jean	1763
Pyrrhon of Elis	1769
Pythagoras	1773
Pytheas	1779
Rabanus Maurus	1784
Rāmānuja	1790
Ramses II	1795
Ratramnus	1801
Raymond of Peñafort	1806
Razi, al-	1810
Rienzo, Cola di	1815
Rudolf I	1820
Rumi, Jalal al-Din	1825
Sa'di	1830
Saladin	1835
Salimbene	1840
Sallust	1845
Samuel	1851

LIST OF BIOGRAPHIES IN VOLUME FOUR

	page
Sappho	1856
Sargon II	1861
Saxo Grammaticus	1866
Scipio Aemilianus	1871
Scipio Africanus	1876
Scopas	1881
Seleucus I Nicator	1885
Seneca the Younger	1890
Sergius I	1895
Sergius I, Saint	1901
Sesostris III	1906
Shapur II	1910
Shōtoku Taishi	1918
Siger of Brabant	1922
Simeon Stylites, Saint	1927
Siricius, Saint	1933
Sluter, Claus	1938
Snorri Sturluson	1943

NIZAM AL-MULK
Abu 'Ali Hasan ibn 'Ali

Born: 1018 or 1019; Tus, Iran
Died: October 14, 1092; near Nahavand, Iran
Area of Achievement: Government
Contribution: The vizier, or principal minister, of the second and third Seljuk rulers of Iran, Nizam was the virtual architect of the Seljuks' Middle Eastern empire, which he administered for thirty years between 1063 and 1092. His *Siyasat-nama* became a classic of medieval Muslim statecraft.

Early Life

Nizam al-Mulk was born in or near the city of Tus, near modern Mashhad, in the northeastern Iranian province of Khorasan, in 1019 or 1019. His full name was Abu 'Ali Hasan ibn 'Ali, but he is invariably referred to by his title of Nizam al-Mulk (Regulator of the State), given to him by the Seljuk sultan Alp Arslan. His father belonged to the ancient class known as *dihqans*, landowning gentry of Iranian stock who, at least in Khorasan, had survived the Arab conquest of the seventh century by demonstrating their usefulness to the invaders as local officials and tax collectors, roles which they continued to play for centuries. Nizam al-Mulk's father was a middle-ranking official in the service of the Ghaznavid sultans Mahmud (reigned 998-1030) and Mas'ud I (reigned 1031-1041), and Nizam al-Mulk's mature views on what constituted an ideal system of administration must have been colored by what he knew at first hand of Ghaznavid rule, as well as by what he had heard of Samanid rule in tenth century Bukhara. He himself received an excellent formal education, probably in Neyshabur, after which he too entered Ghaznavid service. When the Ghaznavids were forced to abandon their territories in eastern Iran to the Seljuk Turks (c. 1040), Nizam al-Mulk transferred to the service of the Seljuks and was employed in a secretarial capacity by the new governor of Balkh, in northern Afghanistan. The governor's superior was the Seljuk sultan's brother, Chaghri Beg, who was quick to recognize the superior abilities of the young official. On his deathbed, Chaghri Beg is said to have strongly recommended Nizam al-Mulk to the attention of his son, Alp Arslan, who took him into his household and eventually appointed him to the post of vizier—in effect, his man of business and general factotum.

Under the rule of their first sultan, Toghrïl Beg (reigned 1038-1063), the Seljuks, originally Turkish nomads from the Central Asian steppes, became masters of a Middle Eastern empire extending from the Mediterranean eastward to the Pamirs, with its center of power on the Iranian plateau. It was to be the historic role of Nizam al-Mulk to condition these steppe warriors to the norms of traditional Irano-Islamic statecraft and to erect an institutional framework by which to administer their far-flung conquests.

When Sultan Toghrïl Beg died in 1063, there was uncertainty over the succession, and the late sultan's vizier, Amid al-Mulk Abu Nasr al-Kunduri, endeavored to prevent the accession of Toghrïl Beg's eldest nephew, Alp Arslan, by advancing the claims of Alp Arslan's younger brother, Sulaiman. In the intrigues which followed, Nizam al-Mulk seems to have played a major role in bringing about Alp Arslan's accession, as well as in effecting al-Kunduri's removal, imprisonment, and eventual murder. Prior to his death, al-Kunduri is said to have sent the following warning to Nizam al-Mulk:

> You have introduced a reprehensible innovation and an ugly practice into the world by executing a minister and by your treachery and deceit, and you have not fully considered what the end of it all will be. I fear that this evil and blameworthy practice will rebound on the heads of your own children and descendants.

In fact, Nizam al-Mulk and several of his sons and grandsons did suffer violent deaths.

Meanwhile, with Alp Arslan now sultan (reigned 1063-1072), Nizam al-Mulk became vizier of the Seljuk empire, head of the civil administration, the sultan's chief counselor, and, for all practical purposes, his deputy. After Alp Arslan's death, Nizam continued to serve as the vizier of Alp Arslan's son, Malik-Shah (reigned 1072-1092), and to such an extent was he perceived to be the presiding genius of the Seljuk empire that the Arab historian Ibn al-Athir long afterward described the thirty years during which Alp Arslan and Malik-Shah reigned (and which was, in fact, the golden age of Seljuk rule) as *al-dawla al-Nizamiya*, the Age of Nizam al-Mulk.

Life's Work

As vizier, Nizam al-Mulk was responsible for the entire administration of the civil affairs of the empire, including the collection of revenue and its disbursement. He was the head of the bureaucracy, and all matters relating to the *diwan* (chancery) were in his charge. As the personal representative and closest adviser of the sovereign, he was also a member of the *dargah* (the sultan's court). The duties of viziers were rarely precisely defined. While many viziers were not involved in military matters, Nizam al-Mulk is known to have campaigned with his master and also to have conducted independent military operations. His involvement in military affairs necessitated the maintenance of good working relations with the great Turkish emirs, or commanders. This involved diplomatic skills of a high order, since the emirs were generally disinclined to take orders from non-Turkish bureaucrats. As vizier, Nizam al-Mulk also maintained close contacts with the leading *'ulama'*, the Muslim clerics. The highest judicial appointments for the Shari'a (religious law) and *mazalim* (equity and arbitration) courts were awarded to members of the *'ulama'*, appointments which, no doubt, would have required Nizam's prior approval. He was also responsible for the distribution of government funds allocated for the support of pious scholars, religious endowments, and education, as well as for alms.

In addition to the day-to-day running of the administration, Nizam al-Mulk seems to have exercised a general oversight with regard to relations with other states and also with regard to cultural policy and propaganda. He contributed markedly to the revival of Sunni Islam which characterized the eleventh and twelfth centuries. Prior to the arrival of the Seljuks in the Middle East, the political fortunes and spiritual vitality of Sunni Islam had been at a very low ebb. Its central institution, the 'Abbasid Caliphate of Baghdad, had long been in decline. In fact, since 945 the caliphs had been virtual captives of a line of Buyid emirs who had made themselves masters of Baghdad. As Shi'ites, the Iranian Buyids displayed scant respect for the orthodox "Commander of the Faithful," as the caliph was officially styled. This period of decline had come to a close in 1055, when Toghril Beg had occupied Baghdad and released the caliphs from ninety years of thralldom to the Buyids, although at the cost of making them clients of the all-powerful Seljuk sultan. Nevertheless, the Seljuks were seriously committed to restoring the spiritual authority of the caliphate, through which their own *de facto* rule could be conveniently legitimized. It was the achievement of Nizam al-Mulk that he was able to harness the raw power of the Seljuks on behalf of both an orthodox religious revival and a restoration of hallowed Iranian traditions of statecraft and autocracy.

The institutional decline of the 'Abbasid Caliphate reflected a deeper spiritual malaise prevailing throughout much of the Islamic world, of which deep sectarian fissures constituted both cause and effect. At the beginning of the eleventh century, Egypt, much of North Africa, Hejaz, Palestine, and Syria were under the rule of a rival, heterodox caliphate, that of the Shi'ite Fatimids. The Fatimids dispatched *da'is* (missionaries) throughout the provinces still nominally loyal to the 'Abbasids to spread revolutionary millennial doctrines which threatened the very foundations of the orthodox Sunni political and social order. Linked with the Fatimids were the so-called Assassins, members of the Isma'ili sect of the Nizaris, with their strongholds in the Alburz Mountains of northern Iran, as well as in the mountains of Syria and Lebanon. Nizam al-Mulk regarded these latter as the most formidable adversaries of the renovated political order, of which he saw himself as the architect. It was to counter such dangerous heterodoxy that he embarked upon the policy of founding well-endowed *madrasas*, or theological colleges (known as *Nizamiyas* in honor of their founder), in such major urban centers as Baghdad, Isfahan, Neyshabur, and Herat. The purpose of these colleges, with their scholarships for needy students, their learned faculties, and their excellent libraries, was to graduate well-educated orthodox *'ulama'*, jurists and bureaucrats who would provide a new administrative elite for the Seljuk empire. The curriculum varied from college to college, but generally it included study of the Koran, the Traditions of the Prophet (Hadith), Muslim jurisprudence (*fikh*), Koranic exegesis (*tafsir*), and theology (*kalam*), as well as grammar and prosody, belles lettres, and, in some cases, mathematics and medicine. There has been keen scholarly debate regarding the origins of the *madrasa* as an educational institution, as well as the innovative role of Nizam al-Mulk himself, but whatever his objectives in founding his *Nizamiyas*, it is unlikely that they made much direct impact upon contemporary methods or modes of administration. What is beyond question is that, from the time of Nizam al-Mulk, the *madrasa* became a ubiquitous feature of urban life throughout the Muslim world.

It may be supposed that throughout the reign of Alp Arslan, Nizam al-Mulk acted as the sultan's representative, well aware that he owed everything to his master's confidence and favor. With Malik-Shah the relationship was rather different. Nizam al-Mulk now acted as the experienced, worldly-wise mentor counseling a youthful, impetuous ward, playing the role of Cardinal Wolsey to the sultan's Henry VIII. It was a role which Malik-Shah did not appreciate. With the passing of the years, the sultan grew increasingly suspicious and resentful of his vizier's enormous authority. Moreover, like most viziers before and after him, Nizam al-Mulk was unable to resist the temptation of gathering excessive wealth and power for both himself and his extended family. Probably, he believed that he could secure his position and be certain that his orders were being carried out only if he surrounded himself with relatives and protégés, appointing them to key positions in the central administration or those of the provinces. Such nepotism bred corruption and the abuse of power and multiplied the vizier's enemies. As the years passed, Malik-Shah came to wonder whether he was still master in his own house. When Jamal al-Din, Nizam al-Mulk's eldest son, brutally murdered a member of the sultan's household, Malik-Shah gave orders for the criminal to be secretly poisoned, but he still did not move openly against his old servant.

In the end, it was the sultan's favorite wife, Terkhen-Khatun, who was to be the cause of Nizam al-Mulk's downfall. Terkhen-Khatun was determined to ensure the succession of her son, Mahmud, while the vizier supported the candidacy of Berk-Yaruq, the sultan's older son by another wife. Thus, Nizam al-Mulk and Terkhen-Khatun were set upon a collision course. The eventual outcome was the vizier's dismissal and his replacement by Terkhen-Khatun's nominee, Taj al-Mulk. Nizam al-Mulk, however, seems to have remained in the sultan's entourage, despite his disgrace. While traveling with the sultan from Isfahan to Baghdad, not long afterward, he was stabbed to death by an assailant near Nahavand on October 14, 1092. The general assumption was that his murderer had acted on behalf of the Isma'ilis, whom

Nizam al-Mulk 1481

Nizam al-Mulk had vigorously persecuted, but suspicion also pointed to the sultan, who may have found the presence of his old minister an embarrassment, and to his supplanter, Taj al-Mulk, who was murdered by Nizam al-Mulk's servants a few months later. Malik-Shah himself died of a fever less than a month after the death of his great minister. With the removal of Nizam al-Mulk's guiding hand, the Seljuk empire entered upon a period of internal strife and struggles for the succession, presaging its eventual dismemberment.

Summary

Nizam al-Mulk enjoys the posthumous reputation of a model statesman and of being the man who provided the administrative framework by means of which the Seljuks could exercise their Middle Eastern hegemony. Within the Persian literary tradition, he is the ideal of the sage minister, the counselor of kings. In reality, his position at the pinnacle of power can never have been wholly secure. His master could dismiss him at a moment's notice. His executive actions must often have provoked resentment on the part of members of the ruling house and of the great emirs. Within the bureaucracy itself, aspiring subordinates and rivals awaited the opportunity to profit by his mistakes.

In the final analysis, Nizam al-Mulk's enduring legacy is not the imperial structure which crumbled so soon after his death, but his single surviving literary undertaking. This work is the *Siyasat-nama* (c. 1091; *The Book of Government: Or, Rules for Kings*, 1960), written not long before his death to instruct Malik-Shah in the art of kingship. Written in a plain, unadorned style and divided into fifty sections, it addresses such matters as the duties and conduct of the ruler, the organization and management of the sultan's household, the recruitment and training of slaves, the control of the army and the bureaucracy, and the evils of innovation, especially in religion. Predictably, it is strongly anti-Shi'ite, but above all, it is a work deeply imbued with nostalgic devotion for the traditions and glories of ancient Iran, as befits a writer who was the embodiment of the Irano-Islamic cultural heritage and of an enduring political philosophy rooted in realpolitik and autocracy. The British Iranologist Edward G. Browne described it as "one of the most remarkable and instructive prose works which Persian literature can boast."

A standing monument to Nizam al-Mulk's fame is the fine prayer hall which he had built in the congregational mosque of Isfahan, and which is still standing. Memorials of a different kind were his numerous descendants. A number of sons and grandsons served as viziers to later Seljuk sultans, but most perished violently; not one displayed any great talent. Nizam al-Mulk himself emerges from the contemporary sources as a harsh, pragmatic realist who does not seem to have inspired the flattering anecdotes attached to the reputations of some medieval Muslim statesmen. A twelfth century belletrist tersely noted that Nizam had no regard for poets, he himself having no skill at the art, and cared little for mystics or men of religion. The record points to a man endowed with great practical abilities and possessing both an enormous appetite for power and all the skills and ruthlessness needed for wielding it.

Bibliography
Bosworth, C. E. "The Political and Dynastic History of the Iranian World (A.D. 1000-1217)." In *The Cambridge History of Iran*, vol. 5, edited by J. A. Boyle. Cambridge: Cambridge University Press, 1968. This chapter provides a masterly and very detailed review of the Seljuk period in which Nizam al-Mulk played so conspicuous a part.
Bowen, H. C. "The *Sar-gudhasht-i sayyidnā*, the 'Tale of the Three Schoolfellows,' and the *Wasaya* of the Nizām al-Mulk." *Journal of the Royal Asiatic Society* (1931): 771-782. This interesting article examines some of the late and spurious legends which collected around the name of Nizam al-Mulk.
Browne, Edward G. *A Literary History of Persia*. 4 vols. Cambridge: Cambridge University Press, 1902-1924. This is still the standard account of classical Persian literature, into which is woven a historical narrative which places authors' lives and works in their contemporary settings. Volume 2 contains rather extensive discussions of various aspects of the career and writing of Nizam al-Mulk.
Klausner, Carla L. *The Seljuk Vezirate: A Study of Civil Administration, 1055-1194*. Cambridge, Mass.: Harvard University Press, 1973. This monograph provides important background material and discussion on Nizam al-Mulk's career as the most famous vizier of the Seljuk sultans.
Lambton, Ann K. S. "The Dilemma of Government in Islamic Persia: The *Siyāsat-nāma* of Nizām al-Mulk." *Iran: Journal of the British Institute of Persian Studies* 22 (1984): 55-66. This article is essential reading for anyone interested in Nizam al-Mulk's ideas concerning government or in more general examination of medieval Islamic political thought.
_____. "The Internal Structure of the Saljuq Empire." In *The Cambridge History of Iran*, vol. 5, edited by J. A. Boyle. Cambridge: Cambridge University Press, 1968. This is the best account of the political and administrative institutions of the Seljuk empire, which were largely molded and then dominated for so long by Nizam al-Mulk.
Makdisi, G. "Muslim Institutions of Learning in Eleventh-Century Baghdad." *Bulletin of the School of Oriental and African Studies* 24 (1961): 1-56. A most interesting discussion of the rise of the *madrasa*, providing useful background information on Nizam al-Mulk's educational policy.
Nizam al-Mulk. *The Book of Government: Or, Rules for Kings, the "Siyasatnama" or "Siyar al-Mulk."* Translated by Hubert Darke. London: Rout-

ledge and Kegan Paul, 1960. This polished translation of the *Siyasat-nama* (the only one ever undertaken in English) is essential reading for an understanding of both Nizam al-Mulk and the workings of government during the Seljuk period.

Tibawi, A. L. "Origin and Character of al-Madrasah." *Bulletin of the School of Oriental and African Studies* 25 (1962): 225-238. As a response to Makdisi's article (listed above), this essay provides the student with useful insights into a significant area of scholarly debate.

Gavin R. G. Hambly

SAINT OLAF

Born: c. 995; west of the Oslo fjord, Norway
Died: July 29, 1030; Stiklestad, Norway
Areas of Achievement: Government, law, and religion
Contribution: By consolidating and unifying Norway under a strong Christian monarchy, Olaf established his country's first national government and permanently influenced the political and religious development of his land.

Early Life

Olaf Haraldsson was the great-great-grandson of King Harald I Fairhair, the legendary warrior chief and first king in southeastern Norway. Olaf's father, Harald Grenske, was a regional king in southeastern Norway and died while Olaf was still an infant. His mother, Áasta, daughter of a prominent man in the Uplands, was remarried to Sigurð Syr, a regional king in Ringerike. An anecdote concerning Olaf's childhood, related by Snorri Sturluson in *Heimskringla* (c. 1220; *History of the Kings of Norway*, 1964), reveals something of the boy's disposition and of his attitude toward his stepfather, Sigurð, an unpretentious, mild-mannered farmer. One day King Sigurð asked Olaf to go to the stable and saddle a horse for him. Olaf returned leading a large goat saddled with the king's harness. Olaf not only thought the menial task unworthy of a chieftain and warrior but also repudiated the unmartial life of his stepfather by suggesting that this animal was as suitable for a farmer-king as horses are for other riders. From an early age, Olaf showed an unswerving desire to become a warrior and demonstrated contempt for any lesser life. He was hot-tempered, imperious, and proud of his birth.

Although the Viking Age was coming to an end and Olaf himself was to be the last great Viking chief, Viking expeditions were still taking place during Olaf's boyhood, and experience as a Viking was still considered a suitable education for a young man of the chieftain class. Thus, at age twelve and in the company of experienced men, Olaf participated in raids off the shores of the Baltic Sea, in Jutland, and in Frisia. From age fourteen to nineteen, Olaf remained in Western Europe, mainly in the service of a king—a fact which suggests that the Viking era was indeed passing and the era of wars between states had begun. In the service of King Ethelred II the Unready of England, Olaf helped to repel the Danish invasions of England from 1009 to 1014. Earlier, he had fought on the side of the Danes against the English while serving King Sven I Forkbeard, but it is clear that Olaf's alliance was with the English and with Ethelred, who became his protector. The influence of the English on Olaf was to prove substantial, and it was probably while in Ethelred's service in Rouen, Normandy, that he was converted to Christianity and baptized in 1013. By the age of nineteen, Olaf had gained wide political and military training, considerable eminence as a warrior and a leader, great wealth through large tribute payments, and a knowledge of European systems of government. By the age of twenty, through skill and some luck, he had gained the throne of Norway.

It is unclear exactly when Olaf decided to conquer Norway. His political fortunes in England worsened when King Ethelred died and Knut of Denmark (son of King Sven I Forkbeard) established his rule in England. Olaf was very conscious of his royal ancestry and his right to the throne, however, and it is reasonable to assume he had some idea of the desirability of a unified Norwegian kingdom. Olaf's namesake and kinsman, Olaf Tryggvason (Olaf I, 995-1000) had briefly unified the country and had attempted through hardhanded methods to impose Christianity on the land, but after his death in the Battle of Svolder in 1000, rule of Norway passed to the earls of Lade Eirik and Svein, in part as representatives of the Danish and Swedish crowns. The unity and independence of Norway had thus been lost, and much of the country had reverted to paganism.

In 1015, Olaf and 120 followers set sail for Norway, not in Viking warships but in two merchant vessels. Olaf clearly expected to win the throne with the help of forces raised within the country itself. In Norway at this time there were many regional kings (such as Olaf's stepfather), each ruling his own little "province." They owed allegiance to a foreign crown and paid tribute, but they were allowed to run their own domestic affairs as they saw fit. The arbitrariness of their rule and the growing differences in wealth and distinction among their subjects were grievances that Olaf was able to exploit. Promising freedom from the tyranny and exactions of local kings, Olaf won the support of the yeoman. He used the prestige of his ancestry and the wealth he had acquired to win many others to his side. He manipulated national sentiment against the Danish and Swedish overlords to lead a rebellion. Finally, he employed his military proficiency and won a decisive naval battle against Earl Svein and established himself as King Olaf II.

Life's Work

Olaf II is remembered as the first effective king of all Norway, a great lawgiver, a zealous Christian missionary, and eventually Norway's patron saint. Certainly there is little in Olaf's early life to suggest that he would become a national saint. Neither his career as ruthless Viking warrior nor his character hints of the saintly. Such varying descriptions of Olaf exist that it is difficult to discern his true nature. One physical characteristic, however, is clear from his nickname, which was variously Olaf the Big, Olaf the Stout, and, as one of his enemies called him, Olaf the Fat. Although he was a large man and possibly inclined toward corpulance, his swiftness and agility as a warrior belies the stereotype, and Snorri records that he was capable of great asceticism. In some verses supposedly written by Olaf, he accuses himself of being too susceptible to the charms of women. Icelandic poets as late as the fifteenth century allude to his many amours, one of whom produced an illegitimate son, Magnús, who succeeded his father as king. Still, his life also gives evidence of the gradual subduing of paganism, both within Norway and within himself.

Some modern historians doubt that Olaf was as devout a Christian as medieval historians stated in their writings, which were somewhat hagiographic in tone. Olaf's devotion to Christianity undoubtedly had practical as well as spiritual motivations. Norway had been Christian in name since the time of Olaf I, but following his death a pagan reaction set in. Olaf, while in England, possibly perceived that national unity through an established church was a politically astute strategy. He undoubtedly intended to establish a state church similar to what he had observed in England, for he brought numerous bishops and priests from England. Certainly Christianity could not be established without law and permanent organization. Olaf abolished the system of petty kings and established the authority of priests to administer the many churches he had had built throughout Norway and to regulate the lives of the people according to fundamental Christian principles. The Church was given authority to regulate marriages, fasts, and feastdays, and to abolish pagan practices. Many of the laws in the *Kristenret* (the name given to Saint Olaf's code of laws) appeared revolutionary to the heathen, for it stated that parents no longer had the right to rid themselves of unwanted children through exposure; that a man would be permitted only one wife, to whom he must be faithful; and that the worship of house gods was forbidden. Other ideas, such as the Sabbath as a holy day of rest even for thralls, or the concept of a fast day even for those who could afford to eat and drink abundantly, were also disturbing and viewed by many pagans as unwarranted intrusions into private life. Thus, many of Olaf's laws were met with fierce resistance, and accordingly, Olaf, despite his desire to treat his people according to principles of mercy and peace, used increasingly harsh methods to enforce the code of laws. He mutilated obdurate heathens and deprived them of their property, and during the last phase of his reign he resorted to burning villages and executing men. Yet Olaf was also capable of great restraint and even of magnanimity in dealing with his enemies, and he was known for his evenhanded treatment of all people, in spite of rank.

Olaf reigned for twelve relatively peaceful years, during which time he established the first national government in Norway and continued his systematic efforts to establish Christianity throughout the land, particularly in the north and in the interior, where resistance was greatest. A foreign war, however, brought about his downfall.

King Knut, who ruled both England and Denmark, began a plan to reclaim Norway. He sent money and gifts to the deposed petty kings and promised to restore their freedom and authority, which Olaf had taken away.

Through his emissaries, he also agitated the many individuals who resented the new faith which had been thrust upon them and all those who found Olaf's strict rule to be too harsh, as well as those who hoped to gain greater independence under a more distant king. Realizing that an erosion of support for him was taking place among his people, Olaf entered into an alliance with the Swedish king, and together they made a precipitous, ill-conceived attack on Knut in Denmark, presumably before he could attack them. The attack failed and instead initiated Knut's conquest of Norway in 1028. Olaf, knowing he had been betrayed by his countrymen, fled to Russia, where he was entertained by King Jaroslav and Queen Ingigerd (to whom Olaf had once been engaged). King Jaroslav offered him authority and dominions in Russia, but Olaf desired only that it might be God's will for him to return to Norway. In 1030, he left his son Magnús at the Russian court and returned to Norway by way of Sweden. The King of Sweden supplied him with four hundred men and authorized him to call for volunteers. Olaf marched through dense forest to Norway, where other kinsmen joined him, mainly ruffians and robbers. According to some accounts, Olaf rejected all heathen volunteers who refused baptism; according to other accounts, Olaf went into battle with three thousand men, Christians on his right and heathens on his left.

King Knut appointed Kálf Árnason, Olaf's former friend, to command the defense of Norway. The opposing armies met at Stiklestad at midday in brilliant sunshine, but after an hour the sky turned red, the sun was obscured, and the battlefield became dark as night. Olaf's army, greatly outnumbered, fought on bravely, but Olaf was wounded. He was leaning against a boulder and calling upon God for help when he received his deathblow, probably from Kálf Árnason. In addition to an eclipse of the sun, other miracles were recorded on this day within a few hours of Olaf's death—wounds were healed and sight was restored to a blind man by contact with Olaf's blood. When Olaf's body was exhumed a year after burial and found to be uncorrupt, he was proclaimed a saint. In 1041, the Church officially declared his sainthood, and his remains were placed above the high altar of Saint Clement's Church, where many more miracles reportedly occurred. The cult of Saint Olaf spread rapidly, and miracles relating to Saint Olaf were reported in places as distant as Constantinople and the British Isles. Churches were dedicated to Saint Olaf throughout Western Europe, and a painting of him appeared in the Nativity Church in Bethlehem around 1170.

Summary

The unusual circumstances of Olaf's death and the events which followed it help to explain how Olaf became a saint within a few years of his death. Neither Olaf's followers nor his detractors could help but associate his death with the death of Christ on Calvary. Another factor was the increasing discontent with the rulers that Knut installed in Norway following Olaf's defeat and death. Svein, son of Knut, was still a child when appointed regent, and power was therefore transferred to his tyrannical mother, Álfífa. The harsh laws, increased taxes, and precedence given to Danes in Norway (in court, the witness of one Dane was regarded as the equivalent of ten Norwegians) roused the people to fury and caused them to view Olaf as a martyr and a champion of national liberty. Ironically, Olaf's enemies led the expedition to Russia to bring back Olaf's ten-year-old son, Magnús, to be king. Additional factors in the reversal of opinion about Olaf II may have been the self-interest of leading aristocrats in establishing a shrine to Saint Olaf, which would attract pilgrims from many lands, and the desire of church prelates for eminence.

The most enigmatic aspect of Olaf's sainthood remains Olaf himself. There is much disagreement and controversy about his personality and his life, especially about the way he could embody Christian principles (humility, forgiveness, and nonviolence) yet at times reveal an almost instinctive cruelty and arrogance. He was a missionary king, continuing the work of Olaf I in bringing lost souls to salvation (even against their will). He was a Viking, punitive, shrewd, and ruthless when necessary. Snorri states that Olaf, while in exile at the Russian court, became increasingly engrossed in prayer and contemplated traveling to Jerusalem to take monastic vows. According to Snorri, Olaf relinquished all desire to rule for the sake of power and wished only to be an instrument of God's will. A dream told him to regain the kingdom. As Olaf drew near his last battle, many signs of sanctity were seen, among them Olaf's immersion in prayers and fasting and his selfless concern for the souls of his men.

In art, Saint Olaf is always depicted holding a battle-ax with a dragon under his foot, representing the heathendom which he destroyed. Gradually, it became customary to depict a face on the dragon resembling the king's own, suggesting that it was also Olaf's own heathen nature that he trampled underfoot. Undoubtedly, by consolidating and strengthening the monarchy in Norway, by upholding law and order, by attempting to be both just and strict, and by promoting passage of laws consistent with Christian principles, King Olaf II was a great civilizing force in a dark time. His martyr's death and subsequent canonization established the concept of Norway as a unified Christian nation under the rule of a single Christian monarch. Thus he is known as the "Eternal King" of Norway.

Bibliography

Gjertset, Knut. *History of the Norwegian People*. Reprint. New York: Macmillan, 1927. A complete history. Three chapters give a full account of Olaf's rise and fall and provide detailed accounts of the social, political, and economic conditions in the land.

Larsen, Karen. *A History of Norway*. New York: Princeton University Press, 1948. A good general account of Norway's history and one of the most readable. Provides a brief overview of Olaf's development and one of the most sympathetic accounts of his life. Includes a brief bibliography of books available in English.

Sturluson, Snorri. *Heimskringla: History of the Kings of Norway*. Translated with introduction and notes by Lee M. Hollander. Austin: University of Texas Press, 1964. A history of the kings of Norway from the quasi-mythic origins of the dynasty to the year 1177 by the thirteenth century Icelandic poet. "Saint Olaf's Saga" (three hundred pages) is one of Snorri's greatest literary achievements and is a major if controversial source for what is known about Olaf II. Includes an introduction and copious notes.

Turville-Petre, Gabriel. *The Heroic Age of Scandinavia*. London: Hutchinson's University Library, 1951. An introductory history of the Norsemen to the year 1030. A chapter devoted to Olaf II emphasizes that the cult and legends of Olaf II have eclipsed the historical figure. Includes a discussion of the confusion about the date of Olaf's death (which does not coincide with the solar eclipse). Brief bibliography of works in English.

Undset, Sigrid. *Saga of Saints*. Reprint. Translated by E. C. Ramsden. Freeport, N.Y.: Books for Libraries Press, 1968. A chapter on Olaf offers interesting insights into the differences between pagan and Christian values and practices. An uncritical presentation of the many legends and miracles which surround Olaf.

Karen A. Kildahl

OMAR KHAYYÁM

Born: 1048; probably Nishapur, Iran
Died: 1131; Nishapur, Iran
Areas of Achievement: Mathematics and poetry
Contribution: Khayyám was a leading medieval mathematician and the author of Persian quatrains made world famous through Edward FitzGerald's *The Rubáiyát of Omar Khayyám.*

Early Life

Omar Khayyám was born in all likelihood in Nishapur, then a major city in the northeastern corner of Iran. At his birth, a new Turkish dynasty from Central Asia called the Seljuks was in the process of establishing control over the whole Iranian plateau. In 1055, when their leader, Toghril Beg (Toghril I), entered Baghdad, the Seljuks became masters of the Muslim caliphate and empire. Of Omar's family and education, few specifics are known. His given name indicates that he was a Sunni Muslim, for his namesake was the famous second caliph under whose reign (634-644) the dramatic Islamic expansion throughout the Middle East and beyond had begun. The name Khayyám means "tentmaker," possibly designating the occupation of his forebears. Omar received a good education, including study of Arabic, the Koran, the various religious sciences, mathematics, astronomy, astrology, and literature.

At Toghril Beg's death, his nephew Alp Arslan succeeded to the Seljuk throne, in part through the machinations of Nizam al-Mulk (1020-1092), another famous man from Nishapur, who was to serve the Seljuks for more than thirty years as a vizier. Alp Arslan, who ruled from 1063 to 1072, was succeeded by his son Malik-Shah, who ruled until 1092.

During this period of rule, Khayyám studied first in Nishapur, then in Balkh, a major eastern city in today's Afghanistan. From there, he went farther northeast to Samarkand (now in the Soviet Union). There, under the patronage of the chief local magistrate, he wrote a treatise in Arabic on algebra, classifying types of cubic equations and presenting systematic solutions to them. Recognized by historians of science and mathematics as a significant study, it is the most important of Khayyám's extant works (which comprise about ten short treatises). None of them, however, offers glimpses into Khayyám's personality, except to affirm his importance as a mathematician and astronomer whose published views were politically and religiously orthodox.

From Samarkand, Khayyám proceeded to Bukhara and was probably still in the royal court there when peace was concluded between the Qarakhanids and the Seljuks in 1073 or 1074. At this time, he presumably entered the service of Malik-Shah, who had become Seljuk sultan in 1072.

Omar Khayyám

Life's Work

Two of Malik-Shah's projects on which Khayyám presumably worked were the construction of an astronomy observatory in the Seljuk capital at Esfahan in 1074 and the reform of the Persian solar calendar. Called *Maleki* after the monarch, the new calendar proved more accurate than the Gregorian system centuries later.

Khayyám was one of Malik-Shah's favorite courtiers, but after the latter's death Khayyám apparently never again held important positions under subsequent Seljuk rulers. In the mid-1090's, he made the *hajj* pilgrimage to Mecca and then returned to private life and teaching in Nishapur. It is known that Khayyám was in Balkh in 1112 or 1113. Several years later, he was in Marv, where a Seljuk ruler had summoned him to forecast the weather for a hunting expedition. After 1118, the year of Sanjar's accession, no record exists of anything Khayyám did. He died in his early eighties.

Some of the meager information available today regarding Khayyám was recorded by an acquaintance called Nizami 'Aruzi (fl. 1110-1161) in a book called *Chahár Maqála* (c. 1155; English translation, 1899). Nizami tells of visiting Khayyám's gravesite in 1135 or 1136. Surprisingly, given Khayyám's reputation as a poet, the anecdotes regarding him appear in Nizami's "Third Discourse: On Astrologers," and no mention of him is made in the "Second Discourse: On Poets." In other words, though in the West Omar Khayyám is known for his poetry, no evidence in Persian suggests that he was a professional court poet or that he ever was more involved with poetry than through the occasional, perhaps extemporaneous, composition of quatrains (*ruba'i* or *roba'i*, plural *rubáiyát*). Because the quatrains first attributed to Khayyám are thematically of a piece and are distinct from panegyric, love, and Sufi quatrains, they can be usefully designated as "Khayyamic" even if authorship of many individual quatrains is impossible to determine definitively.

The following three quatrains are among the most typical and earliest to be attributed to the historical figure of Omar Khayyám:

> There was a drop of water, it merged with the sea.
> There was a speck of dirt, it merged with the earth.
> Your coming into the world is what?
> A fly appearing and disappearing.

> Drink wine: the universe means your demise,
> intends the death of your pure life and mine.
> Be seated on the grass and drink bright wine,
> for here will blooms bloom from your dust and mine.

> This ancient caravanserai called the world,
> home of the multicolored steed of night and day,
> is where a hundred Jamshids feasted and
> a hundred Bahrams ruled in splendor, and left.

In the centuries following Khayyám's death, increasing numbers of quatrains attributed to him appeared in manuscripts. Several of these manuscripts came to the attention of Edward FitzGerald (1809-1883), a serious student of Persian, who found them particularly appealing. His study of them inspired him to compose *The Rubáiyát of Omar Khayyám*, the first edition of which consisted of seventy-five quatrains and appeared in 1859. A second edition, expanded to 110 quatrains, appeared in 1868. The third edition in 1872 and the fourth in 1879 contained 101 quatrains, and the latter is the standard text. By FitzGerald's death, his work had begun to receive favorable critical attention, but its extraordinary fame, making it the single most popular poem of the Victorian Age, did not commence until later. A comparison of *The Rubáiyát of Omar Khayyám* with the Khayyamic Persian quatrains which FitzGerald had read and studied reveals that the themes, tone, and imagery of his poem are very close to those in the Persian quatrains, but that FitzGerald's poem is not a translation in any sense. It was the worldwide popularity of *The Rubáiyát of Omar Khayyám* that drew scholarly attention in Iran to Khayyám as a poet, so that he now is recognized as a leading figure in the Persian literary pantheon, along with Firdusi (c. 940-c. 1020), Jalal al-Din Rumi (1207-1273), Sa'di (c. 1200-c. 1291), and Hafiz (c. 1320-c. 1390).

Summary

The Persian quatrains attributed to Omar Khayyám express the point of view of a rationalist intellectual who sees no reason to believe in a human soul or an afterlife (as in the first quatrain quoted above). The speaker would like to live a springtime garden life, but his continuing awareness of his own mortality and his inability to find answers in either science or religion lead him to a modified *carpe diem* stance: In this far-from-perfect world, in which human beings do not have a decent chance at happiness, one should nevertheless endeavor to make the best of things (as in the second quatrain quoted above). Some slight consolation is offered in appreciating the fact that human beings have faced this situation from the beginning of time (as in the third quatrain quoted above).

In the orthodox Seljuk age, Khayyamic quatrains constituted a bold, individualistic voicing of skepticism. Because literary Iranians throughout history have admired individualists and free spirits, Omar Khayyám has been mythologized into a figure quite different from what the known facts about his biography imply. For example, he was a hero and inspiration to Sadiq Hidayat, Iran's most acclaimed twentieth century author, in whose novel *Buf-i kur* (1941; *The Blind Owl*, 1957) are palpable Khayyamic echoes.

Regardless of the historical facts, the view of Hidayat and many others is that Khayyám bucked the tide of religious orthodoxy and dared to say what many secular-minded people believe: that religion, science, and government fail to give an adequate explanation of the mystery of the individual lives of human beings.

Bibliography

Boyle, J. A. "Omar Khayyám: Astronomer, Mathematician, and Poet." In *The Cambridge History of Iran*, edited by R. N. Frye, vol. 4. Cambridge: Cambridge University Press, 1975. A succinct and careful review of the known facts about Khayyám's life, concluding with a brief review of the dispute over Khayyám's attitude toward Sufism, with which he presumably had little affinity.

Dashti, 'Ali. *In Search of Omar Khayyám*. Translated by L. P. Elwell-Sutton. London: Allen and Unwin, 1971. A translation of the first edition of the most reliable study of Khayyám to date, which includes a review of his age and the known facts of his life, a collection of seventy-five quatrains which Dashti argues can be attributed with some confidence to Khayyám, and Dashti's sympathetic and sensitive identification of themes in the poems.

Elwell-Sutton, L. P. "The *Ruba'i* in Early Persian Literature." In *The Cambridge History of Iran*, edited by R. N. Frye, vol. 4. Cambridge: Cambridge University Press, 1975. A review of the first two centuries of the verse form and its uses for panegyrical, didactic, satirical, amatory, and Khayyamic statements.

FitzGerald, Edward. *The Rubáiyát of Omar Khayyám*. 4th ed. London: Bernard Quaritch, 1879. This is the last edition which FitzGerald saw to press and thus the official, final version of the poem.

Heron-Allen, Edward. *Edward FitzGerald's "Rubáiyát of Omar Khayyám" with Their Original Persian Sources*. Boston: L. C. Page, 1899. A study of FitzGerald's 101 stanzas paralleled with the Persian texts of possible sources, demonstrating that, although FitzGerald was inspired by Khayyamic and other Persian quatrains, *The Rubáiyát of Omar Khayyám* is an original English poem and not a translation.

Hillmann, Michael C. "Perennial Iranian Skepticism." In *Iranian Culture: A Persianist View*. Lanham, Md.: University Press of America, 1988. A treatment of the significance to Iranian culture today of the ideas expressed in Khayyamic quatrains, which are compared to FitzGerald's poem. Extensive notes provide a comprehensive bibliography of writing in English on Khayyám and FitzGerald.

Kennedy, E. S. "The Exact Sciences in Iran under the Saljuqs and Mongols." In *The Cambridge History of Iran*, edited by J. A. Boyle, vol. 5. Cambridge: Cambridge University Press, 1968. Surveys the foundations of mathematics, algebra, trigonometry and computational mathematics, planetary theory, observational astronomy, mathematical geography, specific gravity determination, and rainbow theory, with a discussion of Khayyám's contributions to polynomial equations and balances for determination of specific gravity, and his possible contribution to observational astronomy.

Khayyám, Omar. *The Algebra of Omar Khayyám*. Translated by Daoud S. Kasir. New York: Teachers College, Columbia University, 1931. A work of great interest to students of the history of mathematics and Khayyám's most important extant work, prefaced with a discussion of the state of algebra before his time and Khayyám's methods and significance.

Nizami 'Aruzi. *Revised Translation of the "Chahár Maqála" (Four Discourses)*. Translated by Edward G. Browne. London: Cambridge University Press, 1921. Divided into four sections: "On Secretaries," "On Poets," "On Astrologers," and "On Physicians," with two anecdotes on Khayyám in the third section. This is the most important extant source of biographical and critical data on Persian poetry from the ninth to the middle of the twelfth century.

Michael Craig Hillmann

ANDREA ORCAGNA
Andrea di Cione

Born: c. 1308; Florence, Italy
Died: c. 1368; Florence, Italy
Area of Achievement: Art
Contribution: In paintings and in sculptural and architectural projects combining religious intensity with naturalism, Orcagna extended the expressive range of Italian art in the mid-fourteenth century.

Early Life

Little is known of Orcagna's early life; even the date of his birth is conjectural. In *Le vite de' più eccellenti architetti, pittori, et scultori italiani* (1550; *Lives of the Most Eminent Painters, Sculptors, and Architects*, 1842-1859), Giorgio Vasari states that Orcagna lived to the age of sixty. This fact, together with the reasonable assumption that he died in 1368, is the only basis for claiming 1308 as the year of his birth.

The name "Orcagna" is derived from "Arcagnuolo"; the artist's actual name was Andrea di Cione, and it is known that his three brothers were also artists: Nardo, probably older than Andrea, and two younger brothers, Matteo and Jacopo. While still a child, according to Vasari, Orcagna began to study sculpture under Andrea Pisano and only after some years took up drawing and painting. Orcagna had achieved some recognition as a painter by 1346, but it was not until 1352 that he became a member of the Florentine stonemason's guild responsible for works of sculpture; thus Vasari's claim may be incorrect. The uncertainty is not a matter of very great importance, however, because Orcagna's career, like those of many artists of his time, was based on a variety of artistic endeavors, including the practice of architecture as well as of painting and sculpture.

Orcagna was born in an era when the practice of the visual arts was still based more on traditions of craftsmanship than upon the exploration of individual artists. It was seldom thought necessary by contemporary writers to research and record the details of the lives of even those artists who emerged from the background of the workshops. Few such accounts survive, and much biographical detail is circumstantial. In Orcagna's case, for example, it is known that he was married only from a 1371 reference to his widow; the same document serves as the only dated evidence of his death.

Life's Work

Orcagna's career is documented only between 1343 and 1368. By 1347, he was associated with his brother Nardo, sharing a workshop with him and probably participating in his commissions for paintings. Orcagna's reputation grew rapidly in the early 1350's, leading to major commissions in Florence,

Orvieto, and Siena. In 1354 he was commissioned by the wealthy Strozzi family to paint an altarpiece for the family chapel in the church of Santa Maria Novella in Florence. The subject of the work, which was completed in 1357, is *Christ Conferring Authority on Saints Peter and Thomas Aquinas*. It is a panel painting executed in tempera, a medium which lends itself to precise shapes, deliberate design, and strong colors. In these characteristics, it is a somewhat conservative departure from the successful norms established by Orcagna's great predecessor, Giotto, whom he knew during the latter part of Giotto's life. Giotto's life's work was almost wholly concerned with painting in the fresco medium, which is more successfully employed to render objects as volumes rather than as shapes, and which gives a greater sense of atmosphere as well as harmony of color. These differences in technique relate to differences in artistic objective. Giotto's aim was to humanize the religious content of Christianity, particularly the legend of Saint Francis, in paintings possessing a sense of great physical reality. Orcagna's purpose, more than a generation later, was to reemphasize the institutional authority of the Church by rendering religious topics in a majestically austere style. In the Strozzi altarpiece, the resurgent Dominican order is, in effect, given a vote of confidence over the less-orthodox Franciscan Order—the painting depicts Christ enthroned, bestowing a book on Saint Thomas Aquinas (the second patron of the order after Saint Dominic) while giving the keys of Paradise to Saint Peter, the symbol of the Church of Rome.

For the years 1355, 1356, and 1357, the records of the Florentine church Or San Michele show Orcagna as the capomaestro, or superintendent, of work on a kind of chapel within the arcade of an adjacent grain market. Known as the Tabernacle, it is an ornate structure decorated with a wealth of carving, enclosing a painting of an enthroned Madonna and Child by Orcagna's near-contemporary, Bernardo Daddi. Planning and execution of the Tabernacle called upon Orcagna's varied skills in architecture, sculpture, and even goldsmithing. One authority has called it delightful and sumptuous; another compares its decoration to spun sugar and questions Orcagna's reputation as an architect, which rests solely upon this one surviving, documented example. It is clear, in any case, that Orcagna attempted to blend elements from disparate architectural and sculptural traditions, probably as much in response to demands of his patrons as to his own artistic objectives.

In 1357 Orcagna was employed in the work on the cathedral of Florence, Santa Maria del Fiore; in 1358, he went to Orvieto, where he served as capomaestro until 1362. From 1360 to 1362 his work on the decoration of the Orvieto façade, consisting of a rose window and mosaics, was done in collaboration with his brother Matteo, who remained in Orvieto while Andrea returned to Florence to carry on other work. The last recorded work by Andrea Orcagna, finished in June, 1368, was a Madonna for Or San Michele, now lost. Two months later, he fell ill and presumably died shortly thereafter; a commission for a triptych on the subject of Saint Matthew was turned over to his brother Jacopo for completion.

Summary

Andrea Orcagna was not the leading Italian artist of the fourteenth century, an honor which unquestionably belongs to Giotto. Also held in precedence to Orcagna are Duccio di Buoninsegna, Simone Martini, the brothers Pietro and Ambrogio Lorenzetti, and others. In the realm of Florentine painting, however, possibly only Maso di Banco could be judged to rank with Orcagna, and Maso's painting lies largely within Giotto's sphere of influence. Orcagna inherited the moral seriousness of Giotto and Maso but found it necessary to depart from the sense of equilibrium that characterizes the art of Giotto and his immediate followers. Orcagna's dramatic feeling for active religious faith is different from the simplicity and humanism of Giotto and seems to reflect a sense of spiritual discipline that corresponds to the contemporary preaching of the Dominicans.

There can be little doubt that the nature of the times in which he lived influenced Orcagna's art. In addition to political uncertainty during the early 1340's, there were significant Florentine bankruptcies in 1343 and 1345, followed by a famine in 1346 in Tuscany, the region which includes Florence and Siena. Then, in 1348, a calamitous plague struck in June. The Black Death, as it was called, was thought by many to be a punishment from God; the Dominicans capitalized on this fear by claiming that the order knew the secret of protecting the city from a recurrence of the plague. Much of the populace reacted to the material stresses of the times with increased devotion, but some responded with religious indifference; a tension between the two forms of reaction lent increased importance to the Church, its hierarchy and its rituals, and to the art that supported them. In response to the needs of the Church as well as to his own spiritual inclinations, Orcagna's art assumed a powerful, dedicated character that distinguishes it from the work of less receptive and adventurous artists.

To some degree, one must speculate on the matter of Orcagna's individual achievement in relation to the work of others who might have collaborated with him, including his brothers Nardo and Jacopo; Nardo, in particular, was an artist of great sensitivity. As in the case of many artists of the Gothic period and before, it is best to temper the concept of individual genius with an appreciation of the nature of collective endeavor and of shared artistic traits. Yet even accounting for these factors, Orcagna stands out as a strong figure in the midst of many remarkable artists emerging from the workshops of early and mid-fourteenth century Italy.

Bibliography
Berenson, Bernhard. *The Italian Painters of the Renaissance*. London:

Phaidon Press, 1959. This book consists of the texts of four essays first published from 1894 to 1907, together with an extensive collection of pertinent reproductions. Although Berenson is literally a figure from the past (though he lived until 1959) and his conclusions are much modified by modern scholarship, his characteristic approach to viewing art, referred to as "connoisseurship," has been influential in subsequent appreciation of Renaissance art.

Carli, E., J. Gudio, and G. Souchal. *Gothic Painting*. New York: Viking Press, 1965. This small survey provides a balance between text and good illustrations in black and white and color, but individual artists, with the exception of the universally important ones such as Giotto and Duccio, are dealt with only briefly.

Francastel, P. *Medieval Painting*. New York: Dell Publishing Co., 1967. This diminutive paperback has a particular advantage in that its small, color illustrations allow for telling comparisons among works of various sizes and styles. Contains an excellent reproduction of Orcagna's Strozzi altarpiece.

Hartt, Frederick. *History of Italian Renaissance Art: Painting, Sculpture, Architecture*. Englewood Cliffs, N.J.: Prentice-Hall, 1979. This large volume, the standard survey of this period of the history of art, is both readable and profusely illustrated and offers an authoritative bibliography.

Meiss, Millard. *Painting in Florence and Siena After the Black Death: The Arts, Religion, and Society in the Mid-Fourteenth Century*. New York: Harper and Row, Publishers, 1964. This classic of art scholarship, detailed yet readable, places Orcagna, along with several other artists, in the social and historical context of mid-fourteenth century Italy. The book's small black-and-white illustrations, though essential to understanding the author's arguments, are unlikely to communicate the full power of the works discussed.

Vasari, Giorgio. *Vasari's Lives of the Artists: Biographies of the Most Eminent Architects, Painters, and Sculptors of Italy*. Edited by Betty Burroughs. New York: Simon and Schuster, 1946. Vasari, a painter who lived from 1511 to 1574, wrote his book "not to acquire praise as a writer but to revive the memory of those who adorned these professions." First published in 1550, the work is more colorful than it is useful, since scholarship has overtaken virtually all of Vasari's information; nevertheless, each page of this classic document enlivens its subject as no other source does.

C. S. McConnell

ORIGEN

Born: c. A.D. 185; Alexandria, Egypt
Died: c. A.D. 254; probably Tyre (modern Sur, Lebanon)
Areas of Achievement: Theology and religion
Contribution: Origen is usually considered the greatest of the early Christian thinkers; he was the first not only to write extensive commentaries on most books of the Bible but also to study the main areas and problems within theology. He did so with such intelligence that often what he wrote determined the lines of all subsequent Christian thought.

Early Life

Origen was born at the end of the period that Edward Gibbon, the eighteenth century English historian, called the happiest and most prosperous the human race had known; he died during a time of civil war, plague, economic dislocation, and persecution of the Christian Church. Alexandria, the city of his birth, was one of the great cities of the world; it used Greek as its first language and was the home of the largest library in the Mediterranean basin. There many of the best scholars of the Greek world taught and studied.

Origen was the oldest of nine children. His father, whom tradition names Leonides, was prosperous enough to provide him with a Greek literary education and concerned enough about his Christian formation to teach him the Bible. From childhood Origen was a serious Christian and a learned Greek. The Old Testament from which he studied, the Septuagint, was a Jewish translation of the Hebrew Bible into Greek. It contained, in addition to translations of those Scriptures originally written in Hebrew, books originally written in Greek. Although the canon, or list of books considered properly to be in the Bible, was not completely set in Origen's day, for most purposes his New Testament is that still used by Christians. While young, Origen memorized long passages of the Bible; thus as an adult he could associate passages from throughout the Bible on the basis of common words or themes. He, like other Christians of his day, also accepted as authoritative a body of teaching held to come from the Apostles.

Origen imbibed from his father and the Christian community the dramatic and heroic idea that he, as an individual Christian, was a participant in the drama by which the world was being redeemed. Like many other Christians, he was uneasy about wealth and marriage and tended to see Jesus calling the Christian to poverty and celibacy (that is, to a heroic mode of existence). Although martyrdom was still relatively infrequent, it was exalted in the Christian community, and in many ways Origen saw himself throughout his life as a living martyr doing battle for the spread of Christ's kingdom. At an unknown date, thoroughly instructed in the faith, he was baptized. Around

202, when Origen was seventeen, his father was martyred and the family property was confiscated by the state. It may be argued that for the rest of his life Origen saw himself continuing his martyred father's work.

Life's Work

In the following years, Origen added to his knowledge of grammar and Greek literature a knowledge of Gnosticism, a form of dualism very common in the Greek world of his day, which condemned all things material, especially the appetites and passions of the human body, and celebrated the spiritual, especially the human soul and spirit. Salvation was seen to lie in the separation of the soul from matter, and before Origen's day a form of Christian Gnosticism had developed. After his father's death, a Christian woman had taken Origen into her house so that he could continue his studies, and he subsequently began to teach grammar. In this woman's house Christian Gnosticism was practiced. Although Origen rejected much of what he heard there, he adopted the Gnostics' distinction between literal Christians, who understood only the literal sense of the Bible; psychic Christians, who went beyond this to consider the spiritual meaning of Scripture; and perfect Christians, who understood and followed the deepest meanings of the Bible. Origen also accepted a doctrine that was, after his death, to be condemned as heretical: He believed that ultimately all men, and even Satan himself, would be reconciled with God.

One of the second century Gnostic documents discovered at Nag Hammadi in Upper Egypt in 1945 contains many teachings similar to those found in Origen's writings and represents a form of Gnosticism more acceptable to the Christian tradition in which Origen had been formed. In this work, as in Origen's, Christ was conceived of as very similar to God the Father, although subordinate to Him in being. It also, with Origen, conceived of human existence as a long process of education, in which evil and death prepare man for union with God. Another writer, Marcion, whom Origen classified a Gnostic, provided a foil against which Origen developed the teaching that human suffering can be reconciled with God's power and goodness. Unlike Marcion, Origen held that difficult passages in the Scripture might be allegorized.

Sometime between 206 and 211, Origen added catechetical instruction (explanation of Christianity to those interested in conversion) to his duties as a grammar teacher. This period was again a time of persecution, and although he taught in secret, at one point Origen was discovered and almost killed; some of his students were martyred.

After the persecution, he gave up his work as a teacher of grammar, sold his books of Greek literature, became the chief Christian teacher in Alexandria, and gave himself totally to Bible study. He began to follow what became a lifelong practice of strictly imitating the hardest sayings of Jesus, fasting regularly, sleeping very little (the Bible had said to "pray without ceasing"), and possessing only one cloak; he also castrated himself.

In the years between 211 and 215, Origen learned much of the Platonic tradition, and that had a deep influence on him, especially the Platonists' insistence on both Divine Providence and human freedom and—against the Gnostics—on the fundamental, if limited, good of the created order. Sometime before 217 Origen traveled briefly to Rome, where he was exposed to growing controversies over the definition of the relation of Jesus Christ to God the Father. Also sometime between 215 and 222, Origen met a Hebrew-speaking convert to Christianity who had been trained as a rabbi, with whom he began to study Hebrew and Jewish biblical interpretation. He also met an Alexandrian, Ambrose, who became his lifelong patron. The first problem facing Origen as a biblical scholar was the establishment of a reliable biblical text; his response was to write first *Tetrapla* (third century) and ultimately, after he had settled in Palestine, *Hexapla* (231-c. 245), each of which contained various Greek translations in parallel columns next to a transliterated Hebrew Old Testament. In this task he revealed lifelong characteristics—painstaking interests in textual criticism and historical problems. In his mind these were completely compatible with his interest in mystical interpretation of the Bible. Origen's growing reputation is evident from an incident that occurred about 222, when he was summoned to Arabia by the Roman governor for the discussion of an unknown subject.

Most of his early writings, from between 222 and 230, have been lost, but one of his most important, *Peri archon* (*On First Principles*, 1869), survives. Heavily influenced by Platonism, it espoused the idea, later to be condemned, that the human soul before entering the body has existed eternally. Students were now flocking to Origen's lectures; of these he accepted only the most promising. Ambrose provided a staff of stenographers, who took down Origen's lectures in shorthand as he gave them, and of copyists, who then prepared a more finished text.

Probably in 230, after unspecified conflict with Bishop Demetrius of Alexandria, Origen moved, at first briefly, to Caesarea, in Palestine. Having returned to Alexandria, he again left in 231, summoned by the dowager empress, Julia Mamaea, to Antioch to teach her more about Christianity. After a brief return to Alexandria, he left for Greece, traveling via Caesarea, where he was ordained a priest. In 233 a final break with Bishop Demetrius took place, and Origen moved to Caesarea. Finally, works which he had long been developing, such as a commentary on the Gospel of John and *Peri eykhēs* (c. 233; *On Prayer*, 1954), the first thorough Christian examination of prayer as contemplation of God, were finished.

Even more productive were the years from 238 to 244, when he regularly preached and was consulted in matters of doctrine. Again, although most of his work has been lost, some has survived, above all more than two hundred sermons. Following an estrangement from his bishop, Theoctistus, Origen departed for Athens, where he continued his writing. In 246 or 247, he returned to Caesarea, where he set to work on commentaries on the Gospels of Luke and Matthew and on *Contra Celsum* (c. 249; *Against Celsus*, 1954), a defense of Christianity. During roughly the last eight years of his life, he found himself in the midst of both theological controversy and serious persecution of the Christians by the emperor Decius. By 251, Origen, who had been imprisoned and tortured, was a broken man. The circumstances of his death are uncertain.

Summary

Origen was more important than any other early Christian thinker in assimilating the Jewish and Greek traditions to Christianity. The former he accomplished through his lifelong contact with rabbinic scholars and the latter through his lifelong devotion to the Platonic tradition. His conscious intent was always to be faithful to Christianity whenever there was a direct conflict between it and what he had inherited from the earlier traditions. Nevertheless, he also intended to be open to truth wherever it might be found. That Christians usually think of themselves as the heirs to both the Jewish and the Greek traditions is more his work than any other's. He was the first Christian to discuss at length central problems such as the nature of free will and of God's relation to the world; as the first to do so, Origen did not always arrive at conclusions deemed correct by later standards. Thus, in spite of his genius, he has often been the subject of some suspicion in later Christian tradition. Yet arguably he had as much influence in setting the terms of later Christian theology as any writer, Paul included.

Origen subjected himself to great ascetic discipline, usually surrounded by his community of scribes and students, and his mode of life may be justly described as protomonastic; indeed, it was only about forty years after his death that the monastic movement began. Finally, with his great confidence in the ability of the disciplined intellect to rise above the world of sense to the vision of God, Origen stands near the source of the Christian contemplative tradition.

Bibliography

Caspary, Gerard E. *Politics and Exegesis: Origen and the Two Swords*. Berkeley: University of California Press, 1979. Centers on Origen's thought about the relation of Christianity to the political order but has much useful information about his biblical interpretation and political thought. A structuralist interpretation which mistakenly attributes pacifism to early Christians in general before the time of Constantine the Great.

Daniélou, Jean. *A History of Early Christian Doctrine Before the Council of Nicaea*. Vol. 2, *Gospel Message and Hellenistic Culture*. Translated by John Austin Baker. London: Westminster Press, 1973. Contains fine sections on Origen's catechetical teaching, biblical interpretation, Christology, anthropology, demonology, and understanding of Christian Gnosticism. Daniélou is very precise on the meaning and practice of allegory for Origen.

——————. *Origen*. Translated by Walter Mitchell. New York: Sheed and Ward, 1955. Covers Origen's life and times but is especially strong on his theology, including his interpretation of the Bible, cosmology, angelology, Christology, and eschatology. This Roman Catholic reading of Origen gives a very fair account of scholarly disagreement over Origen's theology of the sacraments.

Origen. *Contra Celsum*. Translated by Henry Chadwick. Cambridge: Cambridge University Press, 1965. The introduction and notes of this translation of one of Origen's most important works are a mine of information. Well indexed.

Trigg, Joseph Wilson. *Origen: The Bible and Philosophy in the Third-Century Church*. Atlanta, Ga.: John Knox Press, 1983. The best general survey of Origen's life and thought in English. Daniélou's explanation (see entries above) of Origen's spiritual exegesis of the Bible is more perceptive than that of Trigg, but Trigg is consistently well-informed. A Protestant reading of Origen.

Glenn W. Olsen

OSMAN

Born: c. 1258; Söğüt, Turkey
Died: 1326; Söğüt, Turkey
Areas of Achievement: Government and warfare
Contribution: Under Osman's patient and steady leadership, the influence and territorial extent of his principality were expanded until it arose as a regional power, which, as the Ottoman Empire, ultimately became one of the great powers of the early modern world.

Early Life

When Osman, the son of Ertuğrul, was born in northwestern Anatolia at Söğüt in about 1258, much of the surrounding area was held by Turkish tribes which had moved into that region in the wake of widespread political upheaval. The Seljuk sultanate, which had displaced Byzantine power, increasingly began to weaken under Mongol pressure from the east, and separate march lords arose in border areas. Ertuğrul, as a leading noble, was granted lands about ninety miles southeast of Constantinople in return for his service as a commander on behalf of the Seljuk sultan. Some Turkish materials maintain that Ertuğrul and his associates were from the Kayı, one of the Oğuz tribes which had earlier played a major role in the settlement of Asia Minor. Relatively little is known specifically about Osman's youth. One explanation of his given name has cited an Arabic form, 'Uthman, which would seem to signify an early acquaintance with Islam; another version has suggested that it was taken from the Turkish name Ataman. Osman succeeded his father in 1281 or 1288; some have speculated that as an octogenarian, Ertuğrul yielded power before his death.

Various quaint tales have been recounted about Osman's early life. It is known that for advice he turned to a certain Edebali, who was respected as a wise and venerable old man. There probably is as much legend as fact to the account that Osman had a dream showing great rivers of the world outlined against a tree, which Edebali interpreted as a sign that his achievements would bring great and lasting renown upon his house. Other claims that Osman's fame as the founder of a mighty dynasty was foretold in portents from his own time may well have been the concoctions of later annalists. As the sheikh of a dervish order, Edebali may have exercised some spiritual influence upon Osman; some accounts maintain that he urged the Koran upon Osman as a condition of marrying his daughter. Osman had two wives, and among the nine children born to his household were Alaeddin, who became an important administrator, and Orhan, his eventual successor.

Life's Work

After he assumed power, Osman began a series of military campaigns which gradually cleared a path for the growth of his state. In the process, Turkish as well as Greek opponents had to be confronted. His first conquest of note was achieved in 1288, when he drove the neighboring Germiyan tribe from Karacahisar, to the south of his birthplace. At about that time he also wrested İnegöl, to the west, from Greek lords. Osman's armies captured outposts such as Bilecik and Körprühisar, which lay northwest of Söğüt in the direction of Nicaea (İznik). When Turcoman chieftains to the north relented in their raids on Byzantine positions, Osman's troops began to operate in that region as well. Some sources suggest that Osman conspired to murder his uncle (or cousin) Dündar, whom he may have regarded as a potential rival within his own ranks. Osman began to assert personal sovereignty by having his name read in the *hutbe*, or religious invocation, which customarily was delivered during Friday services. By 1299, Osman was sufficiently powerful to be able to terminate payments to Seljuk rulers or their Mongol suzerains. It seems more likely, however, that some form of tribute was disbursed during the early fourteenth century until this practice was discontinued after his death.

By this time, Osman's warriors were in a position to disrupt access along routes leading from Constantinople to inland cities; further raids were also mounted across the frontier. A decisive engagement came about when a Byzantine force, determined to check Turkish incursions, embarked on an expedition which marked the first effort on the part of the central government to meet the challenge of Ottoman power. At Bapheus (Koyunhisar), near Nicomedia (İzmit), on July 27, 1301, an army of about two thousand men met a Turkish force later estimated at about five thousand troops. Osman's men, who excelled in cavalry tactics, carried out a series of charges which broke through the lines of their heavily armored adversaries. They were prevented from turning this action into a rout only by the stalwart defense of Slavic mercenaries in the Byzantines' rear guard. Thereafter, Osman was left in a position to consolidate his gains. Although some action was necessary to repel Tatar irruptions in lands to the south, major objectives involved the reduction of Byzantine resistance in areas where Ottoman forces could dominate the countryside. By 1308, several fortresses were captured which brought Osman's armies within range of Prousa (Bursa), northwest of Mount Olympus, or Uludağ. Moreover, Ottoman units had already reached the Black Sea and by this time also ranged as far as the Sea of Marmara. An arc was thus drawn about that corner of Anatolia to hem in Byzantine holdings on their southern and eastern frontiers. Subsequently, Osman remained steadfast in his determination to subdue his opponents by landward expansion leading to the encirclement of local strongholds.

The nature of government under Osman has been represented in several ways, and it may well have been that there were some variations in the practices which he employed. Osman himself has been described as having swarthy features, with dark hair and a dark beard; he had long arms and was well built. He was reputed to have been a good horseman. When centuries later his portrait was made to show him as the first of his dynasty, he was depicted seated on his throne, a regal figure with a solemn and pensive demeanor. Throughout his rule, Osman was known as bey; the title of sultan came into use only during the late fourteenth century. While for a time he had resided in Karacahisar, after about twelve years Osman made Yenişehir his capital, possibly because of its location on a line south of Nicaea and east of Prousa. The extent to which Islamic conceptions of war and administration were important for early Ottoman institutions has been disputed. Different approaches indeed may have been used as Osman and his staff increasingly had to deal with diverse peoples in their vicinity. While in time later historians, both Ottoman and Western, often contended that the new state owed its expansion to the practice of *gaza*, or war for the faith, divisions along religious lines may not have been so sharply drawn as was the case during subsequent periods of struggle. The nucleus of Osman's army was composed of Turkish warriors who had settled in western Anatolia with their leaders.

Disorders and internecine conflict in other parts of Asia Minor probably led to the flight of Turcoman bands, which tended increasingly to settle on the frontier; some of them may have joined Osman's forces. When news of Osman's feats was received in other Muslim lands, men from adjoining areas also enrolled themselves in his armies. The distinction between religious warfare and raids into outlying Byzantine lands, however, may not have been very great, and for that matter villagers involved in local turmoil may have elected to support the Ottomans. Fiscal exactions on the part of Greek authorities quite possibly hastened this process. Some townspeople may also have valued the relative security provided by Ottoman rule. There is also evidence that in some cases lands were obtained by purchase or through marriages involving the families of local seigneurs. Some materials refer to the service of Greek Orthodox Christians with Osman's army. While many of them apparently embraced their commander's Muslim faith, forced conversion was not carried out as a matter of policy among conquered peoples at large. A certain number of renegades rose to important positions in the service of the Ottoman state. One of them, who became known as Köse Mihal, was from a prominent Greek family; after he was captured during an early raid, he became one of Osman's advisers on military matters. Moreover, while political authority was exercised on a local level through Osman's family, particularly his sons, who governed particular cities and towns, religious preferences were not always decisive on more basic concerns. It is known that at times Osman intervened to prevent Christians from being treated unfairly by Muslim merchants, and he also opposed the wholesale depredation of villages in Bithynia.

Apart from the outcome of military undertakings, not much is known about the last years of Osman's rule. In 1317, his son Orhan captured Atranos (Orhaneli), southwest of Mount Olympus. The Ottomans increasingly began to mobilize large armies to provide a show of strength which might daunt beleaguered Byzantine garrisons. A report from about 1330 maintained that the Ottomans could put about forty thousand men into the field. While this estimate may have been exaggerated, it has been taken as indicative of the growing strength of Ottoman forces during that period. In 1321, the maritime city of Mudanya, forty-five miles from Constantinople, was taken, and thus a logistical connection which was vital for the defense of Prousa was severed. While Ottoman armies also encircled Nicaea, preparing for its eventual capture under Orhan in 1331, want and deprivation gradually began to weaken the Byzantine defenders further south. The capture of Prousa, which as Bursa in its turn became the capital of the Ottoman state, was accomplished finally with minimum fighting. When it yielded, on April 6, 1326, Osman evidently had been inactive for some time; it is recorded that he received word from Orhan of the city's fall while he was on his deathbed. The source of his final illness has been described as an infirmity of the limbs. He had returned to Söğüt, and when he died later that year, he left his son an enlarged and strategically situated state with a growing military tradition that had already proved its capacity to endure struggle and conflict.

Summary

During the generations that followed, Ottoman power was established in other parts of Anatolia, and by the late fourteenth century significant conquests had been achieved in the Balkan peninsula as well. After certain setbacks, notably in the wake of Tamerlane's incursions into Asia Minor, sultans of the fifteenth century proceeded to subdue other lands in Europe and Asia. In 1453, Constantinople fell to the Ottomans, while elsewhere further expansion was carried out. Once the Ottoman Empire had become a great power, with its own distinctive ethos and means of government, historians began to trace the origins of the Ottoman state and in many instances attempted to find lofty antecedents and edifying principles in the acts of past rulers. In an early form, this tendency appeared in writers such as the poet-historian Ahmedi (c. 1334-1413). Other chronicles, such as those of Aşıkpaşazade (1400-c. 1484) and Mehmet Neşri (died c. 1520), which also formed the basis for later historical studies, depicted religious themes and doctrines of holy war in ways that were meant to stress the elements of continuity which they contended had existed throughout Ottoman history. Moreover, genealogical claims were added whereby the house of Osman was asserted to have descended from Noah and other illustrious figures. Occasionally, other legends were incorporated into historical writings. As a result, quite apart from obvious overstatements and embellishments, many of the ideals and principles of the ascendant Ottoman state were also attributed to Osman and his immediate successors. Traditions of this sort came to be regarded as part of Osman's heritage, and the epithet *gazi* often accompanied his name. Even during the waning years of the Ottoman Empire, such conceptions were widely accepted. During the first part of the twentieth century, some modifications were introduced, but the importance of religious warfare for the early Ottoman state was propounded in studies which otherwise showed more critical assessments of the sources and evidence that were available. Other scholars, however, have pointed to latitudinarian aspects of politics in frontier areas. Economic and demographic issues, in a broader context, have also been considered significant. There is still much that remains murky about Osman's life and work, however, and many details will perhaps remain beyond the realm of historical knowledge. The importance of his accomplishments, however, remains evident: By the unswerving and methodical pursuit of his objectives, Osman elevated his state to a position of consequence alongside other principalities, and his methods of rule facilitated the transition from Byzantine to Ottoman administration in a vital portion of Asia Minor. Although the success of his endeavors also depended on the lassitude of Byzantine government, and certainly he and his successors benefited from the fragmentation of political authority which affected much of the area, the combination of resolute persistence in military efforts and pragmatic administration of internal concerns was essential in Osman's role as the founder of the state which came to bear his name.

Bibliography
Cahen, Claude. *Pre-Ottoman Turkey: A General Survey of the Material and Spiritual Culture and History, c. 1071-1330*. Translated by J. Jones-Williams. New York: Taplinger, 1968. As an essential contribution to modern understanding of early Turkish states in Anatolia, this study considers political developments alongside an analysis of the social problems which affected the formation of the Seljuk sultanate and later principalities. The author, a noted French specialist, does not deal particularly with matters of personality or biography; rather, his work is useful in pointing to the broader historical forces which led to the eventual emergence of the Ottoman Empire.
Gibbons, Herbert Adams. *The Foundation of the Ottoman Empire: A History of the Osmanlis up to the Death of Bayezid I (1300-1403)*. New York: Century Co., 1916. This work is one of the more useful older studies of Ottoman history. Subsequent research has modified some conclusions, supplied details where formerly these were lacking, and turned away from the author's conceptions about early national and dynastic alignments. Nevertheless, as a narrative account this effort still warrants consideration. Osman's life and rule are discussed in the first chapter.

Inalcik, Halil. *The Ottoman Empire: The Classical Age, 1300-1600*. Translated by Norman Itzkowitz and Colin Imber. London: Weidenfeld and Nicolson, 1973. An important survey by a prominent modern scholar, this work is useful largely for its treatment of Ottoman institutions as they developed during the heyday of the empire. Although historical events are discussed in a cursory fashion, economic relations and the structure of government are considered in specific terms where fundamental patterns of administration are concerned.

_____. "The Question of the Emergence of the Ottoman State." *International Journal of Turkish Studies* 2 (1981): 71-79. A useful and important, though brief, restatement of historical theories regarding the Ottomans' position with respect to neighboring states; some emphasis is placed on population movements and military factors where they affected political developments.

Jennings, Ronald C. "Some Thoughts on the Gazi-Thesis." *Wiener Zeitschrift für die Kunde des Morgenlandes* 76 (1986): 151-161. This article considers problems with the theory of holy war as a factor promoting early Ottoman conquests. The author comments favorably upon arguments that evidence from later times has been taken too readily as applicable also to the period of Osman and his immediate successors.

Lindner, Rudi Paul. *Nomads and Ottomans in Medieval Anatolia*. Bloomington: Indiana University Press, 1983. A number of primary materials and anthropological studies have been used in this important work of scholarship and interpretation. In considering ways in which previous explanations for the Ottoman ascendancy have been inadequate, the author contends that often enough Muslim and Christian peoples worked together, and thus warfare for the faith was not always an inseparable part of Ottoman ideology.

Wittek, Paul. *The Rise of the Ottoman Empire*. London: Luzac, 1938. This brief study, which concisely summarizes many of the conclusions reached by an influential scholar, is significant as an exposition of the thesis that religious warfare supplied major impetus in the advance of Turkish states on the frontiers of the Byzantine Empire.

J. R. Broadus

OTTO THE GREAT

Born: November 23, 912; Saxony
Died: May 7, 973; Memleben, Thuringia
Area of Achievement: Government
Contribution: Otto's decisive victory over the Magyars shaped the fate of Europe; his coronation as emperor determined the course of German policy for centuries to come. Internally, he overcame tribalism by putting central administration in the unifying hands of the Church.

Early Life
In 912, when Otto the Great was born the first son of Matilda, second but first legitimate wife of his father, Henry, the latter was still Duke of Saxony, and the idea of a powerful central kingship in Germany was a rather remote one. Real power was held by the dukes of the various tribes, and the title "King of Germany" did not wield much more than ceremonial influence; it would be up to Otto to seek a change. When his father was elected king in 919 after the death of Conrad I, the last Franconian king from the line of Charlemagne, Henry I relied on his might as Duke of Saxony and did not require more than ceremonial homage to his royal position from his largely independent ducal colleagues.

Nevertheless, Henry I seemed to have planned more for his successor. Against the wishes of his wife, who favored Otto's younger son Henry, who had been born when his father was already king, Henry I promoted Otto as heir apparent and succeeded in winning for him the hand of an English princess. In 930, Otto married Edith, whose dowry, the town of Magdeburg, would play an important role in Otto's later politics.

Henry I had prepared the German nobility to elect Otto I at a council in Erfurt upon his death. Accordingly, a splendid coronation ceremony took place at the chapel of Aachen on August 7, 936. There, the nobles swore Otto an oath of fealty, and three archbishops anointed the king and his wife and crowned Otto on the marble chair which had belonged to Charlemagne. A contemporary illustration of the banquet which followed shows the king with his crown; he has long blond hair, a beard, and an open, intelligent face, and he is sitting elevated at a table where the four dukes of the kingdom are waiting on him, each holding an instrument signifying his ceremonial office of chamberlain, steward, cupbearer, and marshal. It is worth noting that Otto wears ceremonial Franconian clothes, not Saxonian clothes; thus, the illustration shows Otto's awareness of a new status in an office which had its own regal tradition.

Life's Work
The splendor of the coronation and the demonstration of unity and loyalty

Otto the Great

of dukes and nobles soon wore off and left Otto with a series of rebellions at home and increasing danger at the boundaries of his kingdom. In the south, the Magyars were barely held at bay and in the east the Slavs were pressing against the eastern marches; there, Otto relied on the military prowess of his margraves Herman Billung and Count Gero. Because of Otto's grants of land to Count Gero, his own half brother Thankmar, a bastard son of Henry I from his first, annulled marriage, felt slighted and joined Duke Eberhard of Franconia in an open rebellion against the king. Thus, hardly two years after his accession, Otto faced the first challenge to exercise the rights of his royal position.

Initial combat brought victory for Otto when Thankmar fell and Eberhard submitted to the king. In 939, however, his younger brother Henry, whom Otto had installed in Bavaria and who had been captured by the rebels, switched to the side of his captors. Suddenly, the rebellion gathered momentum. Eberhard turned coat again, the French king supported the insurgents, and Giselbert of Lotharingia and even the Archbishop of Mainz closed ranks against Otto. In this precarious position, Otto was saved by a clever attack on the disjointed rebels. A strike by two of his warlords brought the death of Eberhard and the drowning of Giselbert in the Rhine River. Thereafter, the rebellion faltered, and Otto forgave his brother, only to have Henry try to assassinate him in 941. Again, Otto showed largess when his brother approached him, penitent, on Christmas Day in the cathedral in Frankfurt. From that point onward, Henry proved loyal and valuable, and he obtained the duchy of Bavaria in 947.

After these early struggles to bring the quarrelsome and independent-minded German nobles in line, Otto tried to achieve control of the duchies through a series of dynastic marriages of his Saxon princes and princesses. To counteract the accumulation of hereditary privileges by the nobles, the king relied on ecclesiastical administrators and officers, who could have no legal offspring, to govern his royal holdings.

Yet Otto used the Church for more than interior administration. In the east, his biggest project was the establishment of the archbishopric of Magdeburg, which would serve as a base from which the land between the rivers Elbe and Oder could be pacified. This territory had long been dominated by the Slavs, whose belligerence presented a constant danger to the Saxonian lands. (Against the resistance of the Archbishop of Mainz, who feared a diminution of his own power, Otto finally succeeded in creating the new archdiocese in 968.)

In 951, when his authority had grown so much that even the Prince of Bohemia paid tribute to him, Otto had begun to turn his attention to Italy. An occasion to march southward arose with the reception of a distress call from Princess Adelaide of Burgundy, whom Berengar of Ivrea had imprisoned for her refusal to marry his son. Otto, a widower since 946, chased away Berengar, crowned himself King of the Lombards, and married Adelaide in Padua. Many contemporaries believed that they would soon see the imperial crown on Otto's head, and indeed, in 952, Otto was recognized as King of Italy.

Rome, however, did not welcome Otto, and at home his son Liudolf rebelled, fearing the influence and potential offspring of his new stepmother. Immediately, Otto marched north to discover a huge rebellion, which humiliated him. His battles with the insurgents were indecisive at best, but a new attack by the Magyars brought public opinion against the rebels. Under public pressure from the nobles, the uprising faltered, and Liudolf had to submit to his father early in 955.

Finally able to collect and command a great army, Otto attacked the invaders at their camp by the city of Augsburg. The ensuing battle on the Lechfeld was a complete victory for the Germans. Never again would the Magyars threaten Europe; instead, they gave up their existence as nomadic plunderers and settled to live peacefully in their homelands in Hungary.

Six years after his great victory, Otto followed the custom of appointing his heir as coregent and saw Otto II, his six-year-old son by Adelaide, elected and crowned King of Germany. Having regulated his succession, Otto received a call for help from Pope John XII, a rather worldly youth who found himself threatened by Berengar. That was Otto's chance to obtain the imperial crown for himself and thus to fashion himself after the great Charlemagne, who had been the last real emperor. On February 2, 962, after a successful arrival in Rome, Otto was crowned Emperor of the Holy Roman Empire of the German Nation, marking the beginning of a tradition for the German kings which would last almost a millennium—until the rise of Napoleon Bonaparte, who formally abolished the title in 1802.

A few days after his coronation, Otto signed a mutual treaty, the Privilegium Ottonianum, which bestowed land on the Papacy (the grant consisted of territories which were yet to be conquered) in exchange for the emperor's right to ratify papal elections. Theoretically, the popes were placed under imperial control, but in reality the Romans readily deposed officeholders whom they found objectionable. This practice began almost immediately after Otto engineered the deposition of John XII for committing treason with Berengar; the imperial nominee for the succession was himself deposed, then reinstated, but he died soon after. Otto's next choice, John XIII, was chased away by the Romans, who elected an antipope. To protect his candidate, Otto had to spend the years from 966 to 972 in Italy.

During this time, Otto also tried to contact Byzantium, which at first showed only arrogance to the German upstarts. After a new ruler came to power in the East, Otto's diplomatic mission succeeded, and he obtained the hand of the gifted princess Theophano for his son Otto II, who married her in 972.

Otto the Great

At the height of his power, Otto I returned to Germany to hold a great assembly of his court at Quedlinburg in Saxony on March 23, 973. This time, the ceremonies were less perfunctory and reflected the real power of the person venerated as king and emperor. After a reign of thirty-seven years, at age sixty, Otto died a few weeks later in the adjacent town of Memleben and was put to rest beside his first wife, Edith.

Summary

Otto the Great was the first king of Germany to consolidate real power and authority for the kingship and give a clearer sense of national unity to the tribes of Germany. His defeat of the Magyars secured the boundaries of the later empire in the southeast, and his expansion to the Oder River created a stable area for German settlement, the limits of which would mark the eastern frontier for a long time.

Otto's grasping of the imperial throne gave his kingship additional prestige and influence over the rich cities of northern Italy, but it also allowed for direct German involvement in Roman and Italian politics, which had the potential to strain the resources and muddle the interests of the German rulers and their people. Further, Otto's coronation laid the foundation for a mutual dependency and rivalry between emperor and Pope; in a crippling struggle for power, both sides would vie for control over each other, with the Pope claiming superiority over the emperor because of his ultimate spiritual authority and the latter adamantly refusing the Pope's meddling in imperial affairs. Similarly, Otto's reliance on the clergy to administer his kingdom in order to weaken local power would prove to be a double-edged sword, lending unity to the empire at the price of ecclesiastical (and, consequently, Romish) power in Germany.

Culturally, Otto's reign brought Germany in touch with the almost forgotten legacy of the great Mediterranean cultures of antiquity and led to a general intellectual flourishing which has been called the "Ottonian renaissance." The fine arts thrived, some monasteries became true centers of academic life, and the written documents of the era show sophistication of learning.

Bibliography

Fleckenstein, Josef. *Early Medieval Germany*. Translated by Bernard S. Smith. New York: North Holland Publishing Co., 1978. Apart from providing an excellent portrayal of life in Germany around Otto's time, this work provides solid information on Otto's life and puts his achievements and struggles in the larger context of German history.

Haight, Anne Lyon, ed. *Hroswitha of Gandersheim: Her Life, Time, Works, and a Comprehensive Bibliography*. New York: Hroswitha Club, 1965. Contains translations of this medieval chronicler's works. Hroswitha's contemporary account of Otto's reign reads well and is an invaluable source for further studies.

Henderson, Ernest F. *History of Germany in the Middle Ages*. Reprint. New York: Haskell House, 1968. Chapters 8 and 9 offer an informed, readable account of Otto's rule as king and emperor and present his achievements in a larger historic context. Although this work was written in 1894, it is still a useful historical source.

Hill, Boyd H., Jr. *Medieval Monarchy in Action*. New York: Barnes and Noble Books, 1972. The introduction to this collection of translations of selected documents of the period has an informed chapter on Otto I which provides a precise overview of his reign.

——————. *The Rise of the First Reich*. New York: John Wiley and Sons, 1969. A collection of translations of contemporary sources, such as Widukind's chronicles and the writings of Liutprand of Cremona on Otto. Fourteen plates of medieval art works and a map of Germany give the reader an illustrated view of Otto's era.

Reinhart Lutz

OU-YANG HSIU

Born: 1007; Mien-yang (modern Szechwan Province), China
Died: 1072; Ying-chou (modern Anhwei Province), China
Areas of Achievement: Literature and government
Contribution: A political figure and innovative writer of prose and poetry, Ou-yang Hsiu substantially shaped the Confucian tradition which dominated China for almost a thousand years.

Early Life

Ou-yang Hsiu's father held an office in the Chinese civil service system. When Ou-yang Hsiu was a very young child, his father died. His mother undertook his education. As he grew to young adulthood, the Chinese society of the Sung period (960-1279) was undergoing marked change. The previous dynasty, the T'ang (618-907), had been dominated by aristocratic families and influenced by the military. During this period, however, the economy had expanded rapidly, and the gentry, steeped in Confucian learning, were becoming more powerful. To increase their influence, they sought to regularize the civil service system, entrance to which was gained increasingly through a series of examinations in Confucian writings. Because Confucian learning was a step to political power, writing style and the careful selection of classical models in prose and poetry were of utmost importance. The model style of the late T'ang and early Sung, known as "parallel prose," had grown rigid and formalistic, enforcing conventions of length, grammar, and diction upon writers.

Ou-yang Hsiu, studying alone, discovered the works of an influential T'ang period writer, Han Yü (768-824). Believing Han Yü's style, called *ku-wen* (ancient style), to be a much better vehicle for expressing ideas than parallel prose, Ou-yang began to practice it. Because he wrote in the unconventional *ku-wen* style, he failed his first two attempts at the examinations, in 1023 and 1027. The resourceful young man thereupon presented an established scholar, Yen Shu, with samples of his writings in the *ku-wen* style. Yen Shu was so impressed that he began to sponsor Ou-yang, who rose rapidly, gaining his doctorate in 1030 with very high marks.

Life's Work

Ou-yang Hsiu began his career as a prefectural level (county) judge from 1031 to 1034 in Loyang, formerly the capital city. Confucian bureaucrats led lives of studied leisure, with minimal official duties. They vied in writing poetry and prose and engaged in rounds of banquets. Ou-yang wrote many *tz'u* (songs), poems meant to be sung to popular tunes. His *tz'u* were lively songs of love and romance, often performed by the singing girls who attended the fetes. During this period, Ou-yang married, but his wife died in childbirth.

In 1034, his reputation as a writer came to the attention of the court. He was promoted to the position of collator of texts at the capital, K'ai-feng, where he compiled an annotated catalog of the Imperial Libraries. He increasingly distinguished himself as a prose writer in both the *ku-wen* style and the wooden parallel style in which court documents were still written. He remarried, but he lost his second wife to childbirth in 1035.

Ou-yang was drawn into a battle between conservatives and reformers, triggered by an official, Fan Chung-yen, who attempted to make the court and the emperor more responsible to the opinions of the Confucian bureaucrats. The Confucian political system had many merits, such as the great stability and continuity that it provided Chinese society, but it also had many defects. The system was, like Confucianism itself, rigidly hierarchical, based upon differences in gender, age, education, and social status. It was difficult to challenge established authority, and political quarrels often involved vituperative personal attacks. In the increasingly bitter conflict between reformers and conservatives, Ou-yang's patron, Fan Chung-yen, was demoted. Ou-yang courageously came to Fan's defense and was exiled in 1036, as he had expected. In 1037, Ou-yang married his third wife, with whom he would live the rest of his days.

Posted to a remote region of Hupeh Province, Ou-yang wrote a history of the interregnum states (907-960) between the T'ang and Sung dynasties, *Hsin Wu-tai shih* (1036; the new history of the Five Dynasties), which eventually became part of the official corpus of dynastic histories, an unusual honor for a work that was not produced under court direction. Confucians value historical studies as the highest form of intellectual work, believing that history reveals models for human behavior.

The tide at court turned in favor of the reformers, and in 1040 Ou-yang Hsiu was invited back, under the patronage of Fan Chung-yen, but he declined. Henceforth he came to be known as a man who would not trade upon friendship for personal advantage, a rare stand within the Confucian world. He was soon recalled to his former post as collator of texts. By 1042, the reformers were dominant, and Ou-yang became policy critic, then drafting official, both influential posts.

Ou-yang's powerful writing and reputation as an independent thinker made him a key figure in the reform program, but clique fighting sharpened. When Fan Chung-yen was accused in 1043 of forming a "faction," for which there was no place in the Confucian system, Ou-yang wrote a remarkable essay on partisanship in which he argued that it was proper for gentlemen to ally to express positions on political issues. The essay became a classic political statement and was denounced by authoritarian emperors as late as the eighteenth century.

The iconoclastic reformers were very vulnerable, and soon their fortunes declined again; many were sent into exile. Ou-yang was attacked on moral grounds, perhaps because of his reputation as the *bon vivant* author of romantic songs. In 1045, he was accused of having sexual relations with his sister's stepchild, a very serious charge in the family-centered Confucian culture. Although acquitted, he was again exiled, to Ying-chou, where he served in a series of prefectural governorships. One of the values for which Ou-yang was later remembered was his insistence that gentlemen, though in exile, should not be bitter but should cultivate their inner essence and live productive and carefree lives. He lived out these values in Ying-chou.

Ou-yang's mother died in 1052. Although he could have returned to court shortly thereafter, he withdrew for the full two years of formal mourning sometimes practiced at the death of a parent. His mother occupies a special place in Confucian legend, along with the mother of the great philosopher Mencius (c. 372-c. 289 B.C.), who also educated her son under adverse circumstances.

During this exile, Ou-yang's reputation grew. His *shih* (poems), though they were valued for their adherence to classical tradition, had a carefree and lighthearted air which was rare in previous poetry. Their serenity, achieved through Confucian self-cultivation, continued to be influential in later generations. He also compiled an important catalog of archaeological artifacts. Ou-yang was very happy during this period, doing the things that he loved, which included hosting literary gatherings at his "Old Drunkard's Pavilion," where abundant wine was poured by witty and attractive singing girls. In 1054, however, he was recalled to court.

At court, Ou-yang produced another history, *Hsin T'ang shu* (1060; the new T'ang history). In 1057, he conducted the doctoral examinations, insisting that they be written in *ku-wen* and be judged on their substance, not their adherence to classical forms. In 1059, he wrote one of the most beautiful pieces in Chinese literature, "The Sounds of Autumn," a *fu* (rhapsodic prose poem). The *fu*, like parallel prose, was a classical form which had grown stiff and formal. Ou-yang Hsiu and his protégé Su Shih (1037-1101) managed to revivify the genre.

Ou-yang Hsiu next served as Prefect of K'ai-feng, as policy critic, and as assistant chief minister, his highest office. He now counseled gradual reforms to avoid the backlash fatal to earlier efforts. He was instrumental in promoting a period of benevolent rule under two emperors between 1060 and 1066. Problems arose at court, however, and in 1067, enemies charged that Ou-yang had committed incest with his daughter-in-law.

Although the ensuing investigation cleared him, Ou-yang Hsiu, now sixty years old, resigned. He was appointed to a post near his estates in Ying-chou. In 1069, another former protégé, the statesman-poet Wang An-shih (1021-1086), undertook a doomed program of radical reforms. Criticizing the program as ill-advised, Ou-yang repeatedly requested permission to resign. Finally, in 1071, it was granted. He returned to his estate in Ying-chou, but he did not long enjoy his freedom, for in the summer of 1072 he died of unknown causes.

Summary

Ou-yang Hsiu made a lasting mark in many areas of human endeavor. As the "Literary Master" of the Sung period, his prose and poetry became models for later generations. He contributed major works in history and archaeology; his methods for writing genealogies became the standard in China. He was a much sought-after writer of epitaphs, one of the highest Confucian literary pursuits. His prose and poetry have been translated into the world's major languages and may be found in standard anthologies. While achieving these heights, he also had an important political career.

Like many universal minds, Ou-yang Hsiu was not to be the greatest name of his generation in any one field. His friends Su Shih and Mei Yao-ch'ien (1002-1062) surpassed him in writing poetry, his political rival Ssu-ma Kuang (1019-1086) in writing history. Nevertheless, because of the breadth of his abilities and his optimistic and lighthearted attitude, coupled with intense self-cultivation, it was Ou-yang Hsiu who became a model scholar, political figure, and Confucian gentleman for generations of Chinese.

Bibliography

Egan, Ronald C. *The Literary Works of Ou-yang Hsiu (1007-1072)*. Cambridge: Cambridge University Press, 1984. Includes a good critical introduction to Sung literature. An excellent analysis of the writings of Ou-yang Hsiu, with much biographical information. The appendices include translations of some of his prose pieces, and his poetry is reproduced throughout.

Franke, Herbert. *Sung Biographies*. 2 vols. Wiesbaden, West Germany: Steiner, 1976. The standard biographic reference for important Sung figures, including those mentioned in this piece. Unfortunately, many of the entries are in German. The entry for Ou-yang (in volume 2) is by James T. Liu and is a concise statement of material found in his work *Ou-Yang Hsiu*, listed below.

Gernet, Jacques. *Daily Life in China on the Eve of the Mongol Invasion, 1250-1276*. Stanford, Calif.: Stanford University Press, 1970. A description of late Sung China, with a physical and social description of the city of K'ai-feng, the Sung capital where Ou-yang passed so much of his career. Although Ou-yang is mentioned but once, the work gives helpful descriptions of daily life among the urban gentry and of the nature of a great Chinese city.

Lai, Monica, and T. C. Lai. *Rhapsodic Essays from the Chinese*. Hong Kong: Kelly and Walsh, 1979. This work reproduces six essays in the *fu* form, including Ou-yang Hsiu's famous piece "The Sounds of Autumn." The work includes reproductions of paintings depicting Ou-yang writing the piece, as well as facsimiles of the original in his calligraphy and a printed contemporary edition. It also includes another important *fu*, "The Red Cliff," written by Su Shih.

Liu, James T. *Ou-Yang Hsiu: An Eleventh-Century Neo-Confucianist*. Stanford, Calif.: Stanford University Press, 1967. The standard study of Ou-yang Hsiu, with more attention to biography and political life than in the work of Egan, listed above. Based upon a wide reading of classical and modern Chinese sources. Liu should be considered the foremost biographer of Ou-yang.

Nivison, David S. "A Neo-Confucian Visionary: Ou-yang Hsiu." In *Change in Sung China*, edited by James T. Liu and Peter J. Golas. Lexington, Mass.: D. C. Heath and Co., 1969. This essay places Ou-yang Hsiu in the Confucian tradition. Other essays in the volume give much information on the political and social context of Sung China.

Nivison, David S., and Arthur F. Wright, eds. *Confucianism in Action*. Stanford, Calif.: Stanford University Press, 1969. An excellent series of essays on Confucianism, with frequent references to the ideas and influence of Ou-yang Hsiu. Some of the introductory material overlaps with Nivison's essay, above.

Yoshikawa, Kojiro. *An Introduction to Sung Poetry*. Translated by Burton Watson. Cambridge, Mass.: Harvard University Press, 1967. The author places Ou-yang Hsiu in the context of Sung poetry, crediting him with a major poetic innovation: the atmosphere of serenity which distinguishes Sung poetry from that of the T'ang period. Many of Ou-yang's poems are reproduced here.

Jeffrey G. Barlow

OVID
Publius Ovidius Naso

Born: March 20, 43 B.C.; Sulmo, Italy
Died: A.D. 17; Tomis on the Black Sea
Area of Achievement: Literature
Contribution: While his contemporaries Vergil and Horace were glorifying the Roman Empire or harking back to sober republican virtues, Ovid wittily celebrated the senses. He also preserved for later generations many of the classical myths, although he treated the gods with the same irreverence as he did his fellow mortals.

Early Life

Publius Ovidius Naso was born in 43 B.C. in central Italy. As his family was a locally prominent one, he enjoyed the advantages of an education and preparation for an official career. Ovid's youth was a period of political chaos. Rome was still nominally a republic, but Julius Caesar had made himself dictator. When Caesar was murdered in the year before Ovid's birth, the Roman world was plunged into civil war. Peace was not truly restored until fourteen years later.

First, Octavian, great-nephew and adopted son of Julius Caesar, combined with Marc Antony and Marcus Aemilius Lepidus to defeat the chiefs of the republican party, Marcus Janius Brutus and Gaius Cassius Longinus. Then, Lepidus was shunted aside, and Octavian and Antony entered into a protracted struggle for power. In 30 B.C., the year after his disastrous naval defeat at Actium, Antony and his Egyptian ally and lover, Cleopatra VII, committed suicide. Octavian was the complete military ruler of Rome. By 27 B.C., the senate had conferred upon him the official title Imperator, or emperor, and the honorary title Caesar Augustus, or the august one.

The extent to which these wars affected Ovid's family is not known, but the eventual outcome should have proved beneficial for him. He had become a poet, and the Augustan Age was a favorable time for poets. Gaius Maecenas, a chief counselor to Augustus, was the protector and financier of poets. Yet the fun-loving Ovid was destined to squander his advantages and fall afoul of his emperor.

Life's Work

Although Ovid was born one hundred miles east of Rome, he was soon exposed to the atmosphere of the capital. As the scion of an established family, he was sent to Rome at the age of twelve to be trained in the law. His arrival at the capital roughly coincided with Augustus' final victory over Antony. The era of the Pax Romana had begun.

Ovid was twenty-two years younger than Horace and almost thirty years younger than Vergil. Since he had been a child during the civil war, his experience of those terrible times had been less immediate than that of the older poets. Vergil and Horace were conservative in temperament and viewed the emperor, despite his new title, as the embodiment of the traditional Roman virtues. Their approval of Augustus was apparently sincere as well as politically and financially expedient—Horace, who had fallen into poverty as a young man through his support of the ill-fated Brutus, received the gift of a farm from Maecenas in 33 B.C. Ovid, however, was not a member of Vergil and Horace's circle. His companions were young and less closely associated with the regime.

Ovid entered the Roman civil service but quickly abandoned the law for poetry. He was a born poet, who once wrote that whatever he tried to say came out in verse. For one element of patrician Roman society, the new era of peace and prosperity was a perfect time for pleasure seeking. Ovid was soon the darling of this brilliant society. He became a professional poet, and his social success equaled his literary success. His themes were often frivolous, but he treated them with great elegance and wit. Technically, his verse was dazzling. The tone of his work was skeptical and irreverent. He practically thumbed his nose at the official solemnity and high-mindedness of the Augustan establishment. *Gravitas* might be the prime Roman virtue, but it was not the poetic mode for Ovid.

Little is known of Ovid's appearance or personal behavior. A tradition grew up, totally unsubstantiated by evidence, that Ovid was a rake and a womanizer—a sort of ancient precursor to John Wilmot, Earl of Rochester, and George Gordon, Lord Byron. The legendary Ovid, the good-looking playboy, is largely the product of two of his poems. The first, the *Amores* (c. 20 B.C.; English translation), was also his first published work. The *Amores* unblushingly recounts the conquests of a Roman Don Juan. The second, the *Ars amatoria* (c. 2 B.C.; *Art of Love*), is a tongue-in-cheek seduction manual.

The *Art of Love* could hardly have endeared Ovid to Augustus. While the emperor's propagandists were portraying a Rome turning back to the virtuousness, dignity, and piety of its forefathers, the impudent Ovid portrayed an amoral and libertine Rome, where panting ladies were ripe for the plucking. Since generalizations must of necessity distort, both Romes probably existed simultaneously. In addition to being wickedly amusing, the poem reveals many psychologically valid insights into the gamesmanship of love. Ovid recommends the theater, the arena, dinner parties, and large festivals as the most likely sources of pliant females. He artfully plays upon the stereotypes, already centuries old in his day, of man as an unskilled dissembler and woman as a born actress. His advice to the would-be gallant is practical in nature: Bind your mistress to you through habit; it is the most potent thing in life. Never, even playfully, discuss any of her defects. Do not be so foolhardy as to demand her age; this information is not to be had. Last, if she is over thirty-five, do not be distressed; older women are more practiced, and therefore more desirable, lovers.

Ovid's passing reference to pederasty is made without apology and suggests that it was an all too common practice in his society. Perhaps the tone and theme of the poem are crystallized in one line, Ovid's assertion that after dark there are no ugly women. Yet the poem contains self-mockery too. Of the role poetry plays in wooing a woman, the poet says: Send her gold rather than verses for, even if they are perfectly written and perfectly recited, she will consider them a trifling gift at best.

Over the next seven years, Ovid worked on his masterpiece, the *Metamorphoses* (c. A.D. 8; English translation). The poem consists of fifteen books which retell the stories of classical mythology, beginning with the creation of the world. The title means "transformations," especially by supernatural means, but it is only loosely descriptive. Although many of the tales recount the transformation of human beings into animals or inanimate things, others do not. Fortunately for posterity, Ovid retold so many stories that his poem became a principal sourcebook of classical myths. One cannot read the great triumvirate of English literature—Geoffrey Chaucer, William Shakespeare, and John Milton—without noticing how often they allude to the *Metamorphoses* or choose Ovid's version of a familiar myth.

Some ancient writers later accused Ovid, with justification, of lacking a proper respect for the gods. It is clear that the author of the *Metamorphoses* did not believe the stories he was telling or in the deities who populated them. It is equally clear that he had matured artistically since the composition of the *Art of Love*. The *Metamorphoses* is, like the *Art of Love*, witty, charming, and beautifully constructed; still, it is also more comic than frivolous, often seriocomic, occasionally even tragicomic. Ovid modernized the poem in a way that should have pleased the emperor. He portrays the ascension of the murdered Julius Caesar into the heavens, where he becomes a star, and hints that Augustus himself will one day be changed into a god.

By A.D. 8, however, Ovid was in deep trouble with his emperor. Although he was by that time Rome's leading poet, he was tried before Augustus on a charge which history has not recorded and was banished from Rome. Possibly the emperor's disapproval of the *Art of Love* had finally brought about the poet's downfall. Yet that poem was completed about 1 B.C. and had been in published form since A.D. 1. Why would the emperor wait seven years before acting against Ovid? Scholars suggest that the poet's offense may have been his involvement in a scandal, possibly one associated with the emperor's daughter Julia. For whatever reason, he was banished to Tomis (located in modern-day Romania), an outpost on the Black Sea. Tomis was a cultural and intellectual backwater—and dangerous besides, since it was menaced by hostile border tribesmen.

For the next nine years, Ovid pleaded, through a series of epistles in verse known as the *Tristia* (after A.D. 8; *Sorrows*), for the lifting of his punishment. Augustus did not relent, nor did his stepson Tiberius, who succeeded him in A.D. 14. Given the excesses which were eventually to mark that reign, one wonders how corrupting the poet's presence could have been in the Rome of Tiberius. Nevertheless, Ovid died still in exile in A.D. 17.

Summary

Aeneas, Vergil's self-sacrificing Trojan prince, and the manliness and common sense of Horace's odes express one aspect of the Augustan Age. It was probably the dominant aspect, stressing as it does the patriotism of the *Aeneid* (c. 29-19 B.C.) and the traditional religious, moral, and social values of the *Odes* (23 B.C., 13 B.C.). Ovid, however, writing in the sensual tradition of Catullus, reflects another aspect of the age.

The Rome of Vergil and Horace gave to the Western world a legal system and a framework of political unity which only a serious and an industrious people could have devised. Yet there was also in the Roman nature a playfulness, a highly developed aesthetic sensibility, and a *joie de vivre*; these are the qualities found in Ovid's poetry. All men in every age are capable of excesses and base behavior, but the three great Augustan poets reflect the two faces of the Roman Empire at its best.

It is ironic that it was the skeptical Ovid who, in his *Metamorphoses*, breathed life back into the debilitated gods of Rome. Ovid lived at the dawn of the Christian era, and within a few centuries the Christians' monotheism would sweep aside the polytheism of Greece and Rome. Nothing is so dead as a dead idea, but Ovid preserved the gods as intriguing characters in dozens of charming stories told in elegant verse. His compendium of mythological tales has been so influential that few indeed are the great works of Western literature which contain no allusion to Ovid's *Metamorphoses*.

Bibliography

Binns, J. W., ed. *Ovid*. London: Routledge and Kegan Paul, 1973. An entry in the series Greek and Latin Studies: Classical Literature and Its Influence. Composed of seven essays by British and American scholars. The first five address the poetry itself, while the last two address Ovid's influence in the Middle Ages and the sixteenth century.

Brewer, Wilmon. *Ovid's "Metamorphoses" in European Culture*. Boston: Cornhill Publishing Co., 1933. A three-volume companion work to an English translation in blank verse. Begins with a long introductory survey which includes much biographical detail. Very valuable, because every story in the poem is discussed in the light of its cultural and literary antecedents, then of later works for which it served as antecedent.

Hoffman, Richard L. *Ovid and "The Canterbury Tales."* Philadelphia: University of Pennsylvania Press, 1966. Since John Dryden first compared Ovid and Chaucer in 1700, many Chaucerians have remarked that the great English poet studied, imitated, and relied on Ovid above all other authors. This study treats the *Metamorphoses* as a predecessor of *The Canterbury Tales*.

Rand, Edward Kennard. *Ovid and His Influence*. Boston: Marshall Jones Co., 1925. Reprint. New York: Cooper Square, 1963. Part of the series Our Debt to Greece and Rome. A professor of Latin poses the question: What does our age owe to a professed roué, a writer so subtle and rhetorical as to strike some as thoroughly insincere? His 184 pages answer that question.

Syme, Ronald. *History in Ovid*. Oxford: Clarendon Press, 1978. Concentrating on Ovid's latest poems, the author develops a kind of manual designed to cover life and letters in the last decade of Caesar Augustus. Valuable because of the relative obscurity of that period.

Thibault, John C. *The Mystery of Ovid's Exile*. Berkeley: University of California Press, 1964. The author examines various hypotheses about Ovid's exile, describes their content, and evaluates the evidence and the cogency of the arguments.

Patrick Adcock

PACHACUTI

Born: c. 1391; probably Cuzco, Peru
Died: 1471; near Cuzco, Peru
Areas of Achievement: Government and warfare
Contribution: Pachacuti, through personal courage, brilliant political sense, and administrative genius, was primarily responsible for the creation of the Inca Empire in its final form.

Early Life

Pachacuti (Cusi Inca Yupanqui), the ninth emperor of the Inca in a direct line from the perhaps legendary Manco Capac, who founded the dynasty about the year 1200, was, with his son Topa Inca Yupanqui and his grandson Huayna Capac, one of the three greatest Inca emperors. Since he was said to have been about eighty years of age when he died in 1471, he presumably was born in Cuzco, the capital, about 1391, the son of Viracocha Inca and Runtu Coya. As the son of the emperor, Pachacuti was thoroughly educated in military science and the art of administration, but almost nothing is known about his life before the dramatic events of 1437-1438 brought him to the throne.

The Inca had no written historical records, and what is known of their origins is to be found in chronicles written after the Spanish Conquest. These were based on the memory of native historians, however, who used the *quipu*, knotted ropes which served as memory devices, to recall the events of Inca history. Certainly from the beginnings of Pachacuti's reign the chronicles must be considered generally reliable, though it is possible that he may have dictated an account of his accession in order to justify the legitimacy of his claim to the throne.

During the reign of Viracocha, the Inca Empire, an area from the country north of Cuzco to the shores of Lake Titicaca, was threatened by various tribes on its borders to the north and west. In 1437, the Chanca, a warrior tribe in the Apurimac Valley northwest of Cuzco, defeated the Quechua, thus upsetting the balance of power which the Inca had maintained among their enemies, and pushed through the Quechua country to the Inca frontier. Viracocha, apparently assuming that Cuzco could not be held, fled the city, while Pachacuti became the leader of a cabal which was determined to defend Cuzco and to put Pachacuti on the throne. He organized the city's defenses, and, even though the Chanca actually broke into the city itself, he drove them out. In one account he is described as wearing a lionskin as he personally led his troops in battle. Later he won a great victory over the Chanca at their stronghold of Ichupampa, west of Cuzco, virtually destroying them as a tribe, and in 1438 he became emperor. At this time, by one account, his father gave him the name Pachacuti, translated variously as "cataclysm" or "Earth upside down," which suggests that even at that time he was determined to change the Inca Empire completely.

Life's Work

The chronicles do not agree on the exact nature of Pachacuti's claim to the throne. According to some, he was Viracocha's eldest son and thus his legitimate heir but was, in effect, disinherited by his father on behalf of Inca Urcon, a younger brother. By another account he was a younger son, and when Viracocha resigned the throne to Inca Urcon the latter made Pachacuti governor of Cuzco while he retired to the enjoyment of his vices. What is certain is that Pachacuti, after his victory in the Chanca War, made Viracocha his virtual prisoner, was given his blessing, and, by methods which are not clear, brought about the death of Inca Urcon. Viracocha died soon after.

Pachacuti spent the first three years of his reign in Cuzco, consolidating power and creating an entirely new leadership; then, in 1441, he embarked on a three-year tour of inspection of the empire and the reconquest of the territory of those tribes which had rebelled against Inca rule during the Chanca incursion. Only then did he undertake the military campaigns which made him the most remarkable conqueror of any American Indian leader.

His first campaign, in 1444, took him into the Urupampa Valley, in an area now called Vilcapampa, north of Cuzco, and then west into Vilcas. Later he conquered the Huanca tribe in Huanmanca (the modern departments of Junín and Huancavelica) and the provinces of Tarma, Pumpu, Yauyu, and Huarochiri. When Hastu Huaraca, the defeated Chanca leader, organized opposition to the Inca in the Apurimac Valley, Pachacuti again defeated him in battle and achieved his submission and a grant of warriors for the Inca army. Later he won a great victory at Corampa, and in a campaign against the Soras, which culminated in a successful two-year siege of Challomarca, their capital, he achieved virtual control of all central Peru south of Ecuador. He then sent his Chanca auxiliaries south into Collao, followed with his main army, defeated the Canas at Ayavire, at the end of Lake Titicaca, and in a decisive battle at Pucara eliminated Collao power. This military victory was probably in 1450.

Pachacuti's firm control of the imperial administration and of the armies by which it was maintained is indicated by the fact that when he dispatched his general Capac Yupanqui into the province of Chucurpu and then learned that Capac had exceeded his orders and had advanced farther into the lands beyond Chucurpu, he ordered him back to Cuzco and had him executed for disobedience, even though the expedition had added more land to the empire than he had anticipated.

By 1457, Pachacuti had conquered all the territory between the coastal range of Peru and the valley of the Marañón. In 1463, he gave command of the army to his son (and heir), Topa Inca. This force of forty thousand men began in 1464 the subjugation of Chimor, an advanced civilization on the northern Peruvian coast which was, in a sense, Greece to Cuzco's Rome. By 1470, with the fall of the Chimor capital of Chanchan (modern-day Trujillo), this conquest was complete. Other commanders under Pachacuti's orders conquered the territory beyond Lake Titicaca and as far south as the Atacama Desert in northern Chile. In all, these conquests created an empire of sixteen million people, extending from Ecuador to northern Chile and Bolivia.

If Pachacuti were only a conqueror he would be less remarkable. In fact, his supreme achievement was the creation of a political structure which survived with great stability until the civil war which broke out over the question of imperial succession shortly before the arrival of the Spanish. It was Pachacuti who inaugurated the system of populating conquered lands with colonists who eventually intermarried with the local population and gave them identity as Inca, and he created the *mitimaes* system, by which dissident elements in a conquered territory would be moved as colonists to another region where Inca rule had been accepted. He also instituted a system of runners to carry royal messages, which gave the empire the kind of coherence that only rapid communication could make possible.

In religious matters, Pachacuti simplified and redefined the rites of the Incas and incorporated the deities of conquered peoples into the Inca pantheon. Above all, he was determined to make each conquered nation an organic part of a larger whole. Often after conquering a nation he would take its king to Cuzco, bestow upon him lavish gifts and hospitality, and then send him home to rule as his proconsul. He also completely reorganized the imperial school in Cuzco, where not only the sons of the Inca caste but also those of conquered lords studied economics, government, military science, the arts and sciences of the Inca, and Quechua, the language of the empire.

Many of the engineering achievements of Pachacuti are still seen in Peru. In 1440, he began the complete rebuilding of Cuzco, and at about the same time the great fortress of Sacsahuaman, the "house of the sun" north of the city, was begun by twenty thousand laborers, a monument so massive that it was not completed until 1508, during the reign of his grandson. Though scholars no longer agree whether Pachacuti ordered the construction of Machu Picchu, it is probable that he was responsible for its later development as a bastion of Inca defense. He also encouraged terracing to take advantage of the steep Andean terrain for agriculture and is credited with the development of the greatest Inca irrigation systems.

When Topa Inca returned from his conquest of Chimor and Ecuador, Pachacuti partially resigned the throne to him, serving until his death in 1471 as a kind of coregent. This arrangement ensured a smooth transfer of power and enabled Topa to embark on his further conquests when he became emperor, though some accounts suggest that as a result of Pachacuti's declining physical powers, he had no choice but to share power with his son.

Summary

Pachacuti was not only a valiant warrior but also a statesman with a clear understanding of the requirements of imperial administration. The laws and the political structure which he created survived almost a century until his descendants, forgetting the need for imperial unity in their quarrels over the succession to the throne, weakened the empire at precisely the moment that the soldiers of Pizarro landed on the Peruvian coast in 1532. It seems unlikely, in fact, that the Spanish conquest of Peru would have been possible, at least with Pizarro's small force, if it had been attempted when Pachacuti was at the height of his power.

Though Pachacuti's wars with those immediate neighbors who had conspired against the Inca were fought to the death and often culminated in massacre, his conquests through the rest of his empire were followed by liberal treatment of his subjects. For Pachacuti, war was a necessary evil, the last application of political methods to achieve Inca hegemony and the order which, under his leadership, accompanied it. If war in the reigns of his predecessors was a means of personal aggrandizement not unlike hunting or sport, it was for Pachacuti the work of trained professionals and an instrument of public policy. His armies fought aggressively, but their success was in large part a result of Pachacuti's attention to logistic detail. When their victories had been achieved, he directed their energies to the administration of the conquered territory and the creation of those public works that would make them more productive.

For these reasons, Pachacuti must be considered not only the greatest conqueror among all American Indian leaders but also the most brilliant ruler.

Bibliography

Brundage, Burr Cartwright. *Empire of the Inca*. Norman: University of Oklahoma Press, 1963. A thorough discussion of Inca civilization from its origins until the arrival of the Spanish, this study synthesizes all the chronicles and scholarship to provide the most probable account of these events.

Cieza de León, Pedro de. *The Incas*. Edited and translated by Harriet de Onis. Norman: University of Oklahoma Press, 1959. Cieza's account, first published in 1553, is the most objective early account of the Incas. This objectivity and annotations by Victor Wolfgang von Hagen make it a basic text for understanding Inca history.

Cobo, Bernabé. *History of the Inca Empire*. Edited and translated by Roland Hamilton. Austin: University of Texas Press, 1979. Cobo was a Jesuit priest who went to Peru in 1599 as a missionary to the Indians. Most of his manuscript was lost; what remained, published in 1653, was largely concerned with pre-Columbian America. It is based on Cobo's archival research in Mexico City and Lima and on interviews with descendants of the Inca royal dynasty.

Garcilaso de la Vega. *Royal Commentaries of the Incas and General History of Peru*. Translated by Harold V. Livermore. 2 vols. Austin: University of Texas Press, 1966. Complete in 1604 and first published in 1609 as *Primera parte de los comentarios reales*, Garcilaso's history of Peru cannot be ignored but must be used with caution and corrected by reference to Cobo and Cieza de León.

Hyams, Edward, and George Ordish. *The Last of the Incas*. London: Longman, 1963. This work is primarily concerned with the Spanish conquest of Peru and the events which immediately preceded it, but its second chapter is a thorough discussion of Inca civilization and the events of the reign of Pachacuti.

Means, Philip Ainsworth. *Ancient Civilizations of the Andes*. New York: Gordian Press, 1964. A thorough study, originally published in 1931, of all the cultures and civilizations of Peru from the earliest prehistoric times to the Spanish Conquest. Means devotes two chapters to Inca history which are valuable, though partially superseded by later scholarship.

Rowe, John Howland. "Inca Culture at the Time of the Spanish Conquest." In *Handbook of South American Indians*, edited by Julian H. Steward, vol. 2. Washington, D.C.: Government Printing Office, 1949-1959. Rowe's seven-volume study is primarily concerned with social and cultural aspects of Inca civilization, but it is important for the dating of pre-Conquest events generally accepted by later scholars.

Robert L. Berner

PAN KU

Born: A.D. 32; place unknown
Died: A.D. 92; Lo-yang, China
Area of Achievement: Historiography
Contribution: Through his compilation of the *Han shu*, Pan Ku preserved a full, well-documented record for this vital period of Chinese history and set the standard for all subsequent dynastic histories of China.

Early Life
Pan Ku was a member of the illustrious Pan family of Han China (207 B.C. to A.D. 220). Since the generation of his great-great-grandfather, the Pans had distinguished themselves in scholarship, serving the Han imperial government in both court and provincial posts. His grandaunt had been a favorite concubine of Emperor Ch'eng (reigned 32-7 B.C.). Ku's twin brother, Ch'ao, assigned the title of Marquess for Establishing the Remote Regions, won for himself immortal fame by reestablishing Chinese hegemony in Central Asia. His younger sister, Chao, much respected in court circles as the tutor of imperial princesses, was one of China's foremost women scholars; she wrote the *Nü-chieh* (A.D. 106; instructions for women), the first textbook ever written for teaching Chinese women.

Life's Work
Despite having such illustrious forebears and siblings, the young Pan Ku had a hard time finding his niche in the world. The Pan family had no automatic right to high office. Ku's father, Piao, though fairly successful in his official career, died when his sons were still relatively young and unestablished. He did, however, bequeath to Ku a project which was to secure to the Pan family a hallowed place in China's literary tradition: the writing of a complete history of the Former Han Dynasty, the *Han shu*. Ku's efforts in writing the history were brought to the attention of Emperor Ming (reigned 58-75), who appreciated his merits and made him a gentleman-in-waiting (*lang*). In this capacity, Ku had access to government archives which facilitated his writing efforts.

Besides writing the *Han shu*, Ku was given other writing assignments such as to report on the proceedings at the Po-hu Pavilion, in which an enclave of Confucian erudites gathered to deliberate on the correct interpretations of Confucian classics bearing on the ritual aspects of the Chinese monarchy. In addition, he found time to indulge his poetic propensities. His two *fu* (rhymed prose essays or rhapsodies) on the two capitals of the Han Dynasty established him as the foremost poet of his time.

Although other people had a hand in the compilation of the *Han shu*, notably his father, Piao, his younger sister, Chao, and the scholar Ma Hsü, there is no question that the main credit has to go to Ku. He gave the book its definitive form and was personally responsible for writing most of the text. Thus, it is appropriate to credit Pan Ku as the author of the *Han shu*.

Traditionally, Pan Ku's name came to be linked to that of Ssu-ma Ch'ien (often abbreviated to read Ma-Pan) to suggest the highest standard in historiographical writing. There is no denying Ku's indebtedness to Ssu-ma Ch'ien. In fact, the *Han shu* cannot be meaningfully discussed apart from the historiographical context that Ssu-ma Ch'ien and his masterpiece, *Shih chi* (c. 90 B.C.), provided.

Before Ssu-ma Ch'ien's time (c. 145-c. 86 B.C.), historical works had not been formally or conceptually differentiated from other forms of serious literature, which all purported to be authentic words and deeds of the ancients. To the extent that conscious attempts to write history were made, the only available framework into which records of the past could be fitted was the *pien-nien* (annals), as exemplified by the *Ch'un ch'iu* (c. 480 B.C.; *Spring and Autumn Annals*), edited by Confucius. This was a strictly chronological listing of events as they transpired, recorded from the point of view of some court historian. The disadvantages of this format are obvious. In treatments of events that had to be recorded close to the time they occurred, they often appear to be abstracted from their context, unless substantial digression and background materials were incorporated. To catch the attention of the recorder, events had to be of a spectacular nature—battles, diplomatic alliances, and the accession or death of rulers. Long-term changes such as population growth or technological development occurred too slowly to be noticed. Moreover, the format could not accommodate matters such as social or cultural history that had no immediate bearing on the government.

Ssu-ma Ch'ien lived at a time when vast changes had overtaken China. The decentralized feudal China of the time of Confucius had given way to the centralized bureaucratic empire under the Ch'in (221-206 B.C.). The Ch'in Dynasty, ruling over a unified China for the first time in history, was undone by excessive tyranny and was overthrown by a universal revolt. The ensuing struggle to succeed to the throne of China ended with the triumph of the House of Han, which was to rule for more than four hundred years. Meanwhile, the quest for empire was taking the Chinese into Mongolia and Central Asia. The economy was expanding, and enormous fortunes were made. Myriad individuals had played important roles in the unfolding drama. The times called for a new historiography that would be capable of portraying these vast changes and doing justice to these individuals and their contributions.

In writing the *Shih chi*, Ssu-ma Ch'ien overcame the limitations of the old historiography by developing a composite format. The seventy chapters of the *Shih chi* are divided into five sections, each representing a distinct style of historical writing. The first section, known as "Basic Annals" (*pen-chi*), essentially follows the *pien-nien* style of the old historiography, being a chronicle of events recorded from the viewpoint of the paramount ruler of China. The longest section is the "Biographies" (*lieh-chuan*). Here, attention is given to individuals, ranging from successful generals and ministers to unconventional characters such as the would-be assassin Ch'ing K'o, as well as physicians, diviners, entertainers, and entrepreneurs. Ssu-ma Ch'ien chose people who exemplified in their words or deeds patterns of human endeavor which were to be commended. The biographical section also gave the historian the flexibility to reconcile the two moral imperatives of his profession: objectivity in reporting, and praising the worthy and castigating evildoers. Since the annals and the biographies sections together constitute the bulk of the *Shih chi*, the *shih-chi* format of historiography is often known as the *chi-chuan* style.

The section of hereditary houses (*shih-chia*) deals with the history of the *de facto* sovereign states during the period preceding the Ch'in unification. The section on chronological tables (*piao*) traces the genealogy of the prominent families and furnishes a convenient scheme for correlating the chronologies of the various feudal states. The most distinctive section of the *Shih chi* is the one titled "Monographs" (*shu*), which comprises eight chapters dealing with such wide-ranging matters as rites, music, pitched pipes, the calendar, astronomy, state sacrifices, rivers and canals, and the economy.

Ssu-ma Ch'ien lived during the reign of Emperor Wu-ti (140-87 B.C.), during the heyday of the Former Han Dynasty. By A.D. 9, however, Wu-ti's descendants had been edged out of the succession by the usurper Wang Mang, who founded the Hsin Dynasty (A.D. 9-22). Wang Mang, however, was unable to consolidate his regime, and his dynasty fell amid a revolt by starving peasants and disgruntled landlords, precipitating another scramble for the throne of China. The man who emerged triumphant in this contest, Liu Hsiu (reigned as Emperor Kuang-wu, A.D. 25-57), who was descended from the founder of the Former Han Dynasty, claimed that his dynasty was a continuation or restoration of the Great Han. As his capital was located at Lo-yang, to the east of the Former Han capital, Changan (also spelled Sian), historians refer to the restored dynasty as the Eastern or Latter Han.

To scholars living at the court of the Latter Han, the period from the founding of the first Han Dynasty to the final overthrow of the usurper Wang Mang constituted a natural unit of history. Emulating the success of Ssu-ma Ch'ien, several of them (among them Pan Piao, Ku's father) had tried to write its history. Apart from determining the overall design and collecting source materials for the project, however, Piao apparently had done little actual writing. Though Ku received the idea of writing the *Han shu* from his father, and though he was apparently deeply moved by the Confucian value of filial piety, he saw no need to be bound by his father's design. Whereas his father had had no use for the majority of Ssu-ma Ch'ien's innovations, Ku retained almost all the sections of the *Shih chi*, with the exception of "Hereditary Houses" (for the obvious reason that in the centralized bureaucratic polity of Han China there were no authentic hereditary houses apart from that of the imperial family).

Shih chi not only was the model for Pan Ku's *Han shu* but also constituted his single most important source. Materials from the *Shih chi* pertaining to the first hundred years of the Former Han Dynasty, in which the coverage of the two works overlaps, were copied almost verbatim into the *Han shu*. Nevertheless, Ku was no mere imitator; wherever possible, he sought to develop the potentialities of the model he had inherited. Ssu-ma Ch'ien, for example, had invented the category of monographs to expand the scope of historiography to encompass ritual, social, and economic as well as political history. Pan Ku went one step further. In the section on monographs (which he renamed *chih* instead of *shu*), he retained all the *Shih chi* chapters on ritual matters but vastly expanded the scope of administrative history, adding new chapters on penal law and geography. The monograph on geography gives detailed population figures for the administrative subdivisions of the empire, thus yielding the first complete census of China, for the year A.D. 2. In addition, he ventured into the domain of intellectual history. The monograph on literature (*i-wên chih*) was more than a systematic account of Chinese intellectual history; it also contained the first complete catalog of all Chinese books extant at that time.

Although Ku's character was amiable and accommodating, he had the misfortune late in life to be caught up in the factional strife of the Han court. He joined the staff of General Tou Hsien as his confidential secretary on the eve of the latter's punitive expedition against the Hsiung-nu (Huns). Upon his return, the general was impeached for treason, and members of his retinue were also implicated. Ku was cast into prison, where he died before his friends could rescue him.

Summary

Through his *Han shu*, Pan Ku had a great impact on Chinese historiography and on Chinese political consciousness. He developed the possibilities of the *chi-chuan* format, bringing it into the mainstream of Chinese official historiography. His contribution in this regard is twofold. First, he produced a monumental work, in one hundred chapters, in the style of Ssu-ma Ch'ien's new historiography, thus helping to popularize it. Indeed, it is doubtful whether Ssu-ma Ch'ien's legacy could have survived if Pan Ku had not written the *Han shu* in support of it. There is evidence that until the T'ang period (618-907), the *Shih chi* was an extremely rare book and that it was primarily thanks to Pan Ku's *Han shu* that scholars became acquainted with the *chi-chuan* style of historiography. Second, Pan Ku was the one who arranged for the new historiography to be wedded to the salient feature of Chinese history, the dynastic cycle. Although dynasties varied in length and in the circumstances of their rise and fall, generally speaking, each dynasty marked a distinct period, an era with its own characteristics. After the time of Pan Ku, as soon as a new dynasty had consolidated its power, one of the first things its scholars did was to compile an official history of the dynasty which had preceded it, signifying in this way that that dynasty was indeed defunct. The precedent for this practice was established by Pan Ku, who also set the tone for the writing of these official dynastic histories: impersonal, objective, and dignified.

Bibliography
Hughes, E. R. *Two Chinese Poets: Vignettes of Han Life and Thought*. Princeton, N.J.: Princeton University Press, 1960. The author examines two sets of rhapsodies on the two Han capitals, by Pan Ku and Chang Heng, respectively. While the book is informative with regard to the nature of Han rhapsodies and the descriptions of the two capitals, the main purpose of the author is to highlight, through exploring the minds of the two poets, the contrasting style and ethos of the two Han dynasties. Indispensable for understanding Pan Ku's ideology and worldview.
Hulsewe, A. F. P. *China in Central Asia: An Annotated Translation of Chapters Sixty-one and Ninety-six of the History of the Former Han Dynasty*. Leiden, Netherlands: E. J. Brill, 1979. Particularly useful is the seventy-page introductory chapter by M. A. N. Loewe. Loewe comments on the materials on which the original copy of the *Han shu* was written (wood or bamboo slips) and discusses the relationship between the *Shih chi* and the *Han shu*. He argues, contrary to previous assumptions, that at least in one case the *Shih chi* text is not the source for the *Han shu* but indeed derivative from it.
_____. "Notes on the Historiography of the Han Period." In *Historians of China and Japan*, edited by W. G. Beasley and E. G. Pulleyblank. London: Oxford University Press, 1961. A general but authoritative survey on the authors of the *Shih chi* and the *Han shu* and other works of historiography of the Han period.
Swann, Nancy Lee. *Pan Chao, Foremost Woman Scholar of China*. New York: Century Co., 1932. Still the most important source on Pan Ku's life. The author traces the genealogy of the Pan family, discusses the career of some of Ku's forebears, and assesses the contributions which Ku's father and younger sister and others made toward the completion of the *Han shu*. A meticulous scholar, Swann utilizes all available primary and secondary sources in arriving at her conclusions.
Watson, Burton. *Ssu-ma Ch'ien, Grand Historian of China*. New York: Columbia University Press, 1958. Not only the most authoritative study on the *Shih chi* but also indispensable for any serious work on the *Han shu*;

the author often makes insightful comments on the relative merits of the *Shih chi* and the *Han shu* and their respective authors.

Winston W. Lo

PAPPUS

Born: c. 300; Alexandria, Egypt
Died: c. 350; place unknown
Area of Achievement: Mathematics
Contribution: Pappus provided a valuable compilation of the contributions of earlier mathematicians and inspired later work on algebraic solutions to geometric problems.

Early Life
Almost nothing is known about Pappus' life, including the dates of his birth and death. A note written in the margin of a text by a later Alexandrian geometer states that Pappus wrote during the time of Diocletian (284-305). The earliest biographical source is a tenth century Byzantium encyclopedia, the *Suda*. This work lists the writings of Pappus and describes him as a "philosopher," which suggests that he may have held some official position as a teacher of philosophy. Nevertheless, this reference to philosophy may be no more than an indication of his interest in natural science. The geometer had at least one child, a son, since he dedicated one of his books to him. In addition, Pappus mentions two of his contemporaries in his texts: a philosopher, Hierius, although the connection between the two is not clear; and Pandrosian, a woman who taught mathematics. Pappus addressed one of his works to her, not as a tribute, but because he found several of her students deficient in their mathematical education.

Pappus lived at a time when the main course of Greek mathematics had been in decline for more than five hundred years; although geometry continued to be studied and taught, there were few original contributions to the subject. To alleviate this lack, he attempted to compile all available sources of earlier geometry and made several significant contributions to the subject. As the first author in this new tradition, sometimes called the silver age of mathematics, Pappus provides a valuable resource for all of ancient Greek geometry.

Life's Work
Throughout his life, Pappus maintained a lively interest in a number of areas dealing with mathematics and natural science. The bulk of his surviving works can be found in the *Synagoge* (c. A.D. 340; English translation known as *Collection*). Other works either are in fragmentary form or else are no longer extant, although mentioned by other writers. There exists part of a commentary on the mechanics of Archimedes which considers problems associated with mean proportions and constructions using straightedge and compass. There are two remaining books of a commentary on Ptolemy's *Mathēmatikē suntaxis* (c. A.D. 150; *Almagest*) explaining some of the finer

Pappus

points of the text to the inexperienced reader. Pappus continued his interest in the popularization of difficult texts in a work, of which only a fragment survives, on Euclid's *Stoicheia* (c. fourth century B.C.; *Elements*), in which Pappus explains the nature of irrational magnitudes to the casual reader. The lost works include a geography of the inhabited world, a description of rivers in Libya, an interpretation of dreams, several texts on spherical geometry and stereographic projection, an astrological almanac, and a text on alchemical oaths and formulas. Pappus was more than a geometer; he was a person who lived in a world where the search for new knowledge was rapidly declining and where political instability was the order of the day. Yet he expressed a continuing interest in the education of those less fortunate than himself and showed a lively interest in affairs outside his city.

Pappus' claim to historical and mathematical significance is found in a compendium of eight books on geometry. This collection covers the entire range of Greek geometry and has been described as a handbook or guide to the subject. In several of the books, when the classical texts are available, Pappus shows how the original proof is accomplished as well as alternative methods to prove the theorem. In other books, where the classical sources are not easily accessible, Pappus provides a history of the problems as well as different attempts at finding a solution. An overall assessment of these books shows few moments of great originality; rather, a capable and independent mind sifts through the entire scope of Greek geometry while demonstrating fine technique and a clear understanding of his field of study.

A summary of the contents of the eight books shows that some are of only historical interest, providing information on or elucidation of classical texts. Other books, particularly book 7, have been a source of inspiration for later mathematicians. All of book 1 and the first part of book 2 are lost. The remainder of book 2 deals with the problems of multiplying all the numbers between 1 and 800 together and expressing the product in words using the myriad (10,000) as base. Pappus refers to a lost work by Apollonius of Perga which seems to be part of the problem of expressing large numbers in words that began with Archimedes' third century B.C. *The Sand-Reckoner* (translated in 1897). Book 3 deals with construction problems using straightedge and compass: finding a mean proportion between two given straight lines, finding basic means between two magnitudes (arithmetic, geometric, and harmonic), constructing a triangle within another triangle, and constructing solids within a sphere. Book 4 consists of a collection of theorems, including several famous problems in Greek mathematics: a generalization of Pythagoras' theorem, the squaring of the circle, and the trisection of an angle. Book 5 begins with an extensive introduction on the hexagonal cells of honeycombs and suggests that bees could acquire geometric knowledge from some divine source. This discussion leads to the question of the maximum volume that can be enclosed by a superficial area and to a sequence of theorems that prove that the circle has the greatest area of figures of equal parameter. His proof appears to follow those formulated by an earlier Hellenistic geometer named Zenodorus, whose work is lost. In a later section of this book, Pappus introduces a section on solids with a Neoplatonist statement that God chose to make the universe in a sphere because it is the noblest of figures. It has been asserted but not proved that the sphere has the greatest surface of all equal surface figures. Pappus then proceeds to examine the sphere and regular solids. Book 6 is sometimes called "Little Astronomy"; it deals with misunderstandings in mathematical technique and corrects common misrepresentations.

Book 7 is by far the most important, both because it had a direct influence on modern mathematics and because it gives an account of works in the so-called *Treasury of Analysis* or *Domain of Analysis*, of which a large number are lost. These are works by Euclid, Apollonius, and others that set up a branch of mathematics that provides equipment for the analysis of theorems and problems. Classical geometry uses the term "analysis" to mean a reversal of the normal procedure called "synthesis." Instead of taking a series of steps through valid statements about abstract objects, analysis reverses the procedure by assuming the validity of the theorem and working back to valid statements. Through the preservation of Pappus' account of these works it is possible to reconstruct most of them.

His most original contribution to modern mathematics comes in a section dealing with Apollonius' *Kōnika* (c. 250 B.C.; *Conics*), where Pappus attempts to demonstrate that the product of three or four straight lines can be written as a series of compounded ratios and is equal to a constant. This came to be known as the "Pappus problem." Book 8 is the last of the surviving books of *Synagoge*, although there is internal evidence that four additional books existed. In this book, Pappus takes on the subject of mechanical problems, including weights on inclined planes, proportioning of gears, and the center of gravity.

There exist substantial references to various lost books of Pappus; among the lost works is a commentary on Euclid's *Elements*, although a two-part section does exist in Arabic. Several other works fit into this category, surviving only in commentary by later writers or in fragments of questionable authorship in Arabic. One of the more interesting Arabic manuscripts (discovered in 1860) shows that Pappus may have invented a volumeter similar to one invented by Joseph-Louis Gay-Lussac. Pappus was not merely a geometer; he was a conserver of classical tradition, a popularizer of Greek geometry, and an inventor as well.

Summary

The works of Pappus have provided later generations with a storehouse of ancient Greek geometry, both as an independent check against the authenticity of other known sources and as a valuable source of lost texts. For modern mathematics, Pappus offers more than merely historical interest. In 1631, Jacob Golius pointed out to René Descartes the "Pappus problem," and six years later this became the centerpiece of Descartes' *Des matières de la géométrie* (*The Geometry of Descartes*, 1925). Descartes realized that his new algebraic symbols could easily replace Pappus' more difficult geometric methods and that the product of the locus of straight lines generated from conic sections could generate equations of second, third, and higher orders. In 1687 Sir Isaac Newton found a similar inspiration in the "Pappus problem" using purely geometric methods. Nevertheless, it was Descartes' algebraic methods that would be utilized in the future. Pappus also anticipated the well-known "Guldin's theorem," dealing with figures generated by the revolution of plane figures about an axis. It can be argued that Pappus was the only geometer who possessed the ability to work out such a theorem during the silver age of Greek mathematics.

Bibliography
Bulmer-Thomas, I. "Guldin's Theorem—or Pappus's?" *Isis* 75 (1984): 348-352. There exists some question whether the Pappus text is original or if the text was corrupted at a later date. A less significant issue here is the interpretation of the Pappus manuscript—a historical problem concerned with the extent to which Pappus anticipated Guldin.
Descartes, René. *The Geometry of René Descartes*. Translated by Davis E. Smith and Marcia L. Latham. Chicago: Open Court, 1952. It is possible to follow from Descartes' own text the relevant passages from Pappus' work, seeing how Descartes develops his new symbols and why this method would later become the preferred method.
Heath, Sir Thomas. *A History of Greek Mathematics*. Vol. 2, *From Aristarchus to Diophantus*. Reprint. New York: Dover Publications, 1981. This edition contains several long sections from the *Collection* as well as commentaries on the history and contents of these theorems.
Molland, A. G. "Shifting the Foundations: Descartes's Transformation of Ancient Geometry." *Historica Mathematica* 3 (1976): 21-49. This work focuses on how Descartes was able to shift from geometric to algebraic methods. Since Pappus plays a significant part in this transformation, it is possible for the reader to see the differences and similarities of Pappus' and Descartes' mathematical symbols.
Pappus. *Book 7 of the Collection*. Edited by Alexander Jones. 2 vols. New York: Springer-Verlag, 1986. These two volumes contain the most complete rendition of book 7; in addition, there are exhaustive commentaries and notes on every aspect of this text. Contains a detailed account of the history of various Pappus manuscripts and notes on the problems of translating ancient Greek text.

Turnbull, H. W. *The Great Mathematicians*. London: Methuen and Co., 1961. This work covers the major contributors to the history of mathematics, from the ancient Greeks to the late nineteenth century scholars. The section on Pappus is short, but it does place him in the context of the second Alexandrian school.

Victor W. Chen

PARMENIDES

Born: c. 515 B.C.; Elea (also known as Velia)
Died: Perhaps after 436 B.C.; possibly Elea
Area of Achievement: Philosophy
Contribution: By exploring the logical implications of statements which use apparently simple terms such as "one" or "is," Parmenides established metaphysics as an area of philosophy.

Early Life

In the mid-sixth century B.C., as the Persian Empire advanced through Asia Minor toward the Aegean Sea, some of the Greek city-states which were thus threatened accommodated themselves to the invaders, while others attempted to maintain their independence. In the case of one Ionian city, Phocaea, many of the inhabitants left Asia Minor entirely. They migrated to southern Italy, founding Elea around 540. Parmenides' father, Pyres, may have been one of the emigrants, or, like his son, he may have been born in Elea. At any rate, Parmenides' family background was in Ionia.

It is therefore entirely natural that Parmenides would eventually compose verse in the standard Ionic dialect which had earlier been used for Homeric epics. Philosophical influences on the young Parmenides must be more conjectural, but at least some interest in the Ionian philosophers of the sixth century, such as Thales of Miletus and Anaximander, seems entirely reasonable for someone growing up in a Phocaean settlement.

The ancient traditions about Parmenides, on the other hand, connect him with the poet and philosopher Xenophanes. Born circa 570, Xenophanes was from Colophon in Asia Minor, and like the Phocaeans, he fled before the Persians to the western Greek world. Some contact between him and Parmenides is therefore quite likely. It is not so clear, though, that one should regard Parmenides as being in any real sense Xenophanes' student. A better case can be made for a close association of Parmenides with the otherwise obscure Ameinias, to whom, after his death, Parmenides built a shrine, according to Diogenes Laërtius (c. A.D. 200). Ameinias was a Pythagorean, and thus one should add the sixth century philosopher and mystic Pythagoras to the list of early influences on Parmenides.

The date which Diogenes Laërtius gives for Parmenides' birth is around 540 B.C. Plato's dialogue *Parmenides* (c. 370 B.C.), on the other hand, is inconsistent with this date. Most of the dialogue is clearly invented by Plato, since it includes details of argumentation which Plato himself developed in the fourth century. The conversation between Parmenides, Socrates, and others, therefore, can scarcely have taken place as described by Plato; still, the overall setting of the dialogue, which implies that the title character was born around 515 B.C., may be chronologically accurate. Possibly, the date given by Diogenes Laërtius arose from a reference in one of his sources to the founding of Elea around 540 B.C. as a crucial event in Parmenides' background.

Life's Work

Pondering the implications of earlier philosophy, which saw a single unifying principle—such as water, the infinite, or number—behind the various phenomena of the world, Parmenides strove to uncover a paradox residing in any such analysis. He wrote one treatise, in poetic form, in which he set forth his views. This work is generally referred to as *Peri physeos* (only fragments are translated into English), although it is not certain that Parmenides himself so entitled it. Of this poem, about 150 lines are preserved in Greek, along with another six lines in a Latin translation.

Parmenides' central concern, or at least that for which he is best known, lies in the implications of the Greek word *esti*, meaning "is." According to Parmenides, of the two predications "is" and "is not," only "is" makes sense. Merely to say "is not" gives some stamp of evidence to whatever one says "is not" and therefore involves self-contradiction. With "is not" thus rejected, all reality must somehow be single and unified, all-encompassing and unchanging. Such a view would seem to be essentially ineffable, but toward the middle of Parmenides' fragment 8, which gives the core of his argument, what "is" is compared to a well-rounded ball, perfectly poised in the middle, with nothing outside itself.

Despite this thoroughgoing monism, the opening of Parmenides' poem (fragment 1) refers to two paths of inquiry—one of *aletheia* (truth) and one of *doxa* (opinion). The argument about the primacy of "is" over "is not" follows the path of *aletheia*, while the latter part of fragment 8 follows the path of *doxa*. (These sections are generally known as the *Aletheia* and the *Doxa*.) Ancient authors did not, on the whole, find the *Doxa* so interesting. It was therefore not so much quoted in antiquity, and only about forty-five lines from it are preserved. As a result, many modern treatments of Parmenides concentrate on the better preserved *Aletheia*. Such an approach may also find a precedent in Plato's dialogue *Parmenides*. Other scholars, though, acknowledge *Doxa* as having been an integral part of the poem, and this approach is entirely supported by some of the ancient references to Parmenides. Aristotle (384-322 B.C.), for example, refers in *Metaphysica* (335-323 B.C.; *Metaphysics*) to Parmenides as having been constrained by phenomena to acknowledge change and multiplicity in the sensible world.

Aristotle's line of interpretation is probably correct. Despite the paucity of direct information about the *Doxa*, several crucial ideas in ancient science are consistently associated with Parmenides, either as originating with him or as being promulgated by him. For example, the simile which concludes the *Aletheia*—that what "is" resembles a well-rounded ball—may have a more prosaic but still-grander cosmic application to Earth as a sphere, poised in space. Fragment 14 refers to the moon's shining, not of its own accord but by reflected light. Aëtius (c. A.D. 100) and Diogenes Laërtius ascribe to Parmenides the observation that the evening and morning star are the same body (Venus) as it travels through space. Strabo (who flourished during the first century B.C.), quoting an earlier source, refers to Parmenides as having divided Earth into five zones. Such astronomical and geographic interests, along with various references to his treatment of biology, anatomy, and psychology, suggest that Parmenides had a mind more concerned with the investigation of physical phenomena than his austerely logical treatment of "is" and "is not" would suggest.

Nevertheless, Plato's contrary focus on Parmenides as primarily a metaphysician provides the earliest biographical and descriptive vignette of Parmenides. Plato's account places Parmenides in Athens in 450, at the time of a quadrennial festival to the goddess Athena. According to Plato, the Eleatic visitor to Athens was then about sixty-five years old, already white-haired but still of a forceful and commanding appearance and quite capable, as Plato reveals in the rest of the dialogue, of engaging in a complicated philosophical discussion.

Unfortunately, there is nothing very specific in Plato's physical description of Parmenides. One might hope that the picture would be filled out by the bust from the first century A.D. found during excavations at Elea in 1966. The bust matches an inscription, "Parmenides the son of Pyres the natural philosopher," found in 1962; also, the inscription somehow connects Parmenides with Apollo as a patron of physicians. The existence of this statue obviously attests the regard in which Parmenides was held in Elea several centuries after his death. It is unlikely, however, that it actually portrays the visage of Parmenides, since it seems to be modeled on the bust of a later figure, the Epicurean Metrodorus (c. 300 B.C.), who was chosen to represent the typical philosopher.

In his account of Parmenides' visit to Athens, Plato includes the detail that Zeno of Elea, who accompanied Parmenides on that occasion, had once been his lover. Athenaeus (fl. c. A.D. 200) objects to this point as a superfluous addition which contributes nothing to Plato's narrative. Whatever the case may be, Zeno and the slightly later Melissus (born c. 480 B.C.) are often grouped with Parmenides as the founders of an Eleatic school of philosophy. In particular, the intellectual connection between Parmenides and Zeno may be especially close. Both were from Elea (while Melissus was from the Aegean island Samos), and, according to Plato, Zeno's paradoxes, purporting to show the impossibility of motion, were designed to support Parmenides' doctrine concerning the unified nature of reality.

The determination of direct influences of Parmenides beyond the Eleatic school is more tenuous. Theophrastus (c. 372-287 B.C.), however, connects two other fifth century figures with him—the philosopher-poet Empedocles and Leucippus, the founder of atomism. Also, although he is from a later generation, it is generally agreed that Plato himself owed much to Parmenides.

Of Parmenides' life after his possible visit to Athens in 450, nothing definite is known. Theophrastus' implication that Leucippus studied with him at Elea should possibly be dated after 450. Also, Eusebius of Caesarea (who flourished during the fourth century A.D.) implies that Parmenides was still living in 436 B.C.; this information leads scholars to believe Plato's chronology over that given by Diogenes Laërtius. According to Plutarch, Parmenides was a lawgiver as well as a philosopher, and subsequent generations at Elea swore to abide by his laws.

Summary

Some critics see fundamental flaws in Parmenides' reasoning. According to the modern scholar Jonathan Barnes, for example, it is perfectly acceptable to say that it is necessarily the case that what does not exist does not exist, but Parmenides erred in holding that what does not exist necessarily does not exist. Even if this objection is valid, Parmenides' lasting influence on subsequent thought is undeniable. Often, his arguments are presented without quibble in modern treatments of the history of philosophy, as having uncovered difficulties with which any process of thinking must cope.

It is also important to keep in mind the poetic medium which Parmenides used. His sixth century predecessors, such as Anaximander and Anaximenes, had used prose for their philosophical treatises. Parmenides, however, chose verse, perhaps to give some sense of the majesty and dignity of the philosopher's quest. The ineffable quality which Parmenides claims for ultimate reality may also find an appropriate expression in poetry. Above all, the use of verse puts Parmenides in a rich verbal tradition, stretching back to the earliest extant Greek poetry, that of Homer and Hesiod, and to even earlier oral poetry. The most obvious parallels are with Homer's *Odyssey* (c. 800 B.C.). For example, the cattle of the Sun are described in the *Odyssey* as neither coming into being nor perishing, and this idea is also central to Parmenides' concept of what is. A close verbal parallel to Homer's description of the paths of night and day in the *Odyssey* is also found in Parmenides. More generally, one may note that Odysseus, after his manifold adventures in the outer reaches of the world, eventually returns home to Ithaca and to his wife, Penelope, exactly as Parmenides would both partake of and yet somehow eschew the realm of pure thought for the mundane world of *doxa*.

Parmenides thus emerges as a prime mediator between ancient Greek and later philosophy. While casting his thought in terms of the poetic imagery, metaphors, and formulas used by Homer and Hesiod, he still insisted emphatically on the paramount importance of reason that his contemporaries and successors, such as Zeno, Leucippus, and Plato, framed anew.

Bibliography

Barnes, Jonathan. *The Presocratic Philosophers*. London: Routledge and Kegan Paul, 1982. Contains three chapters mainly on Parmenides, along with numerous other references. Barnes puts Parmenides' ideas into a modern philosophical framework, and although his use of technical jargon and symbols is sometimes a bit heavy, he nevertheless handles the ramifications of Parmenides' argument in magisterial fashion. Includes a good bibliography.

Burnet, John. *Early Greek Philosophy*. London: Adam and Charles Black, 1930. A classic work on pre-Socratic philosophy first published 1892. Contains a clear, readable chapter on Parmenides and a chapter on Leucippus which suggests that Parmenides' reference to what "is" as a self-contained sphere may have given rise to atomism.

Finkelberg, Aryeh. "The Cosmology of Parmenides." *American Journal of Philology* 107 (1986): 303-317. Treating the *Doxa* as an important part of Parmenides' poem, this article deals principally with Aëtius' report of Parmenides as referring to various rings which comprise Earth, a fiery region within it, airy rings which are associated with the heavenly bodies, and so on.

Lombardo, Stanley, ed. *Parmenides and Empedocles: The Fragments in Verse Translation*. San Francisco: Grey Fox Press, 1982. A spirited if somewhat free translation, but the best source for getting some sense in English of the fact that Parmenides wrote in verse and that this point is important for understanding the effect he wanted to achieve.

Mackenzie, Mary Margaret. "Parmenides' Dilemma." *Phronesis* 27 (1982): 1-12. Discusses the appearance of second-person verb forms in Parmenides' poem. The use of locutions such as "you think" must inevitably lead to an acknowledgment of plurality, and Parmenides' inclusion of the *Doxa* in his poem may be explained in these terms.

Mourelatos, Alexander P. D. *The Route of Parmenides*. New Haven, Conn.: Yale University Press, 1970. The main thrust of this work is Parmenides' philosophical program, with particular attention to the way in which material in the *Doxa* parallels statements in the *Aletheia*, often through a more or less explicit appeal to paradox. There is also a good introductory chapter on Homeric prototypes for Parmenides' poetic technique. Contains Greek text of fragments of Parmenides but no translation.

Owen, G. E. L. "Eleatic Questions." *The Classical Quarterly* 10 (1960): 84-102. Rejecting Aristotle's assessment of the importance of *Doxa* in *Peri physeos*, Owen maintains that for Parmenides the preceding section of his poem, the *Aletheia*, was all that really mattered.

Parmenides. *The Fragments of Parmenides: A Critical Text with Introduction, Translation, the Ancient Testimonia, and a Commentary.* Edited by A. H. Coxon. Assen/Maastrich, Netherlands: Van Gorcum, 1986. Greek text and English translation of the fragments of Parmenides. The extensive commentary is often hard to follow without at least some knowledge of Greek. Although somewhat technical, Coxon's introduction conveys a good sense of the textual problems which must be solved when establishing Parmenides' meaning.

——————. *Parmenides of Elea, Fragments: A Text and Translation, with an Introduction.* Edited by David Gallop. Toronto: University of Toronto Press, 1984. This volume consists of Greek text and English translation of the fragments of Parmenides, with English translations of the contexts in which the fragments occur. Also contains brief biographies (one to three sentences) of the ancient authors who quote or refer to Parmenides. The most convenient source for getting a general view of the ancient sources concerning Parmenides. Includes a good bibliography.

Plato. *Plato's "Parmenides": Translation and Analysis.* Translated by R. E. Allen. Minneapolis: University of Minnesota Press, 1983. Primarily a translation of Plato's dialogue, with extensive commentary. Several pages deal specifically with Parmenides, however, and there are also other scattered references to his poem. Allen stresses the fundamentally fictional nature of Plato's account of Parmenides' meeting with Socrates—and the corresponding caution with which Plato must be used for biographical information concerning Parmenides.

Edwin D. Floyd

SAINT PAUL

Born: Date unknown; Tarsus, Cilicia (now Turkey)
Died: c. A.D. 64; Rome
Area of Achievement: Religion
Contribution: Through depth of conviction and force of personality, Paul spread the teachings of an obscure Jewish sect throughout the eastern Mediterranean and eventually to Rome. As the educated apostle, he gave Christianity a measure of intellectual credibility and formulated much of what would later become doctrine.

Early Life

Saint Paul was born at Tarsus in Cilicia, a region in southeast Asia Minor, on the Mediterranean. He was a Jew, known during his early years by the name of Saul. Little documentary evidence exists concerning these years, but certain things can be inferred from Paul's status at the time that he appeared on the historical scene.

Paul was trained as a rabbi in the Pharisaic tradition. His background as a Pharisee indicates a close adherence to both the written law and the oral, or traditional, law. This stance would have been a source of constant tension between Paul and the apostles who arose out of the village culture of Palestine. In the Gospels, the term Pharisee takes on connotations of self-righteousness and sanctimony. Further, Paul was a product of the city and of the Diaspora, the settlements of those Jews who had been dispersed throughout Asia Minor. Certain awkward phrases in his writings, when he is trying to be more simple, indicate that he was never comfortable with agricultural or bucolic topics. He was exposed early in life to Greek language, mythology, and culture. In the Hellenistic synagogues where he worshipped as a youth, he would have heard the Jewish scriptures read not in Hebrew but in Greek translation. Paul is identified in the Acts of the Apostles as a Roman citizen, so rare a status for a Jew that his family must have been influential and highly connected. Finally, he was for a time a leading persecutor of the new sect, seeing the followers of Jesus as a grave threat to the Jewish legal tradition.

For all the reasons cited above, it is little wonder that after his conversion many of his fellow Jewish Christians viewed him with suspicion and even with hostility. Yet Paul's conversion was so total and the rejection of his past life so absolute that other writers have felt the need to dramatize it, even though his own letters do not describe it at all.

Life's Work

Paul's great achievement was to take Christianity from Jerusalem throughout the eastern provinces of the Roman Empire and finally to the capital itself. He possessed the vision to see that the new faith had a message and an appeal which were not limited to the Jews.

During the years preceding the conversion of Saul of Tarsus, the future of Christianity was not promising. Rome had imposed a political order upon the eastern Mediterranean and had inculcated its attitudes of tolerance (for the times) and materialism. The relative peace and prosperity of the period, however, apparently proved insufficient to meet the spiritual and psychological needs of the subject peoples. The major ancient religions had ossified and were the source of very little spiritual energy; among the Greeks and Romans, religious practice had become almost purely conventional, and the Jews awaited the great supernatural event which would revitalize them. In response to this state of affairs, philosophical and religious sects sprang up everywhere, including Greek syncretism, Mithraism, Zoroastrianism, and Christianity. The struggles of these and many other sects to win the minds and hearts of the people would continue for the next five hundred years (before Saint Augustine's conversion to Christianity in 386/387, he experimented with virtually all of its competitors). At the middle of the first century after the death of Jesus, Christianity—a provincial religion under the leadership of a small group of unsophisticated and unlettered men—seemed unlikely to be the winner of this great competition. Thus, it is difficult to overstate the impact of the conversion of Saul of Tarsus.

He was a most unlikely apostle of the crucified carpenter from Galilee. Far from being a man of the people, he was a member of the most learned Jewish party. He held Roman citizenship. He had not been personally associated with Jesus of Nazareth and viewed those who had been as a threat to the Jewish Law, which he uncompromisingly supported. His nature was sometimes imperious, as his writings disclose. He did not leave a description of his conversion as Saint Augustine was later to do, but something in his thinking was leading him toward the profound change which would make him history's archetypal Christian convert. He developed a sense of the frailty and corruption of the world's institutions, a disgust for the secular materialism which surrounded him, and a conviction that humanity's only hope lay in dying to all worldly things. He gave up a comfortable, settled life for that of an itinerant preacher and religious organizer. He changed from a defender of the legal tradition of Judaism to the most zealous opponent of those Jewish Christians who sought to retain any part of it.

Saul first appears in the book of the Acts of the Apostles at Jerusalem, as a witness to the stoning of Stephen, the first Christian martyr. His complicity in the execution is strongly suggested, for he is reported to have consented to the death (as if he had some say in the matter), and the witnesses laid their clothes down at his feet. His age at the time is not known, but he is described as a young man. Succeeding chapters paint him as a fierce oppressor of the Christians. His persecutions culminate in a trip to Damascus, where, under authority from the high priests, he is to harry all the Christians he can find. It

Saint Paul

is on this journey that he has his famous conversion experience: He hears the voice of Jesus challenging him, and he is struck blind. After three days, his sight is restored. He is baptized and almost immediately begins to preach in the synagogues that Christ is the Son of God. Scholars who do not subscribe to a literal interpretation of the scriptural account suggest that it results from Paul's having left no account of his own. Presented with the sudden, total, and inexplicable change in Saul's behavior, perhaps his first biographer could not resist romanticizing it.

The remainder of his story in Acts is replete with adventure and conflict. Saul is so skilled in disputation that both his Jewish and Greek opponents plot to kill him; he makes narrow and dramatic escapes. Still the Christians in Jerusalem cannot fully trust him; they remember the old Saul, and send him back to Tarsus. By chapter 13 of Acts, Saul (whose name means "asked of God" in Hebrew) has become known as Paul (meaning "small" in Greek). He has also become the missionary to the Gentiles. He travels widely: preaching, healing, organizing Christian communities, and suffering periods of hardship and imprisonment. The Scriptures hint at but give no account of his eventual martyrdom in Rome; legend would later supply one.

Much of Paul's career as a missionary can only be the object of conjecture. Some of his work and the time of its accomplishment have been verified through seven of his letters whose genuineness is generally accepted—his epistles to the various fledgling Christian communities. The first letter to the church at Thessalonica, provincial capital of Macedonia, was written from Corinth, c. 51. At that time, Paul was in the company of Silvanus (known in Acts as Silas) and Timothy. About three years later, from Ephesus in western Asia Minor, he wrote a stinging letter to the Christians in Galatia. They had been entertaining rival missionaries, who apparently argued that pagan converts were subject to the Jewish Law. In this letter, Paul defends his understanding of the gospel and his teaching authority with occasionally bitter sarcasm. The next year, near the end of his stay at Ephesus, he wrote the first of two extant letters to the church at Corinth, which he had founded c. 50. The church had developed several factions and incipient heresies (in the early church, it was largely Paul who delineated the orthodoxies and the heresies). In addition to responding to these matters, Paul offers sexual advice to husbands and wives, his famous pronouncement that the ideal Christian life is a celibate one, and his beautiful disquisition on love. A second letter to the Corinthians, written c. 56, asserts Paul's credentials and questions with heavy irony those of false prophets who have been wooing the flock. The letter addresses a number of other issues in such a curious chronology that it may well be a composite of several fragments, the work of some ancient editor. Paul's physical appearance is a mystery (early iconography seems based on little more than imagination), but in this letter he does allude to a "thorn in the flesh" from which three separate entreaties to the Lord have not relieved him. The nature of the illness is not known but has been the object of much speculation.

Around 57, during his last stay at Corinth, Paul wrote a long letter to Rome. It was both a letter of introduction and a theological treatise, written in anticipation of his preaching there. His letter to the church at Philippi was long held to have been written at Rome c. 62, during his two years of imprisonment there. Some scholars argue, however, that at least a part of it was written much earlier (c. 56) from a prison in Caesarea or Ephesus. Another letter from prison—a request that Philemon, a Colossian Christian, magnanimously take back a runaway slave whom Paul has converted—is also variously dated, depending upon whether the missionary wrote from Rome or elsewhere. Other letters (such as Timothy and Titus) bear Paul's name, but their authenticity has been disputed.

The last of Paul's many arrests occurred in Jerusalem, where he was attempting to promote unity within the Christian community (ironically, he himself had been one of the divisive factors there). As a citizen, he appealed to Rome and was transported to the capital. His lengthy period of imprisonment there is described in some detail in Acts. It is presumed that around 64 he was executed—legend has it that he was beheaded—just preceding Nero's persecution of the Roman Christians.

Summary

While Saint Peter and the other Palestinian apostles were at first content to limit Christianity to converted Jews, Saint Paul determined to take it to the Gentiles. As the other apostles moved back and forth among the villages of their native region, Paul spread the faith to the bustling cities of Asia Minor and southern Europe. He tirelessly plied the trade routes of the eastern empire, setting up church after church in the major population centers. In his second letter to the Corinthians, he catalogs his sufferings: imprisonments, beatings, floggings, a stoning, shipwreck, assassination plots, hunger, thirst, and—above all else—anxiety for the welfare of his churches.

He believed, as did the other primitive Christians, that he lived at the end of history, that the second coming of his Lord was at hand. Even so, he threw himself into every aspect of church organization—doctrine, ritual, politics. He fought lethargy here, inappropriate enthusiasm there. He constantly sought to make peace between Jewish and non-Jewish Christians. His dictates on such subjects as Christian celibacy and the lesser role of women in the church continue to provoke controversy, thousands of years after they were written.

Paul has been called the man who delivered Christianity from Judaism. He has been called the man who furnished Christianity with its intellectual content. Because of his argument that the Crucifixion represents a covenant superseding the ancient law, he has been called the father of the Reformation,

Saint Paul

and it has been suggested that Protestantism derives from him as Catholicism derives from Saint Peter. He has been called a compulsive neurotic, whose works were instances of sublimation and whose thorn in the flesh was psychosomatic. George Bernard Shaw characterized him as the fanatic who corrupted the teachings of Jesus.

It would be extravagant to claim that Christianity would not have survived without Paul. It is safe to say that it would not have survived in its present form without him.

Bibliography

Bruce, F. F. *Paul: Apostle of the Heart Set Free*. Grand Rapids, Mich.: Wm. B. Eerdmans Publishing Co., 1977. Bruce is perhaps the foremost evangelical among Pauline scholars. This book, which is accessible to the general reader, focuses on Paul's life, though there is also discussion of his writings. Well illustrated, with indexes of names and places, subjects, and references.

Davies, William David. *Paul and Rabbinic Judaism: Some Rabbinic Elements in Pauline Theology*. London: S•P•C•K, 1948, 2d ed. 1955. The author, a professor of New Testament at Princeton, attempts to prove that Paul was in the mainstream of first century Judaism and that Hellenistic influences upon him have been overestimated. The first of ten chapters assesses the degree of difference between Palestinian and Diaspora Judaism. Chapters 5 and 6 discuss Paul as preacher and teacher.

Deissmann, Adolf. *Paul: A Study in Social and Religious History*. Translated by William E. Wilson. New York: Harper and Row, Publishers, 1957. Takes the view that primitive Christianity was more a cult marked by mysticism than a religion marked by doctrine. Interprets the Pauline Christ-mysticism.

Glover, T. R. "The Mind of St. Paul." In *Springs of Hellas and Other Essays*. Cambridge: Cambridge University Press, 1945. A classicist's study of Paul, emphasizing the cosmopolitan nature of his world and his heroic efforts to reconcile Jew and Gentile, Greek and barbarian.

Meeks, Wayne A. *The First Urban Christians: The Social World of the Apostle Paul*. New Haven, Conn.: Yale University Press, 1983. This social history begins with the admission that great diversity existed within early Christianity. The author chooses to study Paul, his coworkers, and his congregations as the best-documented segment of the early Christian movement. The book's first premise is that Paul was a man of the city and that an urban bias informed the Pauline school from the earliest period of evangelizing. The social level of Pauline Christians and the governance and rituals of their communities are discussed at length. Includes notes, indexes, and an extensive bibliography.

_____, ed. *The Writings of Saint Paul*. New York: W. W. Norton and

Co., 1972. A critical edition containing the Revised Standard Version of the undoubted letters of Paul and the works of the Pauline school, heavily annotated. Also contains more than two dozen essays and excerpts evaluating, from diverse points of view, Paul's thought, works, and influence on modern Christianity.

Schoeps, Hans J. *Paul: The Theology of the Apostle in the Light of Jewish History*. Translated by Harold Knight. Philadelphia: Westminster Press, 1961. The author begins by sketching the several approaches to interpretation (for example, the Hellenistic approach and the Palestinian-Judaic approach); then he treats Paul's position in the primitive church, his eschatology, his soteriology (theology of salvation), his views on the law, and his concept of history. Indexed to biblical passages and to modern authors. Heavily annotated.

Stendahl, Krister. *The Bible and the Role of Women: A Case Study in Hermeneutics*. Translated by Emilie T. Sander. Philadelphia: Fortress Press, 1966. This slim volume is composed of Stendahl's essay, a lengthy editor's introduction and author's preface, and a copious bibliography. The essay first appeared in 1958, growing out of a specific controversy over the proposed ordination of women as priests in the Church of Sweden (Lutheran). Part 2 of the essay, "The Biblical View of Male and Female," is devoted largely to an exegesis of Paul's pronouncements on the subject in his epistles.

Patrick Adcock

PAUL OF AEGINA

Born: c. 607; Aegina, Greece
Died: c. 690; place unknown
Area of Achievement: Medicine
Contribution: Paul of Aegina was a celebrated Byzantine physician, surgeon, and medical writer. His *Epitome* summarized nearly all medical knowledge of his time and had a profound influence on Western European, Arabic, and Persian medicine. His treatment of surgery is the best summary of ancient surgery that has survived.

Early Life

Little is known of the life and career of Paul of Aegina. He was born on the Greek island of Aegina in the Saronic Gulf near Athens in the early seventh century. As a young man he studied at Alexandria in Egypt. At this time the eastern Mediterranean world was dominated by the Byzantine Empire, which came into existence in A.D. 395, when the Roman Empire was divided in two. Centered in the great city of Constantinople, named after the emperor Constantine in 330, the Eastern Roman Empire gradually developed a separate identity of its own. Enjoying geographic and economic advantages over the Western Empire, it survived after the fall of Rome in the West. No one thought of it as a new empire, but rather as a continuation of the Roman Empire on a reduced scale.

Alexandria had long enjoyed a reputation as one of the chief centers of learning in the Mediterranean. It was renowned as a center of medical study, particularly the study of anatomy. Late antiquity witnessed a gradual decline in the quality of learning in all fields, but the schools of medicine continued to function at Alexandria well into the Byzantine period, even if their finest days were past. Hence Alexandria continued to attract young medical students, as it had for centuries. Paul seems to have practiced medicine in Alexandria, where he may even have taught, but how long he remained is not known. In 640 the city fell to the Muslims, ending, for all intents and purposes, Alexandria's prominence as a center of science and medicine. Whether Paul remained there after the conquest, and if so how long, are unknown.

According to a later Arab source, Paul had special experience in women's diseases and enjoyed considerable success in their treatment. Midwives are said often to have sought his aid regarding difficult cases and to have received from him much useful advice. For that reason he was given the title of *alqawabeli*, or "the Birth-helper." He wrote on pediatrics and obstetrics and in fact summarized nearly everything that was known at the end of antiquity on these subjects. He does not, however, seem to have specialized in these areas to the exclusion of others, for his writings reveal wide experience in medicine and surgery generally.

Life's Work

Byzantine medicine fell heir to nearly a thousand years of Greek medical development. Greek medicine, after reaching its zenith in the work of Galen in the second century after Christ, began a long period of decline and ossification. In late antiquity, medical writers increasingly abandoned firsthand medical investigation in favor of compiling encyclopedic compendia of medical knowledge in which the great medical writers of the past, whose works were regarded as too extensive to be manageable, were summarized and abridged. Hence much of the earlier Greek medical heritage was passed down to subsequent generations in the form of medical encyclopedias. In the fourth century, Oribasius, the court physician to Emperor Julian, compiled a large medical encyclopedia in seventy books. This practice of systematic compilation was continued by Byzantine physicians such as Aëtius of Amida and Alexander of Tralles in the sixth century. Paul of Aegina, who had Oribasius' work at his disposal, believed that it was too long to be used by most ordinary physicians and so compiled his own abridgment of it, *Epitome medicae libri septum* (*The Seven Books of Paulus Aegineta*, 1844-1877, commonly known as the *Epitome*).

In the preface to his *Epitome* Paul disclaims originality, saying that he has compiled the work from previous authors except for a few things that he has employed of his own. He includes material chiefly from Oribasius, but also from other distinguished medical writers. His statement that earlier writers had said all that there was to say on medicine has been taken to indicate Paul's recognition of the low state of medicine in his own day. In fact, however, it is probably no more than a conventional expression of piety to the great medical writers of the past. Book 1 of the *Epitome* deals with hygiene and regimen. Paul accepts Greek humoral pathology, discusses the temperaments, and recommends dietary therapeutics for different seasons and ages. Book 2 is devoted to fevers, which are symptomatic of acute or chronic diseases, and to the discussion of the value of the pulse (of which Paul classifies sixty-two varieties), urine, and sputum as indications of disease. In book 3 Paul deals with topical afflictions. He begins at the top of the head (with afflictions of the hair) and proceeds downward to the toenails. Included are discussions of diseases of the kidneys, liver, and uterus. Book 4 treats diseases of the skin (such as leprosy and cancer) as well as intestinal worms. Book 5 deals with toxicology and describes the treatment of stings and bites of venomous animals. Book 6 is devoted to general surgery and book 7 to simple and compound medicines (Paul includes some six hundred plants and ninety minerals). There are in the *Epitome* 242 sections that deal with virtually every aspect of medicine and represent a summary of medical knowledge in Paul's day. While relying heavily on Oribasius, he also drew on Galen, Soranus, Aëtius, and Dioscorides, sometimes reproducing them word for word. Yet Paul was no mere copyist. He was critical, providing correctives where necessary. On one occasion, having given the Hippocratic opinion on a particular condition, he added the warning, "Time, however, has demonstrated that this procedure is inadvisable."

Book 6 of the *Epitome* contains the best short treatment of ancient surgery that survives. The book is divided into two sections that deal respectively with manual operations and the treatment of fractures and dislocations. Altogether, Paul provides detailed descriptions of more than 120 operations. In general he describes surgery only on the surface of the body or in its orifices (such as nasal or genital passages), where surgical instruments can be easily inserted. Paul describes lithotomy (surgical removal of bladder stones), trephination (removal of a bone disc from the skull), removal of tonsils, and amputation of the breast. Also included are surgical techniques for tracheotomies, catheterization, and removal of hemorrhoids. The method that he recommends for excision of tonsils remained virtually unchanged in practice for centuries. Paul describes as well venesection, cupping, and the use of ligation for bleeding vessels. Book 6 also contains one of the most detailed treatments of ancient opthalmic surgery extant. Paul records procedures for removal of cataracts, and his treatment of trachoma is especially good for the age in which it was written. His account of military surgery is similarly comprehensive. Paul's treatment of surgery shows him to have been probably the greatest surgeon of his day. Although his accounts of surgical procedures were for the most part derived from the works of earlier medical writers, he reproduced them with clarity and precision. He did not hesitate to reject established procedures when he thought it necessary. Thus, in his treatment of fractures he sometimes contradicts Hippocratic teaching in favor of what he regards as sounder procedures (for example, he recommends the immediate reduction of dislocations).

Among other aspects of medicine treated by Paul are pediatrics (he includes discussion of dentition, convulsions, and constipation), lung diseases, and difficult labor. He provides one of the earliest descriptions in medical literature of lead poisoning. There are also descriptions of encephalitis, apoplexy, and epilepsy. In his discussion of insanity, there are excellent clinical observations as well as sound recommendations for treatment. Paul also gives the first description of hygienic rules for travelers, which became very popular in the Middle Ages.

Summary

Paul of Aegina was the last great physician and surgeon of the early Byzantine period. Following his death near the end of the seventh century, there was little original work done in medicine; few influential Byzantine physicians are known until the eleventh century. Although Paul reflects the tendency of late Roman and Byzantine physicians to substitute the collected wisdom of earlier Greek writers for experimentation and independent judgment, he rose above his contemporaries in rejecting traditional procedures and therapeutics where they conflicted with his personal experience. Since the time of Celsus (who lived in the first century after Christ), it appears that in technical skill Roman and Byzantine surgeons had made considerable advancement. Paul's treatment of surgery represents the culmination of advances made by Greek surgeons. The progress, however, ended with him: There was no one after Paul who equaled him. Hence he became the authoritative writer on surgery for later Byzantine physicians—which had negative as well as positive ramifications. In describing the operation for hernia, for example, Paul recommended that the testicle be removed; as a result of his authority, this unfortunate procedure continued to be practiced until the sixteenth century. His treatment of surgery was long used as a textbook at the University of Paris. In the sixteenth century his works were translated into Latin and quoted extensively by medical writers. His discussion of surgery was extracted by Hieronymus Fabricius ab Aquapendente (the teacher of William Harvey) in his work on surgery published in 1592.

Paul's reputation was at least as great among Muslim physicians as it was among European Christians. Arab and Persian physicians quoted him frequently and regarded him as an authoritative Greek writer on medicine. The famous Persian physician al-Razi borrowed heavily from Paul's surgery. Abu al-Qasim (1013-1106), the great Muslim surgeon, based his well-known treatise, *al-Tasrif liman 'ajaz'an al-Ta'alif*, on the surgical writings of Paul. Inasmuch as Abu al-Qasim remained the leading authority on surgery until the thirteenth century, Paul of Aegina continued to influence surgery in the Muslim world nearly as long as he did in the West.

Bibliography
Gordon, Benjamin Lee. *Medieval and Renaissance Medicine*. New York: Philosophical Library, 1959. A brief discussion of Paul of Aegina together with other leading representatives of Byzantine medicine.
Paul of Aegina. *The Seven Books of Paulus Aegineta*. Translated by Francis Adams. 3 vols. London: Sydenham Society, 1844-1847. An excellent translation into English of the *Epitome* prefaced by a good introduction on Paul of Aegina and his influence on later medicine.
Scarborough, John, ed. *Symposium on Byzantine Medicine*. Washington, D.C.: Dumbarton Oaks, 1984. A collection of papers by specialists that deal with virtually every aspect of Byzantine medicine.
Thomas, Phillip D. "Paul of Aegina," in *Dictionary of Scientific Biography*, vol. 10. New York: Charles Scribner's Sons, 1974. Contains a detailed summary of Paul's *Epitome*.

Gary B. Ferngren

PEISISTRATUS

Born: Early sixth century B.C.; place unknown
Died: 527 B.C.; place unknown
Area of Achievement: Government
Contribution: As tyrant of Athens, Peisistratus saved his polis from internal political turmoil and ensured the future development of democracy while nurturing nationalism and the intellectual brilliance that became the hallmark of Athenian civilization.

Early Life
Though Peisistratus' family originated in Pylos in the Peloponnesus, he himself was probably born in Brauron, in the northeast part of Attica, for his family is often connected with the Philaidai of Brauron, one of the more influential aristocratic families involved in Athenian politics. (Actually, no source says where or when his birth occurred.)

A kinsman of Peisistratus, bearing the same name, was an Athenian archon in 669-668 B.C., and, even though they lived remote from Athens itself, his family must have become somewhat prominent in Athenian affairs. Some confirmation of his position in society perhaps comes from his command against Megara, as well as his association with Solon (to whom Peisistratus' mother was related). It may be that Peisistratus was nurtured early in Athenian politics from this family connection, since Solon, sole archon in 594 B.C., was charged with running the government of Athens during one of its more critical periods. Nevertheless, Peisistratus witnessed the eventual failure on the part of his kinsman. Solon pursued a policy of the middle—pleasing some, alienating others—but he failed to solve the problems which had necessitated his position. Following Solon, political chaos ensued as government fell victim to political strife; though evidence for internal affairs in Athens becomes hazy after 580 B.C., it is probable that the turmoil continued until mid-century. Eventually, two political clubs, the *Pedieis* (Plains) and the *Paraloi* (Coast), further demanded changes to Solonian legislation.

That Peisistratus inherited the rivalry created from Solon's legislation and developed a third faction of pastoral mountaineers also underscores his potential political prowess and some determined calculation on his part. Peisistratus apparently developed skills which would later make him a consummate politician. His political acumen was evident in his disarming manner of speech, moderate and cautious actions in all matters, and love of the poor—traits which suggest a studied response to critical political problems. Beyond this psychological caricature, however, no record of Peisistratus' physical characteristics exists. The so-called Sabouroff Head (c. 540 B.C.) in Berlin is often seen as a portrait of him. If so, the head, so unusual in

Archaic art, of a person with short hair, mustache, and beard was perhaps made to underscore the exceptional personality of the politician.

Peisistratus' popularity, however, stemmed not only from his politics but also from his military career. He was a general in or around 565 in the war with Megara, the neighbor southwest of Attica which had been at war with Athens for some years and had lost the island Salamis to the Athenians under Solon. Peisistratus took Nisaea, Megara's major port on her eastern coast, severely disabling Megarian maritime trade. Tradition has it that his capture of Nisaea involved a ruse. He intercepted Megarian vessels attacking Eleusis, killed the crews, and replaced them with Athenians, including some women who were the objective of the Megarians in the first place. Landing these captured vessels near Megara and waiting until the Megarians came out to greet their returning warriors, Peisistratus defeated them and therefore took control of the port.

Life's Work

The major political achievement of Peisistratus was Athens' first tyranny (a term which for the Athenians lacked opprobrium and merely meant that Peisistratus gained control of Athens by methods other than inheritance). His initial attempts, however, hardly revealed his success in this regard. In 561, in one particular instance of internal feuding, Peisistratus established himself as tyrant by support of his new party, known as *Hyperakrioi* or *Diakrioi*, "the party of the Hills." Confidently, Peisistratus presented himself in the assembly with (self-inflicted) wounds and sought to have bodyguards assigned for his protection. These were granted, which suggests that Peisistratus had votes within the assembly beyond those that he controlled. With his "clubmen," Peisistratus made himself tyrant, though how he did so is unclear, save that he took the Acropolis. Though he governed well for five years, Peisistratus did not win the support of Lycurgus and Megacles, leaders of the Plains and Coast parties, respectively. These leaders and their parties combined to drive Peisistratus out of Athens (perhaps to Brauron or Argos) around 556. This alliance predictably proved disastrous, however, and within that same year, Megacles and Peisistratus joined efforts to put the tyrant back into power. The coalition entailed the marriage of Megacles' daughter and Peisistratus, which Peisistratus took lightly, forcing a reconciliation between Lycurgus and Megacles. This time, Peisistratus voluntarily withdrew beyond Attica for ten years, where he gained support from Argos, Eretria, Naxos, Thessaly, and Thebes, and accumulated money from silver and gold mining operations in Thrace. In 546, Peisistratus forced entry into Attica, landing near Marathon and defeating his opponents at Pallene. His third tyranny lasted until his son Hippias was driven out of Athens in 510.

As tyrant, Peisistratus was no revolutionary, but a pragmatic politician. He inherited the Solonian reforms, which had limited aristocratic privilege and revamped the mechanics of government. Peisistratus wisely kept this system, but he did guarantee its cooperation by using mercenaries, hostages, and his own people. In addition, he solved the problem of the divided aristocracy by using some in the chief magistracies of the state, though his success here is not completely recorded. Certainly some of his opponents—the Alcmaeonids and, ironically, a member of the Philaidai, Miltiades—left Athens in response to Peisistratus' tyranny. Both families, however, eventually cooperated with the system: Cimon, a kinsman of Miltiades, was active in Athenian politics in the 530's, and Cleisthenes, future designer of Athenian democracy and son of the Megacles who had bitterly opposed the tyrant, was archon two years after Peisistratus' death.

In similar fashion, Peisistratus placated the common people. Since his following included both rich and poor, he had to balance the demands of the aristocrats and the expectations of his faithful constituency. His relief system for poor farmers, based on a one-fifth contribution from produce and taxes, brilliantly provided the answer: It swept away the need to confiscate land from the rich, while satisfying Peisistratus' debt to his populist image. The lessening of agricultural distress was coupled with judicial reform which sent district judges into the countryside, where Peisistratus himself made frequent visits. Rural Athens was thus made part of the larger whole, while stability and general prosperity fostered confidence in central government and caused particularism to die.

In matters of foreign policy, Peisistratus was as daring and deliberate as he was in politics. When he reoccupied Sigeum, on the southern side of the entrance to the Hellespont, he secured control of that important link between the Black Sea and the Aegean Sea. This move paralleled the earlier occupation of the opposite northern coastline by Miltiades, who (with the tyrant's blessing) had left Athens for the region early in Peisistratus' reign. In order to facilitate northern shipping and to tap the mineral wealth of the region, Peisistratus occupied a site on the Theramic Gulf at Rhaecalus. As a result of his preparations for his third tyranny, there was the support of many allies, most of whom no doubt continued in their friendship with the tyrant after his return to Athens. Lygdamus, tyrant of Naxos, gave Athens a base on that island, allowing the Athenian sphere of influence to spread farther east. A similar relationship with Samos developed under Peisistratus, and he purified the island of Delos (built a temple there for Apollo), demonstrating most dramatically Athenian interest in the mid-Aegean and the pro-Ionian policy which would characterize the foreign policy of fifth century Athens.

As political crisis gave way to relative calm, other benefits followed. Trade particularly was stimulated under Peisistratus, and production of olive oil and black-figured vases flourished as Athens became the major exporter and the pottery center of Greece. Peisistratus issued heraldic coins, though the exact date of their appearance is in doubt. These paid for local services, goods, and taxes and were the source of the plentiful revenue of Peisistratus' reign. (The variety of types meant rich men participated in their production, accommodating themselves to the tyranny and guaranteeing the weight and quality of the coins.) Public works marched forward with the economic advance. Among Peisistratus' projects in Athens were the beginning of the temple of Olympian Zeus, the Enneakrounos fountain, and a temple of Athena on the Acropolis, from which the pediment survives. This activity bolstered the tyranny since it gave employment to many in Athens, but by building in Eleusis and on Delos it is clear that Peisistratus consciously sought the glorification of Athens in a larger context.

Other activities of Peisistratus equally stressed his desire to foster local pride. The Panathenaea, begun in the archonship of Hippocleides about 565 B.C., was a festival in honor of the unification of Attica. Peisistratus reorganized the festival to suggest subtly his hand in bringing unity and peace once again to Attica: Without doubt, however, under his regime the festival (now famous for its games and poetic contests, especially the recitation of Homer) assumed greater importance as an international event. A text of Homer's poems was perhaps also created under the tyrant. In like manner, Peisistratus developed the Dionysia, to which in 535, on his invitation, Thespis came to Athens, initiating for that city her undying reputation as the center for the dramatic arts. His activity at Eleusis was calculated to make Demeter's mystery religion an Athenian possession. Interestingly, all of these stress nationalism over particularism, the theme so consistent in Peisistratus' political endeavors.

Peisistratus had a flair for the extraordinary, a trait which perhaps first surfaced in his taking of Nisaea from Megara, or in the equally bold ruse he used to secure his initial tyranny. The most famous incident, however, was coupled with his return for his second tyranny. Herodotus records the facts but sees them as somewhat unbelievable. Peisistratus hired a rather stately woman named Phya to play the part of Athena, drive him into Athens, and announce that Athena ordered his recall. Attempts have been made to explain the event away, though minimal consensus exists. These events show at least that Peisistratus understood human nature well: The Athenians needed to be impressed, since impression is one step away from acceptance. Peisistratus also used art to reinforce his image. The Dorian Heracles, the hero of Peisistratus, became the image of the immigrant accepted by the Athenians, much as the tyrant's family had been in the past.

Summary

Aristotle assessed Peisistratus' tyranny as "the life of the days of Cronos," which for the Greek implied an age when the gods lived among men and peace reigned on Earth. That praise was not given to the form of government practiced by Peisistratus, but to the accomplishments of it. The fourth century judgment of Aristotle seems sound, even if the term tyranny has a ring of intolerance. Peisistratus' settlement not only brought an end to the political chaos that had plagued Athens for almost fifty years but also gave a stability to the Athenian state unknown since the coup of Cylon in 623. In every way, the tyranny of Peisistratus was a substantial help to Athens' future development. His policies in foreign fields prefigured the fifth century Athenian Empire; his political balance and tolerance defined the actions of future Athenian leaders; his pursuits in architecture and the arts set the stage for the grandeur of the fifth century B.C.; and his financial policies provided the eventual sources of funds on which all these activities rested. Peisistratus' tyranny was the necessary ingredient for future Athenian greatness and democracy. Plutarch was later to report that Pericles, under whom Athens reached her highest potential, was called the "second Peisistratus," and Thucydides accurately tagged his years in office as "nominally a democracy, but really the rule of one man."

Bibliography
Adcock, F. E. "The Exiles of Peisistratus." *The Classical Quarterly* 27 (1923): 174-181. Establishment of the standard dates for Peisistratus' tyrannies based on analysis of the evidence given by Aristotle and the narrative of the tyrant's career as supplied by Herodotus.
Andrewes, Antony. *The Greek Tyrants*. New York: Harper and Row, Publishers, 1963. Contains an excellent chapter on Peisistratus, covering the many facets of his career; includes bibliography and notes.
Hignett, Charles. *A History of the Athenian Constitution to the End of the Fifth Century B.C.* Oxford: Clarendon Press, 1952. An indispensable work that delineates Peisistratus' political career and especially his relationship with the Philaidai, coupled with bibliography and indexes.
Holladay, James. "The Followers of Peisistratus." *Greece and Rome* 23 (1977): 40-56. An insightful analysis concerning the makeup of the three parties that dominated Athenian politics in the mid-sixth century.
Jeffery, L. H. *Archaic Greece: The City States, c. 700-500 B.C.* New York: St. Martin's Press, 1976. Contains a chapter discussing the problems of the Peisistratean occupation of Sigeum, with additional references and bibliography.
Kraay, Colin M. *Archaic and Classical Greek Coins*. Berkeley: University of California Press, 1976. Contains a discussion on the coinage of Peisistratus and his son Hippias, along with excellent appendices, bibliography, and plates.
Legon, Ronald P. *Megara: The Political History of a City-State to 336 B.C.* Ithaca, N.Y.: Cornell University Press, 1981. A history of Megara, with a chapter focusing on the war with Athens and the historical problems of it, especially the roles of Solon and Peisistratus.

Parke, H. W. *Festivals of the Athenians*. Ithaca, N.Y.: Cornell University Press, 1977. Contains valuable information concerning Peisistratus' use of festivals as part of his unification of Attica.

Ure, P. N. *The Origin of Tyranny*. Cambridge: Cambridge University Press, 1922. Contains a chapter on the tyranny of Peisistratus in Athens, detailing the life of the tyrant drawn from the pertinent ancient sources, with conclusions somewhat dated but still acceptable.

Wycherley, R. E. *The Stones of Athens*. Princeton, N.J.: Princeton University Press, 1978. A full discussion of the buildings in Athens, including those of Peisistratus, with bibliography.

R. Leon Fitts

PETRUS PEREGRINUS DE MARICOURT

Born: Early thirteenth century; place unknown
Died: Thirteenth century; place unknown
Area of Achievement: Physics
Contribution: Petrus was the author of the first Western scientific treatise on the principles of magnetism. His practical inventions included a floating compass and a pivoted compass, both of which were used for finding the meridian and the azimuths of heavenly bodies.

Early Life
Very little is known about the life of Petrus Peregrinus de Maricourt (Peter the Pilgrim of Maricourt). What is known comes from two sources: Petrus' *Epistola Petri Peregrini de Maricourt ad Sygerum de Foucaucourt, militem, de magnete* (*Epistle of Petrus Peregrinus de Maricourt, to Sygerus of Foucaucourt, Soldier, Concerning the Magnet,* 1902), completed on August 6, 1269, at Lucera, and references in Roger Bacon's treatise *Opus tertium* (c. 1266).

The surname "de Maricourt" indicates that Petrus hailed from Méhaircourt, a village in Picardy (an old province in northern France); whether he was born at Méhaircourt or simply lived there is not known. Given his extensive education, it is clear that he was of noble birth. The appellation "Peregrinus" has been a matter of controversy. As "Peregrinus" was an honorary title given to people who had made pilgrimages to the Holy Sepulcher in Jerusalem or who had participated in a crusade, it was formerly conjectured that Petrus was a Templar Knight or was a member of one of Louis IX's Crusades in the thirteenth century. It is now recognized that "Peregrinus" was also bestowed on anyone who fought in an officially sanctioned crusade outside the Holy Land. Thus, Petrus probably received his appellation from his service at the siege of Lucera, where he apparently wrote his work on magnetism.

Frederick II, the Holy Roman Emperor of Germany who was excommunicated three times in his life by the Papacy, had established early in the thirteenth century the town of Lucera in southern Italy as a colony and place of refuge for Saracens. Three times between 1255 and 1269, this town, manned by Saracens and supported by the German emperor, was attacked by the forces of Charles I of Anjou, King of Italy. As the Papacy had declared these assaults official crusades, Petrus received his title "Peregrinus" from his activity in Charles's final siege of the city in 1268-1269. Given his keen interest in mechanical devices, it seems likely that Petrus served as an engineer: Perhaps he constructed machines for breaching walls or hurling objects.

Other information on Petrus' life comes from Roger Bacon. In Bacon's *Opus tertium* (chapter 11), Petrus is referred to as one of the two "perfect mathematicians" and a *magister*, that is, someone who had earned a master of arts degree, perhaps at the University of Paris. In chapter 13, Bacon describes Petrus as the greatest experimental scientist of his time and one completely skilled in alchemy, warfare, agriculture, and the theory and use of all technical arts.

Life's Work

Although Petrus had planned to write a treatise on mirrors and may in fact have composed one on the composition of an astrolabe (a manuscript on such a topic bears his name in the title), his fame rests on the work on magnetism. The work is divided into two parts, theoretical and practical. The first, consisting of ten chapters, is devoted to the properties and effects of magnets and the principles of magnetism; the second discusses the construction of three instruments utilizing magnets (two compasses and a perpetual motion machine).

After an introductory chapter stating the purpose of his work, Petrus sets forth the qualifications of the scientist. Petrus insists that theory and speculation alone are insufficient; one must be good at manual experimentation, for only then can errors, undetected by abstract thinking and mathematics, be corrected. Chapter 3 contains a discussion of the properties of a good lodestone (natural magnet). It should look ironlike, slightly bluish, and pale. It should be heavy, homogeneous in material, and possessing "virtue," or the power to attract the greatest amount of iron. Thus, in the latter instance, Petrus considered the extent of magnetic strength (perhaps the lifting power of the stone) to be of crucial importance.

Chapter 4 is very important in the history of magnetism, for here is the earliest account of magnetic polarity and the methods for fixing the north and south poles. The poles of the lodestone are analogous to the celestial poles. In this respect, Petrus followed medieval thinking. According to the cosmology of the Middle Ages, Earth was the center of the universe, fixed and immobile; around it lay ten heavens, all of which, except the outermost, where God resided, rotated about their common center. The rotation of the heavens was on an axis, the ends of which formed the north and south celestial poles. Petrus believed that the celestial poles attracted the magnet; it was only later that scientists, beginning with William Gilbert in 1600, thought of Earth as having its own magnetic poles.

The theory of the celestial poles led Petrus to form two methods of distinguishing the poles of a lodestone. The first method involves a lodestone that has been polished into a spherical shape. A needle or piece of iron is placed on the stone's surface; a line is then drawn in the direction of the needle, dividing the sphere in half. If this procedure is performed repeatedly, all the lines (meridians) will converge at two points—the poles. This conclusion represents an astounding piece of scientific experimentation: The poles of a spherical magnet are recognized and the magnetic meridians located.

The second method was also revolutionary. Petrus insisted that the poles can also be detected without drawing meridians—simply by noting the greatest attraction of a needle by the magnetic force. Petrus suggested that a two- or three-inch-long needle of iron, if moved around a lodestone, would locate the polar point, the place where the needle stands the most erect. What Petrus observed is the action of the magnetic field of force: At the poles the needles stand erect, and at other points they are more or less inclined.

The next step was to determine which pole is north and which is south (chapter 5). Here Petrus set forth the fundamental law of magnetic polarity. If the magnet is placed in a wooden cup and the cup into a large vessel of water, then the north pole of the lodestone will point toward the north celestial pole and the south pole of the lodestone to the celestial south pole. Even if one forcibly turns the magnet away in a new direction, it will return to its true alignment. Next, the effect of one lodestone upon another was demonstrated. The north pole of a lodestone, when brought close to the south pole of a second lodestone, will cause the latter to try to adhere to it; the same will happen if the south pole of the one is moved to the other's north pole. If the reverse is done, however—that is, if like poles are brought into close proximity—then the poles "flee" each other. Thus Petrus established the law of attraction and repulsion. Petrus then made a further startling discovery: If a magnet is broken into two, each part will act like a magnet and have its own north and south poles; moreover, the opposite poles of the magnets will unite if brought together, thus making again a unified magnet. Petrus' work was the first theory of persistence of polarity in the separate parts of a magnet.

Petrus next showed the action of a magnet on iron: A needle when touched by the north pole of the magnet will turn to the south celestial pole and vice versa. Thus, the south pole of the needle will be attracted to the north pole of the magnet and repelled by the south pole; the north pole of the needle will be attracted to the south pole of the magnet and repelled by the north pole. Polarity, however, can be reversed by touching the north pole of the needle with the north pole of the magnet, causing the needle's north pole to be converted into a south pole. This observation of reversal of magnetic polarity was centuries ahead of its time.

Petrus finished part 1 of his work with a discussion of the cause of the virtue (attractive power) of the lodestone. He rejected the then commonly held view that mines of magnetic stone in the northern region of the world caused a magnet to be oriented on a north-south line. Instead, the poles of a magnet are influenced by the celestial poles. Petrus also refuted the idea that the Pole Star was at the true north; rather, it was Polaris that rotated around that point. (It should be noted, however, that Petrus was not aware of declination, that is, the fact that the compass needle does not point due north but at a small angle which varies from place to place. This effect had long been observed by the Chinese and is mentioned in an eleventh century work by Shen Kua. The discovery in Europe of the declination was formerly attributed to Christopher Columbus during his voyage of 1492 or even to Sebastian Cabot during his voyage to Labrador in 1497-1498; current scholars, however, recognize that European mariners knew of declination long before this.) The chapter closes with a description of a perpetual motion machine with pivoted spherical magnets. The magnet, made with fixed pivots at its poles so that it could freely rotate, would follow the motion of the celestial poles and so rotate. This theory was possible, one must remember, because Petrus believed that Earth was motionless and the celestial heavens rotated around it.

Part 2 is very important for the history of the compass. The Chinese had known about the magnet's properties of pointing north-south and had employed it for geomancy; yet they did not apply this knowledge to the construction of a mariner's compass until the twelfth century. At about the same time, references to the mariner's compass appear in Western literature; whether the compass was introduced from the East by Arab or European sailors or was independently developed is not known. This early compass was a water compass. A needle or piece of iron, after being placed on a magnetic stone, was floated on wood in a vessel of water; it would turn until it pointed in the direction of north. Hardly a sophisticated piece of equipment, this early compass gave only a directional heading and did not permit any bearings.

Petrus made tremendous improvements on this water compass by constructing two compasses—a dry compass and a wet one. The latter consisted of an oval magnet inside a bowl or wooden case and floated on water inside a large vessel. The rim of the vessel was marked into four quadrants by the four cardinal points of the compass. Each quadrant was subdivided into ninety equal parts, or degrees. On top of the container that had the magnet inside it, Petrus placed a light bar of wood, with an upright pin at each end. This device allowed the navigator to determine not only the direction of the ship but also the azimuth of any heavenly body (sun, moon, or star). The innovation, in other words, was a combination of a compass needle and nautical astrolabe that was capable of steering a vessel on any given course.

Petrus proceeded to invent a pivoted compass. In place of the floating bowl and the vessel of water, a circular compass container was constructed with a transparent lid of glass or quartz. The top of the container was divided into the same ninety parts per quadrant as in the floating compass; then, a movable pivot rule with upright pins at each end was fastened on top of the lid. An axis of brass or silver was then fastened below the lid and the bottom of the vessel. Two needles—one of iron, the other of brass or silver—were inserted at right angles through the axis. The iron needle was then magnetized by a lodestone so that it would point north and south. The lid of the

Petrus Peregrinus de Maricourt

vessel was then turned until its north-south points were in line with those of the needle. Azimuthal readings could then be made by rotating the pivot rule to the heavenly body sought. Others later improved this compass by adding the compass card, that is, the thirty-two points of the compass affixed to the compass' pointing needle.

Petrus closes his treatise with yet another attempt at perpetual motion by magnetic power. He conceived of a wheel of silver with a series of iron teeth. A magnet was to be placed at the end of a radial arm within the ring and close to the teeth. Petrus believed that any one tooth of the wheel would be attracted to the north pole of the magnet. Because of its attraction to the north pole, the tooth would gain enough momentum to move onto the magnet's south pole. Here it would be repelled by the south pole, whose momentum would force that tooth beyond the magnet. The next tooth is attracted to the north pole of the magnet, and so on. This alternating attraction and repulsion of the teeth would cause the wheel, to which the teeth are attached, to move in perpetual motion.

Summary

The "letter" on magnetism is the first scientific work on the subject. Petrus Peregrinus de Maricourt found and differentiated the poles of a magnet. He then formulated the laws of magnetic repulsion and attraction and discussed the strength of the magnetic force field by the amount of inclination of an iron needle when brought into close contact with a magnet at various points. He knew that the Pole Star was not at the true north and, therefore, did not affect the magnet. He knew also about reversal of magnetic polarity. Petrus applied this knowledge to practical inventions. His pivoted and floating compasses allowed the determination of the meridian and the azimuths of heavenly bodies and were the first to have the fiducial line and a division of 360 degrees. Finally, he suggested the conversion of magnetic energy into mechanical energy by a perpetual motion machine. Petrus' work exerted considerable influence on later writers and was drawn upon extensively by William Gilbert, who laid the foundation of magnetic science in 1600 in his *De magnete, magneticisque corporibus, et de magnete tellure* (1600; *On the Magnet, Magnetic Bodies Also, and on the Great Magnet the Earth*, 1860).

Bibliography

Benjamin, Park. *History of Electricity*. New York: John Wiley and Sons, 1898. Perhaps the most extensive discussion in English of Petrus' life and work. The style is a bit trying, but this work explains very well the ideas expressed in Petrus' treatise.

Grant, Edward. "Petrus Peregrinus." In *Dictionary of Scientific Biography*, edited by Charles C. Gillispie, vol. 10. New York: Charles Scribner's Sons, 1974. Aside from Benjamin's book, this article is the definitive English treatment of Petrus. Very readable. Contains an invaluable bibliography.

Harradon, H. D. "Some Early Contributions to the History of Geomagnetism-I." *Journal of Terrestrial Magnetism and Atmospheric Electricity* 48 (1943): 3-17. Contains a brief discussion of Petrus' life and work, followed by a translation of the letter. (This journal was subsequently renamed the *Journal of Geophysical Research*.)

Mottelay, Paul Fleury. *Bibliographical History of Electricity and Magnetism, Chronologically Arranged.* London: C. Griffin, 1922. Reprint. New York: Arno Press, 1955. Contains a summation of the letter, with a bibliography on Petrus and the manuscripts and editions of the letter.

Peregrinus of Maricourt, Petrus. *Epistle of Petrus Peregrinus of Maricourt, to Sygerus of Foucaucourt, Soldier, Concerning the Magnet.* Translated by Silvanus P. Thompson. London: Chiswick Press, 1902. Preceding his translation, Thompson includes a good introduction to Petrus' life and theories on magnetism.

Roller, Duane H. D. *The "De magnete" of William Gilbert.* Amsterdam: Menno Hertzberger, 1959. A useful discussion of magnetism in the Middle Ages, with an emphasis on Petrus.

Sarton, George. *Introduction to the History of Science.* Vol. 2, *From Rabbi Ben Ezra to Roger Bacon.* Baltimore: Williams and Wilkins, 1931. Short but very helpful biography of Petrus and a summation of the contents of the letter.

Thompson, Silvanus P. "Petrus Peregrinus de Maricourt and His *Epistola de magnete.*" *Proceedings of the British Academy* 2 (1905-1906): 377-408. Extensive discussion of Petrus' life, his work, and his impact on subsequent times.

Steven M. Oberhelman

PERICLES

Born: c. 495 B.C.; Athens, Greece
Died: 429 B.C.; Athens, Greece
Area of Achievement: Government
Contribution: The Age of Pericles was a crucial period in the history of Athens. Pericles' transformation of the Delian League into the Athenian empire provided the financial basis for the flowering of Athenian democracy.

Early Life

Pericles was born in Athens around 495 B.C., the son of Xanthippus and Agariste (the niece of Cleisthenes). As the son of a wealthy aristocratic family in Athens and possessed of an above-average intelligence, Pericles received an excellent education from private tutors. The two men who had the greatest influence on Pericles' life were the musician Damon and the philosopher Anaxagoras. Damon taught Pericles the moral and political influence of music and Anaxagoras taught him political style, effective speech making, and analytical rationalism.

Although Pericles had prepared himself for a political life, he did not openly side with any of the factions in Athens until 463, when he joined in the prosecution of the Athenenian statesman and general Cimon. During this period, various political factions frequently brought charges against their opponents, with the goal of diminishing the prestige of the accused. Cimon, having recently returned from a two-year military campaign against the island of Thasos, which had rebelled against the Delian League, was brought to trial by the democratic faction on charges of bribery. In this instance, Cimon was acquitted.

In 462, Sparta requested military aid from Athens because of a revolt among the helots (serfs). Sparta, a city-state unfamiliar with siege warfare, needed help in trying to dislodge the helots who had fled to and fortified Mount Ithome in Messenia. Cimon urged the Athenians to cooperate with the Spartans, while the democratic faction, led by Ephialtes and Pericles, opposed any form of cooperation. On this occasion, Cimon won popular support and led an Athenian force to Mount Ithome. The Spartans, however, having reconsidered their request, dismissed Cimon and his men when they arrived. Because of this humiliation, Cimon's influence with the people declined rapidly.

With Cimon in disgrace, the democratic faction now focused its attention on the Areopagus, the council of former archons (magistrates). In 461, Ephialtes and Pericles led the people in stripping the Areopagus of any real power. Cimon, unable to rally the conservative opposition, was ostracized in the same year. Not long after, a member of the conservatives assassinated Ephialtes, and Pericles became the new leader of the democratic faction.

Life's Work

Pericles' main achievement as the leader of Athens was the conversion of the Delian League into an Athenian empire. The Delian League was originally formed in 476 as an offensive and defensive alliance against Persia. Although it was composed predominantly of Ionian maritime city-states individually bound by treaty to Athens, with all member states considered equal, only Athenians were league officials. The league collected annual tribute from its members to maintain a fleet. For all practical purposes, it was an Athenian fleet, built and manned by Athenians but paid for by the allies. Because the allies had been paying tribute every year since 476, the income of the league far exceeded its expenditures. When the league treasury was transferred from Delos to Athens in 454, it contained a vast sum of money which was essentially at the disposal of the Athenians.

Pericles, believing that the Athenians had every right to enjoy the benefits of empire, introduced numerous measures which provided pay to Athenians for their services as soldiers, magistrates, and jurors. An estimated twenty thousand Athenians were on the government payroll. In addition, so that no Athenian would be deprived of the opportunity to attend the plays of the Dionysiac Festival, even the price of admission to the theater was given to the poor.

The city of Athens itself was not to be neglected in Pericles' plans for the Delian League treasury. Pericles was building commissioner for the Parthenon and many other important building projects in Athens. The Parthenon, Propylaea, Odeum, and Erectheum are merely a few of the many temples and public buildings which were built or planned under the direction of Pericles but financed with league funds.

To increase the power of Athens, Pericles attempted to enlarge the Delian League. When the Island of Aegina, located in the Saronic Gulf near Athens, declared war on Athens in 459, Pericles saw an opportunity to expand the league by creating an Athenian land empire which would complement the sea empire already embodied in the league. After the Athenians captured Aegina and forced it to become a member of the Delian League, the Peloponnesian coastal area of Troezen, facing Aegina, joined the league in self-defense. When Sparta tried to counter Athens by helping Thebes to dominate the Boeotian League in 457, Athens sent troops to fight the Spartans in the Battle of Tanagra. Although Athens lost the battle, Sparta soon withdrew her forces, and Athenian troops returned to rally the Boeotian League against Thebes. With the Boeotian League joined to the Delian League, the neighboring areas of Phocis and Locris joined the league, along with Achaea. By 456, the Periclean strategy of creating an Athenian land empire was a success, and the empire had reached its greatest territorial extent.

The Athenian land empire, however, disintegrated almost as quickly as it had been created. In 447, the Boeotian League revolted against Athens. As a result, Athens lost not only control of Boeotia but also the support of Phocis and Locris. When the Five-Year Truce with Sparta expired in 446, Sparta invaded Attica with a Peloponnesian army and encouraged the Athenian allied island of Euboea to revolt. Pericles quickly dealt with the two problems by bribing the Spartan commander of the Peloponnesians to leave Attica and by personally leading the Athenian reconquest of Euboea. While the Athenians were temporarily distracted, Megara broke its alliance with Athens and joined the Peloponnesian League along with Troezen and Achaea. All that remained now of the Athenian land empire was Aegina, Naupactus, and Plataea. Because Athens was in no position to reverse the situation, Athens and Sparta agreed in 445 to the Thirty Years' Peace.

Pericles successfully led the democratic faction in its control of Athenian politics from 461 until his death. He was a political genius in that he was able to provide leadership to the Athenian people without being led by them. The only surviving contemporary evidence of the opposition to Pericles is from Attic comedy. In general, the opponents of Pericles resented his oratorical skill, his family's wealth, and his political successes. Pericles was a very reserved and private individual, and his enemies interpreted these personality traits as signs of haughtiness and arrogance. Having earned the confidence of the people, however, Pericles was frequently elected *strategos* (general) in the 450's. When his chief political opponent, Thucydides, son of Melesias, was ostracized in 443, Pericles led the people virtually unopposed and was elected *strategos* every year until his death in 429.

The Peloponnesian War broke out in 431, when Athens and Sparta found that they could no longer observe the Thirty Years' Peace. Pericles believed that Athens and the Delian League had strategic advantages over Sparta and the Peloponnesian League. While the Peloponnesians had access to greater numbers of troops than the Athenians and had more agricultural land on which to produce food to support those troops, the Peloponnesians lacked a large fleet and so were more or less restricted to conducting a land war. The plan of Pericles was for the Athenians to abandon their property and homes in Attica and withdraw into the city of Athens. With its Long Walls assuring access to the port of Piraeus, Athens could withstand a siege of any length. In addition, Athens controlled the Delian League treasury and possessed a large fleet which could be used for hit-and-run raids on the Peloponnesians. As a safety precaution, however, Pericles set aside one thousand talents from the league treasury and reserved one hundred ships to be used only in the extreme emergency of defending Athens itself.

As Pericles predicted, the Peloponnesians invaded Attica in 431 and ravaged the countryside, trying to lure the Athenians from their walled city to fight a pitched battle. The Athenians, however, held firm. Instead of fighting in Attica, the Athenians, under Pericles' direction, mounted an attack on the

Peloponnese. After they ravaged the territory of Epidaurus and Troezen, the Athenians sailed to Laconia to bring the war directly to the Spartans. After the Peloponnesians had withdrawn their troops from Attica, Athens prepared to bury its dead. It was the custom of the Athenians to choose their best speaker to give the funeral oration for the first men who had fallen in a war. As expected, Pericles was chosen for this honor. Pericles' funeral oration was more a speech extolling the virtues of Athens than a speech of mourning. He clearly wanted to impress upon the living Athenians the greatness of their city and the enlightened life they were privileged to lead.

In the second year of the war, the Athenians continued to follow the Periclean strategy. The people withdrew from Attica into Athens when the Peloponnesians returned to ravage the land. Athenian morale, however, was devastated by a plague which broke out in the city, killing many people. In their anger and frustration, the people blamed Pericles for their suffering and drove him from office. Though he was tried for embezzlement, convicted, and fined, he was soon elected *strategos* once again. Within six months, however, Pericles contracted the plague; he died in 429. The Athenians would have to endure the rest of the Peloponnesian War without the guidance of their greatest leader.

Summary

Pericles was the dominant political figure during the most important period in Athenian history. Rather than being a demagogue who flattered the people and pandered to their base instincts, Pericles won the people over to his policies by his forceful and energetic oratory. While some politicians sought to win a following by agreeing with whatever was currently popular, Pericles used his oratorical skill to lead the people to decisions which he thought were correct. Possessing an incorruptible character, Pericles gained the confidence of the people and knew how to keep it. By respecting their liberties and by offering the Athenians a consistent policy, Pericles prevented the people from making what he considered grave errors in judgment. What Pericles failed to understand, however, was that personal government was, in the long run, harmful to the state because it limited the ability of the people to govern themselves. In addition, while Athens enjoyed its democracy, the Athenians refused to recognize that it was based upon the political, military, and financial oppression of others in the empire.

Although Athens and Sparta did go to war in 431, Pericles had worked for peace twenty years before. In 451, Sparta and Athens agreed to a five-year truce; in 449, Persia and Athens reached an understanding in the Peace of Callias. With Athens assured of peace, Pericles called for a meeting of all Greek city-states to consider the issue of peace throughout the Greek world. According to Pericles, representatives at the proposed meeting were to discuss the rebuilding of all temples destroyed during the Persian Wars, the elimination of piracy, and the promotion of trade and commerce between and among all Greek city-states. Although because of Spartan opposition such a meeting was never held, Pericles' proposal showed that the Athenians were content with the territories they had and that they wanted peace.

Bibliography
Andrewes, A. "The Opposition to Pericles." *Journal of Hellenic Studies* 98 (1978): 1-8. While Plutarch is the main source of information on the struggle between Pericles and Thucydides, son of Melesias, Andrewes shows that he is unreliable because of his anti-imperialist bias. Although there were opponents to Pericles' building program, the argument that it was wrong to use league funds would not have been made, for Athenians viewed the empire as theirs to be enjoyed.
Bloedow, Edmund F. "Pericles' Powers in the Counter-Strategy of 431." *Historia* 36 (1987): 9-27. Bloedow tries to discover the constitutional basis for the power of Pericles through a close study of Thucydides. Although Pericles was only one of ten generals (*strategoi*) who led the state, he wielded authority that went far beyond that of a general. It was Pericles, for example, who decided if and when the assembly could meet.
Cawkwell, George. "Thucydides' Judgment of Periclean Strategy." *Yale Classical Studies* 24 (1975): 53-70. Cawkwell examines Thucydides' belief that the Athenians brought ruin upon themselves when they strayed from Periclean strategy after the death of Pericles. The author shows that, with the exception of the abandonment of Attica and withdrawal into Athens, the Athenians used the same strategies as the Spartans even during the time of Pericles.
Ehrenberg, Victor. *Sophocles and Pericles*. Oxford: Basil Blackwell, 1954. More than a third of this work directly concerns Pericles and his leadership role in Athens. The author provides an excellent analysis of all the dramatic and comedic references to Pericles and the politics of his time. The comments of the author on Plutarch's use of sources are invaluable.
Hignett, C. *A History of the Athenian Constitution to the End of the Fifth Century B.C.* Oxford: Clarendon Press, 1952. Contains three chapters which cover the Athenian democracy from the revolution of 462 to the fall of the Athenian empire. The author covers all Periclean laws and their impact upon the Athenian constitution. An appendix covers Pericles' citizenship law of 451. Although a very specialized study, this work is seminal.
Kagan, Donald. *The Outbreak of the Peloponnesian War*. Ithaca, N.Y.: Cornell University Press, 1969. The author discusses the position taken by Thucydides that the Peloponnesian War was inevitable. By using all available sources, Kagan reexamines the foreign and domestic decisions made by Pericles and the Athenians and concludes that the war was not inevitable, but was the result of poor judgment and bad decisions.

Meiggs, Russell. *The Athenian Empire*. Oxford: Clarendon Press, 1972. This is an attempt to bring together all the available evidence for the Athenian empire and to evaluate it in the light of archaeological and epigraphic evidence. The coverage is comprehensive, thorough, and sound. Seventeen appendices cover controversial points of interpretation.

Plutarch. *The Rise and Fall of Athens*. Translated by Ian Scott-Kilvert. Harmondsworth, England: Penguin Books, 1960. Contains a chapter on Pericles, together with other chapters on some of his political rivals. Plutarch preserves much material regarding Pericles' time; the interpretations, however, are often biased. Still, the work is useful in showing the opinion of the opposition.

Ste. Croix, G. E. M. de. *The Origins of the Peloponnesian War*. Ithaca, N.Y.: Cornell University Press, 1972. An in-depth study of the reasons for the Peloponnesian War, based upon a detailed reexamination and reevaluation of the primary sources. The author attempts to show that Thucydides is a reliable source and a keen observer of events. The work ends with forty-seven appendices and an extensive bibliography.

Thucydides. *History of the Peloponnesian War*. Translated by Charles Forster Smith. 4 vols. Cambridge, Mass.: Harvard University Press, 1919-1923. Books 1 and 2 of the first volume of Thucydides constitute the primary source on Pericles' background, his political career, and his strategy for the transformation of the Delian League into the Athenian empire. While historians may interpret and reinterpret Thucydides, he remains the indispensable beginning point for any study of Pericles.

Peter L. Viscusi

PÉROTIN

Born: 1155-1160; possibly Paris, France
Died: 1200-1205; probably Paris, France
Area of Achievement: Music
Contribution: Pérotin was a pioneer in the evolution of harmony as a principle of Western music. He transformed the nature of early music by first introducing three- and four-voice textures into church music, by developing polyphonic forms with semichordal sequences, and by adapting liturgical forms to secular purposes.

Early Life

Almost nothing is known about Pérotin's life, which in itself reveals the lack of personal esteem accorded artists during the Middle Ages. There is one existing contemporary reference to him, significantly in a treatise on twelfth century composers attributed to a writer designated Anonymous IV. That text associates Pérotin with the then recently built Cathedral of Notre Dame, first begun in 1163; since he cannot be identified as any of the registered principal musicians of the cathedral, the cantors and succentors, he is assumed to have been a choirmaster, though he could have been an organist. The treatise does attribute to him, however, specific compositions by title and others by type.

The named compositions are convincingly dated 1198-1200; the others seem to have been written a bit earlier. His association in the text with the earlier composer Léonin suggests that Pérotin may have begun working under his tutelage, suggesting a possible birth date. Since nothing in his music reflects the changes that took place in music and society after 1203, it is convenient to assume that his death occurred around that time. This date seems more likely since his music was not only admired but widely copied and distributed as well, surviving in several different widely separated manuscripts. Had he written after 1203, his work would have been preserved. All attempts to determine more information about the man and his life have failed. The man lives in his music and in the general information known about life in twelfth century Paris.

Life's Work

Because Pérotin's music is in some ways almost as obscure as his life, it is dismayingly easy to discount his significance. His music is really accessible only to specialists, and specialists often are so mired in minutiae that they lose sight of the larger implications of their enthusiasms. Thus few scholars will say that Pérotin was one of the most important composers in Western music, although in many ways he can be considered the father of harmony;

since harmonic texture and sequence is the major distinguishing quality of Western music, Pérotin was indeed of consequence.

Along with his predecessor Léonin, Pérotin was connected with innovations in music associated with the Cathedral of Notre Dame. Earlier in the twelfth century, composers centered at the Abbey of St. Martial at Limoges in south-central France had developed a new kind of two-part music called florid, melismatic, or Saint Martial organum. Although not the first type of multipart, multivoice music, it was distinct in having the upper voice improvise a free plainchant melody over drawn-out single notes in the lower, like drones. This lower line had originally been a melody itself; now that became unrecognizable. Thus, a new, nonmelodic aspect became added to the texture of music.

Léonin made the first significant changes to this style, developing a form known as Notre Dame organum, though he also worked in the equally important, related form of descant. Much of his work is preserved in the *Magnus liber organi* (c. 1170; great book of organum), a liturgical cycle of two-part settings for Vespers and Matins, as well as Alleluias and Graduals for the Mass. *Magnus liber organi* is the first identified volume of compositions by one master; its importance is attested by its preservation in several manuscripts in Italy, Germany, and Spain, as well as in France. Léonin introduced two new features in his work. One involved composing alternating sections of two-part polyphony and choral unison chant; this alternation becomes the principal formal structure. The second novelty is within the polyphony itself: The upper, "melody" part becomes flexible and semi-improvisatory, seeming to reach climaxes almost accidentally.

Léonin's organum looks and sounds much like chant superimposed on drone, something like unornamented bagpipe music. His descant is much different. Here the lower part moves more quickly, though in equally measured tones; the upper voice moves even faster now in a distinctly rhythmic pattern, almost as if dancing after swaying in the chant of the organum. When combined with organum in this way, the descant sections were called clausulae; they contrasted with the organum sections also in reaching distinct and definite final cadences.

Pérotin continued, expanded, and also transcended these practices. He adopted the basic formal style invented by Léonin but regularized it by establishing more precise rhythms and using clausulae more frequently. The lower part of the organum becomes less dronelike, more rhythmically regular and more melodic. In this respect Pérotin laid the foundation for the later thirteenth century motet, which became the major musical form of the succeeding three centuries. More important, he developed organum in a completely different way by adding first a third and then a fourth voice, creating an entirely new texture in music.

In terms of linear structure, Pérotin's triple and quadruple organum resemble Léonin's—both have alternating sections of slower, more sustained and faster, more rhythmic material, though Pérotin is always more rhythmic and melodic. Yet the difference in horizontal structure, or overlayering, is almost breathtaking. The upper voices dance, intertwine, cross, and resolve over the moving bottom line. Each line is distinct, moving on its own, but all play against the others. Something completely new happens in the process. The accepted intervals for voice doubling in organum were octaves, fifths, and (rarely) fourths. One of the perhaps unexpected results of multiplying upper voices is the regular emergence of thirds; the combination produces what sounds like a sequence of chords for the first time in Western music. These do not yet work together to form a chordal progression to resolution, but they establish the basis for this later formulation. Pérotin himself is still working with the tonal modes of medieval plainsong, so this kind of progression is unthinkable in his work, but the germ of the idea is there.

This foreshadowing is only part of his glory. Another part resides in the new sounds he creates. His music creates shifting webs of sonority and dissonance, in which the voices weave around one another in an unfolding maze centered on the stable lower part, much like mists floating above a mountain valley. A completely different source of beauty arises from Pérotin's practice of reflecting the vowel patterns of the text in the melodies and rhythms to which he sets them. In this he anticipates the text imaging of later composers, though few of them match him in subtlety and delicacy.

Pérotin also invented and popularized another, simpler polyphonic form known as conductus. Conductus seems to have originated in separating clausulae from organum and substituting secular (though still sacred) verses for the original hymn and sequence texts. These new verses were then reset so that all voices moved in nearly equal rhythms. This music, written for two, three, or four voices within a fairly restricted range, rested on cadences on fifths and unisons; since thirds occurred frequently and instrumental doublings were common, the effect was quasichordal, prefiguring later harmonic hymn settings. This type, known as conductus style, was extended to other forms, including completely secular ones.

Compared to Léonin's clausulae, conductus became a considerably expanded form; unlike it, the texts for conductus were commonly set syllabically. Eventually conductus even absorbed certain clausulae—which proved easily detachable from organum—and used them as contrasting melismas, textless and rhythmically varied, within its own structure. These contrasting passages—called caudae—gave conductus a structure parallel to that of organum, though the texts were treated quite distinctly.

One further difference had a major effect on the future of music: Pérotin began composing a new melody for the lower part rather than adopting an ecclesiastical chant. Thus he became the first composer to devise both the melodic and the harmonic aspects of polyphonic compositions.

Summary

Pérotin's final achievement was in laying the foundations of the motet, linked earlier to his practice in organum. In fact his work in both organum and conductus foreshadowed and tended toward the motet; it is not at all surprising that the motet should supersede both in the history of music. No existing motets have been ascribed to Pérotin, but this lack should not be allowed to obscure his significance in this regard. In that preprint age, the identification of composers in manuscripts was haphazard and casual; it is not incidental that the best-known composer until the sixteenth century is Anonymous. Further, secular music was then far from the serious business it later became. For centuries to come a composer would be identified primarily by his religious and liturgical work. Pérotin can be singled out as the most prolific composer of descant clausulae of the early thirteenth century, and these clausulae are barely distinguishable from motets. Thus he is the true father of motets, and hence of formal Western music.

He is equally important for ecclesiastical music. His organum, for example, established the prevailing manner of presenting the Mass for the following 150 years—in itself is a remarkable achievement. Even more remarkable is the recognition that when Guillaume de Machaut introduced innovations in Mass settings, the musical form he used was still the organum of Pérotin. Yet beyond that fact lies Pérotin's almost miraculous anticipation of chordal harmony, since Western music eventually chose to focus almost exclusively on that as a medium of musical expressiveness. In fact, since he worked long before Western composers decided to concentrate on the major-minor axis of tonality, his modal quasichords explore harmonic areas left inaccessible to composers before the twentieth century. Listening to him opens the ear to untrodden regions of sound.

Bibliography

Caldwell, John. *Medieval Music.* Bloomington: Indiana University Press, 1978. This study contains the most current attempt to synthesize reconstructions of Pérotin's music; includes an extensive bibliography.

Grout, Donald J. *A History of Western Music.* 2d ed. New York: W. W. Norton and Co., 1973. Grout's work is the best attempt to place Pérotin in the evolution of Western music; extensive examples and bibliography included.

LaRue, Jan, ed. *Aspects of Medieval and Renaissance Music: A Birthday Offering to Gustave Reese.* New York: W. W. Norton and Co., 1966. LaRue collects a variety of articles, as the title suggests; the work contains much information about the nature and forms of medieval music and its background and includes an excellent biographical sketch by Hans Tischler.

Waite, William. *The Rhythm of Twelfth-century Polyphony.* New Haven, Conn.: Yale University Press, 1954. Much more than the title suggests, this work is primarily an attempt to decipher medieval manuscript musical notation in order to reconstruct actual musical practice. Contains detailed analyses of the various forms practiced by Pérotin.

James L. Livingston

SAINT PETER
Simon

Born: Early first century; Bethsaida of Galilee
Died: A.D. 64; Rome
Area of Achievement: Religion
Contribution: During Jesus' life, Peter was the most faithful and outspoken of the disciples; after Jesus' death he gave leadership to the early Church at Jerusalem and was active in missionary work. In Catholic tradition, he is the founder of the Christian Church and of the Papacy.

Early Life

Peter was born Simon (or Simeon), son of Jonah in Bethsaida; the date is uncertain, but it is believed that he was born in the first few years of the Christian era. The name Peter was given to him later by Jesus; the Greek word *petros* means "rock" and translates into the Aramaic Cepha or Cephas. Nothing is known of Peter's life before his call to discipleship. At the time of the call, he was working as a fisherman in partnership with his brother Andrew; according to the Gospel of Luke, he was also partners with James and John, thus beginning an intimacy with John which continued until both left Palestine.

Peter was a married man; it is recorded that Jesus cured Peter's mother-in-law of a fever. That his wife later accompanied him on missionary journeys is suggested by Paul in 1 Corinthians 9 (King James Version, the version cited throughout this article): "Have we not power to lead about a sister, a wife, as well as other apostles, and as the brethren of the Lord, and Cephas?" According to another tradition, Peter's wife was martyred at the same time as Peter. Concerning Peter's call, there are two accounts. The Synoptics (Matthew, Mark, and Luke) make Peter and Andrew the first to be called as they were fishing (or washing their nets); henceforth, they were to be "fishers of men." According to the Gospel of John, Andrew was the first to follow Jesus and afterward recruited Simon, whom Jesus immediately christened Peter (Matthew's account of the bestowal of the name will be discussed later).

Life's Work

In the accounts given of Jesus' ministry in the four Gospels, Peter plays a more prominent part than any of the other disciples, even John. When the Twelve are listed, Peter is always listed first and is even identified as "the first." He is noted as first, too, of an inner circle which includes James and John. These three were present (with Andrew) at the healing of Peter's mother-in-law and also at the healing of Jairus' daughter. Together they were present at the Transfiguration, where Peter proposed building tabernacles ("shelters" in the New English Bible) for Jesus, Moses, and Elijah (Matt. 17). Of all the Apostles, Peter was the most talkative—or the most often quoted. It was Peter who asked how often he should forgive his brother, who asked for the interpretation of a parable, who commented on the withered fig tree, and who protested that the Apostles had left all to follow Jesus. He also attempted to imitate his master by walking on the water and then lost his faith and had to be rescued. It was Peter who first realized that Jesus was indeed the Christ, "the son of the living God" (Matt. 16). Yet it was Peter who refused to believe that Jesus had to "be killed, and the third day be raised up" (Matt. 16) and earned the rebuke "Get thee behind me, Satan."

Peter was also prominent in the events of the Passion. According to Luke 22, Jesus sent Peter and John ahead to prepare the Passover. When Jesus washed the disciples' feet, Peter alone resisted, and when Jesus insisted, Peter asked that "not my feet only, but also my hands and my head" be washed (John 13). When Jesus foretold that "one of you shall betray me," Peter prompted "the disciple whom Jesus loved" (presumably John) to ask Jesus who it was. When Peter protested that he was ready "to go both to prison and to death," Jesus answered, "Peter, the cock shall not crow this day, before that thou shalt thrice deny that thou knowest me" (Luke 22). In the Garden of Gethsemane, when Jesus went aside to pray for the last time, he took Peter, James, and John with him. Three times he found them sleeping; according to Matthew and Mark, it was to Peter that he directed his reproach: "What, would you not watch with me one hour?" (Mark 14). Yet according to John, when the officers came to arrest Jesus, again Peter alone resisted and cut off the ear of the high priest's servant. He followed Jesus to Caiaphas' house and sat in the court with the officers, warming himself by a fire; it was there that, being questioned by the servants, he denied Jesus thrice.

Though in the First Epistle of Peter, Peter calls himself a witness of Christ's sufferings (implying that he was present at the Crucifixion), he next appears in the Gospels in the aftermath of the Resurrection. According to Luke and John, Mary Magdalene, perhaps with some other women, found the tomb empty and reported the fact to Peter (and "the beloved disciple," according to John); Peter went to the tomb and found only the linen cloths in which Jesus' body had been wrapped. Luke speaks also of an appearance of the Lord "to Simon"; otherwise, aside from the appearance to Mary and to the two on the road to Emmaus, Jesus first appeared to the Eleven (or the Eleven without Thomas); neither here nor in most of the subsequent appearances was Peter particularly distinguished. An exception is John's report of an appearance by the Sea of Galilee. Peter had gone fishing with his old partners, James and John, and some others, when they became aware of a figure on the shore, whom the "beloved disciple" recognized as the Lord. It was then that Jesus gave Peter a pointed commandment, "Feed my sheep," and prophesied "by what manner of death he should glorify God."

In the period following the Resurrection appearances, one sees the Apostles gradually, and perhaps at first not intentionally, forming themselves into a church at Jerusalem, of which Peter was the natural if not the official leader. (Paul speaks of Peter and John and James, the Lord's brother, as "reputed pillars" of the Church.) Peter took the initiative in urging the appointment of a twelfth Apostle to replace Judas. When the Holy Spirit descended on the Apostles at Pentecost and they spoke in tongues, Peter spoke boldly to the astonished multitude, defending the speaking as the fulfillment of prophecy and proclaiming Jesus as the Messiah; thus he added thousands to the Church. When, in company with John, Peter healed a crippled man, he and John were for the first time arrested and brought before the high priest and the Sanhedrin, but they were released after being warned to desist from preaching in the name of Jesus. When further miracles followed, the whole body of Apostles was arrested, and although (it is said) the Apostles miraculously escaped from prison, they appeared before the high priest the next day and might have been executed except for the cautiousness of Gamaliel, a teacher of the law.

After the martyrdom of Stephen, the infant church was dispersed, and adherents carried the Gospel into the country districts. Philip preached in Samaria with such success that Peter and John were sent down to support him. This was apparently the beginning of Peter's missionary work outside Jerusalem. Tours of Lydda and Joppa, which followed, were important to the history of the Church. Peter had performed two miracles; soon afterward, he had a vision which seemed to abolish the Jewish distinction between clean and unclean food. The next day, he received a message from one Cornelius, a Roman centurion and convert to Judaism, who had had a vision urging him to send for Peter. The result was that the Holy Spirit was poured out on Gentiles, and they were baptized; Peter understood that he could no longer reject food as unclean or refuse to eat with the uncircumcised. For the time being, the disciples in Jerusalem seemed to accept Peter's position. It was about this time that Herod Agrippa I executed John's brother James. (He would have done the same with Peter if Peter had not miraculously escaped from prison.)

Meanwhile, Paul had undergone his conversion, and his missionary activity raised again the problem of the status of gentile converts. In Galatians, Paul asserts that three years after his conversion he went to Jerusalem and spent two weeks with Peter, without seeing any of the other Apostles except James, the Lord's brother. Fourteen years later, Paul went again to Jerusalem with Barnabas to discuss the problem raised by those Jewish Christians who would have imposed on gentile converts the burden of observing the Jewish ceremonial law. According to Paul, the meeting concluded amicably, with James, Peter, and John agreeing that they would minister to the Jews and

Saint Peter

Paul would minister to the Gentiles. The account in Acts (assuming that the same meeting is meant) adds that Peter spoke up on behalf of the Gentiles and was supported by James, who, however, made the condition that the gentiles should abstain "from pollutions of idols, fornication, and from things strangled, and from blood" (Acts 15). The fragmentary evidence would suggest that by this time Peter, though apparently still the most outspoken of the group at Jerusalem, had yielded some of his authority to James. (Perhaps influence would be a better word than authority, for neither is described as holding an executive position or having any special title.) The compromise did not prevent further misunderstandings: Later, at Antioch, Peter, under pressure from James, refused any longer to eat with gentile converts and was rebuked by Paul (Gal. 2).

This, except for what can be conjectured from the Epistles of Peter, is the last that Scripture tells of Peter. The episode does not do credit to him, and yet the whole business of the controversy about the gentile converts fits with what is already known about Peter. The Gospels uniformly depict him as loyal, enthusiastic, courageous, and open to change, but he is also depicted as possessing that quality of irresolution which appeared most spectacularly in the episode of the denial.

Summary

Even though Scripture breaks off with the quarrel at Antioch, this does not mean that Peter ceased to serve the Church. Indeed, tradition has much to say about his further career, though some of the statements have proved highly controversial. It seems obvious from Scripture that Peter held a special place among the disciples. Matthew 16 elaborates on this:

> Thou art Peter, and upon this rock I will build my church; and the gates of Hades shall not prevail against it. I will give unto thee the keys of the Kingdom of Heaven: and whatsoever thou shalt bind on earth shall be bound in Heaven: and whatsoever thou shalt loose on earth shall be loosed in heaven.

This passage can be used to support the claims of the Catholic church regarding the authority and infallibility of the Papacy. Connected with this is the question of Peter's residence and martyrdom in Rome. According to an early and persistent tradition, Peter was martyred in Rome in A.D. 64 (or a bit later), after having lived in Rome for as long as twenty-five years, serving as bishop. Tradition also asserts that Peter was in contact with Mark in Rome and furnished material for his Gospel. It is natural for Protestants to deny not only that Peter was in effect the first pope but also that he was ever in Rome at all. The controversy has of late become less intense. It seems to be agreed that Peter was in Rome, though hardly for twenty-five years, and that he was crucified there, in the vicinity of the Vatican Hill; the question of his burial is still uncertain.

Peter showed himself a leader of the Apostles even during the lifetime of Jesus, and he was also a leader of the early Church, though sharing his authority at first with John and later with James and Paul. He almost certainly was martyred in Rome. Whether he had any authority in the Roman church and whether he could transmit that authority to others are questions on which even believers are likely to remain divided.

Bibliography
Alter, Robert, and Frank Kermode, eds. *The Literary Guide to the Bible*. Cambridge, Mass.: Harvard University Press, 1987. Especially relevant on the subject of Acts, which contributor James M. Robinson treats less as history than as "dramatized theology." The section "English Translations of the Bible," written by Gerald Hammond, explains the preference for the King James Version, used in this article.
Brown, Raymond E., Karl P. Donfried, and John Reumann. *Peter in the New Testament: A Collaborative Assessment of Protestant and Roman Catholic Scholars*. Minneapolis: Augsburg Publishing House, 1973. A very learned and reasonable analysis of the evidence—but with cautious conclusions, such as "an investigation of the historical career does not necessarily settle the question of Peter's importance for the subsequent church."
Cullmann, Oscar. *Peter—Disciple, Apostle, Martyr: A Historical and Theological Study*. Translated by Floyd V. Wilson. 2d ed. Philadelphia: Westminster Press, 1962. Although thorough and scholarly, this volume is less a biography than a Protestant criticism of Catholic claims.
O'Connor, Daniel William. *Peter in Rome: The Literary, Liturgical, and Archeological Evidence*. New York: Columbia University Press, 1969. An exhaustive survey of the evidence. The account of the archaeological investigations (heavily illustrated) is particularly interesting.
Reicke, Bo. Introduction and notes to *The English Bible: The Epistles of James, Peter, and Jude*. Garden City, N.Y.: Doubleday and Co., 1964. Accepts that the First Epistle was written by Peter, probably with assistance from Silvanus. The First Epistle was written from "Babylon," by which Rome is almost certainly meant; there is a reference to Mark, presumably the author of the Gospel of Mark.
Smith, Terence V. *Petrine Controversies in Early Christianity: Attitudes Toward Peter in Christian Writings of the First Two Centuries*. Tübingen, West Germany: J. C. B. Mohr, 1985. In his opening statement, Smith confesses, "To talk of the Apostle Peter is to enter into a world of disaccord, polemic, and controversy." Contains an extensive bibliography.

John C. Sherwood

PETRARCH
Francesco Petrarca

Born: July 20, 1304; Arezzo, Italy
Died: July 18, 1374; Arquà, Italy
Area of Achievement: Literature
Contribution: Petrarch's scholarship stimulated a revival of interest in classical studies, and his vernacular poetry created a veritable Petrarchan school of sonneteers.

Early Life

Petrarch's father, Pietro di Parenzo—more commonly known as Ser Petracco—was, like Dante, a member of the White Guelph Party in Florence. Following the victory of the Black Guelphs, he was condemned to a heavy fine and the loss of a hand. He fled with his wife, Eletta Canigiani, to Arezzo in October of 1302, and there, on July 20, 1304, Francesco Petrarca was born. The following year, Petrarch and his mother moved to Incisa, where his brother, Gherardo, was born in 1307.

Because Incisa was under Florentine rule, Pietro could visit his wife and children only surreptitiously, so in 1311 the family moved again, this time to Pisa. There Petrarch saw for the first and only time that other famous Florentine exile, Dante. Apparently it was at Pisa, too, that Petrarch began his studies under yet another exile, Convenevole da Prato. In 1312, the family again relocated, settling in Carpentras, France, fifteen miles northeast of Avignon, to be close to the papal seat. Many years later, Petrarch wrote to Guido Sette, recalling his life in the French village: "Do you remember those four years? What happiness we had, what security, what peace at home, what freedom in the town, what quietness and silence in the country!" Sette, who became Archbishop of Genoa, was to be a lifelong friend and correspondent.

In 1316, Petrarch was sent to the University of Montpellier to study law, the family profession. He was already showing far more interest in the classics than in legal matters; according to his own account, his father discovered his Latin library and threw all but two books, one by Vergil and one by Cicero, into the fire, sparing this pair only because of his son's pleas. Like so many other of Petrarch's autobiographical accounts, this anecdote seems too pat to be true, for throughout his life Petrarch took Vergil and Cicero as his models, seeking to surpass the one in poetry, the other in prose. While Petrarch was still at Montpellier, his mother died; the event called forth his earliest surviving poem, a moving Latin elegy of thirty-eight hexameter lines, one for each year of her life.

To complete his legal studies, Petrarch was sent to the University of Bologna in 1320, the most celebrated law school in Europe. Again, Petrarch showed more interest in Latin literature than in law, recording in February, 1325, his purchase of Saint Augustine's *De civitate Dei* (413-427; *The City of God*); this copy is now at the University of Padua. His father's hostility to classical studies seems to have vanished, if it ever existed, for from Paris he brought his son that compendium of medieval learning, Saint Isidore of Seville's *Etymologiae* (late sixth century to early seventh century). The acquisition of the volume by Augustine also belies Petrarch's claim that in his youth he read only secular works.

The death of his father in April, 1326, freed Petrarch to pursue his own interests. He returned to Avignon and studied literature. In his *Posteritati* (1370-1372; *Epistle to Posterity*, 1966), he describes himself as having been a good-looking youth, with bright eyes and a medium complexion. He had two illegitimate children—a son, Giovanni, born in 1337, and a daughter, Francesca, born six years later—and sustained many enduring friendships throughout his life.

Life's Work

About a year after his return from Bologna, Petrarch had one of the most important encounters of his life. As he wrote in 1348 in his copy of Vergil that served as a diary,

> Laura, illustrious through her own virtues, and long famed through my verses, first appeared to my eyes in my youth, in the year of our Lord 1327, on the sixth day of April, in the church of St. Clare in Avignon, at matins.

Virtually all of his vernacular poetry was to revolve around this woman: The verses of the *Rerum vulgarium fragmenta* (1470, also known as *Canzoniere*; *The Sonnets and Stanzas of Petrarch*, 1879) celebrate his love for her both during her life and after her death; the various *Trionfi* (1470; *Tryumphs*, 1565, best known as *Triumphs*, 1962) reveal her power over Petrarch, Cupid, mortality, and even time itself.

Petrarch's father had left his two sons enough money to free them from the need to work, but by 1330 the peculations of feckless executors and dishonest servants forced the young men to seek some occupation. Since Petrarch despised law and hated medicine, as he would make clear in a later diatribe against the profession (*Invective contra medicum*, 1352-1355), he took minor religious orders, and, in the autumn of 1330, he entered the household of Cardinal Giovanni Colonna. Subsequently, he received various benefices, among them the canonries of Lombez, Pisa, Parma, Padua, and Monselice. Neither pluralism nor nonresidency troubled him; he treated these posts as sinecures, though he was willing to trade them for less lucrative offices to oblige his friends. Though at various times throughout his life he was offered papal secretaryships and even bishoprics, he always refused, preferring the freedom to read and write over power and money.

During the early 1330's, he traveled widely and added to his library. A list of his favorite books, compiled in 1333 (*Libri mei peculiares*), already contained some fifty entries, about twenty of them by Cicero and Seneca. A 1346 letter to Giovanni dell' Incisa makes clear his sentiment: "I am possessed by one insatiable passion, which I cannot restrain—nor would I if I could.... I cannot get enough books."

Among the Ciceronian works he may have owned was *De gloria*, of which no copy is now extant. He certainly owned the *Pro Archia* (62 B.C.), which he found in Liège in 1333; the discovery added an important speech to the known canon, and this defense of poetry treated a subject of lifelong interest to Petrarch himself. Sometime before 1337, his collecting led to his preparing the first scholarly edition of Livy's history of Rome, *Ab urbe condita* (27 B.C.-A.D. 17; *The Roman History*). Originally composed of 142 books arranged in groups of ten (called decades), by the Middle Ages this monumental work had been scattered. During his travels, Petrarch had found manuscripts in Chartres and Verona, and he recognized that they belonged together. His own transcript, now in the British Museum, united the first, third, and fourth decades to create the most complete copy then known. Moreover, his philological knowledge allowed him to complete certain gaps and choose the best among various readings. His text served as the basis of subsequent editions, and his comments remain useful to scholars of the Roman historian.

In these years, he was writing lyrics, sonnets, and canzoni in Italian, as well as a comedy, *Philologia*, now lost. About one hundred of these vernacular poems were to be incorporated into the 366 that constitute the final version of the *Canzoniere*. His Latin works of the period are fewer, but he did address an appeal to Pope Benedict XII to return to Rome. Throughout his life, he regarded the Eternal City as the only fit place for the seat of the papacy and the Holy Roman Emperor, and he repeatedly urged popes and kings to return there.

His own visit to Rome in 1337 marked a milestone in his life, for thereafter he devoted an increasing amount of effort to Latin compositions. He began *De viris illustribus* (1351-1353; reorganized as *Quorundam virorum illustrium epithoma*), a biographical compendium of classical and more recent figures; in 1338 or 1339, he started work on *Africa* (1396; English translation, 1977), an epic about Scipio Africanus. The former was his attempt to create a historical work to rival Livy's, while with the latter he hoped to imitate, indeed surpass, Vergil's *Aeneid* (c. 29-19 B.C.). Neither work was ever finished, but both circulated in manuscript during his lifetime and earned for him much fame. Indeed, by September, 1340, his reputation was such that both the University of Paris and the Roman senate invited him to be crowned poet laureate.

Petrarch rejected the medieval Scholasticism that the university represented, and he regarded Rome as the true center of culture. On April 8, 1341, he was crowned with a laurel wreath in the Senatorial Palace on the Capitoline, where he delivered a speech praising poetry. While in Rome, he began his collection of antique coins, which he treasured not for their monetary value but for their historical information.

He was now living in the country in Vaucluse, not far from Avignon but still removed from crowds and the papal court. Perhaps, again, he was imitating such classical models as Horace, who had retired to his Sabine farm, or his beloved Cicero at Tusculum. Certainly he was the first person since antiquity to retreat from the city to write. He seems genuinely to have loved nature, choosing to live in rural seclusion whenever possible. In a poetic epistle to Giacomo Colonna he wrote, "How delightful it is to imbibe the silence of the deep forest." Elsewhere he speaks of rising at midnight to wander in the moonlit landscape, and in his introspective *Secretum meum* (1353-1358; *My Secret*, 1911), a supposed dialogue between Augustinus (Saint Augustine) and Franciscus (Petrarch) that defends the pursuit of secular literature and scholarship, Augustinus speaks of the days when, "lying upon the grass in the meadows, you [that is, Petrarch] listened to the murmur of the stream as it broke over the pebbles: Now, sitting on the bare hills, you measured freely the plain extended at your feet."

Petrarch's aversion to Avignon was certainly sincere. In one of his metrical epistles he complains of "The uproar that resounds within the walls/ Of the straitened city, where the very ground/ Cannot contain the crowds, nor the very sky/ Contain the clamor." He hated the intrigues of the papal court, and in his *Sine nomine* (1359-1360; *Book Without a Name*, 1973), so called because he deleted the names of the addressees, he described Avignon as a place

> in which no piety, no charity, and no faith dwell; where pride, envy, debauchery, and avarice reign with all their arts; where the worst man is promoted and the munificent robber is exalted and the just man is trampled on; where honesty is called foolishness and cunning is called wisdom; where God is mocked, the sesterce [money] is adored, the laws are trodden under foot, and the good are scorned.

Much as he loved the seclusion of Vaucluse, he frequently traveled through northern Italy on papal missions, and in 1344, he bought and refurbished a house in Parma, apparently with the intention of remaining permanently. He would leave France for good in 1353, and in his letters as well as in *Invectiva contra eum qui maledixit Italiae* (1373) and in poems such as "Italia mia" ("My Italy"), he revealed himself as a true Italian patriot. His residence in Parma was short-lived; in December, 1344, the Marquess of Mantua and the Visconti brothers of Milan laid siege to the city. Petrarch fled the fighting on February 23, 1345, and traveled to Modena, Bologna, and Verona.

In Verona, he found a volume of letters from Cicero to his brothers Quintus and Brutus and to the literary patron and critic Atticus. This discovery marked yet another of Petrarch's contributions to the world's knowledge of the Roman orator, and it led directly to Petrarch's decision to preserve and collect his own letters in the twenty-four books of *Rerum familiarium libri* (wr. 1325-1366; English translation, 1975-1985) and the eighteen of *Senilium rerum libri* (wr. 1361-1374; *Letters of Old Age*, 1966).

Back in Vaucluse, he wrote the first draft of *De vita solitaria* (1346; *The Life of Solitude*, 1924), praising the country life, and began his *Bucolicum carmen* (1364; *Eclogues*, 1974), writing four of the twelve eclogues of this collection modeled on Vergil's pastorals. A visit to his brother at Montrieux, where Gherardo had entered the Carthusian monastery in 1343, prompted *De otio religioso* (1376), a celebration of monasticism. While Petrarch's writings before this date were not exclusively secular, these works suggest a deepening interest in religion.

In 1348, Petrarch was again living in Parma, where he learned of Laura's death. In response to this news, he wrote three more eclogues, two dealing with the Black Plague that had killed Laura and a third specifically treating her death. He also began the third of his six *Triumphs*, the triumph of Death, with Laura once more the theme.

Following several years of travel between France and Italy, Petrarch settled in Milan in 1353, residing there until 1361. There he completed his *De remediis utriusque fortunae* (1366; *Physicke Against Fortune*, 1597). He explained its contents in a letter to Guido Sette:

> All philosophers, all experience, and truth itself agree in this: that in times of adversity... the one remedy is patience... and that in times of prosperity the one remedy is moderation. I have had it in mind, of late, to write at some length about both these remedies, and now have I done so.

In his dedicatory preface, Petrarch notes that of good fortune and bad, the former is the more dangerous.

During this period, Petrarch undertook various missions for the Visconti brothers. In 1354, he attempted to effect peace with the doge of Venice and Genoa, and when that effort failed, he was sent to Emperor Charles IV to enlist his support against the Venetians. Another embassy took him to France to welcome King John back from English captivity; the king was so impressed with Petrarch that he tried to dissuade him from returning to Italy. Emperor Charles IV had also wanted Petrarch to remain with him in Prague, but Petrarch's Italian patriotism impelled him to reply, "In the whole world there is nothing under heaven that can be compared to Italy, in respect either to the gifts of nature or to human worth."

Through his scholarship he was, however, able to serve the emperor. Duke Rudolf IV of Austria was claiming autonomy from the Holy Roman Empire because of certain privileges he claimed that his country had been granted in patents by Julius Caesar and Nero. Charles sent the documents to Petrarch, who exposed them as forgeries.

In 1362, Petrarch moved to Venice, offering to bequeath his extensive collection of books to the city in return for a house during his lifetime. Although the proposal eventually fell through, it marks the first attempt to establish a public library for "those ingenious and noble men... who may delight in such things." Again, one sees that Petrarch was well ahead of his age.

After several years of moving between Venice, Pavia, Milan, and Padua, he settled in Padua in 1368, before moving in 1370 to rural Arquà, about ten miles to the southwest, where he spent the remainder of his life in the care of his daughter. Until his death on July 18, 1374, he continued to revise his earlier works and to add new ones, such as the last of the *Triumphs* and a Latin translation of the story of Griselda by his friend Giovanni Boccaccio.

Summary

In his *Epistle to Posterity*, Petrarch writes, "Perhaps you will have heard something of me." Posterity has, indeed. Rodolphus Agricola, the Dutch Humanist who was Petrarch's first biographer, claimed that Petrarch initiated the study of classical literature, and Boccaccio told him that "because of your example, many within and perhaps without Italy are cultivating studies neglected for centuries." His interest in classical antiquity led to the recovery of many previously lost or obscure works, thus aiding in the modern study of Cicero, Sextus Propertius, and the ancient geographer Pomponius Mela.

Petrarch claimed, "I never liked this present age.... I am alive now, yet I would rather have been born at some other time." One assumes he would have preferred the age of Cicero. Certainly, it was as a classicist that he hoped to earn his reputation. In 1359, he rejected Boccaccio's suspicions that he (Petrarch) harbored any jealousy toward Dante:

> I ask you, is it likely that I should envy a man who devoted his whole life to things to which I gave myself only in the first flush of youth; so that what for him was, if not the only, certainly the most important branch of literary art, has for me been only a pastime and relaxation and a first exercise in the rudiments of my craft.

This dismissal of the *Canzoniere*, which he disparagingly called *Rerum vulgarium fragmenta*, is disingenuous, for he continued to add to these vernacular poems and polish them throughout his life. However Petrarch may have felt about these works, posterity has regarded them as his major literary achievement. These poems have been translated into more than a dozen languages and influenced the poets of the French Pléiade, the English Renaissance, and Italy. Among the progeny of this first sonnet cycle in the West are Sir

Petrarch

Philip Sidney's *Astrophel and Stella* (1591), Edmund Spenser's *Amoretti* (1595), and William Shakespeare's *Sonnets* (1609).

Even as a classicist, Petrarch was more modern than he allowed, for he adapted rather than imitated classical models. His eclogues treat contemporary themes; his epic *Africa* sought to portray Scipio as a fusion of classical heroism and Christian saintliness; his unfinished *Rerum memorandum libri* (1343-1345) classifies the deeds and writings of the ancients under the four cardinal Christian virtues of Prudence, Justice, Fortitude, and Temperance. He was thus the first of the Christian Humanists, as he was the first Humanist to study Greek (though he made little progress in the language), the first modern historian, and, as he repeatedly reveals in his letters, the first person to analyze himself so carefully. In sum, Petrarch may be called the first modern man.

Bibliography
Bergin, Thomas G. *Petrarch*. New York: Twayne Publishers, 1970. A critical biography by a leading translator of Petrarch's Latin writings. Covers the life and works, with detailed discussions of the *Canzoniere* and the *Triumphs*.
Bishop, Morris. *Petrarch and His World*. Bloomington: Indiana University Press, 1963. A lively work that gives much information on the history of the fourteenth century. Includes numerous quotations from Petrarch in Bishop's own elegant translations. Offers a balanced view, neither idolizing Petrarch nor condemning him, but pointing out his failings, such as accepting the patronage of the tyrannical Visconti.
Forster, Leonard. *The Icy Fire: Five Studies in European Petrarchism*. London: Cambridge University Press, 1969. Examines the widespread influence of Petrarch's works, especially the vernacular poetry.
Mann, Nicholas. *Petrarch*. New York: Oxford University Press, 1984. This brief book talks about Petrarch's writings as a lifelong effort to create and explain a self. Includes a useful bibliography of primary and secondary sources.
Potter, Murray A. *Four Essays*. Cambridge, Mass.: Harvard University Press, 1917. Of these four essays, three relate to Petrarch—as author, as creator of his own image, and as critic/reader. Keen insights, elegantly presented. Still useful despite its age.
Wilkins, Ernest H. *The Life of Petrarch*. Chicago: University of Chicago Press, 1961. A detailed biography based on Petrarch's letters. Helpful for the political background of fourteenth century France and Italy that affected Petrarch's life and writing. Includes some discussion of the works and traces the stages of their composition and revision.

Joseph Rosenblum

PHIDIAS

Born: c. 490 B.C.; Athens, Greece
Died: c. 430 B.C.; Elis, Greece
Area of Achievement: Art
Contribution: Phidias' work embodied the high classical ideal in sculpture; his renditions of the gods became standards to which later artists aspired. Director of the sculpture program of the Parthenon in Athens, he was best known for his cult images of Athena in Athens and of Zeus in Olympia.

Early Life

Phidias, the son of Charmides, was born just before the wars which pitted his fellow Athenians against the invading Persians in 490 and 480 B.C. This fact is of great importance in understanding his development and that of his country, for these wars proved to the Athenians that with their own resources and the gods' favor, the fledgling democracy could succeed against overwhelming odds. Phidias' sculptures came to reflect confidence in men and the gods' grace.

After the wars, Athens became the preeminent Greek state and led a confederation that continued to fight the Persians. Athenian leadership led to Athenian domination, and any city that tried to leave the league was disciplined. Pericles led the state during Phidias' adult lifetime and created a strong Athens by pursuing an expansionist policy. Phidias grew up knowing that he lived in one of the most powerful and influential of the Greek states.

Little is known of Phidias' early training beyond the fact that—like other Athenian children—he would have received his education in the gymnasium, learning athletics, music, mathematics, and poetry, including the Homeric epics. The works of Homer in particular were to have a profound impact on Phidias' vision of the gods, which expressed itself in his sculpture. Along with the sculptors Myron and Polyclitus, he received artistic training from Ageladas (also called Hageladas) of Argos, who worked mainly in bronze and is known for a great statue of Zeus which he made for the Messenians.

Phidias attended the dramatic festivals of Dionysus, where he saw performances of Aeschylus' tragedies, including *Persai* (467 B.C.; *The Persians*), a triumphant paean to Athenian success and divine favor, and the *Oresteia* trilogy (458 B.C.), which extols the gods Zeus and Athena and ends with an encomium to justice as practiced in Athens. Phidias grew up to be proud of his land's traditions and the accomplishments of its citizens. The tragic vision revealed in Athenian drama, with the grace of the immortals contrasting with human limitations, was to have a profound effect on the sculptor's works.

Another formative influence on the sculptor was the humanistic teachings of Sophists such as Protagoras, who held that "man is the measure of all things," and Anaxagoras, who insisted on the divine supremacy of reason.

With their notions of subjectivity and emphasis on the potential for human progress, these new thinkers saw people as responsible for their own advancement. Thus, they represented an anthropocentric view of life that encouraged the development of the arts, because to them civilization was advanced by *technē* (artistic skill). Phidias' work was a physical manifestation of this confidence in human accomplishment. At the same time, his statues reflected the measured relationships that Anaxagoras saw as the reflections of the divine world-reason.

Phidias was a product of his age, which was characterized by confidence in human rationality, the tragic notion of human limitation in the face of divine power, and the idea of civilization's triumph over barbarism. His sculptures both reflected his age and recalled epic notions of Homeric gods and heroes.

Life's Work

During Phidias' early years, the temples and sanctuaries which the Persians had destroyed remained untouched because the Greeks, in the Oath of Plataea, had agreed to leave the ruins as memorials to barbarian sacrilege. Consequently, Phidias' earlier sculptures were monuments to the Athenian victory over the Persians at Marathon. In fact, two of them were built with spoils from that battle. One, a colossal bronze statue of armed Athena Promachos (c. 470-460 B.C.; Athena, first in battle), stood prominently on the Acropolis at Athens; approximately fifteen meters high, its shining spear tip and helmet crest could be seen from far out at sea. The other, a bronze group containing Athena, Apollo, the legendary heroes of Athens, and the victorious Athenian general Miltiades, was dedicated at the panhellenic sanctuary at Delphi (c. 465 B.C.).

Phidias' Athena Lemnia was commissioned and dedicated by Athenian colonists settling on Lemnos around 450. This bronze stood on the Athenian Acropolis and had a reputation for extraordinary beauty. Later copies and ancient descriptions indicate that it showed the goddess contemplating her helmet in her right hand.

Pericles respected the Oath of Plataea as long as a state of belligerence with Persia—fostered by the Athenian general Cimon—kept the issue alive. When Cimon died in 449 and a peace treaty was arranged with the Persians, Pericles no longer felt the need to maintain the Athenian temples in ruins. The stage was set for a rebuilding of the sanctuaries on the Acropolis, and the next year, construction of the Parthenon began. Pericles named Phidias general supervisor for the project.

The Parthenon—the temple of Athena the Maiden—was a major synthesis of architecture and sculpture. Phidias coordinated the sculptural program, which consisted of ninety-two metopes with battle scenes (Greeks/Trojans, Greeks/Amazons, lapiths/centaurs, and gods/giants; in place by 443), a 160-meter sculptured frieze (the Panathenaic Procession; complete by 438), the cult statue of Athena Parthenos (complete by 438), and pediments (the birth of Athena and the contest of Athena and Poseidon; complete by 432). The sculpted decoration of the Parthenon was unique: No other temple had both sculpted metopes and a continuous frieze, so Phidias' genius had the maximum opportunity to show itself.

Phidias himself was completely responsible for the chryselephantine (gold and ivory) statue of Athena inside, which stood more than twelve meters high. No original pieces of this statue have survived, but later copies and descriptions give an idea of its appearance. Athena stood with a statue of Nike (victory) in her right hand, which rested lightly on a Corinthian column. She was dressed in her aegis, a magical breastplate surrounded by snakes, and wore a three-crested helmet and a belt of snakes. A spear and shield stood at her left side, the latter decorated with relief figures of gods battling giants (inside) and Greeks fighting Amazons (outside). These motifs reflected those of the Parthenon's other sculptures: the forces of order battling those of barbarity—another sign of Athenian pride in the Persian defeat. Beneath the shield rose the form of a great snake, representing the local god Erichthonius. The statue stood upon a rectangular base showing Pandora being adorned by all the gods.

After the cult image was dedicated in 438, Phidias was accused by Pericles' enemies of having stolen some of the gold from the statue. This charge was proved false when it was revealed that the gold on the statue, weighing more than one thousand kilograms, had been designed to be easily removed. When it was weighed, no gold was found missing. Upon his acquittal on that charge, Phidias was accused of sacrilege, for it was commonly believed that he had represented himself and Pericles on the shield of Athena. This charge provides the circumstances for the description of Phidias: He was shown as a bald old man lifting up a stone with both hands. Upon his conviction, Phidias had to leave Athens, probably around 437.

Fortunately for Phidias, the Elians at this time invited him to come to Olympia to make a chryselephantine cult image of Zeus for the recently completed temple of Zeus. Phidias set up a workshop behind the temple, where he worked for five years, helped by his nephew Panaenus. Pieces of the molds for the golden drapery have been found there, in addition to a cup with the inscription "I belong to Phidias."

Phidias' Zeus at Olympia represented a new conception in Greek art. Until that time, Zeus had been usually depicted striding forward with a thunderbolt in his hand. Phidias portrayed him seated on a throne in Olympian calm, seven or eight times life size (more than twelve meters), his head almost touching the roof. The throne was four-fifths of the height of the whole and was decorated with ebony, gold, and ivory. The golden cloak was decorated with lilies and glass inlay. The majesty of the statue impressed all who saw it. Quintilian asserted that it enhanced traditional religion, Dio Cocceianus

Phidias

(Chrysostomos) that the sight of it banished all sorrow. According to one anecdote, Phidias said that he had been inspired by the image of Zeus in Homer's *Iliad* (c. 800 B.C.), in which the god on his throne nodded and caused all Olympus to shake. Pausanias related that Phidias carved his signature beneath the god's feet and that when the statue was complete, the god sent a flash of lightning to show that he approved of the work. The men in charge of cleaning the great statue were said to be the descendants of Phidias himself.

Phidias died shortly after having completed the Olympian Zeus, probably in Elis around 430. Many other works have been attributed to him, including a bronze Apollo near the Parthenon, a marble Aphrodite in the Athenian Agora, a chryselephantine Aphrodite in Elis, and a famous Amazon in Ephesus. In addition, literary sources indicate that he was skilled in paintings, engraving, and metal embossing. None of these works survives.

Summary

Phidias' life spanned three important periods in the development of Greek art. He was born toward the end of the Archaic period, when sculpture was quite formal, orderly, and stylized, with a quality of aloofness. Phidias lived as a young man in the Early Classical period, a time of artistic transition, when statues were more representational and heavily charged with specific emotions. When he matured, Phidias worked in a style that avoided the extremes of both: the High Classical, whose statues had expressions that were neither overly remote nor involved, but simultaneously detached and aware. This attitude of idealism, congenial to Phidias' strong Homeric tendencies, colored his work and gave it its distinctive quality.

The sculpture on the Parthenon came to embody what later generations considered "classical," and Phidias' style influenced all cult images subsequent to his Athena and Zeus, setting a standard for later sculptors to follow. For example, his pupil Alcamenes was responsible for the cult images in the Hephaesteum and the temples of Dionysus Eleuthereus and Ares in Athens, as well as the Aphrodite of the Gardens. Agoracritus, another pupil, created the cult statue and base for the temple of Nemesis at Rhamnus.

The chief characteristics of Phidias' style were sublimity, precision, and an "Olympian" rendering, showing the gods as detached from the human realm yet still concerned for men. Their expressions were calm and dignified. They were so pure in their conception that stories arose that Phidias had seen the gods themselves. His works brought the divine down to earth and made heavenly forms manifest for mortals; the gods of Homer came alive under his touch.

Since so few of Phidias' works survive—the Parthenon sculptures are most likely his design, but not of his hand—scholars try to re-create his sculptures on the basis of later copies, mostly of Roman date. The Athena Lemnia, for example, has been reconstructed from ancient references, combined with a marble head now in Bologna and a torso in Dresden; the Athena Parthenos from later copies, including the Varvakeion Athena of Roman date; the Olympian Zeus from coins and gems depicting it in Roman times. Identifications of copies of Phidian originals cannot be proved for the most part, but the quest continues to exercise the ingenuity of scholars. For example, some assign to Phidias the bronze warrior statues found in 1972 in the sea off Riace in southern Italy, while others oppose the attribution.

Bibliography
Boardman, John, and David Finn. *The Parthenon and Its Sculptures*. Austin: University of Texas, 1985. The best work on the subject, with hundreds of large, clear photographs and illustrations. Excellent discussion of the history of the building, the role of Phidias, the nature of the sources, historical context, interpretation of the sculpture, and relation to religious festivals. Bibliography and index.
Harrison, Evelyn B. "The Composition of the Amazonomachy on the Shield of Athena Parthenos." *Hesperia* 35 (1966): 107-133. Exhaustive study of literary sources that describe the battle scene said to include a representation of Phidias himself, with an analysis of the ancient copies. Discussion of composition and iconography, including illustrations with discussion of each figure. Extensive bibliography, catalog of figures, and detailed reconstruction. Phidian scholarship at its best.
Leipen, Neda. *Athena Parthenos: A Reconstruction*. Toronto: Royal Ontario Museum, 1971. Devoted to the problem of reconstructing Phidias' Parthenon cult statue, this is a photographic documentation of all relevant artifacts, with a discussion of literary descriptions, the Royal Ontario Museum's own construction of a model of the statue, and a detailed description of each part of the figure, including accessories. Extensive notes and bibliography.
Palagia, Olga. "In Defense of Furtwangler's Athena Lemnia." *American Journal of Archaeology* 91 (1987): 81-84. Discussion of a reconstruction of Phidias' most beautiful statue. Contains an illustration of the most accepted reconstruction and of other sculptures which support that interpretation. A good example of scholarly methodology used to re-create a Phidian original. Bibliography.
Pollitt, J. J. *Art and Experience in Classical Greece*. Cambridge: Cambridge University Press, 1972. The world of classical Greek art, putting Phidias in perspective. Describes the intellectual influences on the sculptor, his own influence on other media, his style and spirit, and the problems with writing his biography. Illustrations. Includes suggestions for further reading.
Richter, Gisela M. "The Pheidian Zeus at Olympia." *Hesperia* 35 (1966): 166-170. Excellent summary of what is known about the statue that was consid-

ered one of the seven wonders of the world. Includes descriptions of the statue as rendered in literature and on gems and coins. Generously illustrated and footnoted.

_____. *The Sculpture and Sculptors of the Greeks*. New Haven, Conn.: Yale University Press, 1929, 4th rev. ed. 1970. Definitive work on the lives and works of Greek sculptors. Treats anatomy, technique, composition, copies. Long and detailed section on Phidias, discussing all of his works, with extensive bibliography of ancient and modern sources. Two indexes, numerous photographs, chronological table of Greek sculptors and their works.

Schefold, Karl. *The Art of Classical Greece*. New York: Crown Publishers, 1967. Contains a significant section on the Mature Classical period, with discussion and appreciation of Phidias' genius, especially in relation to the Parthenon sculptures and statue of Olympian Zeus. Numerous small but useful illustrations.

Daniel B. Levine

PHILIP II

Born: August 21, 1165; Paris
Died: July 14, 1223; Mantes
Area of Achievement: Government
Contribution: Philip II, the strongest of the Capetian kings of France, greatly expanded the royal domain and created an efficient system of political administration.

Early Life

Philip II was born on August 21, 1165, in Paris, the son of King Louis VII and Adela of Champagne. Since he was Louis' only son, his birth was received with great enthusiasm and hailed as the beginning of a new era. In his youth, however, Philip suffered from poor health and timorousness, which alarmed the king so much that in 1179 he made a pilgrimage to Saint Thomas à Becket's shrine in Canterbury. Philip recovered and apparently grew up a strong, well-built young man, though his health declined again after the Third Crusade. He returned with little hair, was extremely nervous, and had good vision in one eye only.

On November 1, 1179, Philip, continuing an old Capetian custom, was crowned at Reims to ensure the succession. Although he was only fourteen years of age, it was a fortuitous move, for King Louis would die shortly thereafter. The youth was plunged almost immediately into a morass of political problems, for his maternal uncles, William, Archbishop of Reims, and the counts of Champagne, Blois, and Sancerre sought an opportunity to control the new king. Philip, like his grandfather Louis VI, was stubborn and determined to send a message to the nobility that he would rule as well as reign. Thus, on April 28, 1180, Philip married Isabella of Hainaut, daughter of Baldwin V, Count of Hainaut, and niece of Philip of Alsace, Count of Flanders; this marriage gave him control over the queen's dowry of Artois and an interest in other family lands. He succeeded in avoiding domination by his wife's family as well. Two months after his marriage, Philip formed an alliance with King Henry II of England which effectively alienated the Counts of Champagne and Flanders. By the time of his father's death on September 18, 1180, Philip was in firm control of the monarchy.

Life's Work

Philip's alliance with Henry drove his disaffected vassals together and precipitated a great revolt. The breach was widened in 1182, when Isabella, Countess of Flanders and wife of Philip of Alsace, died, leaving Vermandois, Amiénois, and Valois to her sister Eleanor, Countess of Beaumont. Since both the king and Philip of Alsace claimed these important lands, the rebellion continued until the two sides reached an agreement in 1186. For his part,

Philip II 1599

the king received the county and city of Amiens, sixty-five castles, the county of Montdidier, and a portion of Vermandois.

At the expense of relatives and truculent nobles, Philip had begun to enlarge the royal domain. The most important story of his reign, however, was the struggle with the house of Anjou to recover French Continental possessions. The Angevin kings had come through the years to rule Normandy, Anjou, Aquitaine, Maine, and Touraine—in sum, most of western and southern France. Although Henry II was Philip's vassal for these lands, clearly the English king was the dominant force in the relationship. Since Philip was no match for Henry on the field of battle, he elected to continue the policy of intrigue begun by his father, Louis VII, with Henry's discontented sons.

There was relative peace between the two sides until 1186-1187, when Richard, Henry's eldest surviving son, failed to keep his promise to marry Alice, Philip's sister. Richard, called the Lion Heart and considered the most able warrior of his day, had little interest in a woman rumored to have been his father's mistress. At any rate, when Henry refused to return either Alice or her dowry, the Vexin, Philip declared war and marched into Berry. As he had done in the past, Philip sought to foment discord in the Angevin house. In November, 1188, Richard threw his support to Philip and rendered homage for the Continental fiefs at Bonmoulins. The alliance proved successful, and in July of the following year Henry submitted near Tours. According to the Treaty of Colombières, Richard was recognized as Henry's successor, while Philip received Auvergne and other territorial concessions. Henry died two days later after learning that John, his favorite, had also turned against him.

For the moment, Richard and Philip were friends, but it soon became obvious that Philip had traded one formidable opponent for another. In 1190, the two kings joined forces and sailed from Europe on the Third Crusade. Philip's mother, Adela, and his uncle, the Archbishop of Reims, were appointed regents in his absence. In Messina, Italy, Richard and Philip quarreled and parted company. Richard, it would seem, had once again refused to marry Alice and, instead, had taken Berengaria of Navarre to be his queen. That necessitated a revision of their earlier agreement. According to the Treaty of Messina in 1191, Richard would retain the Vexin, unless he died without issue, in exchange for Alice, the town of Gisors, and ten thousand marks.

After the settlement, Philip went on to Palestine, where he was eventually rejoined by Richard in the siege of Acre. Philip remained long enough to take the city, and then, supposedly for reasons of illness, he decided to return to France. It is more likely that his departure was hastened by mounting differences with Richard and political concerns at home. Philip of Alsace, Count of Flanders, had died on the Crusade, and Philip was eager to assert his wife's claim to the count's lands. Philip was also determined—though it would be a violation of feudal and canon law—to take advantage of Richard's absence from Europe to attack Angevin holdings in France. When Richard learned that Philip and John, his younger brother, were plotting against him, he left Palestine and attempted to dash incognito across Europe. He was recognized and captured by Leopold V, Duke of Austria, and, at the insistence of Philip, was turned over to Emperor Henry VI to be held for ransom. With Richard out of the way, Philip attacked the Vexin and made plans to invade Normandy. His success, however, was short-lived. In 1194, Richard was released, and thereafter he initiated a series of wars which resulted in the eventual recapture of all lost lands.

Twenty years into his reign, Philip had gained little in his struggle with the Angevins. Moreover, he had become embroiled in a major dispute with the Papacy. In 1193, Philip formed an alliance with Canute VI, King of Denmark, in preparation for an invasion of England. As part of the agreement, Philip, whose first wife had died in 1190, was to marry the Danish king's sister Ingeborg. Almost immediately, Philip developed an aversion to his new bride and tried to have the marriage annulled on grounds of consanguinity. Matters went from bad to worse when, in 1196, Philip took another wife. Eventually Ingeborg's party referred the matter to Pope Innocent III, who placed France under an interdict in 1200. In July of that year, Philip's third wife died, but the rift with the Church continued until 1213, when Philip, preoccupied with more important political considerations, took back his estranged queen.

Although the Ingeborg affair proved distracting and injurious, there were encouraging developments on another front. In 1199, Richard met an untimely death and was succeeded by Philip's fellow conspirator, John. Although John was a better king and administrator than his brother, he was an inept general. He also had a rival claimant for the throne in his nephew Arthur, Duke of Brittany and Count of Anjou, a division which Philip was quick to exploit. All that was needed was an excuse. The opportunity presented itself in August, 1200, when John married Isabella of Angouleme, who was betrothed to Hugh of Lusignan, Count of La Marche. The angry count waged a brief, unsuccessful war against John before referring the matter to Philip's court. John, accordingly, was summoned to answer for his crime, and when he failed to appear, Philip and Arthur prepared for war. In the ensuing struggle, Arthur was captured, imprisoned, and executed, probably on John's orders. Arthur's outraged Breton and Angevin vassals then threw their full support behind Philip. By 1205, Philip had taken control of Normandy, Maine, Anjou, Touraine, and portions of Poitou. Yet John would not concede defeat and was soon at work lining up new allies. The most important of these was his nephew, Otto IV, the Holy Roman emperor. In 1214, the coalition invaded Philip's dominions, but suffered a crushing defeat at the Battle of Bouvines, which put an end forever to John's hopes of reclaiming the lost French lands.

By 1214, Philip's most important battles with the English, his nobles, and the Church were over. He had increased the size and wealth of the French royal domain to such extent that it was necessary to revamp the archaic Capetian system of administration. Royal agents, called bailiffs and seneschals, drawn from the middle class and paid a salary, were sent into the various counties and duchies to collect the king's revenue, administer justice, and occasionally command armies in defense of the realm. In this way, Philip built up an efficient and powerful administrative bureaucracy composed of men whose first loyalty was to the king.

Philip's last years were fairly tranquil. He apparently felt comfortable enough with his conquests and administrative arrangements to eschew the coronation of his son and heir, Louis VIII, in his lifetime, a departure from the Capetian practice of the past two centuries. Nor would he lend anything more than token support to Louis' invasion of England in 1216. As his health failed, Philip's chief concerns were spiritual, namely, the Albigensian Crusade and the defense of the Holy Land. Philip died at Mantes on July 14, 1223.

Summary

The first two centuries of Capetian rule were relatively uneventful. While the great nobles of the realm recognized the king as their feudal overlord, the king's actual authority did not extend much beyond the Île de France, or Paris and its environs. Some gains were made under Louis VI and Louis VII, but when Philip II assumed power in 1180 he was still surrounded by the great magnates of the realm. Over the next forty years, through marriage, political alliances, and war, Philip would more than triple the size of the French royal domain. The additional land and revenue, in turn, necessitated a revision of existing administrative agencies, giving France a more centralized government.

There can be little doubt, then, that Philip was the greatest of the Capetian monarchs. Yet he has received less attention than some of the other historical giants of the era, and has been judged more harshly. Critics point out that he was cruel and treacherous and that he accomplished little while Henry and Richard were alive. His supporters, on the other hand, argue that while he had little interest in education and the arts, he was intelligent, generous, and a great supporter of the Church. He reigned longer than Henry II and was a more accomplished king than Richard; when he died in 1223, his empire was still intact.

Bibliography

Baldwin, John W. *The Government of Philip Augustus*. Berkeley: University of California Press, 1986. A lengthy study of Philip's administration, with detailed footnotes and appendices. Should appeal mainly to a knowledgeable audience, but does provide some biographical information of interest to the general reader.

Davis, R. H. C. *A History of Medieval Europe, from Constantine to Saint Louis.* New York: David McKay Co., 1957, rev. ed. 1970. A general history of the area from the fourth through the thirteenth centuries. A brief section is devoted principally to Philip's attempts to expand the royal domain at the expense of his barons and the English. Very good for the beginning student.

Fawtier, Robert. *The Capetian Kings of France: Monarchy and Nation, 987-1328.* London: Macmillan, 1960, reprint 1962. Perhaps the best study of the Capetian line from beginning (987) to end (1328). Philip, as the strongest member of the family, receives much attention throughout. Students will find it helpful, though the bibliography will appeal more to scholars.

Hallam, Elizabeth M. *Capetian France, 987-1328.* New York: Longman Group, 1980, reprint 1986. An updated version of Fawtier's work reflecting modern scholarship. Maps, genealogies, and detailed bibliographies enhance the book's value. For scholars and students alike.

Luchaire, Achille. *Social France at the Time of Philip Augustus.* New York: A. Holt and Co., 1912. An old work which, although not primarily concerned with Philip, yields valuable background information about the Church, nobility, and peasantry during his day.

Painter, Sidney, and Brian Tierney. *Western Europe in the Middle Ages.* New York: Alfred A. Knopf, 1970, 3d ed. 1978. One of the better surveys of the period. Contains an excellent chapter on the feudal monarchies of England, France, and the empire. Provides a good overview of Philip's career. An excellent introductory work.

Petit-Dutaillis, Charles. *The Feudal Monarchy in France and England from the Tenth to the Thirteenth Century.* New York: Harper and Row, Publishers, 1936, reprint 1964. Intensive study of the political evolution of England and France from the tenth century through the thirteenth. Several important chapters on the Capetians. Scattered references to Philip. Scholars and more knowledgeable students of the period will find it very helpful.

Powicke, F. M. "The Reigns of Philip Augustus and Louis VIII of France." In *The Cambridge Medieval History*, vol. 6, edited by J. R. Tanner, C. W. Previté-Orton, and Z. N. Brooke. Cambridge: Cambridge University Press, 1929. A chapter from the best multivolume survey of the period. One of the best brief studies of Philip's reign, by an eminent British historian. Provides valuable information on his character, marriages, and political struggles. Excellent for all reading audiences.

Larry W. Usilton

PHILIP II OF MACEDONIA

Born: 382 B.C.; Macedonia
Died: 336 B.C.; Aegae, Macedonia
Areas of Achievement: Government and warfare
Contribution: Philip inherited a backward kingdom on the verge of collapse and made it a powerful state. His military innovations revolutionized warfare and created the army that would conquer the Persian Empire.

Early Life

Situated on the northern frontier of the Greek world, Philip's homeland of Macedonia long remained a kingdom without real unity. From their capitals of Aegae and Pella near the Aegean coast, Philip's ancestors had ruled the eastern area of lower Macedonia since the seventh century B.C. They exercised only a tenuous rule inland over upper Macedonia, however, and suffered repeated invasions and interference from their neighbors, barbarian and Greek alike. Philip's direct experience of these problems during the reigns of his father and two older brothers helps explain his determination as king to reverse Macedonia's precarious position.

In 393, Philip's father, Amyntas, suffered his first expulsion at the hands of the Illyrians, his neighbors to the west. Amyntas soon regained his throne, but he secured peace with the Illyrians only by paying tribute. As part of the settlement, he also married an Illyrian princess, Eurydice—the future mother of Philip. Ten years later a second Illyrian invasion forced Amyntas to entrust a portion of this kingdom to the Chalcidian Greeks, who refused to relinquish it. By 382, the year of Philip's birth, they had extended their control westward to include Amyntas' capital, Pella. An intervention by Sparta, then the most powerful of the Greek states, restored Amyntas to his capital in 379, but the Spartans demanded Macedonia's subservience to Sparta.

When Philip's older brother Alexander II assumed the throne in 370, the now-adolescent Philip went as a hostage to the Illyrians, who also demanded tribute as the price of peace. The boy returned home to find Alexander in a civil war that invited intervention by Thebes, the ascendant Greek city-state since the defeat of Sparta in 371. In 368, after the Thebans resolved the conflict in favor of Alexander, Philip and thirty other sons of Macedonian nobles were sent to Thebes as a guarantee of Macedonian obedience to Theban wishes. For three years Philip observed Thebes at the peak of its diplomatic and military power. Later accounts of the military lessons of this visit are probably exaggerated, but this experience must have influenced Philip. At the very least it allowed him to understand how the Greeks conducted their affairs, and it may explain his later severe treatment of Thebes. Following the assassination of Alexander, a second Theban intervention saved the throne for Philip's other brother, Perdiccas III, and brought more hostages to Thebes.

Back in Macedonia after 365, Philip received a district of his own and witnessed seizures of Macedonian coastal territory by the Athenians. In 359 he may have taken part in the disastrous Illyrian expedition that resulted in the death of Perdiccas and four thousand Macedonian soldiers. After the death of his brother, Philip—at age twenty-three—became the eighteenth King of Macedonia.

Life's Work

Philip inherited a kingdom on the verge of disintegration. Rival heirs challenged his right to the throne, the army threatened to collapse, and enemies menaced on all sides. Fortunately, the Illyrians did not choose to follow their victory with an invasion; to the north, however, the Paeonians began to raid Macedonian territory, while a Thracian king supported a pretender who claimed the kingship. Diplomacy and bribery forestalled these threats, while Philip dealt with a more immediate danger: Another pretender, backed by the Athenians, marched on the ancestral capital, Aegae, with three thousand mercenaries. After ensuring the loyalty of the capital, the young king trapped and disposed of his rival. Wisely, he then made conciliatory gestures to the Athenians in order to neutralize them while he returned his attention to the barbarians.

The opportune death of the Paeonian king allowed Philip to force an alliance upon his weaker successor, and by 358 Philip felt secure enough to lead a revitalized Macedonian army west against his most dangerous foes, the Illyrians. The details of his first major battle remain unclear, but Philip won a decisive victory and inflicted unusually severe casualties on his defeated enemy—three-quarters of the Illyrian army reportedly died. Followed by his marriage to an Illyrian princess, this victory secured his western frontier and allowed him to consolidate his position in Macedonia. As part of that consolidation, Philip began the transformation of Macedonia from a largely pastoral society to a more agriculturally based and urbanized state. Less visible than his military activities, these internal changes were equally important to the rise of Macedonia.

His dramatic victory over the Illyrians indicates that Philip had already begun the reorganization of the Macedonian army that would revolutionize warfare and make Macedonia the supreme military power in the Mediterranean. One year after his unfortunate brother had lost four thousand men to the Illyrians, Philip fielded a force of ten thousand foot soldiers and six hundred horsemen. (By the time of Philip's death, the Macedonian army would comprise at least twenty-four thousand infantry and four thousand cavalry, with numerous supporting troops.) As important as the increase in manpower was Philip's use of heavy cavalry as a primary instrument of attack against infantry, a tactic that explains the remarkably high rate of casualties among his foes. Equally significant was his redesign of the traditional Greek phalanx infantry formation, which he used in expert combination with his horsemen. Superbly trained to fight as a unit, Philip's phalangites used a novel fifteen-foot pike, the *sarissa*, and wore minimal defensive armor. Their success depended upon careful coordination with cavalry and lighter armed infantry. Philip's army also included specialists in siege techniques, who introduced the torsion catapult and tall siege towers. The evolution of this fighting force is obscure, but Philip clearly began his military reform early—he suffered only one defeat in his entire career.

With his kingdom more or less secure from barbarian threats, Philip abandoned his conciliatory posture toward the Athenians and moved to eliminate their presence on his eastern frontier. In 357 he seized the strategic city of Amphipolis, founded by the Athenians eighty years previously. This move gave Philip access to the rich gold and silver mines of neighboring Mount Pangaeus, which eventually rendered him an annual revenue of one thousand talents. Philip next took Pydna, one of two Athenian-controlled cities on the lower Macedonian coast. In 354 his successful siege of Methone eliminated the last Athenian base in Macedonia, but at a considerable cost to Philip: During the assault on the city an arrow destroyed his right eye.

Once he had placed Athens on the defensive, Philip moved against two nearby Greek districts that had threatened Macedonia during his youth: Thessaly to the south, Chalcidice to the east. His venture into Thessaly in 353 produced the only serious defeat of his career, but Philip came back the next year to win the Battle of the Crocus Plain, in which six thousand enemy soldiers died. This victory, followed by his election as president of the Thessalian League and his marriage to a Thessalian princess, brought Thessaly, with its renowned supply of horses, securely under Macedonian control. In 349 Philip began his move against the thirty-odd cities of the Chalcidian League, which he subdued one by one. Olynthus, the most important city of the league and the last holdout, fell after a two-month siege in 348. Philip razed the city and enslaved its inhabitants. Having eliminated most threats in the north, Philip now turned his attention to the city-states of central and southern Greece. The former victim of Greek interventions had become the intervener.

In 346, after obtaining a peace with Athens recognizing his right to Amphipolis, Philip in a surprise move came south and forced an end to the so-called Sacred War, which had been waged for nearly a decade. By intervening against the Phocians, whose sacrilegious seizure of the international sanctuary at Delphi had brought them almost universal condemnation, he cleverly played to Greek public opinion. Moreover, his refusal to punish the Athenians, despite their aid to the Phocians, suggests that already Philip had decided to attack Persia and hoped to use the Athenian navy in that effort.

Philip withdrew from Greece late in 346 to continue his work of consolidation in Macedonia.

A shattered shinbone in 345 kept Philip out of military action for a few years, but in 342 he began a systematic attack on Thrace and in 340 laid siege to the strategic cities of Perinthus and Byzantium, which overlooked the sea lane through the Bosporus. This move threatened the grain supply of the Athenians, who responded with aid to Byzantium. When the sieges of these well-fortified cities proved more difficult than expected, Philip abandoned them, declared war on Athens, and in 339 invaded Greece. At Chaeronea in August of 338 Philip faced a Greek army headed by Athens and Thebes. The battle was long, and Philip appears to have won through a controlled retreat of his right wing that created a break in the Greek line. Philip's son Alexander, who would be known later as Alexander the Great, struck through this gap with the cavalry against the Theban contingent, while Philip with his infantry crushed the Athenian wing. The elite Sacred Band of Thebes was completely destroyed, and half the Athenian participants were killed or captured. Greece lay at Philip's mercy, and many city-states anxiously expected the worst.

Philip sought their compliance, however, not their destruction, and with the exception of Thebes and Sparta he treated them leniently. He summoned representatives from all the Greek states to a congress at Corinth, where they swore to a common peace and formed what modern historians call the League of Corinth. Its members accepted Philip as their leader and agreed to provide troops for a common armed force. Early in 337, at Philip's request, the council of the league declared war on Persia and named Philip the supreme commander for the anticipated conflict.

Returning home in triumph, Philip began final preparations for the attack on Persia and took as his seventh wife a young Macedonian noblewoman named Cleopatra. His previous marriages had all shown political shrewdness, but this one was most impolitic and alienated Philip's primary wife-queen, Olympias, and her son, the crown prince Alexander. After a drunken encounter in which Philip drew his sword against Alexander, both mother and prince fled Macedonia.

With advance units of the Persian expedition already in Asia, military and political necessities forced him to arrange a reconciliation of sorts with Alexander, but Philip did not live to lead the invasion. In the summer of 336, as he attended the wedding festival of his daughter, one of his bodyguards, Pausanias, stabbed him to death. Although the murderer was almost certainly driven by a private grievance, the rift within the royal family brought suspicion on Alexander and Olympias, who were the primary beneficiaries of Philip's untimely death. Whatever the truth of this matter, Alexander succeeded Philip as King of Macedonia at a most opportune moment. Using Philip's army, he would make himself the most famous conqueror in history.

Summary

Philip II of Macedonia inherited a backward, largely pastoral kingdom on the verge of disintegration and in his twenty-three-year reign transformed it into a major power. Less visible than his military endeavors, his domestic reforms were no less important. By bringing new areas under cultivation, founding new towns, and resettling upland populations, he made Macedonia a more advanced and cohesive kingdom. His military innovations revolutionized warfare and produced the best army the world had yet seen. With it he won three major pitched battles, suffered only one significant defeat, and successfully besieged nine cities. A general of great bravery and energy, Philip also possessed good strategic sense and never lost sight of his objectives. He saw war as an instrument of policy, not an end in itself, and used it along with diplomacy to achieve realistic ends.

Unfortunately for Greece, Philip's success meant the end of Greek independence, and his victory at Chaeronea effectively ended the era of the autonomous city-state. Philip created the army that Alexander would employ to destroy the Persian Empire. Had he lived, it is likely that Philip would have used it in a more restrained and constructive fashion than did his brilliant son.

Bibliography

Adcock, Frank E. *The Greek and Macedonian Art of War*. Berkeley: University of California Press, 1957. This small volume provides the best brief introduction to Greek warfare, with appropriate references to Philip's innovations.

Bury, J. B., S. A. Cook, and Frank E. Adcock, eds. *The Cambridge Ancient History*. 12 vols. Cambridge: Cambridge University Press, 1923-1939. Chapters 8 and 9 in volume 6 describe Philip's rise to power with emphasis on his relations with the Greeks, especially the Athenians.

Cawkwell, George. *Philip of Macedon*. London: Faber and Faber, 1978. An excellent—though brief—biography, with outstanding maps. References to secondary works are minimal, but the notes contain a full record of the primary sources. The discussion of Greek military practices and Philip's part in their evolution is especially good.

Diodorus Siculus. *Diodorus of Sicily*. Translated by C. H. Oldfather et al. 12 vols. London: Heinemann, 1962. Book 16 in volumes 7 and 8 provides the only surviving ancient narrative of Philip's reign, interspersed with descriptions of activities in other parts of the Greek world. Diodorus must be used with care, because his account is sometimes inconsistent and chronologically confused.

Ellis, J. R. *Philip II and Macedonian Imperialism*. London: Thames and Hudson, 1976. This detailed study analyzes Macedonian expansion in the light of the needs and resources of Macedonia and in the context of fourth century Greek and Aegean politics. It includes a detailed chronology of Philip's reign, an appendix on his coinage, and a full bibliography of relevant modern works.

Hammond, N. G. L., and G. T. Griffith. *A History of Macedonia.* 2 vols. Oxford: Oxford University Press, 1972-1979. Volume 2, chapter 4 (by Hammond) provides a fine picture of Macedonia's weak condition in the forty years before Philip's accession. Chapters 5 through 20 (by Griffith) form the fullest, most authoritative biography of Philip available, with complete discussion of sources and chronological problems.

Hatzopoulos, Miltiades B., and Louisa D. Loukopoulos, eds. *Philip of Macedon.* London: Heinemann, 1981. A collection of thirteen essays by leading scholars of Macedonian history. Included are chapters on Philip's personality, his generalship, his coinage, his foreign policy, his achievement in Macedonia, his death, and the royal tombs at Vergina. This volume is beautifully illustrated and includes excellent maps, a chronological table, and a bibliography.

Perlman, Shalom, ed. *Philip and Athens.* Cambridge: Heffer, 1973. This volume assembles twelve important articles dealing with Philip's relations with the Greek city-states.

Plutarch. "Alexander." In *Plutarch's "Lives,"* translated by Bernadotte Perrin. 11 vols. Cambridge, Mass.: Harvard University Press, 1959-1967. In the absence of an ancient biography of Philip, this brief (fifty-page) biography of his son provides much useful information on Philip's later career and the magnificent army that he created.

James T. Chambers

PHILIP IV THE FAIR

Born: 1267 or 1268; Fontainebleau, France
Died: November 29, 1314; Fontainebleau, France
Areas of Achievement: Government and politics
Contribution: King of France from 1285 to 1314, Philip steadfastly created a strong monarchy in France. He developed a bureaucracy that allowed for firmer central control over raising revenues in the kingdom. His efforts, by accelerating the departure from a feudal form of government, began to modernize the French state.

Early Life

Philip IV, known as "the Fair" because of his supposedly handsome and stately appearance, was born in 1267 or 1268 at the royal castle of Fontainebleau, southeast of Paris. The second son of the weak king Philip III—who succeeded the holy and revered Louis IX—and Isabella of Aragon, young Philip endured a difficult childhood. When he was three years old, his mother died, and in 1274 his father remarried, taking Marie of Brabant as his second wife. Marie, likely hoping to see her own children become the heirs of the French throne rather than her stepchildren, shunned Philip and his older brother Louis. Prince Louis died in 1276, making Philip the next in line to the throne.

Although Philip III did not have a particularly close relationship to his son and heir, the king did provide Philip with an education befitting a royal prince. The king arranged for the famous scholar Giles of Rome to instruct his young son. Giles's clerk, Guillaume d'Ercuis, however, was the one upon whom the task of teaching Prince Philip fell. Guillaume provided the prince not only with the basics of reading and writing but also with the warmth and close companionship which he lacked after his mother's death. At his father's court, Philip also learned about aristocratic life and the business side of government, with its bureaucrats, foreign diplomats, favor-seekers, and feudal barons, whose every demand had to be considered and answered in order to preserve their loyalty and support.

On August 28, 1284, Philip III arranged a brilliant marriage for his son, betrothing him to Jeanne, the heiress to the kingdom of Navarre and the county of Champagne. This marriage arrangement was particularly important because it brought the extremely valuable and strategically located county of Champagne into the lands held directly by the king, thereby providing the Crown with a plentiful income as well as a solid foothold in vulnerable eastern France. Philip was a most devoted husband, who, unlike many other monarchs in medieval Europe, seems truly to have loved the spouse who was provided for him. After his wife's death in 1305, Philip did not remarry.

Shortly after his son's marriage, Philip III became involved in a papal crusade against Pedro, King of Aragon, who had attacked Philip's uncle King Charles I of Sicily, a vassal of the Pope. While on this disastrous mission to conquer Aragon, King Philip became ill, and he died on October 5, 1285. Philip, his heir, became the new King of France later in the month upon receiving the news of his father's death. He inherited a poorly waged war, a massive financial burden, and an Aragonese enemy.

Life's Work

The suddenness with which Philip the Fair ascended the French throne was emphasized by his immediate departure from his predecessor's interests, concerns, and method of government. Abandoning the papally ordered crusade against Aragon, the young king directed his attention toward selecting new advisers and reordering the bureaucratic machinery of his kingdom. Unlike his father, Philip IV strongly desired to make the kingdom of France independent of papal or church influence, control, or interference. Philip believed that his subjects' political concerns were more important than those of the Pope and that whatever was good for the kingdom would necessarily be favorable for the Church.

Although the new king was a pious man, who supported the Church financially within his kingdom, he also knew, as one of his biographers put it, the importance of the "religion of monarchy." This powerful ideology established the king as the most powerful individual within the kingdom, deserving absolute obedience, and permitted him to act autonomously. Philip demonstrated his devotion to this "religion" throughout his reign by strengthening the power of the royal administration, asserting his sovereignty over all subjects, noble and non-noble alike, in his realm, and engaging in struggles with external powers, such as the English King Edward I and Pope Boniface VIII, who encroached upon his territories or rights.

Because the French monarchy under the Capetian dynasty had emerged as a feudal state, the majority of governmental business was undertaken not by the king but by his personal vassals, who resided in the various regions of the realm and loyally provided military and governmental service for their lord. Thus, Paris, the royal capital, was not yet the seat of royal power in the thirteenth century, and vassals, who had pledged to be loyal to the king, provided legal, military, and administrative service as they saw fit in the king's absence. In order to maintain itself as the protector and defender of the French people, the French monarchy, under the guidance of Philip IV, created a new bureaucratic order and uniformity.

As the amount and complexity of legal business in the realm increased in the late thirteenth century, it became increasingly obvious that the king's courts needed to be reorganized. The Parlement, which had initially been an outgrowth of the royal council that heard certain types of important legal cases, was routinely engulfed in work. Under Philip, the court was divided into several lesser courts which held inquests, received petitions for equity cases, heard cases based on the written law used in southern France, or pronounced judgments in suits. The king also relied heavily upon a corps of officers to supervise affairs and administer justice in local jurisdictions.

In addition to this reorganization of the court, Philip's reign witnessed a reorganization of royal finances and the development of effective mechanisms for accounting, auditing, and disbursing royal funds and tax revenues by the Chamber of Accounts. To manage the large bureaucracy needed to rule the kingdom, Philip depended upon a small, permanent royal council—instead of the large council made up of most of the leading aristocrats and prelates of the kingdom. This smaller body was made up of full-time civil servants who could travel with the king throughout his realm and act decisively when called upon. With this large, complex, and powerful army of bureaucrats, Philip was better prepared to know the state of his kingdom and to rule his subjects than his predecessors, who had depended upon their occasionally cantankerous feudal vassals to assist them in the task of governing.

Philip IV's strong assertion of royal power within France is a theme which can be noted throughout his twenty-nine-year reign. From the early years, when Philip cast aside his father's advisers and policies in favor of his own, to the middle years, when he tangled with the most powerful vassal, Edward, Duke of Aquitaine and King of England, to the final weeks of his life, when he taxed his subjects heavily and ignited an aristocratic rebellion, the king appeared determined to shape both his reign and his nation. Unwilling to be a passive observer, the workhorse king played an active role in policymaking, participating in the meetings of the small royal council, drafting letters and pronouncements, and issuing orders to his civil servants.

Although Philip insisted on assuming this dominant role in French politics, he also portrayed himself as the protector of his subjects. When Edward encroached upon the rights of Frenchmen and attacked La Rochelle in 1294, Philip summoned him to appear before the Parlement. When Edward refused to appear as a king suspected of wrongdoing in Philip's court, Philip seized the duchy of Aquitaine and declared war against his English vassal. For several years, the two kings fought in an inconclusive war. Only in 1302, when Edward's ally, the Count of Flanders, inflicted a stunning defeat on Philip's large army at Courtrai, was peace restored.

To finance the war, Philip levied several onerous taxes on the French, regardless of their rank. In the final years of the war, the subjects demanded that they be allowed to give their consent to such extraordinary levies. Philip, always anxious to be seen as a good monarch, obliged them by assembling representatives from various localities to approve taxes and, in 1302, by convoking the Estates General, to endorse the principles of regular royal taxation during wartime. By pursuing his legal claims against the rebellious Duke Edward, plunging the realm into a protracted war to protect his royal powers, and establishing regular taxation to support the royal government and armies, Philip demonstrated not only his desire to rule France firmly but also his sovereign power over his subjects as their king.

Philip's pressing financial need, created by the prolonged war against Edward, contributed to his famous clash with Boniface VIII. In this conflict, the king claimed that as king of all subjects, laymen as well as clergymen, he had the right to tax everyone in order to defend the realm against enemies. The Pope strenuously resisted Philip's effort to tax churchmen. Boniface decreed that it was illegal for a monarch to do so, and, in 1302, he threatened to excommunicate the king and release all of his subjects from their obligation to be loyal to him.

Unwilling to allow Boniface VIII to dictate to him, Philip turned on the Pope. He effectively declared that the Pope could not interfere with what the king regarded as the internal affairs of the kingdom. He condemned the Pope for his actions and threats, spreading propaganda throughout the kingdom about the Pope's unjustified actions and raising questions about the Pope's legitimacy and moral conduct. Shortly before he was due to be banned from the Church, Philip ordered a small band of soldiers to arrest the Pope at his residence in Italy. With the arrest, Boniface had no choice but to capitulate. By this extreme political statement, Philip clearly established that the King of France was the sole ruler of every French person and that, in order to preserve his autonomy, he would not surrender to the orders and threats of the Pope.

Summary

When Philip IV the Fair died in November, 1314, France was in turmoil. His heir, Louis X, inherited a kingdom riddled with rebellions, as noblemen across the northern half of the realm resisted the payment of yet another round of burdensome royal taxes. This uprising, however, revealed the successes which Philip had achieved. A king noted for his steeliness, Philip created during his long reign a mature kingdom, established upon principles of firm royal government and furnished with the courts, professional bureaucrats, institutions, and accepted procedures necessary for maintaining a cohesive nation. It was this very royal strength which the rebels condemned in 1314, as they felt the Crown's grip tighten on what they perceived as their own rights and privileges.

Some years before, when the exasperated Bishop of Pamiers reflected upon the character of the French king, he wrote: "The king stares at men fixedly, without uttering a word.... He is not a man, not a beast, he is a graven image." This owllike monarch, who struck the perfect pose of a determined ruler and did not hesitate to impose his will on subjects and enemies alike, had introduced his realm to effective government between 1285 and 1314. Moreover, the image that the king presented to the bishop reflects the awesomeness that he had cultivated. His subjects, enemies, officers, and fellow monarchs revered the royal majesty as respectful worshippers who acknowledged and trembled before the royal might he wielded. It is not the effective administration of the realm alone for which Philip the Fair deserves credit, but also his creation and practice of the "religion of monarchy."

Bibliography
Fawtier, Robert. *The Capetian Kings of France: Monarchy and Nation, 987-1328*. New York: St. Martin's Press, 1960. In a survey of the first dynasty that ruled France, Fawtier provides a picture of the needs and growth of French monarchy, culminating in the reorganization under Philip IV.
Perroy, Edouard. *The Hundred Years' War*. Translated by D. C. Douglas. New York: Capricorn Books, 1965. Still the best survey of the late medieval conflict between the kings of England and France. The early chapters are devoted to explaining the origins of the struggle, especially during the reign of Philip IV.
Petit-Dutaillis, Charles. *The Feudal Monarchy in France and England from the Tenth to the Thirteenth Century*. New York: Harper and Row, Publishers, 1936. An older, but useful, book for understanding the concept of the feudal state and how it differed from the bureaucratic state created by kings such as Philip the Fair.
Strayer, Joseph R. "Philip the Fair: A 'Constitutional' King." In *Medieval Statecraft and the Perspectives of History: Essays by Joseph R. Strayer*, edited by John F. Benton and Thomas N. Bisson. Princeton, N.J.: Princeton University Press, 1971. In this brief article, Strayer not only outlines the perceptions of monarchy that Philip had but also indicates how Philip implemented his ideas about the function of the king in France.
_____. *The Reign of Philip the Fair*. Princeton, N.J.: Princeton University Press, 1980. Although not a chronological biography of the king, this book examines how Philip totally reformed the government of France by changing the personnel of government, relying more upon professional bureaucrats for the business of rule, and reorganizing the administration of the realm.
Wood, Charles T., ed. *Philip the Fair and Boniface VIII: State vs. Papacy*. New York: Holt, Rinehart and Winston, 1967. This small volume contains many of the primary documents and historical interpretations of the famous struggle between pope and king.

David M. Bessen

PHILIP THE GOOD

Born: July 31, 1396; Dijon, Burgundy
Died: June 15, 1467; Bruges, Flanders
Areas of Achievement: Government and patronage of the arts
Contribution: Despite his failure to build a unified state between France and the German states, Philip created sound administrative policies throughout his territories and established one of the most brilliant and cultured courts in Europe.

Early Life
Philip the Good was the third of four Valois dukes of Burgundy and the ablest among them. He was born in the ducal capital of Burgundy on July 31, 1396, the son of Duke John the Fearless and Margaret of Bavaria. Reared in wealthy circumstances, he was fascinated by the courtly manners of chivalry and ambitious for the future of Burgundy.

He succeeded to his inheritance on September 10, 1419, at the brutal assassination of his father by agents of the heir to the French throne. In 1409, Philip married Michelle of France, daughter of Charles VI and sister to Catherine, the wife of Henry V of England. Philip was involved with both countries as a result of the Hundred Years' War and always conscious of the fact that the duchy of Burgundy had been exploited by the French crown until the days of his grandfather, Philip the Bold.

Because of Philip's interest in art and patronage of artists, as well as his desire to publicize the history of his territory by encouraging official chroniclers, there are portraits and writings which form a clear picture of the duke. He was described as being of medium stature with proportionate weight, slim in arms and legs. His biographer wrote that he was bony rather than fleshy and had a dark complexion with brown hair. His eyebrows were thick above gray eyes and his nose was somewhat long.

In personality, he was said to have been proud, sensitive, and temperate. He had a fear of drunkenness and was abstemious in food and drink. His rather large brood of illegitimate children—numbered at eleven by modern scholarship, more by his contemporaries—indicated that his sexual appetite was not governed by the same moderation.

Although he had a quick temper, he did not hold grudges, and a sincere apology usually sufficed to clear the air after differences with his associates. As a youth he was fond of sports, riding, fencing, jousting, and hunting. He loved reading and tried to read, or be read to, each day. He had inherited a remarkable library of nine hundred volumes; by the end of his reign it had grown to include four times that number.

After his father's assassination, Philip dressed in black, although his simple clothing was of rich material and he had a penchant for fine jewels. He loved

Philip the Good

to hear music but was not very musical himself. Less superstitious than most of his contemporaries, he disliked flattery but demanded much of his courtiers.

Life's Work

The basis of Philip's inheritance was the duchy of Burgundy, roughly equivalent to a sizable portion of southeastern France on a modern map. It had been a holding of the French crown but was given to Philip the Bold, fourth son of John II of France, in 1364. It was a reward from the king to a son who had been captured with him at the Battle of Poitiers in 1356 and who had shared his father's captivity in England.

Although not originally intended, the duchy became virtually independent of the French crown thereafter. Territories of Flanders, Nevers, Artois, and Rethel (all portions of modern northern France and Belgium) were added by 1380. Philip's first marriage brought him additional French territory, and during his reign he added more, namely Namur, Hainaut, Brabant, Holland, Zeeland, and Luxembourg. These territories incorporated much of modern Belgium, the Netherlands, and Luxembourg.

Philip's goal was a firm union of these lands, which he acquired by force of arms, marriage contracts, negotiation, and purchase. The difficulty lay in the fact that they were scattered possessions. Not only were they separated geographically but also they had no linguistic or cultural unity. In spite of the obvious, the duke sought to unify the administrative apparatus, especially the financial chambers. While he had some success, effective union never was a reality. He was spurred on by his knowledge that the Carolingian Empire had been divided into three parts by the Treaty of Verdun (843). Lothair had been granted a middle kingdom, which Philip believed might be re-created if he could gain the duchy of Lotharingia from the German emperor. In this he was to be disappointed. Yet he passed on to his heir the dream of such a state.

His relationship with the leaders of many of his wealthy cities was often stormy. From the 1430's to the 1450's great cities such as Antwerp, Ghent, and Bruges rose in rebellion. These and other communes had developed autonomous control of internal affairs, and the merchant leadership resisted the centralizing efforts of ducal government, while accepting the overall hegemony of the Burgundian power structure.

Efforts toward political union did not deter the duke from spending excessive energy and monies in creating the most lavish court of his age. He was more successful in achieving this goal. His patronage of art brought such names as Hans Memlinc, Rogier van der Weyden, and Jan van Eyck to his court. He encouraged the illumination of manuscripts, which included exquisite miniature painting at the capitals. Tapestries also became art forms of remarkable size and workmanship, sometimes illustrating legends of ancient history as well as contemporary scenes.

Artisans of every kind filled the cities. The gigantic caldron built to heat six thousand gallons of water for the court baths was the talk of Europe. In Dijon, walls were smoothed for murals, a superior tile was developed for roofs, and cloths of the richest material were developed for the prevailing fashions (which were carefully preserved in artists' portraits).

Education was encouraged, and chroniclers such as Georges Chastellain and Olivier de La Marche kept careful records, investigating past history as well as glorifying the House of Burgundy. The search for and the copying of books became an end in itself. Perhaps the duke's perception in choosing qualified men to carry out his governmental and cultural pursuits made much of the work possible. Philip the Good was adept at delegating authority. His chancellor, Nicholas Rolin of Auten, served him loyally for thirty-nine years.

As a psychological effort to strengthen the position and reputation of the Burgundian dukes, nothing was more successful than Philip's establishment of the chivalric order known as the Order of the Golden Fleece. It was established in Bruges on July 10, 1430, at Philip's marriage to his third wife, Isabel of Portugal. It was a chivalric order much like the Order of the Garter in England, extended as a signal honor to a chosen few.

The symbol of the Golden Fleece represented the victory of the mythological Jason over his challengers. Churchmen would have preferred a biblical victor, but wool was a commodity on which the manufacturing towns of Flanders had built a great industry. By dedicating the order to the Virgin, Philip believed that the pagan symbol did not threaten Christianity. The rules of the order demanded loyalty and service of its members, and it is probable that Duke Philip envisioned it as a nucleus for a crusading movement to wrest the property of Christians and the Holy Land from Turkish hands. He also hoped that it would establish a link between noblemen from all parts of his holdings, a link that would increase the possibility for internal union.

The first meeting of the order was held on November 22, 1431, at Lille. There, the sixty-six statutes that established the order were read, and the number of members increased to thirty-one. Saint Andrew, patron of Burgundy, was named sponsor. The Papacy confirmed the order and its goal by three bulls and praised its founder. Standards for admission were based on proven military accomplishment, courage, honor, and devotion to Christian precepts. Treachery, immorality, cowardice, or unbecoming conduct were grounds for expulsion.

To celebrate the order, elaborate and beautiful pageants were created around tournaments. The tournaments, frowned on by the Church as dangerous, became famous throughout Europe. The feasts which attended them were served in splendor by liveried servants in a hall where the labors of Hercules were depicted in priceless tapestries. The duke's order became a

Philip the Good

highly coveted honor, and its value in bringing attention to him and his family was significant.

Philip survived serious illnesses in 1465 and again in 1466. It was said that he maintained his faculties until his death at seventy in 1467. He was succeeded by his son, Charles, the last of the Valois dukes of Burgundy.

Summary

Philip the Good faced insurmountable problems as he proceeded with his grandiose plans for a unified Burgundian state. While his internal problems were legion, the role of his disparate duchy in international affairs was an even greater problem. The wealth of his territories was well-known. England and France, in the throes of struggling national statehood, were very much aware of the role of Burgundy.

Following the assassination of his father, Philip was an ally of the French for a period of time. He was to share the regency of France with John, Duke of Bedford, brother of Henry V of England, after the latter's successful conquest of French forces. Yet Philip refused that responsibility, fearing the growth of English power on the Continent. A wool-producing country, England was interested in its commercial connections to the provinces of Burgundy, where artisans and merchants were masters of woolen manufacture. Therefore, Philip had to be wary of both countries, and he became more aloof in his dealings with them as his reign progressed.

For a period of time Philip had serious concerns as a dynast about producing an heir. His first wife, Michelle of Valois, whom he married in 1409, died childless in 1422. His second wife, Bonne of Artois, also died childless. Finally, Isabel of Portugal, whom he married in 1430, produced the son and heir so necessary for Philip. While Philip did not hesitate to recognize his illegitimate sons and employ them in various ways to serve his state, his legitimate son Charles was his successor.

The lasting contribution of Philip the Good resulted from his patronage of artists whose works still hang in museums from Spain to Vienna and in terms of his desire for the House of Burgundy to be chronicled in song and history. The illuminated manuscripts from his court, now collected in Brussels, are a reminder of his love of beauty and craftsmanship.

His chivalric tendencies, concretized in court etiquette, influenced every European court for centuries. They became, especially in the latter part of his reign, the greater part of his interest. The effort to increase his territories and to improve his administration also flagged as time went by. A modern biographer has said that one of his problems was that he lived too long.

He bequeathed to his son, the last of the Valois dukes of Burgundy, a failing political structure, handicapped by an increasingly cumbersome administration. The heads of the territories he valued had developed varying degrees of distrust, even hatred, for the ducal power. Perhaps Philip was too medieval for the new, Renaissance concepts of national statehood, but his appreciation of civility and beauty have earned for him an important place in European cultural history.

Bibliography

Cartellieri, Otto. *The Court of Burgundy: Studies in the History of Civilization.* London: Kegan Paul, Trench, Trübner, and Co., 1929. Although old, this work can still be read profitably. It is the result of twenty years of research on the Burgundian court. Well-chosen plates add to its usefulness, as well as a detailed genealogical chart. There are chapter notes but no index.

Fowler, Kenneth A. *The Struggle of Plantagenet and Valois.* New York: G. P. Putnam's Sons, 1967. An oversimplified and very basic text on the subject of the Hundred Years' War. Its value lies in its splendid plates, which include portraits, weapons, armors, clothing, buildings, and interiors.

Steward, Desmond. *The Hundred Years' War.* New York: Atheneum Publishers, 1982. A valuable adjunct to an understanding of the complicated period of struggle between France and England, with attention to the Burgundian faction. A clear discussion of a most difficult subject.

Tyler, William R. *Dijon and the Valois Dukes of Burgundy.* Norman: University of Oklahoma Press, 1971. Primarily a social history, this important book helps the reader gain a sense of the wealth and level of expenditure that made Burgundy known throughout the Continent. Includes excellent description of life at court, art, feasts, and tournaments. Contains a short selected bibliography, chronological summary, and family chart.

Vaughan, Richard. *Philip the Good.* New York: Barnes and Noble Books, 1970. Vaughan is the preeminent authority in English on the history of Valois Burgundy. This work, a highly detailed study of the reign of the third duke, is a seminal treatment of the subject in English. Always in command of his overwhelming material, Vaughan includes interesting details that enhance the life and times of Philip. A bibliography and index facilitate the study of individual events.

_____. *Valois Burgundy.* Hamden, Conn.: Shoe String Press, 1975. This volume, an overview of the territories and their four rulers, is clearly written, with sufficient maps to make the territorial problems intelligible. With index and full bibliography.

Anne R. Vizzier

PHILO OF ALEXANDRIA

Born: c. 20 B.C.; Alexandria, Egypt
Died: c. A.D. 45; possibly outside Alexandria
Area of Achievement: Philosophy
Contribution: Philo harmonized Old Testament theology with Greek philosophy, especially Platonism and Stoicism; his thought contributed much to that of Plotinus, originator of Neoplatonism, and to the ideas of the early church fathers.

Early Life
Philo came from one of the richest and most prominent Jewish families of Alexandria. The city had a large Jewish community, with privileges granted by its founder, Alexander the Great, and confirmed by his successors, the Ptolemies. The intellectual climate was Greek, and these Jews read their Scriptures in the Greek Septuagint version. According to ancient sources, the Greek population of Alexandria showed great hostility toward Jews.

Philo's brother Alexander held the Roman post of alabarch and collected taxes from Arab communities. He also managed the financial affairs of Antonia, mother of Emperor Claudius, and supplied a loan to Herod Agrippa, Caligula's choice as Jewish king.

In A.D. 39, anti-Semitism flared in the city, touched off by the visit of Herod Agrippa. The ensuing pogrom, permitted by the Roman governor Aulus Avilius Flaccus, resulted in a mission of opposing delegations to Caligula in Rome; the delegations consisted of three Greeks, led by the famous anti-Semite Apion, and five Jews, of whom Philo was eldest and spokesman. Caligula rudely dismissed the Jews and ordered his statue placed in their temples. In 41, under Claudius, Jewish rights were restored.

Life's Work
At least sixty-four treatises attributed to Philo are known. Only four or five are spurious; a few others, whose names have survived, no longer exist. The dates of the treatises, and even the order of their composition, are not known, except when a treatise refers to a previous one or to a dated event, such as the delegation to Rome. All the treatises have been translated into English (1854-1855), but some retain their original titles.

Foremost among Philo's writings are the exegetical works on the Pentateuch. These were arranged by Philo himself. Of the cosmogonic works, *De opificis mundi* (*The Creation of the World*), an allegorical explanation of Genesis, is most important. The historical works, allegorical commentaries on various topics in Genesis, are known as *Quod Deus sit immutabilis* (*That God Is Immutable*), *De Abrahamo*, *De Josepho*, *De vita Moysis* (*On the Life of Moses*), and *De allegoriis legum* (*On the Allegorical Interpretation of the*

Laws). Philo also wrote legislative works, commentaries on Mosaic legislation, such as *De Decalogo* (*On the Ten Commandments*) and *De praemiis et poenis* (*On Rewards and Punishments*). Philosophical writings, such as *De vita contemplativa* (*The Contemplative Life*), and political writings, such as *In Flaccum* (*Against Flaccus*) and *De legatione ad Gaium* (*The Embassy to Caligula*), are attributed to Philo as well.

As a devout Jew, Philo's intent was to reconcile the prevalent Alexandrian philosophical thought of Platonism and Stoicism with the Sacred Law of Israel (the Old Testament). He wanted to show the identity of the truths of philosophy and of revelation—and the priority of the latter. He thus suggests not only that Moses had been a consummate philosopher but also that the "holy assembly" of Greek philosophers (Philo includes Plato, Xenophanes, Parmenides, and Empedocles—and the Stoics Zeno and Cleanthes) had access to Holy Scripture.

Beyond the notion of the unity of God, on which the Bible, Stoicism, and Plato's *Timaeus* (360-347 B.C.) clearly agree, the Old Testament bears little relation to Greek philosophy. Philo thus adopted for the Old Testament the Stoic technique of reading the Greek myths as allegories illustrating philosophical truths. Even as a Jew he was not original in this, for the Jewish philosopher Aristobulus (fl. mid-second century B.C.) and others had employed this method. Jews, however, could not gratuitously disregard the literal sense of the Old Testament stories. Philo resolved the problem by asserting that Scripture has at least two levels of meaning: the literal, for the edification of simple folk, and a deeper spiritual meaning, of which the literal account was merely an allegory. This higher meaning was available to subtler minds capable of comprehending it. Indeed, the allegorical method seems imperative when the literal sense presents something unworthy of God or an apparent contradiction and when the text defines itself as allegorical.

Philo rejects the anthropomorphism of God in the Old Testament as a concession to weaker minds. His teaching is that Yahweh, God, is perfect existence (*to ontos on*) and absolutely transcendent, that is, outside creation, beyond comprehension, and inexpressible. One can know of His existence but nothing of His essence; one cannot predicate anything of Him, for He is unchangeable. In this Philo went beyond Plato and the Stoics. Having described God in such terms, Philo was compelled to harmonize this with the scriptural concept of Yahweh as a personal God, immanent in the world and intimate with His people.

In order to bridge the gulf between this transcendent God and the created cosmos, Philo adopted the Stoic doctrine of divine emanations, or intermediaries, as the means of God's extension to the physical world. The first emanation and—according to Philo's various terminology—God's firstborn, His mediator, administrator, instrument, or bond of unity, is the divine Logos. The Logos is, in Stoic symbolism, the nearest circle of light (fire) proceeding from God, defined as pure light shedding His beams all around. In the Old Testament, the angel of God is an allegory for the Logos. The Logos is also identified with Plato's Demiurge.

Philo varied his conception of the intermediary beings of creation, including the Logos. Sometimes they are forces, ideas, or spiritual qualities of God; sometimes they are spiritual personal beings, which Philo identifies with the biblical "powers" (*dynameis*, an order of angels). They derive from the Logos as Logos derives directly from god. God created first an invisible, spiritual world as a pattern (*paradeigma*) for the visible world. This is identified as the Logos *endiathekos* (organizer). Thus Logos is the location of Plato's Ideas. From this pattern, Logos *prophorikos* (forward-carrying) created the material world. Like the Greeks, who believed that nothing could be produced out of nothing, Philo assumed primeval lifeless and formless matter (*hyle*) as the substratum of the material world. At the same time, this matter became, for Philo, the source of the world's imperfection and evil.

God made the first preexistent, ideal man through Logos. This was man untainted by sin and truly in the divine image. His higher soul (*nous*, or *pneuma*) was an emanation of the purely spiritual Logos; it permeated man as his true, essential nature. Man's body and lower nature, or soul, with its earthly reason, were fashioned by lower angelic powers, or Demiurges. In a flight of Platonic dualism of body and soul, Philo saw the body as the tomb of the *pneuma*. The soul's unfolding was retarded by the body's sensuous nature, which it must overcome in order to gain salvation.

Philo's ethical doctrine employs the Logos in yet another, Stoic guise: operating as man's conscience and as teacher of the virtues. Men should strive for Stoic *apatheia*, apathy—the eradication of all passions. They should cultivate the four cardinal virtues of the Stoics (justice, temperance, courage, and wisdom). As this is an interior task, public life was discouraged by Philo; man, however, will never succeed by himself in getting free of the passions. God, through His Logos, can help man build virtue in the soul. It follows that man must place himself in correct relationship to God.

For this last and most important task, the sciences—grammar, rhetoric, dialectics, mathematics, music, and astronomy—are helpful. Yet they have never been sufficient to produce the Stoic ideal man of virtue. Contemplation of God alone is true wisdom and virtue. Thus Philo forges a link between Greek philosophy and the world of the mystery religions. He advocates going beyond ordinary conceptual knowledge, which recognizes God in His works, to an immediate intuition of the ineffable Godhead. In this ecstasy, the soul sees God face-to-face. Having passed beyond the original Ideas within the Logos, already beautiful beyond words, the soul is seized by a sort of "sober intoxication." As it approaches the highest peak of the knowable (*ton noeton*), pure rays of divine light come forth with increasing brilliance, until the soul is lost to itself and understands all.

Philo says that he himself had frequently been so filled with divine inspiration but that the ecstasy was indeed available to all the "initiated." These statements lend credence to the possibility that he ended his life as a member of the sect of the Therapeutae, an Essene-like community near Alexandria which he described affectionately in *The Contemplative Life*. Eusebius of Caesarea, quoting Philo, wrote that such communities in Egypt were founded by Mark the Evangelist and that their lives epitomized Christian practice in the seminal days of the new faith.

Summary

Though Photius' remark that Philo of Alexandria was a Christian cannot be accepted, his philosophy exerted a profound influence on early Christian theology. The Logos of John's Gospel certainly seems identical with one or more senses of the Logos in Philo. Ultimately, however, the Christian Logos, meaning the incarnate Word of God, can never be traced to Philo, for whom Logos was always incorporeal. Common to both Philo and many church fathers was the belief that philosophy was a special gift from God to the Greeks, just as revelation was His gift to the Jews. The fathers also used the allegorical method in interpreting Scripture beyond its literal meaning.

Philo's importance in Christian thought is underscored by the extensive commentary on and frequent reference to him by early Christian writers. Eusebius, Jerome, and Photius all provide lists of his tractates. Philo's philosophical language regarding God's transcendence influenced Christian apologists such as Justin, Athenagoras, Clement of Alexandria, and Origen.

Philo's greatest influence extended to Plotinus, founder of Neoplatonism. Though Plotinus may have pursued philosophy in India, many of his principles echo Philo's: that the body is the prison of the soul, that politics is trivial and distracting, that God (the One) is utterly transcendent yet the source of all truth and goodness, that Creation was effected by emanations from the One, and that pure souls may hope to return to the One, though in this life it is possible to encounter the One in a mystical experience. Thus Philo had an impact on the two major theological systems of the Roman Empire.

Bibliography

Colson, F. H., and G. H. Whitaker. *Philo*. 12 vols. London: Heinemann, 1929-1962. These volumes, part of the famous Loeb Classical Library, provide the original Greek with English translation on facing pages. They supply ample introductory sections, copious footnotes, and a complete bibliography addressing all problems of Philo scholarship.

Copleston, Frederick. "Greece and Rome." In *A History of Greek Philosophy*, vol. 1. Westminster, Md.: Newman Press, 1946. Reprint. Garden City, N.Y.: Doubleday and Co., 1962. Contains a short but encyclopedic survey of Philo's chief doctrines. Greek terms and references in Philo's writings are given for each specific teaching of Philo.

Philo of Alexandria. *Philo Alexandrinus: "Legatio ad Gaium."* Translated by E. Mary Smallwood. Leiden, Netherlands: E. J. Brill, 1961. Bilingual text with commentary.

Wolfson, Harry A. "Greek Philosophy in Philo and the Church Fathers." In *The Crucible of Christianity*, edited by Arnold Toynbee. London: Thames and Hudson, 1969. Wolfson isolates the primary similarities and oppositions in the thought of the earliest Christian fathers and Philo. The chapter is fully documented for further research.

_____. *Philo: Foundations of Religious Philosophy in Judaism, Christianity, and Islam*. Cambridge, Mass.: Harvard University Press, 1947. This is the most thorough, complete, useful, and current treatment of Philo available in English.

Zeller, Eduard. *Outlines of the History of Greek Philosophy*. Translated by Wilhelm Nestle. New York: Meridian, 1955. Includes an overview of Philo's key ideas. Zeller defines major differences between Philo and Greek thought.

Daniel C. Scavone

PIANKHI

Born: c. 769 B.C.; place unknown
Died: 716 B.C.; place unknown
Areas of Achievement: Warfare and politics
Contribution: Dynamic and forceful King of Kush, Piankhi invaded a divided Egypt, conquered it, and initiated an almost century-long Kushite rule over the entire Nile Valley.

Early Life

Nothing is known of Piankhi's early life. He was the son of the Kushite chieftain, Kashta, who controlled northern Nubia, the land immediately south of Egypt. Relatively early in its history, the Kingdom of Egypt was attracted to this neighboring territory up the Nile; gold, incense, and slaves, among other things, were obtained there. Nubia also was the corridor through which Egypt traded with lands farther south in inner Africa, Nubian middlemen being essential in this commerce. Beginning in the Old Kingdom (3100-2700 B.C.), Egypt's rulers thought it necessary to control northern Nubia and therefore established permanent bases there. Gradually, as the Egyptian hold weakened through the centuries, local leadership produced a state known as the Kingdom of Kush. The nature of its relationship with the greater power to the north depended on the latter's internal stability and the successive pharaohs' ability periodically to reassert firm imperial control over this outlying territory.

By the seventeenth century B.C., Kush's rulers had their capital at Kerma, just south of the Third Cataract on the Nile River. While they looked to Egypt's impressive culture for inspiration and imported assorted luxury goods, these presumably black kings of Kush enjoyed political independence for long periods. Inevitably, however, the Egyptians took back northern areas near the Egyptian border and sometimes absorbed all of Kush. During the Second Intermediate Period (1785-1580), Egypt itself was invaded for the first time, and much of its territory was conquered by a chariot army of the Hyksos, a people from western Asia. They ruled the country for about 150 years and recognized Kush, independent once again, as an equally great power whose rule extended as far north as Elephantine (Aswan).

Kush clearly was under heavy Egyptian cultural influence from early times, borrowing religious beliefs, architectural styles, and writing from the long-established northern civilization. Not only Egyptian soldiers and merchants worked there; many craftsmen, builders, and priests are also believed to have ventured up the Nile for employment under rich Kushite kings.

Life's Work

By the time Piankhi ascended the throne in 751, Kush's royal capital was

Napata, just north of the Fourth Cataract on the Nile. He inherited a strong kingship, one that had replaced an Egyptian viceroyalty lasting about four hundred years that had been imposed on Kush by pharaohs of the Eighteenth and Nineteenth dynasties (c. 1595-c. 1194). The Kushites, partly emulating Egypt's institution of divine monarchy, believed their king was the adopted son of several deities. A council composed of high priests, the queen mother, clan chiefs, and military commanders determined the royal succession, usually selecting one of the dead king's brothers. Piankhi is an obvious exception here, since he followed his father to the throne.

More than a political capital, Napata also was an important religious center. The seat of Egyptian royal power long had been the city of Thebes in Upper Egypt, which in addition was the principal center for the worship of the sun god, Amon. When the Twenty-second Dynasty of Egyptian kings moved its capital downstream to the delta region and emphasized dedication to the god Ptah rather than Amon, this alienated the latter's priests, who consequently shifted their religious headquarters to Napata, which already was the site of major temples erected by the Egyptians to honor Amon. The extensively Egyptianized Kushite population—or at least its leaders—thus became even more zealous devotees of Amon. It is likely that these newly moved religious authorities, in need of strong support in their new base, established an alliance with local chieftains who in time became the new Kushite monarchs from whom Piankhi descended. It cannot be determined, however, if this new dynasty could trace its bloodline back to the original royal lineage of Kerma.

As Kush became an increasingly centralized state under native rulers by the eighth century B.C., Egypt, in contrast, was experiencing political division. Indeed, ever since the tenth century, Egypt had been torn by dissension. By the eighth century that country was a confusing scene of about eleven major political entities, each under its own local potentate and more or less independent of the central authority of the weak Twenty-second Dynasty (c. 945-c. 730). The next dynasty returned the capital to Thebes, but evidently this did not help it overcome the political turmoil that prevailed with so many regional seats of power contending with one another. Such confusion and disunity eventually would draw Kush into Egyptian politics in a very dramatic way.

A major figure aspiring to leadership in Egypt during the mid-eighth century was Tefnakhte, lord of Sais, a principality in the western delta. He managed to extend his rule over a large part of Lower Egypt. In addition, this aggressive prince brought all the eastern- and middle-delta rulers into an alliance system dominated by him. Tefnakhte was the major power in all Lower Egypt and even a part of Middle Egypt. The man who would resist his efforts to reunify Egypt under a delta monarchy was Piankhi, who now reigned at Napata. This situation was not only one of political rivalry; Piankhi considered the northern Egyptians religiously and culturally inferior and thus unfit to govern Egypt.

When Tefnakhte sent his army south to besiege Heracleopolis, a center in Middle Egypt that had held out successfully against him earlier, the King of Kush recognized that this expanding force might be a potential threat to his own position. Still, he did not yet move against Tefnakhte. Ultimately, though, other Egyptian princes, seeing fellow rulers forced to submit to Tefnakhte's control, appealed to Piankhi to interfere, and he complied. Piankhi dispatched one of his armies, already in Egypt, to liberate the city of Hermopolis. Another force was sent to assist in that task but, having passed slightly north of Thebes, it encountered Tefnakhte's river fleet carrying many troops. The Kushites won a furious battle, inflicting heavy casualties on the enemy and taking many prisoners.

When Piankhi's two contingents joined farther northward, they fell upon Tefnakhte's forces besieging Heracleopolis. Again the men from the south were successful, and the losers were driven out of the area. The victorious Kushites then pushed on to Hermopolis, where they began their own siege of that city. When informed of his army's triumphs, King Piankhi, still in Napata, naturally was pleased. Satisfaction turned to rage, however, when he heard that his antagonist's surviving forces had been allowed to escape toward the delta. Deciding to take personal command of the campaign, Piankhi left for Egypt.

The Kushite ruler was slow to overtake his army. When he arrived in Thebes he spent some time engaged in elaborate ceremonials dedicated to Amon in the great temple complex of Karnak. This monarch was nothing if not a pious servant of his favorite god. It has been suggested that such ostentatious worship also was intended to convince Egyptians that this foreign leader enjoyed divine sanction for his impending conquest of the country. In any case, upon the completion of his devotions, Piankhi reached his army and soon ended the siege of Hermopolis by agreeing to spare its ruler's life if he surrendered. As Piankhi subsequently led his army to the north, his military strength as well as his reputation for clemency toward his enemies encouraged towns in his path to capitulate.

Tefnakhte, now concerned about the approaching Kushites, established his base at Memphis, the ancient city just south of the delta region. It was strongly defended, but Piankhi devised a shrewd plan of attack. Since the eastern side of the city was under water, its defenders thought it unnecessary to worry about an assault from that direction. Grasping the opportunity this presented, the royal commander ordered his men to seize all the enemy's boats in the harbor, which, along with the Kushite's own flotilla, were then utilized quickly to ferry his fighting men to the city walls. These were mounted easily before the opposition could react effectively. When the city fell, Piankhi characteristically gave credit to Amon.

This spectacular victory led to the submission of the surrounding country. In keeping with his religious habits, Piankhi celebrated each of his military successes by publicly worshipping in local sanctuaries, including, especially, those of Memphis. Ptah, the artificer god, was the major deity of that city and believed to be the creator of Amon. The bold conqueror from the distant south could now announce that Ptah had recognized him as the legitimate King of Egypt. All the princes of the delta eventually submitted to Piankhi's authority, demonstrating their homage by delivering their substantial treasures to him. It is interesting that Piankhi, the religious puritan, refused to meet some of these leaders personally, as he considered such "fish-eaters" to be unclean.

The Kushite's principal target, however, eluded him. Even though Tefnakhte's army was destroyed, that ambitious and determined leader defied his adversary, ultimately taking refuge on an island in the northern delta. Piankhi settled for Tefnakhte's pledge of allegiance rather than continuing pursuit in the difficult, unfamiliar swampland. Thus, when the few other notable rulers of outlying territories swore obedience to him, Piankhi, the prince of a longtime colony of Egypt, was now the lord of that great imperial nation by the Nile.

Having achieved such success, the man from Napata packed his accumulated prize wealth aboard his riverboats and made his way up the river to his own desert land. Although it was short-lived, political unity had been restored to Egypt by a foreign conqueror. Nevertheless, Tefnakhte soon resumed his efforts to acquire control of Egypt himself and enjoyed considerable success in the north. Kushite dominance in Upper Egypt was secure, however, during the remainder of Piankhi's reign. That king evidently was content to have imposed his nominal authority over the entire Nile Valley without troubling to remain in Egypt in order to enforce his sovereignty over the long term. As long as Upper Egypt, particularly the holy city of Thebes, was not threatened by the "unclean" northerners, he rested easily. Piankhi's last known accomplishment, which seems fitting for a king so obsessed with pleasing the gods, was his reconstruction of and addition to the great temple of Amon at Napata (Jebel Barkal). It remained for his brother and successor, Shabako, to return to Egypt and firmly establish his dynasty's rule by residing there as pharaoh.

Summary

Piankhi's extended military effort in Egypt was the foundation for Kushite control of that country for almost a century. Although he is not officially listed as such, it is generally accepted that he initiated the Twenty-fifth Dynasty of Egyptian kings, the so-called Nubian or Ethiopian Dynasty, which reigned from about 716 to 656. His achievement, consequently, established Kush as a major power in the ancient world. If the other important states of the time had not noticed inner Africa before, they did after Piankhi's conquest. The Kushites' appearance in force in Egypt undoubtedly was feared by the proud Egyptians as the coming of barbarian hordes, but it was not the calamity they expected. Piankhi and his men represented a culture that was heavily Egyptianized. Admittedly, Kush was an African kingdom and never completely lost its unique identity under the Egyptian façade. Yet the influence of Egypt's long-established and admired civilization had brought Kush within the northern cultural orbit to a considerable extent. These were not savage barbarians but fellow residents of the Nile Valley whose leaders were literate worshippers of Egyptian gods and who expressed themselves in cultivated Egyptian terms. Piankhi, in the twenty-first year of his reign, erected a stela in Napata that recounts his Egyptian expedition. It is acknowledged as one of the most interesting and revealing documents in Egyptian and Kushite history, vividly describing the military exploits of the king and his army as well as clearly communicating details about the fiery temperament, religious piety, and generosity of Piankhi. Now exhibited in the Cairo Museum, it is a fitting memorial to one of the great figures in African history.

Bibliography
Adams, William Y. *Nubia: Corridor to Africa*. Princeton, N.J.: Princeton University Press, 1977. Clearly the most comprehensive account of the region from prehistoric times to the nineteenth century, it provides excellent coverage of the "heroic age" of the Nabatan kings and their rule in Egypt. It also reflects the best of recent scholarship. Extensive end notes and chapter bibliographies are included.
Arkell, A. J. *A History of the Sudan: From the Earliest Times to 1821*. 2d rev. ed. London: University of London, Athlone Press, 1961. By an expert boasting of many years' service in the Sudan, this work is good for a description of the country and its occupation by Egypt. The chapter on Kush's conquest of Egypt is useful but inferior to that found in the Adams book.
Breasted, James Henry. *Ancient Records of Egypt*. Vol. 4, *The Twentieth to the Twenty-sixth Dynasties*. Chicago: University of Chicago Press, 1906-1907. Contains a translation of the Piankhi stela as well as the editor's excellent scholarly summary of it. An essential source.
Emery, Walter B. *Egypt in Nubia*. London: Hutchinson, 1965. A good survey, providing important background on Egyptian-Kushite relations before Piankhi's conquest.
Gardiner, Sir Alan. *Egypt of the Pharaohs: An Introduction*. Oxford: Clarendon Press, 1961. An extensive chapter on Egypt under foreign rule provides a fine historical sketch as background for the Kushite conquest and includes an account of Piankhi's feat.

Hakem, A. A., with I. Hrbek and J. Vercoutter. "The Civilization of Napata and Meroe." In *General History of Africa*, edited by G. Mokhtar, vol. 2. Paris: UNESCO, 1981-1985. Provides little on Piankhi's reign but includes a good discussion of Kushite life and institutions, although the Meroitic period receives most attention. An extensive bibliography also makes the work an important resource.

Lysle E. Meyer

PINDAR

Born: c. 518 B.C.; Cynoscephalae, near Thebes, Boeotia, Greece
Died: c. 438 B.C.; Argos, Greece
Areas of Achievement: Literature and music
Contribution: Pindar proved through his poetry and music that creative aspirations raise humanity to near-perfection; as the greatest lyrical poet of classical times, he influenced literature and culture for centuries.

Early Life

Pindar, the greatest of ancient Greek lyric poets, was born in Cynoscephalae, near Thebes, probably around 518 B.C. A city rich in history and legend, Thebes was located in the region known as Boeotia, north of the Gulf of Corinth. Pindar came from a noble Dorian family whose lineage went back to ancient times and included heroes whom he celebrated in his poems. His uncle was a famous flute player; Pindar, who excelled at that instrument, may have acquired his skills from him. Lyric poems were written primarily for solo or choral singing, with instrumental accompaniment, and Pindar learned his craft in writing poetry from two important lyric poets, Lasus of Hermione and Corinna of Tanagra. It is said (but disputed by some) that Corinna defeated Pindar five times in lyric competition. If the story is true, it is probable that the judges in these contests, all of whom were male, were influenced not only by Corinna's poetry but also by her remarkable beauty.

In the framing of his poetry, Pindar drew from the vast store of myths—many of them associated with Thebes—that he had learned in his youth. To him, the Olympians and other figures from ancient stories were not mythical but real. He accepted reverently, for example, the stories of the oracle of Delphi, and he devoutly worshipped Zeus (even composing a famous hymn to him) and other gods and goddesses all his life. He was also the heir to several priestly offices, which buttressed his natural inclination toward religion. In addition to being educated near Thebes, he is said to have received instruction in Athens, which was a great academic and cultural center. Studying in Athens would account for his having known the Alcmaeonids, a politically active family in Athens for which he wrote laudatory poems—probably, as was customary, under commission.

Pindar was schooled in history, philosophy, religion, music, and literature. His poetry is filled with allusions to those fields as well as to his homeland and relatives. He secured his reputation as a young man, and fabulous legends grew up around him. For example, one story explaining his talent claimed that as he slept out in the fields one day, bees had deposited honey on his lips.

Pindar received a constant flow of engagements to write poems for important figures, including the victors of athletic contests, the odes for which are the only surviving works of the poet. Usually these victory odes (*epinicia*) were performed in processionals welcoming the heroes home. Pindar's odes are named for the particular games at which they were performed—the *Olympian Odes*, *Pythian Odes*, *Nemean Odes*, and *Isthmian Odes*. This celebratory tradition was at one with the Greek belief that great deeds—including the greatest of all, the creation of the world—should be artistically remembered so as not to pass into oblivion. For a time, Hieron, tyrant of Syracuse, was a patron of Pindar and of other poets, such as Simonides, Bacchylides, and the great tragedian Aeschylus. This activity helped Syracuse to rival Athens and Thebes as an intellectual center and helped perpetuate Pindar's already considerable fame.

Life's Work
In the Alexandrian list of the nine best lyric poets, Pindar's name came first. In his own time and in later centuries he was remembered as "soaring Pindar." The fact of music is inseparable from the fact of lyric poetry in Pindar, for it is clear that his poems were written to be sung. What is not known is how to reproduce for modern performance the melody and the meter of his lyrics, all of which were written in celebration of an individual or an event, often an athletic victory. This is to speak only of the four books which have survived, for there are fragments of his other works (or allusions to them) that prove that his genius was not limited to the choral lyric. He produced thirteen books in genres other than the *epinicia*, including hymns, processionals, and dirges.

Another obstacle to the comprehension of Pindar's poetry is its allusiveness. Those people hearing the performance of a victory ode had an immediate awareness of Pindar's allusions, whether to the Olympians, the heroes of myth, the rulers of the times, the athletes or families being honored, or even autobiographical references. Only one who has read widely in Greek history, philosophy, literature, and legend can begin to understand these allusions or the stirring effect they would have had on Pindar's audience.

The poems are, then, locked into a time frame in their references and in their constructions. The themes, however, are accessible. A central theme in Pindar is the emulation of divinity. Humans are of the same race with gods but lack their powers; thus they are ever striving toward perfection, in an effort to be as much like the gods as possible. This view required the poet to overlook or disbelieve scandalous stories in mythology (which, to Pindar, was religion) which belied the perfection of the gods. Remembrance of the greatness of Zeus—Zeus unsullied by rumors about his lust, his violence, his unreasonableness—gave humanity a standard by which to live. Life is the thing of a day—another theme in Pindar—and to live it with constant reverence for the lessons taught by gods and heroes was to give reverence to oneself and to give a degree of permanence to life.

Virtue, bravery, manliness, and competitive physical activities were far more important to Pindar than was (as with Homer) intelligence, and he expressed scorn toward those who displaced these attributes with intellectual measures. The intelligent, resourceful Odysseus, for example, he found less praiseworthy than a man of physical prowess. Physical things—bodily strength and athletic skills and other things of the earth—were the things of heaven. Acquired learning paled beside innate talent, inborn greatness of soul and body.

Pindar always wrote his odes as if those they celebrated were joined with the immortals. Poets were said to have Zeus speaking through them; subjects celebrated by odes were, similarly, raised above the ordinary lot of humankind. There was a mystical link between the human being and divinity, a link that could not, to Pindar's way of thinking, be achieved by education. A basic belief of the aristocracy which Pindar represented was that qualities of goodness—humanistic ideals—could not be taught; universal edification being impossible, therefore, society depended on an aristocracy that was morally and spiritually enlightened. Pindar's place as a poet was to praise heroes in order to raise humankind.

Rooted in tradition as he was, Pindar was conservative; still, he was an innovator and a searcher. He was always seeking profound meanings from human events, ideals and nobility from everyday realities. He supported the rule of Eunomia (law, or good constitution) as a way for a moderate aristocracy to succeed tyranny. Such an aristocracy would be made up not only of those from the traditional aristocracy but also of those from the wealthy class. Those with leisure to contemplate new possibilities for humanity would most likely be those who would bring about new achievements for the betterment of humanity; the wealthy, the aristocratic, had freer minds. Large audiences listened to Pindar, audiences accustomed to hearing Homeric epics recited and therefore prepared for the exceptionally long, whirling passages of Pindar sung by an enthusiastic chorus.

Pindar's fame was even greater after his death than in his own time. His writings proved not to be locked in time; rather, they were one more link of many links in Greek literature going back to a time even before Homer, and extending through Aeschylus to Plato, which, while glorifying aristocratic tradition, pointed the way to the political principle that came to be known as democracy. The highest virtue that elitism had, in other words, was the knowledge that what was available at first to only the privileged few was ultimately accessible to all. Pindar's poetry was one of the main avenues making accessible this Greek ideal: that the commonest individuals have within them resources of divine inspiration, divine identity, divine glory.

Summary

In a chapter devoted to Pindar in *The Greek Way* (1973), Edith Hamilton says, "There never was a writer more proudly conscious of superiority." She provides arguments and examples supportive of his proud consciousness of superiority. As he felt himself superior in his poetry, so he believed that his "race," the aristocracy, could achieve for the good of all what tyranny and other kinds of rule (including democracy) could not. He could not have known that members of the aristocracy who glorified themselves as individuals of the highest order were opening the way for all human beings to see themselves as privileged and knowing aristocrats.

Pindar's complex style as preserved in the *epinicia* challenged later generations of poets to compose "Pindaric odes," in which colorful images shifted rapidly and imaginatively, like rushing water. Although the content of Pindar's surviving works is obscure for the modern reader, his inspired style remains a model of purely beautiful language.

Bibliography
Carne-Ross, D. S. *Pindar*. New Haven, Conn.: Yale University Press, 1985. A brief work addressed to the general reader, with a short but useful bibliography.
Crotty, Kevin. *Song and Action: The Victory Odes of Pindar*. Baltimore: Johns Hopkins University Press, 1982. Devoted to individual examinations of the performances of the odes for which Pindar is most remembered. Includes notes, bibliography, and index.
Finley, John H., Jr. *Pindar and Aeschylus*. Cambridge, Mass.: Harvard University Press, 1955. More than half the book is devoted to Pindar.
Finley, Moses I. *The Ancient Greeks*. New York: Viking Press, 1964. Gives brief but interesting and useful information on Simonides, Bacchylides, and Pindar.
Gerber, Douglas E. *A Bibliography of Pindar, 1513-1966*. Cleveland, Ohio: Case Western Reserve, 1969. A comprehensive bibliography of 160 pages, usefully divided into thirty topical sections.
Grant, Mary A. *Folktale and Hero-Tale Motifs in the Odes of Pindar*. Lawrence: University of Kansas Press, 1967. Straightforward account of the subject, with an index of motifs and an index of mythological characters.
Hamilton, Edith. *The Greek Way*. New York: Avon Books, 1973. The best short book on the Greek way of life; devotes a chapter to Pindar. Bridges scholarship and general readership. Seven pages of references, especially to works of ancient Greek writers.
Highet, Gilbert. *The Classical Tradition: Greek and Roman Influences on Western Literature*. New York: Oxford University Press, 1949. The best work available on the Greco-Roman influences on Western literature. Lengthy discussion—perhaps the most accessible anywhere for general readers—on Pindar's poetical forms and on his direct influences on poetry. Extensive notes in lieu of a comprehensive bibliography.

Norwood, Gilbert. *Pindar*. Berkeley: University of California Press, 1945. A major work based on scholarly lectures. Includes bibliography and index.

Pindar. *The Odes of Pindar*. Edited and translated by Richmond Lattimore. Chicago: University of Chicago Press, 1961. Translation of all the surviving odes. Contains a preface on Pindar and his poetry. Lattimore is one of the most respected modern translators of Greek.

Race, William H. *Pindar*. Boston: Twayne Publishers, 1986. As one of the volumes in Twayne's World Authors series, this work is characteristically comprehensive in biography, criticism, and bibliography. For both scholarly and general audiences.

Snell, Bruno. *Poetry and Society: The Role of Poetry in Ancient Greece*. Bloomington: Indiana University Press, 1961. Focuses on the forms, purposes, and occasions of Pindar's poetry. Snell is also the author of *The Discovery of the Mind: The Greek Origins of European Thought* (New York: Harper and Row, Publishers, 1960), which contains a valuable section on Pindar's hymn to Zeus.

David Powell

ANDREA PISANO
Andrea da Pontadera

Born: c. 1270-1290; possibly Pisa, Italy
Died: c. 1348; probably Orvieto, Italy
Area of Achievement: Art
Contribution: Bronze, unknown as a medium for sculpture in Florence prior to the 1330's, was brought to that city by Pisano, who made an important contribution to art with his baptistery door, which was to be the example to be matched and supremely surpassed during the Florentine Renaissance.

Early Life

Nothing certain is known of Andrea Pisano's early life. His first appearance as a public figure does not occur until 1330, when he received the most important commission of his artistic career. The fine detail and design of his bronze sculptures suggest that he may have had training as a goldsmith. He may also have been trained by Giovanni Pisano, who was a sculptor who had, in turn, been trained by his father Nicola Pisano. The Pisanos, father and son, were natives of Pisa and made important contributions to the development of bronze sculpture in the thirteenth and fourteenth centuries, but they were not related to Andrea Pisano, whose real name is, in fact, Andrea da Pontadera. The fact that he was generally called Pisano and emerges as a worker in bronze, a speciality of Pisan artists, suggests a Pisan connection.

In 1330, he gained the prestigious contract for a set of doors on the baptistery of the cathedral in Florence. Some reputation must have helped to capture this grand opportunity. It is likely that a competition took place, and it is known that Pisano's wax model for the doors had to be redone. He must have been known for prior work of some quality, but nothing has been so identified, and his work in Florence was to be the major source of his modest fame.

Life's Work

The baptistery is a separate building to the west of the cathedral in Florence. It may have been started as early as the fifth century and was probably annexed through the centuries. Local craft guilds took upon themselves the responsibility for major religious buildings, and it was the Guild of Cloth Importers that sponsored the work on the baptistery. In 1329, it was decided that a set of bronze doors should be added to the south face of this octagonal, white-and-green marble building. The obvious subject for decoration of the door was the life of John the Baptist, and the upper series of the twenty-eight panels which Pisano designed for the door took John as their subject, while the lower set depicted Christian virtues. The individual scenes were enclosed by a border of Gothic design.

Both technically and aesthetically, Pisano's door was a great success and provided the example and impetus for the later, even finer work of Lorenzo Ghiberti on two further doors, which were initiated at the beginning of the fifteenth century.

The use of bronze, an extremely expensive material, had died out after the fall of the Roman Empire, and very few examples of Greek and Roman bronze have survived, given its frangible nature and the obvious temptation to melt it down for other uses. Nicola and Giovanni Pisano's example in successfully bringing bronze back into the realm of religious sculpture was to mark the beginning of a renewed, flexible use of the metal which Andrea's baptistery door instituted in Florence. It would be in Florence, in particular, where the use of bronze was to have a glorious future and where so much of the greatest art of the early Renaissance would be produced, after Pisano, by artists such as Ghiberti and Donatello.

Yet Pisano brought something else to Florence. The earlier Pisanos, working with bronze in several cities throughout northern Italy, had also shown in their design an interest in adding to their Gothic roots the more realistic, more sensuous influences of classical sculpture, as well as delicate rhythms of French Gothic design. Giovanni, in particular, had strong connections to northern Gothic artists and seems to have had some considerable influence on Pisano. Working in the last century of the Gothic period, the Pisanos, and Andrea, in their wake, manifested the return to the celebration of the human body which had been central to classical art and was to reach elegant and celebratory expression in the early years of the Italian Renaissance.

Pisano is not, in fact, a Renaissance artist. He was a late Italian Gothic artist who manipulated with considerable success not only his heritage of medieval ideas and preconceptions but also other influences which come together for the first time in his own work. The restrained, flat style of Gothic art is present in the baptistery sculpture, and his use of space is unadventurous, but the compositions and modeling have a reality about them which suggests greater things to come. The influence of Giotto, the most important "link" figure between late Gothic and early Renaissance art, is also apparent in the harmonious juxtapositions, the sense of space in the panels. That is not surprising, since Giotto was responsible for the adjacent campanile. An added dimension of Pisano's work on the panels is his use of drapery, gracefully reminiscent of French Gothic influences which he may have picked up from Giovanni Pisano.

The Giotto influence is even more pronounced in Pisano's own work on the campanile, where he was responsible for a series of reliefs, decorating the lower stories of the tower. There is some opinion that Giotto may have had a hand in the design of these scenes. Whatever the truth may be, it is obvious that the tender sonority and grace of these scenes, as well as the similar aura surrounding a series of marble figures which Pisano carved for niches on the tower, are examples of Giotto's effect on Pisano, who was to succeed him as the supervisor of the campanile project when Giotto died in 1337.

Pisano remained in Florence until 1343 and may have left then simply because of the financial difficulties of that time, which forced the guilds to cut back on their social and religious projects. He seems to have returned to Pisa initially, but he soon moved to Orvieto, where he became the overseer of works at the cathedral. By this time his son, Nino Pisano, who was also a sculptor and would succeed him as overseer at the cathedral, was working with him. It is likely that Andrea Pisano was a victim of the Black Death, which struck at the end of the 1330's. There seems to be little work after the Florence period that can be identified as that of Pisano, so it is to those two projects, the baptistery and the campanile, that his reputation is attached.

Summary

Andrea Pisano's contribution to the history of art is a minor one, but it is not insignificant, in terms of either technique or aesthetic theory. His baptistery work was in itself proof positive of the potential for bronze as a legitimate medium for the new Humanism, and a close study of the technical mastery which he displayed in dealing with the John the Baptist theme reveals a capacity for the subtle manipulation of this difficult metal.

If he was less successful than Ghiberti in infusing psychological subtlety and dramatic breadth into the panels, it is important to remember how far he did go, how much emotional power he did express in his work. Ghiberti comes at the beginning of a new age, a new sensibility, and it has often been suggested that the Renaissance can be dated from the moment at which he presented his design for the second portal of the baptistery in 1401.

Yet the Renaissance did not suddenly spring fully formed from the work of Ghiberti; it had been brewing slowly, sometimes painfully, throughout the preceding century. In sculpture, particularly in bronze sculpture, the Renaissance can be seen working its way out of the aging Gothic sensibility in the work of the Pisanos. Nicola knew that the old ways, the static, flattened, restrained designs of the Gothic, however graced by northern influences, were not sufficient for him, and he was constantly circling the idea that the classical, heathen world holds the answer in its glorification of the human form. He passed that idea on to his son, and it passed, in turn, into the work of Andrea Pisano.

Pisano was, in short, that peculiar kind of artist who comes at the end of one tradition and who may easily fail if he does not possess, as Pisano did, the rare gift for assimilation and absorption of new ideas and the capacity to express the conjunction of the old and new in ways which not only make for art of outstanding quality but also for an example which will lead the greater artists of the new mode.

When Andrea Pisano was asked to design the first door for the baptistery, there was not an artisan in town who could work with bronze. It was necessary to import a bell caster from Venice to work with the artist. When Pisano left town, years later, the tradition was there in proof, in the great door and in his work on the campanile panels. Some years later, again with the financial support of the guild, the great sculptor Ghiberti followed the example set by Pisano and carried the bronze sculpture into the glories of the Renaissance.

Bibliography
Avery, Charles. *Florentine Renaissance Sculpture*. London: John Murray, 1982. A great aid to the untrained reader, beginning step-by-step with a group of chapters which move out of the late Gothic period into the Renaissance. Very good at putting the ubiquitous Pisanos in the right order in time, contribution, and influence. With generous illustration.
Borsook, Eve. *The Companion Guide to Florence*. London: Collins, 1966. The best guidebook to Florence and quite helpful to the reader who needs to know how public sculpture was placed in this city. Succinct, civilized, and sensitive to the needs of a reader studying the birth of the Italian Renaissance.
Crichton, G. H., and E. R. Crichton. *Nicola Pisano and the Revival of Sculpture in Italy*. Cambridge: Cambridge University Press, 1938. Pisano can be understood fully only in the context of the Pisan tradition, reviewed in this volume, and particularly in relation to the oldest Pisano's lead in developing the bronze sculpture as a Pisan skill.
Henderson, George. *Gothic*. Harmondsworth, England: Penguin Books, 1967. A handsomely illustrated paperback in Penguin's Style and Civilization series which addresses the vexing question of exactly what Gothic art means.
Pope-Hennessy, John. *Italian Gothic Sculpture*. 3 vols. London: Phaidon Press, 1955. Pisano makes sense only if he can be seen clearly as both a precursor of the Renaissance and as a late Gothic artist. Pope-Hennessy is one of the finest, most elegant commentators on both elements of Pisano's gift.
Wittkower, Rudolf. *Sculpture: Processes and Principles*. Harmondsworth, England: Penguin Books, 1977. Using 180 photographs, the noted scholar traces the history of the art from antiquity to the present. This book is helpful in putting the Pisano achievement in perspective and in explaining how artistic style changed from the Middle Ages to the Renaissance.

Charles H. Pullen

NICOLA PISANO and GIOVANNI PISANO

Nicola Pisano

Born: c. 1220; Apulia, Italy
Died: Between 1278 and 1284; Pisa, Italy

Giovanni Pisano

Born: c. 1250; Pisa, Italy
Died: Between 1314 and 1318; probably Siena, Italy
Area of Achievement: Art
Contribution: By synthesizing Gothic and classical influences, Nicola and Giovanni Pisano created sculptural styles which are considered proto-Renaissance in their concern with expanded form and space and humanized narrative scenes.

Early Lives

Although Nicola Pisano's earliest known work is the signed and dated pulpit for the baptistery of Pisa of 1260, the style and skill demonstrated there are clearly the work of a mature artist. His history and career prior to 1260, however, are largely a matter of conjecture based upon a few late documents and observable influences on the style of his known works. On the basis of two documents dated 1266 which refer to him as "Nicolas de Apulia," it is thought that he was probably born in southern Italy around 1220. This theory is supported by the strong influence of classical sculpture seen in the marble reliefs of the Pisa pulpit, an influence which suggests a familiarity with the classicized art encouraged in the south during the reign of Frederick II. Nicola may also have passed through Rome while making his way north.

By 1258, Nicola had established himself as an artist in Pisa. Since his son Giovanni is documented as having been born in Pisa, possibly as early as 1248, Nicola most likely arrived in that city around mid-century. Attributions of works whose dates precede that of the Pisa pulpit have been made, but none is certain. A visit to France by Nicola in the 1250's has been suggested, based upon stylistic and iconographic details of the Pisa pulpit, but such a trip is not accepted by all scholars.

Giovanni Pisano was trained as a sculptor by his father. Nicola's contract for a pulpit in the Siena cathedral names Giovanni as a junior member of the studio by 1265. From this evidence, his birth date is placed around 1250. Inscriptions on two of Giovanni's own works mention his place of birth as being Pisa.

Besides the Siena pulpit, it is known that Giovanni assisted his father on the Fontana Maggiore (great fountain) in Perugia and probably on the exterior, second-story sculpture of the Pisan baptistery. The emphatic Gothicism of his mature style can be identified in parts of these earlier commissions, and portions of them have been attributed to his hand. It has been suggested that his knowledge of French Gothic art was acquired during a trip to France between 1270 and 1276, but the evidence for such a visit is strictly stylistic. Alternatively, it is possible that he learned of the French style through a study of portable art works such as ivory carvings and manuscript illuminations.

Life's Work

Nicola Pisano's pulpit for the baptistery of Pisa demonstrates that in 1260 he was working in a heavily classicized style. The classical influence can be seen in his handling of draperies, the sculpting of bodies and heads, the emphasis on the human form, the technical virtuosity, and the sense of classical reserve that permeates the reliefs and statuettes. Specific sources for some of the figures can be found among ancient Greek, Roman, and Etruscan works. Nicola's classicism was neither debased nor pastichelike but extended to the structure of the pulpit itself, the interest in space and form, and the depiction of narrative scenes as human dramas. The Pisa pulpit also reflects other influences, including Italian Romanesque sculpture, Italo-Byzantine painting, and French Gothicism.

The pulpit at Pisa marked a distinct development beyond the Romanesque style prevalent in Italy at the time, a style characterized by flattened forms, shallow cutting, schematic draperies, and little illusion of three-dimensional space. Nicola's talent, however, was not static. Within a few years of the completion of the Pisa pulpit, the French Gothic style began to influence his work heavily. This development can be seen in his next major commission, a pulpit for the cathedral in Siena, completed in 1268. In the relief sculpture and statuettes for this work, Nicola continued his emphasis on volumetric human form and retained an innate classicism, but he exploited the expressive and emotional possibilities inherent in the more fluid naturalism of the Gothic.

Nicola's reputation rests on the achievement of these two pulpits, but he was involved in other commissions as well. He designed the tomb of Saint Dominic in San Domenico Maggiore at Bologna, the execution of which fell to his studio, most notably to Arnolfo di Cambio. In 1273, he built, or reconstructed, the altar dedicated to Saint James in the cathedral at Pistoia. In 1278, he completed work on the Fontana Maggiore in Perugia. He may also have been involved in architectural designs, in particular the arcade and sculpture on the second story of the baptistery in Pisa. There is no mention of him after 1278, and in 1284 he is documented as deceased.

By the time of his father's death, Giovanni Pisano had become one of the most prominent artists in Italy. Sometime after March, 1284, he renounced his Pisan citizenship and became a citizen of Siena, where he worked as an architect and sculptor on the cathedral. By 1290, he is documented as capomaestro (supervisor of works) at the cathedral, a position that he retained until 1296. During this period, he designed a façade for the cathedral, and the lower portion may have been completed according to his plan. He also created sculptures of human and animal figures to decorate the façade. These statues are notable for their plasticity and movement. The figures were conceived with their designated positions on the façade in mind. Proportional distortions were imposed which would be optically resolved when viewed from below at a distance. The poses were planned to complement one another for a unified compositional effect. The figures reveal an expressive intensity which became the hallmark of Giovanni's style.

Giovanni departed Siena under accusations of fiscal irregularities at the cathedral works. By 1297, he was back in Pisa as capomaestro of that town's cathedral works, but he retained his Sienese citizenship and property. In 1301, he completed a pulpit for the Church of San Andrea in Pistoia. The next year, he began a pulpit for the Cathedral of Pisa which was completed in 1310. The sculpted portions of these two pulpits reveal an extreme expressive style and compositions marked by rhythmic patterns and advanced spatial considerations. Deep carving and protruding forms serve to deny the planar surface of the marble panel. In the Pisa pulpit, he once again composed the work with the spectator's viewpoint in mind. Throughout the narrative reliefs of both pulpits, Giovanni manipulated naturalism for expressive purposes but managed to avoid overt distortion.

The supports for the Pisa pulpit include large sculpted figures whose style shows a retreat from the strong Gothic expressiveness of the earlier relief panels. A modifying restraint is evident, quite possibly the result of contact with the works of the early fourteenth century Florentine painter Giotto. This more composed style is also evident in one of Giovanni's free-standing Madonnas, that created circa 1305 for the altar of the Arena Chapel in Padua. The same chapel contains Giotto's greatest fresco cycle, painted between 1304 and 1312. While Giovanni's Madonna is clearly derived from French Gothic types, the emphasis upon more subtle expression and dignified massing heralds a new artistic age.

Giovanni's last known work was a monument to Margaret of Luxembourg in San Francesco di Castelletto at Genoa, undertaken in 1312. It was commissioned by the Hohenstaufen emperor Henry VII, a recent ally of Pisa, in honor of his wife, who had died in Genoa that year. Despite its current disassembled state, the central figure group of Margaret being awakened by two angels displays a subtle poignancy unique to Italian Gothic sculpture.

Documents show that Giovanni was still alive in 1314 but dead by 1318. He was buried in Siena.

Summary

Nicola and Giovanni Pisano are two late medieval Italian sculptors whose works reflect influences, intentions, and explorations that mark them as forerunners of the Italian Renaissance. Nicola's first style demonstrated strongly classical tendencies which were later subordinated to the expressive naturalism of Gothicism. Giovanni's sculpture was more consistently Gothic, but, like his father, he manipulated the Gothic idiom in the interest of naturalism, especially in the exploration of integrated, spatial compositions made up of volumetric forms. Along with the sculptor Arnolfo di Cambio, Nicola and Giovanni Pisano were largely responsible for freeing Italian sculpture from its long subordination to architecture. Their careers also mark the beginning of a noticeable evolution in the status of artists, and their signing of their works symbolically separates them from the anonymous craftsmen-sculptors of the Middle Ages. Both artists stand at the threshold of a new era of art, one that emphasized the personal, human qualities of images and narratives over didactic, symbolic concepts. The Pisanos' compositional and interpretive innovations influenced the pictorial explorations of fourteenth century Italian artists. Along with the fourteenth century painters Giotto and Duccio di Buoninsegna, Nicola and Giovanni Pisano are considered the principal late medieval Italian artists whose works were proto-Renaissance in style.

Bibliography

Ayerton, Michael. *Giovanni Pisano, Sculptor*. New York: Weybright and Talley, 1969. A lavish monograph written from an artist's perspective but reflecting a knowledge of current scholarship. Introduction by the sculptor Henry Moore. More than three hundred photographs reproduce all the known and attributed works, with many detail shots. Diagrams, bibliography, and catalog notes on the plates. Also includes information on and photographs of Nicola Pisano's work.

Crichton, G. H., and E. R. Crichton. *Nicola Pisano and the Revival of Sculpture in Italy*. Cambridge: Cambridge University Press, 1938. An early monograph, but still useful. Includes an extensive discussion of stylistic influences. Places Nicola within a historical and art historical context. An appendix lists and quotes the documents related to the birthplace controversy.

Pope-Hennesy, John. *An Introduction to Italian Sculpture*. Vol. 1, *Italian Gothic Sculpture*. London: Phaidon Press, 1955, 2d ed. 1972. A standard study of the period. The text provides excellent stylistic perspectives on the artists' careers. Includes photographic reproductions, biographical data, catalog entries, and a selective bibliography for Nicola and Giovanni Pisano and other sculptors of the late medieval period in Italy.

Seymour, Charles, Jr. "Invention and Revival in Nicola Pisano's 'Heroic Style.'" In *Studies in Western Art: Acts of the XXth International Congress of the History of Art*, edited by Millard Meiss, vol. 1. Princeton, N.J.: Princeton University Press, 1963. Examines Nicola's relationship with southern Italian art and the influence of classical prototypes.

Weinberger, Martin. "Nicola Pisano." In *Encyclopedia of World Art*, vol. 10. New York: McGraw-Hill, 1965. Like all the contributors to this reference work, Weinberger was a world-class scholar and expert in his field. His article broadens the attributions to Nicola and examines in detail the theories regarding his place of birth and the sources of his style. Accompanied by photographs and a brief bibliography.

_____. "Remarks on the Role of French Models Within the Evolution of Gothic Tuscan Sculpture." In *Studies in Western Art: Acts of the XXth International Congress of the History of Art*, edited by Millard Meiss, vol. 1. Princeton, N.J.: Princeton University Press, 1963. Examines the influence of French Gothic art on the works of Giovanni Pisano and the Siena pulpit of Nicola Pisano.

White, John. *Art and Architecture in Italy: 1250-1400*. Baltimore: Penguin Books, 1966. A basic reference on late medieval Italian art. Contains chapters on Nicola and Giovanni Pisano which discuss all of their principal works as well as some undocumented attributions. Text makes frequent reference to contemporary documents. Includes photographic reproductions, notes, and brief bibliography.

Madeline Cirillo Archer

PITTACUS OF MYTILENE

Born: c. 645 B.C.; Mytilene, Lesbos, Greece
Died: c. 570 B.C.; Mytilene, Lesbos, Greece
Area of Achievement: Government
Contribution: Elected tyrant by the people of Mytilene, Pittacus brought an end to his state's bitter aristocratic party struggles and established a government that remained stable for years after he had relinquished power. Though he was vilified by his political opponent Alcaeus, later Greeks considered Pittacus one of the "Seven Sages."

Early Life
Pittacus, the son of Hyrras (or Hyrrhadius), was reared in Mytilene on the island of Lesbos (famous for its wine), the richest and most powerful of the Aeolian Greek settlements in the eastern Aegean Sea. Mytilene had colonized territories on the mainland (notably Sestos, c. 670), had dealings with the nearby Lydian kingdom, and maintained commercial connections throughout the northeastern Aegean. The citizens of Mytilene were enterprising and bold in their projects and vigorous in defense of their mainland interests. Furthermore, Mytilene's citizens fought in the service of Asiatic rulers, and the city was the only one of its Aeolian neighbors to take part in the Greek trading colony at Naucratis in Egypt. In short, Pittacus was reared in a cosmopolitan city, familiar with merchants, soldiers, and colonists.

In addition to being a progressive and dynamic state, the Mytilene of Pittacus' childhood was steeped in its old Aeolian traditions. Lesbos was within sight of the territory of Troy, and heroic poetry dealing with the Trojan saga was prominent in its early literature. Pittacus' younger contemporary Alcaeus wrote a poem describing with pride a collection of armor that harked back to the heroic age.

In addition, a rich tradition of popular song on the island gave rise to the lyric monodies of Sappho and Alcaeus, performed at *symposia* (drinking parties). The Aeolians valued their descent from the house of Agamemnon, the victor of the Trojan War, and young Pittacus respected the traditions of his ancestors and the hereditary rights of his family. Although Pittacus' father's name was Thracian, there is every indication that the family was a member of the nobility.

The civic strife in the aristocracy at Mytilene is the single most important factor in Pittacus' early life. At that time, his city was involved in bitter quarrels among the nobles vying for control of the state. During his childhood, the Penthilid clan ruled at Mytilene, claiming descent from Agamemnon's son Orestes, whose own son Penthilus was said to have colonized Aeolis. The Penthilids gained a reputation for cruelty and were said to have clubbed their aristocratic rivals. Pittacus witnessed an uprising against that family, led by

Pittacus of Mytilene

Megacles, followed by Smerdis' murder of Penthilus and the establishment of a tyranny by Melanchrus.

During Pittacus' youth, the aristocratic government of Mytilene functioned through a council which submitted its deliberations to an assembly for discussion and approval. As a young man, Pittacus attended the meetings of the assembly and probably became familiar with the council through his father's connections.

Life's Work

There are two main sources for Pittacus' life and work: the poetry of his political enemy Alcaeus, which is hostile, and the writings of other writers, which extol his wisdom and place him among the so-called Seven Sages of the Greeks. From the praise and blame of the two traditions a somewhat coherent picture of his life emerges.

During the forty-second Olympiad (612-608 B.C.), Pittacus and the older brothers of Alcaeus deposed Melanchrus, an aristocrat of Mytilene who had made himself tyrant and become odious to the other noble families of the city. Pittacus' role in the action is unclear, but he must have established a reputation for leadership and daring, for soon afterward the people of Mytilene put him in charge of their army in a military encounter against the Athenians in a territorial dispute over Sigeum, near Troy. One early story records that in the course of this struggle he fought and won a duel with the Athenian general and Olympic victor Phrynon (c. 607 B.C.), killing him with a trident and knife, having first caught him in a net (perhaps a reference to a popular song describing Pittacus as a fisherman hunting his prey).

In the power struggle that ensued after the fall of Melanchrus, Pittacus allied himself with the political coterie of Alcaeus against Myrsilus, another aristocratic claimant to power. After an indeterminate period of maneuvering, Pittacus forsook the coalition which he had pledged to help and gave his support to Myrsilus' party. Alcaeus and his supporters went into exile on Lesbos, where they railed against Pittacus' defection. Pittacus married into the Penthilid family probably during Myrsilus' rule, thereby gaining a larger political base. His wife, a sister of a man named Draco, was said to be the daughter of one Penthilus. Pittacus' son Tyrraeus was murdered in nearby Cyme while sitting in a barbershop. Pittacus was said to have forgiven his murderer.

Myrsilus ruled as tyrant until he died in 590. Alcaeus was overjoyed at his death and wrote a poem calling for everyone to get drunk in celebration. The poet's hopes of repatriation, however, were disappointed, for the people of Mytilene immediately chose Pittacus to succeed Myrsilus. The new tyrant maintained a policy of subduing party strife by forcing Alcaeus and his supporters to leave Lesbos altogether. Although poems of Alcaeus call for his overthrow and mention Lydian support for the rebels, there is no indication that Pittacus' rule was ever seriously threatened from without or within. One anecdote tells of Alcaeus falling into Pittacus' hands during this period. Instead of punishing his enemy for his savage attacks, the tyrant is reported to have freed him and uttered the maxim "Pardon is better than revenge." Pittacus held supreme power in Mytilene until 580, when he voluntarily gave up his post and returned to private life.

Pittacus' rule at Mytilene was benevolent and was probably the source of his excellent reputation in later years. He did not overthrow the traditional constitution but respected its institutions while adding new laws to those already in existence. His respect for the law produced his description of the best rule as one of "the painted wood" (that is, of laws written on wooden tablets). His most famous statute, aimed at curbing alcohol abuse, provided a double penalty for anyone committing a crime while drunk. This law calls to mind both the reputation of Lesbian wine and the poems of Alcaeus extolling its use.

The only physical descriptions of Pittacus come from Alcaeus' abusive poems and therefore can probably be dismissed as rhetorical excess. Alcaeus calls Pittacus flat-footed, dirty, and pot-bellied. Yet everything known about Pittacus from other sources makes doubtful the validity of these slanders. Indeed, Alcaeus also calls Pittacus "base-born," a charge which can also be explained as simply part of the vocabulary of invective.

Several sayings of Pittacus are preserved, including "Even the gods do not fight against Necessity" and "Office reveals the man." Because of the fighting he had witnessed all of his life, Pittacus is credited with a rather un-Greek notion when he urged people to seek "victories without blood." His statement that "It is a difficult thing to be good" was the basis of a poem by Simonides and a long discussion in Plato's *Protagoras* (c. 399-390 B.C.). Numerous other quotations of his are preserved, mostly commonplace sentiments.

A number of stories tell that Pittacus had dealings with the Lydian king Croesus, and although chronology of their lives makes it unlikely that they ever met while both were in power, Croesus was the governor of the Lydian province close to Lesbos before he became king, and therefore it is possible that he could have met Pittacus at that time. It is most likely that stories relating the two are the result of an ancient attempt to create stories analogous to those which connected the Athenian sage and lawgiver Solon with the Lydian king. Pittacus' name has been identified on an inscription of his contemporary Nebuchadnezzar, King of Babylon, providing evidence that Mytilene did have important relations with the great powers to the east.

Pittacus died in 570, having lived over seventy years. He left behind a stable and prosperous city, as well as an enviable reputation—despite the protests of Alcaeus' poetry. Few ancient biographies have such happy endings. His traditional epitaph is:

> With her own tears, Holy Lesbos who bore him
> Bewails Pittacus who has died.

Summary

The work of Pittacus of Mytilene must have been very successful in quelling the party strife that had troubled the state for so long. He felt comfortable enough with the political situation to retire after only ten years, and there is no evidence of further civil disturbances thereafter. Indeed, Pittacus entered the ranks of the traditional Greek Seven Sages for his work. The Seven Sages were contemporaries of Pittacus who held similar positions as lawgivers and tyrants and included Periander of Corinth and Solon of Athens. More is known of them than of Pittacus, although Pittacus is admired as much as the others by later tradition.

Diodorus of Sicily said that Pittacus not only was outstanding for his wisdom but also was a citizen whose like Lesbos had never before produced—nor would produce, until such time as when it would make more and sweeter wine (that is, never). Diodorus called Pittacus an excellent lawgiver and a kindly man who was well-disposed toward his fellow citizens. He released his homeland from the three greatest misfortunes: tyranny, civil strife, and war. In addition, he was serious, gentle, and humble, perfect in respect to every virtue. His legislation was just, public-spirited, and thoughtful, and he himself was courageous and outstandingly free from greed.

Encomiums such as this made up the bulk of the later tradition dealing with Pittacus and form a strong contrast with the poetry of his contemporary Alcaeus. Diogenes Laertius wrote a "Life of Pittacus" in his *Peri bion dogmaton* (early third century A.D.; *Lives of Eminent Philosophers*, 1925), which includes numerous anecdotes illustrating his wisdom and justice. In his "Life of Thales," Diogenes gives various ancient lists of the Seven Sages, and Pittacus appears in each one. Plutarch provided a similar portrait of Pittacus in his work "Banquet of the Seven Sages," in *Moralia: Septem sapientum convivium* (early second century; *Moralia*, 1603). Strabo's *Geōgraphica* (c. 7 B.C.; *Geography*, 1917-1933) twice mentions Pittacus, each time emphasizing that he was one of "The Seven Wise Men," and notes that Pittacus used his monarchic powers to rid the state of dynastic struggles and to establish the city's autonomy. Aristotle wrote that Pittacus' position of elective tyrant was a distinct form of rule called *aesymneteia*, but he gives no other examples of it, and no others are known.

The impression made by Pittacus on his countrymen is revealed in the fact that the rich Lesbian folk song tradition preserves his memory:

> Grind, mill, grind.
> For even Pittacus grinds,
> As he rules great Mytilene.

Historians have few details to illustrate these ancient generalizations about Pittacus' exceptional character and achievements. Further discoveries of ancient evidence about archaic Lesbos and its most admired citizen would help fill in the gaps about Pittacus' life.

Bibliography
Andrewes, Antony. *The Greek Tyrants.* Reprint. New York: Harper and Row, Publishers, 1963. Solid and balanced discussion of the tyrannies at Mytilene, Alcaeus, and Pittacus in the chapter "Aristocratic Disorder at Mytilene." Best comparative material with other archaic tyrannies, and general discussion of the phenomenon. Puts Pittacus in perspective. Notes, index, bibliography.
Burn, A. R. *The Lyric Age of Greece.* New York: Minerva Press, 1960, rev. ed. 1967. Includes "The Lyric Age of Lesbos," with sections on Sappho, Alcaeus, and the "Revolution at Mytilene." Good background for Pittacus' world, explaining its politics, literature, and history. Chapters on contemporary archaic city-states provide comparative material. Index and notes.
Campbell, David A., ed. *Greek Lyric Poetry.* Cambridge, Mass.: Harvard University Press, 1982. Contains all fragments of Sappho and Alcaeus, translations, and brief notes to each poem. Includes an introduction with good discussion of how to date events in the life of Pittacus. Lists ancient evidence for lives of Alcaeus and Pittacus. With an index.
Jeffery, L. H. *Archaic Greece: The City-States, c. 700-500 B.C.* New York: St. Martin's Press, 1976. This work provides background on all the Greek city-states during the ancient period, with a useful section on the Aeolian Greeks and specific discussion of the political and economic status of Lesbos and the place of Pittacus. Comparisons made between Solon and Pittacus. Includes notes, glossary, maps, and index.
Lefkowitz, Mary R. *The Lives of the Greek Poets.* Baltimore: Johns Hopkins University Press, 1982. Includes important perspective on ancient biography, claiming that most material in the lives is fiction—based on the poems, not history. Relevant to Alcaeus' information used for his life and that of Pittacus. With a chapter on ancient lyric poets and an index and bibliography.
Murray, Oswyn. *Early Greece.* Atlantic Highlands, N.J.: Humanities Press, 1980. Good general background on ancient Greece, with a short section on Alcaeus and Pittacus and examples of Alcaeus' poems. Points out the unique political position held by Pittacus. With maps, illustrations, useful chronological chart, and an annotated list of primary sources.
Page, Denys. *Sappho and Alcaeus: An Introduction to the Study of Ancient Lesbian Poetry.* Reprint. New York: Oxford University Press, 1965. A seminal work on the most important source for Pittacus: the poetry of Alcaeus. Complete Greek texts and translations of the political and non-

political poems, with detailed literary, grammatical, and historical commentary. Extensive and comprehensive.

Podlecki, Anthony J. *The Early Greek Poets and Their Times*. Vancouver: University of British Columbia Press, 1984. A substantial chapter on Alcaeus and Sappho offers chronological analysis of Pittacus and his contemporaries on Lesbos, with analysis of the use of Alcaeus' poems in creating the picture of Pittacus. A thoughtful and readable treatment, with good use of all available sources. Includes an index and bibliography.

Romer, F. E. "The *Aisymneteia*: A Problem in Aristotle's Historic Method." *American Journal of Philology* 103 (1982): 25-46. Discusses sources for the rule of Pittacus and Aristotle's definition of the *aisymneteia*, or elective tyranny. Proves that this definition originated in his own philosophical ideas about civil strife and political harmony. Well documented, with many notes and further reading.

Daniel B. Levine

PLATO

Born: 427 B.C.; Athens, Greece
Died: 347 B.C.; Athens, Greece
Area of Achievement: Philosophy
Contribution: Plato used the dialogue structure in order to pose fundamental questions about knowledge, reality, society, and human nature—questions that are still alive today. He developed his own positive philosophy, Platonism, in answer to these questions, a philosophy which has been one of the most influential thought-systems in the Western tradition.

Early Life
There is an ancient story (very likely a true one) that Plato was originally named Aristocles, but acquired the nickname Plato ("broad" or "wide" in Greek) on account of his broad shoulders. Both of Plato's parents were from distinguished aristocratic families. Plato himself, because of family connections and expectations as well as personal interest, looked forward to a life of political leadership.

Besides being born into an illustrious family, Plato was born into an illustrious city. He was born in the wake of Athens' Golden Age, the period that had witnessed Athens' emergence as the strongest Greek power (particularly through its leadership in repelling the invasions of Greece by the Persians), the birth of classical Athenian architecture, drama, and arts, and a florescence of Athenian cultural, intellectual, and political life. By the time of Plato's youth, however, the military and cultural flower that had bloomed in Athens had already begun to fade. A few years before Plato's birth, Athens and Sparta—its rival for Greek supremacy—had engaged their forces and those of their allies in the Peloponnesian War.

This long, painful, and costly war of Greek against Greek lasted until Plato was twenty-three. Thus, he grew up witnessing the decline of Athens as the Greek military and cultural center. During these formative years, he observed numerous instances of cruelty, betrayal, and deceit as some unscrupulous Greeks attempted to make the best of things for themselves at the expense of other people (supposedly their friends) and in clear violation of values that Plato thought sacred.

It was also at an early age, probably in adolescence, that Plato began to hear Socrates, who engaged a variety of people in Athens in philosophical discussion of important questions. It could fairly be said that Plato fell under the spell (or at least the influence) of Socrates.

When, as a consequence of losing the Peloponnesian War to Sparta, an oligarchy was set up in Athens in place of the former democracy, Plato had the opportunity to join those in power, but he refused. Those in power, who later became known as the "Thirty Tyrants," soon proved to be ruthless rulers;

they even attempted to implicate Socrates in their treachery, although Socrates would have no part in it.

A democratic government was soon restored, but it was under this democracy that Socrates was brought to trial, condemned to death, and executed. This was the last straw for Plato. He never lost his belief in the great importance of political action, but he had become convinced that such action must be informed by a philosophical vision of the highest truth. He continued to hold back from political life, devoting himself instead to developing the kind of training and instruction that every wise person—and political people especially, since they act on a great social stage—must pursue. Plato maintained that people would not be able to eliminate evil and social injustice from their communities until rulers became philosophers (lovers of wisdom)—or until philosophers became rulers.

Life's Work

In his twenties and thirties, Plato traveled widely, becoming aware of intellectual traditions and social and political conditions in various Mediterranean regions. During these years, he also began work on his earliest, and most "Socratic," dialogues.

When he was about forty years old, Plato founded the Academy, a complex of higher education and a center of communal living located approximately one mile from Athens proper. Plato's Academy was highly successful. One famous pupil who studied directly under the master was Aristotle, who remained a student at the Academy for twenty years before going on to his own independent philosophical position. The Academy continued to exist for more than nine hundred years, until it was finally forced to close in A.D. 529 by the Roman emperor Justinian I on the grounds that it was pagan and thus offensive to the Christianity he wished to promote.

In 367 B.C., Plato went to Sicily, where he had been invited to serve as tutor to Dionysius II of Syracuse. The project offered Plato the opportunity to groom a philosopher-king such as he envisioned in *Politeia* (388-368 B.C.; *Republic*), but this ambition soon proved to be unrealizable.

One of the main tasks Plato set for himself was to keep alive the memory of Socrates by recording and perpetuating the kind of impact that Socrates had had on those with whom he conversed. Virtually all Plato's written work takes the form of dialogues in which Socrates is a major character. Reading these dialogues, readers can observe the effects that Socrates has on various interlocutors and, perhaps more important, are themselves brought into the inquiry and discussion. One of the explicit aims of a Platonic dialogue is to involve readers in philosophical questioning concerning the points and ideas under discussion. In reading essays and treatises, readers too often assume the passive role of listening to the voice of the author; dialogues encourage readers to become active participants (at least in their own minds, which, as Plato would probably agree, is precisely where active participation is required).

The written dialogue is an effective mode of writing for a philosophy with the aims of Plato, but it sometimes leaves one uncertain as to Plato's own views. It is generally agreed among scholars that the earlier works—such as *Apologia Socratis* (*Apology*), *Euthyphro*, and *Gorgias*, written between 399 and 390 B.C.—express primarily the thought and spirit of Socrates, while middle and later dialogues—such as *Meno*, *Symposium*, *Republic*, *Theaetetus* (all 388-366 B.C.), *Philebus*, and *Nomoi* or *Laws* (both 360-347 B.C.)—gradually give way to the views of Plato himself.

The dialogues of Plato are among the finest literary productions by any philosopher who has ever lived, yet there is evidence that Plato himself, maintaining the superiority of the spoken word over the written word, and of person-to-person instruction over "book learning," regarded the written dialogues as far less important than the lectures and discussions that took place in the Academy. There is, however, very little known about those spoken discussions, and the best evidence available for Plato's views is surely in his many dialogues.

The fundamental thesis of Plato's work is the claim that there are "forms" or "ideas" that exist outside the material realm, that are the objects of knowledge (or intellectual cognition), and that, unlike material objects, do not come into existence, change, or pass out of existence. These forms, rather than material things, actually constitute reality. This is Plato's well-known theory of forms (or theory of ideas).

The theory attempts to take two points of view into consideration and to define their proper relationship. The two points of view give the questioner access to a changing world (of sensible or material things) and an unchanging world (of intellectual objects). From the first perspective, human beings know that they live in a changing world in which things come into existence, change, and pass out of existence. If one tries to pin something down in this world and determine whether various predicates apply to it (whether it is big, or red, or hot, or good, for example), one finds that the object can be viewed from a variety of standpoints, according to some of which the predicate applies and according to some of which it does not apply. Socrates, for example, is big compared to an insect, but not big compared to a building. This train of thought leads one, however, to the other point of view. An insect, Socrates (that is, his body), and a building belong to the changing physical world in which the application of predicates is problematic or changing. In the nonphysical, or intellectual, world, however, there must be some fixed points of reference that make possible the application of predicates at all. These latter fixed points do not change. Whether one compares Socrates with the insect or with the building, when one judges which is bigger one is always looking for the same thing. Bigness or largeness itself, Plato thought, must always exist, unchanging, and it must itself be big. It is this abstract or intellectual element with which a person must be familiar if the person is to be in a position to decide whether various objects in this changing material world are big.

The forms, or objects of intellect, are quite different from (and superior to) physical objects, or objects of sense. Plato thought of knowledge as occurring only between the intellect (or reason) and its objects, the forms. The bodily senses give human beings only belief, he said, not true knowledge.

Plato considered human beings to be composed of a rational aspect and an irrational aspect. The intellect or reason, that which communes with the forms, is rational. The body, which communes with the physical world, is irrational. Plato looked down on the body, considering it merely the seat of physical appetites. Additionally, there is a third, intermediate aspect of people: passions, which may follow intellect (and thus be rational) or follow the bodily appetites (and thus be irrational).

In each person, one aspect will dominate. Reason is best, but not everyone can achieve the state in which his life is under the direction of reason. Thus, communities should be organized in such a way that those who are rational (and not led by physical appetites) will be in command. The philosopher-king is one who both attains philosophical insight into the world of the forms and holds power in the day-to-day changing world.

Summary

Plato defended the role of reason in human life, in opposition to many ancient Greek teachers who were called Sophists. The Sophists traveled from city to city and claimed to be able to teach young men how to be successful in life. They offered such services for a fee. Although the Sophists were never a unified school and did not profess a common creed, certain beliefs are characteristic of them as a group and almost diametrically opposed to the views of Plato. The Sophists mainly taught the art of speaking, so that a person could speak well in public assemblies, in a court of law, and as a leader of men. Plato thought, however, that such speakers were probably more likely to appeal to feelings and emotion than to reason. Such speakers may hold forth and sound impressive, but they tend not to be acquainted with the objects of the intellect, the ground of true knowledge. Plato argued that such speakers may, for example, be persuasive in getting a man who is ill to take his medicine, but it is only a real doctor who can prescribe the right remedy. Plato also compared the Sophist to a makeup artist, who makes only superficial changes in people's looks; the true philosopher, on the other hand, is compared to a gymnastic trainer, who is genuinely able to bring health and soundness to people's bodies.

In Plato's view, however, the stakes are really much higher, for both Sophists and philosophers actually affect people's souls or inner selves, not their bodies, and Plato followed Socrates in thinking of the cultivation of the soul as much more important than the cultivation of the body. Moreover, Plato went beyond the views of other Greek philosophers and beyond the cultural norms of ancient Athens by affirming that women and men had the same potential for philosophical wisdom and community leadership. Many writers in the twentieth century have referred to Plato as the first feminist, although it is also true that the vast majority of ancient, medieval, and modern philosophical Platonists did not follow him in this particular. The Sophists, in any case, were false teachers and false leaders, in Plato's view. True leaders must have wisdom, and the acquisition of such wisdom, he believed, could only come about in a cooperative community of inquirers who were free to follow argument, not carried away by speech making.

Throughout the history of more than two millennia of Western philosophy, Plato has been one of the most influential thinkers. One twentieth century philosopher, Alfred North Whitehead, has said that philosophy since Plato's time has consisted mainly of a series of footnotes to Plato. There have been numerous revivals of Plato's thought in Western philosophy. Platonists, Neoplatonists, and others have made their appearance, but Plato's influence is probably better gauged in terms of the importance of the questions he has raised and the problem areas he has defined, rather than in terms of the numbers of his adherents or disciples. From both dramatic and philosophical points of view, Plato's dialogues are so well constructed that even today they serve well as a student's first encounter with the philosophical practice of inquiry and argument.

Bibliography
Crombie, I. M. *Plato: The Midwife's Apprentice*. London: Routledge and Kegan Paul, 1964. A readable examination of Plato's life, his methods, his character, and his philosophy. Well informed, yet uncluttered by footnotes and other scholarly apparatus.
Grube, George M. A. *Plato's Thought*. London: Methuen and Co., 1935. Reprint. Boston: Beacon Press, 1958. Each chapter is devoted to a single topic and usefully draws quotations and ideas from the entire Platonic corpus. Topics covered are the theory of ideas, pleasure, eros, the soul, gods, art, education, and statecraft.
Guthrie, W. K. C. *History of Greek Philosophy*. Vols. 4 and 5. Cambridge: Cambridge University Press, 1975. A very thorough and scholarly examination of Plato's life and works. Includes notes, bibliography, indexes, and references to specific passages in Plato. The Greek terms and phrases that occur are generally translated and explained.
Shorey, Paul. *What Plato Said*. Chicago: University of Chicago Press, 1933. After a review of the life of Plato, Shorey painstakingly summarizes and

examines each of the dialogues of Plato (as well as some forgeries and some doubtful cases). This survey of Plato's works is followed by detailed notes and references to works of other scholars.

Taylor, Alfred E. *Plato: The Man and His Work*. London: Methuen and Co., 1926. This is a classic work of scholarship that has been reprinted many times in later editions. Taylor discusses Plato's work dialogue by dialogue. He strives to convey the point of each of Plato's inquiries and the force of the arguments that are discussed.

Vlastos, Gregory, comp. *Plato: A Collection of Critical Essays*. 2 vols. Garden City, N.Y.: Doubleday and Co., 1971. Reprint. Notre Dame, Ind.: University of Notre Dame Press, 1978. The first volume contains essays by a variety of students of Plato on metaphysics and the theory of knowledge. The second volume focuses on Plato's theories regarding ethics, politics, eros, the soul, art, and religion. A good source for penetrating readings of Plato by modern thinkers.

Stephen Satris

PLAUTUS

Born: c. 254 B.C.; Sarsina, Italy
Died: 184 B.C.; Rome, Italy
Areas of Achievement: Theater and drama
Contribution: Plautus' action-packed, middle-class comedies, built from a dizzyingly contrived structure of disguises, mistaken identities, and the obligatory revelatory scene, were sensationally popular in his time; they have since influenced or been adapted by such comedic dramatists as William Shakespeare, Richard Brinsley Sheridan, Molière, and Jean Giraudoux.

Early Life

The sparse details of Titus Maccius Plautus' life are drawn from historians and writers such as Livy and Cicero. From his birthplace, Sarsina, a mountainous rural region of Italy, where the native tongue was Umbrian, Plautus escaped, joining a traveling group of players (probably as an actor). He learned the technical intricacies of the profession, acquired a mastery of Latin—and perhaps some Greek—and became the unequaled practitioner of his comedic craft.

In Rome, Plautus worked in the theater, lost money in trade, and eventually became a mill worker, writing in his leisure moments. No record remains of his life except the plays that he wrote, and even some of these claim authenticity only on the basis of ascription. Plautus became so popular that dramas by other writers were attributed to him in order to gain production and popular reception. In his time, it was enough merely that a play bore his name; a generation later, it was enough that the prologue to the play *Menaechmi* (*The Twin Menaechmi*) contain the words "I bring you Plautus"—words that remain in that prologue forever as guarantors of laughter.

Life's Work

Although he may have written more than fifty plays, only twenty-one manuscripts of works attributable to Plautus survive, the oldest of these dating to the fourth or fifth century A.D. Only twenty of these are complete plays. In an age when records were shoddily kept, or not kept at all, and when aspiring contemporary playwrights did not hesitate to attach Plautus' name to their plays, a large number of comedies were attributed to him.

In an attempt to clear up the chaos of authorship, Marcus Terentius Varro, a contemporary of Cicero, compiled three lists of plays: those given universal recognition as being written by Plautus, those identified by Varro alone as plays by Plautus, and those recognized as Plautus' work by others but not by Varro. The first list, labeled by scholars the "Varronianae fabulae," contains the twenty-one plays that succeeding generations of scholars have agreed on as belonging to Plautus. Other plays remain outside the canon.

The dates of Plautus' plays are as speculative as are the details of his life. Only two of them—*Pseudolus* (191 B.C.) and *Stichus* (200 B.C.)—are attached to specific dates, about half the remainder are unidentified chronologically, and the rest are qualified with terms such as "probably early" or "late." Like William Shakespeare nearly fifteen hundred years later, Plautus borrowed his plots and reworked Greek originals; some sources have been identified, but others remain unknown.

Among the most famous stock situations and character types associated with Plautine comedy are the vain soldier-braggart (*miles gloriosus*), which finds its most complex realization in Shakespeare's Falstaff; the farcical chaos caused by mistaken identity, a chaos to which order is eventually restored; the servant who, wiser than his superiors, extricates them from a web of near-impossible entanglements, sometimes of the master's making; and finally, a happy ending. The plays, whether serious—*Amphitruo* (*Amphitryon*)—or farcical—*The Twin Menaechmi*—are always comic in the Aristotelian definition of comedy as a play which begins in an unfortunate situation and ends fortunately.

Like the commercial playwright of modern times, Plautus wrote for a broad audience, basing his appeal on laughter and a good story, love and money forming an integral part of the story. Preceding his plays, as was the custom, with a prologue devoted to a summary of the borrowed story, he then developed his plot by highly improbable complications, witty native dialogue, slapstick scenes, and an infinite variety of jests, all kept within the limits of popular recognition. That recognition is embodied in the characters, the most famous of which in his time and, perhaps, in any time is the *miles gloriosus* figure, the Greek *alazon* or "overstater" (commonly translated as the soldier-braggart), whose vanity and consequent exposure have never failed to entertain. In Plautus' time, the Punic Wars created an audience receptive to fast-paced action and to the adventures of the returning soldier.

On a broader social scale, the element of recognition is drawn from the merchant-class milieu of his time, in which servants, wiser than their masters, extricate their superiors from entrapments of one sort or another, thereby resolving problems and bringing the play to its happy conclusion. Molière's middle-class comic heroes and villains stem from this Plautine tradition. The stories borrowed from Greek comedies became merely the scaffolding for the native Roman ribaldry, schemes, and jests that characterize the famous Plautine humor, and the upper-class characters are frequently a part of that scaffolding. In the course of the play, they give way to the servants or peasants. Thus, in the tradition of the New Comedy of Menander (as opposed to the old Aristophanic satire, which was topical), Plautus opened the comic stage to the common man. What social satire is present is a part of the more broadly based humor, concerned with the outwitting of the upper classes by their inferiors. Like death, humor becomes the great leveler.

Of the twenty-one surviving plays, the two that remain the most famous are *The Twin Menaechmi*—frequently translated as *The Two Menaechmi*—and *Miles gloriosus* (*The Braggart Warrior*), the date and source of the former unknown, the latter dated about 205 B.C. Both are placed by scholars in the early or early middle of the agreed-upon chronology of his writing. Respectively, they are the direct source of Shakespeare's play *The Comedy of Errors* (c. 1592-1594) and of his most famous and complex comic figure, Falstaff. Indirectly, they have influenced both literary style and popular humor in most succeeding comedies. Both plays exude the festive spirit to which C. L. Barber attributes Shakespeare's comedies and which distinguishes Plautine humor, heavily dependent on robust and fast-moving physical actions, from that of traditional satire, invective, or other modes of comedy in which ideas are prominent.

The Twin Menaechmi, more directly imitated perhaps than any other play, builds its comedy on a set of separated twins, whose lives develop complications that, once begun, take on a life of their own in a seemingly endless web of mistaken identities and consequent misunderstandings. Only the most skillful plotting of events by the author can extricate the twins from that web created by disguises and accidental meetings.

The title figure of *The Braggart Warrior* (variously entitled *The Soldier-Braggart*), the soldier Pyrgopolynices, is considered by scholars to be Plautus' most brilliant creation. Convinced of his bravery and appeal to women and recently returned from the wars, Pyrgopolynices (who is characterized by lechery and stupidity as well as vanity) falls victim to the elaborate deceptions of a slave whose master is in love with a woman whom the braggart soldier has brought to Ephesus against her will. The slave concocts a pattern of disguises and misunderstandings that befuddle the vain soldier, and the lovers are reunited. Again, disguises, misunderstandings, and deceptions create a farcically intricate plot, delightful in its escalating complications and ingenious in its resolution.

Summary

In addition to being "the dean of Roman drama," Plautus has directly provided the plots for at least three illustrious successors: Shakespeare's *The Comedy of Errors*, based on *The Twin Menaechmi*; Molière's *L'Avare* (1668; *The Miser*, 1672), based on *Aulularia* (*The Pot of Gold*); and Jean Giraudoux's *Amphitryon 38* (1929; English translation, 1938), based on *Amphitryon*. Edmond Rostand's *Cyrano de Bergerac* (1897; English translation, 1898), Nicholas Udall's *Ralph Roister Doister* (1552), Ben Jonson's *Every Man in His Humour* (1598, 1605), and the contemporary American musicals, *The Boys from Syracuse* (1938) and *A Funny Thing Happened on the Way to*

Plautus

the Forum (1962) are among the popular descendants of Plautus' work.

Erich Segal, writing about Plautine humor, quotes the psychiatrist Ernst Kris, who describes comedy as a "holiday for the superego." A "safety valve for repressed sentiments which otherwise might have broken their bonds more violently," Plautine comedy provides release from the conventions of a socially prescribed life. It produces a resolution of the tension between dreams and actuality, order and chaos, and finally between the vital and repressive forces in life, as it acts out that resolution for the audience. In the end, a kind of ironic equilibrium is achieved, an equilibrium that reconciles dream with reality, providing the release necessary to avoid the violence inherent in the tragic mode.

Bibliography

Beare, William. *The Roman Stage: A Short History of Latin Drama in the Time of the Republic.* London: Methuen and Co., 1950, rev. ed. 1964. A history of Roman drama with illustrations, plates, appendices, notes and sources, bibliography, and general index, as well as an index to Latin lines quoted or discussed in text.

Dorey, T. A., and Donald R. Dudley, eds. *Roman Drama.* New York: Basic Books, 1965. A collection of essays on Latin literature and its influence, focusing on Menander, Plautus, and Seneca, with illustrations and notes.

Duckworth, George E. *The Nature of Roman Comedy: A Study in Popular Entertainment.* Princeton, N.J.: Princeton University Press, 1952. A historical sweep of the Golden Age, including its origins, thematic nature, and stage conventions; includes an extensive bibliography and an index.

―――――, ed. *The Complete Roman Drama.* New York: Random House, 1942. This volume contains four plays by Plautus and three by Terence, with an introduction contrasting the comedic qualities of their plays.

Segal, Erich. *Roman Laughter: The Comedy of Plautus.* Cambridge, Mass.: Harvard University Press, 1968. A sprightly treatment of the social milieu that spawned Plautus' comedies, with extensive notes, an index of passages quoted, and a general index.

―――――, ed. and trans. *Plautus: Three Comedies.* Harper and Row, Publishers, 1969. Includes Segal's translations of *The Braggart Warrior*, *The Twin Menaechmi*, and *Mostellaria* (*The Haunted House*), with an introduction dealing with Plautus' popularity in his time as well as a pronunciation guide and a selected bibliography.

Susan Rusinko

PLINY THE ELDER

Born: Probably A.D. 23; probably Novum Comum, Italy
Died: August 25, A.D. 79; Stabiae, near Mount Vesuvius
Areas of Achievement: Science and natural history
Contribution: Pliny's *Natural History*, though not a work of original natural science, preserved for later times priceless information on the ancients' beliefs in countless areas. His work had great influence on later antiquity, the Middle Ages, and the early Renaissance, and he remains a major figure in the history of science.

Early Life

Gaius Plinius Secundus, or Pliny the Elder, was in his fifty-sixth year when he died during the famous eruption of Mount Vesuvius in August of A.D. 79. He therefore was probably born in late 23. His family was prominent in Novum Comum and most scholars believe that he was born there, although some prefer to use the evidence which points to Verona. Clues to his career are found in his own writing, in a life by Suetonius, and in the letters of his nephew and adopted ward Gaius Plinius Caecilius Secundus, better known as Pliny the Younger.

It can be inferred from certain remarks in his work that Pliny came to Rome at an early age to study, as befitted his status as the son of a prominent northern Italian family. He obtained the normal education of the time and thus would have been thoroughly trained in rhetoric, a discipline to which he would later return, as well as several of the fields which he would cultivate for the next thirty years until he wrote *Historia naturalis* (A.D. 77; *The Historie of the World*, 1601; better known as *Natural History*). The next natural step for a young man in his position was one of military service and therefore, at about the age of twenty-three, he went to Germany as a military officer and, in addition to holding other posts, was put in command of a cavalry troop. Later comments in the *Natural History* lead scholars to believe that he traveled throughout the area and took copious notes on what he saw during his stay there.

Although all Pliny's writings except the *Natural History* are lost, his nephew published a chronological, annotated bibliography of his uncle's works, and the titles from this early period are instructive. His first work was a single-volume book entitled *De iaculatione equestri* (on throwing the javelin from horseback), and his next was a two-volume biography of his patron Lucius Pomponius Secundus. His third book was a twenty-volume history of all the wars Rome had ever waged against Germany. Pliny claimed that he was instructed to begin this work at the behest of the ghost of Drusus Germanicus (the brother of Tiberius and the father of Claudius I), who was concerned that the memory of his deeds would be lost. Scholars also suspect a

Pliny the Elder

certain amount of imperial flattery in this story. It was probably also during this German campaign that Pliny became close to the future emperor Titus, to whom he dedicated the *Natural History*. A belief that he served under Titus later during the campaign in Judaea is somewhat suspect.

After a fairly lengthy stay in Germany, Pliny returned to Rome and began the second phase of his career as a writer and public servant.

Life's Work

During this time, generally thought to begin during the reign of Claudius, Pliny turned to the life of a professional pleader, a natural choice for one of his station and education. There is no record of any great successes in this regard, and none of his speeches survives, but his next book, *Studiosi* (the scholar, sometimes translated as the student), reflects again his tendency to write about matters with which he was concerned. In it, Pliny traced the training of a rhetorician from the cradle onward. The work encompassed three books in six volumes and very likely occupied Pliny during the early years of Nero's reign. It was consulted by Quintilian and earned some cautious praise from that author. The later, more turbulent, years of Nero's reign were occupied with an eight-volume study of grammar. Pliny, who later would call Nero an enemy of mankind, was clearly keeping out of the maelstrom of Neronian politics by retreating to his study. It is therefore not surprising that near the end of Nero's reign Pliny accepted a posting as procurator of Spain, perhaps to remove himself completely from the city during troubled times.

It may have been during this period that Pliny also found time to write a thirty-one-book history which continued the work of Aufidius Bassus. Bassus' history seems to have ended with the events of Claudius' reign, and Pliny began there and ended perhaps with the events of 69. It is likely that this work was published posthumously. It was also at this time that Pliny's brother-in-law died and entrusted the care of his son, Pliny's nephew, to this now-distinguished Roman figure. Pliny could not care for the lad from Spain but chose a guardian for him until he adopted him upon his return to Rome. He held his post in Spain until Vespasian emerged victorious from the turmoil which followed Nero's death in 69, a year of civil war commonly referred to as the Year of the Four Emperors.

Vespasian brought stability to a war-weary city, and for Pliny he represented political patronage as the father of Pliny's army friend Titus. After Pliny's return to Rome, he held several high-ranking posts abroad, and it can be surmised from his first-person reports in the *Natural History* that one of these trips may have taken him to Africa, where he made copious notes on what he saw. At this time, he was also made an official "friend of the court" and thus became an imperial adviser, regularly called to Vespasian's court for meetings at daybreak.

The demands of Pliny's renewed public life were thus intense, and yet he was also finishing the *Natural History* at the same time he held these offices. Pliny had been amassing information for this work for years. His nephew writes that his uncle never read without taking notes and that one of his mottoes was that no book was so bad that he could not find something of use in it. He always read or was read to whenever possible—even while bathing, eating, or sunbathing (one of his favorite pastimes). He read or dictated while riding in a sedan chair, and he once chastised his nephew for walking since it was impossible to read while one did so. He even devised a sort of glove to ensure that his slave could take notes on such trips in cold weather. To find more time for his studies, Pliny retired early and rose even earlier, reading and writing by lamplight in the early morning darkness. So diligent was he that upon his death he left his nephew 160 books of notes written in a tiny hand.

The *Natural History* became the great showcase for these notes. Its thirty-seven books cover virtually every aspect of nature's works and several of those of man. After an entertaining preface, book 1 offers a full table of contents and a list of authorities cited—a rare and welcome practice in antiquity. The remaining books range far and wide across the realms of zoology, entymology, botany, mineralogy, astronomy, geography, pharmacology, anthropology, physiology, folklore, and metallurgy. There are countless long digressions on such subjects as the history of art, the manufacture of papyrus, the growing of crops, religious practices, aphrodisiacs, and magic spells. In his preface, Pliny claims to have studied about two thousand volumes, to have emerged with twenty thousand noteworthy facts, and to have cited one hundred principal authors. In reality, the total number of authors cited by name is almost five hundred. Although it is surmised that the work was published in 77, there are certain signs that it is unfinished; Pliny may well have been revising the work when he met his death.

On August 24, 79, Pliny was on duty at Misenum as prefect of the fleet in the bay of Naples. Upon seeing the volcanic cloud from Vesuvius, he sailed across the bay both to investigate further and to help in possible evacuation plans. Once at his destination, he sought to calm his hosts by a casual attitude and even fell asleep amid the danger, a fact attested by those who overheard his characteristic loud snoring. Yet the volcano intensified, and by the next morning Pliny and his hosts had to flee to the shore with pillows tied over their heads for protection.

The sea was too rough to set sail, and Pliny was exhausted from his labors, being rather obese and prone to heavy and labored breathing. He lay down for a while on a sail and requested cold water, but upon rising fell suddenly dead, the victim either of the foul air or of a heart attack. His body was found the next day, looking, according to his nephew, more like one asleep than one who had died.

Summary

It is fashionable to criticize Pliny the Elder as an uncritical encyclopedist, an assiduous notetaker with little or no discrimination. It is charged that his work is devoid of literary style and is almost completely lacking in organization. It is clear that most of his information came from late-night notetaking and not from fieldwork, a point in which he suffers by comparison to Aristotle.

Yet Pliny's sins are not as great as they may seem. In his own time, he was much consulted. One can see traces of his rhetorical and grammatical works in Quintilian and Priscian and of his histories in Tacitus, Plutarch, and Dio Cassius. The popularity of the *Natural History* is shown in the number of authors who used it as a treasure trove of facts, in its imitators such as Solinus, Martianus Capella, and Isidore of Seville, and by the great number of manuscript versions of the text, in whole or in part, which survived into the Middle Ages.

The work was much used by medieval scholars, who mined it for whatever information they needed. Several produced topical condensations, and in the early 1100's a nine-volume "reader's edition" was prepared. Its traces are frequently to be seen, often cited by name, in such authors as Thomas of Cantimpre, Bartholomaeus Anglicus, Vincent of Beauvais, and Saint Albertus Magnus. Not surprisingly, it was printed as early as 1469 and was so popular that by 1499 six more corrected editions had been printed. It was translated into Italian in 1476 and 1489.

Such popularity merits consideration and should cause the work to be judged on its own terms. In the first place, posterity owes Pliny much for preserving so many intriguing facts and the names of authors otherwise lost. Clearly, it is not meant to be read as literature. It is an old curiosity shop of antiquity, wherein a reader can wander, fascinated, at his leisure. It is a book for browsers and, as such, offers the rewards of hours of pleasurable discovery to those people who, like Pliny, believed that knowledge was inherently good.

Bibliography

Chibnall, Marjorie. "Pliny's *Natural History* and the Middle Ages." In *Empire and Aftermath: Silver Latin II*, edited by T. A. Dorey. London: Routledge and Kegan Paul, 1975. Careful and clear study of the influence of the *Natural History* from late antiquity through the Middle Ages.

French, Roger, and Frank Greenway, eds. *Science in the Early Roman Empire: Pliny the Elder, His Sources and Influence*. Totowa, N.J.: Barnes and Noble Books, 1986. Twelve essays occasioned by a Pliny symposium, with a brief life and studies centering on such subjects as medicine, pharmacy, botany, zoology, metallurgy, and astronomy.

Pliny the Younger. *Letters and Panegyricus*. Translated by Betty Radice.

Cambridge, Mass.: Harvard University Press, 1969. Part of the Loeb Classical Library. Letters 3.5, 6.16, and 6.20 are vivid, firsthand accounts of the elder Pliny, his writings, life-style, and death.

Thorndike, Lynn. *A History of Magic and Experimental Science.* Vol. 1, *The First Thirteen Centuries of Our Era.* New York: Macmillan, 1923. Discusses the place of Pliny in the history of science and his contributions to the belief in magic.

Wethered, H. N. *The Mind of the Ancient World: A Consideration of Pliny's "Natural History."* London: Green and Co., 1937. An elegant defense of Pliny with seventeen chapters on various topics, accompanied by extensive quotes from Pliny, William Shakespeare, Andrew Marvell, and John Milton, among others.

Kenneth F. Kitchell, Jr.

PLOTINUS

Born: 205; possibly Lycopolis, Upper Egypt
Died: 270; Campania, Italy
Area of Achievement: Philosophy
Contribution: As the founder of Neoplatonism, Plotinus has exerted a profound influence on Western philosophical and religious thought, from his own day to the present.

Early Life

Plotinus was born in 205, but there is almost no information about his origins or his early life. His nationality, race, and family are unknown, and information about his birthplace comes from a fourth century source which may not be reliable. Plotinus told his disciples little about himself; he would not even divulge the date of his birth. Only one thing can certainly be said: Plotinus' education and intellectual background were entirely Greek. This fact can be deduced from his writings; Plotinus shows little knowledge of Egyptian religion and misinterprets Egyptian hieroglyphic symbolism. Porphyry, Plotinus' pupil and biographer, reports that Plotinus had a complete knowledge of geometry, arithmetic, mechanics, optics, and music, and he must have acquired some of this knowledge during the early years of his education.

Porphyry reports that in 232, when Plotinus was twenty-seven, he felt a strong desire to study philosophy. He consulted the best teachers in Alexandria, but they all disappointed him. Then a friend recommended a teacher named Ammonius Saccas (c. 175-242). Plotinus went to hear him and immediately declared, "This is the man I was looking for." Little is known, however, of Ammonius' philosophy; he was self-taught, wrote nothing, and made his followers promise not to divulge his teachings.

Beginning in late 232 or early 233, Plotinus studied with Ammonius for eleven years (Plotinus' long stay in Alexandria may be the only reason for the common belief that he was originally from Egypt). Following that, Plotinus wanted to learn more of the philosophy of the Persians and the Indians, and he joined the army of Emperor Gordianus III, which was marching against the Persians.

It is not known in what capacity Plotinus served; he may have been a scientific adviser, or he may have occupied a more lowly position. The expedition, however, did not achieve its objective. Gordianus was assassinated in Mesopotamia, and Plotinus escaped with difficulty to Antioch. He made no attempt to return to Ammonius (nor did he ever return to the East). Instead, in 245, at the age of forty, he traveled to Rome, where he was to remain for twenty-five years, until shortly before his death. The stage was set for him to emerge as the last great pagan philosopher.

Life's Work

For the next ten years, Plotinus established himself in Rome. He accepted private students and based his teaching on that of Ammonius. During this time he wrote nothing, but by the time Porphyry joined him in 264, Plotinus no longer considered himself bound by the restrictions on publication which Ammonius had imposed (other pupils of Ammonius, such as Origen and Erennius, had already published). Plotinus had therefore written twenty-one treatises by 264, although none of them had circulated widely. Porphyry urged him to write more, and twenty-four treatises followed during the six years that Porphyry was his pupil.

Only one story survives about Plotinus' life in Rome before Porphyry's arrival. A philosopher named Olympias, from Alexandria, who was also a former pupil of Ammonius, attempted to "bring a star-stroke upon him [Plotinus] by magic." Plotinus, who apparently believed in the power of magic, felt the effects of this attack, but Olympias found his attempt recoiling on himself. He ceased his attack and confessed that "the soul of Plotinus had such great power as to be able to throw back attacks on him on to those who were seeking to do him harm."

During the time that Porphyry was his pupil, Plotinus lived comfortably in what must have been a large house, owned by a wealthy widow named Gemina. He earned a reputation for kindness and gentleness and was always generous in offering help to others. Many people entrusted their sons and daughters to his care, "considering that he would be a holy and god-like guardian." Although Plotinus was an otherworldly philosopher, he also believed in the importance of the social virtues, that the practice of them contributed to the soul's ultimate liberation. He was therefore practical, wise, and diplomatic in daily affairs, taking good care of the worldly interests of the young people in his charge. For example, they would be encouraged to give up property only if they decided to become philosophers, and even this was a decision that they would have to make for themselves. The same was true of Plotinus' attitude toward the physical body and its desires. Although he believed in self-discipline, he acknowledged that legitimate physical needs must be looked after, and he never advocated the kind of asceticism which was found in some other ancient philosophical schools.

Plotinus often acted as arbitrator in disputes, without ever incurring an enemy. The only opposition he appears ever to have aroused (apart from that of Olympias) was when some Greek philosophers accused him of stealing some of his philosophy from Numenius, a charge which modern scholars have not accepted. Plotinus was also a good judge of character, and his advice was sound. When Porphyry, for example, confessed that he was contemplating suicide, Plotinus told him that the desire was caused by physiological reasons, not by rational thought, and advised him to take a vacation. Porphyry accepted his advice.

Plotinus

Plotinus had a number of aristocratic friends, and members of the senate attended his lectures. One of them, Rogatianus, relinquished his property and became an ascetic after being exposed to Plotinus' teaching. The Emperor Gallienus, sole emperor from 260 to 268, and his wife, Salonia, venerated Plotinus. Plotinus once asked them to found a "city of philosophers" in Campania, to be called Platonopolis, which would serve as a monastic retreat for him and his followers. The scheme failed, however, as a result of opposition in the Roman senate. Gallienus' assassination in 268 must have been a blow to Plotinus, since Gallienus' successors showed no interest in Greek philosophy.

Plotinus' lectures were more like conversations; discussion was always encouraged. One of his pupils once complained that he would prefer to hear Plotinus expound a set treatise and was exhausted by Porphyry's continuous questions. Plotinus replied, "But if when Porphyry asks questions we do not solve his difficulties we shall not be able to say anything at all to put into the treatise." Plotinus was a thoroughly engaging teacher; when he was speaking, "his intellect visibly lit up his face: there was always a charm about his appearance... kindliness shone out from him."

Plotinus would never revise his written work; he complained that writing gave him eyestrain. He was careless in the formation of the letters, and he showed no interest in spelling. Porphyry comments that Plotinus would compose everything in his mind. When he came to write, the thoughts were already fully formed, and he wrote "as continuously as if he was copying from a book." Even if someone engaged him in conversation, he would continue writing and not lose his train of thought. This ability to focus on the inner life enabled him to achieve a high level of mystical experience. He attained complete mystic union four times during Porphyry's stay with him, and in a treatise written before Porphyry's arrival, Plotinus says that he had experienced it often.

In his final years he suffered from a painful illness which may have been leprosy. Although he stopped teaching and withdrew from his friends and pupils, who feared contagion, he continued to write. Nine treatises appeared in his last two years (268-270), bringing the total to fifty-four, which were collected and edited by Porphyry, at Plotinus' request. Finally, Plotinus went away to the estate of his deceased friend Zethus in Campania, where he died alone, except for the presence of his doctor, Eustochius. His last words, according to Eustochius, were "Try to bring back the god in you to the divine in the All!"

Summary

As the last great philosopher of antiquity, and the only one to rank with Plato and Aristotle, Plotinus' philosophy has exerted an enormous influence both on the thought of his own period and on that of later times. Although he probably thought of himself as no more than an interpreter of Plato, Plotinus became the founder of Neoplatonism. His thought lived on in his pupils Porphyry and Amelius, and all later Neoplatonic philosophers regarded him as a respected, although not a supreme, authority.

Plotinus' system was a comprehensive and original one. He brought to the best of Greek philosophy a dimension of mystical thought which in its force, immediacy, and beauty has rarely, if ever, been equaled in the West. The *Enneads* are not merely an ethical or metaphysical system; they are a guide to the soul's liberation, culminating in the experience and contemplation of the One. This experience is seen as the goal of the philosopher's quest, and that of all men.

Plotinus, and Neoplatonism in general, were also major influences on the development of Christian theology. Saint Augustine knew all the six *Enneads* and quotes Plotinus by name five times. The fourth century Cappadocian Fathers, especially Gregory of Nyssa, also came under his spell. His thought emerged again in the Renaissance in the work of Marsilio Ficino (who translated Plotinus into Latin) and Giovanni Pico della Mirandola. In modern thought, Plotinus' influence can be traced in the work of German Idealist philosopher Friedrich Schelling, French philosopher Henri Bergson, and English Romantic poets such as William Blake and William Butler Yeats, whose interest in Plotinus was prompted by the translations made by the English Platonist Thomas Taylor in the late eighteenth and early nineteenth centuries.

Bibliography
Armstrong, A. H. *The Cambridge History of Later Greek and Early Medieval Philosophy*. New York: Cambridge University Press, 1970. This is the best introduction to Plotinus in English. Armstrong's balanced and sensible account of Plotinus' life takes into account the most recent scholarly research. One chapter discusses Plotinus' method of teaching and writing, and three additional chapters provide a concise but rich exposition of his thought. Includes a bibliography.
Bréhier, Émile. *The Philosophy of Plotinus*. Translated by Joseph Thomas. Chicago: University of Chicago Press, 1958. A concise introduction to Plotinus' thought but selective in its focus. Concentrates on Plotinus' philosophy of the three hypostases: the One, Intelligence, and Soul. Contains the best discussion in English of the possible Oriental influence on Plotinus' thought.
Dodds, E. R. *Pagan and Christian in an Age of Anxiety*. New York: Cambridge University Press, 1965. This brief but wide-ranging book by a renowned classical scholar discusses the historical and social background of Neoplatonism, the conflict between Neoplatonism and Christianity, and the many types of religious and psychological experience which flourished

during the period. The section on Plotinus' mysticism is particularly valuable. Well written and scholarly, but accessible to the general reader.

Inge, William R. *The Philosophy of Plotinus*. 3d ed. 2 vols. London: Longmans, Green and Co., 1948. Originally given as the Gifford Lectures at the University of St. Andrews, Scotland, in 1902-1904, this work remains a useful introduction to Plotinus' thought, gracefully written by a Christian Platonist.

Plotinus. *Plotinus, with an English Translation by A. H. Armstrong*. Vol. 1. Cambridge, Mass.: Harvard University Press, 1966. Contains an annotated translation of Porphyry's biography of Plotinus and an annotated bibliography of primary and secondary sources.

Rist, J. M. *Plotinus: The Road to Reality*. New York: Cambridge University Press, 1967. A scholarly work which includes detailed studies of Plotinus on the One, the Logos, free will, and faith. Argues that Plotinus was aware that his philosophy differed from that of Plato. Includes a chapter on Plotinus' mysticism.

Wallis, R. T. *Neoplatonism*. New York: Charles Scribner's Sons, 1972. Covers Neoplatonism from its sources in Plato, Aristotle, the Stoics, and the Middle Platonists, through to Plotinus' successors, Porphyry, Iamblichus, and the fifth and sixth century schools of Athens and Alexandria. Extensive bibliography.

Bryan Aubrey

PLUTARCH

Born: c. A.D. 46; Chaeronea, Boeotia
Died: After A.D. 120; Chaeronea, Boeotia
Area of Achievement: Literature
Contribution: Plutarch was the greatest biographer of antiquity. He taught his successors how to combine depth of psychological and moral insight with a strong narrative that evokes the greatness and excitement of subjects' lives.

Early Life

Most of Plutarch's writing was not accomplished until late middle age. He was born in a Roman province to an old and wealthy Greek family. He received a comprehensive education in Athens, where he studied rhetoric, physics, mathematics, medicine, the natural sciences, philosophy, and Greek and Latin writing. His worldview was strongly influenced by Plato, and he took considerable interest in theology, serving as the head priest at Delphi in the last twenty years of his life. By the time he was twenty, he had rounded out his education by traveling throughout Greece, Asia Minor, and Egypt. Before his writing career began, Plutarch worked in Chaeronea as a teacher and was its official representative to the Roman governor. Later, he undertook diplomatic trips to Rome, where he befriended several important public servants.

The prestige of Greek learning stood very high in the Roman Empire, and Plutarch eventually was invited to lecture in various parts of Italy on moral and philosophical subjects. Sometime in his late thirties, he began to organize his notes into essays. There is evidence to suggest that by the time he was forty, Plutarch enjoyed a highly receptive audience for his lectures. This was a time in which the Roman emperors were particularly favorable to Greek influences.

Although Plutarch could easily have made a career of his Roman lecture tours, he returned to his home in Chaeronea at about the age of fifty. There, he served in many administrative posts with the evident intention of reviving Greek culture and religion. His principal great work, *Bioi paralleloi* (first transcribed c. 105-115; *Parallel Lives*), was written in these years when his sense of civic responsibility and leadership had matured and when he was able to draw on his considerable experience of political power.

Life's Work

In *Parallel Lives*, better known simply as *Lives*, Plutarch chose to write about actual historical figures. The lives were parallel in the sense that he paired his subjects, so that Alexander the Great and Julius Caesar, Demosthenes and Cicero, could be discussed in terms of each other. It was impor-

Plutarch

tant to have a basis of comparison, to show how equally famous men had arrived at their achievements in similar and different circumstances, with personalities that could be contrasted and balanced against each other. Plutarch's aim was not merely to describe lives but to judge them, to weigh their ethical value and to measure their political effectiveness. Clearly, he believed that human beings learned by example. Thus, he would present exemplary lives, complete with his subjects' strengths and weaknesses, in order to provide a comprehensive view of the costs and the benefits of human accomplishment.

Plutarch has often been attacked for being a poor historian. What this means is that sometimes he gets his facts wrong. On occasion he is so interested in making a moral point, in teaching a lesson, that he ruins the particularity and complexity of an individual life. He has also been guilty of relying on suspect sources, of taking reports at face value because they fit a preconceived notion of his subject.

While these faults must be acknowledged and compensated for, they should not be allowed to obscure the enormous value of Plutarch's biographies. In the first place, he realized that he was not writing histories but lives and that some of his sources were questionable. Unlike the historian, he was not primarily interested in the events of the past. On the contrary, it was the personalities of his subjects that had enduring value for him. To Plutarch, there was a kind of knowledge of human beings that could not be found in the close study of events or in the narration of historical epochs. As he puts it, "a slight thing like a phrase or a jest often makes a greater revelation of character than battles where thousands fall, or the greatest armaments, or sieges of cities." Plutarch found his evidence in the seemingly trifling anecdotes about great personages. He was of the conviction that an intense scrutiny of the individual's private as well as public behavior would yield truths about human beings not commonly found in histories.

Plutarch thought of himself as an artist. He was building portraits of his subjects:

> Just as painters get the likenesses in their portraits from the face and the expression of the eyes, wherein the character shows itself, but make very little account of the other parts of the body, so I must be permitted to devote myself rather to the signs of the soul in men, and by means of these to portray the life of each, leaving to others the description of their great contests.

As the founder of modern biography, Plutarch was pursuing psychological insight. Individuals were the expressions of a society, the eyes and face of the community, so to speak. He would leave to historians the description of society, "the other parts of the body."

What makes Plutarch convincing to this day is his keen perception. No biographer has surpassed him in summing up the essence of a life—perhaps because no modern biographer has believed as intensely as Plutarch did in "the soul in men." Each line in Plutarch's best biographical essays carries the weight and significance of a whole life. It is his ability to make his readers believe that he is imagining, for example, Caesar's life from the inside, from Caesar's point of view, that makes the biographer such an attractive source that William Shakespeare and many other great authors borrowed from him.

It has often been said that no biographer can truly penetrate his or her subject's mind. Yet Plutarch perfected a way of reading external events, of shaping them into a convincing pattern, until—like a great painting—his prose seems to emit the personality of his subject. Here, for example, is his account of Caesar's ambition:

> Caesar's successes ... did not divert his natural spirit of enterprise and ambition to the enjoyment of what he had laboriously achieved, but served as fuel and incentive for future achievements, and begat in him plans for greater deeds and a passion for fresh glory, as though he had used up what he already had. What he felt was therefore nothing else than emulation of himself, as if he had been another man, and a sort of rivalry between what he had done and what he purposed to do.

These two long sentences, with their complex clauses, are imitative of Caesar's life itself, for they demonstrate how ambition drove him on—not satisfying him but actually stimulating more exploits. Here was a great man who had set such a high example for himself that his life had turned into a competition with itself. Plutarch manages the uncanny feat of having Caesar looking at himself and thereby gives his readers the sensation of occupying Caesar's mind.

Plutarch was by no means interested only in men of great political and military accomplishment. His pairing of Demosthenes and Cicero, for example, is his way of paying respect to mental agility and the power of the word. Both men prepared for their public careers as orators through long, careful training, but their personalities were quite different. Cicero was given to extraordinary boasting about himself, whereas Demosthenes rarely spoke in his own favor. If Cicero was sometimes undone by his penchant for joking, there was nevertheless a pleasantness in him almost entirely lacking in Demosthenes. That two such different men should have parallel careers is surely part of Plutarch's point. There is no single pathway in life to success or failure, and personal faults—far from being extraneous—may determine the fate of a career. Shakespeare realized as much when he based much of his *Coriolanus* (c. 1607-1608) on Plutarch's interpretation of the Roman leader's choleric character.

Summary

Most of the *Lives* and its companion volume, *Ethica* (*Moralia*), seem to have been written in the last twenty years of Plutarch's life—precisely at that point when he was most seriously occupied as a religious official, statesman, and diplomat. It is likely that his *Moralia*, or moral reflections on life, helped to give him the worldly perspective, tolerance, and acute judgment that are so evident in his masterpiece, the *Lives*. His studies of philosophy and religion surely gave him the confidence to assess the lives from which he would have his readers learn. He died an old man in peaceful repose, recognized for his good services by his fellow Boeotians, who dedicated an inscription to him at Delphi.

It has been suggested that Plutarch was most concerned with the education of his heroes, whose stories proceeded from their family background, education, entrance into the larger world, climax of achievement, and their fame and fortune (good and bad). He exerted a profound influence on the Roman world of his time, on the Middle Ages, and on a group of important writers—chiefly Michel Eyquem de Montaigne, Shakespeare, John Dryden, and Jean-Jacques Rousseau. If his impact is less obvious in modern times, it is probably because there is less confidence in the moral patterns Plutarch so boldly delineated. What modern biographer can speak, as Plutarch did, to the whole educated world, knowing that he had behind him the prestige and the grandeur of Greek literature and religion?

Bibliography
Barrow, Reginald Hayes. *Plutarch and His Times*. Bloomington: Indiana University Press, 1967. Includes map of central Greece. Emphasizes Plutarch's Greek background, with chapters on his role as a teacher and his relationship to the Roman Empire. The bibliography is divided between English and foreign titles.

Gianakaris, C. J. *Plutarch*. New York: Twayne Publishers, 1970. The best short introduction to Plutarch. Includes detailed chronology, discussions of all Plutarch's important works, a selected and annotated bibliography, and a useful index. Gianakaris writes with a firm grasp of the scholarship on Plutarch, corrects errors of earlier writers, and conveys great enthusiasm for his subject.

Jones, Christopher Prestige. *Plutarch and Rome*. London: Oxford University Press, 1971. Several chapters on Plutarch's career, on his lives of the Caesars, and on the sources, methods, and purposes of the *Lives*. Concentrates on the importance of Rome in Plutarch's life and work. With an extensive bibliography and a helpful chronological table.

Russell, Donald Andrew. *Plutarch*. London: Duckworth, 1973. Draws on the best English and French scholarship. Slightly more difficult than Gianakaris as an introduction. Chapters on language, style, and form, on the philosopher and his religion, and on Plutarch and Shakespeare. Contains several appendices, including one on editions and translations, and a general bibliography and index.

Wardman, Alan. *Plutarch's Lives*. Berkeley: University of California Press, 1974. A very detailed scholarly discussion of the *Lives*. Includes chapters on the problems of historical method, politics, rhetoric, and form. The bibliography includes many foreign titles, especially from French and English scholarship.

Carl Rollyson
Lisa Paddock

MARCO POLO

Born: c. 1254; Venice
Died: 1324; Venice
Area of Achievement: Exploration
Contribution: Through his Asian travels and his book recording them, Marco Polo encouraged a medieval period of intercultural communication, Western knowledge of other lands, and eventually the Western period of exploration and expansion.

Early Life

Despite his enduring fame, very little is known about the personal life of Marco Polo. It is known that he was born into a leading Venetian family of merchants. He also lived during a propitious time in world history, when the height of Venice's influence as a city-state coincided with the greatest extent of Mongol conquest of Asia. Ruled by Kublai Khan, the Mongol Empire stretched all the way from China to Russia and the Levant. The Mongol hordes also threatened other parts of Europe, particularly Poland and Hungary, inspiring fear everywhere by their bloodthirsty advances. Yet their ruthless methods brought a measure of stability to the lands they controlled, opening up trade routes such as the famous Silk Road. Eventually, the Mongols discovered that it was more profitable to collect tribute from people than to kill them outright, and this policy too stimulated trade.

Into this favorable atmosphere a number of European traders ventured, including the family of Marco Polo. The Polos had long-established ties in the Levant and around the Black Sea; for example, they owned property in Constantinople, and Marco's uncle, for whom he was named, had a home in Sudak in the Crimea. From Sudak, around 1260, another uncle, Maffeo, and Marco's father, Niccolò, made a trading visit into Mongol territory, the land of the Golden Horde (Russia), ruled by Berke Khan. While they were there, a war broke out between Berke and the khan of the Levant, blocking their return home. Thus Niccolò and Maffeo traveled deeper into Mongol territory, moving southeastward to Bukhara, which was ruled by a third khan. While waiting there, they met an emissary traveling farther eastward who invited them to accompany him to the court of the great khan, Kublai, in Cathay (modern China). In Cathay, Kublai Khan gave the Polos a friendly reception, appointed them his emissaries to the pope, and ensured their safe travel back to Europe: They were to return to Cathay with one hundred learned men who could instruct the Mongols in the Christian religion and the liberal arts.

In 1269, Niccolò and Maffeo Polo finally arrived back in Venice, where Niccolò found that his wife had died during his absence. Their son, Marco, then about fifteen years old, had been only six or younger when his father left home; thus Marco was reared primarily by his mother and the extended Polo family—and the streets of Venice. After his mother's death, Marco had probably begun to think of himself as something of a orphan. Then his father and uncle suddenly reappeared, as if from the dead, after nine years of travel in far-off, romantic lands. These experiences were the formative influences on young Marco, and one can see their effects mirrored in his character: a combination of sensitivity and toughness, independence and loyalty, motivated by an eagerness for adventure, a love of stories, and a desire to please or impress.

Life's Work

In 1268, Pope Clement IV died, and a two- or three-year delay while another pope was being elected gave young Marco time to mature and to absorb the tales of his father and uncle. Marco was seventeen years old when he, his father, and his uncle finally set out for the court of Kublai Khan. They were accompanied not by one hundred wise men but by two Dominican friars, and the two good friars turned back at the first sign of adversity, another local war in the Levant. Aside from the pope's messages, the only spiritual gift Europe was able to furnish the great Kublai Khan was oil from the lamp burning at Jesus Christ's supposed tomb in Jerusalem. Yet, in a sense, young Marco, the only new person in the Polos' party, was himself a fitting representative of the spirit of European civilization on the eve of the Renaissance, and the lack of one hundred learned Europeans guaranteed that he would catch the eye of the khan, who was curious about "Latins."

On the way to the khan's court, Marco had the opportunity to complete his education. The journey took three and a half years by horseback through some of the world's most rugged terrain, including snowy mountain ranges, such as the Pamirs, and parching deserts, such as the Gobi. Marco and his party encountered such hazards as wild beasts and brigands; they also met with beautiful women, in whom young Marco took a special interest. The group traveled through numerous countries and cultures, noting the food, dress, and religions unique to each. In particular, under the khan's protection the Polos were able to observe a large portion of the Islamic world at close range, as few if any European Christians had. (Unfortunately, Marco's anti-Muslim prejudices, a European legacy of the Crusades, marred his observations.) By the time they reached the khan's court in Khanbalik (modern Peking), Marco had become a hardened traveler. He had also received a unique education and had been initiated into manhood.

Kublai Khan greeted the Polos warmly and invited them to stay on in his court. Here, if Marco's account is to be believed, the Polos became great favorites of the khan, and Kublai eventually made Marco one of his most trusted emissaries. On these points Marco has been accused of gross exaggeration, and the actual status of the Polos at the court of the khan is

Marco Polo

much disputed. If at first it appears unlikely that Kublai would make young Marco an emissary, upon examination this seems quite reasonable. For political reasons, the khan was in the habit of appointing foreigners to administer conquered lands, particularly China, where the tenacity of the Chinese bureaucracy was legendary (and eventually contributed to the breakup of the Mongol Empire). The khan could also observe for himself that young Marco was a good candidate: eager, sturdy, knowledgeable, well traveled, and apt (Marco quickly assimilated Mongol culture and became proficient in four languages, of which three were probably Mongol, Turkish, and Persian). Finally, Marco reported back so successfully from his first mission—informing the khan not only on business details but also on colorful customs and other interesting trivia—that his further appointment was confirmed. The journeys specifically mentioned in Marco's book, involving travel across China and a sea voyage to India, suggest that the khan did indeed trust him with some of the most difficult missions.

The Polos stayed on for seventeen years, another indication of how valued they were in the khan's court. Marco, his father, and his uncle not only survived—itself an achievement amid the political hazards of the time—but also prospered. Apparently, the elder Polos carried on their trading while Marco was performing his missions; yet seventeen years is a long time to trade without returning home to family and friends. According to Marco, because the khan held them in such high regard, he would not let them return home, but as the khan aged the Polos began to fear what would happen after his death. Finally an opportunity to leave presented itself when trusted emissaries were needed to accompany a Mongol princess on a wedding voyage by sea to Persia, where she was promised to the local khan. The Polos sailed from Cathay with a fleet of fourteen ships and a wedding party of six hundred people, not counting the sailors. Only a few members of the wedding entourage survived the journey of almost two years, but luckily the survivors included the Polos and the princess. Fortunately, too, the Polos duly delivered the princess not to the old khan of Persia, who had meanwhile died, but to his son.

From Persia, the Polos made their way back to Venice. They were robbed as soon as they got into Christian territory, but they still managed to reach home, in 1295, with plenty of rich goods. According to Giovanni Battista Ramusio, one of the early editors of Marco's book, the Polos strode into Venice looking like ragged Mongols. Having thought them dead, their relatives at first did not recognize them, then were astounded, and then were disgusted by their shabby appearance. Yet, according to Ramusio, the scorn changed to delight when the returned travelers invited everyone to a homecoming banquet, ripped apart their old clothes, and let all the hidden jewels clatter to the table.

The rest of the world might have learned little about the Polos' travels if fate had not intervened in Marco's life. In his early forties, Marco was not yet ready to settle down. Perhaps he was restless for further adventure, or perhaps he felt obliged to fulfill his civic duties to his native city-state. In any event, he became involved in naval warfare between the Venetians and their trading rivals, the Genoese, and was captured. In 1298, the great traveler across Asia and emissary of the khan found himself rotting in a prison in Genoa—an experience that could have ended tragically but instead took a lucky turn. In prison Marco met a man named Rustichello (or Rusticiano), from Pisa, who was a writer of romances. To pass the time, Marco dictated his observations about Asia to Rustichello, who, in writing them down, probably employed the Italianized Old French that was the language of his romances. (Old French had gained currency as the language of medieval romances during the Crusades.)

Their book was soon in circulation, since Marco remained in prison only a year or so, very likely gaining his freedom when the Venetians and Genoese made peace in 1299. After his prison experience, Marco was content to lead a quiet life in Venice with his family and bask in his almost instant literary fame. He married Donata Badoer, a member of the Venetian aristocracy, and they had three daughters—Fantina, Bellela, and Moreta—all of whom eventually grew up to marry nobles. Thus Marco seems to have spent the last part of his life moving in Venetian aristocratic circles. After living what was then a long life, Marco died in 1324, roughly seventy years of age. In his will he left most of his modest wealth to his three daughters, a legacy that included goods which he had brought back from Asia. His will also set free a Tartar slave, Peter, who had remained with him since his return from the court of the great khan.

Summary

The book that Marco Polo and Rustichello wrote in prison was titled *Divisament dou monde* (description of the world), although in Italian it is usually called *Il milione* (the million), and it is usually translated into English as *The Travels of Marco Polo*. The original title is more accurate than this English title, which is somewhat deceptive, since after its prologue the book is actually a cultural geography instead of a travelogue or an autobiography.

The book was immediately popular. Numerous copies were made and circulated (this was the age before printing), including translations into other dialects and languages. Some copyists were priests or monks who, threatened by descriptions of other religions and the great khan's notable religious tolerance, made discreet emendations. These changes may in part account for the emphasis on Christian miracles in the book's early sections and even for its anti-Muslim sentiments. The numerous manuscripts with their many variants have created a monumental textual problem for modern editors of the work, since Marco and Rustichello's original manuscript has disappeared.

Modern readers might be surprised by the book's impact in Marco's time and for centuries afterward, but to readers of the early fourteenth century descriptions of Asia were as fantastic as descriptions of outer space are today. Unfortunately many people then tended to read it as though it were science fiction or fantasy, perhaps in part because of its romantic style (including Rustichello's embellishments). The title *Il milione*, whose origin is obscure, could refer to the number of lies the book supposedly contains. (Some readers considered Marco Polo merely a notorious liar.) Yet, allowing for textual uncertainties, modern commentators have judged the book to be remarkably accurate; thus, it was a valuable source for those readers who took it seriously. For centuries it was the main source of Western information about Asia, and it exercised a tremendous influence on the Western age of exploration (Christopher Columbus carried a well-marked copy with him). It has also continued to influence the Western imagination—inspiring plays, novels, and films, as well as unrestrained scholarly speculation about Marco's life and travels. In short, Marco Polo has become a symbol of Western man venturing forth.

Yet in large part the meaning of Marco Polo's experience has been misinterpreted. His sojourn in the East has too often been seen as the first probe of Western man into unknown territory (a viewpoint which is shamefully ethnocentric), with Marco as a kind of spy or intelligence gatherer identifying the locations of the richest spoils, the first example of Western man as conquerer. While he did influence the Western age of exploration, conquest, and colonization, this was hardly his intent. Instead, Marco can best be seen as an exponent of intercultural communication who lived during a period when communication between East and West opened up for a brief time.

Bibliography

Calvino, Italo. *Invisible Cities*. Translated by William Weaver. New York: Harcourt Brace Jovanovich, 1974. Originally published in 1972 as *Le città invisibili*, this postmodernist novel by one of Italy's leading writers is a fascinating example of an imaginative work inspired by Marco Polo. Consists of conversations between Marco Polo and Kublai Khan and Marco's descriptions of imaginary cities.

Li Man Kin. *Marco Polo in China*. Hong Kong: Kingsway International Publications, 1981. Although poorly written and edited, this volume is a good example of a freely speculative work about Marco from a non-Western point of view. Includes good illustrations, although they are not closely related to text.

Olschki, Leonardo. *Marco Polo's Asia: An Introduction to His "Description of the World" Called "Il milione."* Translated by John A. Scott. Berkeley: University of California Press, 1960. The best scholarly introduction to

Marco Polo and his book. Discusses in detail the book's treatment of such topics as nature, politics, religion, Asian history, historical and legendary figures, and medicine.

Polo, Marco. *The Travels of Marco Polo*. Translated by Ronald Latham. Harmondsworth, England: Penguin Books, 1958. The best translation into English of Marco's book. Based on modern textual scholarship. Contains a brief but good introduction by the translator.

Power, Eileen. "Marco Polo: A Venetian Traveler of the Thirteenth Century." In *Medieval People*. 10th ed. New York: Barnes and Noble Books, 1963. A colorfully written account of Marco's travels, with descriptions of cities and rulers and quotations from other European travelers of the time who visited Asia.

Harold Branam

POLYBIUS

Born: c. 200 B.C.; Megalopolis, Arcadia, Greece
Died: c. 118 B.C.; Greece
Area of Achievement: Historiography
Contribution: Through the advancement of sound historical methodology, Polybius contributed to the development of history as a significant area of inquiry having primarily a didactic rationale.

Early Life

Polybius was born in about 200 B.C. in Megalopolis, Arcadia, in Greece. He was the son of Lycortas, a prominent Achaean diplomat and political leader; nothing is known of Polybius' mother. His family's wealth was based on extensive and productive land holdings. During his youth Polybius developed an interest in biography, history, and military topics. He wrote a biography of Philopoenen, a legendary leader in Arcadia, and a military treatise, *Tactics*, which has not survived. As a young nobleman, Polybius complied with the expectation that he be trained as a warrior in order to support the policies of the Achaean League. At the age of twenty, Polybius was named a hipparch, a commander of cavalry, in the army of the League, and he remained in that position for a decade. Shortly after 170, the fragile tranquillity of the Greek world was disrupted by the Roman war against Perseus of Macedonia. Amid this crisis, which saw a heightened Roman distrust of the various Greek states, Polybius declared his support for the Romans and offered his cavalry to assist the Roman forces, which were under the leadership of Quintus Marcius Philippus. Not only did the Romans not accept Polybius' offer of support, which was a result of their lack of trust, but they also seized Polybius and about a thousand other Achaeans and transported them to Italy. This episode marked a transformation in the life and work of Polybius.

Life's Work

Upon arriving in Rome, Polybius came under the protection of Scipio Aemilianus, a prominent Roman general who had befriended the exiled Achaean. Polybius traveled with Scipio to Spain, Africa, and southern France; they witnessed the destruction of Carthage in 146 at the close of the Third Punic War. In the same year, Polybius was in Corinth, which had been destroyed by the Romans. Polybius exhibited effective diplomatic skills as he arranged an end to hostilities and a reasonable settlement for the Achaeans.

Throughout his travels and contacts with the Romans, Polybius developed his interest in history and formulated a plan to write a history of the emergence of Rome to a position of hegemony in the Mediterranean world. At first, Polybius intended to conclude his work in 168 with the victory of the Romans over Perseus in the Battle of Pydna. He later decided, however, to continue the history through to the fall of Carthage and Corinth in 146. It appears that his history was published in forty books; although only the first five books have survived intact, fragments and collaborative evidence provide considerable information on the remaining thirty-five books.

In *The Histories*, Polybius clarified and expanded the role of the historian and the importance of the study of history. He maintained that historians must be familiar with the geography of the regions they cover, knowledgeable about the practice of politics, and informed of the appropriate documentary sources relating to their topic. Polybius viewed history as an analysis of political developments which would better equip leaders to increase political wisdom. He advanced a philosophy of history which was based on the frequency of constitutional changes or revolutions in societies and cultures. Polybius argued that in the earliest years of a society's history, people banded together and designated a leader whose primary purpose was to provide protection for the group; the consequence of this action was the appearance of despotism. As the society expanded and the concept of law emerged, the despotism was transformed into monarchy, which eventually led to tyranny and an aristocratic reaction. The aristocratic regime yielded to oligarchy, which was then replaced by democracy. The democracy survived for a few generations until the memory of the oligarchy passed and democracy was corrupted to mob rule, during which the conditions that first resulted in the emergence of despotism were re-created. A despot would again seize power and the politically oriented and driven process would resume. Polybius argued that Rome would be exempt from the processes of decay because of the fluid nature of the constitution of the Roman Republic.

In collecting his sources, Polybius exercised a thoroughness and discrimination which were revolutionary in the study of history. He relied heavily upon the use of oral testimony; indeed, he structured the chronological limits of his study so that he could emphasize the material which he gathered from oral sources. These sources could be used as collaborative evidence and were capable of being verified. In addition to oral history, Polybius had access to and made use of a wide range of written sources. From Achaean and Roman official records to earlier histories, Polybius effectively utilized all the available sources.

The Histories constitute an apologia, an explanation for the emergence of Rome as the leader of the Mediterranean world. Polybius contended that Rome deserved its preeminent position because the Roman leaders and people had developed a progressive political system; the other Mediterranean peoples, Polybius believed, did not possess the realistic political worldview of the Romans and, as a consequence, lost their independence. In the development of this notion as well as others, Polybius demonstrated his concern with causation. On several occasions he discussed the concept of cause and effect and noted contrasts between the larger causes of a development and the immediate activities which resulted in it. It should be noted, however, that Polybius also ascribed to Tyche (the Greek goddess of chance) developments which were inexplicable. Throughout his writings Polybius repeated that history should be instructive,

> ... for it is by applying analogies to our own circumstances that we get the means and basis for calculating the future; and for learning from the past when to act with caution, and when with greater boldness, in the present.

Polybius repudiated partisan histories, such as the writings of Timaeus, the Greek antiquarian, and warned against the worthlessness of deliberately biased works. He was interested in determining the truth and, once it was determined, learning from it.

Both in his own time and in subsequent generations, critics noted the shortcomings of Polybius' style, which in many ways appears to have been as tedious as modern bureaucratic English. Polybius was repetitious, exercised a penchant for ambiguity, and developed his arguments in such an indirect fashion that his principal points were frequently submerged. Nevertheless, Polybius, along with Herodotus and Thucydides, raised the study and writing of history to a new level of serious inquiry. Polybius' emphasis on proper methodology, his vision of a universal political historical process, and his advocacy of history as a didactic art resulted in the enhancement of the Greco-Roman historical tradition. Polybius allegedly died at about the age of eighty-two in approximately 118 B.C. in Greece, as a result of injuries suffered when he was thrown from a horse.

Summary

While Polybius was a leading Achaean during his lifetime and used his abilities and connections to develop an accommodation with Rome for his native Arcadia, his more significant legacy consisted of his contributions to the development of the study and writing of history. In the tradition of the earlier Greek historians Herodotus and Thucydides, Polybius considered the multitude of issues relating to historical methodology and developed an expanded notion of historical evidence. His use of oral history and his approach to collaborative evidence were significant contributions to his craft. Polybius' methodology and his concept of history influenced Roman historians such as Livy and Tacitus.

While much of *The Histories* of Polybius has been lost, the first five books provide the reader with more than a glimpse of Roman history at a time when the Mediterranean world was in a state of crisis. In this context, Polybius' contributions to the study of constitutions and political cycles should be emphasized; his thesis on the progression from despotism to monarchy to tyranny to aristocracy and then on to democracy and the return to despotism via mob rule not only advanced a historical analysis but also provided a framework for the discussion of constitutionalism. Twentieth century historiographers such as Harry Elmer Barnes and Eric Breisach have sustained Polybius' place in the first rank of ancient historians.

Bibliography
Barnes, Harry Elmer. *A History of Historical Writing*. 2d ed. New York: Dover Publications, 1963. A standard historiographical analysis which identifies Polybius as being in the tradition of Herodotus and Thucydides. Barnes credits Polybius with the advancement of historical writing during the classical period; Polybius' methodology and organizational skills are discussed in the context of Greek historiography.
Breisach, Ernst. *Historiography: Ancient, Medieval, and Modern*. Chicago: University of Chicago Press, 1983. Breisach discusses Polybius' work in the context of early Roman historiography, emphasizing his concept of political history. The author also provides a schema for Polybius' cycle of constitutional revolutions. This work constitutes one of the best single-volume reviews of historiography available. Includes an excellent bibliography.
Magie, D. *Roman Rule in Asia Minor*. Princeton: Princeton University Press, 1950. An excellent introduction to the expansion of Rome in the eastern Mediterranean, this volume provides a valuable insight into the world and writing of Polybius.
Robinson, Charles Alexander. *Ancient History, from Prehistoric Times to the Death of Justinian*. New York: Macmillan, 1962. A somewhat dated but still excellent introduction to the study of ancient history. Polybius is presented as one of the progressives of antiquity whose contribution to the development of civilization was substantive.
Scullard, H. H. *Scipio Africanus in the Second Punic War*. Cambridge: Cambridge University Press, 1930. A classic study of the Second Punic War and the emergence of Rome as the major power in the Mediterranean region. This book provides an excellent examination of Roman policy at the end of the third century.
Walbank, Frank A. *A Historical Commentary on Polybius*. 3 vols. Oxford: Clarendon Press, 1957-1958. This is the preeminent scholarly study of Polybius by one of the major classical scholars of the twentieth century. The work includes extensive details on Polybius, textual commentary, and criticism on *The Histories*.
_____. *Polybius*. Berkeley: University of California Press, 1972. Walbank's volume treating the life of Polybius and his work stands as a significant contribution to biography and historiography as well as to the study of this particular historian. The work is well documented and includes a useful bibliography.

William T. Walker

POLYGNOTUS

Born: c. 500 B.C.; Thasos, Greece
Died: c. 440 B.C.?; Thasos or Athens, Greece
Area of Achievement: Art
Contribution: Innovative, brash, confident in his skills, Polygnotus was the first great Greek painter. His murals at Delphi and in Athens established his reputation as the preeminent painter of the fifth century B.C. and probably the most famous in antiquity.

Early Life

Little is known about Polygnotus' early life. He was born on the Greek island of Thasos, near Thrace, and was the son and pupil of the prominent painter Aglaophon. His brother Aristophon was also an artist; a later painter named Aglaophon may have been his son or nephew. Polygnotus' family appears to have been politically active, and he may have been related to the famous seventh century poet Archilochus, whose family had colonized Thasos.

Polygnotus was already being employed as a painter, and probably also as a sculptor, for major projects on the Greek mainland during the first quarter of the fifth century. He eventually made his way to Athens, where he spent much of his life, and became the first known artistic adviser to an Athenian politician—Cimon, whom he recognized as his patron. Cimon was the dominant political figure in Athens from the late 470's to 461, and it was undoubtedly through his influence that Polygnotus became an Athenian citizen, a rare honor. Cimon's free-spirited sister, Elpinice, was Polygnotus' lover and model.

Polygnotus may have been persuaded to enter Cimon's service when the latter conquered Thasos, which had revolted from Athens and the Delian League in 465, but it is more likely that the association had begun in the previous decade. There is plausible evidence to suggest that Polygnotus helped decorate the Theseum in Athens, the shrine for the bones of the hero Theseus which Cimon had discovered and returned to the city in the mid-470's. The relationship could have begun as early as 479, when Polygnotus was painting in a shrine commemorating the Battle of Marathon, in which Cimon's father, Miltiades the Younger, had been the hero.

Life's Work

The destruction of Athens in 479 during the Second Persian War left the city in ruins; the necessity of rebuilding and beautifying the city provided an opportunity for artists such as Polygnotus. Polygnotus' friend Cimon was responsible for an extensive building program, and the artist was actively employed in decorating Cimon's structures. The most significant of these was the Stoa Poikile (painted stoa), which was funded by Cimon's brother-in-law and probably completed by 460. Polygnotus (who may have been the artistic director for the building) and other prominent artists created a "Cimonian" picture gallery in the Stoa Poikile, choosing mythological and historical themes which could call attention to Cimon's family and his accomplishments. Like many ancient murals, these paintings were executed not directly on the walls but on wooden panels which were pinned to the walls with iron pegs.

Polygnotus was responsible for the *Iliupersis*, a mural depicting Troy fallen. The theme evoked memories of Cimon's great victory at the Eurymedon River in Asia Minor in 469, where the Athenian general had inflicted so crushing a defeat upon the Persians that, at the time, it seemed as final as the legendary Greek triumph over the Trojans. Polygnotus also used the opportunity to paint the face of Elpinice on Laodice, the most prominent Trojan woman in the mural, further indication that the mural honored Cimon.

Among other works in Athens attributed to Polygnotus was a depiction of the marriage of Castor and Pollux to the daughters of Leucippus, a painting which appeared in the sanctuary of the Dioscuri, another building associated with Cimon. In the Propylaea on the Acropolis, his murals of Achilles among the virgins on Scyros and Odysseus' encounter with Nausicaa were displayed. What he painted in the Theseum cannot be determined.

Polygnotus' greatest works were not in Athens but at Delphi, in the Cnidian Lesche (clubhouse), which had been dedicated to the god Apollo by the people of Cnidus, a Greek city in Asia Minor, soon after the Battle of the Eurymedon. In that structure, the artist painted what would become the most famous murals of antiquity—the *Iliupersis* (Troy fallen), a much larger and earlier version of the painting with the same name in Athens, and the *Nekyia*, or "Odysseus' Visit to the Underworld."

The paintings were gigantic by contemporary standards and covered the interior walls of the clubhouse, which measured 55 feet long and 25 feet wide. Their dozens of mythological figures, which were arranged on at least three different levels on a surface perhaps fifteen feet tall, were almost life-sized, and the themes of the murals, like the themes of most of Polygnotus' paintings in Athens, related directly to Cimon—in this case, his victory at the Eurymedon. The Cnidians, devotees of Apollo, had themselves participated in the battle. They had been among the forces led by Cimon, whose fleet had departed for the final engagement from their harbors and whose triumph at Eurymedon guaranteed their freedom from further Persian domination. Nothing would have been more appropriate for them than to celebrate the victory by making a thank-offering to Apollo at Delphi and commissioning paintings whose symbolism would reflect favorably upon the god's agent at the battle—Cimon. The fact that Polygnotus, Cimon's close friend and client, was chosen to execute the paintings in the Cnidians' clubhouse is further evidence of the political intent of the paintings—though, politics aside, the artistic merits of the two great murals were so impressive that the artist was voted free food and lodging for life by the Amphictionic Council (the "common council" of Greece). Since Athens was a member of that council, the patriotic tradition that Polygnotus painted in the city without fee becomes understandable. He had no reason to charge, since Athens was already contributing to his upkeep, and, certainly, Cimon saw to it that his material needs were met.

Polygnotus' later life is largely a subject for conjecture. When Cimon was ostracized from Athens in 461, there is no reason to believe that the artist was adversely affected or forced to leave. He was, after all, an Athenian citizen. He may have continued to work on the Stoa Poikile; it is known that other artists who had worked on Cimonian projects or were close to Cimon were able to remain in Athens. One was the great sculptor Phidias, who became the intimate friend of Pericles, the man who had helped engineer Cimon's exile and became the single dominant politician in Athens after him. The Polygnotean paintings displayed in the Propylaea, built by Pericles in the 430's, may be indication that the artist stayed, though it is not known whether these murals were actually painted while Pericles was in power or were earlier works collected from other places and deposited there.

When and where Polygnotus died is uncertain. He held political office on Thasos sometime after 450, as did his brother Polydorus, but whether he remained there for the rest of his life cannot be determined.

Summary

Polygnotus was the first great Greek painter. A friend and client of the powerful Athenian politician Cimon, he painted murals in Athens which reflected favorably upon his patron. His *Iliupersis* and *Nekyia* at Delphi were the two most famous paintings of antiquity, and their mythological themes celebrated Cimon's crushing victory over the Persians at the Eurymedon River in 469.

Polygnotus represented a break from the conventions of earlier times, freeing painting from its archaic stiffness. He did not confine his figures to a single ground line but arranged them on several levels, scattering them about at various points in space and adding landscape elements such as rocks and trees to give an additional feeling of depth.

Among other innovations attributed to him were painting women in transparent drapery, representing their heads in multicolored headdresses, depicting the mouth open and teeth showing, and more natural treatment of the face. There was an emotional quality to his work, with figures or groups of figures reacting to events. Aristotle, at least, came close to assigning Polygnotus a didactic intent, saying that he represented men as better or more virtuous than they were and was concerned with portraying good character.

Later critics maintained his greatness but considered him almost a primitive, citing his simplicity of color and lack of shading. The assertion by Cicero that Polygnotus painted in only four colors is probably erroneous. He is said to have been among the first to paint with yellow ochre.

During the early years of the Roman Empire, Quintilian averred that any serious survey of art must begin with Polygnotus, and his work was considered meritorious enough over the centuries to justify frequent restorations. Pausanias, who provides the most complete account of Polygnotus' paintings, was still impressed by them in the second century A.D., about six hundred years after they were painted. Some of Pausanius' descriptions are corroborated in the surviving work of ancient potters, who borrowed Polygnotus' themes, figure groupings, and figure poses and applied them to their own work.

Bibliography
Barron, J. P. "New Light on Old Walls: The Murals of the Theseion." *Journal of Roman Studies* 92 (1972): 20-45. A detailed discussion of the murals in the Theseum in Athens, attempting to reconstruct their content and identify who painted them. The fullest discussion of Polygnotus' role in the decoration of this building.
Jeffery, L. H. "The *Battle of Oinoe* in the Stoa Poikile: A Problem in Greek Art and History." *Annual of the British School at Athens* 60 (1965): 41-57. A discussion of the paintings in the Stoa Poikile, including Polygnotus' *Iliupersis*.
Kebric, Robert B. *The Paintings in the Cnidian Lesche at Delphi and Their Historical Context.* Leiden, Netherlands: E. J. Brill, 1983. This study is the most complete analysis of the political content of Polygnotus' major paintings and his relationship with Cimon. The major historical and chronological questions surrounding the paintings at Delphi, in particular, are discussed fully. An extensive bibliography is provided.
Meiggs, R. *The Athenian Empire.* Oxford: Clarendon Press, 1972. A thorough study of the Athenian Empire which provides a detailed analysis of the period of Polygnotus' activity and of Cimonian Athens. Polygnotus himself is given a three-page treatment.
Pollitt, J. J. *The Art of Greece, 1400 B.C.-31 B.C.* Englewood Cliffs, N.J.: Prentice-Hall, 1965. An accessible sourcebook which contains relevant passages from ancient writers about Polygnotus and his work.
Robertson, Martin. *A History of Greek Art.* 2 vols. New York: Cambridge University Press, 1976. This survey of ancient Greek art contains the best single introduction to Polygnotus' art and paintings.

Robert B. Kebric

POMPEY THE GREAT

Born: September 29, 106 B.C.; probably near Rome
Died: September 28, 48 B.C.; Pelusium, Egypt
Areas of Achievement: Government and warfare
Contribution: As a military leader and imperial proconsul, Pompey greatly extended the bounds of the Roman Empire during the late republic and, with Julius Caesar and Marcus Crassus, was one of the three leading figures whose careers and ambitions coincided with the final downfall of the Roman Republic.

Early Life

Little is known of the early years of Pompey the Great, or Gnaeus Pompeius. His family rose to prominence in Rome only during the second century B.C. and thus was not among the ancient patrician nobility. Pompey's father, Pompeius Strabo, was an ambitious and successful general during the Social War (circa 91 to 87 B.C.). As a result of his military success, Strabo extended his political influence, gaining many supporters, or *clientela*, which he then used in advancing his own career.

The centuries-old Roman Republic was dominated by a number of ancient aristocratic families who ruled the state through the senate with individuals from the plebeian class who had achieved wealth. This government had been under tension for some time, however, as it proved to be less suitable for the great empire which Rome had become. In the resulting political instability, victorious generals and their armies often played a prominent role; Strabo, like his contemporaries Gaius Marius and Lucius Cornelius Sulla, hoped to parlay his military conquests into ruling strength. Many were relieved when he died suddenly of a plague.

Pompey had served under his father during the Social War, but after the unpopular Strabo's death, he had to forge new connections to advance his own political career. When Sulla, victorious in the east, returned to Italy at the head of his army in 83, Pompey raised an army from his own clients and took Sulla's part. After Sulla was elected dictator, Pompey divorced his first wife, Antistia, and married Sulla's stepdaughter, Aemilia. Through Sulla's influence, Pompey was given a military command to pursue opponents of the new regime. He did so, bloodily and efficiently, in Africa and Sicily. After his victories, his troops hailed him *imperator* and *magnus*, but when Sulla attempted to retire Pompey, he resisted disbanding his army. He returned to Rome and demanded a triumph, a recognition of his military exploits. Sulla reluctantly granted his request, and by 80 Pompey had become one of the most significant figures in the unstable landscape of republican Rome.

Because of his handsome looks, his youth, and his military accomplishments, Pompey was compared by his contemporaries to Alexander the

Great, the Macedonian king who had conquered Persia and much of the known world. Yet Pompey's wars and his political machinations were directed toward placing himself among the first citizens of the Roman Republic. He was obsessively concerned with his own dignity and honor but not with absolute power for its own sake, and although he was a military hero, he often resorted to charm and tact rather than the threat of force.

Life's Work

From 80 B.C., when he was in his mid-twenties, until the end of his life, Pompey remained among the leading figures in the republic. After Sulla resigned his dictatorship, there was another period of civil war, directed against Sulla's system of reformed oligarchy. Pompey supported the government against attack in Italy, and then he was awarded an important military command in Spain. From 76 to 72, he pursued Quintus Sertorius, who had fled Rome during the events which had brought Sulla to power and had subsequently established control over much of Spain. Pompey succeeded militarily and also added to his influence by increasing the number of his personal supporters, or clients, in Spain.

Pompey returned to find Italy in the throes of a slave uprising led by a Thracian gladiator, Spartacus. The Servile War led to several defeats of the Roman armies until Crassus took charge. Although the war was almost over when he arrived, Pompey claimed to have attained the final victory, much to the disgust of Crassus. The two rivals were elected consuls in 70 despite Pompey's youth and political inexperience; the exception was made because of his previous heroic accomplishments.

After Pompey's year as consul, he stepped down, but he remained a major figure, one of the *principes civitatis*. Then, in 67, he was granted the authority to eliminate the threat posed by pirates to Mediterranean shipping, particularly to the grain supply necessary to Roman peace and survival. Although there was considerable senate opposition to giving such power to one individual, the price of bread dropped in Rome in anticipation of Pompey's success. Beginning in the west, Pompey swept the pirates east, successfully ending the campaign in three months.

Using his still-increasing popularity and political influence, Pompey next obtained a military command against the continuing threat from Mithradates the Great, ruler of the eastern kingdom of Pontus. Again, his selection was controversial, partially because it would add to Pompey's stature and power. Turning down a peace initiative by Mithradates, Pompey pursued him ruthlessly, forcing Mithradates to retreat into the Crimea region of the Black Sea. Pompey then successfully brought the kingdom of Armenia into the Roman orbit. With the threat from Pontus and Armenia ended, Pompey turned south, into Syria, ending the Seleucid kingdom which had been founded in the aftermath of the conquests of Alexander. He conquered Jerusalem and created a client kingdom in Judaea, as he did elsewhere in the Middle East. By the time he returned to Rome in 62, Pompey had successfully extended the boundaries of the Roman Empire almost to the Euphrates River. Pompey had emulated Alexander and had justly earned the title of Pompeius Magnus, Pompey the Great.

In Rome, Pompey was awarded another triumph, during which he wore a cloak once worn by Alexander. By then, he was probably the richest individual in the empire. His conquests in the east and his wealth, however, did not easily translate into political power. The senate, led by Cato the Censor, denied his demands for rewards for his soldiers and himself. To avoid even the appearance of wishing to assume dictatorial power, Pompey disbanded his armies on reaching Italy. He divorced his wife, Mucia, on grounds of adultery, and planned to marry Cato's niece, but Cato refused to accept an alliance with someone he believed was a threat to the republic. Pompey expected honors and respect, but his return was anticlimactic.

His failure to gain senate ratification of his proposals coincided with a demand by some of Crassus' supporters for changes in the tax collection laws in the east. Pompey and Crassus had been rivals, but the senate's opposition forced the two together. Caesar, returning from campaigning in Spain, desired both a triumph in Rome and to be elected consul; his ambitions were also blocked. To gain the support of Pompey and Crassus, Caesar promised both what they had failed to receive from the senate. By the end of 60, the somewhat misleadingly named First Triumvirate had come into being; formed for practical short-term goals, it was not intended to subvert the government of the republic.

With Caesar as consul and with the public support of Pompey and Crassus, the desired legislation was passed. As a further reward, Caesar received a military command in Gaul. Yet Pompey's own popularity declined; he had returned from Asia, expecting to be accepted as Rome's principal citizen, but in order to achieve his other goals, he had been forced into an alliance with Caesar and Crassus which cast doubt on Pompey's republican patriotism. The alliance soon began to experience difficulties in Rome because of the ambitions of others, such as Clodius Pulcher. Although Pompey had to maintain the coalition for fear that his long-desired legislation might be reversed, Caesar, concerned about the possibility of Pompey's abdication, forged a new bond between them; Caesar's daughter, Julia, was married to Pompey.

Clodius soon became Pompey's chief threat. Through his own clients and his ability to manipulate the city mobs, Clodius neutralized Pompey's authority by threatening violence. Yet Pompey's successful solution to a grain shortage—perhaps the single greatest political issue in the lives of most Romans—restored much of his lost popularity by 57. When it appeared that the triumvirate might end, Pompey and Caesar met and renewed the alliance, with Pompey and Crassus becoming joint consuls for the second time in 55;

they, in turn, ensured that Caesar's command in Gaul would be extended for another five years. Only with bribery and violence, however, were Pompey and Crassus able to defeat their opponents in the senate.

As a reward, Crassus gained a military command in Syria in anticipation of a war against Parthia which would add to his fame. In Rome, Pompey sponsored a large building program, culminating in the Theatrum Pompeii, Rome's first stone-built theater. The traditionalists objected to still another departure from the republican past; again, it was rumored that Pompey wished to become dictator, and again he denied it.

By 53, the triumvirate had collapsed. Julia died in childbirth, removing one bond between Pompey and Caesar, and Crassus met death in his armies' defeat by the Parthians at Carrhae. When Pompey married again, to Cornelia, daughter of Metellus Scipio, it was an alliance not with Caesar but with another ancient family. Renewed violence in Rome bolstered Pompey's position as the only person with the necessary authority who might save the state, and even Cato, defender of the republic, proposed that Pompey become sole consul in order to deal with the emergency.

In Gaul, Caesar desired a second consulship for himself, but he was unwilling to give up the military *imperium* to return to Rome in order to seek election. Pompey was not opposed to having Caesar stand for consul while still keeping his command in Gaul, but he supported legislation which might reduce the period Caesar could keep control of his province. Pompey stated that it was not directed against Caesar, but Pompey was still committed to maintaining his position as the first citizen. He had positioned himself so that Caesar depended on him for protection from the senate, and the senate depended on Pompey for protection from Caesar.

Pompey's position between Caesar and the senate was inherently unstable. In the summer of 50, Pompey suffered a serious illness, and public prayers and declarations of sympathy and gratitude at his recovery indicated to Pompey that his support was both wide and deep. When in December it was rumored that Caesar had already invaded Italy, Pompey was given the command to mobilize the necessary legions and defend the republic. He hoped that a show of strength would cause Caesar to back down, ensuring Pompey's own position of superiority. Pompey became convinced that Caesar was a threat to Rome itself, but even then Pompey hoped to avoid war; only pressure sufficient to stop Caesar, but not destroy him, would maintain Pompey's own position.

Pompey proved to be wrong on two counts: Caesar reacted more quickly than was anticipated, invading Italy in early January, 49, and Pompey's support was less than expected. In reaction to Caesar's invasion, Pompey abandoned Rome. He had not been given supreme power and continued to face the possibility of senate opposition. Both Caesar and Pompey probably wished to avoid war, but the senate, particularly Cato and his faction, opposed any compromise. In March, 49, Pompey left Italy for the east and public opinion began to turn against him. Caesar wisely pursued a policy of clemency, and some began to claim that Pompey had intended all along to establish a dictatorship on the model of Sulla.

Pompey and a majority of the senate retreated to Greece. When Caesar later arrived in Greece, Pompey had three possibilities: He could return to Italy ahead of Caesar, he could retreat and allow Caesar to exhaust his resources, or he could fight a pitched battle. Pompey's supporters demanded a confrontation, and on August 9, 48, both sides met at Pharsalus, where Caesar was victorious. Pompey fled to Egypt but on the day he landed, September 28, 48, the day before his fifty-eighth birthday, he was stabbed to death. His head was presented to Caesar, and his ashes were returned to Italy.

Summary

Two of Pompey the Great's sons continued the struggle against Caesar. After Pompey's murder, they retreated first to Africa and then to Spain, where they had much success in an area of their father's earlier conquests. The elder, Gnaeus, however, met defeat at the hands of Caesar in 45 and was executed. The younger, Sextus, continued the family's battles and survived Caesar's assassination in 44. Yet during the conflicts of the next decade, Sextus took sides against Caesar's heir, Augustus, and was eventually executed in 36.

The verdict on Pompey's career is divided between claims that both Caesar and Pompey sought the same thing—supreme power—and arguments that Pompey was the last of the republicans, a man who gave his life for the ideals of ancient Rome. Perhaps the best estimate is that Pompey was a man of his own time, reflecting the ambiguous politics of the late republic, when the institutions of the past no longer proved entirely adequate. Following the example of his father and others, he used his military conquests to influence politics. He wished to be honored as the premier citizen of Rome, but it is doubtful that he ever intended to replace the senate as the governing body of the republic. Still, Pompey's personality, his ambitions, his conquests, and his ultimate position in Roman society undoubtedly played a part in the fall of the republic.

Bibliography

Greenhalgh, Peter. *Pompey: The Roman Alexander*. Columbia: University of Missouri Press, 1980. The first volume of a two-volume study of the life and times of Pompey, this work carries the subject's biography to the formation of the triple alliance between Pompey, Caesar, and Crassus. The story is presented in a theatrical style, as the author is writing for a wide audience, not simply for academic specialists.

_____. *Pompey: The Republican Prince*. Columbia: University of Missouri Press, 1982. The second and concluding volume of the author's study of Pompey. Like its predecessor, it is written in dramatic form and is especially strong on Pompey's military conquests as well as on the pageant and spectacle of Rome.

Gruen, Erich S. *The Last Generation of the Roman Republic*. Berkeley: University of California Press, 1974. An important revisionist study. The author's thesis is that there was nothing inevitable about the end of the republic and that there was no predestined decline which led to the triumph of Caesar. Instead, Gruen focuses on the continuity and the traditions of the earlier republic which were still viable during Pompey's era.

Leach, John. *Pompey the Great*. London: Croom Helm, 1978. This brief biography praises Pompey's military abilities and accomplishments. The author also admires Pompey's political talents. Leach predicts that if Pompey had defeated Caesar, he would have more likely pursued the later path of Augustus, as *princeps*, instead of Caesar's more dangerous road to the dictatorship.

Scullard, H. H. *From the Gracchi to Nero*. New York: Methuen and Co., 1959. One of the standard works on the late republic and the principate through Nero, this volume is scholarly but well written and naturally includes considerable information on Pompey and his peers. The author's judgment of Pompey is that he excelled in the battlefield but lacked forcefulness in the political arena, always preferring glory to power.

Seager, Robin. *Pompey: A Political Biography*. Berkeley: University of California Press, 1979. One of many biographies of Pompey, it is both brief and scholarly and concentrates primarily on the political and constitutional issues of the late republic rather than on Pompey's activities and conquests in Spain and in the east. The author maintains a balance between Pompey and Caesar in attempting to understand the motives and actions of both without praising or blaming either.

Syme, Ronald. *The Roman Revolution*. London: Oxford University Press, 1939. The author of this classic work on Roman history written during the twentieth century places the actions and activities of Pompey, Caesar, and Augustus in the wider context of Roman politics, including family, clan, and faction, and not simply the individual deeds and ambitions of a few at the top.

Eugene S. Larson

PORPHYRY
Malchus

Born: c. 234; Tyre, Phoenicia
Died: c. 305; probably Rome
Areas of Achievement: Philosophy and scholarship
Contribution: As the loyal and devoted disciple of Plotinus, who is credited as the founder of Neoplatonic thought, Porphyry undertook to compile and edit his master's philosophical works, the *Enneads*, and to write a unique biography of his teacher. He also wrote extensive commentaries on Greek philosophers and on the allegorical interpretation, or exegesis, of the Homeric myths.

Early Life
Porphyry was born of well-to-do Syrian parents in the Phoenician city of Tyre, where he spent most of his early years. His original name was Malchus, which in the Syro-Phoenician language signifies a king. He first Hellenized his name to Basileus, the Greek word for king. Later, at the suggestion of one of his teachers, Cassius Longinus, he changed it to Porphyry, which alludes to the royal purple color of the regal garments.

Sometime in his teens, Porphyry went to Athens to continue his education. There, he attended the lectures of the erudite critic and philosopher Cassius Longinus. From Longinus, he first learned of and was influenced by the Platonism of the time. At the age of thirty, he went to Rome to become the pupil of Plotinus. He remained with Plotinus for six years, during which time he gained his confidence and respect, enjoying prolonged private discussions with him. He was entrusted by Plotinus with the arrangement and editing of his writings. At the end of his six years with Plotinus, Porphyry suffered an acute depression and was contemplating suicide. Plotinus persuaded him to leave Rome. He traveled to Sicily and remained there for several years. He was in Sicily when Plotinus died in 270.

Life's Work
During his stay in Sicily, Porphyry wrote some of his most important philosophical works. He wrote commentaries on the Platonic and Aristotelian systems of philosophy, none of which survives. One of his works, the *Isagoge* (*The Introduction of Porphyry*, 1938), a commentary on Aristotle's *Categoriae* (fourth century B.C.; *Categories*), served as an introduction to the elementary concepts of Aristotelian logic. The *Isagoge* was translated into Latin and interpreted by the medieval philosopher and theologian Boethius. The work's views on the ontological status of universals, stated in the beginning, exercised great influence on the early medieval controversy between realism and nominalism, as well as being the subject of many commentaries.

In Sicily, Porphyry also composed, in fifteen books, the polemic *Kata Christanōn* (against the Christians), written about 270. It was not a particularly philosophical work but a defensive reaction against the growing popularity of Christianity. This work was often imitated in later years, but it also provoked a number of Christian replies and brought upon Porphyry much slander and verbal abuse.

Very little is known of the remainder of Porphyry's life. He returned to Rome several years after the death of Plotinus, supposedly to take over Plotinus' school. It was in Rome that he edited the works of Plotinus, wrote his biography, and gained a reputation as teacher and public speaker by his expositions of Plotinus' thought. At the advanced age of seventy, circa 304, he married Marcella, the widow of a friend with seven children. As he states in *Pros Markellan* (*Porphyry, the Philosopher, to His Wife, Marcella*, 1896; better known as *Ad Marcellam*), the letter he sent to his wife while on a trip away from home, they married so that he could help to rear and educate her children.

Porphyry was very successful in popularizing the thought of Plotinus and in expounding it in a clear, concise, comprehensible manner. It was the Porphyrian version of Neoplatonism that influenced Western thought, both pagan and Christian, until the ninth century. His views are basically those of his master Plotinus. History does not credit Porphyry with any original views. Still, Porphyry did not follow Plotinus slavishly. The main emphasis of his thought was on the salvation, or ascent, of the individual soul, and he wanted to find a universal way of salvation that could be practiced by all individuals. Thus, he placed a greater emphasis on the moral and ascetic aspects of Neoplatonism, was much more interested in the popular religious practices than his master, and introduced the idea of theurgy into Neoplatonism. Porphyry's views on the ascent of the soul are found in the following works: *Aphormai pros ta noēta* (*Auxiliaries to the Perception of Intelligible Natures*, 1823; better known as *Sententiae*), a disjointed collection of ideas; *Peri apochēs empsychōn* (*On Abstinence from Animal Food*, 1823; better known as *De abstinentia*), a treatise defending vegetarianism; and the *Ad Marcellam*, which deals with the practice of virtue and self-control.

Like Plotinus, Porphyry believed that the soul of an individual is of divine origin and has fallen into matter—the body. While in the body, the soul must purify itself by turning its attention from the bodily and material things to contemplation of the absolute supreme deity—the One, or God. Contemplation, or love of God, cannot be combined with concern for or love of the body. Thus, the soul must purify itself by liberating itself from the bonds of the body. This liberation is not attained by death only but by freeing the soul from its bodily concerns. The soul's purification is achieved through the practice of the virtues. Systematizing Plotinus' treatise on the virtues, Porphyry classifies them into four main types: the political (or civic), the purifying, the contemplative, and the paradigmatic. The political/civic and purifying virtues are acquired on the conscious level, while the soul is still aware of and concerned with matters of the material world, and are preparatory to the other virtues, which are acquired purely through the intellect, when the soul has entered the realm of true being or intellect.

The first and lowest class of virtues, the political/civic, produce moderation and free the soul from excessive bodily concern and indulgences, tempering the individual's behavior toward his fellow humans. Mastery of that leads to the purifying virtues. These virtues completely free the body from all bodily and material attachments and lead the soul toward contemplation of true being. Porphyry believed that the soul's purification and ascent were facilitated by the practice of asceticism. In *De abstinentia*, he stressed the abstinence from animal food, as well as from all external pleasures and desires, and the practice of celibacy. At the third stage of the ascent, the soul is directed toward the world of the intellect, is filled by it and guided by it; the soul has realized its true self, its divinity. Finally, in the fourth and last stage, the soul completely discards all the qualities of a mortal or material nature and its affection for them and becomes pure intellect, living by reason alone and becoming one with the supreme being: God.

Porphyry believed that philosophy was the best means by which the soul could achieve salvation. Yet he realized that the discipline of philosophy as a means of salvation was not possible for all. His interest in and search for a universal way of salvation common to all nations and levels of mankind led him to accept external aids that would lead an individual to that end. He acknowledged the religious practices, rites, and superstitions of the popular polytheism of the time and accepted their gods as symbols, giving their myths an esoteric interpretation. Unlike his master, Plotinus, he upheld the worship of the national gods, claiming that it is important to show respect for the ancient religious practice of a nation.

The early centuries of the Christian era were times of increasing insecurity and anxiety that led individuals to long for salvation, a release from the misery and failure of human life. People turned to the practice of magic and the utterances of the oracles or inspired prophets for answers to their everyday concerns and solutions to their spiritual needs. Astrology and the mystery cults with their purification rites, their enthusiasm and ecstasy, and their rewards of immortality through deification enjoyed immense popularity. The Chaldaean Oracles in particular, composed about A.D. 200 in hexameter verse, were purported to be a divine revelation containing both a theology and a way of salvation communicated by the gods through an entranced medium or prophet. They presented a sure method of salvation through ritual magic, by means of which a divine force could be incarnated in a human being, resulting in a state of prophetic trance. This approach to salvation and union with the divine was known as theurgy. Porphyry acknowledged theurgy as an alternative approach to salvation. Theurgy became one of the major influences in the development of later Neoplatonism from the time of Porphyry to the eleventh century. Porphyry believed that theurgy had some validity and in some way connected the individual with the gods—but only on the lower, or conscious, level. Remaining basically loyal to the philosophy of Plotinus, Porphyry maintained that it is only philosophy that can lead the soul to final union with God.

Summary

Although Porphyry has been considered an unoriginal and uncritical thinker, his contributions to learning are far from insignificant. He had an insatiable intellectual curiosity and thirst for knowledge that led him to delve into and become well-versed in many subjects. In addition to the preservation and intelligible interpretation of Neoplatonism, his main contribution, Porphyry wrote on numerous and varied subjects: rhetoric, grammar, numbers, geometry, music, philology, and philosophy. History credits him with seventy-seven titles. Unfortunately, many of his works are either no longer extant or available only in scanty fragments. Being a detailed scholar, he quotes his authorities by name in his works and thus has preserved numerous fragments of scholarship that otherwise would not have been maintained.

His *Isagoge* became a standard medieval textbook of logic. Of his nonphilosophical works, *Homērika zētēmata* (Homeric questions) is considered a milestone in the history of Homeric scholarship concerning the meaning and exegesis of the Homeric works and reveals his vast knowledge of the epics. The essay on the Homeric cave of the nymphs in the *Odyssey* (c. 800 B.C.) is an excellent example of the type of mystical allegorizing of the Homeric epics that was prevalent at the time and is the oldest surviving interpretive critical essay. In the field of religion, his polemic against the Christians is a study in biblical criticism that was not equaled until modern times, and he anticipated modern scholars in discovering the late date of the biblical Book of Daniel through sound historical scholarship. Although the text was condemned by the Christian church in 448, sufficient fragments remain to show Porphyry's expert knowledge of Hebrew and his wide and accurate knowledge of both Hebrew and Christian Scriptures. Applying the standards of historical criticism to the Scriptures, he denied the authenticity and prophetic character of the Book of Daniel, disputed the authorship of the Pentateuch, and pointed out the discrepancies within the different Gospel narratives and the Epistles of Saint Paul. He is believed to have been the first individual to apply the rules of historical criticism to the Scriptures.

Porphyry stands at the end of the creative phase of Greek philosophical thought. After him, Neoplatonism became more a religion than a philosophy. In an attempt to rescue pagan religion and culture from the overwhelming strength of Christianity, Neoplatonism sacrificed Greek rationalism for occult magico-religious practices which were meant to secure the salvation of the soul.

Bibliography

Lamberton, Robert. *Homer the Theologian.* Berkeley: University of California Press, 1986. Contains an excellent study of Porphyry's work on the Homeric epics. It analyzes in detail the surviving fragments of *Homērika zētēmata* and presents an in-depth study of Porphyry's essay on the cave of the nymphs. An unusual study, because most studies on Porphyry deal only with his philosophical work.

Porphyry. *Life of Plotinus.* Edited and translated by A. H. Armstrong. London: Heinemann, 1966. A major source of information for the life of Porphyry, this work is part of the Loeb Classical Library. Although primarily a biography of Plotinus, it contains many facts of Porphyry's own early life and discusses his association with Plotinus and with Longinus. It also presents an interesting profile of Porphyry's personality.

_____. *On the Cave of the Nymphs.* Translated by Robert Lamberton. Barrytown, N.Y.: Station Hill Press, 1983. An example of Porphyry's method of allegorically interpreting the poetic mythology current at that time. The work is a mystical interpretation of the cave of the nymphs in Homer's *Odyssey.* This work is important not only because it demonstrates the mystical allegorical reading of Homer at that time but also because it is the oldest surviving commentary on a literary text.

_____. *Porphyry, the Philosopher, to His Wife, Marcella.* Translated by Alice Zimmern. London: George Redway, 1896. An old work, but invaluable. It is the only translation of Porphyry's *Ad Marcellam* in English. The lengthy introduction, comprising more than half of the book, includes a summary of the development of Neoplatonism, a review of Porphyry's emphases, and a discussion of the letter to Marcella, showing its religious character and its emphasis on the practice of virtue.

Smith, Andrew. *Porphyry's Place in the Neoplatonic Tradition.* The Hague: Martinus Nijhoff, 1974. A study in post-Plotinian Neoplatonism. It presents an analysis of Porphyry's views of the soul and its means of salvation and compares them with those of Plotinus and Iamblichus, Plotinus' pupil and successor. There is an extensive bibliography of ancient and modern sources and an appendix listing the works of Porphyry relevant to the doctrine of the soul.

Antonía Tripolitis

POSIDONIUS

Born: c. 135 B.C.; Apamea of the Orontes, Syria
Died: c. 51 B.C.; Rome
Area of Achievement: Philosophy
Contribution: Though virtually none of his writings survives, it is clear that Posidonius was one of the most influential thinkers of the ancient world. He made important contributions in the fields of philosophy, history, astronomy, mathematics, natural history, and geography.

Early Life

Posidonius was born in Syria around 135 B.C. Some ancient writers refer to him as "The Apamean," from his birthplace in Syria, which, at that time, was part of the Roman Empire. This vast empire had greatly facilitated the international exchange of knowledge. The dominant philosophy which emerged under the empire was Stoicism, named for the *stoa poikile* (the "painted porch") of the building in Athens where the originators of the doctrine taught. The earliest expression of Stoic philosophy comes from Zeno of Citium (c. 335-261) in Cyprus and Cleanthes of Assos (c. 331-c. 232) in Asia Minor; they were of the Early Stoa, the first period of this doctrine, which lasted from 300 B.C. to the beginning of the second century B.C. The thinkers of the Middle Stoa introduced this philosophy to Roman culture during the second and first centuries B.C. Panaetius of Rhodes (185-109) and his prize student, Posidonius, were the most important figures of the Middle Stoa. Though Stoicism was to remain the dominant philosophy until the second century A.D., Posidonius was the last of the Greek Stoic philosophers.

Posidonius left his home country early in his life and traveled to Athens, where he studied philosophy under Panaetius. After his teacher died in 109, Posidonius traveled for several years throughout North Africa and the western Mediterranean, including Spain, Italy, and Sicily. During these travels he conducted extensive scientific research. He returned to Greece and settled in Rhodes, the largest island in the Dodecanese group, off the southwest coast of Asia Minor. In Rhodes, he was appointed head of the academy which he would later make the center of Stoic philosophy. Posidonius also became involved in local politics and influenced the course of legislation on more than one occasion. In 87, the Rhodians sent him as an envoy to Rome with the charge of appeasing Gaius Marius. The result of this visit was that Posidonius developed an extreme dislike for Marius and later heavily criticized him in his historical writings.

The Stoic philosophy which Posidonius studied at Athens and taught at Rhodes consisted of three domains of concern: logic, physics, and ethics. Stoic logic included the study of grammar but emphasized the formal nature of reasoning, that is, relations between words, not between words and what

Posidonius

they stand for. The relations in rational discourse (as studied by logic) were regarded as reflecting the processes of the cosmos (as studied by physics). The dominant theme of Stoic physical theory was that the universe is an intelligent living being. The physical theory of the Stoics was equivalent to their theology, for the rational totality was equated with God, Zeus, the logos, or the ordering principles of the universe (all these terms being synonymous within their philosophy). In the physical theory of the Stoics, matter is inert or passive and is acted upon by God, the rational active cause. All gradations of being in the universe were regarded as having been formed by this action. According to this philosophy, the action of the rational cause upon the matter is cyclical. Throughout the aeons, each cycle begins with the pure active cause organizing the four fundamental elements and ends with a universal conflagration in which all created matter is consumed and the totality reverts to its purified state. Stoic ethical doctrines were perhaps the most famous element of their philosophy and were connected to their cosmological conceptions.

The basic precept of the Stoic ethical system was to live according to the order of the universe. The ultimate goal of ethical action was to achieve self-sufficiency, the only guarantee of happiness. Happiness was regarded as possible only through that which was entirely within the individual's control, and this state was to be achieved through the practice of the virtues. The most important of the virtues were wisdom, courage, justice, and self-control. The Stoics emphasized two ways of acquiring the virtues: the imitation of exemplary lives and the study of ethics and physics.

It was in the context of these broad doctrines that Posidonius developed his conceptions of man and the universe. Though only a few fragments of Posidonius' writings have survived, he is mentioned by more than sixty ancient writers, and it is through their comments that scholars have been able to reconstruct his philosophy. He is mentioned primarily in the works of Cicero, Strabo, Seneca, and Galen.

Posidonius differed from the Stoic tradition in which he was educated in his concern with empirically oriented scientific investigations. He did, however, adhere to the Stoic division of philosophy into the branches of logic (or dialectics), ethics, and physics. His teacher, Panaetius, admired Plato, and it was with the development of Posidonius' philosophy that the influence of Plato upon Stoicism truly began. Posidonius also emphasized his agreement with the doctrines of Pythagoras, and, in general, he argued for the reconciliation of all opposing philosophies.

Life's Work

While developing his own version of Stoic philosophy at his academy in Rhodes, Posidonius became quite famous. In 78, the famous Roman orator Cicero attended his school. In fact, Cicero requested of Posidonius that he edit his account (in Greek) of the conspiracy of Catiline. Posidonius declined the request.

Posidonius' most famous visitor was the Roman general Pompey the Great, who visited Posidonius' school on two different occasions in order to attend lectures: in 72, when Pompey returned from the eastern part of the empire after action in the Mithradatic War, and again five years later, after a victorious campaign against pirates in the Mediterranean Sea. As a gesture of respect for the great philosopher, Pompey ordered his officers to lower their fasces (bundles of rods with axes in them, which were used as scepters by Roman leaders) at the door of Posidonius' school. Posidonius greatly admired Pompey and added an appendix to his *Histories*, which was devoted exclusively to Pompey's campaigns in the East.

Posidonius' history of the world began with the year 146 B.C. (the point at which the famous history of Polybius ended) and continued up to the dictatorship of Lucius Cornelius Sulla around 88 B.C. Virtually none of this work has survived, but its influence was tremendous, both at the theoretical level (that is, in the conception of history) and in terms of the sheer mass of factual information which the work contained. All the following historians were influenced by it: Sallust, Julius Caesar, Cornelius Tacitus, Plutarch, Timagenes, Pompeius Trogus, and Diodorus Siculus. Posidonius' *Histories* was noteworthy for including the histories of the Eastern and Western peoples with whom the Romans had come into contact, such as the Germans and the Gauls. His study of primitive cultures led him to hypothesize that these cultures represented the original state of the more advanced cultures. The work was written from a standpoint which favored the nobility and opposed the Gracchi and the equestrian party. It was also opposed to the independent Greeks, who were supported by Mithradates. In short, the work was strongly pro-Roman, and in it Posidonius attempted to show that Roman imperialism embodied the commonwealth of all mankind and ultimately reflected the commonwealth of God. To this latter commonwealth only those statesmen and philosophers who had lived worthy lives were to be admitted after their stay on earth. In addition, Posidonius argued that lesser civilizations should accept and even welcome Roman domination for the sake of their own self-betterment. This theory had a tremendous influence upon Cicero and provided the foundations for the eventual development of the doctrine of natural law.

Posidonius' conception of the history of the human race was intimately linked to his conceptions of ethics. Politics and ethics were fused within his system, since political virtue consisted in attempting to bring back the natural condition of humanity. In this condition, the philosopher-statesman apprehends the world of God (from which morality is derived) and conveys this vision to the rest of humanity living solely in the material world. Morality and religion were fused in Posidonius' view, since any moral or political duty was also a religious duty. In a work entitled *On Duty*, Posidonius argued that by adhering to duty, the philosopher-statesman gained knowledge of the spiritual world and freedom and was prepared for the superior forms of existence after death. The highest state to be achieved by a man in this life was regarded by Posidonius as contemplation of the truth and order of the universe (without distraction by the promptings of the irrational part of the soul). Posidonius parted with Stoic orthodoxy on the connection between virtue and happiness, however, and argued that the former was not a sufficient condition for the latter and that external bodily goods were also needed to achieve happiness.

Posidonius also made modifications of Stoic psychological doctrines. The most significant of these was his reaffirmation, in *On the Soul*, of the division of the soul into rational and irrational parts (the latter being the source of the emotions and appetites). Stoic tradition held to the essential unity of the soul. Posidonius claimed, in *On Emotion*, that the emotions of the irrational part of the soul have two distinct origins: the body, and judgments of good and evil. He took as evidence for this view the fact that animals, which are irrational creatures, experience emotion. This doctrine also parted from the standard Stoic conception of emotion as based solely on false judgments about good and evil. In this theory, Posidonius drew a connection between the union of the soul and the body and the external influences upon that union. He argued that some conditions of the human being are predominantly bodily, whereas others are predominantly spiritual or mental. Some influences pass from the body to the soul and others pass from the soul to the body. He based a system of character on the idea that permanent modifications of character can be caused by certain bodily organizations.

More fundamental aspects of Posidonius' psychology are contained in his metaphysical system, in which he followed the standard Stoic conception of two fundamental principles governing the universe: the passive principle (matter) and the active principle (God). God, for Posidonius, did not create the human soul, though the soul was believed to be composed of the same stuff out of which the heavenly bodies are composed. As a result, upon the death of the body the soul "escapes" and returns to the heavens. In addition, for Posidonius, God was not the creator of matter, and matter was endowed with its own form and quality. The divine principle merely shaped and modeled this matter (that is, God does not endow matter with form). As part of this cosmology, Posidonius posited, in *On Heroes and Daemones*, the existence of beings which were intermediary between God and man. These beings were regarded as immortal and were revealed to mortals in visions, divinations, and oracles. Posidonius also regarded the gap between reason and matter as bridged by mathematical forms. Of all the Stoics, only Posidonius was a realist with regard to mathematical entities. In *On the Void*, he argued that the vacuum beyond the universe was not infinite (a standard Stoic conception) but only large enough to allow for the periodic dissolution of the universe. He also argued that the end of the universe would occur not by fire but by this dissolution.

Among the scientific achievements of Posidonius which were related to his metaphysics was his construction of a model of the celestial system. This planetarium allowed the apparent motions of the sun, moon, and planets around the earth to be exhibited. An important inference he made concerning astronomy, in a work entitled *On the Sun*, was that the sun is larger than the earth because the shadow cast by the earth is conical. He rejected the heliocentric conception of the solar system in favor of a geocentric conception. He also succeeded in calculating the distance between the earth and the sun at 502 million stadia (one stadium equals approximately six hundred feet). The diameter of the sun he calculated at four million stadia, and the circumference of the earth at 180,000 stadia, figures that were generally accepted by thinkers in his day. Posidonius also considered the moon to be larger than the earth and to be composed of matter that is transparent. Because of the moon's size, light does not pass through it during eclipses. In another work on astronomy, *On Astronomical Phenomena*, Posidonius argued that the Milky Way is composed of igneous material and is intended to warm those parts of the universe which the sun cannot warm. This view was also widely accepted by other thinkers. He had collected considerable geographical data on his various travels, and in *On the Ocean* he charted the currents of the ocean and pointed out the connection between the tides and the moons.

In about 51 B.C., Posidonius left Rhodes on another trip to Rome, where he died soon after arriving. Upon his death, the school in Rhodes was taken over by his grandson Jason.

Summary

Posidonius had an extremely influential personality—he was reported to have a good sense of humor and was known as a man of dignity. He also developed a reputation as the most learned man in the world and was especially known for his dialectical skills, shrewd powers of observation, and love of poetry. Though he was extremely influential in his own time and for two centuries afterward, his writings disappeared at some point and he is not mentioned after the second century A.D. Virtually all the important Roman philosophers and historians were influenced by Posidonius. His disciples and students included Phanias, Asclepiodotus, C. Velleins, C. Cotta, Q. Lucilius Balbus, and perhaps Marcus Junius Brutus. His influence on thought in the ancient world has been compared to that of Aristotle. He was the last compiler of the Greco-Roman heritage, furthered the development of Greek rationalism, and was influential in the development of Neoplatonism. Nevertheless from the Renaissance through the nineteenth century, Posidonius was considered to be only a minor figure in the history of Stoicism. It was not until the beginning of the twentieth century that his influence was attested and classicists began to discover references to Posidonius in many of the writers of his time.

Bibliography
Dobson, J. F. "The Posidonius Myth." *Classical Quarterly* 12 (1918): 179-191. Attacks the source criticism method of assessing Posidonius' influence, suggesting that Posidonius' achievements have been exaggerated.
Edelstein, Ludwig. "The Philosophical System of Posidonius." *American Journal of Philology* 57 (1936): 286-325. Reconstructs the philosophical system of Posidonius from the existing fragments. Written by the foremost authority on Posidonius of the twentieth century.
Kidd, I. G. "Posidonius on Emotions." In *Problems in Stoicism*, edited by A. A. Long. London: Athlone Press, 1971. Contains a detailed analysis of Posidonius' modification of the standard Stoic conception of the emotions.
Mattingly, John Robert. "Cosmogony and Stereometry in Posidonian Physics." *Osiris* 3 (1937): 558-583. Contains an extensive explication of the cosmological system developed by Posidonius.
Rist, John Michael. *Stoic Philosophy*. London: Cambridge University Press, 1969. Contains a chapter devoted to the ethical system of Posidonius.
Solmsen, Friedrich. *Cleanthes or Posidonius? The Basis of Stoic Physics*. Amsterdam, Netherlands: Noord-Hollandsche Uitg. Mij., 1961. The best available discussion of the relative influence of Cleanthes and Posidonius on developments in Stoic thought concerning science and the relation between science and the cosmos.

Mark Pestana

PRAXITELES

Born: c. 390 B.C.; Athens, Greece
Died: c. 330 B.C.; place unknown
Area of Achievement: Art
Contribution: The subtle expression of personal emotions, such as tenderness and laziness, through marble statuary is the trademark of Praxiteles. His most famous work, the *Aphrodite of Knidos*, established Western civilization's standard of perfection in the female figure.

Early Life

Although very little is known of his early life, Praxiteles came from a long line of Greek sculptors. His grandfather and father were both sculptors, as were his two sons and perhaps a nephew. At least seven of the line were also named Praxiteles.

Praxiteles' father was the Athenian sculptor Kephisodotos (sometimes spelled Cephisodotus), whose most famous sculpture is entitled *Peace and Wealth*. The original statue, which was probably erected soon after Athens' victory over Sparta in 375 B.C., depicts a mother, the goddess Peace, fondly holding her infant son, Wealth. The tenderness of the mother and the playfulness of the child display a marked departure from earlier Greek statues, which expressed such public virutes as courage and honor. Also, the subject, a family scene, is very different from the usual subjects of Olympian gods and heroic humans. Praxiteles carried on and far surpassed the subtler, intimate tradition established by his father.

In addition to *Peace and Wealth*, Kephisodotos carved another statue, *Hermes Carrying the Infant Dionysus*, which had a more direct effect on the son. Kephisodotos' *Hermes* and Praxiteles' *Hermes* share both subject matter and arrangement. Although the original is lost, the fact that there are several Roman copies attests the popularity of Kephisodotos' statue. On the other hand, most historians agree that the *Hermes* found in the Olympia excavations is indeed the original work of the son. Fortunately, the condition of the statue is quite good, as it is missing only the right forearm and the two legs below the knee. Since the *Hermes* is the most muscular of Praxiteles' known statues, it is probably an early work. The smooth, sensuous young men appear to belong to a later period, during which Praxiteles was sculpting his famous female figures.

No statues of Praxiteles can be dated with absolute certainty, but his major works were carved between about 370 and 330. Early, dated works include portions of the *Altar of Artemis* at Ephesus, which was begun around 356, and the *Artemis at Brauron*, around 346.

Life's Work

Although ancient writers mention almost sixty works by Praxiteles, the surviving originals include only three heads and the major portion of one statue, the aforementioned *Hermes*. The *Hermes* was found on May 8, 1877, at the temple of Hera at Olympia. In Greek legend, Hermes, the messenger of the gods, is charged with taking young Dionysus back to the nymphs of Crete. Dionysus is a great embarrassment to Zeus, as the baby is the result of Zeus's indiscretion with a human woman. In banishing Dionysus to Crete, Zeus hopes to escape the jealousy of his wife, Hera. In Praxiteles' conception, the statue is a masterpiece of psychological complexity. Hermes, gazing tenderly at the young god, is clearly in no hurry to leave Olympus. Leaning lightly against a tree, he has placed the babe in his left arm and amuses himself by dangling in his right hand something, probably a bunch of grapes, for Dionysus. The fact that the infant Dionysus, who is eagerly grabbing at the grapes, will grow up to be the god of wine and intoxication is evidence of Praxiteles' urbane sense of humor.

Another statue which illustrates the Praxitelean sense of humor is the *Apollo Sauroctonos*, or *Lizard Slayer*. Here Praxiteles makes fun of the Greek legend in which the fierce young sun god Apollo slays Pythus, a fire-breathing dragon, in order to win control of Delphi. Leaning dreamily against a tree trunk and holding an arrow in his right hand, Praxiteles' Apollo seems to have barely enough energy to swat an everyday lizard which is climbing up the trunk. While the original bronze statue is lost, reproductions occur on the coins of several city-states and in several Roman replicas, notably a marble statue in the Louvre and one in the Vatican.

Related to the *Lizard Slayer* in stance is the *Satyr*. Both statues bear Praxiteles' personal stamp. In fifth century statuary, satyrs were savage half-goat, half-man beasts with large tails and devilish eyes. Praxiteles' satyr is instead a strong and active youth with pointed ears and a small stub of a tail. There is in his face, however, a strong sensual expression which suggests that some of the old animal instinct still lingers.

The original *Satyr* of Praxiteles, which stood in a temple of Dionysus at Athens, was a favorite collector's piece among the Romans, as more than seventy copies still exist. One of the best is the copy in the Capitol Museum in Rome. It is this statue that Nathaniel Hawthorne saw in 1858 and that inspired him to write his novel *The Marble Faun* (1860). Hawthorne, intrigued by the possibility of a real man who actually embodied all the characteristics he saw in the faun or satyr, created a character whose combination of total innocence and animalistic instincts made him unprepared to exist in the real world. The Louvre has a fragmentary version of the *Satyr*, but the execution of that statue is generally considered to be quite good. A few writers have theorized that it might be the original. Although the *Satyr* in the Capitol is complete, it is clearly a Roman copy.

Evidence that the *Satyr* was one of Praxiteles' personal favorites is related by the ancient historian Pausanias. According to the story, Phryne, Praxiteles' mistress, asked for the most beautiful of the sculptor's works. Praxiteles agreed, but he refused to say which one of his works he thought the most beautiful. Phryne secretly arranged for one of her slaves to run in and declare that Praxiteles' studio was on fire. On hearing the news, Praxiteles ran for the door, claiming that all of his labor was lost if the flames had taken the *Satyr* and *Eros*.

Phryne chose the *Eros*, god of love, and gave it to her native town of Thespiae in Boeotia. This statue made Thespiae famous. Unfortunately, the very popularity of the statue may have led to its destruction. Pausanias explains that the Roman emperor Gaius (Caligula) took it, but when Claudius assumed power, he restored the sacred statue to Thespiae. Then the Emperor Nero took it away a second time. Pausanias believes that the *Eros* eventually perished by fire in Rome. On the other hand, some art historians theorize that the *Eros* of Thespiae may survive in a headless statue which was excavated from the Palatine in Rome and is now held in the Louvre. Others have speculated that a torso in the Museum of Parma may, in fact, be the original.

What is certain is that the *Eros* once more illustrates Praxiteles' distinctive style. As Greek legend developed over the centuries, the character of Eros grew younger. In his *Theogony* (c. 700 B.C.), Hesiod describes Eros as one of the oldest gods. In that version, Eros comes into existence before Aphrodite and even accompanies her at her birth from the sea to Mount Olympus. After Praxiteles, third century artists would conceive of Eros as the child of, rather than the companion to, Aphrodite. Eventually, the child becomes a mischievous, winged baby, the Cupid on a Valentine's Day card. In the Praxitelean conception, Eros stands between those surface interpretations. He is a delicate, dreamy youth, symbolizing the power of love to capture the soul, a fitting gift from the artist to his mistress.

All the works discussed have been statues depicting male figures. Yet it is Praxiteles' conception of the female form for which he is best known and most admired. His most celebrated work was the *Aphrodite of Knidos*, for which Phryne was the model. About 360, the city of Kos commissioned the sculptor to carve an *Aphrodite*, but the citizens were scandalized when they found that their statue of Aphrodite was nude. Praxiteles then made a clothed goddess of love, but the city of Knidos (sometimes spelled Knidus or Cnidus) was delighted to buy the nude *Aphrodite*. It was an enormously popular statue. Tourists came from all over the Mediterranean to see the work of Parian marble, and the elder Pliny pronounced it the finest statue yet made in Greece. King Nicomedes of Bithynia offered to buy the statue and in return excuse the city's huge public debt, but the Knidians refused. A number of ancient poets composed verses honoring the statue, and legend has it that men were crazed with desire upon viewing it.

The statue, which is thought to have been the first free-standing female nude, was put in an open shrine so that the goddess could be seen and admired from all sides. *Aphrodite* stands in a graceful pose, one hand held in front of her, the other grasping her drapery which falls on a water jar. The goddess is represented at the moment that she steps into her bath. Her gaze is turned to the left, supposedly to see an intruder. Only her right hand makes any effort to cover up and the slight smile displays a hint of welcome.

Reproductions of the *Aphrodite* are found on Roman coins of Knidos as well as in small, practically complete statuettes. The best replicas of the head are those in the Louvre and in Toulouse. Full-sized Roman copies exist in the Vatican, Brussels, and Munich museums, the most-often photographed and reprinted one being the Vatican version.

As a result of the *Aphrodite of Knidos* and other sculptures of Aphrodite by Praxiteles, the nude female figure became one of the most common forms of statuary, but the goddess was increasingly portrayed as a mortal. One example is the statue entitled *Venus of Medici*, which may have been carved by Kephisodotos and Timarchos, the sons of Praxiteles, but here the magnificent Praxitelean ideal woman has been transformed into a mere coquette.

Summary

Coming from a long line of sculptors, Praxiteles stands at the climax of a family of distinguished artists. Inspired by his father's softer, subtler treatment of subjects that the fifth century artists had treated with monumental but impersonal dignity, Praxiteles imbued statues with psychological complexities which give his work its universal appeal. The fleet-footed Hermes pauses for a moment of tenderness, the infant Dionysus turns greedy, the mature Eros becomes a sensual young man, and the heroic Apollo loses his fighting spirit so that he seems to lack the energy even to engage in lizard slaying, a popular Mediterranean boy's sport.

The crowning achievement of Praxiteles' work is his series of Aphrodites, especially the famous nude which he sold to the Knidians. The fifth century sculptors tended to carve nude males and clothed females. For example, the *Peace* by Kephisodotos is weighted down with heavy drapery. Praxiteles' female nude created a sensation and a whole new style of artistic expression. The intricately worked hair, the finely chiseled facial features with their play of emotions, and the perfectly proportioned body of the *Aphrodite of Knidos* set the standard for female beauty. Although Praxiteles did not invent the concept of a statue's standing free in order to be seen in a three-dimensional space, the success of the *Aphrodite*'s backside (her dimpled buttocks were especially admired) inspired other artists to carve free-standing nude females also.

Another Praxitelean innovation, although certainly not an invention, was the expanded employment of the S-curve or *contrapposto* for the body outline, which allows for a more natural, animated stance. The S-curve allows the *Apollo Sauroktonos* to lean casually against his tree trunk and the *Hermes* to hold the babe in one arm while he raises the other arm over his head.

Also, the surface of Praxitelean statues was technically outstanding. Ancient writers who saw the original, painted statues remarked that the body surfaces were smoothly polished and that the modeling of the hair was particularly realistic. Unfortunately, the *Hermes* is the only fairly complete work that can be taken to be an original, and many historians and archaeologists dispute even that attribution. It is so far superior to any of the Roman copies of other works by Praxiteles that the more admired original statues must have been exquisite indeed.

The many facets of Praxiteles' work meant that his work was difficult to copy accurately. While many contemporaries and the sculptors of the third and second centuries were able to capture the outward forms of the statues, they were unable to evoke the complex human emotions. The effect of the Praxitelean style in the hands of inferior artists seems to be merely mannered and elegant.

Bibliography
Furtwängler, Adolf. *Masterpieces of Greek Sculpture.* Edited by A. L. N. Oikonomides. Chicago: Argonaut, 1964. Takes a close look at the original monuments in order to reevaluate generally held theories of attribution and dating.
Kjellberg, Ernst, and Gösta Säflund. *Greek and Roman Art: 3000 B.C. to A.D. 550.* Translated by Peter Fraser. New York: Thomas Y. Crowell, 1970. Catalogs all the major examples of the Greek and Roman art forms. Dates, sizes, and describes included works.
Paris, Pierre. *Manual of Ancient Sculpture.* Edited by Jane E. Harrison. New Rochelle, N.Y.: Aristide D. Caratzas, 1984. Chapter on Scopas and Praxiteles discusses the works of both sculptors at length. Of particular interest is a reproduction of the *Aphrodite of Knidos* seen on a Knidian coin.
Pollitt, J. J. *Art and Experience in Classical Greece.* Cambridge: Cambridge University Press, 1972. Focuses on the period between c. 480 and 323 B.C. and seeks to integrate art styles with historical experience. Particularly useful in describing the emotional states depicted in various statues by Praxiteles.
Richter, Gisela. *A Handbook of Greek Art.* London: Phaidon, 1965. For many years curator of Greek and Roman art in the Metropolitan Museum in New York, Richter presents one of the most authoritative accounts of Greek architecture and sculpture. Traces the historical evolution of Greek sculpture and adds biographical information wherever possible. Includes extensive bibliography and lucid chronology.
_____. *The Sculpture and Sculptors of the Greeks.* Rev. ed. New Haven, Conn.: Yale University Press, 1950. Contains a consecutive, chrono-

logical study of the human figure, drapery, and composition. Includes extensive footnotes and bibliography.

Waldenstein, Charles. "Praxiteles and the Hermes with the Infant Dionysus." In *The Art of Pheidias*. Cambridge: Cambridge University Press, 1885. Published only seven years after the discovery of the *Hermes*, this article contains an in-depth study of the state of the statue when it was first excavated, its importance to the Greeks for whom it was carved, and its relation to other sculptors' versions of the messenger god.

Sandra Hanby Harris

PRISCIAN

Born: Second half of the fifth century A.D.; Caesarea, Mauretania, Africa
Died: First half of the sixth century A.D.; Constantinople
Areas of Achievement: Language and linguistics
Contribution: Priscian's *Institutiones grammaticae* preserved and abridged several earlier works of classical Latin grammar in a form so useful that it was copied and annotated and became the standard work in its genre until the end of the Middle Ages.

Early Life

Few details of Priscian's life are known. He was a native of the Vandal kingdom in North Africa and at some time before A.D. 503 moved his residence to Constantinople, capital of the Eastern half of the Roman Empire. His presence in Constantinople is attested by Cassiodorus (c. 490-c. 585), who asserts that in his own time Priscian was a teacher of Latin grammar there. From Priscian's words in his *De laude imperatoris Anastasii* (panegyric to Emperor Anastasius) it is clear that he disliked barbarians, such as the Ostrogoths, who ruled Italy from about 489 to 568: "My hope is that both Romes may be obedient to you [Anastasius] alone."

It is possible that the Symmachus to whom Priscian dedicated three minor works was the same man who was put to death with his son-in-law Boethius for plotting against Theodoric the Ostrogoth in 524; if so, that would provide additional motivation for Priscian's political leanings and distaste for the Goths. Judging from the fact that in his panegyric Priscian makes no mention of Anastasius' war against the Persians from 503 to 505, it is likely that he wrote it before the war. In addition, since his chief book on grammar was revised or copied by his pupil, Theodorus, "in the consulship of Olybrius" in 526, it is possible that Priscian was dead by that year. Theodorus' copy is the original of all the extant manuscripts of Priscian's *Institutiones grammaticae* (526; grammatical foundations), in eighteen books.

Life's Work

Eleven writings are attributed to Priscian. Their order of composition is not known and only estimates of their dates can be made. Priscian's most important work is clearly his *Institutiones grammaticae*. He certainly completed this large work, formatted in two volumes today, before 526, when it was copied by Theodorus. In its dedication, to one "Julianus, consul and patrician," Priscian states that he has translated from the Greek treatises of Apollonius Dyscolus and his son Herodian (Aelius Herodianus). Priscian chose his sources well, for Apollonius has been called "the father of scientific grammar," and Herodian continued his father's work. They lived in Alexandria and Rome serving the emperors Antoninus Pius and Marcus Aurelius,

Priscian

respectively. Priscian follows Apollonius closely in his treatment of pronouns, adverbs, conjunctions, and syntax, as can be determined from the extant parts of the latter's work. Apollonius' most original contribution to grammatical studies was in the area of syntax. Nevertheless, Priscian believed his own book to be brief compared to the "spacious scrolls" of Apollonius or the "sea" of Herodian. Indeed, the success of Priscian's *Institutiones grammaticae* may derive from its relative brevity.

A valuable feature in Priscian's grammatical work is his inclusion of copious quotations from both Greek and Latin authors to exemplify particular grammatical principles. Thus he preserved much that would otherwise have been lost: precious passages of Quintus Ennius, Marcus Pacuvius, Accius, Cato the Censor, and Marcus Terentius Varro. Most often quoted are Cicero and Sallust, but other Latin writers such as Plautus, Terence, Vergil, Horace, Ovid, Lucan, Statius, Persius, and Juvenal also appear. Priscian's Greek examples come chiefly from Homer, Plato, Isocrates, and Demosthenes. In the first sixteen books of the *Institutiones grammaticae*, often called *Priscianus major* (the great Priscian), he concentrates on grammar itself; the last two books, *Priscianus minor* (the little Priscian), are devoted to syntax. Here Priscian was more original because there existed fewer works on syntax from which to borrow. In one manuscript, the last two books are referred to as a distinct book called *De constructione* (on constructions). A table of contents would include book 1, on the letters and their sounds; book 2, on syllables, words, sentences, and nouns; book 3, on comparatives, superlatives, and diminutives; book 4, on interrelated forms such as verbals and participles used as nouns; book 5, on the gender, number, and case of nouns; book 6, on the endings of the nominative case and the formation of the genitive case; book 7, on the remaining cases—dative, accusative, and ablative; books 8, 9, and 10, on verbs—the general rules for their conjugations and especially the formation of the perfect tense of the four conjugations; books 11 through 16, each devoted to one of the parts of speech—participles, pronouns, prepositions, adverbs, interjections, and conjunctions; and books 17 and 18, on syntax (word order, construction of sentences).

During the Middle Ages, each branch of the trivium (grammar, logic, and rhetoric) and quadrivium (arithmetic, geometry, astronomy, and music) had its own "classic" textbook. For grammar, two treatises of Aelius Donatus (mid-fourth century) known as the *Ars minor* and *Ars maior* (elementary and advanced grammar), which formed the *Ars grammatica*, were used in elementary schools. The more advanced *Institutiones grammaticae* of Priscian served as the classic text in the universities. His minor works include a treatise on the initial lines of the twelve books of Vergil's *Aeneid* (c. 29-19 B.C.), important as an illustration of the exercises demanded of schoolchildren in Priscian's day, and treatises on accents, on the declensions of nouns, and on the meters of Terence (dedicated to Symmachus). Priscian wrote a prose treatise on the symbols used to denote numbers and on weights and measures (*De figuris et nominibus numerorum, et de normis et ponderibus*), also dedicated to Symmachus. In addition, he wrote a poem devoted entirely to weights and measures (*De ponderibus et mensuris carmina*), which is incomplete. Of the extant 162 lines, fifty-five concern weights, the rest the standards of measure for fruits and liquids.

His free translation of the *Progymnasmata* (preparatory rhetorical exercises, or, first steps in rhetoric), written by the Greek Hermogenes of Tarsus in the second century A.D., is significant because with it Priscian supplemented his own grammar and brought to the Latin Middle Ages the elements of Greek rhetorical theory. His translation, *Praeexercitamina rhetorica*, comprised the last section of Hermogenes' major work on rhetoric. The section *De laude* (on panegyrics) contains examples and suggestions for extolling almost anything, from the sport of hunting to horses, doves, and trees. Priscian's use of mythological material ignores the intellectual struggle then dividing Christianity and paganism. This work too was dedicated to Symmachus.

The panegyric in honor of Emperor Anastasius has been dated about 503. It contains 334 iambic and hexameter lines. In about A.D. 100 the panegyric, or praise for a ruler, had been introduced into rhetoric as a genre separate from persuasive and judicial oratory. Priscian's panegyric may have served as his classroom model. Priscian's poem *De sideribus* (on the stars) contains about two hundred lines and is a simple and dry naming of stars and planets. He also produced a poetic free translation of the *Oikumenes periegesis* (description of the earth) by Dionysius, a geographer of the early Roman Empire. Priscian's version, called *De situ* or *Descriptio orbis terrarum*, was likely intended for the instruction of pupils.

Summary

The list of scholars throughout the Middle Ages who studied, quoted, or copied Priscian reads like a Who's Who of medieval intellectual history. Indeed, the modern reader may find it difficult to understand the durability of Priscian's influence over the field of grammatical studies. It should be remembered that, while language is constantly changing, grammar, the underlying structure of language, changes slowly. In addition, reverence for the correctness of past usage kept Priscian's book from early obsolescence.

Priscian was one of the sources used by his younger contemporary Flavius Magnus Aurelius in the latter's *De orthographia* (on spelling). The scholars Aldhelm (639-709) and Bede (673-735) quoted Priscian, indicating that a manuscript of the *Institutiones grammaticae* had reached England by their day. Alcuin (735-804) names Priscian among the authors available in the York library, and the substance of his second dialogue on grammar is borrowed from Priscian. As headmaster of Charlemagne's Palace School at

Aachen, Alcuin relied on Priscian among the other stock authors, including Donatus, Cassiodorus, Bede, Saint Isidore of Seville, and Phocas. Alcuin's pupil Rabanus Maurus (c. 776-856) made a copy of Priscian's *Institutiones grammaticae* and introduced it into Germany at the monastery of Fulda, whose library he founded. Servatus Lupus of Ferrieres, Rabanus' pupil, quoted frequently from Priscian in his letters on literary and grammatical matters. His own disciple Remigius wrote commentaries on Priscian while teaching at Auxerre, Rheims, and Paris. Meanwhile, Priscian's work was favored among Irish scholars in monastic centers, where an interest in Greek was kept alive. Sedulius Scottus (fl. c. 848-c. 860) and possibly John Scotus Erigena wrote commentaries on Priscian's grammatical foundations. At least three (of more than one thousand extant) of Priscian's manuscripts are written in the Irish minuscule script of the ninth century, including that which came to Saint Gall around 860.

Between the times of Alcuin and Peter Abelard (1079-1142), Donatus and Priscian continued to be the principal grammar authorities followed by scholars. From the twelfth century on, however, the emphasis on theology, philosophy, and natural history at the University of Paris brought about significant changes, and literature and grammar were reduced in importance. The new authorities for grammar were the scholars at that university who continued to produce commentaries on or abridgments of Priscian. As late as 1141, Theodoric, chancellor of the school at Chartres, wrote a treatise on the seven liberal arts, liberally quoting Donatus and Priscian for his section on grammar.

It was during the thirteenth century that Priscian gradually lost the place of honor to his commentators, Petrus Helius, professor at Paris about 1142, and Robert Kilwardby, Archbishop of Canterbury from 1272 to 1279. In that period of changing curricula, some scholars regretted the neglect of the study of authors such as Homer, Claudian, Persius, Donatus, and Priscian. One such person was John of Garland, an English scholar at Paris, who wrote fourteen books on Latin grammar. Another was Henri d'Andeli, a master at Rouen whose poem *The Battle of the Seven Arts* (1259) depicts a war between the authors on the side of grammar and those defending logic (Plato and Aristotle). In one episode, Priscian is made to hold his own in combat with Aristotle. In the fourteenth century, Priscian was superseded by the modern compilations of Alexander de Villa Dei, author of a hexameter poem on syntax, grammar, and the figures of speech, called *Doctrinale puerorum* (c. late twelfth century), which drew largely from Priscian. Another who was preferred to Priscian was Evrard of Béthune (fl. c. 1212), who also presented a grammar, called *Graecismus* (c. late twelfth century), in verse format. Presumably, their use of verse as a memory aid was a key to their success.

Besides the rise of logic and other arts, which started to claim precedence over grammar in the schools, another reason must be noted for the demise of grammar and the eclipse of Priscian. Throughout the Middle Ages, Latin was still a living language in the Church and the schools, undergoing the dynamic changes common to living languages. New vocabulary, however, included technical terms and the names of things unknown to antiquity. As Latin departed more and more from classical Latin, the huge and precise grammatical foundations of Priscian became less useful. On the southwest doorway of Chartres Cathedral, which is decorated with personifications of the seven arts and their leading representatives, Grammar and Priscian are found together. The two are also identified in the representation of the Seven Earthly Sciences in the chapter house of Santa Maria Novella Church in Florence. The Renaissance thus paid its homage to Priscian, greatest of all Latin grammarians.

Bibliography
Cameron, A. D. E. "Priscian's *De laude Anastasii.*" *Greek, Roman, and Byzantine Studies* 15 (1974). Discussion of the date and circumstances of Priscian's panegyric to Emperor Anastasius. Concludes that the events not mentioned in the work provide evidence that it must have been written before 503.
Curtius, Ernst R. *European Literature and the Latin Middle Ages*. Translated by Willard R. Trask. New York: Harper and Row, Publishers, 1963. A modest treatment of Priscian himself, the volume provides excellent information on Priscian's later influence.
Keil, Heinrich, ed. *Grammatici Latini*. 7 vols. Leipzig, Germany: Teubner, 1855-1860. Hard to find, but an excellent Latin text of Priscian's *Institutiones grammaticae*. English translations of Priscian's works are essentially nonexistent.
Sandys, John Edwin. *A History of Classical Scholarship*. Vol. 1, *From the 6th Century B.C. to the End of the Middle Ages*. Cambridge: Cambridge University Press, 1903. Encyclopedic coverage of grammatical writing from Greece and Rome through Priscian to the fourteenth century. Shows Priscian's place in the large picture essentially as summarized in this biography.
Wilson, Henry A. "Priscianus Caesariensis (Priscian of Caesarea)." In *A Dictionary of Christian Biography, Literature, Sects, and Doctrines*, edited by William Smith, vol. 4. New York: Kraus Reprint Co., 1967. The most thorough and generally available treatment of Priscian and his writings. Reprinted from the original edition of 1840.

Daniel C. Scavone

PRISCILLIAN

Born: c. 340; Spain
Died: 385; Trier
Area of Achievement: Religion
Contribution: Priscillian provides an example not only of the popularity of ascetic practices in the Christian church but also of what can happen when such activities are carried to extremes and challenge established Church beliefs and lines of authority.

Early Life

The latter half of the fourth century was a great age of Christian ascetics. These individuals withdrew from the secular world and practiced a life of fasting, deprivation, nightly vigils, and spiritual contemplation. Churchmen such as Saint Antony in Egypt, Saint Martin of Tours in Gaul, Saint Jerome in Italy and Palestine, and many others popularized this style of asceticism. In theory, these practices were merely part of the ideal Christian life. Groups of ascetics could become very influential; their members often were chosen as bishops. Extreme forms of ascetism, however, especially those which rejected established church practices and teachings, were looked upon with less favor.

Priscillian was a well-educated Spanish nobleman said to have been versed in secular and Christian literature as well as in astrology and the occult. He was possessed of a keen intellect and was an eloquent speaker. After his conversion to Christianity, he, like many others of his day, adopted an ascetic life. He also claimed to have prophetic powers. He became a wandering lay preacher and assumed the title "doctor." During the 370's, he began to teach his own peculiar brand of Christianity.

Life's Work

Insight into just what Priscillian's teachings were can be gained not only from his contemporary detractors but also from eleven treatises which were first published in 1889. Although only a few of them may have been written by Priscillian himself, or by his supporter Instantius, they do reflect Priscillian's teachings. The Priscillianists were very ascetic, recommending vegetarianism and abstinence from wine. On Sundays, they fasted. They generally walked barefoot. They also were opposed to marriage and to other aspects of the organized Church. They preferred, for example, to meet in secret, either in their own country villas or in mountain retreats. They held communion outside the established Church. At some times of the year, such as during Lent and in the days before Epiphany, which was then recognized as the day of Christ's birth, they seemed simply to disappear from sight.

As to their theological beliefs, the Priscillianists had a marked preference for the New Testament and for some of the apocryphal writings, such as the lives of the apostles Peter, John, Andrew, and Thomas. They also believed in direct, divine inspiration. Aspects of Priscillian's works do in fact seem to reflect a Manichaean dualism: He distinguished, for example, between darkness and light and saw Satan not as a fallen angel but as having an independent existence. His denial of the preexistence of Christ could have been tinged with Arianism. As a result, great controversy soon arose over Priscillian's teachings and practices. The contemporary Gallic writer Sulpicius Severus, in his chronicle, noted, "there followed portentious and dangerous times of our age, in which the churches were defiled and everything was disturbed by an unaccustomed evil."

Priscillian soon gained a large following in Galicia and Lusitania (the northern and western parts of Spain). A large number of women were attracted to him; they held meetings of their own apart from the regular church services. He also was joined by two western Spanish bishops, Instantius and Salvianus. He initially was opposed, however, by more worldly bishops such as Hyginus of Cordova and, in particular, Hydatius of Emerita. Some of his detractors accused him of Manichaeanism. It also was rumored that two of his followers, the noblewoman Agape and the rhetorician Helpidius, had infected him with the Gnostic teachings of Mark of Memphis, an Egyptian who had moved to Spain. The Priscillianists soon were joined by another bishop, Symphosius of Astorga in Lusitania (modern Portugal). Hyginus of Cordova also changed his mind and withdrew his initial objections.

In 380, a council was assembled at Saragossa to consider Priscillian's case. Ten Spanish bishops attended, as well as two Gallic bishops, Delphinus of Bordeaux and Phoebadius of Agen, the latter presiding over the meeting. Priscillian himself, however, did not attend, although he did submit a written reply. The council declined to condemn him by name, although it did denounce some Priscillianist practices, such as the speaking and teaching of women in religious "conventicles" (gatherings), the activities of lay preachers, and the absence from church during Lent. Perhaps in response to the second of these, Priscillian was consecrated shortly thereafter as Bishop of Avila in Lusitania by Salvianus and Instantius. The Priscillianists then made scandalous accusations of their own against Hydatius. In 381, Priscillian's opponents, who had been joined by Bishop Ithacius of Ossonoba, appealed to the Emperor Gratian with the help of Bishop Ambrose of Milan. Gratian then issued a decree condemning "false bishops and Manichees."

Priscillian himself realized the efficacy of such a tactic, noting, "with our names disguised [Hydatius] sought a rescript against pseudobishops and Manichees, and of course obtained it, because there is no one who does not feel hatred when he hears about pseudobishops and Manichees." The Italian writer on heresies Philastrius of Brescia made similar connections, referring to the "so-to-speak ascetics in Gaul, Spain, and Aquitania, who likewise fol-

Priscillian

low the most pernicious belief of the Gnostics and Manichees," despite Priscillian's own explicit anathematization of Manichaeanism.

It was a popular tactic in ecclesiastical debates of this time, however, to attempt to associate one's opponents with some other universally detested heresy. Priscillianism was related to Origenism, for example, by the Spanish writer Paulus Orosius in his *Commonitorium de errore Priscillianistarum et Origenistarum* (c. 414; reminder about the error of the Priscillianists and Origenists). Other heresies by which the Priscillianists also were accused of being influenced included Gnosticism, Montanism, Novatianism, Ophitism, Patripassianism, Photinianism, and Sabellianism.

Priscillian, Instantius, and Salvianus, though the imperial edict had not specifically named them, left Spain seeking additional support. At Eauze in southwestern Gaul, they made many converts. After being expelled from Bordeaux by Bishop Delphinus, they were received by the noblewoman Euchrotia and Procula, the widow and daughter of the professor Attius Tiro Delphidius. They then continued on to Italy. At Rome, where Salvianus died, they were rebuffed by Pope Damasus. Thereafter, they received a similar response from Ambrose of Milan. They were successful, however, in gaining the help of Ambrose's enemies at the imperial court, and they obtained an imperial rescript of their own authorizing them to reclaim their sees, which they then did. Ithacius even was forced to go into exile in Trier.

Soon thereafter, however, in 383, Gratian was murdered by the usurper Magnus Maximus, who subsequently was baptized as an orthodox Christian. Ithacius proceeded to place his case before the new emperor, with whom the Priscillianists had no influence. Maximus, desiring to conciliate the established Gallic and Spanish clergy, ordered a council to be convened in 384 or 385 at Bordeaux under the presidency of Priscillian's enemy Delphinus. Instantius, whose case was heard first, was declared deposed, but before Priscillian could be tried, he appealed to Maximus himself.

A hearing was therefore convened before the praetorian prefect of Gaul at Trier. Priscillian's principal accuser, Ithacius, took the lead in the prosecution. Priscillian was accused, according to Sulpicius Severus, "of witchcraft, of studying obscene teachings, of organizing nocturnal gatherings of shameful women, and of praying in the nude." Some of these crimes were capital offenses. Two other influential bishops who coincidentally happened to be in the city at the time, Martin of Tours and Ambrose of Milan, refused to take part and argued that a bishop should be tried before his fellow bishops. Other bishops, however, supported the proceedings.

In the end, Priscillian and six of his followers, including Euchrotia and the Spanish nobleman Latronianus, were condemned to death and executed. Others, such as Instantius, were sent into exile. Martin was able to prevent the sending of an imperial commission to root out the Spanish Priscillianists, but purges did take place. The aged Hyginus, for example, was sent into exile, and ascetics in general continued to be harassed.

The role of Maximus is seen especially in his letter to Bishop Siricius of Rome informing him of the affair: "Our arrival found certain matters so contaminated and polluted by the sins of the wicked that, unless foresight and attention had quickly brought aid, great disturbance and ruin immediately would have arisen, . . . but it was then disclosed how great a crime the Manichees recently had committed, not by doubtful or uncertain rhetoric or suspicions, but by their own confession." According to the emperor, the Priscillianists were Manichees: In fact, he never referred to Priscillian or Priscillianists by name at all. He may have seen no need to try to define a new heresy when Manichaeanism, a perfectly good, universally detested one, was available. An accusation of Manichaeanism would have allowed Priscillian to be tried under the statutes which made it a capital crime.

This heavy-handed secular interference in church activities led to a split in the Gallic church. Bishops such as Felix of Trier, who associated themselves with Priscillian's accusers, were seen as responsible for his execution by others, such as Martin, who had declined to participate. Thus arose the so-called Felician controversy, in which bishops of the two sides excommunicated each other.

The anti-Felicians, who had opposed the executions, came back into imperial favor in 388, when Maximus was defeated and Valentinian II, Gratian's younger brother, was restored to the throne. Both Ithacius and Hydatius were exiled and imprisoned at Naples. The remains of Priscillian and his followers were returned to Spain and buried with great ceremony. Priscillian was venerated as a martyr and saint, and his teachings continued to have many followers. Subsequently, a number of Priscillianists were chosen as bishops in Galicia, with Symphosius as one of their leaders.

The Council of Toledo in 400 was able to reconcile some of the Priscillianists, such as Symphosius, but Priscillianism continued to have many adherents. Outbreaks are attested in the 440's, mid-530's, and as late as the Councils of Braga in 561 and 572, when seventeen supposed Priscillianist teachings were condemned. Some Priscillianist practices were reflected even later in those of the medieval Albigensians (c. 1200), southern French ascetic, anticlerical dualists, and Adamites, who practiced nudity. The Priscillianist preference for clerical continence, moreover, did eventually become standard Catholic practice.

Summary

The Priscillianist controversy did not concern ecclesiastical dogma as much as it did church authority. Even in the modern day, scholars have a difficult time finding obvious heresy in Priscillian's writings. Nevertheless, his advocacy of uncontrolled scriptural interpretation, lay ministry, the participation of women, and the carrying out of the sacraments outside the established structure excited much opposition from the existing church hierarchy. His and his followers' acquisition of episcopal office, and their attempts to take over the church hierarchy themselves, only served to arouse more opposition against them. The result was a power struggle in which both sides sought assistance from the secular government. Priscillian was the loser, and paid with his life. In the future, the state would become more and more intimately involved in church activities and controversies.

Bibliography
Birley, A. R. "Magnus Maximus and the Persecution of Heresy." *Bulletin of the John Rylands Library* 66 (1983): 13-43. A detailed discussion of the part played by the emperor Magnus Maximus in the Priscillianist controversy. This incident illustrates the increasing interference of the imperial government in the operation of the Church. Includes references to recent scholarship on Priscillian and notes.

Chadwick, Henry. *Priscillian of Avila: The Occult and the Charismatic in the Early Church*. Oxford: Clarendon Press, 1976. The standard, English-language biography of Priscillian. Concentrates on the religious and theological aspects of Priscillian's teaching. Includes thorough documentation and bibliography, with references to many other sources, especially in foreign languages.

D'Alès, A. *Priscillien et l'Espagne chrétienne à la fin du IVe siècle*. Paris: G. Beauchesne et Ses Fils, 1936. A biography of Priscillian which places him and his movement into the broader temporal and geographical context. Includes good documentation of the earlier scholarship.

De Clercq, V. C. "Ossius of Cordova and the Origins of Priscillianism." *Studia patristica* 1 (1957): 601-606. A brief discussion of the background of the Priscillianist controversy; De Clercq seeks to identify possible forerunners of Priscillian's beliefs and theology in earlier Christian teachings, especially those of Ossius of Cordova.

Schepss, G., ed. *Orosius: Commonitorium de errore Priscillianistarum et Origenistarum*. Vienna: F. Tempsky, 1889. The Latin text of Orosius' anti-Priscillianist invective. Orosius, an early fifth century Spanish writer, attempted to convict Priscillian of heresy by associating his teachings with those of the third century writer Origen. Such use of "guilt by association" was a common tactic at this time.

_____. *Priscilliani quae supersunt, maximam partem nuper detexit adiectisque commentariis criticis et indicibus*. Vienna: F. Tempsky, 1889. A Latin edition of the works of Priscillian and his followers. It is still debated just how many of the works which survive under Priscillian's name actually were written by him.

Ralph W. Mathisen

PROCLUS

Born: c. 410; Constantinople, Byzantine Empire
Died: 485; Athens, Greece
Area of Achievement: Philosophy
Contribution: Proclus is known for his detailed systematization of the various theological and philosophical doctrines that he inherited from his predecessors and for his immense commentaries on the works of Plato, which consumed most of his activity.

Early Life

Proclus was born of patrician Lycian parents from the city of Xanthus. They wanted him to be educated in their city; thus, he was sent to Xanthus at a very early age. Later, he went to Alexandria to study rhetoric and Roman law in order to follow his father's profession, law. He soon became interested in philosophy and abandoned the study of law, choosing instead to attend lectures on mathematics and the philosophy of Aristotle. About the age of twenty, he went to Athens and studied under the Athenian Plutarch and his successor, Syrianus, at the Academy, the Athenian school that traced its ancestry to Plato's Academy. There, he continued his study of Aristotle and was introduced to Plato's philosophy and to mystical theology, to which he became a devotee. Proclus was such an intense, diligent student, with extraordinary powers of comprehension and memory, that by the age of twenty he had read the whole of Aristotle's *De anima* (335-323 B.C.; *On the Soul*) and Plato's *Phaedo* (388-366 B.C.), and by twenty-eight he had written several treatises as well as his commentary on Plato's *Timaeus* (360-347 B.C.).

Although a devoted disciple of Platonic thought, which he considered his main influence and inspiration, Proclus was a great enthusiast of all sorts of religious practices, beliefs, and superstitions and a champion of pagan worship against Christian imperial policy. He practiced all the Orphic and Chaldean rites of purification religiously, was a celibate, pursued a strict vegetarian diet, observed the fasts and vigils for the sacred days (more than was customary), devoutly revered the sun and moon, faithfully observed all the Egyptian holy days, and spent part of each night in prayer and in performing sacrifices. He believed that he was in complete possession of the theurgic knowledge, that he was divinely inspired, and that he was a reincarnation of the neo-Pythagorean Nichomachus. Through the practice of theurgy, a type of ritual magic, it is claimed that he caused rainfall in a time of drought, prevented an earthquake, and was able to persuade the god Asclepius to cure the daughter of his friend Archiadas. Proclus had a vast and comprehensive knowledge of philosophy, mythology, religious practices, and cults, and he attempted to harmonize all these elements into a comprehensive system.

Marinus, his biographer, who was also his pupil and successor, describes Proclus as having lived the perfect life of a philosopher, a model of all the virtues, both social and intellectual, the life of a divine man. His only shortcomings were a quick temper and a fiercely competitive nature. Upon the death of Syrianus, Proclus succeeded him as the head of the Academy. Because of his position as the head of the Academy, and his devotion to Platonic thought, he has often been called "diadoches," or successor of Plato.

Life's Work
Proclus believed that his philosophy was a further and necessary development of Plato's thought. In reality, his views are a systematization of those found in other Neoplatonists' interpretations of Plotinian thought, and most can be traced to the teachings of Iamblichus, a follower of Plotinus. Of the many works that Proclus wrote, the most important and the one that best displays his schematizaōsis of Neoplatonic thought is *Stoikheiōsis theologikē* (*The Elements of Theology*, 1933). This work, which anticipates Benedictus de Spinoza's expositions of Cartesianism, is basically a doctrine of categories. It consists of a series of 211 propositions with deductive proofs. Each succeeding proposition follows on the basis of the preceding one, following the Euclidean procedure in geometry.

At the head of Proclus' system is the One, the ultimate First Principle existing beyond being and knowledge, ineffable and incomprehensible. Proclus often identifies God with the First Principle or One. From the One emanates or radiates innumerable lesser independent realities, reflecting the multiplicity of the world order, which strive to return to union with it. Unlike Plotinus, who held that the process of emanation was continuous and equal in degree, Proclus believed that all things emanate by triads and return to the One by triads. Every emanation is less than that from which it evolves but has a similarity or partial identity to its cause. In its emergence from its cause, the derived is also different. Yet, because of its relation to and dependence on its cause, it attempts to imitate its cause on a lower plane and return to and unite itself with it. It is only through the intermediate existences in triadic aspects that an existence can return to the highest reality, the One.

Although not original with him, Proclus was the first to emphasize and apply throughout his system the principle of universal sympathy, the view that everything is in everything else, each according to its proper nature. According to this, every reality in the universe is mirrored in everything else, but appropriately, in accordance with its nature. Eternal things exist in temporal existences temporally, and temporal things exist in eternal things eternally. This principle unifies and interweaves every part of the universe with every other part, from the One to the last stage of being or matter. In his attempt to unify the totality of the universe, Proclus also effects a total synthesis of religion with philosophy. His system is a chain of many carefully constructed links which include the traditional pagan gods, heroes, and other supernatural beings of late pagan syncretistic mythology and cult, as well as the divine principles of Greek philosophy.

Similar to his Neoplatonic predecessors, Proclus believed that the ultimate goal of the individual soul was to lose its identity and return to union with the One, or God. Although he accepted the Neoplatonic view that philosophy was important in the attainment of this goal, he added that theurgy provided an even better avenue. Philosophy is intellectual activity, is discursive and, as such, divided. Thus, it is impossible to achieve union with the undivided One through philosophy alone. Philosophy serves only as a preparation. Union with God is best achieved through the method of theurgy, or, as Proclus calls it, the sacred art, a collection of magical practices based on the principle of universal sympathy, a common sympathy existing between all earthly and divine things. According to this, there can exist in herbs, stones, and other material substances a magical or divine property. On a higher level, divinity could also be found in the names of gods, certain symbols, and even numbers. A skilled theurgist, by placing together the materials that possess divine properties and effacing others, could set forth a chain reaction of sympathies proceeding upward through a whole series of things to a divine being. The result would be a divine illumination, by means of which an individual could come into external communion with a god. Thus, theurgy was considered by Proclus superior to philosophy, for, unlike philosophy, theurgy can lead an individual to the gods themselves.

Proclus posited two types of theurgy, a lower and a higher. The lower uses the unities found in specific material things to stimulate the soul toward self-knowledge, an understanding of its unity and divinity. Union with God, Himself, however, is attained only through a higher theurgy, the power of faith. Faith, according to Proclus, is when the individual goes beyond words, ritual actions, and conceptual thought and arrives at a state of simplicity, or self-unity. That leads to an unexplainable and incomprehensible belief in and love of God. When that occurs, the soul finds itself in a mystical silence before the incomprehensible and ineffable Supreme Being, and to the degree that a soul can, it becomes God.

In its later years, Neoplatonism came to be more a religion than a philosophy in order to compete with Christianity, which was becoming increasingly popular. Neoplatonism's followers were concerned with matters similar to those of their Christian counterparts: constructing a theology and interpreting and reconciling sacred texts. They also adopted some of the tenets fundamental to Christianity and other religions. Since faith is indispensable for salvation in any religion, it became for the later Neoplatonists a basic requirement for salvation or union with God. Proclus understood the problem of combating Christianity and attempted to construct a system that would bring into harmony elements of religion and Greek thought.

Proclus

Summary

Proclus is considered the last of the major pagan Greek philosophers. His works represent the culminating point of Neoplatonic philosophers and the final form of its doctrines. It is in the Proclian form that Neoplatonic doctrines had considerable influence on Byzantine, Arabic, and early medieval Latin Christian thought. Proclus exerted the greatest influence, indirectly, on Latin Christendom through the writings of Dionysius, or Pseudo-Dionysius, as he is now called. It is not known who Dionysius was or when he lived. All that is known is that sometime in the late fifth or early sixth century a Christian follower of Proclus adopted his philosophy in toto, disguised it as apostolic teaching, and claimed it to be that of Dionysius the Areopagite, Saint Paul's first Athenian convert and disciple. Despite the fact that they were fraudulent, the works of Dionysius were highly regarded in the West, and beginning in the early sixth century to the eighth, elaborate commentaries were written defending both their orthodoxy and their genuineness. They soon acquired authority second only to those of Saint Augustine. Through the Dionysian corpus, Proclus' Neoplatonism influenced the thought of Western theologians for many centuries.

In the Byzantine world, the Dionysian theology had influence on the eighth century Eastern theologian Saint John of Damascus, but in general the works of Proclus were not as widely accepted as in the West, although they were well-known and often refuted. The main reason for their non-acceptance was that the Christian East considered Proclus' views on the eternity of the world heretical. It was not until the eleventh century, with the revival of Platonism, that Proclus' philosophy became widely known, studied, quoted, and commented upon in the East. The Muslim world was also influenced by Proclus. His works were translated into Arabic and influenced the thought of Arabic thinkers, especially those mystically inclined, such as al-Ghazzali and the Sufis, Ibn Gabirol and the Cabalists.

Proclus' influence on both the East and the West continued down to the eighteenth century and was especially prominent during the Middle Ages and the Renaissance, when he was considered the great pagan master. His works were translated into many languages, and his influence can be found in the philosophies of John Scotus Erigena (c. 810-c. 877), Thomas Aquinas (1225-1274), Meister Johannes Eckhart (c. 1260-1327), Nicholas of Cusa (1401-1464), René Descartes (1596-1650), Gottfried Wilhelm von Leibniz (1646-1716), and others. Traces of Proclus' philosophy can also be found in many modern works, literary and philosophical.

Bibliography

Lowry, J. M. P. *The Logical Principles of Proclus' "Elements of Theology" as Systematic Ground of the Cosmos*. Amsterdam: Rodopi, 1980. A study of the development of a logical structure of the cosmos as set forth in the logical systematic construction of the 211 propositions in Proclus' *The Elements of Theology*. It contains a good introductory chapter that includes a synopsis of Greek philosophy, Proclus' place in the history of philosophy, his relation to Iamblichus and Plotinus, and his influence on medieval and Renaissance thought.

Proclus. *The Elements of Theology*. Translated by E. R. Dodds. Oxford: Clarendon Press, 1933, 2d ed. 1963. Greek text and English translation, with an excellent introduction and commentary on *The Elements of Theology*. The introduction includes a general description of the work, its place in the philosophical works of Proclus, a summary of Proclus' place among his Neoplatonic predecessors, and his influence during the Middle Ages. The commentary is a detailed critical discussion and historical study of each of the 211 propositions in *The Elements of Theology*. There is also a complete index of Greek terms.

Rosán, Laurence Jay. *The Philosophy of Proclus: The Final Phase of Ancient Thought*. New York: Cosmos, 1949. A compendium of Proclus' writings, with a detailed discussion and annotated bibliography. It also includes a translation of Marinus' life of Proclus, an analysis of Proclus' philosophy, and an annotated list of books, articles, and chapters on Proclus' thought or writings. A valuable book, but somewhat outdated.

Wallis, R. T. *Neoplatonism*. New York: Charles Scribner's Sons, 1972. The study is intended as an updated account of Neoplatonism. It is a summary of Neoplatonic thought from Plotinus to the end of the Athenian Academy, but it also includes two brief but informative chapters on the aims and sources of Neoplatonism and a lengthier chapter on the influence of Neoplatonism through the years. A chapter on the Athenian School contains a good summary of the development of Proclus' thought and its basic tenets. With an extensive bibliography.

Whittaker, Thomas. *The Neo-Platonists*. Cambridge: Cambridge University Press, 1918, 4th ed. 1928. A study in the history of Hellenism, with emphasis on Neoplatonic philosophy, from Plotinus to Proclus, and its influence. Chapter 9 contains a study of Proclus' life and a descriptive account of many of the propositions found in *The Elements of Theology*. At the end of the book, there is a supplementary section of summaries on Proclus' extant commentaries. The work is largely outdated, but it is still valuable for its supplement on Proclus' commentaries.

Antonía Tripolitis

SEXTUS PROPERTIUS

Born: c. 57-48 B.C.; Assisi?, Umbria
Died: c. 16 B.C.-A.D. 2; place unknown
Area of Achievement: Literature
Contribution: Propertius expanded the scope and power of the Roman love poem in the passionate poems to and about Cynthia.

Early Life

Sextus Propertius was born between 57 and 48 B.C. in Umbria, perhaps in the small town of Assisi. He was the son of a knight who was a well-off landowner. Propertius' father died while Propertius was still a child, and his world was further dislocated by the appropriation of land in Umbria to settle the soldiers of Marc Antony and Octavian (later, Augustus).

Propertius grew up under the shadow of the continuing civil wars among Antony, Octavian, and Pompey the Younger—and the early consolidation of power by Augustus. His first book of poems was published about 30 B.C., and it attracted the attention of Gaius Maecenas, the patron of Vergil and Horace. This support improved Propertius' financial situation, but he continued to refuse to write poems in celebration of Augustus.

Life's Work

Propertius' poetry came at the end of the great period of the Roman love poem. His work does not have the passion of Catullus or the polish of Horace, but it does have a complexity and an intensity not found in the poetry of his predecessors. Some critics have complained about Propertius' heavy use of myth, but the allusions in his poetry are well employed—especially the contrasting of the distant gods to the immediate relationship with a woman he called Cynthia.

Propertius' poetry survives in four books. At the heart of the poems are those on Cynthia, and while commentators have been unsuccessful in discovering an autobiographical sequence the poems do give one of the fullest portrayals of an intense relationship in all literature. The first poem (book 1, elegy 1) immediately evokes this intensity: "She was the one to enslave me, and she did it with her eyes;/ till then I'd never felt love's poison arrows." Love is not a pleasant or a sentimental state but a terrible visitation and a loss of control. Propertius contrasts his subject state to mythic figures and urges the powers of love to visit his mistress with the same poison. The poem shifts at the end, as Propertius becomes adviser rather than victim and warns his friends to avoid this sorry state of unrequited love by sticking "to your own love."

In the poems that follow, Propertius frequently complains about Cynthia's mistreatment, yet in book 1, elegy 7, the poet defends his choice of the love poem over the more traditional and valued epic. Propertius' poems are his "life's work" and come from bitter and joyful experience, while the epic of one Ponticus—according to Propertius—is straight out of books. Propertius writes that when Ponticus falls in love, in vain he will try to turn his hand to love poems, while Propertius will be celebrated as "the greatest poet of them all."

In book 1, elegies 21 and 22, Propertius addresses war, not love. The speaker in elegy 21 is a dead man who advises a fleeing soldier. The dead man urges the soldier not to be brave but to "Save yourself/ and bring your parents joy." He also asks the soldier to bring a message of "tears" to his sister. The poem ends ironically, for the dead man was also a soldier and had escaped "the swords of Caesar" only to fall to robbers. It is a personal and a political poem; it evokes the sorrow of the dead soldier and points unmistakably to its cause, the wars of Antony and Octavian.

Elegy 22 is also a political poem. It begins with a question from a man named Tullus about Propertius' origins. The answer is that he comes from "the graveyard of our fatherland/ when civil war set Roman against Roman...." Once more he evokes a landscape littered with "my kinsman's bones" but ends with an opposite image, life and birth: "where the fertile plain touches the foothills/ Umbria gave me birth."

The first poem in book 2 is not addressed to Cynthia but to Propertius' patron, Maecenas. Once more, he contrasts the supposedly trivial love poem to the great epic, but since Cynthia is his inspiration "each trivial incident begets/ a mighty saga." Even if he had the power to write an epic, he would avoid the usual subjects, since they are all clichés. If he had the power he would write about "your Caesar's wars" (another example of the distancing of the poet from the emperor). Yet he has no such power or ability; he can only write "of the battles I fight in bed." The poem ends in an amusing fashion, as Propertius asks Maecenas to visit his obscure tomb, drop a tear, observe the burial rites, and say, "Here lies one for whom destiny/ Was a Cruel mistress." As the poems show, Propertius' destiny was a cruel mistress, Cynthia.

Most of the poems in book 2 complain about Cynthia's ways or lack of faithfulness. Elegy 5 is the most interesting of these. It begins with a series of accusations as Cynthia is called a "whore" and the poet looks forward to following her example and acquiring a new love. The focus of the poem shifts, however, as Propertius looks not to the future but to past moments they shared like "tender sacraments." He then lists all the brutal things he will not do to her; he will, instead, "mark" her with his poetic curse that will last to her dying day.

Book 2, elegy 7, speaks of a more tender relationship between the poet and Cynthia, as well as of the complex relationship he has with Augustus. It

Sextus Propertius

begins with relief that some "law" was not put into operation by Augustus that would separate the poet and his beloved. The relief is tinged with defiance, as the poet declares that "mighty Caesar cannot conquer love." Nor is the poet a fit candidate to be a husband or a breeder of sons for Rome; the only war he will fight is in the name of his mistress. The last lines of the poem are an affirmation of the poet's love, "which is greater to me than the name of father."

In book 2, elegy 10, Propertius seems to have reversed his earlier position and now wishes to sing of "war and war's alarms," since "Cynthia's song is sung." By the end of the poem, however, he sees poems about war as beyond his reach, like a statue that "towers too high." He will, instead, write of and from the lower strain of love. Propertius is very clever in praising Augustus, but, finally, he relocates his art in a private rather than a public arena.

Elegy 34, the last poem in book 2, brings together many of the themes of the earlier poems. It is addressed to another poet, Lynceus, who has attempted to steal the poet's beloved. Lynceus is identified as a student of the "Socratic books," but they will be of no help to a man in love—nor will the usual epic themes. Lynceus must make himself into a love poet in the manner of Propertius if he wishes to succeed. The second section contrasts Propertius' poems with the political and nationalistic ones of Vergil and the pastoral ones of Lynceus. In the end, however, the epic and pastoral poets are left behind, as Propertius places himself in the line of Catullus and Calvus. If he is allowed to join that company, both he and Cynthia will live forever. So the poem is both a disguised love poem that praises Cynthia and a defense of lyric poetry against the epic and the pastoral.

Book 3 continues the themes of Cynthia and the championing of the love poem over the epic. Elegy 4, however, seems to be a surrender to the claims of Rome. The poem praises the new victories of Augustus against the Parthians. Propertius even prays to see "the wheels of Caesar heaped with the spoils of war." Yet where will the poet be while this triumph is celebrated? He will be lying in his "sweetheart's arms watching the sights" rather than taking an active role or even writing about war. The last two lines define the difference between the two areas: "Let those who earned it bear the spoil away,/ and leave me to stand and cheer on the Sacred Way." The role of the poet is to sing and cheer rather than to take part in public life.

Elegy 11 deals with the power that women have over men. It begins with Propertius speaking of his bondage to Cynthia and asserting that it should be no "surprise." He cites Medea and others as examples of this same situation, but the main comparison is to Cleopatra VII. She has "brought into disrepute" the "walls of Rome" and made senators slaves. According to Propertius, however, Augustus was not awed by this woman and has recently defeated and destroyed her; the poet sings out "your triumph, Rome" over these forces. The subjection to women that seemed to be universal at the beginning is now broken and the poet tells the reader to "remember Caesar."

Elegy 22 also discusses Rome, but from a more personal perspective. It is addressed to Tullus, who has been roaming among the various wonders of the world. After listing those exotic sights, however, the poet reminds Tullus that "all the wonders of the world/ are not a patch on Rome." Not only is Rome victorious, but also it is free from the crimes and vices common in other places. So Tullus is welcomed back to a Rome that is "worthy of your eloquence," where children and "a wife to match your love" await. It is clearly a Rome in which there is no mention of Cynthia and her destructive passion.

Book 4 also begins with a celebration of Rome, in the first elegy. A "stranger" is invited to look around at "the grandeur of Rome." He is reminded of Roman history and myth from Romulus and Remus through the founding of Rome by the Trojans, as the poet offers up his song " to the service of my country." He imagines his homeland, Umbria, now proud as the birthplace of "Rome's Callimachus." In the second part of the poem, however, Horus, a god of time and an astrologer, appears and criticizes Propertius' new project. He tells him that he should be fashioning love poems to "provide a model for the scribbling mob," since Apollo "banned you from thundering in the frantic forum." Propertius' fate is Cynthia and the creation of poems about her: "It's she who tells you whether it's day or night; your teardrops fall at her command."

In book 4, elegy 6, however, Propertius returns to the subject of Augustus' wars. After listing the triumphs of his emperor, the poet focuses on the victory over Cleopatra which has made Augustus into a god.

There is one more poem on Cynthia in book 4. It speaks of her as a ghost who is "very much alive," snapping her fingers at the poet and ordering him around. She accuses him of not attending her funeral and of sleeping soon after her death. She has come, however, not to accuse but to bring information about the underworld and to instruct the poet. She tells him, first, to "burn" all the poems he has written about her and to place "this poem" on her tombstone: "Here in the fields of Tivoli/ Lies golden Cynthia/ Adding a new glory/ To the banks of the Anio." She then leaves him to other women until they can be reunited in the afterlife. It is a fitting end to the sequence.

Summary

The poems of Sextus Propertius portray the growth, flowering, decay, and death of an intense love relationship with the elusive Cynthia. From the very first, it is seen as an unconquerable obsession. There are moments of union between the two, but, for the most part, he complains about her neglect and unfaithfulness. The Cynthia sequence can be compared to the one dealing with Lesbia in the poems of Catullus. Catullus goes through a similar wrenching experience of hate and love that defines his existence.

There is, however, another side to the poetry of Propertius. He accepted the patronage of Maecenas, but he did not become an official spokesman for Augustus as Vergil and Horace did. Instead, he defended his right to a private life and a private art, the love poem. The tension created by the struggle to remain free without insulting the emperor gives another dimension to the passionate love poems and adds subtlety to their structure.

Bibliography
Highet, Gilbert. *Poets in a Landscape*. New York: Alfred A. Knopf, 1957. Contains an evocative discussion of Propertius and other Roman poets that concentrates on the poets' biographies and societies. Well written, providing background information but no interpretation.
Luck, G. *The Latin Love Elegy*. London: Methuen and Co., 1969. A useful early study of some of the techniques and concerns of the Roman love poem. It is quite good on the literary tradition but not much of a guide to individual poems.
Propertius, Sextus. *The Poems of Propertius*. Edited by Ronald Musker. London: J. W. Dent, 1972. A brief and adequate introduction to the poetry of Propertius with an excellent translation. A good introduction to Propertius for readers without knowledge of Latin.
Stahl, Hans-Peter. *Propertius: Love and War, Individual and State Under Augustus*. Berkeley: University of California Press, 1985. A superb study of Propertius' ambiguous relationship with Augustus and the themes of love and war. It is written primarily for an academic audience, but other readers will find it clear and informative.
Williams, Gordon. *Tradition and Originality in Roman Poetry*. New York: Oxford University Press, 1968. A scholarly treatment of many aspects of Propertius' thought and interests. The book is very good on the background and tradition of the poems but assumes knowledge of Latin.

James Sullivan

PROTAGORAS

Born: c. 485 B.C.; Abdera, Greece
Died: c. 410 B.C.; place unknown
Areas of Achievement: Philosophy and education
Contribution: Protagoras was among the first and was possibly the greatest of the Greek Sophists, itinerant teachers who professed to be able to teach men virtue for a fee. His ideas on learning, morality, and the history of human society have influenced the system of education since the fifth century B.C.

Early Life

Most of what is known of Protagoras comes from select writings of Plato, Aristotle, Aristophanes, and certain later authors. Protagoras was born about 485 B.C. in Abdera, a coastal town of Thrace to the east of Macedonia. The town was remarkable for producing several famous philosophers, including Democritus, and as the third richest city in the Delian League, a fifth century alliance established to expel the Persians from Greece.

Protagoras' father, Maeandrius (or by some accounts, Artemon), was said to have been one of the most affluent citizens of Abdera and was thus able to obtain a good education for his son. When Xerxes I, King of the Persians, stopped in the town with his army prior to invading Greece, Maeandrius supposedly gained permission for his son to be educated by the magi who were part of Xerxes' retinue. The magi were supposed to have been the source of Protagoras' well-known agnosticism. No trace of their influence, however, can be seen in his work, so the story is largely discounted.

A story arose that Protagoras invented the shoulder pad that porters used, because he himself had been a porter in his youth. A longer version of the tale claims that his fellow citizen, the philosopher Democritus, saw him working at a menial task and was so impressed by his methodical arrangement of firewood that he first made the boy his secretary, then trained him in philosophy and rhetoric. Since Democritus was actually younger than Protagoras, this story must also be rejected. Yet he may have been a "hearer" of Democritus, as some accounts claim.

The numerous stories from ancient times which have largely been discounted by later generations prove that nothing certain can be said about Protagoras' early life. It is stated authoritatively, however, that at the age of thirty Protagoras began his career as a Sophist, traveling up and down the peninsula of Greece, and into Sicily and southern Italy, giving lessons to wealthy young men for a fee.

Life's Work

Prior to the mid-400's no schools or professional teachers existed, yet the city-states experienced an increasing need for well-educated, informed leaders. The older Sophists, Protagoras, Prodicus, Hippias, and Gorgias, filled this need by teaching upper-class young men how to acquire political and personal success. They held similar views on education and had similar aversions to the objective scientific doctrines of their day. They claimed: superiority in wisdom, the ability to teach that wisdom, and the right to charge a fee for their lessons. In this atmosphere Protagoras gained fame by lecturing and by writing books.

Many disapproved of the Sophists' methods, especially Socrates and Plato. Socrates argued that wisdom was a quality which could not be taught. Plato, who disparaged the rhetorical tricks used specifically by Protagoras, brought ill repute to all the Sophists. A generation later, Aristotle branded their teaching as the furthering of the appearance of wisdom without the reality, and the Sophists as men who made money on this pretense.

Still, Protagoras was clearly more than a specious philosopher. Plato consistently portrayed him as witty, intellectual, moral, and sincere in his praise of Socrates—and thought Protagoras' ideas important enough to refute in several dialogues. Aristotle's extensive refutation of Protagoras' beliefs attests the fact that he, too, took Protagoras seriously.

Protagoras' instruction was practical. He emphasized skill in persuasive speaking and effective debating. He taught his students the importance of words by the study of grammar, diction, and poetic analysis. He may have been the first to emphasize the importance of proper timing. Armed with these skills, Protagoras believed, his students would excel as civic leaders and political advisers. The Athenian orator Isocrates and Protagoras' fellow Sophist Prodicus were two of his most famous students. He also influenced Aristophanes and Euripides.

On his journeys, Protagoras no doubt stayed with influential families and read his speeches to select audiences. His most famous visits were to Athens, which he first saw in 444 B.C., when the Athenian ruler Pericles asked him to write the constitution for the new Panhellenic colony of Thurii in southern Italy. This assignment probably required him to live in Italy for some years. He spent enough time in Sicily to have won fame as a teacher. He returned to Athens about 432, when he engaged in the debate with Socrates described in Plato's dialogue *Protagoras* (399-390 B.C.). He may have visited the city once more in 422 or 421.

Protagoras' high fee of one hundred minae was notorious; according to Plato, Protagoras earned more money in his forty years of teaching than did the famous sculptor Phidias and ten other sculptors combined. Protagoras claimed that a student was not compelled to pay the fee if he did not think the instruction worth the price.

Protagoras was known to have written at least two books, though many more titles have survived. *Aletheia* (*The Truth*) was an early, and his most important, composition. He wrote another titled *Antilogion* (*Contrary Argu-*

ments) and may also have written a third called *Peri theon* (*On the Gods*).

Only two substantial fragments of his writing remain. In conjunction with numerous shorter fragments, they reflect the two main philosophies of Protagoras' life and portray him as a person interested in philosophy, rhetoric, grammar and syntax, and literary criticism. The statement for which he is most famous introduces *The Truth*: "Man is the measure of all things, of the things that are, that they are, of the things that are not, that they are not." The saying, perhaps a reply to the mathematicians, has been interpreted since Plato to mean that what a man perceives to be true for him is true for him. A new fragment discovered in 1968 expounds further on the remark.

Protagoras' subjectivism, as it was called, was not well received by philosophers. Aristotle declared the statement absurd. Plato argued that a pig or a baboon was equally capable of being the measure. The flaw in Protagoras' argument was that if others believed the maxim to be false, then by that very maxim their perceptions must be true for them and his maxim was false for them. Despite these objections, the dictum represented an original contribution to fifth century philosophy.

On the Gods is said to have opened with the following statement:

> With regard to the gods, I cannot know whether they exist or do not exist, nor what they are like in form; for the factors preventing knowledge are many: the obscurity of the subject, and the shortness of human life.

Such agnosticism shocked Protagoras' contemporaries. The Athenians reportedly expelled him from the city for impiety. Nearly seven hundred years later, Sextus Empiricus labeled Protagoras an atheist for this remark, as did Diogenes Laërtius.

In *Contrary Arguments*, Protagoras stated that two contradictory propositions existed for every issue. Aristotle rejected the saying as contradicting Protagoras' own belief that all views were equally true, and Aristophanes lampooned the idea in his comedy *Nephelai* (c. 423 B.C.; *The Clouds*). Modern views of sophistry stem from the comic playwright's portrayal of these rhetorical tricks.

Minor fragments reveal Protagoras' interest in speech, grammar, and education in general. He wrote on existence, he refuted mathematics, and he discussed such varied topics as wrestling, ambition, virtues, laws, human error, and the underworld. Protagoras' influence on his contemporaries is apparent from later authorities. Porphyry claims that Plato plagiarized substantial passages from the *Contrary Arguments* for his work, the *Politeia* (388-366 B.C.; *Republic*). Protagoras' personal friend Pericles may have chosen him to draft laws for Thurii, partly because he respected the Sophist and partly because Protagoras was already familiar to Western Greeks. The drafting of the laws may have brought him into contact with the historian Herodotus, who was also involved in founding Thurii. Protagorean influence has been noted in part of Herodotus' *Historiai Herodotou* (c. 425 B.C.; *The History of Herodotus*, 1709).

The circumstances of Protagoras' death remain shrouded in mystery. By one account, he died in a shipwreck. Diogenes believed he died fleeing Athens when he was banished for impiety. Probably closest to fact is Plato's statement that he died after forty years of teaching, that is, about 410 B.C.

Summary

Protagoras' importance in the realm of Greek philosophy has been largely underrated because of the refutations of Plato and Aristotle and the lampoons of Aristophanes. He and his fellow Sophists initiated the practice of instructing students. Before this time young men had had to rely on the dramatists and their plays for lessons in how to be good citizens. After the Persian War, this brand of instruction was inadequate for the demands of the city-states, especially Athens. The Sophists provided a necessary service by establishing a definite curriculum.

Yet the system was not without flaws. The aim from the beginning was to educate only the leaders of society, not the general populace. Protagoras' claim to teach virtue was too weak an assertion to support, as Plato, Aristotle, and others clearly saw. Still, it is interesting that after the death of Socrates, who vehemently protested that he taught nothing and never charged a fee, his student Plato founded the Academy, where he lectured to paying students in the area of philosophy. In this respect, Plato much more closely resembled Protagoras than Socrates.

Protagoras' influence has spanned generations. He was known in the Middle Ages and early Renaissance through the writings of Cicero, Seneca, and Aulus Gellius—and in the Latin translations of Aristotle. Some scholars have seen evidence for sophistic origins of Renaissance Humanism. Greek Sophists founded the type of intellectual movement with which the Italian humanists are identified. There seems to have been a Humanist character to the Sophists, a character that arguably makes the Sophists, through Cicero and his knowledge of them, the progenitors of the thoughts and ideas expressed in Italian Humanism of the 1400's. Protagoras' myth on the origin of human society corresponds to the Humanists' concepts of their own moral and educational role in society.

As W. K. C. Guthrie so aptly claims:

> Protagoras' innovation was to achieve a reputation as a political and moral thinker without supporting any political party, attempting political reform, or seeking power for himself, but simply by lecturing and speaking and offering himself as a professional adviser and educator. . . .

Protagoras made men think about their lives in relation to society and sparked some very strong objections from philosophers regarding the direction of learning. In this way, he helped advance education.

Bibliography
Barnes, Jonathan. *The Presocratic Philosophers*. Vol. 2, *Empedocles to Democritus*. London: Routledge and Kegan Paul, 1979. The author's special contribution is interpreting Protagoras' sayings according to ancient commentators. The extensive bibliography, endnotes, and index will be helpful to general and advanced readers.
Freeman, Kathleen. *Ancilla to the Pre-Socratic Philosophers: A Complete Translation of the Fragments in "Diels, Fragmente der Vorsokratiker."* Cambridge, Mass.: Harvard University Press, 1983. This volume provides a translation of all the existing fragments written by Protagoras. One could have wished that the author had also translated the fragments from ancient authors about Protagoras.
_____. *The Pre-Socratic Philosophers*. 2d ed. Cambridge, Mass.: Harvard University Press, 1959. Still the best discussion in English of all the fragments of Protagoras, fact and fiction. Freeman puts him in historical perspective with his predecessors, contemporaries, and successors. Clear and concise for general readers.
Guthrie, W. K. C. *A History of Greek Philosophy*. Vol. 3, *The Fifth-Century Enlightenment*. Cambridge: Cambridge University Press, 1969. Compiles all the ancient evidence on Protagoras and presents it in a clear, straightforward manner. Also provides a good historical background to the Sophists and a discussion of their importance. Citations of ancient authors are in the footnotes.
Jaeger, Werner. *Paideia: The Ideals of Greek Culture*. Vol. 1, *Archaic Greece: The Mind of Athens*. Translated by Gilbert Highet. New York: Oxford University Press, 1945, reprint 1979. Jaeger's evaluation of the role and importance of the Sophists and of Protagoras' role is one of the best critical accounts. Includes extensive endnotes.
Plato. *Plato's "Protagoras": A Socratic Commentary*. Edited by B. A. F. Hubbard and E. S. Karnofsky. London: Duckworth, 1982. This translation of Plato's dialogue provides a clear portrayal of Protagoras as Sophist and as intellectual. In the commentary, the translators refer to sections of the dialogue which reveal bits of Protagoras' life, and a succinct biography appears in one of the indexes. Includes a short bibliography.

Joan E. Carr

PSAMTIK I

Born: c. 684 B.C.; place unknown
Died: 610 B.C.; place unknown
Area of Achievement: Government
Contribution: Psamtik carved out political independence for Egypt after almost a century of foreign rule, inaugurating a renewal of its society and culture.

Early Life

Little is known about the early life of Psamtik I (also known as Psammetichus I); even the date of his birth is based on conjecture. He was the son of Necho I, a local Egyptian ruler in the western Delta region. For nearly a century, after the kingdom of Egypt had fragmented into several small principalities, Cushite invaders had held the Nile Valley, calling themselves the Twenty-fifth Dynasty. Assyria was beginning to expand westward; under Assarhaddon and Ashurbanipal, it vied for control of the valley, which led to confrontations with the Cushites.

Psamtik's ancestors, especially his great-grandfather Tefnachte, had unsuccessfully tried to reunite the land. Necho, his father, pursued a precarious course between the Assyrians and Cushites, trying to carve out a maximum of independence for himself and the principality of Sais, which he controlled. This political game would prove fatal: He later died on the battlefield in 664.

Life's Work

A year earlier, Psamtik had participated in a mission to Nineveh together with his father; at that time, Ashurbanipal appointed the two his vassals in Egypt. Necho became King of Memphis and Sais, while Psamtik (in the Assyrian records called "Nabu-shezibanni") was to rule Athribis in the central Delta. Upon the death of his father, Psamtik became ruler of Memphis and Sais. An invasion of the Delta by the Cushites forced him to flee to the Assyrians.

He returned in 664 when Ashurbanipal conducted a campaign against Tanatami, a Cushite ruler, which led to the expulsion of the latter and the sacking of Thebes by the Assyrians. Psamtik was reinstated and had to pay tribute to his Assyrian overlord. With both great powers removed, Psamtik craftily worked to consolidate his position and to expand his rule. A major step toward this goal was the reorganization of his army; with the help of Gyges of Lydia, he hired Carian and Ionian mercenaries—the "bronze men who would make their appearance from the sea" of the Greek historian Herodotus' romantic account. For these soldiers, the first coins were struck in Egypt.

By 657, Psamtik had gained full control over the various principalities of the Delta and Middle Egypt. How he accomplished this is not known in detail. Herodotus relates a fictitious tradition: An oracle had foretold that the one who would perform the divine libation from a bronze helmet would become king of all Egypt. At a ceremony in the temple of Ptah-Hepaistos—so the story goes—the golden cups for the ritual libation were one short and Psamtik quickly took his helmet to perform for the god.

The final unification of Egypt under Psamtik was completed in 656, when Thebes peacefully accepted him. This development was negotiated for Thebes by a local dignitary named Menthuemhet and was formalized by the appointment of Psamtik's daughter Nitocris as "Wife of Amon," the priestess who controlled the economic resources of the temple of the Theban god Amon at this time. With great pomp and lavish gifts, the young Nitocris, probably in her teens at the time, sailed to Thebes. Since Psamtik refrained from any interference in prevailing political situations, he did not stir up any opposition; Thebes remained an integral part of Egypt for the next 130 years.

Following the expansion into Thebes, Psamtik was faced with an attack from Libya; some of the invaders were former Delta princes who had fled there. In 655 he repelled this last challenge to his rule. To prevent any recurrence of outside attacks, he set up garrisons at Egypt's borders, such as Elephantine in the South and Daphne in the Northeast. The troops stationed there were foreign mercenaries, including Greeks, Hebrews, and Carians.

By 655 Psamtik not only had consolidated his rule over Egypt but also was able to shed his dependence on an Assyria exhausted from years of incessant warfare and growing internal tensions. A period of peace and economic renewal was inaugurated for Egypt. Memories of Egypt's former greatness were carefully cultivated, leading to a conscious antiquarianism which found its most visible expression in the arts, where the style of the Old Kingdom, the Pyramid age, served as model. This interest in the past also had its impact on the administration of the country, as indicated by the reappearance of official titles after an absence of fifteen hundred years. The motive seems to have been a desire to emulate the achievements of the past, an illusion sustained by the prosperity following half a millennium of internal strife, political insignificance, and economic stagnation. Despite the antiquarian mold, there were numerous intellectual impulses. The traditional way of writing became increasingly replaced by a smoother, more cursive script called demotic. Medicine flourished, especially in Sais. There was religious fervor, and the cults of Isis and Amon, among others, profited.

The long reign of Psamtik coincided with major shifts in the balance of power in the eastern Mediterranean basin. Assyria, which at the beginning of his reign had been the dominant nation, was losing its importance. Following years of external and internal strife, it was no longer able to exercise influence in Syria and Palestine. In return for military assistance to Assyria,

Psamtik was able to expand Egypt's political might northward, filling the vacuum which developed in the Levant as a result of Assyria's withdrawal. By 612 Egypt's control over parts of Lebanon and Palestine was reestablished, while Psamtik joined the Assyrians in their fight against the Babylonians under Nabopalassar in 616 and 610. Ashdod was seized by Psamtik, but the Egyptian did not concern himself with the affairs of Judah, which under Josiah was concentrating on religious reforms. Being landlocked at the time, Judah did not fall into the overall political plan Psamtik followed at this time in the Levant.

Unlike any of his predecessors on the throne, Psamtik was interested in making Egypt into a naval power on the Mediterranean and later also on the Red Sea. It is not clear from where the technical expertise came, but some Greek participation is feasible. These naval plans coincided with the political expansion into Palestine. Psamtik prepared the basis for Egypt's subsequent role as a truly international power, not only in its traditional land-based form but also as a naval force, culminating in the construction of a canal linking the Mediterranean—via the Nile system—to the Red Sea and the first known circumnavigation of Africa, which took place under his son and successor Necho II.

Summary

When Psamtik I died in 610, he left an entirely different Egypt from the one with which he began his reign fifty-four years earlier. Caught between the Cushites and the Assyrians, the political ambitions of the local ruler of Memphis and Sais faced considerable odds, which were overcome. Since the unification of Egypt was achieved peacefully, however, it did not generate new tensions; instead, it marked the beginning of a period of political, cultural, and economic flowering, known as the Saite Renaissance, which lasted until the Persian invasion in 525. Marked by a reawakened national spirit, which took the glorious past, especially the Pyramid age, as its model, Egypt's last fully indigenous period was a time when the land of the pharaohs exerted considerable cultural influence, on the Greeks especially. Egypt developed its Hellenic contacts, in the process entering the Mediterranean theater. A void in the international political structure not only gave Egypt the opportunity to consolidate its newly attained national identity but also offered the country the chance to become once more a major power, bringing the coastal regions of part of Syria and Palestine under Egyptian authority.

Bibliography
Gardiner, Alan, Sir. *Egypt of the Pharoahs*. New York: Oxford University Press, 1961. This volume is a fine general account of the history of ancient Egypt. Includes a short bibliography, some illustrations, and an index.
Kitchen, K. A. *The Third Intermediate Period in Egypt, 1100-650 B.C.* War-

minster, Pa.: Aris and Phillips, 1973. A well-documented, authoritative study; discusses the Twenty-sixth Dynasty, beginning with Psamtik, extensively. General bibliography.

Spalinger, Anthony. "Psammetichus, King of Egypt: I." *Journal of the American Research Center in Egypt* 13 (1976): 133-147. The only scholarly treatment of Psamtik written in English. Includes citations.

Hans Goedicke

MICHAEL PSELLUS

Born: 1018; Nicomedia
Died: c. 1078; Constantinople
Areas of Achievement: Government, religion, philosophy, and historiography
Contribution: Psellus infused both Byzantine state theory and Orthodox theology with a revived classical tradition, while preserving a history of the personalities and events of his times.

Early Life
Constantine Psellus, who took the name Michael only when he withdrew to a monastery in 1054, was born in 1018 into a family with imperial connections but only modest means. The coemperors at the time were the elderly brothers Basil II (reigned 976-1025) and Constantine VIII (reigned 976-1028). Psellus' own family is but poorly known. Although nothing is recorded about his father, his mother, Theodote, was the subject of one of Psellus' seven extant elegies. In addition to introducing her son to the Orthodox faith and the study of Scripture, she secured the Platonist John Mauropus, later the Archbishop of Euchaita, as his tutor. Under Mauropus' influence, Psellus made several lifelong friends: Constantine Ducas, Constantine Leichudes, and John Xiphilinus. These friends would later assist one another amid the intrigues of the Byzantine court.

Before Psellus reached the age of sixteen, his education in rhetoric had progressed far enough to bring him into the imperial circle. At the court, the youth regularly saw "and on one occasion actually talked with" the elderly emperor, Romanus III. Psellus also attended the imperial funeral; in writing of this period, he would describe himself as one who "had not yet grown a beard" and was just beginning the study of the classical poets.

Psellus' studies were extensive: He memorized Homer's *Iliad* (c. 800 B.C.), and the frequency with which various phrases from the *Odyssey* (c. 800 B.C.) were used in his later writing demonstrates his educational base. He also knew the works of Greek and Latin historians and debated constantly the distinction between true history and panegyric or scandalmongering. Astrology, auguries, soothsaying, and magic practices used for sexual potency ("arts" accepted at the imperial court) as well as arithmetic, geometry, music, and astronomy received his attention. He learned enough medicine to practice. Finally, he read enough on military strategy and equipment of war to go into the field.

Because of his family's financial difficulties, which included the need to provide a dowry for his elder sister, Psellus was forced to curtail his education for a time. He briefly became a tax collector and judicial clerk in Philadelphia, before resuming his studies at the age of twenty-five. Although he was married, nothing is known about his wife. In his own works, he refers to the loss of his beloved daughter, Styliane.

Once back at his studies, Psellus trained his tongue with rhetoric, shaped his mind with philosophy, and integrated the two so that he might give voice eloquently to the art of reasoning. This oratorical ability would take him directly into the service of Emperor Constantine IX.

Life's Work

The death in relatively quick succession of three aged emperors—Basil II, Constantine VIII, and Constantine's son-in-law Romanus III—left in control Constantine's daughters, Zoë and Theodora, who both, by imperial law, held the title of augusta. Romanus, while married to Zoë, in his old age had preferred a mistress; Zoë was left to engage in an affair with a younger court official. She secured the crown for her lover, whom she married; he reigned as Michael IV from 1034 to December 10, 1041. Although he died prematurely, in anticipation of his death, a nephew was adopted to establish the succession. When this heir took control as Michael V and exiled Zoë, the populace revolted and Theodora had him executed. Alexis, the patriarch, then permitted a violation of church and state law so that the empress Zoë could marry a third time; she chose Constantine IX, who was one of the last members of the ancient family of Monomachi. Constantine, who became coruler with the sisters, brought directly into his service Michael Cerularius as patriarch, Constantine Leichudes as president of the senate, and Constantine Psellus as secretary.

Psellus relates that under Michael V he had been "initiated into the ceremonies of entry into the imperial presence." He witnessed, from the outer porch of the imperial palace, the uprising of the people on behalf of Theodora. Psellus had no difficulty surviving the short interlude when the *gynaikonitis* (women's quarters) served as the imperial council chamber and the two empresses continued the business of administration. According to his later account, however, "they confused the trifles of the harem with important matters of state."

A major event in the reign of Constantine IX was the establishment of faculties of law and philosophy for an imperial university at Constantinople in 1045. The faculty of law was to be headed by a salaried *nomophylax* (law professor), which was assigned to John Xiphilinus. There was also established a chair of philosophy for Psellus. Only the barest hint of these events appears in *Chronographia*, apparently written after 1071 (English translation, 1953), and the dimensions of his scholarship must be deduced from the orations and treatises which have survived. Latin had been the language of "Old Rome"; "New Rome" had lost its use. It was being revived in the late tenth century, however, and Romanus III could speak it. The study of law required it, and Psellus gave some time to its study.

As a rhetorical philosopher, Psellus was a master of words and the boundaries of their meaning. He saw everything in terms of Orthodox theology and the mysteries of Scripture. Military victories were accomplished by "the Mother of the Word" carried into battle as the "ikon of the Savior's Mother." Although religious subjects raised many unresolved questions, his mastery of words prevented any accusation of heresy against him as he taught the relationship of classical philosophy to Christian faith.

Psellus perceived that certain Platonic allegories and Aristotelian doctrines related to dialectic or proof by syllogism had received no proper explication. His own studies led him from the teachings of Plato and Aristotle through those of the Neoplatonists Plotinus, Porphyry, and Iamblichus to the writings of Proclus in the fifth century. In his studies, he found a mean between material nature and pure ideas, which he proceeded to synthesize in the manner of geometrical proofs so that he could give logical demonstration in elegant oration. He carried these studies full circle back to "the mystery of our Christian religion"; thus, its dualities—of human and divine nature, of finite and infinite time, and of faith capable of proof yet divinely inspired—could receive the same logical, elegant demonstration.

He produced commentaries on the Song of Songs, on Plato's doctrine of ideas, on *Timaeus* (360-347 B.C.) and *Phaedrus* (388-368 B.C.), and on Aristotle's *De interpretatione* and *Categories*. He paraphrased the *Iliad* and studied Homer's poems allegorically. Two composites gathered up his broadly defined "scientific" thinking: In the "Dialogue on the Operation of the Daimons," considered his literary masterpiece, he opposed a variety of heretical movements; "On Teaching Miscellany" was written for his young pupil, the future Michael VII Ducas. This latter work began in Orthodox fashion with Christian propositional dogmatics, but it climaxed with Neoplatonic interpretations of reality.

Psellus also wrote on Athenian judicial terminology and the topography of Athens, as well as on the "character" of church fathers Gregory of Nazianzus and John Chrysostom. Some five hundred letters remain extant, filling out glimpses of his time and personality.

Zoë died in 1050 at age seventy-two. Constantine IX reigned on, but he appeared to have switched loyalties from Psellus and his friends—learned, self-made men—back to their opponents of the old aristocracy and the military establishment. Constantine Leichudes and John Xiphilinus turned to the Church and underwent monastic tonsuration. Psellus followed their example, receiving the monastic name Michael before retiring to the monastery on Mount Olympus.

When Constantine IX died in 1055 without leaving an heir, power passed again to the empress Theodora. Having never married, she chose no man as a coruler, but she required the rhetorical and literary services of Psellus. Even early in the reign of Constantine IX, Psellus had been consulted by the empress in dispatching confidential letters and conducting other private business. Such services may have contributed to his departure; they certainly brought him back to power.

Theodora's reign did not last. Her death in 1056 at the age of seventy-six precipitated a search for a successor. Michael VI (called "the Aged") was at best a temporary choice, although Psellus continued to support him. All interests—those of the people, the senate, and the army—had to be satisfied by any selection. The army acclaimed Isaac Comnenus in 1057; a battle with the emperor's men followed shortly thereafter at Hades, near Nicaea. After Isaac's victory, Psellus led an embassy of three, including Theodorus Alopus and Constantine Leichudes, which negotiated the transfer of power. Isaac was proclaimed emperor by the populace in September of that year, and Michael VI abdicated, intending to die in peace. As a result of their efforts, Constantine Leichudes became patriarch and Psellus was honored as the president of the senate. Despite (or because of) his success, however, Isaac fell ill; to preserve the fragile peace, he was tonsured by the new patriarch and went to live in a monastery. Constantine Ducas, Psellus' other longtime friend, was chosen by Isaac (on his apparent deathbed) as the new emperor.

In 1064, John Xiphilinus was forced to leave his abbacy to become the new patriarch, while Psellus functioned as prime minister. Psellus stayed on under Constantine X's wife, Eudocia, who ruled briefly with her two young sons until she remarried. When Constantine's successor was captured at the Battle of Manzikert in 1071, Eudocia's older son, Michael, became emperor as Michael VII Ducas. He was the product of Psellus' teaching, and a contemporary chronicler, John Scylitzes, condemned the philosopher for having made Michael unfit to rule.

Psellus finished *Chronographia* with a panegyric to Michael VII and his family. The history abruptly ends with a comment upon the role of Divine Providence, stating that the dictates of Fortune for even the most important men are reversed. The chronicler Attaleiates simply records the death in 1078 of "Michael, monk and *hypertimos*" (most honorable).

Summary

Michael Psellus began his *Chronographia* with a discussion of the reign of Basil II to link it to the earlier historian Leo the Deacon. Psellus' work was later overlapped, supplemented, copied, or continued by numerous others. Psellus explicitly rejected the chronicle form, saying that unlike Thucydides, he had neither numbered his work by Olympiads nor divided it into seasons.

John Italus, one of his students and his successor to the chair of philosophy, was tried for heresy, having too fully revived the ancient notions of the soul and its transmigration, as well as of the eternalness of matter and ideas. An anonymous satire of the twelfth century contrasts Psellus' favorable reception by philosophers in the underworld with that given to Italus. Because of the energy he spent on the re-creation of the university in Constantinople, Psellus came to be viewed as a harbinger of the Renaissance, and renewed study of him has continued. Not all of his works in manuscript have yet received publication, however, and only a few have been translated.

The Schism of Eastern and Western churches of 1054 left no mark on *Chronographia*, though a treatise written by Psellus against the Latin theologians survives. His denunciation in late 1058 of the patriarch Michael Cerularius, who was subsequently removed by the emperor, was not unrelated to the events of the Schism. Yet its force was blunted within a few months by the necessity for Psellus to give a laudatory oration at Cerularius' funeral.

This species of elegy, like his speeches of imperial panegyric, clearly illustrates how in his public conduct Psellus was a man of his time, with the ability to survive, accommodate himself, be of service with increasing influence, and provide criticism of the past in each new administration. Psellus thought highly of himself, as is clear from *Chronographia*, and he was genuinely convinced that he was well regarded by the many rulers under whom he served.

Bibliography
Hussey, Joan M. *Church and Learning in the Byzantine Empire, 867-1185*. London: Oxford University Press, 1937. The context and function of both university and monastery in the Byzantine Empire, in particular the life of Psellus, are treated thoroughly.

_____, ed. *The Cambridge Medieval History*. Vol. 4, *The Byzantine Empire*. Cambridge: Cambridge University Press, 1967. While Psellus is cited intermittently, the sections included on his scholarship and literary achievements are particularly valuable, and the bibliography is prodigious.

Pelikan, Jaroslav J. *The Christian Tradition: A History of the Development of Doctrine*. Vol. 2, *The Spirit of Eastern Christendom (600-1700)*. Chicago: University of Chicago Press, 1974. Pelikan perceives Psellus as the central figure among the eleventh century Orthodox theologians who rose to the defense of classical philosophy within a Christian Hellenism.

Psellus, Michael. *Fourteen Byzantine Rulers: The Chronographia*. Translated with an introduction by Edgar R. A. Sewter. Baltimore: Penguin Books, 1966. The only major work by Psellus translated into English, *The Chronographia* provides his character sketches, in varying length and degree of partisanship, of the imperial figures, both male and female, from Basil II to Michael VII.

Runciman, Steven. *The Eastern Schism*. New York: Oxford University Press, 1955. The Schism is dated to 1054; its relative lack of mention in Psellus' writings makes this historical discussion important, especially that on the role of the patriarchs of Constantinople with whom Psellus was closely associated.

Vasiliev, A. A. *History of the Byzantine Empire, 323-1453*. 2 vols. 2d ed. Madison: University of Wisconsin Press, 1952. With extensive notes and bibliography, this account of the Eastern "Roman" state discusses political, dynastic, social, literary, scholarly, and artistic events and achievements. Chapter 6 covers the times and life of Psellus, though his impact appears throughout other discussions.

Clyde Curry Smith

PTOLEMY

Born: c. 100; Ptolemais Hermii, Egypt
Died: c. 178; place unknown
Areas of Achievement: Astronomy, mathematics, and geography
Contribution: Ptolemy's scientific work in astronomy, mathematics, geography, and optics influenced other practitioners for almost fifteen hundred years.

Early Life
Very little is known about the life of Ptolemy. He was born in Egypt at the end of the first century A.D., but his birth date and birth place and his life thereafter are subjects of speculation. It is thought that he might have been born in the Grecian city of Ptolemais Hermii in Upper Egypt and that he might have lived to the age of seventy-eight. It has been suggested that he studied and made astronomical observations, staying for more than half of his life among the elevated terraces at the temple of Serapis in Canopus near Alexandria, where pillars were erected with the results of his astronomical discoveries engraved upon them. He was probably the descendant of Greek or Hellenized ancestors and obtained Roman citizenship as a legacy from them.

Much more is known about the age in which Ptolemy lived. It was a century during which Rome ruled the Mediterranean world and during which four successive Roman emperors, Trajan, Hadrian, Antoninus Pius, and Marcus Aurelius, built roads and bridges, opened libraries and colleges, and maintained Rome's power and peace. It was a time when educated men spoke Greek as well as Latin, when Athens was still honored for its cultural traditions, when Marcus Aurelius wrote his *Meditations* in Greek, and Greek was still the language of science and the arts.

Ptolemy, who probably used the libraries at Alexandria, was strongly influenced by a Greek scientist, Hipparchus (fl. 146-127 B.C.), who propounded the geocentric theory of the universe. As far back as the fourth century B.C., the leading view of the nature of the universe had the sun, moon, and planets revolving around the fixed Earth in concentric spheres. The competing theory was first advocated by Aristarchus of Samos (fl. c. 270 B.C.). Aristarchus discovered that the sun was much larger than Earth, and this discovery was the basis for his argument that Earth and all other planets revolved around a fixed sun and stars in circles. Yet the heliocentric theory could not be demonstrated by observable phenomena as long as it was thought that the sun was the center of a circle rather than of an ellipse. Hipparchus rejected the contention of Aristarchus, insisting on "saving the phenomena," that is, adhering to the observations. His further scientific speculations founded on the geocentric theory were the legacy to Ptolemy some two centuries later.

Life's Work

Some historians maintain that Ptolemy merely plagiarized from Hipparchus; others have said that Ptolemy superseded Hipparchus and made the work of the earlier scientist superfluous. In fact, it could be said that Ptolemy immortalized Hipparchus by acknowledging the debt he owed to his distant predecessor and by frequently quoting from him.

Whatever historical assessment is more correct, there is no doubt that Ptolemy's work in astronomy alone lasted for more than fourteen hundred years, until the great scientific achievements of Nicholas Copernicus and Johannes Kepler. Ptolemy used new instruments or improved upon old ones to make his observations. In the *Mathēmatikē suntaxis* (c. 150; *Almagest*), one of his most significant books, he utilized the mathematical methods of trigonometry to prove that Earth was a sphere and went on to postulate that the heavens were also spheres and moved around an immobile Earth in the center of the solar system. He dealt with the length of the months and the year—and the motion of the sun; he covered the theory of the moon; and he figured out the distance of the sun, and the order and distances of the planets from Earth. Much of this was not new, not original; the *Almagest* was essentially a restatement of astronomical knowledge available three hundred years earlier. Yet Ptolemy was able to synthesize that scientific information into a system and to expound it in a clear and understandable manner. He was a teacher, and he taught well.

Ptolemy's contribution to mathematics was even more significant. Hipparchus had invented spherical and plane trigonometry for the use of astronomers. Ptolemy then perfected this branch of mathematics so that, unlike his astronomical system, which was finally discredited, the theorems that he and Hipparchus devised form the permanent basis of trigonometry.

The *Almagest*, in which trigonometry was utilized to measure the positions of the sun, Earth, moon, and planets, was later translated into Arabic and then Latin, and so also was Ptolemy's *Geōgraphikē hyphēgēsis* (*Geography*). Ptolemy attempted with considerable success to place the study of geography on a scientific foundation. His book, written after the *Almagest*, was modeled after the work of Marinus of Tyre, but Ptolemy added a unique dimension by placing his predecessor's information into a scientific structure. He assumed that Earth was round, that its surface was divided into five parallel zones, and that there were other circles from the equator to the poles. He was the first geographer to write of "parallels of latitude" and "meridians of longitude." Ptolemy, however, did make one crucial mistake. Along with other ancient geographers, he underestimated the circumference of Earth, and as a consequence few latitudes were established correctly (and, since the means were not available, no longitudes were established).

What most attracted the interest and attention of earlier geographers and of Ptolemy was the size of the inhabited world: in the north, Thule (the present Shetland Islands); in the west, the Fortunate Islands (the Canary Islands and Madeira); and in the south and east, the vast continents of Africa and Asia. Although they overestimated the size of both the eastern and southern continents, Ptolemy's findings, and Marinus' before him, were based on new knowledge derived from travelers' accounts of the silk trade with China and from sea voyages in the Indian Ocean. Ptolemy revised some of Marinus' estimates of the length and breadth of Asia and Africa, and by extending Asia eastward and Europe westward, more than a thousand years later, Christopher Columbus, who relied on Ptolemy's *Geography*, was led to believe that it was possible to reach Asia by a direct route across the Atlantic Ocean.

Ptolemy's *Geography* is restricted to mathematical calculations; he did not write about the physical attributes of the countries he charted or the people who inhabited them. His tables, stating the location of places in terms of latitude and longitude, gave a false impression of precision; he made frequent errors because of his basic misestimate of the size of Earth. Still, Ptolemy's objective to draw a world map was noteworthy. His educated guess as to the location of the sources of the Nile River was remarkable, and his use of the terms "latitude" and "longitude" was a distinct contribution to the advancement of geographical knowledge.

While Ptolemy is well-known among historians of science for his volumes on astronomy and geography, it is also necessary to consider his writings on astrology, which in the ancient world was the "science" of religions. His volume *Apotelesmatika* (*Tetrabiblos*, which means "four books") is important partly because it was more famous than the *Almagest* and partly because it reflects the popular thinking of his age. The *Tetrabiblos* is a summary of Egyptian, Chaldean, and Greek ideas. It attributes human characteristics to the planets, such as masculine and feminine, beneficent and malevolent. It predicts the future of races, of countries and cities, and speaks of catastrophes, natural and human: wars, famine, plagues, earthquakes, and floods. It also expounds on such subjects as marriage, children, the periods of life, and the quality of death. Translated into Arabic, Latin, Spanish, and English, it influenced generations of Europeans (and, later, Americans) and formed the basis of modern astrological beliefs.

There are many historians of science who deplore the superstitions that pervade the *Tetrabiblos* and dismiss it as an unfortunate effort. The great historian George Sarton believes, however, that "we should be indulgent to Ptolemy, who had innocently accepted the prejudices endemic in his age and could not foresee their evil consequences...."

Summary

It would be unreasonable to expect great scientific breakthroughs during the second century A.D., and they did not happen. What did occur was the gradual advancement of knowledge to which Ptolemy contributed. Not only did Ptolemy write the *Almagest* and the *Geography*, adding new and significant materials to that of his predecessors, but he also attempted to illuminate the science of optics and the art of music. In the first case, although little was known about the anatomical and physiological structure of the eye, he devised a table of refraction, and his book reveals that he understood that a ray of light deviates when it passes from one medium into another of a different density. He addressed the role of light and color in vision, with various kinds of optical illusions and with reflection. Ptolemy's volume on music theory, known as the *Harmonica*, covers the mathematical intervals between notes and their classification. He propounded a theory that steered a middle ground between mathematical calculations and the evidence of the ear. Observation was again a guiding principle of his art as well as his science.

Other work on mechanics, dimensions, and the elements was done but has not survived. What did survive had great influence on the Arabic science of astronomy, led to the rise of European astronomy, and influenced the work of Copernicus himself in the fifteenth century. The *Geography*, also translated into Arabic in the ninth century, was amended to describe more accurately the territories under Islamic rule; in the West, where the work became known in the fifteenth century, it was a catalyst of cartography and to the work of the Flemish cartographer Gerardus Mercator. Ptolemy's work on optics inspired the great improvements made by the Arabic scientist Ibn al-Haytham (died 1039), and his work became the foundation of the *Perspectiva* of Witelo (c. 1274), the standard optical treatise of the late Middle Ages.

Just as there is no exact knowledge of Ptolemy's birth date, there is no reliable information about when and where he died and under what circumstances. Yet those biographical facts are not that important; what is significant is the scientific legacy which was transmitted through the centuries. Ptolemy was not, as one expert has argued, an "original genius"; his forte was to take existing knowledge and to shape it into clear and careful prose.

Bibliography
Neugebauer, Otto. *The Exact Sciences in Antiquity*. 2d ed. Providence, R.I.: Brown University Press, 1957. A study of Babylonian and Egyptian mathematics and astronomy, with a chapter describing the Ptolemaic system and comparing it with modern astronomical theory. The book was also issued in a paperback edition by Dover Press in New York in 1969.
Newton, Robert R. *The Crime of Claudius Ptolemy*. Baltimore: Johns Hopkins University Press, 1977. The "crime," according to the author, is that Ptolemy fabricated observations to confirm his theories and that his work in astronomy is basically fraudulent. Newton concludes that Ptolemy was not a first-rate astronomer, even in terms of the period in which he lived.

Ptolemy. *Ptolemy's "Almagest."* Translated by G. J. Toomer. London: Gerald Duckworth and Co., 1984. For students and readers who may want to sample the scientific work of Ptolemy in one of the most recent English translations of his mathematical astronomy. The translator has also provided a twenty-six-page introduction and lengthy annotations.

Sarton, George. *Ancient Science and Modern Civilization.* Lincoln: University of Nebraska Press, 1954. The great Montgomery lecture on "Ptolemy and His Time" takes up thirty-six pages of this book. The paper describes Ptolemy's work in astronomy, geography, astrology, and optics but does not help place Ptolemy in historical context.

Toomer, G. J. "Ptolemy." In *Dictionary of Scientific Biography*, edited by Charles C. Gillispie, vol. 11. New York: Charles Scribner's Sons, 1975. A careful dissection of Ptolemy's contributions, an assessment of his importance as a scientist, and a tracing of the transmission of his work to Islam and to Western Europe. The article includes an extensive bibliography.

David L. Sterling

PTOLEMY PHILADELPHUS

Born: February, 308 B.C.; Cos
Died: 246 B.C.; Alexandria, Egypt
Area of Achievement: Government
Contribution: Under Ptolemy, the domestic institutions and the foreign policy characteristic of Hellenistic Egypt matured. His patronage of the arts and sciences established Alexandria as the most important cultural center of the Greek world.

Early Life
In 308, Ptolemy Soter (fighting to secure his place among the Macedonian dynasts eager to claim their share of Alexander the Great's legacy) personally led an expedition into the Aegean in order to anchor his influence in the region through alliances and a series of naval bases. Along with Ptolemy Soter went his third wife, Berenice, who gave birth to Ptolemy Philadelphus on the island of Cos. Berenice was the least well connected of the polygamous Ptolemy's three wives. She had come to Egypt in the retinue of Eurydice, when that daughter of Antipater came as Ptolemy's bride. Despite her political insignificance, Berenice was Ptolemy's favorite spouse, and her son Ptolemy Philadelphus became heir to Egypt over the claims of an older son of Eurydice, Ptolemy Ceraunus, meaning "thunderbolt."

Ptolemy Philadelphus was not to be the man of action his father had been. Reared at an urbane court in the greatest city of the Greek world, he was a devotee of a softer, if more culturally inclined, life. He had the best of educations under the likes of the Aristotelian Straton and became a king who preferred to rule from his capital, rather than personally oversee his varied foreign interests.

In order to facilitate the transfer of authority to his chosen son, Ptolemy Soter elevated Ptolemy Philadelphus to the throne in 284, and they ruled jointly until Ptolemy Soter died about two years later. On the accession of his half brother, Ptolemy Ceraunus fled Egypt to the court of Lysimachus in Thrace, where his sister, Lysandra, was married to the son of Lysimachus named Agathocles. Also in Thrace, however, was Arsinoe II, the sister of Ptolemy Philadelphus and the wife of the much older Lysimachus. Probably to foster the inheritance of her own young sons, Arsinoe II convinced her husband that Agathocles was engaged in treason. Lysimachus subsequently had Agathocles executed, and, as a result, both Lysandra and Ceraunus fled to the Asian court of Seleucus. When Seleucus defeated and killed Lysimachus in 281, Ceraunus fought for the victor.

The true nature of Ceraunus' loyalty, however, revealed itself when he soon after assassinated Seleucus and seized Thrace. Arsinoe II fled to Macedonia on the death of Lysimachus, to secure it for her children. Not sat-

Ptolemy Philadelphus

isfied with the murder of Seleucus, Ceraunus aspired to add Macedonia to his realm, which he surprisingly accomplished by marrying Arsinoe II. For reasons which are not entirely clear, Ceraunus eventually butchered two of Arsinoe's three sons. Perhaps Ceraunus limited his wife's freedom, but she remained in Macedonia until he was killed fighting Gauls in 279. With Macedonia overrun by barbarians, Arsinoe II and her surviving son, Ptolemy, again fled, this time home to Egypt.

Ptolemy Philadelphus' queen was another woman named Arsinoe (a daughter of Lysimachus), by whom he already had three children. Nevertheless, not long after Arsinoe II came to his court, Ptolemy exiled his first wife, and sometime before 274, he married his sister. It was this union which later earned for Ptolemy the name "Philadelphus." (Arsinoe II alone bore the title in life.) The marriage scandalized many of Ptolemy's Greco-Macedonian subjects, but royal brother-sister unions were known in Egypt, and its consummation had the effect of drawing the Europeans in Egypt closer to native tradition.

Life's Work

Ptolemy ruled Egypt at the height of its Hellenistic power, but before the return of Arsinoe II to Egypt, little is known of Ptolemy's foreign ambitions. In the early 270's he was interested in fostering a regular spice trade with Arabia and as a result recut a neglected ancient canal from the Nile's delta to the Gulf of Suez. Ptolemy subsequently patronized the exploration of the Red Sea (complete with colonies along the African coast) and voyages to India. His desire to tap the exotic luxuries of the East found a counterpart in his interests in sub-Saharan Africa. In fact, the only known foreign expedition personally led by Ptolemy went to Ethiopia in order to strengthen trade to the south. Perhaps Ptolemy's most interesting foreign policy initiative came in 273, when he sent an embassy to Rome and became the first Hellenistic monarch to establish friendly relations with the Republic, which had only recently unified peninsular Italy.

Arsinoe II's holdings in the Aegean (a legacy from her days as Macedonian queen) expanded the interests of Egypt in that region and eventually pitted Ptolemy against Antigonus I Gonatas, whose victories over the Gauls won for him Macedonia. Perhaps prompted by his wife's more assertive personality, in the 270's Ptolemy initiated an aggressive foreign policy which challenged not only Antigonus Gonatas, but the Seleucids as well.

His first conflict of note, the First Syrian War (circa 276 to 271), was fought against the Seleucid Antiochus I over the Phoenician coast. This land not only lay astride the best approach to Egypt but also was an important terminus for trade which stretched eastward along several routes. In this war, Antiochus secured Damascus and successfully incited Magas (Ptolemy's half brother and governor of Cyrene) to rebellion, but Ptolemy's superior fleet was a scourge to Seleucid coastal settlements and eventually won the war for him. By its end, Ptolemy had regained Cyrene and extended his control of the coast northward into Syria. Arsinoe II was probably instrumental in planning the war, since soon after its conclusion, Ptolemy approved worship of her under the auspices of a state-cult, the first attested worship of a living human being since Alexander the Great. Indeed, Arsinoe's political clout must have been enormous, since her portrait appeared with that of Ptolemy on Egyptian coins—an honor exclusively reserved for Hellenistic monarchs. Arsinoe died in July, 269.

In the Balkans, Ptolemy was a party to the Chremonidean War (from 266 to 261, named for an Athenian) in which Athens, expecting strong Egyptian backing, led a Greek coalition against Macedonia. Accounts of this war are extremely fragmentary, making a reconstruction of its significance difficult. The reason Ptolemy did not order his forces in the Aegean to exploit the war more effectively is not known, but by and large they remained on the fringes while Antigonus Gonatas defeated his opponents. Perhaps there is more than a grain of truth in the hypothesis that Ptolemy was an indecisive strategist when not influenced by the forceful Arsinoe II.

Whether the Egyptian success in the First Syrian War was because of Arsinoe, the Second Syrian War (circa 260 to 253) saw Ptolemaic losses. Not long after his accession, the Seleucid Antiochus II attacked Ptolemaic possessions along the coast of Asia Minor. A complicated and elusive struggle followed, until Ptolemy conceded much of the Syrian coast under his garrison. The resulting peace was fixed by the marriage which joined Ptolemy's daughter, Berenice, to Antiochus II.

At home, Ptolemy II faced a brief challenge to his authority in the 270's from a brother, Argaeus, and was forced to recognize the semi-autonomy of Magas in Cyrene. Ptolemy was very successful, however, in establishing a variety of institutions which anchored the legitimacy of his dynasty in Egypt. For example, for the Macedonians who still remembered their native land and its traditions, at the beginning of his reign, Ptolemy established a royal cemetery in Alexandria around the remains of Alexander the Great and Ptolemy Soter. This foundation re-created in Egypt an institution from the homeland and provided a focus for the loyalties of the Macedonians in Egypt. It also acted as a bridge between the legitimacy of the extinct house of Alexander and the new authority of Ptolemy's dynasty. Its political purpose is manifest: Ptolemy laid first claim to the authority of Alexander.

It was under Ptolemy that the apparatus which ruled Hellenistic Egypt matured. The native pharaonic system was too efficient a revenue producer to be abandoned, but the Ptolemies could not afford to trust their security to the loyalty of native Egyptians. As a result, the Ptolemies grafted an immigrant Greco-Macedonian ruling class onto the stock of Egyptian society and tried as much as possible to maintain the distinctiveness of the two social orders (for example, by severely limiting native Egyptian access to the city of Alexandria). Such a policy was doomed at least in the Egyptian countryside, but in the time of Ptolemy it worked. Egypt was the sole possession of the Ptolemaic kings. Except for those estates alienated by the Ptolemies to attract European settlement, it remained their private property. The geographical isolation of Egypt made it possible to sever all but officially sanctioned foreign trade, and its economy was monopolized in the interests of the dynasty. Native Egyptians were compelled to render to Ptolemy at a fixed rate a percentage of their grain, which he thereafter sold abroad at a huge profit, while the immigrants paid significant taxes for the use of their land. In turn, these profits paid not only for such things as cultural patronage and the construction of a city which was home to about one million people but also for the domestic and foreign security ensured by Ptolemy's sizable Greco-Macedonian military establishment.

Like his father before him, Ptolemy elevated his heir, Ptolemy Euergetes (a son of Arsinoe I), to royal authority before his own demise. Ptolemy Philadelphus, having no sons by Arsinoe II, seems originally to have selected as his heir Arsinoe II's only son to have survived Agathocles, but this Ptolemy apparently died in 258. Ptolemy Philadelphus died shortly after passing on the burdens of his office to his son.

Summary

The domestic and foreign policies which made Ptolemy Philadelphus' Egypt the most stable Hellenistic power of his day were very expensive and pushed Egypt to its financial limit. Although an adequate defense of Egypt proper was maintained, the rivalries with Antigonid Macedonia and Seleucid Asia drained the treasury greatly. Arsinoe II may have been responsible for unleashing an aggressive foreign policy, but without her decisiveness to carry the stratagem through, Ptolemy's remote interests languished, taking second place to Alexandrian pleasures.

Evidence suggests that Ptolemy was both intellectually curious and self-indulgent. He was a renowned cultural patron, attracting outstanding poets such as Theocritus and Callimachus to his court. Although Ptolemy patronized the greatest Hellenistic poets, perhaps his greatest cultural legacy resulted from his support of scientific and technological investigation. Ptolemy encouraged such investigation through the great museum and library in Alexandria, which were to be the cultural mainstays of the Hellenistic tradition for the rest of antiquity. The concentration of talent attracted to Alexandria by royal patronage brought the city a luster which drew intellectuals who did not directly enjoy Ptolemy's largess. Jews in large numbers took advantage of the city's resources and there produced a Greek version of their sacred texts, which was to begin the process whereby the Jewish and Hellenistic traditions would intermingle. Ptolemy personally enjoyed the artistic fruits of his patronage, but he also benefited in practical ways: Figures such as the poet Apollonius gave him political advice, and his engineers constantly improved the technological efficiency of the Ptolemaic navy, thus enabling the fleet to remain competitive while Ptolemy was occupied elsewhere.

It is unfair to describe Ptolemy as either lazy or hedonistic, for he was very much concerned with the administration of his kingdom at a time when his dynasty's hold on Egypt was anything but traditionally anchored. Nevertheless, his talents were hardly those of his Macedonian predecessors. He did not feel comfortable leading troops into battle as had Philip II, Alexander the Great, Ptolemy Soter, or even men such as his own contemporary, Pyrrhus. His style of kingship—surrounding himself with elaborate layers of court officials and a well-oiled administration—tempered the martial spirit which underscored the foundation of Alexander's Macedonian empire and its division. A new age had dawned, an age which based its legitimacy on conquest but aspired to more peaceful pursuits.

Bibliography
Bevan, Edwyn R. *The House of Ptolemy*. London: Methuen and Co., 1927. A standard account of the Ptolemaic dynasty. Includes a chapter on the reign of Ptolemy Philadelphus.
Burstein, Stanley. "Arsinoe II Philadelphos: A Revisionist View." In *Philip II, Alexander the Great, and the Macedonian Heritage*. Washington, D.C.: University Press of America, 1982. Argues that Arsinoe II should not be credited with single-handedly devising Ptolemy's foreign policy.
Cary, M. *A History of the Greek World, 323-146 B.C.* 2d ed. London: Methuen and Co., 1951. Includes not only a useful outline of Ptolemy's domestic and foreign affairs but also a review of the cultural importance of Alexandria.
Fraser, Peter Marshall. *Ptolemaic Alexandria*. 3 vols. Oxford: Clarendon Press, 1972. The authoritative study of the Ptolemaic capital and virtually every institution associated with the Ptolemaic dynasty. An essential work for anyone interested in the development of Ptolemaic society.
Macurdy, Grace Harriet. *Hellenistic Queens*. Baltimore: Johns Hopkins University Press, 1932. Includes excellent reviews of what is known of the careers of Arsinoe I and Arsinoe II and, in connection with the latter, a standard summary of her influence over her brother and husband, Ptolemy.
Turner, E. G. "Ptolemaic Egypt." In *The Cambridge Ancient History*. Vol. 7, *The Hellenistic World*. 2d ed. Cambridge: Cambridge University Press, 1984. A review of the Ptolemaic system in Egypt. Includes a good discussion of the social structures harnessed and exploited by Ptolemy.

William S. Greenwalt

PTOLEMY SOTER

Born: 367 or 366 B.C.; the canton of Eordaea, Macedonia
Died: 283 or 282 B.C.; Alexandria, Egypt
Area of Achievement: Government
Contribution: A companion of Alexander the Great during the conquest of the Persian Empire, Ptolemy came to rule Egypt shortly after Alexander died—first as a satrap under Philip III and Alexander IV and after the extinction of the Argead royal family as a king in his own right. Ptolemy thereby founded the dynasty which ruled Egypt until the death of Cleopatra VII in 30 B.C.

Early Life

Ptolemy Soter's origins are obscure—and were so even in his lifetime, when jokes were made about his grandfather's lack of distinction. Ptolemy's father was named Lagus, although in order to enhance his legitimacy among the Macedonians he later ruled in Egypt, rumor maintained that he was an illegitimate son of Philip II and thus that he was the half brother of Alexander the Great. Ptolemy's mother was named Arsinoe, and she may have been distantly related to the Argead royal house. Ptolemy was born in Eordaea, a region in western Macedonia which was firmly brought within the political orbit of the Argead royal house only during the reign of Philip II.

Ptolemy probably came to live at the Argead court in the 350's (after Philip's victory over an Illyrian coalition which threatened Macedonia from the northwest), as Eordaea then fell under direct Argead rule. In order to control the newly incorporated cantons of Upper Macedonia, Philip invited the sons of aristocratic western families to his court at Pella. These youths served as royal pages, responsible for (among other things) the protection of the king's person. The honor associated with becoming a member of the pages was augmented by the educational opportunities (military, political, and cultural) available at court. The selection of royal pages, however, served not only to redirect the loyalty of young aristocrats but also to provide the king with hostages in order to secure the good behavior of their families.

Ptolemy is first mentioned in ancient sources with respect to the so-called Pixodarus Affair. In 337, as Philip was searching for political connections in Asia as a prelude to his proposed attack on the Persian Empire, he made diplomatic contact with the satrap of Caria, Pixodarus, to whose daughter he betrothed his handicapped son, Arrhidaeus. At the time of this initiative, Alexander the Great was temporarily alienated from his father as a result of Philip's last marriage and was in self-imposed exile.

When Alexander learned of Philip's move, he was afraid that Philip had jeopardized his status as heir to the throne. As a result, Alexander rashly interfered with Philip's plans by offering himself to Pixodarus in lieu of

Arrhidaeus. The Carian was delighted with the proposed substitution, but Philip was not. Upon learning of Alexander's obstruction, Philip both broke off diplomatic contact with Pixodarus and severely chastised his son. In the wake of Philip's anger, several of Alexander's associates, including Ptolemy, were exiled from Macedonia.

Many have seen Ptolemy's exile as a result of his long-standing intimacy with Alexander, but such a close friendship between the two is doubtful since Ptolemy was eleven years older than Philip's heir—almost as close in age to Philip as he was to Alexander. By the 330's Philip seemed to have appointed Ptolemy as a counselor to Alexander, with a responsibility to advise the son according to the interests of the father. When Alexander embarrassed Philip in the Pixodarus Affair, the king drove out of Macedonia those who had failed him. Fortunately for Ptolemy, Philip was assassinated not long thereafter (336), and when Alexander became king, he brought home those who had suffered exile.

Life's Work

Although Ptolemy accompanied Alexander into Asia, he did so initially in a minor capacity—proving that Ptolemy had not been an intimate of Alexander. Ptolemy's first command came in 330, when he led one of several units at the battle which gave the Macedonians access to Persia proper. Ptolemy became a figure of the first rank shortly afterward, when he replaced a certain Demetrius as one of Alexander's seven eminent bodyguards, whose duty it was to wait closely on the king in matters of consequence. Ptolemy further distinguished himself in 329, when he personally brought to Alexander Bessus, Alexander's last rival for the Persian throne.

Having attained Alexander's confidence, Ptolemy's service at the side of the king alternated with independent assignments. In 328 he commanded one of five columns as Alexander drove into Sogdiana, in 327 he was instrumental in the capture of the fortress of Chorienes, and, while the Macedonians campaigned along the Indus River (327-325), Ptolemy often led both Macedonian and mercenary troops. The return of Alexander to Susa in 324 brought Ptolemy military honors, his first wife (the Persian Artacama), and additional commands in coordination with Alexander.

The death of Alexander at Babylon in 323 precipitated a constitutional crisis, since the only male Argead living was the mentally deficient Arrhidaeus. Alexander's son by Roxane, Alexander IV, would be born several months after his father's passing. Perdiccas, the officer to whom the dying Alexander had given his signet ring in a gesture of unknown significance, dominated the discussions concerning succession and advised the Macedonians to accept an interregnum until it could be determined whether Roxane would give birth to a son. Among others, Ptolemy objected to the unprecedented leadership role Perdiccas had delegated himself. Dissension infected the Macedonian army until a compromise averting civil war was adopted. It was agreed that the throne should go to Arrhidaeus (who was given the throne name of Philip III), until such time as Roxane gave birth to a son. When that eventuality occurred, a dual monarchy was established. Since neither king was competent, both were put under the protection of Perdiccas. There followed a general distribution of satrapies in which Ptolemy received Egypt.

Once in Egypt, Ptolemy asserted control over the satrapy and extended his authority to incorporate the region around Cyrene. He then used his considerable resources to challenge the authority of Perdiccas. His first open act of defiance concerned the body of Alexander the Great. Whether the Macedonians originally meant to bury Alexander in Macedonia or at the oracular shrine of Ammon located at the oasis of Siwah in the Egyptian desert, when Alexander's funeral procession reached Syria, Ptolemy diverted the remains to Memphis, where they were enshrined until the late 280's, when they were transferred to a complex in Alexandria. Perdiccas saw the appropriation of Alexander's corpse as a rejection of his own authority and in 321 led an expedition to Egypt against Ptolemy.

By this time, others had begun to question the ambitions of Perdiccas, and a coalition including especially Ptolemy, Antipater, and Antigonus formed to strip Perdiccas of his office. In the resulting war, Perdiccas failed miserably in an attempt to force his way into Egypt and was assassinated by his own men for his failure. Ptolemy thereafter successfully appealed to the Macedonians of Perdiccas' army and persuaded many of them to settle in Egypt. One option—that of replacing Perdiccas as the guardian of the kings—Ptolemy refused, preferring to retain his Egyptian base.

Although Perdiccas was dead, Eumenes, his most important ally, remained free in Asia. In response to this new situation, a redistribution of satrapies occurred at Triparadisus. Ptolemy again received Egypt, while Antipater returned to Macedonia with the kings and Antigonus waged war against Eumenes. Ptolemy anchored an expanded influence by taking Antipater's daughter, Eurydice, as a second wife. (A third—Berenice I—was culled from Eurydice's retinue. Ptolemy's polygamy had a precedent in the Argead house.)

The death of Antipater in 319 initiated a new era. The royal family split behind the claims of the two kings, and a civil war erupted. Eventually, both kings were murdered: Philip III by Olympias in 317, and Alexander IV by Cassander in 311 or 310. Through inscriptions and coins, however, it is known that Ptolemy remained loyal to the kings of the Argead house until they were no more. Despite his professed Argead loyalties, Ptolemy continued to secure Egypt at the expense of rivals. In particular, he seized the coast of Palestine in order to safeguard the only viable access to Egypt by land.

In addition to these problems, Antigonus' success and ultimate victory over Eumenes in 316 destabilized the balance of power which had been established among the Macedonian officers at Triparadisus. High-handed actions, such as Antigonus' expulsion of Seleucus from his Babylonian satrapy, created a fear of a second Perdiccas. An alliance consisting of Ptolemy, Cassander, Lysimachus, and Seleucus demanded that Antigonus surrender his authority. When Antigonus refused, war erupted anew. This conflict continued intermittently until Antigonus was killed at a battle near Ipsus in 301. Ptolemy saw action in Palestine (where he defeated Demetrius, the son of Antigonus, at a battle near Gaza in 312) and amid the confusion built the beginnings of a maritime empire in the eastern Mediterranean.

Although this period saw the expansion of Ptolemy's influence, most of his early gains beyond Egypt were tenuously held and setbacks occurred. For example, in 306, Demetrius defeated the Ptolemaic navy off the island of Cyprus in an action so decisive that both he and his father subsequently claimed the title of "king." Once Antigonus and Demetrius claimed the royal mantle from the defunct Argead house, others followed suit, including Ptolemy in 305.

After Ipsus, Ptolemy reestablished influence abroad, retaking Cyprus and actively engaging in Aegean affairs. His occupation of Palestine after 301, however, precipitated a series of wars with the Seleucids in the third century. These civil wars established a rough balance among the emerging powers of Macedonia, Egypt, and Seleucid Asia. This balance was constantly under strain and ever shifting in its precise makeup, composed as it was of infant dynasties seeking legitimacy and leverage.

Egypt also claimed Ptolemy's attention. He inherited an efficient bureaucratic apparatus of great antiquity, capable of funneling great wealth to his coffers. Nevertheless, Ptolemy could not afford to rely on the loyalty of native Egyptians. Rather, he grafted a new Greco-Macedonian aristocracy onto the existing political structure. Recruitment was a major concern, and Ptolemy made every effort to attract Greek mercenaries, military colonists, and professionals accomplished in administration. The wealth of Egypt made possible these initiatives, and each recruit was guaranteed a respectable status as long as Ptolemy remained secure.

In part to unify these enlistees of varied background, Ptolemy combined elements of the Egyptian worship of Osiris and Apis to manufacture the cult of a new deity: Serapis. Traditionally, religion helped to define the parameters of Greek political communities, and the invented Serapis successfully drew Ptolemy's immigrants together. In addition, in an age of emerging ruler cults, Ptolemy posthumously was worshipped as a god (indeed, to the Egyptians, who worshipped him as pharaoh, he was naturally considered divine), receiving the epithet "Soter" (savior) from the Rhodians for his naval protection.

Under Ptolemy, Alexandria became the foremost city of the Hellenistic world. Planned on a grand scale, it held architectural wonders and became

Ptolemy Soter

the greatest literary and intellectual center of the age, with its focus being the great museum and library complex. In 284, after decades of molding Egypt to his liking, Ptolemy shared royal authority with a son by Berenice, Ptolemy II, better known as Ptolemy Philadelphus. Ptolemy Soter died shortly thereafter (in 283 or 282) at the age of eighty-four.

Summary

Ptolemy Soter was the one great link between Greece's classical age—characterized by its narrow geographical orientation and exclusive appreciation of the Greek cultural heritage—and the Hellenistic age, with its expanded horizons. He took advantage of the opportunities presented by the moment to rise as far as hard work could take him and was instrumental in combining Hellenistic traditions with those of the Orient—a mixture which was a hallmark of the Hellenistic period. Not the most talented of Alexander's successors in military affairs, Ptolemy nevertheless understood, even better than Alexander himself, how long-term stability depended on the careful selection of a defendable base coupled with a steady consolidation of resources. His success can be appreciated best once it is realized that he alone of the officers who received assignments in Babylon in 323 passed his legacy on to his descendants. He did more than politically anchor Egypt in a time of unprecedented change: Because of his patronage, which brought so many fertile minds to Alexandria, he was also able to shape the cultural experience which would dominate the civilized Western world for hundreds of years.

The range of Ptolemy's talents is not fully appreciated until it is realized that he was not only an active ruler and a cultural patron but also a historian of note. Late in life, he wrote an account of Alexander's conquests based not only on his own observations but also on important written sources (including a journal which detailed the king's activities on a daily basis, at least for the end of Alexander's reign). Although Ptolemy's account was slanted in his own favor, no other eyewitness account of the Macedonian conquest can claim greater objectivity. No longer extant, Ptolemy's work was one of the principal sources used in the second century of the Christian era by Arrian, whose history is the best extant account of Alexander's life. Without Ptolemy's attention to detail, present knowledge about Alexander would be considerably less accurate.

Bibliography

Bevan, Edwyn R. *The House of Ptolemy*. London: Methuen and Co., 1927. The standard English history of the Ptolemaic dynasty. The chapter devoted to Ptolemy I breifly reviews his pre-Egyptian career but concentrates on his achievements after 323.

Bowman, Alan K. *Egypt After the Pharaohs*. Berkeley: University of California Press, 1986. This work is a broad introduction to Egypt between the conquests of Alexander and the Arabs. As such, it covers the Ptolemaic period, especially insofar as its political and social institutions evolved.

Fraser, Peter Marshall. *Ptolemaic Alexandria*. 3 vols. New York: Oxford University Press, 1972. The authoritative study of the Ptolemaic capital and virtually every institution associated with the Macedonian presence in Egypt. An essential work for anyone interested in how Ptolemy developed the infrastructure of his realm.

Pearson, Lionel. *The Lost Histories of Alexander the Great*. New York: American Philological Association, 1960. A chapter is devoted to Ptolemy's lost history of Alexander.

Tarn, W. W., and G. T. Griffith. *Hellenistic Civilization*. New York: Meridian, 1961. Chapter 1 provides a historical outline of the period (including Ptolemy's contributions), which is unsurpassed in its concise political and military coverage.

Turner, E. G. "Ptolemaic Egypt." In *The Cambridge Ancient History*. Vol. 7, *The Hellenistic World*. 2d ed. Cambridge: Cambridge University Press, 1984. A review of Ptolemy's accomplishment in Egypt, with special attention devoted to the domestic difficulties associated with stabilization of Macedonian authority.

Walbank, R. W. *The Hellenistic World*. Cambridge, Mass.: Harvard University Press, 1981. One of the best introductions to the period in English, especially insofar as it traces the emergence of Hellenistic kingdoms.

William S. Greenwalt

JEAN PUCELLE

Born: c. 1290; Paris or northern France
Died: 1334; Paris
Area of Achievement: Art
Contribution: Pucelle's manuscript illuminations, which depicted three-dimensional spatial settings and the emotional interaction of figures, influenced the direction of artistic developments in northern European painting in the late Middle Ages and the early Renaissance.

Early Life

Although more documents can be connected with Jean Pucelle than with most medieval artists in northern Europe, they reveal comparatively little information about his personal life. Because he begins to appear in documents with an important commission—indicating that he was a mature artist—in 1319, his birth probably occurred around the end of the thirteenth century. One characteristic feature of his illumination is the lively quality of border ornament, which shows close observation of nature and inventive, often humorous grotesques. These stylistic traits, which were particularly developed in north French illumination, may point to a birthplace in this region.

It is likely that he was trained in the traditional medieval manner as an apprentice to one or more artists—probably in Paris, which was a major artistic center in the Gothic period. Another possible influence on Pucelle's formative background was the intellectual milieu of the University of Paris, one of the main universities in the later Middle Ages. As a center for theological studies, its faculty was primarily drawn from the mendicant orders of Dominicans and Franciscans. Most of the manuscripts that Pucelle illuminated were for either Dominican or Franciscan usage. In addition, Pucelle's complex and original iconographic programs, accompanied in *The Belleville Breviary* (1323-1326) by a written explanation likely composed by the artist, suggest that Pucelle was both literate and receptive to intellectual currents in theology.

Life's Work

Pucelle was primarily an illuminator of manuscripts. The first documented reference to his work as an artist, however, is a payment listed in the 1319-1324 accounts of the Confraternity of St. Jacques-aux-Pèlerins in Paris for the design of the group's great seal. The importance of this confraternity's membership demonstrates Pucelle's high standing as an artist. It also shows that the range of his artistic endeavors extended beyond manuscript illumination to include various aspects of design in other media.

Pucelle's manuscript illumination, on which his artistic reputation is based, is generally divided into two phases: early works dating around 1320 and mature works done from about 1323 until his death in 1334. The Italian influences in the illumination of his mature period suggest that a trip to Italy intervened between these two stages. The early works, especially *The Breviary of Blanche of France* (c. 1320) and *The Hours of Jeanne of Savoy* (c. 1320), show several important characteristics of Pucelle's illumination. Both manuscripts, which were intended for young women of the French nobility, are an indication of Pucelle's continued patronage by members of the French royal family. The illumination, executed by several artists, demonstrates how Pucelle often collaborated with other illuminators. Also, the style of Pucelle's painting in these manuscripts shows connections with Parisian illuminators of the early fourteenth century. At the same time, however, his miniatures evidence new interest in modeled figures painted in lighter color tonalities, spatial effects, and inventive border drolleries.

Miniatures in Pucelle's manuscripts from around 1323 on give indications of inspiration from Italian art of the early Trecento. From study of the *Maestà* altarpiece by Duccio di Buoninsegna in the Cathedral of Siena, painted between 1308 and 1311, Pucelle was attracted to the depiction of three-dimensional spatial settings and emotional interaction of figures in narrative scenes. In *The Hours of Jeanne d'Evreux*, the Virgin of the Annunciation stands within a room while the angel approaches through an antechamber in a composition very similar to *The Annunciation of the Death of the Virgin* from the *Maestà*. In Pucelle's *The Entombment* in this book of hours, the Virgin embracing Christ's body and the lamenting figure of Mary Magdalene behind the tomb repeat poses from the *Maestà*'s depiction. Similarly, emotional scenes combined with sculptural plasticity of figures show Pucelle's adaptation of aspects of Giovanni Pisano's sculptured pulpit at the church of San Andrea in Pistoia, completed in 1301: The *grisaille* painting technique of *The Hours of Jeanne d'Evreux* gives the painted figures a sculpturesque solidity. Other manuscripts with illuminations by Pucelle continue these Italian-inspired visual interests. A miniature in *The Miracles of Notre Dame* (executed before 1334), for example, depicts a Tuscan fortress much like the Palazzo Vecchio in Florence. The varied types of artistic borrowing, from three-dimensional spatial settings to iconographic motifs, suggest that Pucelle's knowledge of Italian art was based on firsthand observation.

Documentary evidence connects Pucelle with three illuminated manuscripts that represent the artistic achievement of his mature painting. *The Hours of Jeanne d'Evreux* is a small book of hours done for Jeanne d'Evreux, the wife of Charles IV, between her marriage in 1325 and her husband's death in 1328. This manuscript has been identified with a book of hours described in a codicil to Jeanne d'Evreux's testament in 1371 as being illuminated by Pucelle. It was willed to her nephew, Charles V, and is mentioned in an inventory of his private collection of treasures at Vincennes. Finally, it was owned by Charles V's brother, the great bibliophile Jean, Duke of Berry; it appears in inventories of his library in the early fifteenth century described as "Heures de Pucelle" (hours by Pucelle). The Billyng Bible, copied by an English scribe named Robert Billyng, contains a colophon which dates the manuscript's completion in 1327 and names Jean Pucelle, Anciau de Cens, and Jaquet Maci as illuminators. *The Belleville Breviary* was first owned by Jeanne de Belleville. Liturgical evidence from this Dominican breviary, including the absence of the office of Saint Thomas Aquinas—which the Dominicans adopted in 1326—dates the manuscript between 1323 and 1326. It contains marginal records of payment by Pucelle to other illuminators and decorators. Two other manuscripts have been attributed on stylistic grounds to the last years of Pucelle's career, *The Breviary of Jeanne d'Evreux* and *The Miracles of Notre Dame*. Other manuscripts are associated with Pucelle's shop.

The primary characteristics of Pucelle's illumination are depicting figures in unified, often three-dimensional spatial settings; portraying the psychological reactions of figures in narrative scenes; and presenting abstract theological concepts through visual iconography. *The Hours of Jeanne d'Evreux*, which is considered a masterwork done entirely by Pucelle, shows many of these artistic features. The three-dimensional enclosure in which the Annunciation takes place shows the depiction of spatial surroundings. In other miniatures, figures are tightly grouped, but the *grisaille* painting technique in shades of gray heightens the impression of plastically rendered forms. Many of the miniatures, especially in the Passion cycle, depict strong emotional reactions as seen when the Virgin swoons at the Crucifixion. In addition, the borders are enlivened with *bas-de-page* scenes which, as in the Annunciation to the Shepherds, extend the theme of the miniature. The crouching figures that support the architectural frames of some miniatures as well as the drolleries and grotesques that emerge from line endings reflect the observation of nature and lively humor characteristic of northern sculpture and illumination. *The Belleville Breviary* is especially outstanding for its complex iconographic program. Although parts of its illumination are now missing, the written exposition of the iconography prefaced to the manuscript along with surviving portions permit reconstruction of a program that includes Old Testament prophets revealing a prophecy as a New Testament article of faith in the calendar, three full-page miniatures that complete and expand on these relationships between Old and New Testaments, and in the Psalter, the idea of Virtues overcoming Vices, all culminating in the Last Judgment.

In most manuscripts associated with Pucelle, some variations in style and quality of illumination show that he usually worked with other miniaturists and decorators. The illumination of the Billyng Bible, for example, generally displays more conservative and traditional stylistic and compositional features, although it is contemporary with the aesthetically innovative hours of Jeanne d'Evreux. While such collaboration was a typical practice in Gothic manuscript illumination, it raises questions about Pucelle's artistic movement. Some view him as the head of a workshop, planning iconographic and illustrative elements and executing major parts of the illumination. Another interpretation suggests that he was one of several independent illuminators working on commission for a Parisian stationer. Regardless of the amount of his personal painting in any single manuscript with which he is connected, however, at his death in 1334, Pucelle had participated in, and probably directed the illumination of, many of the most outstanding French manuscripts of the first half of the fourteenth century.

Summary

While further study will continue to clarify Jean Pucelle's precise artistic role in the manuscripts with which his name is associated, his connection with these prominent artistic works shows him to have been a major innovating force in northern European art of the fourteenth century. By merging qualities of Italian and northern painting and sculpture, his illumination introduced new aesthetic concerns. He is the first painter in northern Europe to use coherent, three-dimensional spatial settings. His narrative scenes show a psychological interaction of figures with heightened emotion. The borders and expanded *bas-de-page* scenes in many of his manuscripts are enlivened with a naturalism and keen observation characteristic of northern Gothic art. His personal iconographic invention, particularly evident in *The Belleville Breviary*, demonstrates his intellectual grasp of theological concepts. Throughout his illumination, these creative artistic ideas are presented with an exquisite refinement characteristic of the Parisian court style.

As a recognition of his achievement as an artist, Pucelle's illumination continued to influence developments in French painting into the early fifteenth century. His immediate successor, the illuminator Jean le Noir, repeated Pucelle's compositional innovations with some modifications throughout a career that extended from the 1330's to the 1370's. Pucelle's stylistic interests influenced late fourteenth century painters, as seen, for example, in *Parement de Narbonne*, which also adopts the *grisaille* technique. The identification of manuscripts illuminated by Pucelle in *Jeanne d'Evreux's Testament* and in the Duke of Berry's inventories, unusual during this period, also attests this artist's continued reputation. The quality, creativity, and influence of his illumination make Jean Pucelle one of the most significant artists of the later Middle Ages.

Bibliography

Avril, François. *Manuscript Painting at the Court of France: The Fourteenth Century, 1310-1380*. New York: George Braziller, 1978. A survey of Parisian fourteenth century illumination with a good discussion of Pucelle and his relation to French manuscript painting throughout this century. Excellent color plates and a good bibliography. No index.

Deuchler, Florens. "Jean Pucelle—Facts and Fictions." *Bulletin of the Metropolitan Museum of Art* 29 (1971): 253-256. Reviews the evidence about Pucelle's life and the attribution of works to this artist. This article is skeptical about the relationship of documentary evidence to firm attribution of *The Hours of Jeanne d'Evreux* to Pucelle.

Ferber, Stanley. "Jean Pucelle and Giovanni Pisano." *Art Bulletin* 66 (1984): 65-72. This article presents the case that Pucelle must have studied the sculptured pulpit by Pisano at Pistoia. A good overview of the evidence supporting a trip by Pucelle to Italy and the relationships of Pucelle's illumination to Italian early Trecento art.

Hamburger, Jeffrey. "The Waddesdon Psalter and the Shop of Jean Pucelle." *Zeitschrift für Kunstgeschichte* 44 (1981): 243-257. A discussion of the Waddesdon Psalter which contains some illumination by Pucelle and other miniature painting by a collaborator in a style close to Pucelle's. The article raises issues about the nature of Pucelle's workshop.

Meiss, Millard. *French Painting in the Time of Jean de Berry: The Late Fourteenth Century and the Patronage of the Duke.* 2 vols. London: Phaidon, 1967. Pucelle's work as an illuminator is discussed in the context of the background for French manuscript painting of the late fourteenth century. The book shows Pucelle's influence throughout the century.

Morand, Kathleen. *Jean Pucelle.* Oxford: Clarendon Press, 1962. This monograph covers Pucelle's life and career as an illuminator. Because it was published before the date of Pucelle's death in 1334 was discovered, some of the later manuscripts attributed to Pucelle in this book are now seen as works by his followers.

_____. "Jean Pucelle: A Re-examination of the Evidence." *Burlington Magazine* 103 (1961): 206-211. This article analyzes in detail the documentary evidence connecting Jean Pucelle with the Billyng Bible, *The Belleville Breviary*, and *The Hours of Jeanne d'Evreux*. It supports the interpretation of Jean Pucelle as illuminator of *The Hours of Jeanne d'Evreux*.

Nordenfalk, Carl. "Maître Honoré and Maître Pucelle." *Apollo* 89 (1964): 356-364. This article is, in part, a review of Morand's monograph on Pucelle. As a review essay, it adds perceptive observations and interpretations of Pucelle's illumination.

Panofsky, Erwin. *Early Netherlandish Painting.* 2 vols. Cambridge, Mass.: Harvard University Press, 1953. Although this book concentrates on northern Renaissance painting of the fifteenth century, Pucelle's illumination is discussed from the standpoint of his contribution as an innovator of and precursor to the northern Renaissance style.

Randall, Lilian M. C. "Games and the Passion in Pucelle's *Hours of Jeanne* d'*Evreux.*" *Speculum* 47 (1972): 246-257. This article explains the meaning and relevance of several of the *bas-de-page* scenes to the iconographic program of the miniature cycle in *The Hours of Jeanne d'Evreux*.

Sandler, Lucy Freeman. "Jean Pucelle and the Lost Miniatures of *The Belleville Breviary.*" *Art Bulletin* 66 (1984): 73-96. This article reconstructs the three lost full-page miniatures from the important and unusual iconographic cycle illustrating *The Belleville Breviary*. It provides an edition and translation of the text prefaced to the manuscript which explains this iconographic program.

Karen Gould

PYRRHON OF ELIS

Born: c. 360 B.C.; Elis, Greece
Died: c. 272 B.C.; buried in village of Petra, near Elis
Area of Achievement: Philosophy
Contribution: The founder of skepticism, Pyrrhon, a companion of Alexander the Great, taught that the nature of things is inapprehensible; his attitude greatly influenced science and philosophy throughout antiquity.

Early Life

Few details about the life of Pyrrhon have been preserved. Born in Elis, Pyrrhon was the son of Pleistarchus or, by other accounts, Pleitocrates. Apparently of humble background, Pyrrhon first studied painting, no doubt influenced by the master Apelles in nearby Sikyon, then briefly turned his hand to poetry. Pyrrhon's early philosophical training must have begun soon thereafter; he studied under Bryson and Anaxarchus (a pupil of Democritus and adviser to Alexander the Great), whom he joined in the Macedonian invasion of Persia and India in 331 B.C. During that invasion, Pyrrhon gained a reputation for high moral conduct among the quarrelsome Macedonians. After returning to his native Elis, he was awarded a high priesthood and was exempted from taxes; he also received honorary Athenian citizenship and knew Aristotle, Epicurus, the Academic Arcesilaus, and Zeno of Citium. A tradition that Alexander had provided Pyrrhon with a comfortable endowment may help to account for the philosopher's high social standing. Although probably a man of some means, he was renowned for his modest and withdrawn life.

Pyrrhon's Greece witnessed a major revolution in philosophical thinking as the old political order of independent city-states yielded to the Hellenistic empires. Pyrrhonistic philosophy joined the Epicurean and the Stoic in seeking ways to achieve *ataraxia*—a personal state of freedom from worldly cares. Pyrrhon differed both from his contemporaries and from the previous skeptical trends of Xenophanes, Heraclitus, Democritus, and the Sophists, in that he held no dogmatic position concerning the nature of truth. According to Pyrrhon and his followers, the phenomena of sense experience are neither true nor false, and there is no access to any proof of reality beyond the empirical world. The wise and happy man takes an agnostic stance on the nature of reality.

Pyrrhon did not establish a formal school as did Epicurus and Zeno, though he was the mentor of Philo of Athens, Nausiphanes of Teios, and Timon of Phlius, his only true successor. In his third century A.D. *Peri biōn dogmatōn kai apophthegmatōn tōn en philosophia eudokimēsantōn* (*Lives and Opinions of Eminent Philosophers*, 1688), Diogenes Laërtius quotes extensively from the writings of Timon and from the life of Pyrrhon written by Antigonus of Carystus shortly after the philosopher's death. Diogenes Laërtius' account, together with Cicero's somewhat problematic references, provides an important check on the portrait presented by later skeptical thinkers, including the major work of second century A.D. skeptic Sextus Empiricus.

Life's Work

The second century A.D. Peripatetic philosopher Aristocles of Messana quotes Timon, saying that the happy man must examine three questions: What is the nature of things, what attitude should one adopt with respect to them, and what will be the result for those who adopt this attitude?

Pyrrhon held that things by nature are inapprehensible (*akatalypsias*) and indeterminate (*adiaphora*). Making use of the established distinction between appearances and reality, Pyrrhon elaborated, stating that sense experiences and beliefs are neither true nor false because the true nature of things, if one exists, cannot be known.

Pyrrhonistic skepticism is summed up in the following formula: The nature of things no more is than is not, than both is and is not, than neither is nor is not. Shortened to the phrase "no more," the indeterminability of nature leads the wise man to withhold judgment (*aprosthetein*). According to Pyrrhon, "That honey is sweet I do not grant; that it seems so, I agree." The objective world cannot be perceived, and no ultimate truth can be assigned to subjective observations.

Pyrrhon did not urge the cessation of inquiry into the natural world. On the contrary, he held that the skeptic should continue to seek truth; this position influenced the development of medicine and science in Cos and in Alexandria. A suspension of judgment for Pyrrhon was a system (*agoge*) which leads to the desired goal of mental imperturbability, *ataraxia*.

While the essential origins of Pyrrhonism clearly are to be found in a purely Greek philosophical dialogue, it is possible that Pyrrhon's epistemology had been influenced by Buddhist thought. Contemporary accounts of Alexander show that the Greeks did have access to interpretations of Indian gymnosophists (literally, "naked wise men"). Alexander and his men, presumably including the youthful Pyrrhon, watched a certain Sphines (called "Calanus" in Greek) voluntarily mount his own funeral pyre, declaring that it was better for him to die than to live. The extent to which Pyrrhon was aware of Buddhist agnosticism or the dictum that happiness was freedom from worldly desires cannot be determined. Pyrrhon's penchant for wandering in deserted places searching for knowledge and his attempt to achieve that state of mind he called "silence" (*aphasia*) may well have had their roots in the asceticism of India.

Given the dominance of ethical questions in Greek thought after Plato, it is not surprising that Pyrrhon also addressed the problem of virtue. The testi-

Pyrrhon of Elis

mony of Timon and Cicero shows that Pyrrhon was a stern moralist who led an exemplary life. Rejecting all definitions of virtue, Pyrrhon declared that without any true guide to moral conduct, one must observe traditional laws and customs. Withdrawn from active life though he may have been, Pyrrhon nevertheless was a good citizen.

It is unfortunate that testimony on Pyrrhon reveals little else about his positions. It may be surmised that the debate between Stoics and later skeptics over possible criteria of right conduct had its origin in Pyrrhon's thought. A poem by Timon mentions a right standard (*orthon canona*) by which he can question those who hold that the nature of the divine and the good makes men live most equably. In this poem, Timon inserts the qualification "as it seems to me to be," perhaps to indicate that the Pyrrhonic standard is the incommensurability of appearance and reality.

Pyrrhon was not original in doubting the ultimate truth of sensory experiences. His true contribution to Greek philosophy lay in his denial of the possibility that true knowledge can be gained by pure reason: If the only access to the world is through phenomena, there is no way to judge these phenomena against any objective model. Pyrrhon thus turned away from the monumental intellectual systems of Plato and Aristotle and helped to usher in an age of empiricism.

Summary

Pyrrhon's empirical skepticism did not outlive his pupil Timon. Skeptical thought did persist, however, in the new Academy of the Aeolian Arcesilaus (315-240 B.C.) and of Carneades (214-129 B.C.). This Academic skepticism was more a second version of skepticism than a direct continuation of Pyrrhonism. The Academics used the Platonic dialectic as their basis for a suspension of judgment on the true nature of things. This Academic skepticism was a direct attack on the Stoic position, which held that some sense impressions were true. Unlike the Pyrrhonists, however, the Academic skeptic did maintain that sense impressions can be representative of an objective, external world.

After Carneades, the next important skeptical thinker was the enigmatic Aenesidemus, who lived sometime between the first century B.C. and the second century A.D. in Alexandria. Aenesidemus reorganized skeptical sayings into ten "tropes," a not-too-original attack on the possibility of deriving true knowledge from perceptual experiences.

The last major figure in the history of ancient skepticism was Sextus Empiricus, a Greek physician who lived sometime between A.D. 150 and 250. The large corpus of Sextus' writing that has been preserved provides the most complete statement of ancient skepticism. A true disciple of Pyrrhon, Sextus used the Pyrrhonistic suspension of judgment in his attacks on the dogmatic positions of contemporary philosophers and physicians. Through

Sextus Empiricus, the original philosophy of Pyrrhon of Elis has been saved from oblivion.

Bibliography

Long, A. A. *Hellenistic Philosophy: Stoics, Epicureans, Sceptics.* New York: Charles Scribner's Sons, 1974. A general work on the three main philosophical schools of the Hellenistic age. Includes a chapter on Pyrrhon and the later skeptics.

Patrick, Mary Mills. *The Greek Sceptics.* New York: Columbia University Press, 1929. A standard work on the skeptics. Includes a somewhat speculative account of the antecedents of Pyrrhon's philosophy.

Schofield, Malcolm, Myles Burnyeat, and Jonathan Barnes, eds. *Doubt and Dogmatism: Studies in Hellenistic Epistemology.* Oxford: Clarendon Press, 1980. This work is a collection of ten essays from a 1978 Oxford conference. Presents detailed studies on Hellenistic theories of knowledge.

Stough, Charlotte. *Greek Skepticism: A Study in Epistemology.* Berkeley: University of California Press, 1969. A thorough investigation of the epistemology of the skeptics. Stough includes a chapter on early Pyrrhonism.

Tarrant, Harold. *Scepticism or Platonism? The Philosophy of the Fourth Academy.* Cambridge: Cambridge University Press, 1985. An original investigation of the first century B.C. philosophies of Philo and Charmadas. Discusses the influence of early Pyrrhonists.

Zeller, Eduard. *The Stoics, Epicureans, and Sceptics.* Translated by Oswald Reichel. New York: Russell and Russell, 1962. Part of Zeller's massive nineteenth century history of Greek philosophy, this work contains a useful chapter on Pyrrhon. Includes bibliographical footnotes.

Murray C. McClellan

PYTHAGORAS

Born: c. 580 B.C.; Samos, Greece
Died: 504 B.C. or 500 B.C.; Croton or Metapontum
Areas of Achievement: Philosophy, mathematics, astronomy, and music
Contribution: Pythagoras set an inspiring example with his energetic search for knowledge of universal order. His specific discoveries and accomplishments in philosophy, mathematics, astronomy, and music theory make him an important figure in Western intellectual history.

Early Life

Pythagoras, son of Mnesarchus, probably was born about 580 B.C. (various sources offer dates ranging from 597 to 560). His birthplace was the Greek island of Samos in the Mediterranean Sea. Aside from these details, information about his early life—most of it from the third and fourth centuries B.C., up to one hundred years after he died—is extremely sketchy. On the other hand, sources roughly contemporary with him tend to contradict one another, possibly because those who had been his students developed in many different directions after his death.

Aristotle's *Metaphysica* (335-323 B.C.; *Metaphysics*), one source of information about Pythagorean philosophy, never refers to Pythagoras himself but always to "the Pythagoreans." Furthermore, it is known that many ideas attributed to Pythagoras have been filtered through Platonism. Nevertheless, certain doctrines and biographical events can be traced with reasonable certainty to Pythagoras himself. His teachers in Greece are said to have included Creophilus and Pherecydes of Syros; the latter (who is identified as history's first prose writer) probably encouraged Pythagoras' belief in the transmigration of souls, which became a major tenet of Pythagorean philosophy. A less certain but more detailed tradition has him also studying under Thales of Miletus, who built a philosophy on rational, positive integers. In fact, these integers were to prove a stumbling block to Pythagoras, but would lead to his discovery of irrational numbers such as the square root of two.

Following his studies in Greece, Pythagoras traveled extensively in Egypt, Babylonia, and other Mediterranean lands, learning the rules of thumb that, collectively, passed for geometry at that time. He was to raise geometry to the level of a true science through his pioneering work on geometric proofs and the axioms, or postulates, from which these are derived.

A bust now housed at Rome's Capitoline Museum (the sculptor is not known) portrays the philosopher as having close-cropped, wavy Greek hair and beard, his features expressing the relentlessly inquiring Ionian mind—a mind that insisted on knowing for metaphysical reasons the *exact* ratio of the side of a square to its diagonal. Pythagoras' eyes suggest an inward focus even as they gaze intently at the viewer. The furrowed forehead conveys solemnity and powerful concentration, yet deeply etched lines around the mouth, and the hint of a crinkle about the eyes, reveal that this great man was fully capable of laughter.

Life's Work

When Pythagoras returned to Samos from his studies abroad, he found his native land in the grip of the tyrant Polycrates, who had come to power about 538 B.C. In the meantime, the Greek mainland had been partially overrun by the Persians. Probably because of these developments, in 529 Pythagoras migrated to Croton, a Dorian colony in southern Italy, and entered into what became the historically important period of his life.

At Croton he founded a school of philosophy that in some ways resembled a monastic order. Its members were pledged to a pure and devout life, close friendship, and political harmony. In the immediately preceding years, southern Italy had been nearly destroyed by the strife of political factions. Modern historians speculate that Pythagoras thought that political power would give his organization an opportunity to lead others to salvation through the disciplines of nonviolence, vegetarianism, personal alignment with the mathematical laws that govern the universe, and the practice of ethics in order to earn a superior reincarnation. (Pythagoras believed in metempsychosis, the transmigration of souls from one body to another, possibly from humans to animals. Indeed, Pythagoras claimed that he could remember four previous human lifetimes in detail.)

His adherents he divided into two hierarchical groups. The first was the *akousmatikoi*, or listeners, who were enjoined to remain silent, listen to and absorb Pythagoras' spoken precepts, and practice the special way of life taught by him. The second group was the *mathematikoi* (students of theoretical subjects, or simply "those who know"), who pursued the subjects of arithmetic, the theory of music, astronomy, and cosmology. (Though *mathematikoi* later came to mean "scientists" or "mathematicians," originally it meant those who had attained advanced knowledge in a broader sense.) The *mathematikoi*, after a long period of training, could ask questions and express opinions of their own.

Despite the later divergences among his students—fostered perhaps by his having divided them into two classes—Pythagoras himself drew a close connection between his metaphysical and scientific teachings. In his time, hardly anyone conceived of a split between science and religion or metaphysics. Nevertheless, some modern historians deny any real relation between the scientific doctrines of the Pythagorean society and its spiritualism and personal disciplines. In the twentieth century, Pythagoras' findings in astronomy, mathematics, and music theory are much more widely appreciated than the metaphysical philosophy that, to him, was the logical outcome of those findings.

Pythagoras

Pythagoras developed a philosophy of number to account for the essence of all things. This concept rested on three basic observations: the mathematical relationships of musical harmonies, the fact that any triangle whose sides are in a ratio of 3:4:5 is always a right triangle, and the fixed numerical relations among the movement of stars and planets. It was the consistency of ratios among musical harmonies and geometrical shapes in different sizes and materials that impressed Pythagoras.

His first perception (which some historians consider his greatest) was that musical intervals depend on arithmetical ratios among lengths of string on the lyre (the most widely played instrument of Pythagoras' time), provided that these strings are at the same tension. For example, a ratio of 2:1 produces an octave; that is, a string twice as long as another string, at the same tension, produces the same note an octave below the shorter string. Similarly, 3:2 produces a fifth and 4:3 produces a fourth. Using these ratios, one could assign numbers to the four fixed strings of the lyre: 6, 8, 9, and 12. Moreover, if these ratios are transferred to another instrument—such as the flute, also highly popular in that era—the same harmonies will result. Hippasus of Metapontum, a *mathematikos* living a generation after Pythagoras, extended this music theory through experiments to produce the same harmonies with empty and partly filled glass containers and metal disks of varying thicknesses.

Pythagoras himself determined that the most important musical intervals can be expressed in ratios among the numbers 1, 2, 3, and 4, and he concluded that the number 10—the sum of these first four integers—comprehends the entire nature of number. Tradition has it that the later Pythagoreans, rather than swear by the gods as most other people did, swore by the "Tetrachtys of the Decad" (the sum of 1, 2, 3, and 4). The Pythagoreans also sought the special character of each number. The tetrachtys was called a "triangular number" because its components can readily be arranged as a triangle.

By extension, the number 1 is reason because it never changes; 2 is opinion; 4 is justice (a concept surviving in the term "a square deal"). Odd numbers are masculine and even numbers are feminine; therefore, 5, the first number representing the sum of an odd and an even number (1, "unity," not being considered for this purpose), symbolizes marriage. Seven is *parthenos*, or virgin, because among the first ten integers it has neither factors nor products. Other surviving Pythagorean concepts include unlucky 13 and "the seventh son of a seventh son."

To some people in the twentieth century, these number concepts seem merely superstitious. Nevertheless, Pythagoras and his followers did important work in several branches of mathematics and exerted a lasting influence on the field. The best-known example is the Pythagorean Theorem, the statement that the square of the hypotenuse of a right triangle is equal to the sum of the squares of the other two sides. Special applications of the theorem were known in Mesopotamia as early as the eighteenth century B.C., but Pythagoras sought to generalize it for a characteristically Greek reason: This theorem measures the ratio of the side of a square to its diagonal, and he was determined to know the *precise* ratio. It cannot be expressed as a whole number, however, so Pythagoras found a common denominator by showing a relationship among the *squares* of the sides of a right triangle. The Pythagorean Theorem is set forth in book 1 of Euclid's *Stoicheia* (*Elements*), Euclid being one of several later Greek thinkers whom Pythagoras strongly influenced and who transmitted his ideas in much-modified form to posterity.

Pythagoras also is said to have discovered the theory of proportion and the arithmetic, geometric, and harmonic means. The terms of certain arithmetic and harmonic means yield the three musical intervals. In addition, the ancient historian Proclus credited Pythagoras with discovering the construction of the five regular geometrical solids, though modern scholars think it more likely that he discovered three—the pyramid, the tetrahedron, and the dodecahedron—and that Theaetetus (after whom a Platonic dialogue is named) later discovered the construction of the remaining two, the octahedron and the icosahedron.

The field of astronomy, too, is indebted to Pythagoras. He was among the first to contend that the earth and the universe are spherical. He understood that the sun, the moon, and the planets rotate on their own axes and also orbit a central point outside themselves, though he believed that this central point was the earth. Later Pythagoreans deposed the earth as the center of the universe and substituted a "central fire," which, however, they did not identify as the sun—this they saw as another planet. Nearest the central fire was the "counter-earth," which always accompanied the earth in its orbit. The Pythagoreans assumed that the earth's rotation and its revolution around the central fire took the same amount of time—twenty-four hours. According to Aristotle, the idea of a counter-earth—besides bringing the number of revolving bodies up to the mystical number of ten—helped to explain lunar eclipses, which were thought to be caused by the counter-earth's interposition between sun and moon. Two thousand years later, Nicolaus Copernicus saw the Pythagorean system as anticipating his own; he had in mind both the Pythagoreans' concept of the day-and-night cycle and their explanation of eclipses.

Like Copernicus in his time, Pythagoras and his followers in their time were highly controversial. For many years, the Pythagoreans did exert a strong political and philosophical influence throughout southern Italy. The closing years of the sixth century B.C., however, saw the rise of democratic sentiments, and a reaction set in against the Pythagoreans, whom the democrats regarded as elitist.

Indeed, this political reaction led either to Pythagoras' exile or to his

Pythagoras

death—there are two traditions surrounding it. One is that a democrat named Cylon led a revolt against the power of the Pythagorean brotherhood and forced Pythagoras to retire to Metapontum, where he died peacefully about the end of the sixth century B.C. According to the other tradition, Pythagoras perished when his adversaries set fire to his school in Croton in 504 B.C. The story is that of his vast library of scrolls, only one was brought out of the fire; it contained his most esoteric secrets, which were passed on to succeeding generations of Pythagoreans.

Whichever account is true, Pythagoras' followers continued to be powerful throughout Magna Graecia until at least the middle of the fifth century B.C., when another reaction set in against them and their meetinghouses were sacked and burned. The survivors scattered in exile and did not return to Italy until the end of the fifth century. During the ensuing decades, the leading Pythagorean was Philolaus, who wrote the first systematic exposition of Pythagorean philosophy. Philolaus' influence can be traced to Plato through their mutual friend Archytas, who ruled Taras (Tarentum) in Italy for many years. The Platonic dialogue *Timaeus* (360-347 B.C.), named for its main character, a young Pythagorean astronomer, describes Pythagorean ideas in detail.

Summary

"Of all men," said Heraclitus, "Pythagoras, the son of Mnesarchus, was the most assiduous inquirer." Pythagoras is said to have been the first person to call himself a philosopher, or lover of wisdom. He believed that the universe is a logical, symmetrical whole, which can be understood in simple terms. For Pythagoras and his students, there was no gap between the scientific or mathematical ideal and the aesthetic. The beauty of his concepts and of the universe they described lies in their simplicity and consistency.

Quite aside from any of Pythagoras' specific intellectual accomplishments, his belief in universal order, and the energy he displayed in seeking it out, provided a galvanizing example for others. Sketchy as are the details of his personal life, his ideals left their mark on later poets, artists, scientists, and philosophers from Plato and Aristotle through the Renaissance and down to the twentieth century. Indirectly, through Pythagoras' disciple Philolaus, his ideas were transmitted to Plato and Aristotle, and, through these better-known thinkers, to the entire Western world.

Among Pythagoras' specific accomplishments, his systematic exposition of mathematical principles alone would have been enough to make him an important figure in Western intellectual history, but the spiritual beliefs he espoused make him also one of the great religious teachers of ancient Greek times. Even those ideas of his that are seen as intellectually disreputable have inspired generations of poets and artists. For example, the Pythagorean concept of the harmony of the spheres, suggested by the analogy between musical ratios and those of planetary orbits, became a central metaphor of Renaissance literature.

Bibliography
Bell, Eric T. *Men of Mathematics.* New York: Simon and Schuster, 1937. Includes a chapter on the intellectual challenges that led to Pythagoras' discovery of irrational numbers and the theorem named for him.
Burkert, Walter. *Lore and Science in Ancient Pythagoreanism.* Translated by Edwin L. Minar, Jr. Cambridge, Mass.: Harvard University Press, 1972. This study, translated from the German, attempts to disentangle Pythagoreanism from Platonism and to describe the various aspects of Pythagoreanism, from music theory to what is called shamanistic religion. Includes notes, indexes, and an extensive bibliography.
Kirk, Geoffrey S., and John E. Raven. *The Pre-Socratic Philosophers.* New York: Cambridge University Press, 1957. Provides a good account of Pythagoras and his followers, in their historical context, from a philosopher's point of view.
Muir, Jane. *Of Men and Numbers.* New York: Dodd, Mead and Co., 1961. Simply written for lay readers. Contains a chapter on Pythagoras' mathematical work and its influence on later scientists, especially Euclid.
Philip, J. A. *Pythagoras and Early Pythagoreanism.* Ann Arbor: University of Michigan Press, 1966. Attempts to separate the valid information from the legends surrounding Pythagoras and his teachings. Includes notes and a selected bibliography.
Plato. *Timaeus.* Translated by Thomas Taylor. Princeton, N.J.: Princeton University Press, 1944. An unusual Platonic dialogue, in that here Socrates is not a central figure but a listener. It portrays Timaeus, an energetic Pythagorean astronomer, expounding his teacher's ideas about the origin and character of the universe.

Thomas Rankin

PYTHEAS

Born: c. 350-325 B.C.; Massalia, Gaul
Died: After 300 B.C.; perhaps Massalia, Gaul
Areas of Achievement: Science and exploration
Contribution: Pytheas undertook the first lengthy voyage to the North Atlantic and may have circumnavigated England. This knowledge of the West, together with his astronomical observations, provided the basis for centuries of study.

Early Life

It is a special characteristic of the study of antiquity that the fewer facts scholars know about a figure, the more they seem to write about him. So it is that an enormous bibliography about Pytheas of Massalia, the first known man to explore the far reaches of the North Atlantic, has evolved.

The time period of Pytheas' voyage has been determined with some certainty. Pytheas seems to have used a reference work which dates to 347 B.C., but since he is not mentioned by Aristotle, perhaps the voyage had not occurred before Aristotle's death in 322 B.C. Also, according to Strabo, Pytheas is quoted by Dicaearchus, who died circa 285 B.C. Thus, the voyage most definitely occurred between 347 and 285 B.C. At this time Carthage was the leading city of the western Mediterranean and controlled all traffic in and out of the Pillars of Hercules (Gibraltar). It is, therefore, sometimes claimed that Pytheas could have escaped this blockade only while Carthage was distracted in the war with Syracuse. If these assumptions are correct, the voyage took place between 310 and 306 B.C. Further, since Pytheas was surely a mature adult when he undertook the journey, scholars place his birth roughly between 350 and 325 B.C.

The date for the voyage is important, for it is believed that Pytheas opened the world of the West to Greek exploration at the same time that the wonders of the Far East were trickling back to the Mediterranean as a result of the conquests of Alexander the Great. The cosmopolitan Hellenistic age was being born and a quest for knowledge of far-off lands and their marvels was to play a large role in it. Apart from this tenuous but probable date, only two firm facts about Pytheas' life—his financial condition and his place of origin—are known. Polybius, also quoted by Strabo, sneers at Pytheas' voyage, asking if it was likely that a private citizen, and a poor one at that, ever undertook such a venture. Although Polybius was far from impartial, this comment may indicate that the voyage was state-sponsored.

Ancient authors are unanimous in calling him "Pytheas of Massalia," modern Marseilles. Modern texts often call him "Pytheas of Massilia," using the less accurate Roman form of the name. This place of origin is not unexpected, for Massalia, founded circa 600 B.C. by Phocaea in Asia Minor, was one of the most ambitious seafaring Greek towns. It soon controlled the coast, from its fine harbor down to modern Ampurias, seventy-five miles northeast of Barcelona. A Massaliote named Euthymenes was said to have sailed south along Africa until he saw a river filled with crocodiles (possibly the Senegal), and Massalia had early trading connections with metal-rich Tartessus in Spain. Friction with Carthage was inevitable as the two powers sought control of these rich trade routes. Into this tradition of Massaliote adventurism Pytheas was born, poor but ambitious.

Life's Work

Not a word of Pytheas' works remains. It has even been suggested that Pytheas' own works were not available to such authors as Diodorus Siculus (who wrote under Julius Caesar and Augustus), Strabo (who wrote under Augustus), and Pliny the Elder, who preserved for posterity meager fragments of Pytheas' research by quoting from or citing his works. Very often the information is secondhand, preceded by such phrases as "Polybius says that Pytheas claims that. . . ."

Nevertheless, it is clear that Pytheas was remembered fondly as an astronomical scientist. Using only a sundial, he calculated the latitude of Massalia with remarkable accuracy. He noted first that the pole star was not really at the pole and was also the first to notice a relationship between the moon and the tides. Much of the information on latitudes and geography that he brought back from his voyages was deemed sufficiently accurate to be used by such famous ancient scholars as Timaeus, Hipparchus, and Ptolemy.

Pytheas the explorer, however, had another reputation entirely, neatly summed up by Strabo's calling him "the greatest liar among mortals." The nature and name of the work which reaped such abuse are unknown. The work may have been called "On the Ocean," "The Periplus" (meaning "voyage"), or "Travels Around the World." Modern scholars generally believe that it was a single work and that it recounted Pytheas' voyage. There is much to be said, however, for the theory that it was a general work of geography in which he reported his own firsthand observations, along with the rumors and reports he heard from others. If this is so, the scorn of later antiquity, relying on a spurious text, is more understandable. One can imagine the same comments being directed at Herodotus if only the more marvelous passages of his work had survived in this fashion.

With all that as warning, it is still customary to take the scattered references to Pytheas' voyage and reconstruct his route. If this approach is valid, his travels are impressive indeed. He left the Pillars of Hercules and cruised around Spain and the coast of France to the coast of Brittany and Ushant Island. Instead of continuing his coastal route as was customary for ancient mariners, he apparently struck out across the channel to Land's End, at the southwest tip of Britain at Cornwall. Here he described local tin mining. It is often asserted that Pytheas then circumnavigated the entire island of Britain. This belief is based on the fact that he describes the shape of the island correctly, describes its relationship to the coast better than did his critic Strabo, and, although doubling their true lengths, still correctly determines the proportion of the three sides. He probably made frequent observations of native behavior, and he may have conducted investigations inland. Diodorus, probably relying on Pytheas, reported correctly that the natives' huts were primitive, that they were basically peaceful but knew the chariot used for warfare, that they threshed their grain indoors because of the wet climate, and that they brewed and consumed mead.

Pytheas undoubtedly passed by Ireland, although no specific mention of this is found. It is often claimed, however, that his observations on the island enabled subsequent ancient geographers to locate it accurately on their maps. He apparently moved on to the northern tip of Britain, where he blandly described incredible tides eighty cubits (120 feet) high. Modern scholars see in this the gale-enhanced tides of the Pentland Firth.

It is the next stop on Pytheas' voyage which causes the greatest discussion. Pytheas claims that the island of Thule lay six days to the north of Britain and only one day from the frozen sea, sometimes called the Cronian Sea. Here, he states, days have up to twenty hours of sunlight in summer and twenty hours of darkness in winter. As if that information were not sufficiently incredible, he claims that the island lay in semicongealed waters in an area where earth, sea, and air are all mixed, suspended in a mixture resembling "sea lung" (perhaps a sort of jellyfish).

Where, if anywhere, is this Thule? Pytheas only claims that he saw the sea lung, getting the rest secondhand. Some parts of his tale ring true, such as long northerly days of light or darkness and a mixture of fog, mist, and slush so thick that one cannot tell where sea ends and sky begins. Scholars variously identify Thule as Iceland, Norway, the Shetland Islands, or the Orkney Islands, but no one solution is entirely satisfactory.

Pytheas soon turned south and completed his circumnavigation until he recrossed the channel. Here, again, there are problems, for he claims to have visited amber-rich lands as far as the Tanais River, acknowledged as the boundary between Europe and Asia. Scholars claim either that Pytheas reached the Vistula River and thus, remarkably, the heart of the Baltic Sea or that he stopped at the Elbe River. In either case, it is generally assumed that from there he retraced his steps along the European coast and returned home. Even by the most conservative estimates, he had traveled a minimum of seventy-five hundred miles in ships designed for the Mediterranean and manned by sailors unfamiliar with the rigors of the northern seas.

Summary

How can one assess a man and voyage so beset with problems of historicity? Did Pytheas in fact make a voyage at all? Was it a single voyage or were there two—one to Britain and one to the land of amber? In either case, how far did he go and how much information is from his own experience and how much is from what he learned through inquiry?

Barring the remarkable discovery of a long-lost Pytheas manuscript, these questions will never be answered. A coin from Cyrene, found on the northern coast of Brittany and dating to this time, has been cautiously set forth as evidence of Greek intrusion at this date, but the caution is well deserved.

Yet, despite the poor evidence and the hostility of the ancient authors, scholars can gauge Pytheas' importance from the impact he had on those who came after him. Pytheas opened Greek eyes to the wonders of the West, and it was his reports, for better or worse, which formed the basis for all writers on this area of the world for two centuries to come. In the same way, his scientific observations were respected and used by the best geographical minds of antiquity.

Still, it is highly likely that Pytheas did undertake a voyage himself and that he pushed fairly far to the north. Several thorny problems are solved if one believes that many of his wilder statements were not based on firsthand information but on tales he heard along the way. Much of the difficulty regarding Thule, for example, disappears when one views Pytheas' "discoveries" in this light.

The purpose of this voyage is also unclear. Some have hailed it as the first purely scientific voyage known to humankind. Yet if Pytheas was in fact a poor man and thus had public funds behind him, it is highly unlikely that the elders of Massalia would have found reports of sea lung proper repayment for their investment. It is wiser to see the voyage as primarily commercial, aimed at rivaling Carthaginian trade routes to lands rich in tin and amber, although Pytheas clearly lost no opportunity to engage in scientific enquiry along the way. (To be sure, his entire trip north of Cornwall seems guided more by a sense of adventure than of mercantilism.)

The world soon forgot about Pytheas' contribution to Massaliote trade routes. In fact, there is no evidence that an increase in trade followed his maiden voyage. Less ephemeral were Pytheas' tales of gigantic tides, sea lung, or Thule. His appeal extends into modern times, as the term "ultima Thule" remains a synonym for "the ends of the earth."

Bibliography
Bunbury, E. H. *A History of Ancient Geography Among the Greeks and Romans from the Earliest Ages Till the Fall of the Roman Empire.* 2d ed. Mineola, N.Y.: Dover Publications, 1959. A very sensible and cautious reconstruction of the probable circumstances surrounding Pytheas' voyage.
Carpenter, Rhys. *Beyond the Pillars of Heracles.* New York: Delacorte Press, 1966. A very lengthy section devoted to Pytheas treats several issues in

great detail. An unorthodox date for Pytheas' life is to be rejected but the discussion of Thule is very well done.

Cary, Max, and E. H. Warmington. *The Ancient Explorers.* London: Methuen and Co., 1929. Rev. ed. Baltimore: Penguin Books, 1963. A somewhat uncritical re-creation of the voyage, with a tendency to gloss over several of the thornier questions.

Whitaker, Ian. "The Problem of Pytheas' Thule." *Classical Journal* 77 (1982): 148-164. A fine, careful study not only of Thule but also of most of the crucial problems surrounding Pytheas. Contains excellent documentation and bibliography, with translations of crucial passages from ancient authorities.

Kenneth F. Kitchell, Jr.

RABANUS MAURUS

Born: c. 780; Mainz
Died: February 4, 856; Winkel, Rhineland
Areas of Achievement: Religion, monasticism, and politics
Contribution: As one of the leading scholars of the ninth century Carolingian revival of learning, Rabanus' voluminous writings interpreted and introduced generations of medieval students to the wisdom of the Bible and the church fathers and to the practical skills they would need as priests and monks. As abbot of Fulda and later as Archbishop of Mainz, he played a leading role in church governance at a time when the leaders of the Church helped to shape society.

Early Life

Very little is known about Rabanus Maurus' early life. He was born in Mainz circa 780, apparently to an aristocratic Frankish family. He became a monk at the monastery of Fulda, where he was ordained a deacon in 801. Young monks who showed intellectual promise often were sent to other monasteries for additional reading and study under the tutelage of famous masters. Rabanus was sent to study with Alcuin, an Anglo-Saxon scholar who was a close friend and adviser of Charlemagne. Alcuin was one of the leading figures in Charlemagne's attempt to improve intellectual, cultural, and spiritual life in the Frankish kingdom. As abbot of the monastery of St. Martin in Tours, Alcuin established Tours as an important intellectual center and trained an entire generation of future abbots, bishops, and scholars there. Rabanus was especially close to his mentor. It was Alcuin who gave him the name "Maurus," which was the name of the most beloved disciple of Benedict of Nursia, the founder of Benedictine monasticism. Rabanus was Alcuin's Maurus.

After Alcuin's death in 804, Rabanus Maurus returned to Fulda. He was ordained a priest in 814 and named master of Fulda's monastic school in 819. When the abbot died in 822, Rabanus succeeded to that office and added the duties of an administrator of an important monastery to his work as a scholar. In 847 he became Archbishop of Mainz.

Life's Work

Rabanus was born at an important moment in the political and cultural history of Western Europe. Charlemagne had become King of the Franks in 768, and on Christmas Day in the year 800, he was crowned emperor by the Pope. Charlemagne's empire was an ambitious experiment. Charlemagne, who died in 814, and his son, Louis the Pious, who reigned from 814 to his death in 840, tried to maintain political unity in a Europe that had been fragmented ever since the decline of the Roman Empire in the West during the fourth and fifth centuries. Family rivalries and attempts by the military aristocracy to usurp royal power always threatened political stability and unity.

Charlemagne and his successors were not merely fighters and politicians. With the aid of their ecclesiastical advisers, men such as Alcuin, they broadened the role of the ruler to include in it the moral and spiritual regeneration of society. The interest of Frankish leaders in education and culture was part of a practical program to improve society by inculcating Christian practices and principles in the Frankish people.

The bishops and abbots of cathedrals and monasteries throughout Francia were the point men in the effort to reform society. Often the loyalties of church leaders such as Rabanus were compromised. As monks, they pursued lives of contemplation and distance from the world, an ideal difficult to achieve when kings and emperors sought their help and advice. As bishops, they tried to manage the responsibilities of their provinces and to supervise the clergy and people while sometimes called upon to choose sides in dynastic disputes by committing the moral and fiscal resources of their bishoprics to one side or the other.

Rabanus' career started off simply enough at Fulda when he composed a series of poems entitled *De laudibus sanctae crucis* (in praise of the Holy Cross), which he dedicated to Louis the Pious. The poems were a great success, for they revived the classical practice of joining text to pictures. Rabanus' "figural poems," copied over the design of the Cross or over a full-length drawing of the emperor holding the Cross in his hand, delighted both mind and eye. While still a master at Fulda, Rabanus wrote *De institutione clericorum* (c. 810; on the training of clergy). The book was dedicated to Archbishop Haistulf of Mainz but owed its inspiration to Rabanus' students, who wanted him to put his lectures into written form. *De institutione clericorum* is a manual which covers all the topics a priest needed to know in the ninth century before beginning his ecclesiastical duties. Its various chapters range widely over the books of the Bible, vestments, rituals, festivals, ceremonies, church hierarchy, and many other topics.

His next work, *De computo* (on computation), dates from 820, when Rabanus responded to the plea of a monk named Macharius to explain the very technical subjects of determining dates and numerical reckoning. In the absence of a uniform calendar, it was critical that the clergy be able to determine when feast days were to take place. *De computo* considered various calendar systems, defined seconds, minutes, hours, days, weeks, months, and years, and even broached astronomical topics, since fixing dates depended on the positions of the celestial bodies.

The last work Rabanus wrote before he became abbot of Fulda was a commentary on the biblical book of Matthew. His interest in explaining the Bible was a natural outgrowth of his function as a teacher. Students of the Bible in the Middle Ages needed commentaries to help them understand the many difficult terms used to describe biblical people, animals, plants, places, money, clothing, and rituals. Readers also had to know something about the historical contexts of the various books. Mostly they had to be helped to understand the mystical and sacred meaning which was believed to lie behind the literal meaning of the biblical text. Rabanus was a skilled expositor not so much because he was clever and original, but because he had mastered much of the work of earlier authors and could synthesize it effectively for his own audience. His success at explaining Matthew led to requests throughout his life to comment on other books of the Bible. Soon he had produced commentaries on almost all the books of both the Old and New Testaments.

When he became abbot of Fulda in 822, Rabanus became deeply involved in managing the estates of the monastery, which apparently had been neglected by his predecessors. Fulda was a rich monastery and controlled properties scattered all over the eastern, Germanic part of the Carolingian Empire. Rabanus' first literary work of his abbacy indirectly concerned the landed wealth of his monastery. Gottschalk, a monk of Fulda who had been given to the monastery as a child by his father, wished to be released from his monastic vows. Gottschalk argued that the practice of giving children to monasteries, or oblation, was invalid because children could not freely assent to their vows. More was at stake in Gottschalk's challenge than the life of one monk. Parents often gave grants of land to the monastery in order to help support the abbey which sheltered their children. If Gottschalk succeeded in overturning the practice of oblation, he would thereby threaten not only the sanctity of vows but also the landed wealth of the monasteries. Rabanus' *De oblatione puerorum* (on the oblation of boys), written in 829 at the request of Louis the Pious, represented a stout defense of oblation. Gottschalk was defeated at subsequent church councils in his attempt to renounce his vows, and child oblation continued as a practice in the medieval Church until the twelfth century.

Rabanus' next work, *De reuerentia filiorum erga patres* (834; on the reverence of sons for their fathers), was also inspired by controversy. Louis' sons had revolted against him when it appeared to them that the emperor was diminishing their power for the benefit of a son born of a second marriage. Rabanus' essay defended Louis and sought to remind his sons of their obligation of filial piety toward their father. Though Louis was restored to power, the revolt deeply troubled a society that professed Christian values and tried to implement them even in the political arena. Rabanus' *De uirtutibus et uitiis* (on virtues and vices) is a product of the 830's and represents the abbot's attempt to call Carolingian society back to moral principles of behavior.

When Louis died in 840, a brutal struggle for power and for the rights of succession broke out among his sons. Rabanus supported the eldest son, Lothair. The choice was unfortunate, since by 842, Lothair was defeated by his brother, Louis the German. Rabanus, who by this time was sixty years old and in poor health, retired from his abbacy, probably fearing that his advocacy of Lothair would bring harm to his beloved monastery. He removed himself to Petersberg, close by Fulda, and continued his scholarly and pedagogical activities. His monumental *De natura rerum* (840's; on the nature of things) belongs to this period. This work was an encyclopedic survey of all the things one had to know in order to interpret Scripture. It was modeled on the *Etymologiae* (c. late sixth or early seventh century) of Saint Isidore of Seville and owed much to it. Yet Rabanus' purpose was different, since his work in addition to providing factual information was concerned with revealing the mystical significance of things.

Rabanus' retreat from public life was short-lived. When he responded to Louis the German's request to prepare a biblical commentary, the volume Rabanus produced was a visible sign that the estrangement between monk and king had come to an end. After Archbishop Otgar of Mainz died in 847, Rabanus, undoubtedly with the king's support, became the new archbishop. Rabanus threw himself with his usual energy into the administrative tasks of his new responsibilities. He presided over a number of important church councils, supported Louis and Louis' son, Lothair II, and all the while continued to write.

Among the major works from this period is the *Martyrologium* (martyrology). This book lists the saints whose feast days were celebrated throughout the year and provides brief historical notes about each one. Even as he approached the end of his life, Rabanus was concerned to write books that were useful in the practice of the Christian religion. In this vein, he also prepared two penitentials, books which listed sins and prescribed the appropriate penance for each; a collection of sermons; and *De sacris ordinibus, sacramentis diuinis, et uestimentis sacerdotalibus* (850's; on sacred orders, the divine sacraments, and priestly vestments). His last work was probably the *Tractatus de anima* (treatise on the soul), to which he appended excerpts from the military manual of the Roman author Vegetius as a useful gift to Lothair.

Summary

Rabanus Maurus, despite a busy and sometimes tumultuous public life, was a prolific scholar whose works helped to transmit the learning of earlier Christian authors to a new audience of Frankish Christians in the ninth century. Rabanus' learning and skills as an author helped to train the priests and monks who attempted to implement the Carolingian vision of a Christian society.

Rabanus wrote most of his works at the request of students, fellow bishops, abbots, kings, and emperors. Although he often modestly remarked in the prefaces to his works "I did what I could," his blending of a broad range of earlier authors, some of whom contradicted one another, into a pedagogically effective format was a considerable achievement. Rabanus did not try to be original in fields where traditional truths were more to be authenticated and explained than to be superseded by new insights. Nevertheless, his compilations were, in effect, new works that presented their readers with insights from many texts.

His works were copied many times over in the Middle Ages and continued to be influential even into the age of the printing press, when most of them were published for the first time. Dante placed Rabanus in Paradise with other medieval scholars in his *La divina commedia* (c. 1320; *The Divine Comedy*, 1802). Many modern writers, perhaps with only minor exaggeration, have dubbed Rabanus Maurus the *praeceptor Germaniae*, the teacher of Germany.

Bibliography
Duckett, Eleanor Shipley. *Carolingian Portraits: A Study in the Ninth Century*. Ann Arbor: University of Michigan Press, 1962. Rabanus is not the subject of one of Duckett's portraits, but she does provide chapters on Lupus of Ferrières and Walahfrid Strabo, two Carolingian scholars who studied with the great master. This book succeeds in providing some of the flavor of Carolingian intellectual life.
Laistner, M. L. W. *Thought and Letters in Western Europe, A.D. 500 to 900*. 2d ed. Ithaca, N.Y.: Cornell University Press, 1957. This work is a good introduction to the Carolingian renaissance and to the world of literature and scholarship in which Rabanus moved. Laistner emphasizes the influence of the classical literary heritage on medieval thought and literature.
McCulloh, John. Introduction to *Rabani Mauri "Martyrologium."* Turnhout, Belgium: Brepols, 1979. This is the best discussion of Rabanus' life and work available in English. Although parts of it are directed to the edition of the martyrology which McCulloh edited for this volume, readers will benefit from McCulloh's discussion of Rabanus' career and his useful bibliography.
McKitterick, Rosamond. *The Frankish Kingdoms Under the Carolingians, 751-987*. White Plains, N.Y.: Longman, 1983. This is the best general account of Carolingian history available in English. It is particularly good on the Carolingian reform program and on the close links between intellectual life and politics.
Raby, F. J. E. *A History of Christian-Latin Poetry*. Rev. ed. London: Oxford University Press, 1957. This is a general, handbook discussion of medieval poetry. The section on Rabanus is slight but important.
Spelsberg, Helmut. "Hrabanus-Maurus-Bibliographie." In *Hrabanus Maurus und seine Schule: Festschrift der Rabanus-Maurus-Schule 1980*, edited by Winfried Böhne. Fulda, West Germany: Rindt-Druck Fulda, 1980. This bibliography lists everything published before 1980 about Rabanus, or

Hrabanus as he is sometimes known. It also contains references to printed editions of Rabanus' works. The volume in which the bibliography appears was published to commemorate the twelve hundredth anniversary of Rabanus' birth. It contains excellent photographic reproductions of some of Rabanus' figural poems and some of the manuscripts with which he was associated at Fulda.

Stevens, Wesley M. "*Compotistica et astronomica* in the Fulda School." In *Saints, Scholars, and Heroes: Studies in Medieval Culture in Honor of Charles W. Jones*. 2 vols. Collegeville, Minn.: St. John's University Press, 1979. This is a fine study of the art of *computus* and also of the Fulda school.

―――――. Introduction to *Rabani Mauri "De computo."* Turnhout, Belgium: Brepols, 1979. This introduction to Stevens' edition of the Latin text of Rabanus' *De computo* contains much valuable information as well as a bibliography.

John J. Contreni

RĀMĀNUJA

Born: c. 1017; Śrīperumbūdūr, southern India, near Madras
Died: 1137; Śrīraṅgam, southern India
Area of Achievement: Religion
Contribution: Rāmānuja expounded a theistic interpretation of Vedanta philosophy and led the Śrī Vaiṣṇavas community in its formative period.

Early Life

The dates of Rāmānuja's life are somewhat controversial, because the 120-year life span attributed to him by Śrī Vaiṣṇavas tradition seems exceptionally long; it is also possible that he was born some sixty years later than the traditional date. Particularly noteworthy about the time and place of his life, however, is that most of the region of Tamil Nadu in southern India was at this time a single powerful state, the Cōla kingdom. Śrīraṅgam, which would figure so prominently in Rāmānuja's life, was at the center of a prosperous, highly organized state, the rulers of which often lavishly supported the various religious traditions within their realm.

Rāmānuja was born into a Brahman family—apparently Smārtas Brahmans—who had inclinations toward Vishnu worship but were not members of the Śrī Vaiṣṇavas sect. Traditionally, males of his family were scholars of the Vedic texts and rituals. Rāmānuja was married early in his life, then went to study with Yādavaprakāśa, a local scholar of the Upanishads and Vedanta. Disagreements with his teacher's interpretations of the sacred texts, combined with his increasing interest in the devotional practices of the Śrī Vaiṣṇavas sect, finally led to a decisive break with his teacher and to Rāmānuja's initiation into the sect.

The last great leader of the Śrī Vaiṣṇavas community, Yāmuna, had died immediately prior to Rāmānuja's initiation, denying Rāmānuja the opportunity of serving and being instructed by the living master of the tradition. Still, Rāmānuja regarded himself as Yāmuna's disciple and was acclaimed as Yāmuna's successor by devotees in the Śrī Vaiṣṇavas center of Śrīraṅgam. Detailed instruction in Śrī Vaiṣṇavas doctrine followed Rāmānuja's initiation; this instruction was provided in Rāmānuja's home by a devotee named Periya Nambi. After six months, Rāmānuja's wife quarreled with Nambi's wife regarding their relative status in the caste system; although all of them were Brahman, Rāmānuja's wife believed that Nambi and his wife were members of a subcaste lower in status and that contact with them was polluting. Nambi and his wife left Rāmānuja's home, terminating his instruction. Rāmānuja was so infuriated with his wife's behavior that he sent her back to her parents and shortly thereafter became an ascetic. This incident illustrates Rāmānuja's attitude that the social order of caste hierarchy was less important than the spiritual rank of devotees within the Śrī Vaiṣṇavas community.

Life's Work

After becoming an ascetic, Rāmānuja lived in a small monastery he had established near the temple in Kāñcī. Several of Rāmānuja's younger relatives and other Brahmans came to him for instruction, were initiated into the Śrī Vaiṣṇavas community, and became Rāmānuja's disciples. Among these disciples was his former teacher, Yādavaprakāśa, who composed a manual of rules for ascetics of the Śrī Vaiṣṇavas community at Rāmānuja's request, a work which still exists.

Soon the devotees in Śrīraṅgam heard of these developments and asked Rāmānuja to assume leadership of the community and administration of the temple at Śrīraṅgam. He did so, and during the next few years he thoroughly reorganized the administration of the temple. Since the worship of the lay followers of Śrī Vaiṣṇavism centered on the temple, its administration was a matter of great concern to the whole community. Rāmānuja was able to introduce new procedures and new temple personnel without alienating members of the prior regime. It is noteworthy that these reforms were accomplished despite the fact that several temple officers were displaced while disciples of Rāmānuja (some of whom were his relatives) who came from a different group of Brahmans and from a different area were given positions. Rāmānuja's changes necessitated the peaceful coexistence not only of different subcastes of Brahmans but also of Brahmans and non-Brahmans, for many different groups helped administer the temple. The relatively liberal attitude toward status distinctions based on caste within the Śrī Vaiṣṇavas community is a striking feature of Rāmānuja's tenure as the community's leader.

Since Rāmānuja had not had the opportunity of being taught by Yāmuna, the previous master of the tradition, he sought out five of Yāmuna's disciples to transmit some portion of the master's teachings. Receiving from one the secret meaning of the sacred mantra (prayerlike holy words), Rāmānuja then revealed the teaching to a group of Śrī Vaiṣṇavas publicly. He justified violating the prohibition against publicizing this doctrine on the grounds that even if he went to Hell for doing so, others would be saved by his action. Śrī Vaiṣṇavas tell this story because it illustrates vividly Rāmānuja's compassion for his fellow devotees and his desire to spread the teachings of the doctrine, with all of their saving power, to a wider audience.

Nine works have been attributed to Rāmānuja. Three of these works are commentaries on the *Vedānta-sūtras*, the best known and longest of which is the *Śrībhāṣya*; the shorter ones are entitled *Vedātadīpa* and *Vedāntasāra*. Also attributed to Rāmānuja is a commentary on the Bhagavad Gita. Perhaps his earliest work is a summary statement of his philosophical position entitled *Vedārthasaṃgraha*. (These writings have all been translated widely and are best known by their original titles.) The other four works traditionally ascribed to Rāmānuja are devotional in mood and somewhat different in content from the works above; for this reason, some modern scholars have questioned whether Rāmānuja actually composed them. One work is a ritual manual to be used in one's daily worship. The other three are prose hymns in praise of God (Vishnu). Śrī Vaiṣṇavas have preserved these nine works, which have become the basis of the distinctive theology and practice of their community.

Rāmānuja accepted the traditional Hindu concept of reincarnation and the law of Karma, which determines the nature of one's rebirth based on one's actions in one's previous life. For Rāmānuja, ultimate reality is God, a personal lord who reveals himself to those who acknowledge their dependence on him. The traditional Vedanta is concerned with knowledge of ultimate reality as the means of attaining emancipation from the cycle of rebirth. Rāmānuja's interpretation of Vedanta incorporates knowledge of ultimate reality with the performance of one's ritual duties and social duties as secondary means of attaining liberation, but the primary means is devotion (bhakti). Devotion in the Śrī Vaiṣṇavas community is a recollection of the attributes of God with an attitude of love, so that the devotee feels the presence of God constantly and vividly. Most bhakti traditions regard this devotion as the means to the attainment of God's presence; for Rāmānuja, the devotee who feels a need for God's presence discovers that God needs the loving devotion of his devotee as well. Bhakti in Śrī Vaiṣṇavism is thus the mutual participation of God and his devotees.

Rāmānuja traveled through much of India, taking the doctrines and practices of the Śrī Vaiṣṇavas sect to all who would listen. His influence was particularly strong in southern India, where many converts were won. Late in his life, however, Rāmānuja was forced to flee from Śrīraṅgam when a newly installed king demanded that he declare obeisance to Siva. Rāmānuja fled north to the Hoyśala kingdom, where he was free to practice Śrī Vaiṣṇavism. After the death of the fanatical King of Cōla, Rāmānuja was able to return to Śrīraṅgam and spend his remaining years peacefully in the company of many disciples.

Summary

Rāmānuja emerged as the leader of the small Śrī Vaiṣṇavas community between the eleventh and twelfth centuries and was instrumental in transforming this sect into one of the largest devotional religious movements in India. Rāmānuja's leadership was twofold: He was both the chief administrative officer of the Śrīraṅgam temple and the authoritative teacher of the community of devotees for whom Śrīraṅgam was the center. Since the twelfth century, Rāmānuja has been seen as the most important teacher and leader of the Śrī Vaiṣṇavas community. In fact, Rāmānuja has been regarded by his followers as the means by which salvation was to be attained. Through the teachings which he enunciated and by worshipping at the temple which he reorganized and supervised, the blessed state was attainable. Rāmānuja was thus regarded as the mediator between God (Vishnu) and his community of devotees.

Rāmānuja's leadership established Śrī Vaiṣṇavism as a dynamic and growing tradition in southern India. His reforms of the temple's administrative procedures, and the example of his own life, served to integrate within one religious community Brahmans and non-Brahmans. Subsequent leaders of Śrī Vaiṣṇavism have followed the procedures for temple administration which he instituted and have relied on the writings of Rāmānuja as the official doctrines of the sect. One of the most significant aspects of Rāmānuja's thought is that it provided a theistic interpretation of Vedanta in opposition to Śankara's monism, which was very much the dominant interpretation. In so doing, Rāmānuja contributed to the establishment of devotional theism as acceptable to even the most orthodox Brahmans. Devotional theism has become the most popular kind of worship in India, in part because of Rāmānuja's intellectual and organizational skills.

Bibliography
Buitenen, J. A. B. van. *Rāmānuja on the Bhagavadgītā.* 2d ed. Delhi, India: Motilal Banarsidass, 1968. An excellent condensed rendering of Rāmānuja's commentary on a very important devotional scripture, the Bhagavad Gita. A useful introduction of forty-one pages precedes the text. The work includes an appendix (a translation of a work by Yāmuna) and an index of references to the Bhagavad Gita and other texts, as well as an index of Sanskrit terms.
Carman, John B. *The Theology of Rāmānuja: An Essay in Interreligious Understanding.* New Haven, Conn.: Yale University Press, 1974. This is one of the best sources on the life of Rāmānuja, as well as a detailed study of his major ideas. The work includes an extensive bibliography, index, and a photograph of a metal sculpture of Rāmānuja thought to have been made during his lifetime. The most comprehensive study of Rāmānuja's theology.
Lester, Robert C. *Rāmānuja on the Yoga.* Madras, India: Adyar Library, 1976. A fairly brief (185 pages) but excellent study of Rāmānuja's writings on Yoga. It shows how the classic Yoga system of Patañjali was adapted by Rāmānuja to suit his own devotional religion. The work includes both the philosophy and the practical application of these ideas to one's religious life. There is a bibliography but no index.
Lott, Eric J. *God and the Universe in the Vedāntic Theology of Rāmānuja.* Madras, India: Adyar Library, 1976. This work is a clear and concise study of the religious thought of Rāmānuja, with particular attention to his doctrines regarding God and humanity's relationship to God. For Rāmānuja, the soul is dependent on God much as the body is dependent on the soul

which it contains. The work includes a bibliography.

Thibaut, George, trans. *Vedantasutras, with the Commentary of Ramanuja.* Vol. 48 in *The Sacred Books of the East.* Oxford: Clarendon Press, 1904. This is a very clear translation of the most important text of the Vedanta philosophy—together with the commentary on the Vedanta composed by Rāmānuja. In his commentary, Rāmānuja forcefully presents a theistic interpretation of Vedanta that contrasts with the well-known monism (Advaita) of Śankara. The work includes an index and a bibliography.

Bruce M. Sullivan

RAMSES II

Born: c. 1300 B.C.; probably the Eastern Delta of Egypt
Died: 1213 B.C.; probably Pi-Ramesse (Qantir), Egypt
Area of Achievement: Government
Contribution: Renowned for his statesmanship, military leadership, administrative abilities, and building activity, Ramses set a standard by which subsequent rulers of Egypt measured themselves.

Early Life
Born of Egypt's great god Amon (personified by King Seti I) and Queen Tuya, Ramses was designated "while yet in the egg" as Egypt's future king: Such is Ramses II's account of his own birth. The period into which he was born, that of the New Kingdom, was a time when Egypt was attempting to maintain control of an extensive empire which ranged from the Fourth Cataract of the Nile in the Sudan to the provinces of North Syria. Some fifty years prior to his birth, during the Eighteenth Dynasty, Egypt had undergone a period of turmoil. Akhenaton (Amenhotep IV, who reigned from 1379 to 1362 B.C.), reacting against the ever-growing power of the Amon priesthood, had abandoned the traditional religion and proclaimed the sun god, represented as the sun disk Aton, as sole god of the country. He worshipped the Aton at the virgin site of Amarna. He died without heirs; after his demise, a series of relatively ineffectual kings, including Tutankhamen, ruled for brief periods as the Amon priesthood set about reestablishing religious domination and refurbishing Amon's temples. Meanwhile, using this period of uncertainty in Egypt to best advantage, vassal states in Syria held back their tribute and fomented revolt. When Tutankhamen died without living heirs, a military man of nonroyal birth, Aye, assumed the throne. He was followed only four years later by another, the general Horemheb, who also ruled only a short period before his death, but not before designating another man with a military background, his vizier Pa-Ramessu, as his heir. Pa-Ramessu (Ramses I, first king of the Nineteenth Dynasty) had what rulers since Akhenaton had lacked: viable male descendants. Thus, when Ramses I died after only a two-year rule, his son, Seti I, assumed the throne. Immediately, Seti began an active program of military campaigns in Canaan, Syria, and Libya. During many of these excursions, his son, the young Ramses II, was at his side, learning the art of warfare.

Seti I instructed his son in civil and religious affairs as well, and Prince Ramses accompanied his father or acted as his deputy on state occasions and at religious festivals. As prince-regent, Ramses received the rights of Egyptian kingship, including his titulary (five royal names attributing to him divine power and linking him with Egypt's divine past) and a harem.

When his father died, after a rule of between fifteen and twenty years,

Ramses II oversaw Seti's burial in the Valley of the Kings and assumed the throne. At that time, he was probably in his mid-twenties. He was about five and a half feet tall and had auburn hair. Many children had already been born to him and his numerous wives.

Life's Work

With great ceremony, on the twenty-seventh day of the third month of summer, 1279, Ramses II acceded to the throne of Egypt. Following an age-old tradition, the great gods of Egypt, in the persons of their high priests, placed the crowns of Upper and Lower Egypt (Nile Valley and Delta) on his head and presented him with other symbols of rulership: the divine cobra (uraeus) to protect him and smite his enemies, and the crook and flail. At the sacred city of Heliopolis, his name was inscribed on the leaves of the sacred *ished* tree, and birds flew in all directions to proclaim his names to all Egypt. With this ceremony concluded, the divine order (or balance) in the universe, a concept known as *Ma'at*, was once again in place. It would be Ramses' duty, as it had been of every king before him, to maintain *Ma'at*, thereby guaranteeing peace and prosperity for all.

Ramses II set out with determination to ensure the preservation of *Ma'at*. He was a shrewd politician from the start; one of his first acts as king was to journey south to Thebes to act as high priest in the city's most important religious event, the Opet Festival. Amid great and joyous celebration, Amon's cult image was carried from his home at Karnak to the Luxor temple. There, through a reenactment of his divine conception and birth, the ceremonies of Opet Festival assured the divinity of Ramses' kingship and promoted his association with the god Amon, whose cult image was recharged with divine energy during its stay at Luxor.

Afterward, Ramses II headed north to Abydos, restored that city's holy sites, and promoted a member of the Abydos priesthood to the position of high priest of Amon at Thebes, the highest and most powerful religious office in the land. In this way, he kept Amon's priesthood under his control and averted the power struggles that had beset earlier kings.

From Abydos, Ramses continued his northerly journey to the eastern Nile Delta. There, in his ancestral homeland near Avaris, he established a new capital, naming it Pi-Ramesse (the house of Ramses). Scribes extolled its magnificence, likening the brilliant blue glaze of its tile-covered walls to turquoise and lapis lazuli.

Not only at Pi-Ramesse but also at Memphis, Egypt's administrative capital, at Thebes, her religious capital, and at numerous other sites throughout Egypt and Nubia, Ramses II built extensively and lavishly. Indeed, few ancient Egyptian cities were untouched by his architects and artisans. Monuments which Ramses II did not build he often claimed for his own by replacing the names of his predecessors with his. Colossal statues of the king erected outside temples were considered to function as intermediaries between the villagers and the great gods inside. They also reminded every passerby of Ramses' power.

The territorial problems and general unrest which had compelled Seti I to travel to the Levant continued during Ramses II's rule. When the growing Hittite empire annexed the strategically important city of Kadesh in northern Syria, an area formerly under Egyptian sovereignty, Ramses rose to the challenge.

In April of the fifth year of Ramses' reign, he led an army of about twenty thousand men to meet about twice as many enemy soldiers. As the Egyptian army neared Kadesh, two Hittites posing as spies allowed themselves to be captured. The main Hittite army, they assured the Egyptians, was still far to the north. Thinking that he had nothing yet to fear, Ramses marched ahead, accompanied by only his personal guard. Two more captured Hittites, this time true spies, revealed, upon vigorous beating, that the Hittites were encamped just on the other side of Kadesh, a few miles away. Suddenly, the enemy attacked the Egyptian line, sending surprised soldiers fleeing in confusion and fright.

With valor and courage, Ramses succeeded virtually single-handedly in holding the Hittite attackers at bay. Relief came at a critical moment in the form of the king's advance guard arriving from the north. Gradually, the rest of Ramses' army regrouped and joined battle. The day ended with no clear victor. The second day also ended in a stalemate, and both sides disengaged.

Ramses headed home in triumph, having, after all, saved his army (and himself) from great disaster. Although during the next fifteen years Ramses returned frequently to the Levantine battlefield, no battle made as great an impact as the Battle of Kadesh. For decades following, on temple walls throughout the land, the king's artists told the story of this battle in prose, poetry, and illustration, with each telling more elaborate than the one before. What the chroniclers neglected to mention each time was the battle's outcome: The disputed city, Kadesh, remained a Hittite possession.

Sixteen years after the Battle of Kadesh had made Ramses a great military leader, at least in his own eyes, it cast him into the role of statesman as well. A new generation of leadership in the Hittite empire, the lack of military resolution with Egypt, and the rising power of Assyria made the prospect of continued warfare with Egypt unattractive to the Hittites. Accordingly, a peace treaty was proposed (by the Hittites according to Ramses and by Ramses according to the Hittites). Its terms are as timely today as they were in 1258 B.C.: mutual nonaggression, mutual defense, mutual extradition of fugitives, and rightful succession of heirs. A thousand gods of Egypt and a thousand gods of Hatti were said to have witnessed this treaty, which survives today in both the Egyptian and Hittite versions.

Former enemies became fast friends following the treaty's execution, as king wrote to king and queen to queen. In Year 34, the Hittite king even sent his daughter to Ramses. Chronicles of Ramses' reign indicate his pleasure upon his first sight of her, accompanied by her dowry of gold, silver, copper, slaves, horses, cattle, goats, and sheep.

Matnefrure, as Ramses II named his Hittite bride, joined a harem that was already quite large. In the course of his long rule, the king had at least eight great royal wives and numerous lesser wives. To Nefretari, who must have been his favorite wife, he dedicated a temple at Abu Simbel, and upon her untimely death he buried her in a tomb whose wall paintings are the finest in the Valley of the Tombs of the Queens. Ramses II fathered at least ninety children (some fifty sons and forty daughters), who were often represented in birth-order procession on temple walls or sculpted knee-height beside images of their father.

In 1213, nearly ninety years old and after more than sixty-six years of rule over the most powerful country in the world, King Ramses II died. His carefully mummified body was laid to rest in a splendidly carved tomb in the Valley of the Kings, and he was succeeded on the throne of Egypt by his thirteenth son, Merneptah.

Summary

Military leader, statesman, builder, family man, and possibly pharaoh of the biblical Exodus, Ramses II left a legacy which history never forgot. He distinguished himself in battle in the early years of his reign, and during the remainder of his lengthy rule—the second longest in Egyptian history—he maintained an interlude of peace in an increasingly tumultuous world. Egypt under his leadership was a cosmopolitan empire. Foreigners were free to come to Egypt to trade or settle; others were taken as prisoners of war and joined Egypt's labor force. It was an era of religious permissiveness, and foreign gods were worshipped beside traditional Egyptian deities. The cultural climate of Ramses' Egypt is similar to the one described in the Bible just prior to the Exodus (an event for which no archaeological record has been found).

The monuments Ramses II built to Egypt's gods (and to himself) are larger and more numerous than those of any other Egyptian king. Nine kings named themselves after him and patterned their lives after his. During his own lifetime, he promoted himself as a god, and he was worshipped as such for the next thousand years.

Greek and Roman tourists marveled at his monuments and immortalized them in their writings, just as the poet Percy Bysshe Shelley did hundreds of years later in his poem "Ozymandias." (The name Ozymandias is the Greek rendering of *User-Ma'at-Ra*, throne name of Ramses II.) When the greatest of all Ramses' monuments, Abu Simbel, was threatened by the rising waters of the Aswan High Dam in the 1960's, ninety countries around the world

Ramses II

contributed funds and expertise to save it. In this way, they too paid homage to Ramses, as do millions of tourists who travel thousands of miles to visit his monuments.

Although his tomb was plundered and his body desecrated, Ramses II has gained the immortality he sought. His monuments and his actions bear testimony to his importance and justify the appellation Ramses the Great.

Bibliography

Bierbrier, Morris. *The Tomb Builders of the Pharaohs*. New York: Charles Scribner's Sons, 1984. A delightfully written description of the community of workmen who built the tombs of the New Kingdom kings, including that of Ramses II. An intimate picture of their day-to-day lives. Includes a description of how they built the tombs.

Freed, Rita. *Ramesses the Great*. Memphis, Tenn.: City of Memphis, 1987. Profusely illustrated survey of Ramses II and the Egyptian Empire under his reign. Includes information about religion, daily life, and burial practices during Egypt's New Kingdom. The second part of the book is a catalog of the objects included in the North American showing of the Ramses the Great exhibition.

Gardiner, A. H. *The Kadesh Inscriptions of Ramesses II*. Oxford: Griffith Institute, 1960. Translation of and commentary on Ramses' own description of his most famous battle.

Kitchen, K. A. *Pharaoh Triumphant: The Life and Times of Ramesses II*. Warminster, England: Aris and Phillips, 1983. The best all-around survey of Egypt's most famous king, by a renowned scholar. Includes historical background information, a detailed report of his military career and international dealings, and a discussion of Egypt's contemporary administrative and social history. Includes an extensive bibliography.

MacQuitty, William. *Ramesses the Great: Master of the World*. New York: Crown Publishers, 1978. Brief but well-written and well-illustrated overview of Ramses II and his monuments.

Murnane, William. *The Road to Kadesh*. Chicago: University of Chicago Oriental Institute, 1985. Background for the understanding of Egypt's far-flung empire. Consideration of Egypt's relations with Syria and the Hittites through the reign of Ramses' father, Seti I, and detailed analyses of Seti's military campaigns.

O'Connor, D. "New Kingdom and Third Intermediate Period, 1552-664 B.C." In *Ancient Egypt: A Society History*, by B. G. Trigger, B. J. Kemp, D. O'Connor, and A. B. Lloyd. Cambridge: Cambridge University Press, 1983. Insightful description of the administrative structure of Egypt at the time of Ramses II.

Schmidt, John D. *Ramesses II: Chronological Structure for His Reign*. Baltimore: Johns Hopkins University Press, 1973. Translation of and commentary on monuments of Ramses II in a chronological framework.

Steindorff, G., and K. Seele. *When Egypt Ruled the East*. Chicago: University of Chicago Press, 1947. Still the best overview for the general reader of the history of Egypt during the New Kingdom.

Wildung, D. *Egyptian Saints: Deifications in Pharaonic Egypt*. New York: New York University Press, 1977. A discussion of the meaning of kingship in ancient Egypt and the mechanism by which a pharaoh was thought to cross the boundary from humanity to divinity. Written for the general reader by an expert in the field. Well illustrated.

Rita E. Freed

RATRAMNUS

Born: Early ninth century; near Amiens, France
Died: c. 868; Corbie, France
Areas of Achievement: Literature and religion
Contribution: Ratramnus was one of the leading theological writers of the first Eucharistic controversy, and his treatise on the subject has been cited in every subsequent occurrence of that debate.

Early Life
Little is known concerning the life of Ratramnus except that he entered the Benedictine abbey of Corbie in about 825, was ordained a priest, involved himself in the doctrinal controversies of his time through his writings, and died about 868. All that is known of him comes from his own writings.

The abbey of Corbie, where Ratramnus spent his entire adult life, was located near Amiens in northern France. It had been founded in the seventh century by the Frankish king Chlothar III and his mother Bathilda and was set up under the Benedictine rule by a monk of Luxeil. By the ninth century, Corbie was held in high regard by scholars because of its scriptoria, library, and school. As a center for the study of the liberal arts, Corbie, like a number of other Carolingian monasteries, served as a bridge between the learning of the ancient world and the modern period in European history. Some of the earliest documents written in the Carolingian script were prepared there by monks assigned the task of copying Roman and patristic manuscripts.

The writings of Ratramnus indicate that he was an extremely well-read scholar, one who was held in high regard by his contemporaries, such as the bishops Hildegard of Meaux and Odo of Beauvais and the theologians Gottschalk of Orbais and Lupus of Ferrara. Pope Nicholas the Great called upon him to write a treatise in defense of the primacy of the bishop of Rome. In addition, the Frankish king Charles the Bald on two occasions petitioned him to write tracts on doctrinal matters. Yet, were it not for his first treatise, *De corpore et sanguine Domini* (*Concerning the Body and Blood of the Lord*, 1549), written sometime between 844 and 850, Ratramnus would probably not be remembered, since he left no disciple to keep his memory alive.

Life's Work
Ratramnus was drawn into the first Eucharistic controversy in the history of the Church when he was called upon sometime between 844 and 850 by Charles the Bald to prepare a treatise on Eucharistic doctrine. Charles had already received a book on that subject written by Saint Paschasius Radbertus, Abbot of Corbie, but since Charles disliked the abbot—grave political differences existed between them—it is likely that the king desired a treatise on the subject that would be significantly different. The choice of Ratramnus

for this task indicates that he already had a reputation as a scholar and that his view on the Eucharist was known to be at variance with that held by his abbot.

Paschasius, a pupil of the former abbots of Corbie Saint Adalhard and Saint Wala, claimed that his treatise *De corpore et sanguine Domini* (831; concerning the Body and Blood of the Lord) was based on the writings of many of the Greek and Roman church fathers, including Saint Ambrose, Saint John Chrysostom, Saint Jerome, Saint Augustine, and Gregory the Great. In his work, Paschasius considered two questions concerning the Eucharist: First, does the sacrament contain something hidden, which can be known only by faith, or is the whole reality present? Second, is the body of Christ that was born of the Virgin Mary and suffered and died on the Cross the same body which is received in the Eucharist by the faithful? According to Paschasius, there is a strict identity between the historical body and the Eucharistic body of Christ:

> And therefore, O man, whenever you drink this cup or eat this bread, you should keep in mind that you are not drinking any other blood than the one that was poured out for you and for all for the forgiveness of sins, and that this is no other flesh than the one that was given up for you and for all and that hung on the Cross.

Paschasius believed that the substance of the bread and wine was changed into the actual body and blood of Christ although the elements retained the outward appearance as bread and wine. The presence of the historical body of Christ at many places at the same time in the Eucharist is explained by a creative act on the part of God on each occasion. The presence of Christ's body and blood in the Eucharist is an objective reality; thus, even someone who received them in an unworthy manner would still receive the true body and blood of the Lord.

Ratramnus, in his treatise of the same title as that of Paschasius, attacked the latter's position by making a distinction between the words *figura* and *veritas*. *Figura* denotes something that is set forth under a veil, as when Christ speaks of Himself as the Bread or the Vine or the Door. The word *veritas*, however, means the showing of a thing unveiled or as it really is, as when it is said that Christ was born of a virgin. The bread and wine exhibit one thing to the senses but present something altogether different to the minds of the faithful. Thus, there is no material miracle in the Eucharist; the elements are the same outwardly as before, but inwardly they are Christ's body and blood. In their bodily nature, the elements are, even after consecration, bread and wine, but in power and spiritual efficacy they are the mysteries of the Body and Blood of Christ.

In addressing the second question as to the relationship between the historical and the Eucharistic body of Christ, Ratramnus argued that though there was a resemblance between the bodies, they were not identical as Paschasius had said. While the historical body could properly be called "the real flesh of Christ," the Eucharistic body was "the sacrament of the real flesh." Existing between these two bodies was a difference "as great as that which exists between a pledge and the thing for which it is pledged, between an image and the thing of which it is an image, appearance and reality." The believer does receive the Body and Blood of Christ in the Eucharist but not as a historical and empirical reality. In maintaining this position on the Eucharist, Ratramnus could claim a long tradition that could be traced back to Augustine, while Paschasius was more clearly indebted to Ambrose.

In addition to his major writing on the Eucharistic questions, Ratramnus wrote several other treatises at the request of friends and influential men. In 849-850, he wrote an essay *De praedestinatione* (on predestination), dedicated to Charles the Bald but written in defense of his friend Gottschalk, who was under attack for his views by Hincmar, Bishop of Reims. In 853, Ratramnus wrote *De nativitate Christi* (concerning the birth of Christ). In this controversy, he once again had Paschasius as an opponent. The abbot had written a work in which he not only defended the idea of the virgin birth of Christ but also argued that Christ had not been born like other men, that his birth had taken place without the sorrow or pain which were the consequences of the curse placed on Eve for her sin. Ratramnus, while agreeing that Mary was "virgin before giving birth, virgin while giving birth, virgin after giving birth," nevertheless insisted that Christ's birth was like that of other men, for to say otherwise was a threat to Christ's true humanity, and it was theologically necessary that Christ be both God and man.

In 863, at the request of Odo, Bishop of Beauvais, Ratramnus wrote an essay in which he challenged the heretical view of a monk who claimed that there existed a single spirit that was shared by all men. His final treatise was written in 867 at the request of Pope Nicholas I. Entitled *Contra graecorum opposita* (against the opposition of the Greeks), it was one of several written on the subject by Frankish clergymen, but it was by far the fullest and most logically argued. In this work, Ratramnus defended the claims of the bishop of Rome to primacy over the whole Church against the rival claims of the patriarch of Constantinople. With this work, the pen of Ratramnus was stilled by death, which came in 868, although there was no eulogy to record the precise date.

Summary

Despite the high regard of his contemporaries, had it not been for his role in the Eucharistic controversy, Ratramnus would likely have been forgotten soon after his death. During the next two centuries, his book on the Eucharist received only sporadic attention, while that of Paschasius won great favor among the influential thinkers of that time. In the middle of the eleventh century, another Eucharistic controversy erupted when Berengar, head of the school of Tours, promoted the Eucharistic views of Ratramnus although erroneously attributing the book containing them to John Scotus Erigena. Ratramnus' book was condemned and destroyed under the name of Erigena at the synod held in Vercelli in 1050.

With the definition of the doctrine of transubstantiation at the Fourth Lateran Council in 1215, which in general affirmed the Eucharistic position of Paschasius, it might be thought that Ratramnus' treatise would have been relegated to oblivion. In the course of the Reformation, however, many of the reformers (with the notable exception of Martin Luther) embraced the ideas of Ratramnus as anticipations of their own Eucharistic views. His book was printed for the first time in 1532 and was widely circulated in Protestant circles; in 1559, the censors of the Council of Trent placed it on the Index of proscribed books. By the twentieth century, a number of Catholic theologians had concluded that Ratramnus was not clearly heretical in his views and may indeed have been closer in his Eucharistic views to Augustine than had been traditionally thought.

Bibliography
Bouhot, Jean-Paul. *Ratramne de Corbie: Histoire litteraire et controverses doctrinales*. Paris: Études Augustiniennes, 1976. This work contains a thorough analysis of all the manuscript materials that pertain to the life and work of Ratramnus as well as a detailed analysis of all of his writings.
Fahey, John F. *The Eucharistic Teaching of Ratramn of Corbie*. Mundelein, Ill.: Saint Mary of the Lake Seminary, 1951. A doctoral dissertation which is the only monograph in English devoted exclusively to the Eucharistic views of Ratramnus. Contains a very useful historical introduction. Supports the view that Ratramnus may have been closer to the orthodox view of the Eucharist than has traditionally been thought. Extensive bibliography.
Harnack, Adolf von. *History of Dogma*. Edited by Alexander Balmain Bruce. Vols. 5 and 6. London: Williams and Norgate, 1898, 1899. This translation of the classic German work is extremely useful but rather esoteric. Provides an excellent background to the writing of Ratramnus. Bibliography.
Morrison, Karl F. *Tradition and Authority in the Western Church, 300-1140*. Princeton, N.J.: Princeton University Press, 1969. Valuable for explaining the political and religious climate existing in the Frankish kingdoms at the time Ratramnus was writing. Extensive bibliography.
Pelikan, Jaroslav. *The Christian Tradition: A History of the Development of Doctrine*. Vol. 3, *The Growth of Medieval Theology, 600-1300*. Chicago: University of Chicago Press, 1978. This work has already become the standard for the exposition of Christian doctrine. All Ratramnus' writings

are discussed and evaluated. Draws extensively on all available primary sources. Excellent bibliography.

Ratramnus. "Opera omnia." In *Patrologiae Cursus Completus*, edited by Jacques Paul Migne, vol. 121. Paris: J. P. Migne, 1852. The only source for all the extant theological writings of Ratramnus. In Latin.

Paul E. Gill

RAYMOND OF PEÑAFORT

Born: c. 1175; Peñafort, near Villafranca del Panadés, Catalonia
Died: January 6, 1275; Barcelona, Catalonia
Area of Achievement: Religion
Contribution: Raymond of Peñafort compiled the decretals (the official code of church law) promulgated by Pope Gregory IX in 1234 and wrote a penitential handbook used throughout the Middle Ages.

Early Life
Raymond was born into the Spanish noble family of Peñafort, whose castle was on a high rock above the village of Villafranca del Panadés, not far from Barcelona. It is probable that he was educated in the school of the Cathedral of the Holy Cross in Barcelona, the city to which he kept returning and in which he spent the last part of his life. He was evidently a brilliant student, for he is said to have begun teaching philosophy in Barcelona at the age of twenty (which might have been as early as 1195). Both here and later, in Bologna, Raymond shared his learning out of love and charged nothing for his services as a teacher.
Around the year 1210, Raymond joined with a canon of the cathedral at Barcelona, Peter the Red, and journeyed to Bologna to study canon law. After six to eight years of study there, he was recognized as a master of canon law, and from 1218 to 1221, he taught in Bologna. Again refusing payment from his students, he was given a salary by grateful citizens of Bologna. During this period he wrote his first treatise in canon law, *Summa juris canonici* (1218-1221; a summation of canon law), only part of which is preserved in a unique manuscript.

Life's Work
The turning point in Raymond's life came when he was persuaded by the Bishop of Barcelona to return to Barcelona to help in the founding of a convent of the newly established Dominican Order (also known as the Order of Preachers) by being the teacher for the friars in Barcelona. Raymond was earnest in his service to God and to the Church, and within a short time he had been made canon and then provost of the Cathedral of the Holy Cross. Yet he was not content to be merely on the periphery of the Dominican Order, and on Good Friday, 1222, Raymond became a Dominican friar, and for the rest of his life he was associated with the convent of Saint Catherine in Barcelona.
From 1222 to 1229, Raymond concerned himself with various activities having to do with counteracting the presence of the Moors and the Islamic religion in Spain. In about 1223, he helped found (with Peter Nolasco) the Order of Our Lady of Ransom (the Mercedarians), an organization dedi-

cated to the rescue and rehabilitation of Christians held prisoner by the Muslims. From 1227 to 1229, he was the chief assistant to John of Abbeville, Papal Legate, who was in charge of restoring ecclesiastical discipline in Spain according to the principles laid down at the Fourth Lateran Council of 1215. It was Raymond's task to go into towns before the legate and prepare them for his message. Raymond also joined with the legate in preaching a crusade against the Moors, and in 1229 he was appointed directly by Gregory IX to enlist warriors for the Crusade in the towns of Narbonne and Arles. Also in this year, Raymond had his first direct involvement with James I the Conqueror, a champion of the Crusade; Raymond was ecclesiastical judge in an investigation concerning the king's marriage and the legitimacy of the rights of succession of his eldest son. Raymond's relationship with the king, although sometimes stormy, was to endure for the rest of his life.

Notwithstanding all these activities, Raymond found time during this period to write the most popular of his treatises, *Summa de casibus poenitentiae* (1222-1229; summary of cases of penitence). It was a handbook for priests that went beyond the usual matching of sins with appropriate penances; it provided a systematic discussion of problems of Christian conscience and (in accordance with Raymond's expertise in canon law) also dealt with appropriate church practices in regard to particular sins. The first three books treated, respectively, sins against God, sins against one's fellowman, and miscellaneous questions of church discipline and canon law. The fourth book, on marriage (added in 1235), was largely a redaction of the *Summa de matrimonio* (c. 1214) by Tancred. Raymond's work was circulated both in its entirety and in condensed form throughout the later Middle Ages. One of the best-known restatements of it was in portions of "The Parson's Tale," actually a sermon on penitence (c. 1395) in Geoffrey Chaucer's *The Canterbury Tales* (1387-1400).

When Raymond's assignment with the papal legate in Spain was done, Gregory IX, greatly impressed with Raymond's abilities, called him to Rome in 1230 and appointed him his personal confessor; quickly added to this honor were the offices of chaplain and penitentiary, the latter function giving Raymond the opportunity to render decisions on canon law on behalf of the Pope. As the Pope's confessor, Raymond is said to have imposed penances on Gregory which required him to give special attention to the petitions of the poor. Raymond was often addressed by Pope Gregory as "Father of the Poor," and he was styled by a contemporary as "Promoter of the Petitions of the Poor." There was, however, a severe side to Raymond, shown perhaps most obviously in his work while in the papal court to establish the Inquisition in the region of Aragon in Spain, using his influence with James I.

Raymond's most significant accomplishment in the service of Gregory was to draw up a condensation of canon law from the time of Gratian (whose *Decretum* of 1150 had formed the core of canon law for the last eighty years), up to and including the first part of Gregory's papacy. Gregory's purpose was for Raymond to edit, condense, and catalog these laws to produce a comprehensive, indexed digest of the accepted rules for church governance. The completed work of Raymond was authorized and promulgated in 1234 under the papal bull *Rex pacificus*; this landmark codification of canon law came to be known as the *Decretals* of Gregory IX and remained a key part of canon law in the Roman Catholic church until the modern overall revision in 1917.

Pope Gregory wished to install Raymond as Bishop of Tarragona in 1235, but Raymond begged to be released from this appointment, and, indeed, he became ill at the prospect. He was allowed to return to Spain in 1236, after complying with Gregory's insistence that he at least nominate someone else to fill the vacant bishopric. He was not allowed to rest for long in his beloved Barcelona; in 1238, he was elected the third master general of the Dominican Order. Although he served in this post for only two years (once again managing to get himself relieved of it), his talents for codifying and reorganization were once more exercised in revising the rules of the order. Testifying to the effectiveness of his revision was the longevity of the Raymundian Code for the Dominicans, which was not superseded until 1924.

After Raymond resigned his post, he returned to Barcelona, and there is no record of his leaving Spain again, although he might have done so in order to found a Dominican convent among the Moors in Tunis in northern Africa. He also founded a Dominican house in the midst of Moors in Murcia, in southeastern Spain. The last thirty-five years of his life were dedicated to the conversion of Moors and Jews in Spain. To this end, he established the teaching of Arabic and Hebrew in several Dominican convents, continued his work to rescue Christian prisoners through the Mercedarians, and encouraged Saint Thomas Aquinas to write a treatise directed at persuading pagans of the truth of the doctrines of Christianity. It seems that Raymond was also instrumental during this period of his life in establishing the Inquisition in Catalonia. His name is associated with a guidebook for inquisitors drawn up under Esparrago, Bishop of Tarragona, in 1241.

Summary

Raymond of Peñafort is surprisingly little known for one who lived so long and was continually active. Even his two most influential writings (the *Decretals* of Gregory IX and the *Summa de casibus poenitentiae*) did not bring him fame. Raymond was evidently self-effacing and preferred to work behind the scenes. These qualities of character are seen in his refusal to take fees for his teaching, his faithful service to his superiors, and his eagerness to avoid appointment to prominent offices. Yet in spite of his relative anonymity, his life had a tremendous influence: His revisions and compilations of canon law for Gregory IX and for the Dominican Order lived into the twentieth century; his writings on penitence were widely circulated and were used by Chaucer; his efforts toward the conversion of the Jews and Moors in Spain were a catalyst for the study of Hebrew and Arabic by Dominicans; and he was the instigator of one of the important writings of Saint Thomas Aquinas. The continuing respect in which he was held by his contemporaries was evidenced by his being visited in his last illness by two kings, James I and Alfonso of Castile. Raymond's holiness of life, as well as his service to his church, was recognized in his canonization in 1601.

Bibliography
Kuttner, Stephan. "The Barcelona Edition of St. Raymond's First Treatise on Canon Law." *Seminar* 8 (1950): 52-67. A review by the leading modern authority on the works of Raymond of the only printed edition of the unique fragmentary manuscript of the *Summa juris canonici*. Gives a brief summary of Raymond's other important writings at the beginning.
_____. "Raymond of Peñafort as Editor: The 'Decretales' and 'Constitutiones' of Gregory IX." *Bulletin of Medieval Canon Law* 12 (1982): 65-80. Examines the method by which Raymond revised and edited the materials at his disposal for his major canonical work. Shows the extent to which Raymond exercised his own judgment and drew on uncirculated letters from Gregory in his final compendium. Has a few references to English articles in footnotes.
Pennington, Kenneth. "Summae on Raymond de Pennafort's 'Summa de Casibus' in the Bayerische Staatsbibliothek, Munich." *Traditio* 27 (1971): 471-480. A survey of thirteenth and fourteenth century adaptations and summaries of Raymond's work on penitential principles. Shows the popularity of this work by Raymond. Footnotes are nearly all to Latin sources.
Richardson, H. G. "Tancred, Raymond, and Bracton." *English Historical Review* 59 (1944): 376-384. Treats the interrelationship of the writings of the three authors. Little specifically about Raymond.
Schwertner, Thomas M. *Saint Raymond of Pennafort*. Edited by C. M. Antony. Milwaukee, Wis.: Bruce Publishing Co., 1935. The only complete English-language biography of Raymond. Schwertner is a Dominican, and some of his material comes from miracles of Raymond attested in the document of canonization. His other major source is the Latin *Raymundiana*, a collection of early accounts of Raymond's life.

Elton D. Higgs

AL-RAZI

Born: c. 864; Rayy, Iran
Died: c. 925; Rayy, Iran
Areas of Achievement: Medicine and philosophy
Contribution: The most original thinker and the keenest clinical observer of all the medieval Muslim physicians, al-Razi produced the first clinical account of smallpox and measles, a twenty-four-volume compendium of medical knowledge, and set new standards for medical ethics, the clinical observation of disease, and the testing of medical treatment.

Early Life

There is little authentic information about the life of al-Razi. He was born around 864 in Rayy, a few miles from modern Tehran, administered a hospital in that town as well as in Baghdad, and died in his hometown about 925. In his youth, music was his chief interest; he played the lute and studied voice. Upon reaching adulthood he rejected this pursuit, however, asserting that music produced by grown men lacked charm. He then turned to the study of philosophy, a lifelong interest, and developed decidedly egalitarian views, a keen interest in ethics, and a profoundly questioning stance toward received dogmas, both religious and scientific. In his thirties he began to pursue medical studies and a career as a physician.

His interest in medicine reportedly arose after a visit to a sick home in Baghdad, where he was so moved by the suffering of the sick and maimed patients that he determined to devote the rest of his life to alleviating human misery through the practice of medicine. Exactly where he acquired his medical training is unknown, although it was most likely in Baghdad, where he lived from 902 to 907. At that time the city was the leading center of learning in the Middle East and contained fully equipped hospitals, well-stocked libraries, and a sound tradition of research. Successive 'Abassid caliphs, from al-Mansur (754-775) and Harun al-Rashid (786-809) to al-Ma'mun (813-833), had generously endowed institutes for the study of ancient Greek arts and sciences as well as those of Persia and India. Some scholars suggest that al-Razi, who spent most of his life in Iran, probably studied medicine at the University of Jondisabur, a Sassanid-founded institution, which remained a major medical center in the medieval Muslim East.

Life's Work

Al-Razi, an outstanding clinician and a brilliant diagnostician and medical practitioner, was probably the most learned and original of all the medieval Muslim physicians. His scientific and philosophical writings total some 113 major and twenty-eight minor works, of which twelve discuss alchemy. While chief physician and master teacher of the hospital in Rayy, he produced the ten-volume encyclopedia *Kitab al-tibb al-Mansuri* (c. 915), named for his patron Mansur ibn Ishaq al-Samani of Sijistan; a Latin translation, *Liber Almansoris*, was first published in Milan in the 1580's. Al-Razi was invariably described as a generous and gracious man with a large head, full beard, and imposing presence. His lectures, which attracted full-capacity crowds of students, were organized so that his senior students handled all questions they could answer, deferring to him only those issues beyond their knowledge.

Early in his career he earned a reputation as an effective and compassionate healer, which resulted in his appointment in 918 by the 'Abbasid caliph al-Muqtadir as physician in chief of the great hospital at Baghdad. In choosing a new site for this main hospital, al-Razi is said to have had pieces of meat hung in different quarters of Baghdad, finally selecting the spot where the meat was slowest to decompose, which he deemed the area with the healthiest air. As a result of his compassion for the sick and his contributions to medical ethics, al-Razi is justifiably compared to Hippocrates. In his Baghdad hospital he provided patients with music, storytelling, recitations of the Koran, and separate convalescent quarters. He not only treated poor patients free of charge but also supported them with his own funds during their convalescence at home. He emphasized a holistic approach to treating illness—that the mind as well as the body must be treated—but above all insisted that the art of healing must rest on a scientific basis. In his treatise on medical ethics, *Upon the Circumstances Which Turn the Head of Most Men from the Reputable Physician* (c. 919), al-Razi warns physicians that laymen think doctors know all and can diagnose a problem with a simple examination. He laments that frustrated patients turn to quacks who may alleviate some symptoms but not effect a cure. Al-Razi advises reputable physicians not to despair or promise cures but to use their critical judgment, apply tested treatments to appropriate cases, and be thoroughly familiar with the available medical literature.

Al-Razi, like Hippocrates, based his diagnoses on observation of the course of a disease. In administering treatments, he paid serious attention to dietetics and hygienic measures in conjunction with the use of closely monitored drug therapy. His fine powers of observation and detailed clinical descriptions are evident in his best-known monograph, *al-Judari w-al-hasbah* (c. 922; *A Treatise on the Smallpox and Measles*, 1848), which is the first clinical account of smallpox. In this work he describes the types of human bodies most susceptible to each disease, the season in which each disease most often occurs, and the varied symptoms indicating the approaching eruption of smallpox and measles. These symptoms included fever, back pain, nausea, anxiety, itching in the nose, and nightmares. Since al-Razi believed that these diseases were caused by fermentation of the blood, his remedy was purification of the blood. The therapeutic measures he employed were based upon his readings of the ancient Greeks and his own clinical trials. He devised two different approaches to treatment: to counteract the disease with antidotes such as camphor mixtures, purgatives, bloodletting, and cooling with cold sponges or baths; and to effect a cure with heat, especially steam, to stimulate the eruption of pustules and hasten healing. The choice of treatment depended on the degree of fever and the patient's general condition. Bloodletting, which was a common practice, he recommended using with caution and not on the very young, the very old, or those with a weak constitution. Al-Razi also developed detailed measures for preventing secondary effects from these diseases, such as damage to the eyes, ears, and throat and scarring of the skin.

Possessing an extensive knowledge of pharmacology and therapeutics, al-Razi claimed to have acquired much valuable information from women healers and herbalists in his own country and from his travels to Syria, Palestine, Egypt, and Muslim Spain. Other medieval physicians added little to his vast knowledge of drugs. His drug therapy was similar to contemporary practice in that dosage was based on age and weight. Drugs with which he was acquainted included nux vomica, senna, camphor, cardamom, salammoniac, and arrack as well as other alcoholic drinks. He used oils, powders, infusions, syrups, liniments, plasters, suppositories, compresses, and fumigations. His diligent search for drugs of therapeutic value and his methods of clinical observation laid the foundation on which future physicians would build.

Al-Razi's extensive medical and pharmacological knowledge is contained in his most important work, *al-Kitab al-hawi fi'l tibb* (c. 930; *The Comprehensive Book*), a twenty-four-volume encyclopedia which summarized the medical knowledge of the time, that is, the knowledge of the Greeks, Persians, Indians, and Arabs. It was completed posthumously by his students. First translated into Latin in 1279, it was repeatedly printed from 1486 onward under the title *Continens Medicinae* and exercised considerable influence in the Latin West. Medieval Muslim knowledge of anatomy and physiology was limited by the Koranic prohibition against dissection of the human body. Thus, most information on anatomy and surgery in *al-Kitab al-hawi fi'l tibb* was drawn from Greeks such as Galen and Hippocrates. Al-Razi provided numerous descriptions of his own surgical procedures, however, including those for intestinal obstructions, various forms of hernia, vesical calculi, tracheotomy, and cancer. In treating cancer he stressed that there should be no surgical removal of cancerous tissue unless the entire cancer could be removed.

Much of al-Razi's philosophical thinking can be gleaned from two of his treatises on ethics: *Kitab al-tibb al-ruhani* (c. 920; *The Book of Spiritual Physick*, 1950) and *Sirat al-faylasuf* (c. 920; *The Philosopher's Way of Life*, 1926). He propounded egalitarian views, rejecting a contemporary argument that humans can be stratified according to innate abilities. Rather, he believed that all people possess the capacity to reason and do not need the discipline imposed by religious leaders. The latter he accused of deception, and the miracles of prophets he regarded as trickery. His critical attitude toward religious authority carried over to the established dogmas of science. Only by questioning and testing received knowledge, he argued, could there be continuing progress in science.

Al-Razi asserted that he did not accept Aristotle's philosophy and that he was a disciple of Plato, with whom he shared certain ideas on matter; his egalitarianism, however, was antithetical to Plato's political ideas. Al-Razi's attitude toward animals was also part of his ethics. He believed that only carnivores and noxious animals such as snakes should be killed, for he endorsed the doctrine of transmigration, according to which a soul may pass from an animal to a person. Killing an animal set the soul on a path of liberation, while al-Razi maintained that only souls occupying human bodies should be liberated. Toward the end of his life, al-Razi became blind from cataracts. He reportedly rejected surgery, remarking that he had seen too much of the world already. Some biographers have argued that his interest in alchemy contributed to his blindness; others ascribed it to his excessive consumption of beans. He died around 925 in abject poverty, having given all of his wealth to his impoverished patients.

Summary

Al-Razi's antireligious attitude and his interest in alchemy caused other Muslim intellectuals to criticize his work and question his medical competence. To his credit, his principal work on alchemy, *Kitab al-asrar wa-sirr al asrra* (c. 916; *The Book of Secrets*), which was translated into Latin in 1187 (*De spiritibus et corporibus*), was a chief source of chemical knowledge through the fourteenth century. Later, more talented medieval physicians such as Moses Maimonides found fault with his philosophy but not with his medicine. As Aristotelians they were intolerant of his disavowal of Aristotle and his readiness to accept empirical evidence that upset established doctrines. It was in his insistence on rigorous scientific research and valid evidence, however, that al-Razi anticipated the position of modern medicine. Moreover, as a conscientious practitioner who stressed qualitative medicine—devising the best therapy, based on an evaluation of the patient's physical and mental condition—he set high standards for physicians and paved the way for modern medical practice.

As a result of his many achievements—the application of chemistry to medical treatment, the earliest study of smallpox and other epidemiological studies, the elaboration of medical ethics and scientific trials, the invention of the seton for surgery—al-Razi secured the historical reputation of the medieval Muslim Arab world as the primary center of science and medicine. His Muslim predecessors introduced clinics, hospitals, and pharmacies, but al-

Razi established more rigorous ethical, clinical, and scientific standards, free from dogmatic prejudices, which foreshadowed those of modern science. For that reason, al-Razi's portrait is one of only two portraits of Muslim physicians (the other being that of Avicenna) which were hung long ago in the great hall of the School of Medicine at the University of Paris as permanent testimony to the West's debt to the science of medieval Islam.

Bibliography
Browne, Edward G. *Arabian Medicine*. Reprint. Westport, Conn.: Hyperion Press, 1985. Contains separate sections on al-Razi's life, writings and influence, and his pharmacological contributions.
Campbell, Donald E. H. *Arabian Medicine and Its Influence on the Middle Ages*. Vol. 1. London: Kegan Paul, Trench, Trübner, and Co., 1926. Focuses on medieval Muslim contributions to medical history and contains a sympathetic section on al-Razi.
Gordon, Benjamin L. *Medieval and Renaissance Medicine*. New York: Philosophical Library, 1959. A readily available volume containing a summary of al-Razi's career and a concise summary of his clinical work in the chapter on smallpox.
Hitti, Philip K. *History of the Arabs*. 10th ed. New York: St. Martin's Press, 1974. Still the best and most available text with extensive coverage of the 'Abbasid period; it contains a discussion of al-Razi's work within the context of 'Abbasid scientific and literary accomplishments.
Razi, al-. *The Spiritual Physick of Rhazes*. Translated by Arthur J. Arberry. London: John Murray, 1950. An excellent example of al-Razi's thinking, this slender volume provides clinical information and treatment advice on various issues such as alcoholism, anxiety, and mendacity.
_____. *A Treatise on the Smallpox and Measles*. Translated by William Alexander Greenhill. London: Sydenham Society Publications, 1848. A translation of the classic work, the volume provides an excellent example of al-Razi's medieval Muslim thinking, scientific methodology, and medieval Muslim thought in general.

Kathleen K. O'Mara

COLA DI RIENZO
Nicola di Lorenzo

Born: 1313; Rome
Died: October 8, 1354; Rome
Area of Achievement: Government
Contribution: Though his reign as tribune of Rome was short-lived, Rienzo put in place genuine reforms that effectively broke the power of nobles and barons who had been plundering the city in the manner of warlords.

Early Life
Little is known about the early life of Cola di Rienzo. The anonymous fourteenth century biography to which modern sources are much indebted concentrates mostly on Rienzo's meteoric rise to power and his rule as tribune of Rome. Though scant, evidence suggests that he was born the son of a poor innkeeper and his wife in a Roman slum in 1313. Because his mother was dying while he was still a small boy, Rienzo was brought by his father to relatives in the town of Anagni, where he was reared.

Like so many great men and women, Rienzo exhibited a love of learning early in his life. He was a zealous youth who read avidly Livy's history of Rome, acquainted himself with the classical poets Vergil and Horace, and patterned his own rhetorical style on the works of Cicero. Exactly how Rienzo gained access to these writings and exactly who these relatives in Anagni were to have afforded the boy the opportunity for such study are matters that remain unresolved. It is clear, however, that by the time he was twenty years old, Rienzo had returned to Rome a master of classical literature.

At this time, the dawn of the Renaissance, Rome was a virtual armed camp. The Papacy—a unifying force of medieval society—had abandoned the city in 1305, when the new pope, Clement V, a Frenchman, determined to make the town of Avignon his seat of government. For more than seventy years, this small village in the Rhone River valley was the center of Western Christendom. Meanwhile, Rome itself was left as political carrion. Two great families, the Colonna and the Orsini, ruled as medieval barons. Living in their fortified estates, they plundered at will like gangsters. The city was dangerous, falling into decay. Marble from the ancient public buildings was taken as booty. The air was rank from the surrounding Campagna di Roma, a morass that in summer bred the plague. Cattle and pigs grazed in the streets, and beggars were everywhere.

Into this setting of urban rot and political chaos Rienzo returned sometime in the early 1330's. He married the beautiful daughter of a notary, and Rienzo became a public notary himself, soon gaining the reputation for being a clever, efficient, and honest public servant.

For the next decade, Rienzo pursued the modest duties of his office. He also spent time studying the ancient Roman inscriptions, talking to the peasants, perfecting his knowledge of Latin and the classics, and above all becoming deeply imbued with the glories of the past, when Rome was the center of Western civilization.

Life's Work

This deep love for the Roman past had become a guiding principle for Rienzo. He dreamed of making Rome the supreme city it had once been. Inspired by a brief popular uprising in 1339 which had failed for lack of papal support, Rienzo was convinced that the first step in bringing Rome out of its desperate condition was to gain the support of the Pope, whose influence was indispensable. The Pope could raise an army in those days, and the Church's territorial and political claims rivaled those of the Holy Roman Emperor. Although he resided in Avignon, the new pope, Clement VI, would claim Rome as part of his traditional see. Rienzo aligned himself with those men in Rome who saw that the Pope should be coaxed into declaring a Jubilee for 1350, thus making Rome a commercial and cultural locus for travelers, pilgrims, and all other Christians. In 1342, having persuaded the Romans that only he could sell Clement on the idea, Rienzo left Rome, alone, for Avignon.

There, in 1343, Rienzo secured a papal audience. He denounced the noble oppressors of Rome and sought the pontiff's favor with such stunning rhetoric that Clement—himself a scholar and orator—was deeply impressed by the young notary. In Avignon Rienzo also became acquainted with the famous poet and Humanist Petrarch (1304-1374), whose work was ushering in a new literary movement. Having been appointed to the papal staff, Petrarch, like Clement, was struck by Rienzo's eloquence. He was to become an enduring supporter of Rienzo and at this time took him into the papal court, introducing him to influential and powerful men. Rienzo stayed at the court for more than a year, but in 1344 he returned to Rome, having been given the office of papal notary, a steady income, and an entrée into the political fabric of his city.

For the next three years, Rienzo, now financially secure, continued to engage in scholarship. Though genuine, his studies were only a temporary resort; he was waiting for an opportunity to fulfill his dream of bringing Rome to greatness. Meanwhile, he gathered about him loyal supporters, men who were impressed with his learning and shared his dream.

Rienzo's opportunity arose in 1347, with one of those events in which chance and natural ability conjoin, shaping a turning point in the career of a great man. In pursuit of his studies, Rienzo happened upon a bronze plate virtually buried among the debris of a rebuilt church. As he began to decipher the timeworn inscription, he discovered that he had unearthed the

Cola di Rienzo 1817

original text of the Lex Regia, the ancient law by which the rights of the Roman people were transferred to Vespasian, who ruled the Roman Empire from A.D. 69 to 79. Though the law was well-known and had been the subject of academic discussions throughout the Middle Ages, Rienzo saw his discovery of the plate as an opportunity to give his own interpretation on the law. In his best rhetorical style, he called a public meeting and read the law, indicting the barons, the members of the aristocratic families who were in control of city government, as subversives.

When the leaders of these families, the Orsini and the Colonna, left Rome on business, taking with them their militia, Rienzo saw the time as ripe. Gathering his own forces, he organized an uprising in May, 1347, and quickly took power. Speaking before the assembled populace, he denounced the nobles and proclaimed Rome free of their tyranny. Showing the tact for which he was famous, Rienzo declared himself Tribune of Rome—a title redolent of ancient honor—and installed as his partner in government the Pope's vicar, the Bishop of Orvieto, thus preempting any military intervention by the Pope by showing deference to papal authority.

For the next seven months, Rienzo was the master of Rome. He had broken the power of the barons and now put forth a new constitution which contained several notable reforms, among them the dismissal and punishment of all corrupt judges and the establishment of civil programs protecting the poor and the weak. Rienzo also initiated a program of taxation and trade which gave Rome a fiscal stability it did not have under the barons.

Rienzo's next move was to make Rome the acknowledged capital of the Italian peninsula, as it had once been the center of the Western world. To this end, he arranged to give himself a triumph, a magnificent procession through the city to the steps of the Capitol, where he would be crowned. Designed to evoke the ancient Roman custom in which a great leader would be carried through the streets in glory, Rienzo's triumph was more than a sop to his vanity: It was a dramatic rite, a political symbol of Roman sovereignty. Rome's preeminence was promoted by scores of letters which Rienzo, as tribune, addressed to major Italian cities, urging them to forge informal alliances with Rome; such letters always showed tact and diplomacy so as not to incite either the emperor or the Pope.

Yet Rienzo's effective rule was to be short-lived. The opulence and pomp with which he played the role of tribune—his triumph culminating in a lavish feast reminiscent of the decadent caesars—scandalized many of his loyal followers. In addition, Rienzo's complete humiliation of the barons, his cruelty and severity in dealing with them, made him enemies among those relatives of the barons who held powerful positions in the papal court—including Cardinal Orsini.

By September, 1347, the Pope's vicar arrived in Rome with orders to plumb Rienzo's true fealty to the Holy See. Distrustful of Rienzo's pledges of obedience, the Cardinal Legate called for the popular leader's immediate resignation. The Pope, meanwhile, had already issued an edict of excommunication against him. Bereft of any appeal and facing pressure from the barons, Rienzo resigned his tribunate on December 15, 1347.

Abandoned, Rienzo fled to Naples, where he sought aid from King Louis. Yet the Black Death, which was then ravaging the city, forced Louis to leave, and Rienzo saw the last of his allies withdraw from Italy. Fearing death—either from the papal forces or from the plague—Rienzo fled once again, this time to the mountains of central Italy, where he joined an order of Franciscan monks. The Franciscans accepted Rienzo as a kindred spirit, for they had called for a purging of the impurities of the Church (as Rienzo had sought to cleanse the civil government of its abuses). He stayed in this mountain retreat for about a year, returning briefly to Rome in his Franciscan robes before fleeing to Prague, where he hoped to persuade the emperor, Charles IV, to support his cause.

Charles, however, was not disposed to help Rienzo when such aid might antagonize the Pope. The emperor wished to maintain a balance between the papal jurisdiction and his own attempts to consolidate his power. Rienzo was a threat to that balance, and Charles thus kept him imprisoned for several years, forestalling any commitments to the Pope. In 1351, the Pope's envoys officially ordered the extradition of Rienzo, and Charles released him to the papal authorities. In Avignon once again, this time as prisoner, Rienzo was to be tried for heresy when Clement VI died in 1352. The new pope was Innocent VI, whose administration, seeking reforms, believed that it could use Rienzo as a stabilizing force in the chaos of Roman politics. Through Rienzo, the Papacy hoped to regain jurisdiction over Rome.

Reinstated, Rienzo again rode into Italy, this time as a senator in support of the Pope. After months of rebuilding friendships and raising money, Rienzo took control of the city in September, 1354. His time, however, had clearly passed. Those years of absence had irrevocably lost for him any hold on the civil government. The irascible barons had regrouped, and the economy of the city had once again fallen prey to mismanagement. Unable to raise enough money to pay his mercenaries, who had formed the largest portion of his army, Rienzo imposed taxes on food, wine, and salt. Prompted by the Colonna family, a mob stormed Rienzo's palace. On October 8, 1354, they dragged him to the steps of the Capitol and murdered him, hanging him from his feet for two days while children threw stones at his corpse. The following year, Innocent VI absolved all persons involved in the assassination of Cola di Rienzo.

Summary

Cola di Rienzo's career can be evaluated from several points of view. To some historians, he was a dictator, a proto-Fascist whose self-glorification helped to bring him down. To others, such as Victorian novelist Edward Bulwer-Lytton (1803-1873) and the composer Richard Wagner (1813-1883), both of whom treated Rienzo as the subject of a major work, the popular leader was a hero, a patriot sacrificed on the altar of freedom. Yet Rienzo's career is more clearly understood in the broader context of fourteenth century European history—a period of economic stagnation and political divisiveness, when the Church was struggling to remain whole in spite of an "expatriated" Papacy and an enervating secularism.

Rienzo viewed himself as a dreamer, and his apologists, such as Petrarch, commended his patriotism in support of his dreams. Yet his ambition for Rome, and for himself, was of necessity thwarted by the political and social turbulence that signaled the end of the Middle Ages and the dawn of the Renaissance. Last, his devotion to classical studies certainly puts him in the position of harbinger of the new age.

Bibliography
Barzini, Luigi. "Cola di Rienzo: Or, The Obsession of Antiquity." In *The Italians*. New York: Bantam Books, 1964. A well-balanced account of the popular leader, emphasizing his dream of Roman greatness and its effect on his "theatrical" behavior and love of ceremony.
Cosenza, Mario Emilio. *Francesco Petrarca and the Revolution of Cola di Rienzo*. Chicago: University of Chicago Press, 1913. A seminal source, discussing Rienzo's concept of a united Italy and the political thought of Petrarch. Drawn largely from the letters of Rienzo and Petrarch, the study concludes that both men were centuries ahead of their time.
Fleischer, Victor. *Rienzo: The Rise and Fall of a Dictator*. London: Aiglon Press, 1948. A good—though somewhat biased—account which emphasizes the duplicity of Rienzo rather than his sincerity. Published directly after World War II, the study sees Rienzo as a despot in the tradition of Adolf Hitler and Benito Mussolini, though it does not ignore some of Rienzo's genuine accomplishments.
Gregorovius, Ferdinand Adolf. *History of the City of Rome in the Middle Ages*. Translated by Annie Hamilton. 8 vols. London: G. Bell, 1894-1902. An example of the nineteenth century view which perceived Rienzo as a nationalist and a precursor of Giuseppe Garibaldi. Long and overly detailed, it is still an interesting and valuable work.
The Life of Cola di Rienzo. Translated by John Wright. Toronto: Pontifical Institute of Mediaeval Studies, 1975. The anonymous fourteenth century biography which is the primary source of information on Rienzo. Contains an excellent introduction by the translator, who provides a concise historical background of the period and the various critical views of Rienzo's character.

Edward Fiorelli

RUDOLF I

Born: May 1, 1218; Limburg-im-Breisgau
Died: July 15, 1291; Speyer, Germany
Area of Achievement: Government
Contribution: Rudolf, as the first of his family to achieve eminence, founded a dynasty that was to remain one of the most important royal families in Europe for more than six centuries.

Early Life

Until the age of fifty-five, when events were to raise him to the German throne as King of the Romans, Rudolf I was a relatively insignificant noble in northern Switzerland. His family originated in Alsace, near Mulhouse, and his lands included areas of Swabia, Alsace, and Switzerland that lie in modern southern Germany, eastern France, and northwestern Switzerland. He oversaw these possessions from Habichtsburg (goshawk's castle) in Aargau Canton. As was usual at the time, the family name was taken from the castle, and Habichtsburg came to be known as Habsburg. This area became so important to the Habsburgs as the site of their origin that Emperor Francis-Joseph I tried to buy it from the Swiss just prior to World War I. The Swiss refused, as they considered themselves well rid of the Habsburgs. In fact, Switzerland still celebrates its national holiday on August 1, which is the anniversary of the day in 1291 when news of the death of Rudolf I arrived.

Until his election, Rudolf had been quite active in disputes with the Bishop of Basel and other quarrels within Switzerland. In 1254, he had been involved in a crusade against the Prussian Slavs and had gained a good reputation as a military leader. While all this sounds impressive, he was actually rather unimportant in comparison to several other German nobles who controlled more land and were more powerful. He ranked only as a count in the feudal hierarchy.

Despite his comparatively low status, or rather because of it, he was elected to the throne in 1272. The reasons for this apparently extraordinary election are to be found in the conditions prevailing in Europe after the fall of the Hohenstaufen imperial dynasty in the middle of the thirteenth century. The trouble had begun with Emperor Frederick II. Although Frederick was a Hohenstaufen, his interests were in Sicily and Italy. In fact, he had never been to Germany before his election in 1212. His absence from Germany and his involvement in a feud with the Papacy over control of Italy meant that the German nobles were free to strengthen their own territories and establish their independence from imperial control. The situation continued to deteriorate under Frederick's successors; between 1250 and 1272, there was a succession of weak emperors, some of whom never entered Germany. The German nobles believed that it was in their interest to perpetuate this situation, since it afforded them opportunities to increase their personal power. They very willingly exchanged support for one imperial candidate or another in return for concessions, such as control of cities, the right to collect tolls, and grants of land.

It also appeared to be in the interest of various foreign powers to prevent the election of a strong emperor. The French, in particular, were interested in obtaining territory in Alsace, Lorraine, Burgundy, and other areas west of the Rhine River that were controlled by the emperor. The English were usually interested in opposing French ambitions, and the Papacy was interested in these struggles as well as in increasing its temporal power in Italy. Moreover, some popes were very eager to see a new crusade to the Holy Land. Opposing foreign powers championed candidates who would further their causes, and there were often two claimants each of whom maintained that he had been elected. The result was minor wars and a state of near anarchy within Germany.

With the death of the latest nominal ruler, Richard of Cornwall, in 1272, Pope Gregory X determined that something had to be done to change the situation. He was primarily alarmed at the growing power of France. There had been suggestions from the French that the King of France should be made Holy Roman Emperor, since France was the most powerful country in Europe and could do most for the position. The Papacy was not interested in having an emperor who was too strong or too independent of the Pope. With the territorial encroachments by France into Germany becoming increasingly bold, Gregory feared that France would soon be too powerful to resist. He therefore threatened the electors with a candidate of his own choice if they did not elect a suitable German noble. The German aristocracy did not want a strong emperor, so they turned to someone who posed little threat to their independence.

Life's Work

Rudolf's main ambition from the beginning of his reign in 1272 was to acquire as much land as possible for himself and to establish a hereditary monarchy for his descendants. He was always willing to sacrifice some abstract imperial right or some advantage in a distant part of the empire in return for recognition of the hereditary principle or for territorial additions to his own possessions.

His first task was to defeat the powerful nobles who questioned his election to the throne. Soon after he was elected, the Diet of Speyer gave him the authority to take back all the imperial lands that had been usurped by nobles during the previous twenty-five years. He was unable to carry out any general plans he might have had to confiscate such lands for his own use, because he was too dependent on the support of nobles who controlled them. The authorization did, however, give him an excuse to proceed against some of his most dangerous enemies.

The most important of these enemies was Otakar II, King of Bohemia. Otakar had not been allowed to vote in the election of Rudolf and had other grievances, but his real motive for rebellion was the desire to be elected emperor himself. Rudolf laid siege to Vienna in 1276 and quickly obtained the surrender of Otakar. As punishment, Otakar was dispossessed of many of his lands, including Austria. Vienna thus became the new seat of Rudolf and remained the Habsburg capital until the twentieth century. Otakar received assistance from some of his Slav dependents and resumed his opposition to Rudolf in 1278. He was killed after one of the ensuing battles, and the major threat to Rudolf ended. After the defeat of Otakar, Rudolf's position was stronger, and he granted fewer exceptions to the prohibition against nobles retaining imperial lands.

The defeat of Otakar was the key event in establishing Rudolf's credibility. He was not directly challenged afterward, although there were numerous threatening incidents in addition to the usual refusal of individual knights and nobles to recognize his authority. There were, for example, several impostors who claimed to be either Frederick I Barbarossa or Frederick II, despite the fact that both had been dead for many years. The legend persisted that one or the other of them was not dead, but merely sleeping, and would return in an hour of need. In 1285, Rudolf had one of the most significant of these impostors, Dietrich Holzschuh, burned at the stake. The impostors were a real threat, because they could become focal points for revolt. Rudolf's execution of Holzschuh demonstrated that he was able to deal with such threats.

Rudolf's power and prestige grew to such an extent that he was able to field a large and impressive army against Otto IV, Count Palatine of Franche-Comté. This rebel count had conspired with the King of France to gain independence from the empire. His scheme failed in 1289 with the arrival of the imperial army, and Rudolf was left firmly in control.

Although Rudolf had been elected and had shown that he could exercise power, he was never crowned Holy Roman Emperor by the Pope. Gregory X promised to perform the ceremony on several occasions but died before he could carry out his promise. One of his successors, Pope Nicholas III, was less cooperative. The negotiations between him and Rudolf over this issue are an indication of how weak the empire had become and how far Rudolf was willing to go to secure the succession of his family. In return for the imperial crown, Rudolf was prepared to give up all the historic claims by previous emperors to territory in Italy. He also recognized the temporal superiority of the Pope. These great concessions produced no results, as death intervened again. Nicholas died in 1280, before the negotiations were complete. Again, in 1287, the death of Pope Honorius IV prevented the coronation. By the time arrangements had been made with the new Pope, Nicholas IV, Rudolf himself was too ill to make the journey to Rome. When he died, he still had not received the imperial crown. Without recognition as emperor, he could not have his son crowned King of Rome during his own lifetime; thus, Rudolf could never ensure the royal succession of his family.

The second feature of Rudolf's reign was his determination to increase his family's territorial holdings and pass them on to his sons. Soon after taking the defeated Otakar's lands, Rudolf made the acquisition permanent by naming his eldest son, Albert, Duke of Austria and Styria. He attempted to extend his influence to the east by marrying the fourteen-year-old Isabella of Burgundy himself in 1284. Apparently, he hoped to carve out another duchy for his younger son, Rudolf, in Burgundy or Swabia. He also married his daughter to Wenceslaus II of Bohemia in a continuing effort to establish as many dynastic ties with important families as possible.

Clearly, the object of these maneuvers was to obtain recognition of his younger son as his successor to the throne. It appeared that he might succeed in that ambition, as a significant number of nobles agreed to recognize Rudolf's son as legitimate successor if Rudolf were crowned Holy Roman Emperor. With the death of the younger Rudolf in 1289, at the age of twenty, these hopes were dashed. The elder Rudolf's recent marriage had produced a third son, Johann, but he was still a baby, so the only remaining hope was his oldest son, Albert. In the eyes of most German nobles, Albert was too strong to be a safe king. His father had been too successful at acquiring territory for him. As usual, the German nobles preferred someone who was less of a threat to their independence.

By 1291, Rudolf's health was so bad that he was unable to make the trip to Rome to receive the imperial crown from the hands of the Pope. In any case, there seemed little point in such an exercise after the death of the younger Rudolf. He considered abdicating in favor of Albert, but he had first to obtain recognition of Albert as his successor from the nobles. To that end, he called a diet at Frankfurt-am-Main in May, 1291. As expected, the nobles were unwilling to recognize Albert, and Rudolf left the diet for Speyer, where he wanted to be buried alongside previous emperors. He died there on July 15.

Summary

Although Rudolf I was willing to trade privileges and concessions for recognition of his authority and for advantages to his family, he did maintain order throughout most of Germany and restore much of the lost prestige of the Crown. He used force successfully when necessary, as shown by his campaigns against Otakar of Bohemia and Otto of Burgundy. This appearance of military prowess, his ability to deal with the complaints of cities and nobles, and his forceful suppression of insurrections gained a higher degree of respect for the throne than had existed for the past forty years.

Nevertheless, Rudolf was unable to accomplish any lasting constitutional changes that would alter the course of German history. The pattern of weak central authority and strong nobles that was to prevent the emergence of a German state on the model of France or England had been set. Without a hereditary monarch, those elected to the throne were mainly interested in gaining what they could for their families rather than strengthening the monarchy itself. In other words, in a feudal age when family meant everything, unless the monarchy could be seen as a family possession it would remain secondary in the policy of any king. Rudolf was no exception to this general pattern. He was able to restore something of the Crown's prestige, but his gains in power were traded away by his successors in return for support for their election.

Bibliography
Barraclough, Geoffrey. *The Origins of Modern Germany.* New York: W. W. Norton and Co., 1984. This volume is probably the best English-language discussion of Rudolf in the context of his times.
Crankshaw, Edward. *The Habsburgs: Portrait of a Dynasty.* New York: Viking Press, 1971. A readily available, popularized account of the Habsburgs, from Rudolf to the twentieth century. Many illustrations, including contemporary pictures of Rudolf. With anecdotes about his military campaigns.
Heer, Friedrich. *The Holy Roman Empire.* New York: Praeger Publishers, 1968. Translated from the German edition of 1967. Rudolf receives some attention in this account of the development of the Holy Roman Empire.
Wilks, Michael J. *The Problem of Sovereignty in the Later Middle Ages: The Papal Monarchy with Augustinus Triumphus and the Publicists.* Cambridge: Cambridge University Press, 1963. This work provides a context for Rudolf, focusing on the relations between king and nobles.

Philip Dwight Jones

JALAL AL-DIN RUMI

Born: c. September 30, 1207; Balkh
Died: December 17, 1273; Konya, Asia Minor
Areas of Achievement: Poetry and religion
Contribution: Rumi is the leading poet of Sufism (Islamic mysticism), the eponymous founder of the Maulawiyah Sufi order (which is still active in Konya), and a direct inspiration for almost all subsequent Gnostic writing in the Islamic world.

Early Life
Jalal al-Din Rumi, also known as Maulānā (Our Master), was born in the fall of 1207 in Balkh, a major eastern city in what is now Afghanistan. His father, a well-known Sufi preacher and scholar, moved his family from Balkh across Iran and into Turkey shortly before (and perhaps in anticipatory fear of) the Mongols' devastating westward incursion into the Islamic world. Neyshabur, the home of 'Attar, the leading Sufi poet before Rumi, fell to the Mongols in 1219-1220. A generation later, in 1258, Hülegü, Genghis Khan's grandson, overran the Islamic capital of Baghdad and ended the caliphate.

Rumi's family settled in Konya, in Turkish Anatolia, a region then called Rum, from which the poet later got the name "Rumi," by which he is best known in the West. Rumi studied the Koran, religious sciences, and literature. He was expert in Arabic, but Persian was to be his literary language. When his father died, Rumi, then twenty-three or twenty-four and married, assumed his position as a teacher in a religious school in Konya. Also at this time, Rumi began further study of Sufi doctrine and further initiation into Sufi practice with Burhan al-Din Muhaqqiq, a former pupil of Rumi's father. Burhan al-Din died in 1239 or 1240, by which time Rumi was being referred to as "Shaykh," the title indicating his standing as a Sufi mentor with students and followers.

To this point in his life, Rumi was presumably an orthodox Sufi and had demonstrated no special interest in poetry or in music and dance as vehicles for or accompaniments to religious devotion and expression of faith. All this was to change in the fall of 1244, when he met a peripatetic and charismatic Sufi called Shams-e Tabrizi. Rumi felt mystical love for Shams of Tabriz, who introduced the latter to wholehearted love as the true Sufi's requisite attitude and who became Rumi's chief "sun" and source of illumination. Rumi had apparently found in Shams the image of the Divine Beloved, a focus which would inspire the rest of his life. The intensity of the relationship caused Rumi to begin to express himself in Persian lyric verse and to find special meaning and joy in music and dance.

The attraction of Shams for Rumi and the former's influence on the latter did not please Rumi's family and students. Presumably as a result of verbal abuse, perhaps including threats, Shams suddenly left Konya without telling anyone of his plans. This event brought Rumi great sorrow and inspired the composition of Sufi verse lamenting the separation of lover from beloved. Nearly two years later, after hearing that Shams was in Syria, Rumi sent his older son to bring the wandering dervish back to Konya.

The reunion of the two Sufis inspired Rumi to compose further Sufi poems, this time on the union of lover and beloved. Yet again, however, some of Rumi's followers and family members were vexed at Shams's presence in their community and his hold on Rumi. Shams disappeared for good in late 1248 (reportedly murdered by Rumi's son and disciples). Rumi was again inconsolable and set out for Syria to find his mystical guide and beloved. The poet gradually came to realize, however, that the spirit of Shams was with him, that his poems were really Shams's voice. He consequently chose "Shams" as his own nom de plume.

Life's Work

Rumi's life after the disappearance of Shams became as creative and inspirational as that of any literary-religious figure in history. He composed the bulk of the much-loved and inimitable Sufi lyrics in Persian that comprise the *Divan-e Shams-e Tabriz*. The following is an especially appreciated example of these lyric poems, in a version by Reynold Nicholson, Rumi's foremost Western editor and translator.

> This is love: to fly heavenward,
> To rend, every instant, a hundred veils.
> The first moment, to renounce life;
> The last step, to fare without feet.
> To regard this world as invisible,
> Not to see what appears to one's self.
> "O heart," I said, "may it bless thee
> To have entered the circles of lovers,
> To look beyond the range of the eye,
> To penetrate the windings of the bosom."

Not long after Shams's disappearance, Rumi entered into a Sufi relationship with another man in whom he saw something of Shams. Called Salah al-Din Zarkub, this man was reportedly illiterate and also not to the liking of Rumi's other disciples. Nevertheless, Rumi dedicated some poems to Salah al-Din (who died in 1258), and Rumi's eldest son married the latter's daughter. After Salah al-Din's death, Rumi became interested in a disciple of his called Chalabi Husamuddin Hasan, of whom Shams had presumably thought highly. Rumi and Husamuddin lived together for ten years, and it was the latter who prevailed upon Rumi to compose a didactic and inspirational Sufi verse guide for his disciples. Thus began Rumi's most famous work, called

Masnavi-ye ma'navi (*The Mathnawi*, 1926-1934), which grew into some twenty-six thousand Persian couplets and is an encyclopedic compendium of Sufi lore, combining anecdotal narratives, didactic commentary, and passages best described as ecstatic reflections and outbursts.

The Mathnawi begins with the most famous metaphorical representation of the human condition in Middle Eastern literature. In Talat S. Halman's translation, the passage reads:

> Listen to the reed, how it tells its tales;
> Bemoaning its bitter exile, it wails:
> Ever since I was torn from the reed beds,
> My cries tear men's and women's hearts to shreds.
> Let this separation slit my sad breast
> So I can reveal my longing and quest.
> Everyone is my friend for his own part,
> Yet none can know the secrets of my heart.
> The flames of love make the reed's voice divine;
> It is love's passion that rages in the wine.
> The reed cries with the lovers who fell apart,
> It rends the chest and tears open the heart.
> Nothing kills or cures the soul like the reed;
> Nothing can crave or console like the reed.

For Rumi, then, the proper life is the mystic's quest through dedication to love to return to the original condition of proximity to God, the Divine Beloved. *The Mathnawi* offers Rumi's vision through precept and anecdote for the life lived for love. The work is not formally structured or unified; rather, the poet proceeds as inspiration strikes him, often inspired by verbal association to mystical association. He may have composed large parts of it extemporaneously or orally, with Husamuddin transcribing passages. According to tradition, Rumi composed or recited some tales while dancing around a column at his school.

Rumi died in December, 1273, before finishing *The Mathnawi*, which stops in the middle of a tale in book 6. His death was cause for great mourning in Konya, where his mausoleum is still visited yearly by thousands of pilgrims.

Husamuddin thereafter assumed leadership of Rumi's disciples. At his death in 1283 or 1284, Sultan Walad, Rumi's eldest son, became their leader and organized them into a formal Sufi order called the Maulawiyah, for Rumi's title; its members are now known throughout the world as the Whirling Dervishes. Sultan Walad also composed a spiritual biography of his father in verse.

Summary

Collections of Jalal al-Din Rumi's sermons, letters, and sayings have survived. It is his chief works, *Divan-e Shams-e Tabriz* and *The Mathnawi*, however, which put him in the first rank of Persian poets and which make him the chief poetic voice of Sufism in history.

In Persian poetry, Rumi's intensity of feeling and sure sense of rhythm give him a place in classical Persian *ghazal* poetry alongside his contemporary Sa'di, the supreme technical virtuoso of the Persian *ghazal* (short ode verse), and Hafiz, the master of ambivalent lyric expression in the *ghazal*. At the same time, as a master of the Persian quatrain, Rumi stands at the opposite end of the thematic spectrum from Omar Khayyám, whose verses question the very existence of God and the immortality of the human soul.

Rumi also stands apart from the mainstream of classical Persian poets because he was not involved with the court system of patronage. He apparently had good relations with rulers in Anatolia, because of which he was able to be of great service to the poor and needy. Whereas the majority of Persian poets praised kings and mundane beloveds, however, Rumi praised God and his Divine Beloved, and felt no attraction to temporal power or material wealth.

In addition, as knowledgeable as Rumi was in the craft of Persian poetry, he had little patience for technically and rhetorically correct verse, but concentrated mainly on the development of rhythms that would complement his message. His passionate love of God was filtered through his creativity into a unique Persian style of musical, expressive, spontaneous verse, combining his heartfelt views, his deepest feelings, his abundant knowledge and experience, and his feel for the everyday. The following verses, translated by Annemarie Schimmel, exhibit Rumi's recognition of the spontaneity of his art, which may sometimes not withstand prolonged scrutiny for theological content or technical niceties of verse:

> My poetry resembles Egyptian bread:
> When a night passes over it you cannot eat it anymore.
> Eat it at this point when it is fresh
> Before dust settles on it!

If Rumi was not a professional Persian poet in a conventional sense, he was also not a philosopher or theologian. His special place as a religious thinker and Sufi does not depend upon originality or complexity of thought, but upon his intense personal and artistic dedication to his convictions and his ability through word and deed to communicate those views to others. Among the themes that surface in his verse are a sense of God's transcendence, a perception of nature as offering a hint of God, and a concept of man as the highest creature, who, beyond body, soul, and mind, possesses a yet deeper spirit that partakes of divine revelation. Prophets and saints are special in this respect because God speaks through them. In death, man will be absorbed into God, but some residue of the individual may remain. Still, though these elements of a theological system can be extracted from Rumi's writings, Rumi is not to be appreciated as a systematic thinker; he is to be experienced as an inspired man of great vitality, virtue, and love, whose writings attest the nobility of the human spirit.

Bibliography

Halman, Talat S. "Jalal al-Din Rumi: Passions of the Mystic Mind." In *Persian Literature*, edited by Ehsan Yarshater. Albany, N.Y.: SUNY Press, 1988. An engaging, sympathetic portrait with stylish translations from Rumi's poetry. Another essay in this volume, "Lyric Poetry" by Heshmat Moayyad, provides a background and context for appreciation of Rumi's achievements as a poet.

Rumi, Jalal al-Din. *The Mathnawi of Jalalu'ddin Rumi*. Translated and edited by Reynold A. Nicholson. Vols. 2, 4, 6. London: Luzac, 1926-1934, reprint 1972. A complete scholarly verse translation of Rumi's most important poetic work.

—————. *Mystical Poems of Rumi*. Translated by Arthur J. Arberry. Chicago: University of Chicago Press, 1968.

—————. *Mystical Poems of Rumi, Second Selection*. Translated by Arthur J. Arberry. New York: Bibliotheca Persica, 1979. These two volumes contain translations of four hundred of Rumi's shorter poems.

—————. *Tales from "The Masnavi,"* and *More Tales from "The Masnavi."* Translated by Arthur J. Arberry. London: Allen and Unwin, 1961-1963. Prose retellings of two hundred anecdotal stories from *The Mathnawi*.

Schimmel, Annemarie. *As Through a Veil: Mystical Poetry in Islam*. New York: Columbia University Press, 1982. Five densely annotated essays (originally lectures) titled "The Development of Arabic Mystical Poetry," "Classical Persian Mystical Poetry," "Maulana Rumi and the Metaphors of Love," "Mystical Poetry in the Vernaculars," and "Poetry in Honor of the Prophet." The author demonstrates the centrality of Rumi to all subsequent Sufistic literary expression. Her chapter on Rumi reviews his life, suggests a chronology of his lyrics, and describes images and symbols for love in his verse.

—————. *The Triumphal Sun: A Study of the Works of Jalaloddin Rumi*. London: East-West Publications, 1978. The standard study by the leading Rumi scholar, with emphasis on Rumi's poetic vocabulary and thought. Includes extensive quotations from Rumi's works and a comprehensive bibliography.

Michael Craig Hillmann

SA'DI

Born: c. 1200; Shiraz, Iran
Died: c. 1291; Shiraz, Iran
Area of Achievement: Literature
Contribution: Sa'di's literary works, particularly his worldly-wise and entertaining classics, *The Orchard* and *The Rose Garden*, have made him one of the leading writers of Iran, where he is fondly known as "Shaykh Sa'di" or simply "the Shaykh."

Early Life
Like the expedient morality of his writings, the facts of Sa'di's life are difficult to pin down. Much information about him is available but untrustworthy; most of it tends to be legendary or to come from autobiographical passages in his writings, where Sa'di indulged the common human impulse to invent or correct oneself and in addition needed to make his stories fit his points (though not all do). As one of his characters puts it, "a man who has seen the world utters much falsehood." Moreover, G. M. Wickens, one of his translators, warns that "Sa'di is most often portrayed with shrewd and subtle features, enlivened by a wicked, enigmatic smile." The intermingling of fact, fiction, and uncertainty about Sa'di leaves his biography undependable but ontologically correct, since his main point is that one can never "know" oneself, anybody else, or anything with certainty.

Not even Sa'di's real name is certain. The best opinion is that his true name was Mosharrif al-Din ibn Moslih al-Din or some variation of this (sometimes with "Abdullah" or "Sa'di Shirazi" tacked on). Sa'di is a *takhallus* (pen name) taken from the rulers of Fars Province during Sa'di's lifetime—Sa'd ibn Zangi, his son Abu Bakr ibn Sa'd, and his grandson Sa'd ibn Abu Bakr. In Persian, which uses the Arabic alphabet, the name Sa'di contains an *'ayn* (here indicated by a turned comma, or reverse apostrophe), a separate sound or tightening of the throat for which there is no exact equivalent in English. To indicate this pronunciation, the name is sometimes transliterated as "Saadi."

Sa'di was born in Fars Province, a southern region whose ancient name, Persis, the early Greeks extended to all Iran (which was thus known in the West until recently as Persia). As this etymology suggests, Fars Province has played a central role in Iranian history, and such was especially the case during Sa'di's lifetime. Sa'di's father was a minor official at the court of the provincial ruler, Sa'd ibn Zangi. When Sa'di's father died, Sa'd ibn Zangi assumed responsibility for the young Sa'di's care and education. After schooling in Shiraz, Sa'di attended the Nizamiya College in Baghdad, then perhaps the world's best educational institution. According to some accounts, Sa'di spent his time there carousing and having a good time. In the *Bustan* (1257;

The Orchard, 1882), Sa'di says that he had a teaching fellowship requiring hours of instructional drudgery. In any case, he apparently had the opportunity for an excellent education, even if he was not himself cut out for the academic life.

Following his university studies, Sa'di entered upon the second of three main periods in his life, each of which represented a drastic change. He now began a period of wandering and adventure that, by the standard accounts, lasted for some thirty years. What motivated him to take to the road is not known, but it could have been any of a number of things—his desire to leave university life, the appeal of roaming, the influence of the dervishes or Sufis, or the approach of the conquering Mongol hordes. The Mongols, known as "the Scourge of Islam," were then devastating whole territories, leaving mountains of skulls piled up outside burned cities. In strange ways, Sa'di's fate intertwined with theirs, much as his achievement stands in opposition to what they represented. If the Mongols caused him to flee, they thereby brought about the period of wandering that constituted his real education and the source of his wisdom.

Life's Work

Sa'di's travels ranged throughout the Muslim lands, including Iran, Iraq, Syria, Anatolia (now Turkey), Palestine, Egypt, and other parts of North Africa. He visited the holy city of Mecca in Arabia numerous times. Sometimes he stayed with or traveled in the company of dervishes, members of the mystical Sufi fraternal orders, then at their height in the Islamic world. It is possible that he joined one of the Sufi orders for a time, even if his easygoing, skeptical temperament was not really compatible with Sufi discipline and emotionalism (ecstasy induced by various practices—such as chanting or whirling—to celebrate an all-embracing love). He did enjoy the singing, dancing, and company. Wandering about as a mendicant dervish also enabled him to travel more safely and to get handouts and hospitality, sometimes by preaching sermons that were good practice for writing his great didactic works.

His travels were naturally not without incident and occasionally perilous adventure. For example, in the *Gulistan* (1258; *The Rose Garden*, 1806), Sa'di says that he was captured in Palestine by Christian Crusaders and put to work digging moats. What most offended him about the experience was that the other prisoners in his work gang were "infidels" (or "Jews," depending on the translation); unfortunately, Sa'di displays the typical Muslim bigotry of his time. Eventually, a friend from Aleppo came by, recognized Sa'di, and ransomed him from the Crusaders for ten dinars. Then the friend gave his daughter to Sa'di in marriage, along with a dowry of one hundred dinars. The new wife proved so shrewish, however, that soon Sa'di was wishing himself back among the Christians and Jews. When she pointedly reminded him of how her father had saved him, Sa'di replied that it had cost her father only ten dinars to ransom him from the Crusaders but a hundred dinars to marry him to her. Later Sa'di might have married another woman in Arabia, where they had a child who died. There is no indication of what happened to either woman or that either returned with him to Iran; it is possible that he left them both behind.

Outside Muslim territory, Sa'di seems to have traveled in Armenia and possibly India, though his travel in India has been disputed. In *The Orchard*, Sa'di tells how he got into trouble in India over religion. While watching a temple crowd worship an idol, he commented on the crowd's superstition to a friend. The friend, who turned out to be a believer himself, angrily got up and denounced Sa'di to the crowd, which became ugly. Sa'di saved himself by pretending to be an ignorant foreigner eager to learn more about their worship. The head Brahman instructed Sa'di by making him spend all night with the statue, and the next morning the statue rewarded Sa'di and other worshippers by raising its hands in salute. Apologizing and kissing the statue, Sa'di claimed to be convinced, but a few days later he slipped behind the scenes and caught the Brahman operating levers that raised the statue's hands. Sa'di says that he killed the Brahman by throwing him down a well and dropping a rock onto his head. Then Sa'di got out of India as fast as he could.

Such incidents might have helped persuade Sa'di, sometime during the 1250's, to enter his third major phase—to return to Shiraz and take up a life of seclusion and writing. In addition, as his introduction to *The Rose Garden* shows, Sa'di was impelled by a feeling (although he had already established a literary reputation by then) that he had wasted his life and accomplished nothing of importance. Sa'di's retreat also coincided with another Mongol invasion of the eastern Muslim world, which could have lent urgency to his feelings by threatening both him and the world he knew. He was relatively safe, however, in Fars Province, whose ruler, Abu Bakr ibn Sa'd, had made peace with the Mongols by submitting and paying tribute before the province was invaded. Around the time Sa'di finished writing *The Orchard* and *The Rose Garden*, the Mongols (in January, 1258) devastated Baghdad, the center of Muslim culture for the previous five centuries, and killed its one and a half million inhabitants. Sa'di mourned the occasion in a famous lament.

If the Islamic world had suffered a crushing blow, Sa'di's fortunes dramatically improved. *The Orchard* and *The Rose Garden* found an eager audience. Numerous copies were made and circulated, and Sa'di's literary fame spread. Abu Bakr ibn Sa'd invited him to come and stay in the court, but Sa'di graciously declined the offer, content to live out his years in his "rose garden." After finishing his masterpieces, Sa'di lived on for some thirty more years, aware of his gradually diminishing literary powers but already venerated by his countrymen as "the Shaykh" (wise old man). He died sometime in the early 1290's, probably in 1291.

Summary

While admiring Sa'di as a "wise old man," his Victorian translators and editors were distressed by his casual acceptance of pederasty and by his *khabisat* (obscene poetry and prose). Readers today might be more offended by his bigotry, especially toward Jews and blacks, and by his numerous *qasidas* (long poems of fulsome praise for patrons or rulers). These offending features illustrate some of the more obvious cultural barriers that stand in the way of Westerners reading Sa'di with full understanding. More subtle barriers are posed by the allusions, imagery, and play with language, some of which cannot be translated.

Yet in his own country Sa'di has been revered for more than seven centuries. He has entered the culture and become part of the language, much like Shakespeare in the English-speaking world. Only the Koran has been quoted more in Iran than Sa'di, even if some Iranians now consider him old-fashioned. The British were acting on the right instincts when, during the colonial period, they adopted *The Rose Garden* as a Persian text for training civil servants going to India (Persian was the official language of the Moguls, who ruled parts of India before the British arrived). Anyone hoping to understand the Iranians, and indeed other groups in the Islamic world, could hardly find a better place to begin than with Sa'di. Few writers have so thoroughly defined a culture as Sa'di, both as the culture existed in the past and as it still to some extent persists.

Although Sa'di's *qasidas*, *ghazals* (love poems), and *ruba'iyat* (quatrains) need to be read more by Westerners, *The Orchard* and *The Rose Garden* remain his main works and the most accessible ones. Both works are in the Eastern didactic tradition (not entirely unknown in the West), combining literary, folk, and religious elements. *The Orchard*, written in verse (the *mathnavi* or rhymed couplet form), is a bit more serious and formal than the lighter, looser *The Rose Garden*, written in prose and verse (mostly quatrains). *The Rose Garden* might consist of leftovers from *The Orchard*, since both works are blends of stories, anecdotes, homilies, maxims, and folk sayings purportedly illustrating the virtues or moral topics of the chapter headings (for example, "On Love, Intoxication, and Delirium," "The Morals of Dervishes," "On the Advantages of Silence"). The easy but artful mixture of material tends to grow on the reader, as does Sa'di's slightly warped approach to life. After all, who can resist an author who makes the scorpion say, "What renown do I have in summer that I should also come out in winter?"

Bibliography

Arberry, A. J. *Classical Persian Literature.* New York: Macmillan, 1958. One of the leading introductions to Iran's greatest period of literature (ninth through fifteenth centuries). The chapter on Sa'di gives an excellent idea of his range. Includes generous quotations of his lyrical poetry in translation.

Levy, Reuben. *An Introduction to Persian Literature.* New York: Columbia University Press, 1969. Another good introduction to the literature of Iran, concentrating on the classical period. Includes useful information on the historical setting and Persian verse forms. Sa'di is covered in a separate chapter with Hafiz, another writer from Shiraz.

Sa'di. *The "Gulistan" or Rose Garden of Sa'di.* Translated by Edward Rehatsek. New York: G. P. Putnam's Sons, 1965. A reprint of "the complete and unexpurgated translation printed in 1888 for [the] Kama Shastra Society." The best English translation, done by a nineteenth century Hungarian who found his way to India. Good introductions by W. G. Archer and G. M. Wickens.

_____. *Morals Pointed and Tales Adorned: The "Bustan" of Sa'di.* Translated by G. M. Wickens. Toronto, Canada: University of Toronto Press, 1974. The best English translation, in verse, with a brief but good introduction. The text and notes at the end reflect the latest scholarship up to 1974.

Zand, Michael I. *Six Centuries of Glory: Essays on Medieval Literature of Iran and Transoxania.* Translated by T. A. Zalite. Moscow: Nauka Publishing House, 1967. A compact work examining Iran's classical period of literature from a Communist point of view. The brief but interesting essay on Sa'di comments on his treatment of social issues.

Harold Branam

SALADIN

Born: 1138; Tikrit, Iraq
Died: March 4, 1193; Damascus, Syria
Areas of Achievement: Government and religion
Contribution: In a period of disunity in the Muslim world, Saladin conquered and unified warring factions. Then, as Sultan of Syria, Saladin defeated King Richard I of England in the Third Crusade and drove the Christian rulers from Jerusalem.

Early Life

Al-Malik al-Nasir Salah al-Din aba 'l-Mussafer Yusuf ibn Ayyub ibn Shadi—or Saladin, as he has been known since his own time—learned diplomacy at his father's knee. Born in the town of Tikrit on the banks of the Tigris River, Saladin was the third of eight children of the Kurdish Najm al-Din Ayyub. Ayyub had risen to prominence in the decade before Saladin's birth in the service of the Seljuk Empire and was ruler of Tikrit. As an ethnic outsider, Ayyub had developed administrative skills that made him useful to his overlord, but he was also ambitious for wealth and power. After performing a favor for a rival leader, Ayyub was forced—on the very night of Saladin's birth—to flee Tikrit with his family. Despite this episode, Ayyub's status as an outsider made him a logical compromise candidate for later positions in an atmosphere of jealousy and intrigue; later, Saladin would be elevated for similar reasons.

Ayyub became governor of Baalbek, in Syria, and it was here that Saladin spent his childhood. Like many other well-born youths of his era, Saladin became an accomplished horseman and hunter—lion and gazelle were favored prey—and he learned hawking. He was a highly skilled polo player. Following the accepted educational program for young ruling-class men, Saladin studied the Koran and learned poetry, grammar, and script. He spoke Kurdish, Arabic, and probably Turkish. Also in his early years he drank wine.

Saladin early followed his father and brothers in a military career. His brother Shahan Shah fought in the Second Crusade and was killed in 1148. During this period, Ayyub attained leadership of Damascus, and even before his brother's commander, Sultan Nur al-Din, conquered that city, Saladin became a member of Nur al-Din's military establishment.

When he was only fourteen, Saladin had his own fief, and at sixteen he had considerable property holdings. He may have had a wife by this time, according to some historians, but others say there is no evidence of his marriage before age thirty.

At the beginning of his military career Saladin was posted near Nur al-Din in Aleppo, but at age eighteen he became a deputy in Damascus, responsible for administrative and judicial matters. There Saladin cultivated a love for the fairness and impartiality of Koranic law, and he rendered judgments with loyalty and compassion. When he found that his chief accountant was dishonest, Saladin resigned his position and returned to Nur al-Din as an aide-de-camp.

Their close relationship led to a turning point for Saladin, one of importance to the entire Islamic world for a century: He was sent to Egypt, a major battleground of Islam in the Middle Ages. There he gained his vision for unification of the Muslim world and expulsion of the Christian Crusaders.

Life's Work

The Muslim world was rent by religious differences. The Seljuk caliphate, ruled by Nur al-Din, was of the more liberal Sunni sect and had its seat of power in Baghdad. The Fatimid caliphate of Egypt, which had embraced the more orthodox Shi'a sect, was a volatile agglomeration with weak rulers. Like a splinter between them was the Latin Kingdom, a Christian stronghold along the eastern Mediterranean coast, ruled by a Frank, Amalric I. Nur al-Din believed that if Amalric were able to join forces with the Byzantine emperor to conquer Egypt, the whole Islamic world would be threatened. The stakes were great: Rich trade routes to the Orient, religious and educational centers, and plentiful agricultural lands could be lost.

Saladin, as one of Nur al-Din's principal advisers, helped plan three Syrian invasions of Egypt between 1164 and 1169 to conquer the Fatimid caliphate. During part of this period, Amalric had a treaty to defend Cairo against Syrian invaders. Saladin's first command came at Alexandria, where he was in charge of one thousand men under difficult conditions. After a short time back in Damascus, Saladin returned on Nur al-Din's orders to Egypt after the Fatimid alliance with Amalric broke down.

Saladin had grave misgivings about returning to Egypt, in part because he distrusted the motives of his powerful uncle Shirkuh, who was leading the return. The political situation there was dangerous and unstable. When Shirkuh suddenly died, however, Saladin was well placed to assume Shirkuh's place as vizier of Egypt commanding Nur al-Din's forces there; in this case, he was the compromise candidate among many factions.

Now thirty years old, Saladin drew strength from Koranic exhortations to fulfill God's purpose. Saladin, like Nur al-Din, was pious. He kept little money, acting instead as custodian for the whole Muslim community; the proper function of wealth, he believed, was to further the aims of Islam. Both men saw stable leadership in Egypt as a key to preserving Muslim unity. Still, Nur al-Din was suspicious when Saladin insisted on autonomy to do this—including lessened payments of tribute. Not only did Saladin have military bases on the Egyptian front, but he also had to fight political battles at his rear.

Saladin consolidated power in Egypt by getting rid of Fatimid commanders and substituting loyalists; uprisings continued in the provinces for some years, but finally Fatimid rule was abolished. Now Saladin built up the military and raided nearby areas. His strength was growing just when Ayyub, Nur al-Din, and Amalric died in quick succession. Both Nur al-Din's and Amalric's successors were young boys; thus, both kingdoms were weakened.

Saladin swore fealty to al-Salih, Nur al-Din's successor, but quickly moved to consolidate the empire under his own rule, citing the need for a unified Islam. He struck quickly at the Frankish Kingdom, taking a string of small towns, but the important town of Aleppo did not fall and remained a refuge for al-Salih. Mosul, too, was a holdout, but with other victories Saladin became Sultan of Syria, succeeding Nur al-Din.

The Damascus-Cairo axis was all-important to Saladin as he set out on a *jihad* (holy war) to drive the Franks from the region. After 1176, he undertook major public works, religious, and educational projects in Egypt, but at the same time he needed military action to convince his critics that the *jihad* was not a fraud merely intended to further his personal power.

After a serious reverse at the strategic outpost of Ascalon, he quickly returned to the attack. Angered by the Franks' breaking of a truce, Saladin was successful against them in southern Lebanon, and he consolidated troops from Syria and Egypt in order to destroy the fort at Jacob's Mill. In capturing Frankish defenses, Saladin often destroyed them so they could not be recaptured. He hoped to win strategic territory in Mesopotamia as a base from which to move against Christian-held Jerusalem, his ultimate target.

With the death of young al-Salih in 1180, Saladin had to contend with more Muslim infighting. Aleppo finally surrendered to Saladin, and eventually Mosul did too. Struggling with a serious illness, the conqueror tried to fix the succession among some of his seventeen sons. He managed, however, to recover.

The Latin Kingdom, on the brink of civil war, was rocked when Saladin's forces captured the walled city of Hattin, along with many Frankish leaders. The Christian defenses were weakened, and Jerusalem surrendered after a two-week siege.

Saladin's troops were tired now and not easily disciplined; the European forces were regrouping for a Third Crusade, led by the dashing Richard I (the Lionhearted) of England. Muslim-held Acre, after a long siege, was finally given up in 1191. Yet the cost was high for the Crusaders, and Richard did not want to be gone too long from England.

The final confrontation between Saladin and Richard came in July, 1192. After a day of prayer, Saladin and his troops were ready to face the Crusaders as they poised for an attack on Jerusalem. Suddenly, the Crusaders withdrew. Saladin attributed the retreat to divine intervention, but military historians say that Richard had decided to attack Egypt instead. Such an attack, however, was not undertaken. The Third Crusade was over.

Saladin retired to Damascus to spend time with his wives and children. In the winter of 1193, he rode out in bad weather to meet a group of pilgrims returning from Mecca. He became ill and died a short while later at age fifty-five, penniless by choice.

Saladin's title, al-Malik al-Nasir, or "Strong to Save the Faith," was appropriate in his lifetime. Within a hundred years of his death, however, the many tensions beneath the Muslims' surface unity split apart what Saladin had accomplished.

Summary

Saladin stands out in Western accounts of the Middle Ages because his beliefs and actions reflected supposedly Christian characteristics: honesty, piety, magnanimity, and chivalry. Unlike many Muslim rulers, he was not cruel to his subordinates; Saladin believed deeply in the Koranic standard that all men are equal before the law. He set a high moral tone; for example, he distributed war booty carefully to help maintain discipline in the ranks.

As an administrator, Saladin showed great vision. He altered the tax structure in Egypt and elsewhere to conform to Koranic instructions, and he supported higher education. It was his vision—together with luck and military skill—that enabled him to begin a quest for Muslim unification that would bear fruit many years later.

The failure of Saladin's empire to survive him was a result of factors beyond his control: polygamy and the lack of primogeniture. The inevitable fighting for political inheritance caused ruptures again and again in the Muslim world.

Bibliography

Ehrenkreuz, Andrew S. *Saladin*. Albany: State University of New York Press, 1972. Presents details of Saladin's early life and of his first years in Egypt not included elsewhere. A chapter on Saladin in historical perspective gives a dissenting view—highly critical—concerning his efficacy as a leader. Detailed bibliography.

Gibb, H. A. *The Life of Saladin*. London: Oxford University Press, 1973. A short account of Saladin's life, this densely footnoted book is based on two famous accounts of Saladin by men who knew him. There is no discussion of his fiscal or administrative policies.

_____. *Saladin: Studies in Islamic History*. Edited by Yusuf Ibish. Beirut, Lebanon: Arab Institute for Research and Publishing, 1974. Collection of some of Gibb's earlier articles and chapters, including material on the caliphate, the Ayyubids, and Saladin's military career and translations of contemporary chronicles.

Hindley, Geoffrey. *Saladin*. New York: Barnes and Noble Books, 1976. General biography traces Saladin's rise to power. Emphasis on historical context. Many fine illustrations of desert locations and artifacts of the era. Index and notes on sources.

Hodgson, Marshall G. *The Venture of Islam*. Vol. 2, *The Expansion of Islam in the Middle Period*. Chicago: University of Chicago Press, 1975. This seminal work places the dynamic of Islamic culture in the world context. Glossary of terms and names, bibliography (which includes coverage of visual arts), maps, and timetables.

Lane-Poole, Stanley. *Saladin and the Fall of the Kingdom of Jerusalem*. New York: G. P. Putnam's Sons, 1898. This is the forerunner of other modern biographies of Saladin, and draws extensively on original chroniclers; includes discussions of major campaigns. Illustrations and maps.

Newby, P. H. *Saladin in His Time*. London: Faber and Faber, 1983. A concise and readable account of the Muslim and Christian background to Saladin's accomplishments. Presents major battles and Saladin's methods of government. Contains convenient map of the Middle East circa 1170. Bibliography and index.

Nan K. Chase

SALIMBENE
Balian de Adam

Born: October 9, 1221; Parma, Italy
Died: c. 1290; Montefalcone, Italy
Area of Achievement: Literature
Contribution: A wandering Franciscan friar, priest, preacher, and writer, Salimbene met and wrote about the most important figures of his age—popes, emperors, kings, and prelates—as well as ordinary people and their daily lives.

Early Life

Salimbene was born Balian de Adam on October 9, 1221, in Parma, in northern Italy. His father, Guido de Adam, was a handsome and gallant Crusader who headed a wealthy, well-connected bourgeois family which aspired to nobility. In his *Cronica* (1282-1288; *The Chronicle of Salimbene de Adam*, 1986, commonly known as the *Chronicle*), Salimbene recounts a revealing story about his infancy. In 1222, a powerful earthquake shook northern Italy. The baptistry of Parma, which stood next to the de Adam house, seemed about to collapse on the house. Salimbene's mother grabbed her two daughters and carried them to safety but left her baby boy in his cradle at home. After he learned later about this incident, Salimbene could never trust his mother's love. She had rejected him for his sisters, he believed, but God had saved him. As a result, Salimbene's attitude toward his family was ambivalent, guarded, and emotionally distant. Moreover, he was at odds with his father, whose worldly desires for his son clashed with Salimbene's more reserved temperament. On February 4, 1238, when he was only sixteen years old, Salimbene renounced his prospects of material success and entered the Franciscan Order. Angered, Guido never forgave his son and tried in both devious and violent ways to snatch Salimbene away from the order. Salimbene remained a Franciscan, however—traveling to such places as Lyons, Troyes, Paris, Sens, Geneva, Bologna, Genoa, Modena, and Ravenna; on his travels in Genoa, in 1248, he was ordained a priest. He was dubbed "Salimbene" (meaning "good move" or "good leap") by an elderly friar who took issue with the boy's nickname, Ognibene ("all good"), regarding it as an affront to God; "Salimbene" commemorated the young man's wise move away from the worldly and toward the monastic life.

Salimbene soon found a new family and new, otherworldly hopes in the Franciscans (or Friars Minor or Minorites). Saint Francis of Assisi (1181-1226) had founded his Order of Friars Minor in 1209 and provided its Rule in 1123 and more guidance in his Testament of 1124. After the death of Saint Francis, his order split into the Spirituals, who followed strictly his Rule and Testament and idealized poverty, and the Conventuals, who compromised

Salimbene

with what they saw as social and human realities and rejected the ideal of poverty. Both Spirituals and Conventuals found their inspiration in Francis' spirituality but differed about how best to realize the saint's religious vision. Salimbene admired the Franciscan Spirituals and men such as John of Parma and Hugh of Digne. He despised the politician Elias of Cortona and Frederick II.

Life's Work

Shortly after entering the Franciscan Order, Salimbene came under the influence of the writings of Joachim of Fiore (c. 1135-1202), a saintly hermit and Cistercian abbot of Calabria whose prophecies influenced medieval thought tremendously. Joachim taught that history consists of three ages corresponding with the three aspects of the Trinity. The first age, that of God the Father, had ended with the new dispensation of Jesus Christ. The second age, that of the Son, would soon end with the new dispensation of the Holy Spirit, forty-two generations, or 1260 years, from the birth of Christ. In 1260 would begin an age of perfection, peace, and freedom, which Joachim termed the Sabbath of the Faithful under Christ the King, and a new religious order.

The thirteenth century was perhaps the greatest medieval century, the age of Gothic architecture and Scholasticism, but it was also a time of troubles, with deadly conflict between the Papacy and the Hohenstaufen, civil wars in Italy between the Guelphs and the Ghibellines, heresy, persecution, the decline of the Crusades, and the new menace of the Mongol invasions. This seemed to many to be the time of troubles that Joachim had predicted would occur immediately before the millennium, and the Franciscans to be the new religious order that would officiate at the Sabbath of the Faithful. Joachism appealed to the finest, holiest men of the time, but also to many of the worst sort, who used prophecy as pretext for gross indecency and wild radicalism.

Shortly after the fatal year 1260 had passed without the Joachist apocalypse, Salimbene began his life's work. He had been a Joachist but later would write, "After the death of Frederick II [the Antichrist figure to the Joachists] and the passing of the year 1260, I completely abandoned Joachimism and, from now on, I intend to believe only what I can see." From about 1262 until 1288, the disillusioned Salimbene compiled his *Chronicle*, writing its final draft at Reggio and Montefalcone between 1282 and 1288. Salimbene remained interested in Joachist prophecy as a philosophy of history and futurist orientation, but he loathed the literal-minded Joachism of vulgar heretical millenarians. Often in his *Chronicle*, Salimbene remarks on events which occurred exactly as Joachim of Fiore had foretold but stresses that he saw them "with my own eyes." His objective as a chronicler was not to discover signs of the Last Days but instead to hold up a mirror to his age.

Salimbene was a keen observer of the human comedy. His *Chronicle* is an affectionate album of candid verbal portraits of thirteenth century humanity. In it, Salimbene gently reveals human foibles and contradictions between people's self-images and real characters. He writes, for example, of a Dominican friar who was so puffed up with self-importance that when he had a haircut he demanded that friars collect the clippings as holy relics; of a star-bedazzled nun who is so entranced by the beautiful singing of the musical friar Vita of Lucca that she jumps out of her convent window to follow him on tour, but breaks her leg in the fall; and of the bizarre and cruel scientific experiments that Frederick II performed on human subjects.

Like the Florentine poet Dante, the Parmesan chronicler Salimbene had the gift of presenting the telling detail—the anecdote, saying, gesture, mannerism, or incident which reveals, by a sort of epiphany, the essential character of its subject. Salimbene captured the vicious hypocrisy of the millenarianist heresiarch Gerard Segarelli, who claimed to be like Christ, lying in a manger and shamelessly sucking the breasts of an obliging maiden. The *Chronicle* also contains Salimbene's copious biblical quotations and commentary, as well as curious trivia which some squeamish translators have deleted as extraneous or undignified.

Salimbene's principal activity in the Franciscan Order was writing chronicles, histories, and treatises. He wrote a history of the Roman Empire, miscellaneous chronicles, *XII scelera Friderici imperatoris* (c. 1248; *The Twelve Calamities of the Emperor Frederick*), books on Joachim's prophecies regarding the Franciscan and Dominican orders, works on the correspondences between the lives of Christ and Saint Francis of Assisi, on Elisha, and on Pope Gregory X, and many other treatises. None of these other works is extant except Salimbene's "Book of the Prelate," attacking Elias of Cortona, which he incorporated in his *Chronicle*.

Salimbene traveled widely in France and Italy, conversing, collecting tales, and pausing here and there, sometimes for a few years, to write. He wandered more extensively than the usual friar and was taken to task once by the minister general of his order for being a gadabout. Salimbene's wanderlust seems to have been the outgrowth of innocent curiosity and amiability, however, and he was a good and loyal Franciscan who was intrigued by Joachism, not a revolutionary chiliast. The atrocities wrought by Frederick II were bearable if indeed he was Antichrist, as the Joachists held, and the tribulation would usher in the happy Sabbath of the Faithful. Ominous portents, such as the Mongol invasions and setbacks in the Holy Land and at Constantinople, could be rendered understandable, given a Joachist interpretation. In his own order, Salimbene admired the saintly Spiritual John of Parma and loathed the political realist and opportunist Elias of Cortona. Although Salimbene regarded Joachism as illuminating historically and true figuratively, he prudently dissociated himself from the Joachist movement within the Franciscan Order. His fondness for Joachism and the Spirituals is nevertheless clear.

Salimbene died at Montefalcone, probably in 1290; the last entry in his *Chronicle* is dated 1288. The *Chronicle* remained virtually unknown until its publication in several scholarly editions in the nineteenth century. G. G. Coulton's English translation in 1906 brought Salimbene to the attention of a wider audience. The *Chronicle*'s charm, vividness, wit, candor, humanity, and range of observations make the work indispensable reading for all serious students of medieval civilization. Coulton called Salimbene's *Chronicle* "the most remarkable autobiography of the Middle Ages," historian Maurice Keen called it "perhaps the best gossip of the Middle Ages," and other medievalists have appropriately used the superlatives "greatest" and "finest" to describe this unique, wonderful, charming work.

Summary

Salimbene was an amiable and loquacious itinerant Franciscan friar who chronicled the history of his contemporary Italy and France. His lively sketches of people, great and lowly, reveal their characters, foibles, human nature, and details of everyday life and popular culture. His *Chronicle* is a valuable historical source. He recounts the conflict in the Order of Friars Minor after the death of Saint Francis, the influence of Joachism, the struggle between the Papacy and the Hohenstaufen, and other momentous events, as well as matters of everyday life.

Bibliography
Brentano, Robert. *Two Churches: England and Italy in the Thirteenth Century*. Princeton, N.J.: Princeton University Press, 1968. Contains illuminating comparison and contrast between Salimbene and his older contemporary the English Benedictine historian Matthew Paris (c. 1200-1259).
Brooke, Rosalind B. *Early Franciscan Government: Elias to Bonaventure*. Cambridge: Cambridge University Press, 1969. An authoritative and detailed discussion of Salimbene's "Book of the Prelate" and his hostility toward Elias of Cortona.
Cohn, Norman. *The Pursuit of the Millennium: Revolutionary Millenarians and Mystical Anarchists of the Middle Ages*. Rev. ed. New York: Oxford University Press, 1970. Contains a provocative discussion of medieval chiliasm; important cultural and social background in chapters on Joachim of Flora, Frederick II, and the Flagellants; and examination of other matters relevant to Salimbene's literary flirtations with millenarianism. Cohn argues the controversial thesis of continuity between medieval chiliasm and modern totalitarianism.
Gebhart, Émile. *Mystics and Heretics in Italy at the End of the Middle Ages*. Translated by Edward Maslin Hulme. London: George Allen and Unwin,

1922. A classic history that captures the spirit of thirteenth century Italy. Though general in scope, it contains fascinating specific discussions of Salimbene.

Hermann, Placid, trans. *XIII Century Chronicles*. Introduction and notes by Marie-Thérèse Laureilhe. Chicago: Franciscan Herald Press, 1961. Selections from Salimbene's *Chronicle* relating to France only, but useful for comparison with some of his contemporary Franciscan chroniclers.

Moorman, John. *A History of the Franciscan Order from Its Origins to the Year 1517*. Oxford: Clarendon Press, 1968. The standard history of the medieval Friars Minor. Many citations of Salimbene. Essential for the Franciscan context.

Reeves, Marjorie. *The Influence of Prophecy in the Later Middle Ages: A Study in Joachimism*. Oxford: Clarendon Press, 1969. A magisterial study of medieval and Renaissance attitudes toward the future stimulated by the prophetic writings of Joachim of Fiore.

Ross, James Bruce, and Mary Martin McLaughlin, eds. *The Portable Medieval Reader*. New York: Viking Press, 1949. The standard anthology of medieval source materials. Includes three well-chosen selections from "the ubiquitous friar Salimbene": his sketches of Friar Berthold of Rogensburg, of Emperor Frederick II, and of the two musical friars, Henry of Pisa and Vita of Lucca.

Salimbene. *The Chronicle of Salimbene de Adam*. Translated and edited by Joseph L. Baird, Giuseppe Baglivi, and John Robert Kane. Binghamton, N.Y.: Medieval and Renaissance Texts and Studies, 1986. A magnificent scholarly edition of Salimbene's *Chronicle*, unabridged in translation, with exemplary critical apparatus and important commentary.

_____. *From St. Francis to Dante: A Translation of All That Is of Primary Interest in the Chronicle of the Franciscan Salimbene, 1221-1288*. Translated and edited by G. G. Coulton. 2d rev. ed. Philadelphia: University of Pennsylvania Press, 1972. A reprint of Coulton's 1907 edition, with a new introduction by Edward Peters. Heavily edited and abridged, a hodgepodge of translated passages, paraphrase, commentary, and illustrative passages from other chronicles. Passages that the Victorian Coulton regarded as too racy are provided in Latin in an appendix. Although superseded by the edition of Baird et al., this volume is of value where the better edition is unavailable.

Terence R. Murphy

SALLUST

Born: October 1, 86 B.C.; Amiternum (modern San Vittorino), Italy
Died: 35 B.C.; probably Rome
Area of Achievement: Historiography
Contribution: Sallust's most important accomplishments were influential works of history composed after his retirement from a checkered political career. The tone, style, and subject matter of his writings reflect the perils and disenchantments of his earlier career.

Early Life

Gaius Sallustius Crispus was born in 86 B.C. in the town of Amiternum in the Sabine uplands, some fifty-five miles northeast of Rome in the central Italian peninsula. Though likely a member of a locally eminent family, Sallust was in Roman terms nonaristocratic, that is, a plebeian. As a politician, he was thus a *nouus homo* (new man). Although by the first century B.C. plebeians regularly attained political office and senatorial rank, the highest offices—the praetorship and especially the consulship—remained almost exclusively the preserve of a few wealthy, aristocratic families and such men as they chose to support. To fulfill his political ambitions, the new man needed skill, sagacity, tact, perseverance, luck, and, most particularly, powerful friends. This helps to explain both Sallust's general dislike of the entrenched conservative aristocracy and his affiliation with Julius Caesar.

Sallust was elected quaestor (a junior official with financial responsibilities) around 55 and tribune of the people in 52. In the latter position, he was involved on the side of the prosecution in the murder trial of a notorious right-wing politician (defended by Cicero) who habitually used intimidation and mob violence. This involvement, along with various other anticonservative actions, gained for Sallust numerous political enemies, who retaliated by having him expelled from the senate in 50 on apparently trumped-up charges of sexual immorality.

Hoping for a restoration of status, Sallust sided with Julius Caesar against Pompey the Great in the civil war that broke out in the year 49. He was rewarded with a second quaestorship (c. 49), a praetorship (47), and various military commands. His service in these posts was undistinguished and occasionally incompetent. He failed to quell a troop mutiny, for example, and was not entrusted with a battle command during Caesar's African campaign. Caesar did, however, see fit to appoint Sallust as the first governor of the province of Africa Nova in 46, a fact that implies at least minimal faith in his administrative abilities. After his governorship, Sallust was charged with abuse of power—extortion and embezzlement—but saved himself from conviction by sharing his spoils with Caesar, who was by then dictator. Still, the scandal severely limited Sallust's political prospects and forced him into an early retirement, from which the assassination of Caesar in 44 made it impossible to return.

Life's Work

Sallust's inglorious political career was marred by factional strife, sensational scandals, sporadic ineptitude, and outright misconduct. Whatever he may have lost in public esteem, however, Sallust handsomely recouped in property and possessions. The wealth he amassed in office ensured an opulent style of retirement. Sallust purchased a palatial villa at Tivoli, said to have been owned at one time by Caesar himself. At Rome, he began construction of the famed Horti Sallustiani (gardens of Sallust), in which an elegantly landscaped complex of parklands surrounded a fine mansion. The loveliness of this estate in the capital city later attracted the attention of Roman emperors, whose property it eventually became.

Sallust did not, however, simply settle into a genteel life of disillusioned and indolent leisure. He used his knowledge of the dynamics of Roman government as a lens through which to examine the gradual disintegration of the political system in the late republican period.

The men and events in Sallust's historical works are typical of a period of decline and fall. His first work, *Bellum Catilinae* (c. 42 B.C.; *The War with Catiline*), is a historical monograph devoted to the failed conspiracy of Lucius Sergius Catilina, a disgruntled, impoverished aristocrat who intended to make good his electoral and financial losses by resorting to armed insurrection. The planned coup d'état was quashed by the actions of Cicero during his consulship in 63. The story of the exposure of the plot and of the measures taken by consul and senate to eliminate the threat—ultimately in battle—is familiar from Cicero's four Catilinarian orations.

Sallust's telling of the Catiline story differs from Cicero's in several respects. He sees the conspiracy in the context of a general moral deterioration within the governing class in Rome. Many in the senatorial nobility placed their own advancement ahead of concern for the common weal. Catiline found supporters not only among disaffected political have-nots, but also among members of the ruling elite who—at least for a time—saw in his machinations opportunities for furthering their own selfish interests. This was not surprising in an era that had seen the bloodshed and confiscation of property that marked the dictatorship of Lucius Cornelius Sulla Felix. In *The War with Catiline*, two men of strong moral character—Marcus Porcius Cato (Cato the Younger) and Julius Caesar—stand out in contrast to the surrounding moral decay. Though representing very different political persuasions, both men are portrayed as admirable for their integrity. Sallust is sometimes accused of being an apologist for his erstwhile patron, Julius Caesar, but his favorable portrait of Cato argues a more nonpartisan outlook. Cicero, too, though not the triumphant savior paraded in his own writings, is given his due by Sallust.

Sallust's second work, *Bellum Iugurthinum* (c. 40 B.C.; *The War with Jugurtha*), recounts the war between Rome and an upstart king of Numidia (now eastern Algeria) between 111 and 105. This was an apt subject, in part because of Sallust's familiarity with North Africa and because of the many hard-fought battles, but especially because it afforded another case of mismanagement and corruption among the Roman ruling elite. In *The War with Jugurtha*, the handling of the conflict by the senate and its representatives is portrayed as ineffective, again largely because of divisions among the aristocrats who had allowed their own lust for power or money to displace their obligation to govern well. Some in the government were willing to accept bribes in return for their support of Jugurtha over other claimants to the Numidian throne. The phrase "everything at Rome has its price" rings like a death knell in the monograph. It was finally a new man—Gaius Marius—who succeeded in gaining victory for Rome. Yet Marius, too, in Sallust's account, had flaws of character: He is depicted as a demagogue who connived to damage the reputation of his predecessor in command. Furthermore, though he would have other spectacular military successes (against invading Germanic tribes on Italy's northern frontier), Marius' long career ended in civil war against Sulla.

Sallust's other major work, his *Historiae* (*Histories*), begun around 39, unfortunately survives only in fragments. It was more extensive in scope than the monographs, covering in annalistic fashion the years from 78 apparently to the early 60's; a continuation to perhaps 50 may have been envisaged, but Sallust's death in 35 prevented it.

Sallust does not meet the standards of modern historical scholarship. His chronology is sometimes awry; he neglected or suppressed relevant information, while including long digressions. He sometimes perpetuated patently distorted reports of personalities and events and, in general, did not assess available sources with sufficient care. Still, no ancient Greek or Roman historian is entirely free from such shortcomings, and Sallust's works are historically valuable despite them, particularly as a check against the record furnished by Cicero, who has so colored the modern picture of the late republic.

Sallust is most compelling and influential as a stylist and moralist. His language is deliberately patterned on the ruggedly direct and archaic syntax of the stern Cato the Censor and, among Greek precedents, on the brevity and abnormal grammatical effects of the greatest Greek historian, Thucydides. His terse sentence structure contributes to a forceful and dramatic progression of thought. This style is well suited to the moral outlook of a historian of decline and fall. Like Thucydides, Sallust wrote from the vantage point of a man of wide experience forced out of an active political life into that of an analyst of the causes of deterioration of character and commitment in the ruling elite of a great imperial power. This analysis is achieved by remarkably concise and trenchant sketches of, and judgments upon, persons and motives. The historical figures who are Sallust's subjects act out of clearly defined and exhibited passions—sometimes noble, mostly base, never lukewarm.

Summary

Sallust's qualities as stylist and moralist have always won for him readers, admirers, and imitators. In classical antiquity, he was recognized as the first great Roman historian; the eminent teacher and critic Quintilian even put him on a par with Thucydides. This judgment is a literary one. The most brilliant classical Roman historian, Cornelius Tacitus, was profoundly influenced by the Sallustian style of composition. The poet Martial concurred with Quintilian's high estimation of Sallust, and Saint Augustine's favorable opinion helped to ensure the historian's popularity in the Middle Ages. German and French translations of his work appeared by the fourteenth century, the first printed edition in the fifteenth, and the first English versions early in the sixteenth. The great Renaissance Humanist, Desiderius Erasmus, preferred Sallust to Livy and Tacitus for use in school curricula. In modern times, Sallust has appealed to many, including Marxist readers who find in him an indictment of decadence in a corrupted aristocracy.

Sallust produced the first true masterpieces of historical writing in Latin. His political career served as preparation, in the school of hard experience, for his work as a writer. In modern times, some have charged him with hypocrisy, noting the glaring inconsistency between his own quite dismal record as a public servant and the lofty moral tone he adopts in his histories. Moreover, doubts tend to arise regarding the presentation and interpretation of facts in the writings of a retired politician. Nevertheless, these considerations do not detract from the worth of Sallust's writings in and of themselves. His works are valuable inquiries into and reflections on sociopolitical developments in an exciting and critically significant period in Roman history.

Bibliography

Broughton, T. R. S. "Was Sallust Fair to Cicero?" *Transactions of the American Philological Association* 67 (1936): 34-46. Broughton answers "yes" to the question in his title. Sallust was neither so malicious nor so ironic in his references to Cicero as scholars often claim. Broughton shows that, in fact, Sallust gave Cicero his due in a generally appreciative, though sometimes backhanded, fashion.

Earl, D. C. "The Early Career of Sallust." *Historia* 15 (1966): 302-311. Speculates on the significance of Sallust's origins in the township of Amiternum for his political career at Rome. Traces the likely course of Sallust's shifting allegiance to Caesar and others during his service as an elected or appointed official.

_____. *The Political Thought of Sallust*. Cambridge: Cambridge University Press, 1961. Earl discusses Sallust's views of the political environment of the late Republic, in particular his attitude toward moral degeneracy (declining *virtus*) as a fatal element. Explicates the individual works as reflective of this political perspective.

Laistner, M. L. W. *The Greater Roman Historians*. Berkeley: University of California Press, 1947. Contains a chapter on Sallust giving a harsh assessment of his worth as a historian: "Sallust's merits as an artist have obscured, or made his readers willing to forget, his faults. As a historical authority he is at best in the second rank."

Leeman, A. D. *A Systematical Bibliography of Sallust (1879-1964)*. Leiden, Netherlands: E. J. Brill, 1965. This very thorough and lucidly organized bibliography contains brief annotations and summaries and an index of authors. References to more recent studies of Sallust may be found in the annual volumes of the bibliographical reference work *L'Année philologique*.

MacKay, L. A. "Sallust's *Catiline*: Date and Purpose." *Phoenix* 16 (1962): 181-194. Argues for a first edition of Sallust's monograph in 50, after his expulsion from the senate. The attitudes Sallust evinces toward Pompey, Cicero, Caesar, and others are most consistent with an effort to regain his senatorial rank.

Marshall, B. A. "Cicero and Sallust on Crassus and Catiline." *Latomus* 33 (1974): 804-813. Argues that Sallust inherited from Cato the view of Marcus Licinius Crassus (triumvir with Caesar and Pompey beginning in 59) as having abetted the Catilinian conspirators out of enmity with Pompey the Great.

Paul, G. M. "Sallust." In *Latin Historians*, edited by T. A. Dorey. London: Routledge and Kegan Paul, 1966. Another brief description and assessment of the works of Sallust, more favorable than that given by Laistner.

Syme, Ronald. *The Roman Revolution*. Oxford: Clarendon Press, 1939. An extremely important and influential scholarly work on "the transformation of state and society at Rome between 60 B.C. and A.D. 14." Syme's "pessimistic and truculent tone" (his own words) make him the modern historian most like Sallust in style of presentation.

_____. *Sallust*. Berkeley: University of California Press, 1964. The best and most authoritative work on the life, times, and writings of its subject: "Sallust, who had been a failure more times than one in his career as a senator, enjoyed luck and a supreme felicity. . . . He exploited the flaws and limitations of his own temperament, transmuting ambition into literary excellence."

Waters, K. H. "Cicero, Sallust, and Caesar." *Historia* 19 (1970): 195-215. Sees Sallust's monograph as a valuable corrective to distortions in Cicero's version of the Catiline conspiracy. In particular, Sallust's account proves that Cicero exaggerated or invented many details regarding the actions, motives, and state of preparedness of the conspirators.

James P. Holoka

SAMUEL

Born: c. 1090 B.C.; Ramathaim-Zophim (or Ramah)
Died: c. 1020 B.C.; Ramah
Areas of Achievement: Religion and government
Contribution: Though famed as a priest and prophet, Samuel is chiefly remembered as the instrument by which the monarchy was established in Israel.

Early Life
When Samuel was born, the twelve tribes of Israel had conquered and settled the greater part of the Promised Land but had as yet no unified government. The tribes occasionally united against a common enemy and submitted their disputes to judges, but leaders such as Gideon and Jephthah brought victory in battle without establishing any office or administration.

Samuel's birth followed a pattern common in the Old Testament. He was the son of Elkanah, who had two wives. One, Hannah, was barren; though she had the love of her husband, she was mocked for her barrenness by her sister wife. When the family went to sacrifice at Shiloh, Hannah vowed that if the Lord gave her a man-child, she would dedicate the child to divine service for "all the days of his life." Thus, her son, Samuel, after he had been weaned, became servant to Eli, the priest at Shiloh.

One night Samuel thought that he heard Eli calling; after the third time, Eli realized that the Lord was calling to the boy. Samuel learned that God's favor was withdrawn from the house of Eli because of the misconduct of Eli's sons; shortly thereafter, these sons were killed in battle against the Philistines and Eli died. The ark of the covenant was captured, but it was soon restored when it occasioned plagues among the Philistines. Samuel was now the priest and was also recognized as a prophet who received direct revelations from God, as Eli had not.

Life's Work
Twenty years later, Samuel decided that aggressive action was needed against the Philistines, a people from overseas who had settled on the coast of Palestine. The Philistines were a constant threat to Israel, since they were technologically more advanced, especially in the use of iron. In order to regain divine favor, Samuel persuaded the Israelites to abandon their worship of "strange gods" (the Baalim and Ashtoreth, Canaanite fertility gods). When the Israelites gathered at Mizpeh, and the Philistines attacked them, Samuel sacrificed, and

> as Samuel was offering up the burnt offering, the Philistines drew near to battle against Israel: but the Lord thundered with a great thunder that day upon the Philistines, and discomfited them; and they were smitten before Israel.

Several cities were recovered from the Philistines, and Samuel returned to his priestly and judicial duties, traveling "from year to year in circuit to Bethel, and Gilgal, and Mizpeh, and judged Israel in all those places; and his return was to Ramah; for there was his house" (1 Sam. 7).

In the Book of Judges, there are several examples of leaders, such as Gideon, who might have established a monarchy, but they either refused or behaved so badly that the Israelites repudiated them. Samuel seems almost to have been thought of as a king, but he could not have been accepted as one because his sons, like Eli's, were unworthy: They "turned aside after lucre, and took bribes, and perverted judgment." At this point, Samuel became less a judge or military leader and more a kingmaker, one who as prophet communicated the Lord's intentions to make or unmake a particular monarch. (The narrative of 1 Samuel shows certain inconsistencies which are thought to be the result of combining two accounts, one friendly and one hostile to the idea of a monarchy. Note that the idea of monarchy implies not only authority in war and peace but also succession, the orderly passing of rule from father to son.)

"When Samuel was old," the elders of Israel asked him to give them a king "to judge us like all the nations," to "go out before us, and fight our battles." Samuel consulted the Lord, Who answered, "They have not rejected thee, but they have rejected me, that I should not reign over them." Nevertheless, He directed Samuel, after listing all the forms of oppression which a king might inflict, to give them a king.

Thus Samuel became involved in the tragic career of Saul. The younger son of a Benjaminite named Kish and a "choice young man and a goodly," Saul had been sent with a servant to find some lost asses. They were ready to abandon the search when the servant suggested that they consult a man of God, a seer in the city of Zulph, who might advise them about the asses for a present of one-fourth of a shekel of silver. They went to the seer, who was Samuel. Having been forewarned by the Lord, Samuel entertained Saul cordially and anointed him. This anointing did not imply that Saul would immediately become king. Instead, he was sent home; on the way, he met a company of ecstatic prophets and prophesied with them (perhaps an alternative account is again being presented). Samuel called the people to Mizpeh and by a drawing of lots again chose Saul king. Yet Saul did not begin his reign but went home to Gibeah; he could not even collect taxes, for the sons of Belial "despised him and brought him no presents."

The crisis came when the Ammonites besieged Jabesh-gilead. Saul behaved like a king at last: "And he took a yoke of oxen, and hewed them in pieces, and sent them throughout all the coasts of Israel by messengers, saying, Whosoever cometh not forth after Saul and after Samuel, so shall it be done to his oxen" (1 Sam. 11:7).

According to the phrase "after Saul and after Samuel," Samuel was still a power in Israel when Saul "slew the Ammonites until the heat of the day." Samuel's response to this victory was twofold. First, he conducted a formal coronation ceremony for Saul. Second, Samuel gave a formal abdication speech, stressing his function as judge: "Whom have I defrauded? whom have I oppressed? or of whose hand have I received any bribe?" Samuel further reminded the people of all that the Lord had done for them since He delivered them from Egypt. Emphasizing his point by calling down thunder and rain in the midst of harvest, he concluded grimly, "But if ye shall still do wickedly, ye shall be consumed, both ye and your king."

Saul's reign started auspiciously; he and his son Jonathan were victorious in their campaigns against the Philistines and other enemies of Israel. Yet there were two occasions when Saul acted in ways that caused him to forfeit divine favor. Saul had mobilized the people to meet a Philistine invasion and expected Samuel to meet him and offer sacrifices. When, after seven days, Samuel had not appeared, Saul, seeing his army melting away, offered the sacrifice himself. Immediately thereafter, Samuel arrived and told Saul that because of his disobedience to the Lord, his kingdom, which otherwise would have been established forever, would not continue but would be given to another, a man after the Lord's own heart. Nevertheless, afterward, Samuel ordered Saul, in the name of the Lord, to attack the Amalekites, who had interfered with the Israelites during the Exodus, and massacre them, "both man and woman, infant and suckling, ox and sheep, camel and ass." Saul defeated the Amalekites, but he spared their king, Agag, and kept the best of the sheep and oxen for later sacrifice. This, to Samuel, was another sin of disobedience; the Lord, he said, repented having made Saul king. "And Samuel came no more to see Saul until the day of his death: nevertheless Samuel mourned for Saul."

The Lord had one more duty for Samuel to perform before his death; he was to go to Bethlehem and anoint David as Saul's successor. Saul, meanwhile, was troubled by an evil spirit sent from the Lord; the modern reader may recognize symptoms of paranoia and depression. The remainder of 1 Samuel has little to do with Samuel; it primarily concerns David's rise and Saul's decline. It is recorded simply that Samuel died; "all the Israelites were gathered together, and lamented him, and buried him in his house at Ramah."

Summary

Whether Samuel is considered a prophet or a judge, the Bible portrays him playing a variety of roles in Israel. He was, first, a priest, presiding over a shrine and offering sacrifices there; on special occasions, such as war, he may have offered sacrifices elsewhere. His powers as a prophet varied greatly; he was apparently not insulted at the idea of finding lost cattle for a small sum in silver. He also claimed, however, to receive divine communications regarding the public welfare: In this he resembled the classic prophets, such as Jeremiah and Isaiah. Samuel enforced the lesson that national prosperity meant obedience not merely to general moral principles but also to direct instruction from the Lord, as communicated through His prophets. One form of prophecy Samuel seems not to have practiced: He was not one of the ecstatic prophets who performed in bands and in whose performances Saul twice joined. Samuel also occasionally performed secular functions. At least once, he commanded the armies of Israel, and his function as a judge should not be forgotten.

Samuel's influence did not end with his death. The modern reader does not automatically side with Samuel but asks whether Saul's premature sacrifice was such a fatal piece of disobedience and whether it was necessary to carry out such a ruthless sacrifice of the Amalekites. In part, the Bible answers these doubts: After Samuel's death, Saul's depression deepened, and his jealousy and persecution of David must have weakened him politically. When the Philistines gathered their army once more, Saul "was afraid, and his heart greatly trembled." Unable to gain divine guidance, Saul, who had driven the witches and wizards from the land, in his desperation sought out a woman who had a familiar spirit and asked her to call up Samuel. Samuel appeared, an old man covered with a mantle, and pronounced a grim sentence: "The Lord will also deliver Israel with thee into the hand of the Philistines: and to morrow shalt thou and thy sons be with me." Thus it happened, but the author or last editor of 1 Samuel must have had compassion for Saul; he recorded that the men of Jabesh-gilead recovered Saul's body from the Philistines and gave it honorable burial.

Bibliography
Alter, Robert, and Frank Kermode, eds. *The Literary Guide to the Bible.* Cambridge, Mass.: Harvard University Press, 1987. Contains an essay on 1 and 2 Samuel by Joseph Rosenberg which emphasizes Samuel's role in the establishment of the monarchy. See also Gerald Hammond's "English Translations of the Bible," which justifies the continued use of the King James Version.
Blenkinsopp, Joseph. *A History of Prophecy in Israel.* Philadelphia: Westminster Press, 1983. Places Samuel in the context of Old Testament prophecy and in the context of other Near Eastern cultures.
Kuntz, J. Kenneth. *The People of Ancient Israel: An Introduction to Old Testament Literature, History, and Thought.* New York: Harper and Row, Publishers, 1974. Useful for the historical context and for chronology. Extensive bibliographies.
Pfeiffer, Robert H. *Introduction to the Old Testament.* New York: Harper and Row, Publishers, 1948. Gives an analysis of Samuel's story with an emphasis on its composite character.

Sternberg, Meir. *The Poetics of Biblical Narrative: Ideological Literature and the Drama of Reading*. Bloomington: Indiana University Press, 1985. The final chapter contains a very interesting study of the literary strategies used to handle the downfall of Saul.

John C. Sherwood

SAPPHO

Born: c. 612 B.C.; Lesbos, Greece
Died: Unknown
Area of Achievement: Literature
Contribution: Regarded by ancient commentators as the equal of Homer, Sappho has poetically expressed the human emotions with honesty, courage, and skill.

Early Life

Sappho was born about 612 in either Eresus or Mytilene on the island of Lesbos, just off the western coast of Turkey. Her father was probably a rich wine merchant named Scamandronymus, and her mother was called Cleis, as was Sappho's daughter. The poet had three brothers: Charaxus and Larichus, who served in aristocratic positions in Mytilene, and Eurygyius, of whom no information remains. Charaxus, the oldest brother, reportedly fell in love with and ransomed the courtesan Doricha, which displeased Sappho. Conversely, she often praised her other brother, Larichus, whose name, passed down in Mytilenian families, was the same as that of the father of a friend of Alexander the Great.

About 600, when the commoner Pittacus gained political power in Lesbos, Sappho reportedly went into exile in Sicily for a short time. She was already well-known. She married Cercylas, a wealthy man from Andros, by whom she bore her daughter, Cleis.

Although much of the information available regarding the Aeolian culture of seventh century Lesbos derives only from the poetry of Sappho and her contemporary Alcaeus, scholars have described the society as more sensual and free than that of the neighboring Dorians, Ionians, Spartans, and Athenians. Political unrest, freedom for women, and enjoyment of the senses appear to have characterized the aristocratic circle with which Sappho mingled.

Life's Work

Sappho's poetry, her principal life's work, consisted of nine books, which the grammarians of Alexandria arranged according to meter. The earliest surviving texts date from the third century B.C. Because the first book contained 1,320 lines, it can be surmised that Sappho left approximately twelve thousand lines, seven hundred of which have survived, pieced together from several sources. Only one complete poem remains, quoted by Dionysius of Halicarnassus, the rest ranging in completeness from several full lines to one word. Many of the lines lack beginning, middle, or end because they have survived on mummy wrapping in Egyptian tombs, the papyrus having been ripped crosswise of the roll, lengthwise of the poem. The long rolls of papyrus, made from the stalks of a water plant, also survived in battered condition in the dry Egyptian climate in garbage dumps and as stuffing in the mouths of mummified crocodiles.

Other lines remain because ancient grammarians used them to illustrate a point of grammar or comment on a text; literary critics quoted them to praise Sappho's style or talk about her metrics; and historians, orators, and philosophers used brief quotes from her work to illustrate their points. One fragment was recorded on a piece of broken pottery dating from the third century B.C. Important discoveries of eighth century manuscripts near Crocodilopolis were made in 1879, and two Englishmen made comparable finds in 1897 in an ancient Egyptian garbage dump. One nineteenth century German scholar who rescued Sappho's poetry from its battered condition lost his eyesight, and one of the English scholars temporarily lost his sanity during the arduous process of transcription.

The surviving poetry consists primarily of passionate, simple love poems addressed in the vernacular to young women. "Ode to Aphrodite," the only remaining complete poem, pleads with the goddess to make the object of the poet's passion return her love with equal intensity, which Aphrodite promises to do. Sappho's equally famous poem, "Seizure," is usually interpreted as an objective description of the poet's extreme jealousy when she sees her beloved conversing with a man. She writes that her heart beats rapidly and "a thin flame runs under/ [her] skin"; she cannot speak or see anything and hears only her "own ears/ drumming"; she sweats, trembles, and turns "paler than/ dry grass." Her jealousy can also burst into anger, as when she warns herself

> Sappho, when some fool
>
> Explodes rage
> in your breast
> hold back that
> yapping tongue!

Or she can restrain her emotions, stating quietly, "Pain penetrates/ Me drop/ by drop." The intensity of Sappho's passion becomes clear in the brief metaphor "As a whirlwind/ swoops on an oak/ Love shakes my heart." In a quieter mood, she can reveal another facet of her feelings:

> Really, Gorgo,
>
> My disposition
> is not at all
> spiteful: I have
> a childlike heart.

Sappho's subject matter helps explain the low survival rate of her poetry. Her reputation reached such greatness during the Golden Age of Greece that Solon of Athens reputedly remarked that he wished only to learn a certain poem by Sappho before he died, and Plato referred to her as the "Tenth Muse." The writers of the urbane and sophisticated Middle and New Comedy of Greece in the fourth and third centuries B.C., however, six of whom wrote plays they titled "Sappho," ridiculed Sappho's simplicity and openness, depicting her as an immoral, licentious courtesan. Although the Romans Theocritus, Horace, and Catullus praised and imitated her, Ovid referred to her both as a licentious woman lusting after a young man and as one who taught her audience how to love girls, characteristics which the Christian church did not value.

Consequently, in A.D. 180 the ascetic Tatian attacked her as whorish and love-crazy. Gregory of Nazianzus, Bishop of Constantinople, in about 380, ordered that Sappho's writings be burned, and eleven years later Christian fanatics partially destroyed the classical library in Alexandria, which would certainly have contained her work. In 1073, Pope Gregory VII ordered another public burning of her writings in Rome and Constantinople. The Venetian knights who pillaged Constantinople in April, 1204, further decimated her extant poetry. Thus, no single collection of her work survived the Middle Ages.

During the Renaissance, however, when Italian scholars recovered Longinus' *Peri hypsous* (first century A.D.; *Essay on the Sublime*) and Dionysius of Halicarnassus' treatise on style, they found "Hymn to Aphrodite" and "Seizure." At this point, scholars began to collect all the remaining words, lines, and stanzas by Sappho.

During the nineteenth century, English and German scholars began to idealize Sappho and her work. Many of them viewed her as a moral, chaste woman, either a priestess of a special society of girls who devoted themselves to worship of Aphrodite and the Muses, or as the principal of a type of girls' finishing school. Although they sometimes acknowledged the intensity of her passion for her "pupils," they denied that it resulted in physical expression, a sentiment which persisted in the work of Maurice Bowra in 1936, and which Denys L. Page began to challenge in 1955. Succeeding critical works have increasingly accepted and explored the existence of Sappho's physical love for her young female companions. Although Sappho's expressed lesbian feelings and/or practice have little bearing on her skill as a poet, the stance almost doomed her work to extinction in a predominantly Christian society, in which sexual values differed significantly from those accepted in the ancient world, especially in seventh century Lesbos.

Summary

The poetry of Sappho provides its reader with a direct experience of intense, stark emotions. Its unadorned honesty allows readers from various cultures and time periods a glimpse of the culture in which she lived, but, more important, into the human heart at its most vulnerable. Sappho loves and hates, feels jealousy and anger, and is able to transmit her emotions so immediately that the reader must respond to her stimuli.

Sappho defends the private sphere and shows the power of love within the individual heart. She has caused succeeding cultures to express their values in relation to her openness. To examine the history of Western civilization in reaction to Sappho's work is to stand back and observe as succeeding generations gaze into the mirror which she provides. Many have smashed the mirror, unable to confront the naked human heart. Some have seen themselves as they would like to be, and a few have learned more fully what it means to be feeling, passionate human beings.

Bibliography
Barnard, Mary. *Sappho: A New Translation.* Berkeley: University of California Press, 1958. Contains one hundred of Sappho's poems divided into six sections, a laudatory foreword by Dudley Fitts, and a lengthy footnote by Barnard which provides cultural background, biographical information, summaries of interpretations by Maurice Bowra and Denys L. Page, and notes on the process of translation and the ways the poems have survived the onslaught of time.
Barnstone, Willis. *Sappho: Lyrics in the Original Greek.* Garden City, N.Y.: Anchor Books, 1965. Includes Greek text with translation of 158 poems and fragments, arranged arbitrarily according to the subject and the chronology of the poems' speaker. Also contains major references from both Greek and Latin texts to Sappho and her poetry, metrical tables and metrical indexes, and concordances to three other major translations of her work.
Bowra, C. Maurice. *Greek Lyric Poetry: From Alcman to Simonides.* Oxford: Clarendon Press, 1936, 2d ed. 1961. A classic review of seven Greek lyric poets stressing their historical development and critiquing important works. Offers groundbreaking theories of the poets as a group and as individual writers. Views Sappho as the leader of a society of girls which excluded men and worshipped the Muses and Aphrodite.
Burnett, Anne Pippin. *Three Archaic Poets: Archilochus, Alcaeus, Sappho.* Cambridge, Mass.: Harvard University Press, 1983. Rejects theories of ancient Greek lyrics as either passionate outpourings or occasional verse. Describes Sappho's aristocratic circle and critiques six major poems. Stresses Sappho's acceptance of sexuality and believes that the poet was providing her young female friends with ideals of beauty to sustain them during married life as second-class citizens.
Jenkyns, Richard. *Three Classical Poets: Sappho, Catullus, and Juvenal.*

Cambridge, Mass.: Harvard University Press, 1982. Stresses the relativistic view that no one theory can elucidate ancient poetry. Interesting observations about nineteenth century views of Sappho. Detailed analysis of principal poems and fragments, concluding that Sappho is a major poet and her body of work is unified while emphasizing that each poem must be judged individually.

Page, Denys L. *Sappho and Alcaeus: An Introduction to the Study of Ancient Lesbian Poetry*. Oxford: Clarendon Press, 1955. Includes Greek text, translation, lengthy commentary, and detailed interpretation of twelve Sapphic poems. Views the poet as private, apolitical; regards her epithalamiums as a minor portion of her canon; pictures women in Aeolian Lesbos as uncommonly liberated; and regards Sappho as lesbian in feeling but not practice. Includes an appendix on meters.

Robinson, David M. *Sappho and Her Influence*. New York: Cooper Square Publishers, 1963. A lightweight account of Sappho's life, legends, and writings which offers unsubstantiated conclusions. Surveys her depiction by western artists and chronicles her influence on Greek, Roman Medieval, Renaissance, Italian, Spanish, French, English, and American literature. Views her as a pure, diligent teacher. Twenty-four plates showing paintings, sculpture, and coins associated with Sappho. Selected bibliography.

Shelley A. Thrasher

SARGON II

Born: Second half of eighth century B.C.; Assyria
Died: 705 B.C.; north of Assyrian empire
Areas of Achievement: Warfare and government
Contribution: Through incessant, successful warfare and widespread resettlement of conquered populations, Sargon II brought an embattled Assyria to a late zenith of power and reshaped the structure of its empire; the dynasty he founded would last until the fall of Assyria.

Early Life

There exists no known record of his life before Sargon II assumed the title of King of Assyria from his predecessor, Shalmaneser V, in December, 722, or January, 721. Because he never followed the royal custom of mentioning his father and grandfather by name in his annals, but simply utilized the formula of referring to his ancestors as "the kings his fathers," historians believe Sargon to have usurped the throne, although some insist that he was a son of the successful king Tukulti-apal-esharra (Tiglathpileser III). In any case, he must have been born to a noble family of some renown; after surviving infancy—no small achievement in a society plagued by high infant mortality—the young warrior most likely pursued the customary education for his class: archery, horseback riding and chariot driving, and perhaps reading and writing.

From the ninth century B.C. on, Sargon's royal predecessors had worked to reverse the decline of Assyrian power which had begun with the death of the powerful king Tukulti-Ninurta I in 1208. Their expansionist policy had given birth to the Neo-Assyrian empire, a state which found a most able leader in Tiglathpileser III from 744 to 727.

During his reign, Egypt in the southwest and Urartu in the northeast were defeated, and Palestine, Syria, and Babylonia were conquered and subjected to political reorganization. Indeed, Tiglathpileser bequeathed to Assyria a legacy which defined the direction of that country's interest and armed struggle for more than a century.

During a prolonged punitive mission in Samaria, when the absence of the king paralyzed official life and the work of justice at home, Tiglathpileser's successor, Shalmaneser V, lost his throne to Sargon. The name which the young king took for himself at his accession shows some clever political maneuvering and suggests the need to legitimize this succession, or at least to stress its rightfulness. In its original Semitic form, Sharru-kin, Sargon's name means "established" or "true and rightful king." In addition to this literal claim, there is the implicit reference to the Mesopotamian king Sargon of Akkad, who had reigned more than a thousand years before and whose fame had given rise to popular myths.

Life's Work

Sargon's kingship placed him at the helm of an embattled empire to whose expansion he would dedicate his life. Immediately after his succession, Sargon reaped unearned fame abroad when the city of Samaria fell and 27,290 Israelites were captured and resettled eastward in Mesopotamia and Media; this event has always been well-known, since it is mentioned in the biblical book of Isaiah. At home, the new king secured his position by supporting the priesthood and the merchant class; his immediate reestablishment of tax-exempt status for Assyria's temples was the first demonstration of Sargon's lifelong policy of supporting the national religion.

During the first year of his reign, Sargon had to face opposition in the recently conquered territories. His annals, written in cuneiform on plates at his palace, record how Sargon first marched south against Marduk-apal-iddina II or "Merodach-Baladan, the foe, the perverse, who, contrary to the will of the great gods, exercised sovereign power at Babylon," a city which this local potentate had seized the moment Sargon became king. In league with Ummannish, King of the Elamites to the east of Babylon, the rebel proved able to prevent Sargon's advance through a battle in which both sides claimed victory; Merodach-Baladan remained ruler over the contested city for the next twelve years.

Turning west toward Syria and Palestine, Sargon's army defeated the usurper Ilu-bi'di (Iaubid), who had led an anti-Assyrian uprising, in the city of Karkar. Sargon's revenge was rather drastic; he burned the city and flayed Ilu-bi'di before marching against an Egyptian army at Raphia. There, Sargon decisively defeated the Egyptians and reestablished Assyrian might in Palestine. For the next ten years, neither Egypt nor local rebels would contest Assyrian power in the southwestern provinces, and Sargon began to look north toward another battlefield. There, at the northeastern boundary of the Assyrian empire around the Armenian lakes, King Urssa (Rusas I) of Urartu and King Mita of Mushki (the Midas of Greek legend) habitually supported Sargon's enemies and destabilized the Assyrian border. For five years, between 719 and 714, Sargon battled various opponents in mountainous territory and waged a war of devastation and destruction on hostile kingdoms and their cities. Once they had overcome their enemies, the Assyrians plundered and burned their cities, led away the indigenous population, hacked down all trees, and destroyed dikes, canals, and other public works. In neighboring territories which Sargon intended to hold, a new population of Assyrians would follow the wave of destruction and deportation and settle in the land, and a new city with an Assyrian name would be founded at the site of the ruined old one.

In 714, Sargon finally defeated King Rusas and, upon its ready surrender, plundered the city of Musasir, the riches of which were immense. A year later, a minor campaign against his son-in-law Ambaridi, a northern chieftain, showed the extent of resistance which Assyrian officers and nobles encountered in dealing with their neighbors and the populations of their provinces. The Assyrian response was swift and successful, and after Ambaridi's defeat and the leading away of his family and supporters, a large number of Assyrians settled in the pacified country, as was the usual pattern by then.

The next year saw a new campaign in the west, where pro-Assyrian rulers had been murdered or replaced with anti-Assyrians, who sometimes commanded considerable local support. In all cases, Sargon proved successful. The siege of Ashdod, where an Egyptian contingent was captured as well, is the second of Sargon's exploits mentioned in the Bible.

After his successful conquests and campaigns of pacification in the north and the southwest, Sargon prepared himself for a new showdown with his old enemy Merodach-Baladan. Marching southward, the Assyrian king wedged the two halves of his army between Babylon and the Elamites; his strategy proved successful when Merodach-Baladan left his capital for Elam. In 710/709, Sargon triumphantly entered the open city and became *de facto* king of Babylon, where he "took the hand of Bel," the city's deity, at the New Year's celebration. Again, Sargon showed himself profoundly sympathetic to the cause of the priesthood and made large donations to the Babylonian temples; in turn, priests and influential citizens celebrated his arrival. Merodach-Baladan, in contrast, failed in his attempt at persuading the Elamites to fight Sargon and retreated south to Yakin, close to the Persian Gulf. In April, 709, Sargon defeated him in battle there but let him go in return for a large payment of tribute.

After the fall of Yakin, Sargon ruled over an empire which stretched from the Mediterranean to the mountains of Armenia and encompassed Mesopotamia up to the Persian Gulf in the east. He left the remaining military missions to his generals, made his son and heir apparent, Sennacherib, commanding general in the north, and dedicated his energy to the building of his palatial city at what is now Khorsabad in Iraq. There, besides commissioning his annals to be written on stone plates, Sargon had his artists create impressive reliefs of the Assyrian king. These reliefs show a strong, muscular man taking part in various royal ceremonies and functions, among which is the blinding of prisoners of war. Sargon's head is adorned with an elaborately dressed turban and bejeweled headband; as was the fashion among the Assyrians, he wears a golden earring and a long, waved beard which is curled at the end. On his upper arms he wears golden bands, and his wrists sport bracelets. His multilayered garment bears some resemblance to a modern sari; the cloth has a rich pattern of rosettes and ends in tassels which touch the king's sandals at his ankles.

In 705, Sargon died under circumstances which are as mysterious as is his rise to kingship. Some historians believe that he died in an ambush during a campaign in the north when he led a small reconnaissance unit, as he was wont to do; according to others, he died at the hands of an assassin in his newly built capital, Dur-Sharrukin, a city which was abandoned after his death.

Summary

For all of his aggression against neighboring states, which was the accepted mode of national survival in his times, Sargon showed statesmanship when it came to domestic politics and the treatment of the vast populace of his empire. He was a fair ruler who showed care for the material and spiritual well-being of his subjects. His annals make proud mention of how he paid fair market price for confiscated private land and strove "to fill the storehouses of the broad land of Asshur with food and provisions... [and] not to let oil, that gives life to man and heals sores, become dear in my land, and regulate the price of sesame as well as of wheat." Sargon was also well aware of the fact that his nation, in which resettlement of conquered people and colonization by Assyrians eradicated older national structures, possessed no real racial or religious unity. To achieve a sense of national homogeneity and coherence, he employed the Assyrian language. Dur-Sharrukin, his new capital, was the best example of Sargonian domestic policy. His annals record how he populated the new metropolis:

> People from the four quarters of the world, of foreign speech, of manifold tongues, who had dwelt in mountains and valleys... whom I, in the name of Asshur my lord, by the might of my arms had carried away into captivity, I commanded to speak one language [Assyrian] and settled them therein. Sons of Asshur, of wise insight in all things, I placed over them, to watch over them; learned men and scribes to teach them the fear of God and the King.

Thus, Sargon's successful wars and domestic policy firmly established the power of the Neo-Assyrian empire and left behind a great nation which would last for a century and help fight the northeastern barbarians who were beginning to threaten the ancient civilizations of the Middle East.

Bibliography

Goodspeed, George Stephen. *A History of the Babylonians and Assyrians.* Cambridge: Cambridge University Press, 1902. Chapter 5 deals with Sargon and critically discusses his reign and achievements. Special attention is given to the question of Sargon's legitimacy and to a careful reading of his annals. Good and accessible overview of Sargon's campaigns.

Luckenbill, Daniel David. *Ancient Records of Assyria and Babylonia.* 2 vols. Chicago: University of Chicago Press, 1926-1927. Reprint. New York: Greenwood Press, 1969. This work contains a fine translation of Sargon's letter to the god Ashur, in which the king reports on his northern campaign against Urartu. Sargon's text, far from dry, reveals a remarkable poetic bent.

Olmstead, Albert T. E. *History of Assyria.* New York: Charles Scribner's Sons, 1923. Reprint. Chicago: University of Chicago Press, 1960. Chapters 17 to 23 deal with Sargon in a detailed discussion which closely follows original sources and points out where Sargon's reign connects with biblical events. Richly illustrated with maps and photographs of Assyrian artifacts, ruins, and the present look of the country.

_____. *Western Asia in the Days of Sargon of Assyria.* New York: Holt and Co., 1908. Historically accurate and highly readable book on Sargon and his times which brings alive the Assyrians and their king. Illustrated and with helpful maps.

Ragozin, Zenaide A. *Assyria from the Rise of the Empire to the Fall of Nineveh.* London: T. Fisher Unwin, 1887. 3d ed. New York: G. P. Putnam's Sons, 1891. Chapter 8 is a popular account of Sargon which views his reign partially in the light of corresponding biblical events. Good etchings of Assyrian artifacts, some of which show Sargon in fine detail.

Saggs, H. W. F. *The Might That Was Assyria.* London: Sidgwick and Jackson, 1984. Pages 92-97 deal directly with Sargon. An account of Assyrian history and culture by an author who enjoys his subject. Relatively short on Sargon, but invaluable for its modern insights into Assyrian life. Has maps and interesting illustrations, including representations of both kings and everyday objects. Very readable.

Reinhart Lutz

SAXO GRAMMATICUS

Born: c. 1150; probably Zealand, Denmark
Died: c. 1220; place unknown
Areas of Achievement: Historiography and literature
Contribution: Saxo Grammaticus, who wrote one of the earliest chronicles of Danish legend and history, was Denmark's most prominent medieval scholar. The only great writer of Latin prose in Denmark before the Reformation, and acclaimed as that country's first national historian, Saxo is the most important source of information about early Danish literature and history.

Early Life

The meager details known of Saxo Grammaticus' life have been gleaned from his own history and from the writings of others. Since the accuracy of the external accounts is questionable, however, Saxo himself remains a scholarly mystery.

Based on careful research, scholars have concluded that Saxo was born in about 1150 into a noble family on the island of Zealand in Denmark. If the thirteenth century Zealand chronicle's mention of a Saxo Longus (the Tall) alludes to the historian, height is the only physical characteristic known about him. Saxo himself tells his readers that his grandfather and father served as soldiers in the army of Valdemar I, who reigned from 1157 to 1182.

It is from other, much later, sources that the name Grammaticus (the Lettered) arises. The fourteenth century Jutland chronicle is the first to assign Saxo the title. The writer of his epitome (1431) and the first edition of his work both retain the reference. This surname apparently refers to Saxo's conspicuous scholarship and elaborate style of Latin composition.

Saxo's complex Latin sentences have led scholars to conjecture that his education must have been meticulous, for in his day Latin was the language of the learned. Saxo was no doubt educated in the three major areas of grammar, dialectic, and rhetoric. His stories, literary allusions, and themes suggest that he studied the classics and Vergil's poetry, as well as such authors as Livy, Martianus Capella, Plato, Cicero, Boethius, and Valerius Maximus. He may also have had formal training in law. He seems to have been slightly familiar with spoken Icelandic and marginally acquainted with German. He may have gone to Paris to complete his education, or perhaps to Germany or England.

Scholars have also debated Saxo's profession. Saxo describes himself as one of the retinue of Absalon, Archbishop of Lund from 1179 to 1201, but fails to say what services he actually performed, no doubt assuming that his readers would understand. Sven Aggesen, a slightly older contemporary, mentions Saxo as his *contubernalis* (literally, tent mate), but Sven's exact

Saxo Grammaticus

meaning is unclear, since he may have meant anything from a military comrade to a fellow member of Absalon's retinue. In his will Absalon mentions a clerk by the name of Saxo, but even if this reference is to Saxo Grammaticus (and it has been debated), scholars are uncertain whether this designation was applied to clerics or to laymen. To add to the confusion, the first edition of Saxo's work lists him as "sometime Head" of the cathedral church at Roskilde. One scholar has even suggested that he may have been Absalon's official historian. Such uncertainty has divided scholars; some believe that he was a monk serving as the archbishop's secretary and some argue that he was a secular clerk. What is certain, and what Saxo himself tells his readers, is that his patron, Absalon, encouraged him to record in Latin the history of Denmark, the work for which Saxo is famous.

Life's Work

In *Gesta Danorum* (1514; *The History of the Danes*, 1894, 1980-1981), sometimes called *Historia Danica*, Saxo traces the lives of the Danes and their kings from their eponymous founder, Dan, to 1187 and Gorm III. The composition of the text occupied him from about 1185 until 1208; he spent from about 1208 until his death revising it and writing the preface.

Saxo had many reasons for composing *The History of the Danes*. His primary purpose, stated in the first sentence of his preface, was to glorify his country, then approaching the zenith of its political influence. Aware of Vergil's glorification of Rome, Saxo was eager to present his countrymen with a similar monument to their own great past and recent accomplishments. Furthermore, the appearance of his history some fifty years after Denmark's civil war (1147-1157) was designed to reconcile peoples only lately reunified. Comments on his fellow Danes reveal that he also hoped to civilize his country and to provide evidence of its rich culture to the rest of the world.

Saxo did not use only one source for his history. He drew upon ancient epic poems, folk tales, popular tradition, inscriptions, lists of Danish kings, and oral lays of Denmark. He also borrowed from Icelandic sagas and Norse mythology. Some scholars have even recognized borrowings from Russian stories in the early books. For contemporary history, Saxo's chief source was probably his mentor, Absalon. Saxo also borrowed from foreign colleagues, directly quoting Dudo, the Venerable Bede, and Paul the Deacon, all medieval historians. He may also have known of Jordanes, Gregory of Tours, Wittekind, Helmold, Giraldus Cambrensis (Gerald de Barri), and Geoffrey of Monmouth. It is clear that Saxo reworked everything he borrowed in order to shed greater glory on Denmark.

In literary style Saxo again made use of others, this time pagan Latin authors of the Silver Age and of late antiquity. Justin and Curtius Rufus were important to him. Martianus Capella provided the Latin meters he used. His favorite author, however, was Valerius Maximus. Saxo's writing, characterized by moralizing and artificial cleverness, imitates the pointed style of Silver Age Latin.

Saxo's style, in fact, is another point of contention among scholars. Some say the style is vigorous and compelling; others accuse him of pomposity. Some find him biased against the early kings, the Norwegians, Germans, and Swedes, and prejudiced in favor of Icelanders and Zealanders. Others argue that far from being naïve and uncritical, he contrived to use his stories to give meaning to the ancient past as the precedent for his glorious contemporary Denmark. Still others have discovered an elaborate four-part division to *The History of the Danes*: Books 1 to 4 deal with the world before Christ; books 5 to 8 discuss the period up to Denmark's conversion to Christianity; books 9 to 12 examine the growth of the new church; and books 13 to 16 tell of events after the church is firmly established. Another scholar has shown that Saxo inserts a visit to the Underworld halfway through his history, much as Vergil did in the *Aeneid* (c. 29-19 B.C.).

The story of most interest to students of English literature in Saxo's chronicle has to do with how a Danish prince named Amleth wreaked vengeance on his uncle for the murder of his father. This tale represents the earliest known form of the plot of William Shakespeare's *Hamlet* (c. 1600-1601), and Saxo was the first to set it down in writing. All the evidence indicates that Saxo's tale is not literary fiction but a literary reworking of a Danish oral legend dating from at least the tenth century. Saxo expanded it with details of the story which were known in Iceland.

Though many scholars have admired his pioneer achievements, Saxo has also been sharply criticized for his Latin style, his naïve recounting of fables and fantasies, and even his choice of Latin as a linguistic medium. Historians have found little of value in the first nine books and have disputed the historic reliability of the later ones.

Yet Saxo has left his mark on literature and history for a number of reasons. First, *The History of the Danes* exemplifies the literary renaissance of the twelfth century. Saxo's chronicle is one of only two important sources for this period, the other being the account of Sven Aggesen. The latter's history of Denmark, however, is inferior to Saxo's in its scope, its Latin, and its literary background, and thus is of less importance. Prior to Saxo, Danish heroic poetry had been preserved only by oral tradition. Many of the tales in *The History of the Danes* are unrecorded elsewhere. Some of Saxo's sources are known only through allusions in his work. Consequently, mythologists and folklorists are indebted to Saxo for his preservation of all of these.

Saxo may have had little effect on his own time. His work was not immediately popular; in fact, it was mostly forgotten for three hundred years, surviving only in an epitome and a few manuscripts. The epitome reveals that Saxo's writing was considered to be difficult to comprehend. In the early sixteenth century, however, Christiern Pedersen, Canon of Lund and Denmark's greatest Humanist, prepared a manuscript of Saxo which was published in 1514 in Paris by the renowned printer Jodocus Badius Ascensius. The Renaissance writers were greatly interested in Saxo. As a consequence, editions of Saxo became popular, and libraries throughout Europe boasted copies of his history. Desiderius Erasmus praised Saxo's force of eloquence. One of François de Belleforest's translations of Saxo is generally considered to have been Shakespeare's immediate source for *Hamlet*. Shakespeare himself may have had some knowledge of Saxo's work.

Saxo's work is now known almost completely from the first printed version. No complete manuscript survives. The most important fragment, four quarto leaves on parchment with fifteen lines to a page, is from Angers. Notes and corrections on these pages have been argued to have been written by Saxo's own hand or by the hand of one of his scribes.

Saxo's death probably occurred about 1220. Evidence in his history shows that he died before he completed the revision of his work.

Summary

Saxo Grammaticus was ideally suited to write the history of Denmark. He was well educated in the ways of the Church, in the language and literature of the Romans, and in the culture and literature of his native land, and he used all these resources to praise his people. Like Absalon, Saxo favored a strong, nationalistic monarchy, with the king controlling the legislative, military, and ecclesiastical branches. Through his *The History of the Danes* he was able to emphasize the Church's—and especially Absalon's—importance in national reunification. His knowledge of Latin and the genre of the medieval history allowed him to choose a medium ideal for his purpose of tracing the royal family to the founding of the kingdom, much as Vergil had done in the case of Caesar Augustus in the *Aeneid*. By showing the king to be one with his countrymen, Saxo hoped to reconcile hostile factions of people and to instill national pride. Though he despised all foreign influence and praised ancient Norse ideals, Saxo was so well versed in the literary culture of his age that he could construct a work using a Latin (and therefore foreign) framework and intertwine cultural and literary features from other peoples with his own country's heritage. In this way he hoped to create a work that would place Denmark among the learned civilizations of the world.

Medieval scholars and historians have also benefited from Saxo's history. Because Saxo chose to borrow from many different sources, many of which no longer exist, mythologists and students of folklore have a clearer picture of the evolution, transmission, and migration of certain legends and sagas. Students of Shakespeare gain a deeper appreciation of *Hamlet* through the story of Amleth. Finally, Saxo Grammaticus reveals important information about his own time, observations which would have been lost to subsequent generations if not for *The History of the Danes*.

Bibliography

Dumezil, Georges. *From Myth to Fiction: The Saga of Hadingus.* Translated by Derek Coltman. Chicago: University of Chicago Press, 1973. The introduction provides a clear synopsis of Saxo's life. Though the book deals with only one personage from *The History of the Danes*, the arguments provide insight into other Saxonian legends as well. Not everyone will be convinced by all the interpretations. The book's footnotes are only moderately useful for the general audience.

Hansen, William F. *Saxo Grammaticus and the Life of Hamlet: A Translation, History, and Commentary.* Lincoln: University of Nebraska Press, 1983. While the main part of the book is concerned with Saxo's style and the story of Hamlet, significant parts also deal with Saxo's entire work. The general reader will find the work informative and easy to read. Includes useful notes, bibliography, and index. Illustrated.

Mitchell, P. M. *A History of Danish Literature.* 2d ed. New York: Kraus-Thomson Organization, 1971. A reproduction of the Angers fragment is included in this volume. The author places Saxo in perspective with the other writers of Danish literature. Appropriate for the general reader. Illustrated; includes an extensive bibliography.

Oakley, Stewart. *A Short History of Denmark.* New York: Praeger Publishers, 1972. Though Saxo is not treated extensively, the author puts him in historical perspective. Contains illustrations, an index, and helpful suggestions for further reading.

Saxo Grammaticus. *The First Nine Books of the Danish History of Saxo Grammaticus, with Some Considerations on Saxo's Sources, Historical Methods, and Folk-Lore.* Translated by Oliver Elton. Edited by Frederick York Powell. London: David Nutt, 1894. Elton's is a dated translation. Footnotes in the introduction will help mainly the specialist. Footnotes in the text of the translation will be more valuable to the general reader.

_____ . *The History of the Danes.* Translated by Peter Fisher. Edited by Hilda Ellis Davidson. 2 vols. Cambridge: D. S. Brewer, 1979-1980. The translation is lively and eminently readable. The introductions in both volumes will be extremely helpful for the general reader as well as the more advanced researcher. The reader will find summarized Saxo's life, his place in Danish literature, the history of his text, and the history of scholarship on his work. Useful bibliography.

Taylor, Marion A. *A New Look at the Old Sources of Hamlet.* Paris: Mouton, 1968. The author deals only with Saxo's story of Hamlet but is conscientious in showing more than Danish and Roman influence. The footnotes are fairly specialized. The bibliography, however, will be of some use to the general reader.

Joan E. Carr

SCIPIO AEMILIANUS

Born: 185 B.C.; probably Rome
Died: 129 B.C.; Rome
Areas of Achievement: Warfare, government, and patronage of art
Contribution: Combining a genius for military conquest with an appreciation for literature and the arts, Scipio Aemilianus embodies—perhaps better than any other figure of his day—the paradoxical forces which swept through Rome during the central years of the Republic.

Early Life

Publius Cornelius Scipio Aemilianus Africanus Numantinus, also known as Scipio the Younger, was born into Roman society in 185, about the time that Cato the Elder was beginning his famous censorship. Scipio's earliest years were thus spent during one of the most interesting periods of the Roman Republic. From his vantage point as a member of the distinguished Aemilian *gens* (family), the young Scipio was in a perfect position to witness events which would shape the course of Roman history. In addition to this, because of his father Lucius Aemilius Paullus' interest in Greek culture, Scipio was surrounded almost from birth by Greek tutors, orators, and artists. Together, these two factors—the political distinction of his family and his father's philhellenism—were to inspire in Scipio his interest in a military career and his lifelong enthusiasm for Greek civilization.

Scipio's mother, Papiria, was a member of one of Rome's leading families: Her father had been a victorious general, the first general, in fact, to hold a triumphal procession on the Alban Mount because he had been denied an official triumph back in Rome. Scipio's father had also served as a general and had already been elected to the curule aedileship and the Spanish praetorship; at the time of Scipio's birth, Paullus was only a few years away from the consulship, the highest political office in Rome.

Ironically, at about the same time that Paullus' tenure as consul began, his marriage ended. He divorced Papiria, remarried, and soon had two other sons by his second wife. Perhaps as a result of conflicts between these two families, Paullus decided to allow Scipio and his brother to be adopted into other households. Scipio, as his name implies, was adopted by Publius Cornelius Scipio, the son of Scipio Africanus, who had won his greatest fame as victor over the Carthaginians at Zama during the Second Punic War. His elder brother was adopted into the household of Quintus Fabius Maximus Cunctator, perhaps by a son or grandson of the famous general himself. Yet both Scipio and his brother, now known as Quintus Fabius Maximus Aemilianus, remained close to their birth father. Indeed, they both accompanied Paullus on an important expedition against Macedon in 168, during Paullus' second consulship.

The climactic battle of this expedition, at Pydna in 168, was both the crowning glory of Paullus' career and, quite possibly, Scipio's own first battle. The Macedonians, led by King Perseus, were defeated, and Paullus, in accordance with his literary tastes, chose only one prize for himself out of the spoils: Perseus' library. This mixture of military and literary interests was also apparent in Scipio himself at this time. It was during his stay in Greece that Scipio met the future historian Polybius, an author who would come to be his lifelong friend.

Life's Work

In 151, nearly a decade after the death of his father, Scipio was finally given a chance to develop a military reputation of his own. He was offered the position of military tribune under the consul Lucius Licinius Lucullus, who was about to assume command of the Roman forces in northern Spain. Though the campaign against the Celtiberian tribesmen would nearly be over before Lucullus finally arrived, Scipio did manage to win the *corona muralis* (an honor awarded to the first soldier who scaled the wall of an enemy), and, on a mission to obtain reinforcements in Africa, he witnessed a major battle between the Numidians and the Carthaginians. Thus, in this single campaign, Scipio journeyed to both of the regions which would one day see his greatest victories: Spain and Africa. Later, in 149 and 148, during the Third Punic War, Scipio served again as military tribune. The high honors which he won during the early campaigns of this war prompted his election to the consulship of 147, though neither in age nor in magistracies already held did he meet the requirements for the office.

The task assigned to Scipio during the final campaigns of the Third Punic War was to besiege the city of Carthage itself. Despite fierce opposition from the local inhabitants, Scipio managed to breach the fortifications of the city; six days of bitter fighting from house to house ensued. The Carthaginians resisted the Romans with unexpected vigor, though they had only makeshift weapons with which to defend themselves. While the battle raged in the streets below, the Roman soldiers were surprised to discover that they were being pelted with rocks and roofing tiles cast down from the houses above. Yet, in the end, Carthage was set ablaze, and the Romans proceeded to demolish all remaining structures; as these orders were being carried out, many Carthaginians were trapped and buried alive in their own homes.

Some days later, as the final task of razing Carthage was completed, Polybius noticed tears in Scipio's eyes. When asked the reason for these tears, Scipio replied that he was afraid lest someday the same order might be given for his own city. He then quoted a famous passage of Homer's *Iliad* (c. 800 B.C.): "There will come a day when sacred Ilium shall perish/ and Priam and the people of Priam of the fine ash-spear." Scipio's sentiments notwithstanding, the site of Carthage was declared accursed and its fifty thousand survivors were sold into slavery.

The years following the destruction of Carthage brought Rome once again into conflict with an old enemy: the Celtiberian tribesmen of Spain. For nearly ten years, from 143 until 134, a succession of Roman commanders had tried unsuccessfully to capture a Celtiberian fortress located on the hill settlement of Numantia. In the end, the Romans elected Scipio to be consul for a second time with the hope that he might bring this prolonged campaign to a successful conclusion. Scipio collected a force of nearly sixty thousand men, far outnumbering the four thousand Celtiberians who still remained at Numantia. He then adopted the plan of surrounding the fortress with a ring of seven camps. The ploy was successful, although once again at an appalling cost to human life. The inhabitants were starved out, and some of them had even been reduced to cannibalism before their surrender. In any case, when Numantia finally capitulated to the Romans in 133, Scipio ordered the fortress to be destroyed and its survivors sold into slavery. Once again, this general who had been steeped in Greek culture since childhood felt compelled to resort to extreme measures in his efforts to subdue a Roman enemy. In order to understand this event, however, it is necessary to realize how formidable an opponent Numantia must have seemed at the time: Nearly a century after the fall of the city, Cicero could still refer, without fear of contradiction, to Carthage and Numantia as having been "the two most powerful enemies of Rome."

While these military conquests were still under way, however, Scipio's reputation was also on the rise because of his support for a group of artists and intellectuals who would come to make up the most famous "salon" in Roman history. The group was later to be known as the Scipionic Circle, though it is doubtful that this title was ever used in Scipio's own lifetime. The discussions of the Scipionic Circle covered a wide range of issues, and one of these discussions was later dramatized by Cicero in his dialogue entitled *De republica* (54-51 B.C.; *On the State*). Though the membership in the Scipionic Circle varied from year to year, it eventually came to include such figures as Scipio himself, Polybius, the comic playwright Terence, the Roman legate Gaius Laelius, and the philosopher Panaetius. Membership in the group seems to have been based not only on these individuals' talents but also upon Scipio's genuine affection for those with whom he discussed the issues of the day. Indeed, Scipio's friendship with Laelius became so renowned in later generations that Cicero based his philosophical dialogue *De amicitia* (45-44 B.C.; *On Friendship*) upon Laelius' supposed recollections of Scipio shortly after his death.

In 129, Scipio, on the verge of being given an important new position in the Roman government, was found dead in his bed. He had been in perfect health, it was said, only the night before. As a result, no one knew whether he had been murdered or had died of an illness. Indeed, the question was so vexing that it was still being debated even in the time of Cicero. At first, suspicions fell upon Gaius Papirius Carbo, a keen supporter of the reformer Tiberius Gracchus and a politician well-known for his oratorical ability. Carbo had been tribune in 131 and had proposed that tribunes be eligible for reelection year after year. Scipio had opposed this measure and had led the fight against it. It is possible, therefore, that this political struggle eventually cost Scipio his life.

Summary

While his contemporaries probably believed that Scipio Aemilianus would best be remembered for his military conquests and the political reputation of his family, scholars of later ages have come to view Scipio in a different light, as the center of the Scipionic Circle more than as a conquering general. Though Scipio destroyed Carthage, it was his adoptive grandfather, the defeater of Hannibal, whose name became tied to that city. Though Scipio consolidated Roman rule in Spain, it was Cato the Elder—who had tried and failed to accomplish the same task—whose military vision for Rome has remained clearer throughout the succeeding generations.

The Scipio who is recalled today is thus the Scipio of Cicero's dialogues: the student of Greek civilization, the friend of Polybius and Laelius, the magnet for Roman intellectuals of his time. While this is not an inaccurate picture, it is a picture that is largely incomplete. It is important, therefore, that Scipio Aemilianus be remembered not only as the man who wept and quoted Homer at the fall of Carthage but also as the victorious strategist who brought about the city's destruction.

Bibliography

Astin, A. E. *Scipio Aemilianus*. Oxford: Clarendon Press, 1967. A most complete and accurate study of Scipio Aemilianus. Contains complete biographical data on Scipio, including references to all ancient sources. Family trees of the Aemilii Paulli and the Scipiones are provided. Appendices are included regarding various discrepancies between the accounts of different authors and other difficulties facing the historian who attempts to reconstruct the life of Scipio. Extensive and well-chosen bibliography.

_____. "Scipio Aemilianus and Cato Censorius." *Latomus* 15 (1956): 159-180. Astin explores the possibility that an unusual friendship may have existed between these two very different personalities.

Brown, Ruth Martin. *A Study of the Scipionic Circle*. Scottdale, Pa.: Mennonite Press, 1934. Still the most complete and readable analysis of the Scipionic Circle. Includes information on the history and nature of the Scipionic Circle, its members during various periods in its development, and its influence in Roman society. Though not as systematically annotated as Astin's work, Brown's book is useful in tracking down many primary sources. The bibliography is mostly out of date, but two appendices listing the members of the Scipionic Circle in tabular and chronological form are still useful.

Earl, D. C. "Terence and Roman Politics." *Historia* 11 (1962): 469-485. Earl demonstrates that the political views—or lack thereof—of Terence can be traced directly to his participation in the Scipionic Circle and the Hellenic influence upon that body.

Scullard, H. H. "Roman Politics." *Journal of Roman Studies* 50 (1960): 59-74. Scullard examines the policies of Scipio and those in his immediate circle. The article is valuable for those interested in tracing the rise of the Roman reform movement before the time of Tiberius Gracchus.

Walbank, F. W. "Political Morality and the Friends of Scipio." *Journal of Roman Studies* 55 (1965): 1-16. A study, by the world's foremost authority on Polybius, of the political philosophies of such figures as Polybius, Panaetius, and other members of the Scipionic Circle. The work is useful for the insight it provides into political views current in the central years of the Roman Republic and the attitudes toward imperialism in the period preceding the Roman Empire.

Jeffrey L. Buller

SCIPIO AFRICANUS

Born: 236 B.C.; Rome
Died: 184 or 183 B.C.; Liternum, Campania
Areas of Achievement: Warfare and government
Contribution: Scipio's military victory over Carthaginian forces in Spain and North Africa, brought about by his genius as strategist and innovator of tactics, ended the Second Punic War and established Roman hegemony in the Western Mediterranean.

Early Life
Publius Cornelius Scipio, known as Scipio Africanus or Scipio the Elder, was born to one of the most illustrious families of the Roman Republic; his father, who gave the boy his name, and his mother, Pomponia, were respected citizens of the patrician dynasty of the gens Cornelii. At Scipio's birth, Rome had begun to show its power beyond the boundaries of Italy, and the young nation was starting to strive for hegemony west and east of the known world. Coinciding with expansion outward was Rome's still-stable inner structure; nevertheless, the influence of the Greek culture had begun a softening, or rounding, of the Roman character.

Scipio's early life clearly reflects this transition. His lifelong sympathy with Greek culture made him somewhat suspect in the eyes of his conservative opponents, who accused him of weakening the Roman spirit. On the other hand, as a patrician youth, he must have received early military training, for Scipio entered history (and legend) at the age of seventeen or eighteen, when he saved his father from an attack by hostile cavalry during a skirmish with the invading forces of Hannibal in Italy in 218.

His military career further advanced when Scipio prevented a mutiny among the few survivors of the disastrous Battle of Cannae in 216. As a military tribune, the equivalent of a modern staff colonel, he personally intervened with the deserters, placed their ringleaders under arrest, and put the defeated army under the command of the surviving consul.

In 211, another serious defeat for Rome brought Scipio an unprecedented opportunity. In Spain, two armies under the command of his father and an uncle had been defeated, and the commanders were killed. Although he was still rather young—twenty-seven according to the ancient historian Polybius—and had not served in public office with the exception of the entry-level position of *curulic aedile* (a chief of domestic police), Scipio ran unopposed in the ensuing election and became proconsul and supreme commander of the reinforcements and the Roman army in Spain.

His election attests the extraordinary popularity which he enjoyed with the people of Rome and later with his men. So great was his reputation, which also rested partly on his unbounded self-confidence and (according to

Scipio Africanus 1877

Polybius) a streak of rational calculation, that people talked about his enjoying a special contact with the gods. A religious man who belonged to a college of priests of Mars, Scipio may himself have reinforced these adulatory rumors. Whether his charisma and popularity were further aided by particularly "noble" looks, however, is not known. Indeed, all the extant representations of him, no matter how idealized, do not fail to show his large nose and ears, personal features which do not detract from the overall image of dignity but serve to humanize the great general.

His marriage to Aemilia, the daughter of the head of a friendly patrician family, gave Scipio at least two sons and one daughter, who would later be mother to the social reformers Gaius and Tiberius Gracchus.

Life's Work

Arriving in Spain, Scipio followed the strategic plan of continuing the offensive warfare of his father and uncle and thus trying to tear Spain, their European base, away from the Carthaginians. After he had reorganized his army, Scipio struck an unexpected blow by capturing New Carthage, the enemy's foremost port, in 209. A year later he launched an attack on one-third of the Carthaginian forces at Baecula, in south central Spain. While his light troops engaged the enemy, Scipio led the main body of Roman infantry to attack both flanks of the Carthaginians and thus win the battle. Hasdrubal Barca, the Carthaginian leader, however, managed to disengage his troops and escape to Gaul, where Scipio could not follow him, and ultimately arrived in Italy.

The decisive move followed in 206, when Scipio attacked the united armies of Hasdrubal, the son of Gisco, and Mago at Ilipa (near modern Seville). Meanwhile, his generous treatment of the Spanish tribes had given him native support. Scipio placed these still-unreliable allies in the center of his army, to hold the enemy, while Roman infantry and cavalry advanced on both sides, wheeled around, and attacked the Carthaginian war elephants and soldiers in a double enveloping maneuver which wrought total havoc.

Scipio's immediate pursuit of the fleeing enemy succeeded so completely in destroying their forces that Carthage's hold on Spain came to a de facto end. After a punitive mission against three insurgent Spanish cities, and the relatively bloodless putting down of a mutiny by some Roman troops, Scipio received the surrender of Gades (Cádiz), the last Carthaginian stronghold in Spain.

When Scipio returned to Rome, the senate did not grant him a triumph. He was elected consul for the year 205, but only his threat to proceed alone, with popular support, forced the senate to allow him to take the war to Carthage in North Africa rather than fight an embattled and ill-supported Hannibal in Italy. In his province of Sicily, Scipio began with the training of a core army of volunteers; uncharacteristically for Roman thought, but brilliantly innovative in terms of strategy, he emphasized the formation of a strong cavalry.

In 204, Scipio landed in North Africa near the modern coast of Tunisia with roughly thirty-five thousand men and more than six hundred cavalry. He immediately joined forces with the small but well-trained cavalry detachment of the exiled King Masinissa and drew first blood in a successful encounter with Carthaginian cavalry under General Hanno.

Failing to capture the key port of Utica, Scipio built winter quarters on a peninsula east of the stubborn city. One night early the next spring, he led his army against the Carthaginian relief forces under Hasdrubal and King Syphax, who had broken an earlier treaty with Scipio. The raid was successful, and the camps of the enemy were burned; now Scipio followed the reorganized adversaries and defeated them decisively at the Great Plains. The fall of Tunis came soon after.

Beaten, Carthage sought an armistice of forty-five days, which was granted by Scipio and broken when Hannibal arrived in North Africa. Hostilities resumed and culminated in the Battle of Zama. Here, the attack of the Carthaginian war elephants failed, because Scipio had anticipated them and opened his ranks to let the animals uselessly thunder through. Now the two armies engaged in fierce battle, and, after the defeat of the Carthaginian auxiliary troops and mercenaries, Scipio attempted an outflanking maneuver which failed against the masterful Hannibal. In a pitched battle, the decisive moment came when the Roman cavalry and that of Masinissa broke off their pursuit of the beaten Carthaginian horsemen and fell upon the rear of Hannibal's army. The enemy was crushed.

After the victory of Zama, Scipio granted Carthage a relatively mild peace and persuaded the Roman senate to ratify the treaty. When he returned to Rome, he was granted a triumph in which to show his rich booty, the prisoners of war (including Syphax), and his victorious troops, whom he treated generously. It was around this time that Scipio obtained his honorific name "Africanus."

There followed a period of rest for Scipio. In 199 he took the position of censor, an office traditionally reserved for elder statesmen, and in 194 he held his second consulship. An embassy to Masinissa brought Scipio back to Africa in 193, and in 190 he went to Greece as a legate, or general staff officer, to his brother Lucius. In Greece, the Romans had repulsed the Syrian king Antiochus the Great and prepared the invasion of Asia Minor. Because of an illness, Scipio did not see the Roman victory there.

At home, their political opponents, grouped around archconservative Cato the Censor, attacked Scipio and his brother in a series of unfounded lawsuits, known as "the processes of the Scipios," concerning alleged fiscal mismanagement and corruption in the Eastern war. Embittered, Scipio defended his brother in 187 and himself in 184, after which he left Rome, returning only

Scipio Africanus

when the opposition threatened to throw Lucius in jail. Going back to his small farm in Liternum in the Campania, Scipio lived a modest life as a virtual exile until his death in the same year or in 183. His great bitterness is demonstrated by his wish to be buried there instead of in the family tomb near the capital.

Summary

The military victories of Scipio Africanus brought Rome a firm grip on Spain, victory over Carthage, and dominion over the Western Mediterranean. Scipio's success rested on his great qualities as a farsighted strategist and innovative tactician who was bold enough to end the archaic Roman reliance on the brute force of its infantry; he learned the lesson of Hannibal's victory at Cannae. His newly formed cavalry and a highly mobile and more maneuverable infantry secured the success of his sweeps to envelop the enemy.

On the level of statesmanship, Scipio's gift for moderation and his ability to stabilize and pacify Spain secured power for Rome without constant bloodletting. His peace with Carthage would have enabled this city to live peacefully under the shadow of Rome and could have prevented the Third Punic War, had the senate later acted differently.

Finally, Scipio never abused his popularity to make himself autocratic ruler of Rome, although temptations to do so abounded. At the height of his influence in Spain, several tribes offered him the title of king; he firmly refused. After his triumph, the exuberant masses bestowed many titles on the victor of Zama, but he did not grasp for ultimate power. Unlike Julius Caesar, Scipio Africanus served the Roman state; he did not master it. He is perhaps the only military leader of great stature who achieved fame as a true public servant.

Bibliography

Dorey, T. A., and D. R. Dudley. *Rome Against Carthage*. London: Secker and Warburg, 1971. Chapters 3 to 7 deal with the Second Punic War and place Scipio's conquests in context. Useful discussion of his campaigns, Roman policy toward Carthage, and the origins of the conflict. Contains many illustrations and maps and an adequate bibliography.

Eckstein, Arthur M. *Senate and General*. Berkeley: University of California Press, 1987. Generally scrutinizes who had the power to make political decisions. Chapter 8 illuminates various aspects of Scipio's struggle with the senate. Includes a good, up-to-date bibliography.

Haywood, Richard M. *Studies on Scipio Africanus*. Baltimore: Johns Hopkins University Press, 1933. Reprint. Westport, Conn.: Greenwood Press, 1973. Revises the account by Polybius, who rejected old superstitions about Scipio but made him more calculating and scheming than Haywood believes is justified. The bibliography is still useful.

Liddell-Hart, B. H. *A Greater Than Napoleon: Scipio Africanus*. Boston: Little, Brown and Co., 1927. Reprint. New York: Biblo and Tannen, 1971. Popular account of Scipio's life, with emphasis on his military achievements. Scipio is judged sympathetically and praised for tactical innovations and rejection of "honest bludgeon work." Contains many helpful maps.

Scullard, Howard H. *Roman Politics 220-150 B.C.* 2d ed. Oxford: Clarendon Press, 1973. Chapters 4 and 5 deal with Scipio's influence on Roman politics and place his career in the context of political and dynastic struggle for control in the Roman Republic. Shows where Scipio came from politically and traces his legacy. Contains appendix with diagrams of the leading Roman families.

_____. *Scipio Africanus: Soldier and Politician*. Ithaca, N.Y.: Cornell University Press, 1970. General study and excellent, comprehensive biography. Carefully balanced and well-researched work. Written with a feeling for its subject, which makes it interesting to read. Contains useful maps.

_____. *Scipio Africanus in the Second Punic War*. Cambridge: Cambridge University Press, 1930. An in-depth study of Scipio's campaigns and military achievements, highly technical but readable and with good maps. Brings alive Scipio while dealing exhaustively with its subject.

Reinhart Lutz

SCOPAS

Born: Possibly as early as 420 B.C.; Paros, Greece
Died: c. late fourth century B.C.; place unknown
Area of Achievement: Art
Contribution: A leader of the evolution in late classical sculpture away from the powerful but emotionally detached balance of fifth century art, Scopas created works of relaxed gracefulness on the one hand and strong emotion, stress, and turbulence on the other. With Praxiteles of Athens and Lysippus of Sicyon, his work dominated the art of the fourth century B.C.

Early Life

No biographical information survives. Scopas may have been the son of the Parian sculptor Aristander, who was working in 405 B.C.

Life's Work

Scopas of Paros worked as an architect and sculptor. His most celebrated works are sculptures designed to fit into a specific architectural setting. Ancient sources report that he worked on three important monuments of the early and mid-fourth century B.C.: the temple of Athena Alea at Tegea, the temple of Artemis at Ephesus, and the Mausoleum of Halicarnassus. It is indicative of his prominence that the last two of these three projects became famous as two of the Seven Wonders of the World.

Modern students of Scopas consider the temple of Athena Alea at Tegea the most important of his achievements because its fragments are the basis of whatever judgments can be made about his style. Pausanias (fl. A.D. 143-176) says that he was the architect of the building as a whole; judging from the consistent style of the surviving pieces, it is likely that the temple sculptures were executed by a team of artisans working under Scopas' supervision. The original temple, in southern Arcadia, had been destroyed by a fire in 394 B.C. The rebuilding took place about a generation later, on a scale of size and magnificence designed to overshadow all other temples in the Peloponnese. The central image of the temple, an ivory carving of Athena Alea, had been saved from the earlier temple. Everything else was for Scopas to create, and it is likely that he conceived of the temple itself as a vehicle for the display of the ornamental sculptures he designed. Pausanias, who saw the building intact, reports that the sculptures of the front pediment represented the Calydonian boar hunt referred to in the ninth book of Homer's *Iliad*; the figure of Meleager on this pediment, though lost, is believed to survive in copies, of which the best two are in the Vatican and Berlin. The rear pediment showed the duel between Telephus (the local Arcadian hero) and Achilles which took place just before the Trojan War. Of these sculptures, only fragments of the heads and various body parts survive. Scopas also created the freestanding statues of the healer Asklepios and the health goddess

Hygieia, which flanked the ivory figure of Athena that stood in the interior. A marble head of a woman which may be that of Hygieia was found by French excavators of the site in the early 1920's.

Scopas' role in the creation of the Artemisium at Ephesus is more problematical. There is only the authority of Pliny the Elder that he executed one of the thirty-six ornamented columns which were commissioned for this colossal structure, one of the Seven Wonders of the World. The sixth century B.C. temple of Artemis had burned in 356, reportedly on the night of Alexander the Great's birth, and construction began immediately on what would be (like Athena's temple at Tegea) considerably grander than its predecessor. The remains of this larger second temple are now in the British Museum. Of the three surviving ornamented column bases, one is dubiously attributed to Scopas. It shows Hermes leading the soul of Alcestis, who had offered to die in place of her husband, Admetus, toward a winged figure representing Thanatos, or death.

Scopas' third major work in architectural ornamentation was the Mausoleum of Halicarnassus, ordered by Queen Artemisia as a monumental tomb for her husband Mausolus, Satrap of Caria, who died in 353. This building, constructed entirely of white marble, stood until the fifteenth century, when it was brought down by an earthquake. It was excavated by the British in 1857, and many of its best pieces were taken to the British Museum. Though not its chief architect, Scopas was one of four famous artists brought in to decorate the four sides of the building with relief sculpture. His colleagues in this project, according to Pliny the Elder and Vitruvius, were Bryaxis, Timotheus, and Leochares. The best preserved of the three friezes found near the site by the British team represents an Amazonomachy, any of a number of legendary battles between Greeks and Amazons. Seventeen slabs, more or less defaced, represent this scene. Numerous attempts to attribute sections of the frieze to Scopas himself have been made, but they are problematical as a result of the lack of a single distinctive style which can serve as a signature of the master's work. Four slabs found near the northeast corner are commonly attributed to Scopas, but the touchstone of Scopadic style remains the fragments from Tegea.

Other works by Scopas are known through descriptions in ancient sources, which have led to the attribution of copies that seem to fit the ancient descriptions. A poem by Callistratus describes a Bacchante in ecstasy, carrying a kid she has killed. This image has been identified with a Maenad in the Dresden Sculpture Museum whose head is thrown up and back over her left shoulder. Her light dress, fastened over her right shoulder and held in place by a cord knotted above her waist, is blown by the wind, laying bare her left side, and her back is arched sharply backward as she strides, right leg forward. The Dresden Maenad, commonly attributed to Scopas, is representative of the late Classical and Hellenistic fondness for figures in action, gripped by powerful emotion. One of his most popular sculptures was a statue of Pothos (Longing), a young male nude leaning on a pillar or thyrsus with a cloak over his left arm and a goose at his feet. He stands with his weight on one foot, his left leg relaxed and crossing in front of his right. He looks upward in an abstracted way, as if thinking of an absent lover. Although the original of this masterpiece no longer survives, there are many Roman copies (and gemstone engravings) which testify to its popularity. This work represents the late classical departure from the powerfully built, erect, and concentrated figures of the earlier severe style. The body lines are gentle, the geometry of the figure is sloping rather than erect, the effect one of grace rather than power. Pausanias mentions a bronze Aphrodite Pandemos in a precinct of Aphrodite at Elis; the image has survived on Roman coins. Other works believed to show Scopas' influence are Roman reproductions of his statue of Meleager and the Lansdowne Herakles at the Getty Museum in Malibu, California, thought to be modeled on an original made for the gymnasium at Sikyon. Nearly all these derivative pieces are statues of gods and goddesses: Asklepios and Hygieia, Aphrodite, Apollo, Dionysus, Hestia, and Hermes.

Summary

Scopas must remain an enigmatic figure because no existing work of sculpture can safely be attributed to him; indeed, not much is known about the man or his work. Nevertheless, the testimony of ancient writers such as Pausanias, Pliny the Elder, and Vitruvius affirms that he was famed in the ancient world as both sculptor and architect, that his work was in great demand, and that he was widely imitated. The consensus of ancient opinion represents him as the preeminent sculptor of passion.

Modern students of ancient art are also unanimous in attributing to Scopas an individuality of manner which they perceive in works closely associated with his name. While the best authorities are reluctant to make dogmatic attributions of specific works, they agree in attributing to his style an impetuous force in the rendering of figures, delicate workmanship, and the rhythmical composition of a master sculptor.

Scopas' technical virtuosity is perhaps less important than the human content of his work, which reveals an emotional fervor and a sensitivity to the sadness of life. This interpretation was one of his great contributions to Hellenistic culture. Vergil's *sunt lacrimae rerum* (tears attend trials) is visually anticipated in the Scopadic style. Another aspect of his contribution is the representation of the human form under stress, where the body's tension symbolizes a turbulent emotional state. Hellenistic mannerism grows naturally out of this style. Scopas' unique achievement in recording the deeper recesses of human experience has been appropriately compared to that of Michelangelo in the Renaissance.

Bibliography

Ashmole, Bernard. "Skopas." In *Encyclopedia of World Art*. New York: McGraw-Hill Book Co., 1967. An excellent summary in English supplemented by an extensive bibliography of books and articles in English, French, German, and Italian.

Barron, John. *An Introduction to Greek Sculpture*. New York: Schocken Books, 1984. This volume is brief but well illustrated.

Bieber, Margarete. *The Sculpture of the Hellenistic Age*. New York: Columbia University Press, 1961. A detailed account of the major works still surviving, those described by ancient sources, and existing sculptures in Scopas' style. Finely illustrated and includes a bibliography and references to museum catalogs.

Lawrence, A. W. *Greek and Roman Sculpture*. London: Cape, 1972. This work concentrates on the Tegea figures, with notices of several pieces attributed to Scopas. Limited bibliography.

Richter, G. M. A. *The Sculpture and Sculptors of the Greeks*. 2d ed. New Haven, Conn.: Yale University Press, 1950. Attentive to the ancient sources, which are quoted freely, and most sensitive to the problems of identification. Well documented with references to ancient and modern sources.

Stewart, Andrew F. *Skopas of Paros*. Park Ridge, N.Y.: Noyes Press, 1977. The only full-length study in English, this work was developed from a 1972 University of Cambridge doctoral thesis. Detailed attention to features of style, based chiefly on the Tegea fragments. Richly illustrated, with a full set of ancient testimonia and detailed references to modern scholarship. Likely to remain the standard authority for some time.

Daniel H. Garrison

SELEUCUS I NICATOR

Born: 358 or 354 B.C.; Europus or Pella, Macedonia
Died: Summer, 281 B.C.; near Lysimachia, Thrace
Areas of Achievement: Government, warfare, and conquest
Contribution: By his courage and practical common sense, Seleucus created the Seleucid Empire, maintaining the loyalty of a heterogeneous population by fair government.

Early Life

Seleucus was born in 358 or 354 B.C. in either Europus or Pella, Macedonia. Although ancient sources do not agree on where or when he was born, no one disputes that he was the son of a man named Antiochus and his wife, Laodice. Nothing is known of Seleucus' early life, but both Diodorus Siculus and Appian indicate that he was with the army of Alexander the Great which marched against the Persians in 334. He must have distinguished himself in the following years, for by 326 he had assumed command of the royal hypaspists (elite infantry) in the Indian campaign and had gained a position on the king's staff. When Alexander crossed the Hydaspes River, he took with him in the same boat Ptolemy (later Ptolemy I Soter), Perdiccas, Lysimachus, and Seleucus.

One of Alexander's final acts was to preside over the festival at Susa during which his generals married Persian brides. His two fiercest opponents had been Oxyartes and Spitamenes. Alexander had already married Oxyartes' daughter Roxane; he gave Apama, daughter of Spitamines, to Seleucus. It was a lifetime marriage which provided Seleucus with his son and successor, Antiochus. According to Appian, he named three cities after Apama.

When Alexander died in 323, Perdiccas took over as regent for Alexander's retarded half brother and his unborn child. The empire was divided among the generals, who were to serve as satraps (governors). Seleucus was named chiliarch (commander of the Companion cavalry), a position of extreme military importance but with no grant of land. For this reason, he played a relatively unimportant role for the next ten years, although he led the cavalry rebellion which resulted in the death of Perdiccas in 321. When a new appointment of satraps was made shortly after this, Seleucus gave up his position as chiliarch to become governor of Babylonia.

Babylonia, in the center of what had been Alexander's empire, was the perfect position from which to dominate the entire empire, but its security was threatened by the arrogant satraps of Media (Pithon) and Persia (Peucestas). Pithon seized Parthia to the east, was driven out by Peucestas, and subsequently sought an alliance with Seleucus. Meanwhile, Eumenes, the outlawed former satrap of Cappadocia, appeared in Babylonia with an elite Macedonian force far superior to Seleucus' army. Seleucus was forced to call on Antigonus I, the most powerful of the satraps, for help. Although Antigonus, Seleucus, and Pithon started the campaign together in 317, once they had taken Susiana, Seleucus was left behind to besiege the citadel of Susa while the other two pursued Eumenes. In rapid succession, Antigonus defeated and killed Eumenes, ordered the execution of Pithon, and masterminded the "disappearance" of Peucestas. When he returned to Babylonia, Seleucus tried to appease Antigonus with the treasure from Susa, but it was only a short time later, in 316, that he wisely fled Babylon and sought refuge with Ptolemy in Egypt.

Life's Work

Seleucus would seem to have lost everything at this point, but this was actually the beginning of his climb to even greater power. Antigonus was now the dominant figure among Alexander's successors, but he wanted the whole empire. The three other powerful leaders—Ptolemy in Egypt, Lysimachus in Thrace, and Cassander in Macedonia—formed a coalition against him. In the first phase of the resulting war, Seleucus served as commander in Ptolemy's navy, seeing action in both the Aegean Sea and the eastern Mediterranean around Cyprus. In the beginning of the second phase, he took part in the attack on Gaza by the Ptolemaic army. Antigonus had sent his son Demetrius to hold this strategically important fortress, and his defeat was a severe blow to Antigonus' plans. According to Diodorus (c. 40 B.C.), Ptolemy showed his gratitude to Seleucus by giving him a small army, which he then led to Babylonia.

The troops at first were fearful of their mission, but Seleucus convinced them that an oracle of Didymean Apollo had proclaimed him king. The Seleucids would eventually claim Apollo as an ancestor. Better than the oracle, however, was the fact that during his previous governorship Seleucus had ruled wisely and well. Reinforcements flocked to him as he marched into the territory, and he took the city of Babylon with little trouble. This feat launched the Seleucid Empire.

Seleucus regained Babylonia, but not without antagonizing Nicanor, the satrap of Media, who proceeded to march on Babylon. Seleucus, however, swiftly leading an army out to meet him, surprised and routed Nicanor, whose troops deserted to the victor.

The East was now open to Seleucus. He rapidly took Susiana and Persia before turning to Media, where, according to Appian, Nicanor was killed in battle. Between 311 and 302, Seleucus gained control of all Iran and the lands extending to the Indus River. At the Indus, he reestablished contact with the Indian chieftains of the region and returned home finally with 480 elephants.

Meanwhile, in the West, Alexander's family had been exterminated. In 306, Antigonus proclaimed himself king, and the other four satraps, Ptolemy, Lysimachus, Cassander, and Seleucus, followed suit. Antigonus still had designs on all of Alexander's empire, and by 302, the other kings considered his power so threatening to their own security that they formed a coalition against him.

The armies met at Ipsus in 301, where Seleucus' elephants played a major role in the defeat of Antigonus, who died in battle. In the redivision of land which followed, Seleucus gained Syria and Lysimachus was awarded Asia Minor. A new war could have started between Seleucus and Ptolemy, since the king of Egypt had previously occupied Coele-Syria (Palestine) and now refused to give it up, but Seleucus, remembering that Ptolemy had stood by him in a difficult time, decided to ignore the issue, although he did not give up his claim to the land.

Seleucus now held more land than any of the other kings, and that made them uneasy. In order to balance the power, Ptolemy and Lysimachus joined in marriage alliances; this, in turn, disturbed Seleucus. Although his marriage to Apama was still firm, Seleucus sent word to Demetrius to ask for his daughter Stratonice in marriage (Macedonian kings practiced polygamy). Demetrius agreed, and the marriage took place, but although Stratonice bore him a daughter, Seleucus eventually gave her in marriage to his eldest son, Antiochus, and sent them to Babylon to reign as king and queen in the East. Seleucus ruled in the West from his new capital city of Antioch, named for his father.

Seleucus spent most of the twenty years following the Battle of Ipsus consolidating his empire. One of his major policies was the division of the empire into East and West, with the heir to the throne ruling from Babylon; this would become a standard policy of the Seleucids. His major problem throughout most of this period was Demetrius, who had become king of Macedonia but would not be satisfied until he had regained his father's lost kingdom. Demetrius invaded Asia Minor in 287, but two years later, Seleucus held him captive. At first, Demetrius believed that he would soon be set free, but as that hope faded, so did his self-control. By 283, he had drunk himself to death.

There might have been a peaceful old age for Seleucus if it had not been for Ptolemy's disinherited eldest son, Ptolemy Keraunos. After causing the death of Lysimachus' son in Thrace, Keraunos fled to Seleucus, thus precipitating war between the two former allies. The two met at Corypedium in Asia Minor in the spring of 281. Lysimachus was killed in the battle. Seleucus, who was now in his seventies, suddenly saw himself as Alexander reuniting his empire. He pressed onto Thrace, only to meet death treacherously at the hand of Ptolemy Keraunos outside the capital city of Lysimachia in the following summer. His common sense had deserted him in the end, but he left behind an heir who was experienced in ruling and a well-established empire based on sound government.

Summary

Seleucus I Nicator ruled an empire made up of many diverse ethnic groups. He had inherited the Persian system of administration and was wise enough to realize its value. He continued the Persian policy of respecting the cultures and religions of the people he ruled at the same time that he proceeded to establish a governmental system entirely made up of Greeks. Unlike most of Alexander's generals, Seleucus retained and respected his Persian wife, but there were few, if any, non-Greeks in his administration. His son and successor, who was half-Persian, married a Macedonian woman. Seleucus spread Hellenism throughout the major parts of his empire by the typical Greek method of founding colonies. Antioch, his capital in the West, became one of the great cities of the ancient world.

The first of the Seleucids was a man of honor. He gained his position in Alexander's army through hard work and his empire in the same way. He was able to reclaim Babylonia because he had ruled well throughout his first governorship, and he refused to fight Ptolemy over Coele-Syria out of gratitude for past favors. Later, when he held Demetrius prisoner, Seleucus declined to turn him over to Lysimachus, who had offered a large sum of money in exchange. Demetrius was treated honorably during his imprisonment, but Seleucus realized that he was too troublesome ever to be released. Seleucus was loyal to his friends and treated his enemies fairly. Unfortunately, Ptolemy Keraunos had none of these attributes, and Seleucus died as the result of a cowardly attack by a man who had first called on him for help and then killed him to gain a kingdom he was not wise enough to keep.

Bibliography

Bar-Kochva, B. *The Seleucid Army: Organization and Tactics in the Great Campaigns*. Cambridge: Cambridge University Press, 1976. This study addresses only military affairs, but Bar-Kochva points out Seleucus' courage and tactical ability. Part 1 concentrates on manpower and organization.

Bevan, Edwyn Robert. *The House of Seleucus*. Vol. 1. London: Edward Arnold, 1902. Analytical account of Seleucus' rise to power based on the ancient sources. Still the only comprehensive account of the Seleucids in English.

Cohen, Getzel M. *The Seleucid Colonies: Studies in Founding, Administration, and Organization*. Wiesbaden, West Germany: Steiner, 1978. Contains information on the founding, administration, and organization of new colonies. Attempts to answer questions on the nature of the poorly documented Seleucid colonization program. The answers are tentative but thought-provoking.

Cook, S. A., F. E. Adcock, and M. P. Charlesworth, eds. *The Cambridge Ancient History*. Vol. 7, *The Hellenistic Monarchies and the Rise of Rome*.

New York: Macmillan, 1928. Chapter 5 contains a systematic account of the organization of both the central and satrapy governments in the Seleucid Empire.

Seyrig, H. "Seleucus I and the Foundation of Hellenistic Syria." In *The Role of the Phoenicians in the Interaction of Mediterranean Civilizations*. Beirut, Lebanon: American University Press, 1968. Part of a series of articles edited by W. A. Ward. (Phoenicia was a part of the satrapy of Syria claimed by Seleucus in 301 B.C.)

Linda J. Piper

SENECA THE YOUNGER

Born: c. 4 B.C.; Córdoba
Died: April, A.D. 65; Rome
Areas of Achievement: Government, philosophy and literature
Contribution: An influential intellectual, Seneca also showed great abilities as coadministrator of the Roman Empire during the first years of Nero. In literature, Seneca's essays and tragedies were influential from the Middle Ages to the Renaissance, when English playwrights took his dramas as models.

Early Life

Although Seneca the Younger was born in Córdoba, his father, known as Seneca the Elder, was a conservative Roman knight who had achieved fame as an orator and teacher of rhetoric in Rome. His mother, Helvia, was an extraordinarily intelligent, gifted, and morally upright person whose love for philosophy had been checked only by her husband's rejection of the idea of education for women.

The familial conflict was handed down to the next generation: The oldest of the three brothers, Gallio, pursued a splendid political career, but the youngest, Mela, spent his life making money and educating himself (the poet Lucan was his son). Lucius Annaeus Seneca, the second child and bearer of his father's name, was torn between public life in the service of a corrupted state and life as philosopher and private man.

Coming to Rome at a very early age, Seneca received an education in rhetoric, which was the first step toward becoming an orator with an eye to public offices. Yet the youth also saw teachers of Stoic philosophy who taught a life of asceticism, equanimity in the face of adversity, and an evaluation of the daily work of the self, which laid the foundations of Seneca's eclectic philosophical beliefs.

In Rome, Seneca lived with an aunt; she guarded the precarious health of the thin, feeble boy. His physical deficiencies and what were perhaps lifelong bouts with pneumonia almost led the young man to suicide; only the thought of how much this act would hurt his aging father stopped him. Since intense studies distracted his mind from his sufferings, Seneca would later state that he owed his life to philosophy. In the light of his physical afflictions and his own description of himself as small, plain, and skinny, scholars doubt the veracity of the only extant antique copy of a bust of Seneca, which shows the philosopher and statesman as a corpulent old man with sharp but full features and receding hair.

Seneca's ill health apparently caused him to spend a considerable portion of his youth and early manhood in the healthier climate of Egypt. It was not before A.D. 31 that he permanently left the East for Rome.

Life's Work

As a result of the lobbying of his aunt, Seneca successfully entered public service as quaestor (roughly, secretary of finances), in A.D. 33. Although it is no longer known which positions Seneca held during this period, it is most likely that he continued in ever more prestigious offices.

Besides serving the state under the two difficult emperors Tiberius and Caligula, Seneca began to achieve wealth and fame as a lawyer. From the later works which have survived, one can see how his witty, poignant, almost epigrammatical language fascinated Seneca's listeners and how his pithy sentences, which reflected his enormous active vocabulary, must have won for him cases in court. Further, Seneca's consciously anti-Ciceronian style, which avoided long sentences and ornamental language, established his fame as an orator. Early works (now lost) made him a celebrated writer as well. Seneca's first marriage, dating from around this time, cannot have been a very happy one; he fails to mention the name of his wife, despite the fact that they had at least two sons together, both of whom he writes about in the most affectionate terms.

Under the reign of Caligula (A.D. 37-41), Seneca's ill health proved advantageous. His oratorical success had aroused the envy of the emperor, who derogatorily likened Seneca's style to "sand without lime" (meaning that it was worthless for building), and Caligula sought to execute Seneca. Seneca was spared only because one of the imperial mistresses commented on the futility of shortening the life of a terminally ill man; later, Seneca commented tongue in cheek, "Disease has postponed many a man's death and proximity to death has resulted in salvation."

In 41, the first year of the reign of Claudius I, a struggle for power between Empress Messalina and Caligula's sisters Agrippina and Julia Livilla brought Seneca into court on a trumped-up charge of adultery with Princess Julia. Found guilty, Seneca escaped death only because Claudius transformed the sentence into one of banishment to the barren island of Corsica. There, for the next eight years, Seneca dedicated his life to philosophy, the writing of letters, and natural philosophy; he also began to draft his first tragedies. The most powerful nonfiction works of this era are his letter of advice to his mother *Ad Helviam matrem de consolatione* (c. A.D. 41-42; *To My Mother Helvia, on Consolation*) and the philosophical treatise *De ira libri tres* (c. A.D. 41-49; *Three Essays on Anger*). Both works are deeply influenced by Stoic philosophy and argue that to deal with misfortune is to bear the adversities of life with dignified tranquillity, courage, and spiritual strength; further, violent passions must be controlled by the man who is truly wise.

The execution of Messalina for treason in 48 and the ensuing marriage of Claudius to Agrippina brought the latter into a position of power from which she could recall Seneca. Intent on using the famous orator and writer, Agrippina made Seneca the tutor of her son by a previous marriage, a young boy whom Claudius adopted under the name of Nero. Rather than being allowed to retire to Athens as a private man, Seneca was also made a member in the Roman senate and became praetor, the second highest of the Roman offices, in 50. Further, his new marriage to the wealthy and intelligent Pompeia Paulina drew Seneca into a circle of powerful friends—including the new prefect of the Praetorian Guard, Sextus Afranius Burrus.

The death of Claudius in 54 brought highest power to Seneca and Burrus. Their successful working relationship began when Burrus' guard proclaimed Nero emperor, and Seneca wrote the speech of accession for the seventeen-year-old youth. For five years, from 54 to 59, during the *Quinquennium Neronis*, the statesmen shared supreme authority and successfully governed the Roman Empire in harmony, while Nero amused himself with games and women and let them check his excesses and cruelty. Internally, the unacknowledged regency of Seneca and Burrus brought a rare period of civil justice, harmony, and political security. Seneca's Stoicism led him to fight the cruelty of gladiatorial combat and to favor laws intended to limit the absolute power of the master over his slaves. At the frontiers of the Empire, the generals of Burrus and Seneca fought victoriously against the Parthians in the East and crushed a rebellion in Britain, after which a more reformatory regime brought lasting peace to this remote island.

Seneca's fall was a direct result of Nero's awakening thirst for power. Increasingly, Seneca and Burrus lost their influence over him and in turn became involved in his morally despicable actions. In 59, Nero ordered the murder of his mother, Agrippina, and Seneca drafted the son's address to the senate, a speech which cleverly covered up the facts of the assassination.

Burrus' death and replacement by an intimate of Nero in 62 led to Seneca's request for retirement, which Nero refused; he kept Seneca in Rome, although removed from the court. Seneca's best philosophical work was written during this time; in his remaining three years, he finished *De providentia* (c. A.D. 63-64; *On Providence*) and wrote *Quaestiones naturales* (c. A.D. 62-64; *Natural Questions*) and his influential *Epistulae morales ad Lucilium* (c. A.D. 62-65; *Letters to Lucilius*), in which he treats a variety of moral questions and establishes the form of the essay.

Early in 65, a probably false accusation implicated Seneca in a conspiracy to assassinate Nero, who ordered him to commit suicide. With Stoic tranquillity and in the tradition of Socrates and Cato the Younger, Seneca opened his arteries and slowly bled to death. Fully composed, and with honor, the Roman noble ended a life in the course of which he had wielded immense political power and enjoyed great status as statesman and writer.

Summary

Consideration of the life and work of Seneca the Younger remains controversial. On a professional level, critics have attacked his philosophical work as eclectic and unoriginal, but it is through Seneca that more ancient ideas were handed down before the originals became known. For example, Seneca's tragedies are easily dismissed as static, bombastic, lurid, and peopled by characters who rant and rave; still, English Renaissance works such as John Webster's *The Duchess of Malfi* (1613-1614) could not have been created without their authors' knowledge of Seneca.

The reputation of Seneca the man has suffered from his political alliance with Nero, one of the most monstrous creatures of popular history. The ancient historian Cornelius Tacitus is among the first to censure Seneca for his complicity in the cover-up of Agrippina's murder: "It was not only Nero, whose inhuman cruelty was beyond understanding, but also Seneca who fell into discredit."

A final evaluation of Seneca cannot overlook the fact that his public service ended in moral chaos after a period of doing much good for the commonwealth. It is interesting to note, however, that Seneca's most mature writing came after his de facto resignation from political power and responsibility; it is for his brilliantly written letters to Gaius Lucilius that Seneca achieves the status of philosopher, and these words have been with Western civilization ever since.

Bibliography
Griffin, Miriam Tamara. *Seneca: A Philosopher in Politics*. Oxford: Clarendon Press, 1976. Definitive study of Seneca; a modern, informed reevaluation of the man who had so many lofty ideas and whose life is so full of nasty facts. Dramatizes the problem of public service for a corrupted state. Clearly written. Contains a good bibliography.
Gummere, Richard Mott. *Seneca, the Philosopher and His Modern Message*. Boston: Marshall Jones Co., 1922. Reprint. New York: Cooper Square, 1963. Emphasis on Seneca's philosophical works and their relevance in modern times. Scholarly but not overly dry, this volume makes Stoic philosophy accessible.
Henry, Denis, and Elisabeth Henry. *The Mask of Power: Seneca's Tragedies and Imperial Power*. Chicago: Bolchazy-Carducci, 1985. An interpretative study of Seneca's tragedies, placing them in their cultural context. Occasionally, dramatic conflicts which arise out of a time of corruption are related to the twentieth century. Includes a good, up-to-date bibliography.
Holland, Francis. *Seneca*. London: Longmans, Green and Co., 1920. Reprint. Freeport, N.Y.: Books for Libraries Press, 1969. For a long time, this work was the only biography on Seneca available in English. Still useful and readable, Holland's study is thorough and aware of the problematic status of its subject.
Motto, Anna Lydia. *Seneca*. New York: Twayne Publishers, 1973. Introductory but complete presentation of Seneca's life and work. Written for a

general audience, with a strong focus on Seneca's philosophical and dramatic work.

Sevenster, J. N. *Paul and Seneca*. Leiden, Netherlands: E. J. Brill, 1961. A theological comparison of the thoughts of the two men. Sevenster rejects the medieval myth that Seneca met or corresponded with Saint Paul and was a "closet Christian" and sees the two philosophers as contemporaries trying to answer the problems of their time.

Sorensen, Villy. *Seneca: The Humanist at the Court of Nero*. Translated by W. G. Jones. Chicago: University of Chicago Press, 1984. A well-written, scholarly work which, nevertheless, is understandable to a general audience. Brings alive the man, his time, and his political and philosophical achievements. Includes interesting illustrations.

Sutton, Dana Ferrin. *Seneca on the Stage*. Leiden, Netherlands: E. J. Brill, 1986. This volume argues against tradition that Seneca's tragedies were not merely written to be read, but crafted to be performed. Supports its claim with its discovery of stage directions which are "clues" hidden in the text of the dramas.

Reinhart Lutz

SERGIUS I

Born: Date unknown; place unknown
Died: Early December, 638; Constantinople
Area of Achievement: Religion
Contribution: As head of the Orthodox Christian Church, Patriarch Sergius of Constantinople made a major if unsuccessful effort to resolve the vexing Monophysite controversy by advancing the Monothelete doctrine. At the same time, he became the loyal and invaluable partner of the Emperor Heraclius, helping him save the Late Roman (or Byzantine) state in a time of dire crisis.

Early Life
Virtually no information is available regarding the early life of Sergius. He is said to have been Syrian in origin. He is recorded as holding the office of dean of the clergy of Haghia Sophia, the cathedral of Constantinople, and was also in charge of the church's ministries of charity, at the time of the death of the Patriarch Thomas in 610. Sergius was chosen to succeed to the patriarchal chair himself at this point.

His elevation came in a period of upheaval, strain, and crisis, in both immediate and long-range terms. He was enthroned during the reign of the bloody usurper, the Emperor Phocas, against whom a revolt was brewing. More broadly, he assumed the status of ecumenical patriarch—prelate of the Byzantine Empire's capital and one of the five great ecclesiastical leaders who were recognized as partners in the rule of the larger Christian community—during a time when the Christian world was torn by continuing doctrinal dissent. Various positions in the debate over the understanding of Christ's nature as both a divine and a human being had become identified with divergent cultural traditions and political loyalties as well as spiritual commitments. Fiercely held dissident beliefs among the inhabitants of certain regions of the Empire posed political as well as theological problems, threatening the loyalty of those regions. Whether, left to his own impulses, Sergius would have developed the doctrinal positions that he came to espouse cannot be known, but his career as patriarch was to force him to develop them.

Life's Work
Sergius became Patriarch of Constantinople while the tyrant Phocas was fighting to retain the throne he had won by rebellion and murder in 602. Sergius was barely installed when Heraclius, son of the Exarch (viceroy) of Africa, sailed to Constantinople at the head of a fleet in the autumn of 610 to lead the uprising against Phocas. With the help of dissidents in the city, Phocas was overthrown and executed, and Heraclius was acclaimed as his successor. On October 5, 610, Sergius presided over not only the coronation

of Heraclius but also his marriage.

The patriarch was soon drawn into a close understanding and partnership with the new emperor, a relationship that was not to be without its tensions and trials. After less than two years of marriage, Heraclius was shattered by the loss of his wife, her weak health undermined further by bearing two children. In his bereavement, Heraclius was urged by his mother to take as his second wife the intelligent and devoted Martina. Several objections to such a union were immediately raised: Martina was ambitious, she was twenty-three years younger than Heraclius, and she was his niece—the daughter of his own sister. This last fact prompted outrage and indignation on the part of populace and clergy alike. Sergius is reported to have attempted personally to dissuade the emperor from this plan, but Heraclius became determined to take Martina as his wife. Apparently judging it best not to destroy what must have become an important trust between prelate and sovereign, Sergius capitulated and performed the marriage a year or so later.

Trust and supportive understanding were needed between Sergius and Heraclius as the emperor had to deal with the mounting crises that faced the Empire. While the Turkish Avars ravaged the Balkan provinces, the Persians to the east had begun a program of systematic conquest of imperial territories. In 611, they invaded Syria-Palestine, and their bloody conquest of Jerusalem in 614 was carried out as a calculated humiliation of the Christian faith. Between 616 and 620, the Persians went on to conquer Egypt, and their armies began to penetrate Asia Minor and threaten the approaches to the capital.

With shattered military forces and rapidly dwindling resources, Heraclius seemed paralyzed, despite his best efforts to cope, and must at times have felt despair. It is reported that, by 619, the emperor had decided to withdraw from Constantinople and to transfer his residence to the safer distance of Carthage, from which he might launch a counteroffensive. It is said that, in response, Sergius confronted the emperor on behalf of the panic-stricken citizens of the capital and compelled him to swear a public oath that he would not abandon Constantinople. Historically accurate or not, this story does seem to reflect an understanding reached between Sergius and Heraclius in a time of crisis. For his part, Sergius agreed that the impoverished state should be allowed to draw upon the vast wealth of the Church, at least as a loan, to replenish its depleted coffers. With these new funds, Heraclius was able to finance the recruitment and training of a new and expanded military force to meet the Persian menace.

Meanwhile, Sergius had already been working to assist the emperor in other ways. The demoralizing speed with which the Persians had been conquering Syria-Palestine and Egypt pointed up the added urgency of a problem that had long undermined the stability and loyalty of those regions under the Empire: the large popular adherence there to the Christological heresy known as Monophysitism—the doctrine of the single (divine) nature of Christ—which had been condemned by the Council of Chalcedon in 451 but still remained attractive to many. As patriarch, Sergius was pledged to uphold the Chalcedonian doctrine of the two natures of Christ. Though past attempts at bridging the gap between the two positions had failed, Sergius recognized the desperate need to try again if the Empire's population was to be restored to unity. Moreover, if the report is true that his own parents had been Monophysites of the Syrian Jacobite church, he must have been able to understand the heretical position well.

Sergius therefore drew upon some earlier theological arguments to propose a compromise: a doctrine that bypassed the issue of one or two natures and stressed the concept of a single motivating Energy (*energeia*), "one activity and one will," in Christ. Apparently, the emperor approved this doctrine of "monoenergism" as one with which both Monophysites and dyophysite Chalcedonians might agree. From about 618, Sergius began a round of contacts with prelates and theologians around the Empire, finding much support and encouragement from them. This theological olive branch, as a basis for sectarian pacification and reunion among dissident populations, was as important as the Church's financial support for Heraclius' struggle to save the Empire.

On April 4, 622, all was ready, and Sergius presided with the emperor over a solemn ceremony of public consecration to the new enterprise—one that later generations in Western Europe would hail as a veritable crusade on behalf of the Christian faith, as much as a political and territorial counteroffensive. Crossing to Asia Minor, Heraclius began his initial campaigns with great success. His route took him into the areas of the Caucasus and Armenia, where Monophysite doctrine was strong, so that discussions of the monoenergist doctrine were important components of the emperor's efforts to win allies and recruits for his military operations.

In the midst of the emperor's campaigns, the Persians persuaded the Avars to attack Constantinople as a countermeasure to distract Heraclius. Though repeatedly bribed by tributes to keep the peace, the greedy Avars were only too glad to mount a ferocious and determined siege of the capital, beginning on June 29, 626. Heraclius had entrusted the command of the city in his absence to able civil and military officials, under the general supervision of Sergius himself, and the emperor's confidence in them was not tested as he boldly decided not to end his campaigning to return to the besieged city, as the Persians had hoped. To Sergius in particular fell the task of keeping up the spirit of resistance during this trial. In this he succeeded: The Avars were repulsed and abandoned the attack by August 8, amid stories that the Virgin Mary herself had intervened miraculously to drive off the pagan attackers. Sergius led celebrations of joy and thanksgiving, and this deliverance of Constantinople is still commemorated in one of the most famous hymns of the Greek Orthodox liturgy, the great "Akathistos" hymn. Indeed, it was once thought that the entire hymn dated from this event, perhaps being a composition of Sergius himself; it is now known that the bulk of it was the work of Romanos the Melode of a century earlier, but the prologue, with its explicit reference to the Virgin's intervention against the Avars to save her city, was apparently an addition dating from this episode of 626.

Vindicated by the deliverance of Constantinople, Heraclius renewed his campaigning, and, within the next two years, brought the Persian kingdom to its knees. In September, 628, Heraclius was welcomed back to the capital as a victorious hero, and at some time thereafter he ceremonially restored to Jerusalem the True Cross which had been carried off by the Persians. As part of his restoration of imperial government in the recovered territories, Heraclius continued to promote the doctrinal compromise developed by Sergius. It met with mixed receptions. Among its most determined opponents were the aged and dogmatic Palestinian monk Sophronius and the brilliant young theologian Maximos (later to become known as "the Confessor"). Sergius strove to convince them by theological arguments, and, in his correspondence with the Bishop of Rome, he was able to win qualified acceptance from Pope Honorius I. In the process, the wording of the compromise doctrine began to shift to the concept of Christ having a single Will (*thelēma*) rather than a single Energy: Hence the doctrine's eventual label of Monothelism.

The quest for religious unity acquired new urgency as the areas of greatest sectarian dissent became the target of unexpected and sudden onslaughts of the Arabs, who between 634 and 636 effectively destroyed the Empire's capacity to control Syria-Palestine. Sophronius himself was elected Patriarch of Jerusalem in 634, amid the scramble, and used his position to renew opposition to the Monothelete doctrine. Its failure to win back popular loyalty in Syria-Palestine and the apparent collaboration of the dissidents with the tolerant conquerors made the emperor and patriarch only more anxious to use it to save Egypt from the same fate, as well as to silence the opposition of Chalcedonian loyalists. With help from his advisers, Sergius drew up a doctrinal statement, or *ekthesis*, formally propounding the dogma of the One Will of Christ and forbidding further debate over the one or two natures. It was finally approved by Heraclius and issued about October, 638. This *ekthesis* was Sergius' last service to his emperor. In early December of that year, the old patriarch died, leaving the struggle to his heirs.

Summary

The year of Sergius' death witnessed the deaths of several other central figures in the religious controversy. In March, 638, shortly after negotiating the capitulation of Jerusalem to the Arabs, the adamant Sophronius had died. Pope Honorius I died in October, about the time the *ekthesis* was promulgated. Despite the ruthless Monothelete policies of Cyrus, the Patriarch of Alexandria, Egypt remained unreconciled, and it soon submitted to the Arab invasion of 639-641. Broken and disillusioned, the aged Heraclius died in February, 641. Sergius' Monothelete doctrine was subsequently repudiated by Rome and, after decades of bitter ecclesiastical strife, it was abandoned by the imperial government at the Sixth Ecumenical Council in 681, though some support for it survived in the provinces.

The failure of Monothelism should not, however, tarnish Sergius' achievement. His formulation was the product of a sincere desire to end religious controversy, of a flexible and pragmatic theological learning, and of a noble spirit of service to his church and faith. It must be placed also in the context of Sergius' service to sovereign and people, including his supreme moments of glory in supporting Heraclius and in leading the defense of Constantinople in 626. In a tradition in which the patriarch was often either the subordinate or the opponent of the emperor, Sergius was one of the few prelates to be a genuine partner to his sovereign and to make the theoretical harmony between church and state in Byzantium actually work.

Bibliography
Bury, J. B. *A History of the Later Roman Empire, from Areadius to Irene (395 A.D. to 800 A.D.)*. 2 vols. London: Macmillan, 1889. Bury later (in 1923) published a two-volume replacement of this history, but it extended only to 565, so that volume 2 of this earlier set was not superseded. If a little outdated in its coverage of the early seventh century, it includes a still-useful treatment of the ecclesiastical history of the period, including the career of Sergius.
Every, George. *The Byzantine Patriarchate, 451-1204*. London: Society for the Propagation of Christian Knowledge, 1947, 2d ed. 1962. There is no study focusing specifically on Sergius' life or on the See of Constantinople in this period. Every's very general survey is useful, however, for its broad perspective, even though he includes only a few pages on the epoch of Sergius.
Frend, W. H. C. *The Rise of the Monophysite Movement: Chapters in the History of the Church in the Fifth and Sixth Centuries*. Cambridge: Cambridge University Press, 1972. Written by a leading historian of the early Christian Church and its heretical movements, this is an excellent treatment of this particular sectarian controversy. The latter part of its final chapter gives an excellent account of the doctrinal efforts of Sergius.
Hussey, Joan M. *The Orthodox Church in the Byzantine Empire*. Oxford: Oxford University Press, 1986. A volume in the Oxford History of the Christian Church series, this book covers the time span from the early seventh century through 1453. The treatment of Sergius' era is brief but useful, and set in good context.

Ostrogorsky, George. *History of the Byzantine State*. Translated by J. M. Hussey. New Brunswick, N.J.: Rutgers University Press, 1957, rev. ed. 1969. Though now showing its age, still the most comprehensive one-volume treatment of the Byzantine Empire's history and institutions, from the early fourth through the mid-fifteenth century, with an excellent perspective on the sixth century era in general.

Stratos, Andreas N. *Byzantium in the Seventh Century*. Vols. 1 and 2, translated by Marc Ogilvie-Grant and Harry T. Hionides. Amsterdam: Adolf M. Hakkert, 1968, 1972. The opening volumes (of six in the original Greek version, of five in the English translation) of a remarkably comprehensive study of seventh century Byzantium. These two volumes cover the age of Heraclius, including the career of Sergius. The approach involves often distracting discursiveness on the problems encountered in the sources, but Stratos displays great admiration and sympathy for Sergius and offers up-to-date scholarly information.

John W. Barker

SAINT SERGIUS I

Born: 635; Palermo, Sicily
Died: September 8, 701; Rome, Italy
Area of Achievement: Religion
Contribution: During his reign as pope, Sergius greatly strengthened relations between Rome and the churches in the Anglo-Saxon west and maintained the Western church's independence from the emperors of Constantinople. He introduced the Agnus Dei into the Mass and was responsible for the restoration and embellishment of churches throughout Rome.

Early Life

The father of Sergius, a merchant named Tiberius, migrated from the Syrian town of Antioch to Sicily. It was on this island, in the town of Palermo, that the young Sergius received his early education. Little else is known of this part of his life, except that he journeyed to Rome and entered the priesthood under the papacy of Adeodatus II. During his training for the priesthood, Sergius revealed an enthusiasm for music and was allowed to study under the head cantor. His interest in music would persist throughout his papacy. In either 682 or 683, he was ordained by Pope Leo II and became the titular priest of the town of Santa Susanna, located on the Quirinal. As a priest he developed a reputation for his love of saying Mass in the catacombs, a practice which, though once common, had become rare by his time. In 687, Pope Conon died after a long illness, and a bitter struggle for the papal successor ensued. It was out of this struggle that the humble priest from Santa Susanna emerged as leader of the Church.

Life's Work

While Pope Conon was still upon his deathbed, his archdeacon Paschal had offered a bribe of one hundred pounds of gold to the new Byzantine imperial exarch John Platyn, in order to guarantee the papal chair for himself. John Platyn was at Ravenna at the time and proved to be more than obliging in this request. When the pope finally died, Platyn managed to secure the nomination of Paschal for the papal succession. Platyn was successful in this because the faction which nominated Paschal was composed of officials whom Platyn himself had earlier appointed to govern Rome.

Such treachery would probably have passed unnoticed and Paschal would have become pope had not a larger rival faction nominated the archpriest Theodore as Conon's successor. That created a stalemate. In fact, the opposing factions barricaded themselves in separate parts of the Lateran Palace, each refusing to back down. The group backing Theodore occupied the interior section of the Lateran Palace which contained the private apartments of the pope, while the group backing Paschal occupied the exterior sections.

In the midst of this turmoil, a meeting of leading civic authorities, army officers, and clergy was held in the Palatine Palace with the aim of selecting a third candidate to break the deadlock. The priest of Santa Susanna was unanimously chosen by this group to become the pope. Upon the nomination of Sergius, the gates of the Lateran were stormed and the rival groups ousted. When Sergius himself entered the palace, Theodore immediately renounced his pretensions to the throne. Paschal, too, renounced his designs and recognized the legitimacy of Sergius, but did so grudgingly and only under compulsion. In fact, Paschal continued with his machinations against Sergius and offered more money to John Platyn if the latter would come to Rome and overturn the election.

Platyn went secretly to Rome. Probably to the surprise of Paschal, however, Platyn gave his approval to Sergius when he realized that the installment in power had been carried out regularly and enjoyed massive popular support. Unfortunately, Platyn demanded of Sergius the money that had been promised him by Paschal. Sergius refused—on the grounds, first, that he had not been partner to any such deal and, second, that he simply did not have the money. Nevertheless, Platyn insisted on being paid, and Sergius offered to pledge as payment the candelabra and crowns which stood in front of the altar of Saint Peter. This offer did not satisfy Platyn, and he refused to permit Sergius to be consecrated until the money had actually been raised and paid. Sergius relented, paid Platyn, and was finally consecrated on December 15, 687. Paschal continued, however, to intrigue against the new pope until he was finally arraigned, deprived of the position of archdeacon, and imprisoned. He remained unrepentant and died in prison five years later.

The first noteworthy act of Sergius in his position as leader of the Catholic church was of a housekeeping nature. He had the remains of Leo the Great moved from their relatively inconspicuous burial ground and housed in a newly constructed ornate tomb in the basilica.

The reign of Pope Sergius I was primarily noteworthy for his refusal to endorse the Second Trullan Synod (also known as the Quinisext Council), called in 692 by the Eastern emperor Justinian II. This meeting, of more than two hundred bishops of the Eastern church, was convened by Justinian II with the ostensible purpose of supplementing the work of the Fifth (held in 553) and Sixth (held in 680) general councils. Yet, though the Trullan Synod legislated for the entire Church, only one bishop of the West was present, and the 102 disciplinary and ritual canons enacted by the council were actually motivated by a degree of hostility toward and defiance of the Western church.

The canons banned practices which were established in the West (such as the celibacy of the clergy and fasting on Saturdays in Lent), ignored Western canon law, and reestablished the Twenty-eighth Canon of Chalcedon, which granted patriarchal status to Constantinople (second only to Rome). The lat-

Saint Sergius I

ter canon had been vigorously and continuously resisted by Rome. Representatives of the pope in Constantinople were forced to sign the acts of the council, and in the year after the synod Justinian II sent the canons to Sergius for his signature and approval. Sergius not only refused to sign the acts, he even refused to let them be read out loud. Justinian II responded by arresting two of the pope's councillors stationed in Constantinople and by sending the commandant of his personal bodyguard, Zacharias, to Rome to arrest Sergius and bring him back to Constantinople.

Zacharias arrived in Rome to an extremely inhospitable welcome. Before Zacharias' arrival, Sergius had appealed to the exarch for assistance, and troops were sent from Ravenna to Rome. Though Zacharias managed to corner the pope in the Lateran, he in turn became the hunted. The troops from Ravenna, aided by the Pentapolis and Roman citizens, stormed the Lateran and pursued Zacharias. The commandant of the bodyguard fled in terror from his pursuers and ended up hiding under Sergius' bed in the papal apartments. Sergius was then forced to plead with the people for the life of Zacharias, who was arrested and forced to leave the city. This humiliating defeat for Justinian II would have precipitated serious consequences for Sergius, but the former was himself deposed within two years by Leontius. The major result of the incident was that it served to deepen the existing gulf between the Eastern and Western churches. Since that time, the only response of the Papacy to the Trullan Synod has been tacit approval of the canons for the Eastern church.

Sergius promulgated relations of an entirely different ilk with the Western church. The first major event in the papacy of Sergius concerning the Western churches occurred in 689 on the vigil of Easter. On that date he baptized Caedwalla, the once-pagan King of the West Saxons. Caedwalla, "the strongarmed," had been converted the year before by Saint Wilfrid, whereupon he abandoned his kingship and made the royal pilgrimage to Rome. Caedwalla died only ten days after his baptism by Sergius, who ordered the remains of this notable convert to be buried on the grounds of Saint Peter's itself.

Another well-known Englishman who visited Sergius was the abbot Aldhelm, who was later appointed Bishop of Sherburne by Sergius. Aldhelm was the founder of Malmesbury Abbey and had visited Sergius in order to gain a charter of privilege for the abbey. The charter, which placed the monasteries of Malmesbury and Frome under the immediate jurisdiction of Rome, was granted by Sergius and greatly fortified the power of Rome over the English churches. Sometime around 700, Sergius ordered Saint Wilfrid to be restored to the See of York as bishop. Sergius also approved of the appointment of Brithwald, as the successor of Saint Theodore, to be Bishop of Canterbury.

Connections between Rome and England were further strengthened by Sergius when he authorized the missionary work to the Continent of Saint

Willibrord. Willibrord had trained at the monastery of Saint Wilfrid in Ireland and went as a missionary in 691 to Frisia, a country which lay between the Rhine and the Elbe. After four successful years in that country he was sent to Rome and was consecrated Bishop of the Frisians by Sergius. Inspired by the achievements of Willibrord, Sergius sent Saint Chilian and Saint Swibert to do further missionary work in Germany.

Toward the end of his tenure as pope, Sergius was active in rectifying the schism of Aquileia. This schismatic group, in existence since the condemnation of the "Three Chapters" by Vigilius in 553, consisted of a collection of suffragan bishops under the leadership of the Patriarch of Aquileia, in northern Italy. In order to bring about a rectification of the schism, the King of the Lombards, Cunibert, invited the schismatic bishops to a synod at Pavia. The council was an overwhelming success, and the renegade sect was brought back into the Catholic fold. After the reunion, Sergius commanded that all the works of the schismatic sect be burned to ward off the possibility of ideological contamination.

During the closing days of Sergius' reign, monks were sent to him by Saint Ceolfrid from the monasteries of Saint Peter and Saint Paul (of Wearmouth in England) in order to secure yet another charter for English monasteries. The pope gave his approval to the monasteries and, more important, learned from these men of the great erudition of their fellow monk Bede. Bede would later become known as the greatest historian of early England. Sergius later requested Bede's presence in Rome to help solve certain problems. Unfortunately, Sergius died shortly afterward and Bede never made the pilgrimage.

Sergius' early musical talent was not wasted during his reign as pope. An alumnus of the Schola Cantorum, he was an accomplished singer. Most important, he was responsible for the introduction of the singing of the Agnus Dei into the Mass. He also introduced the practice of making processions to the various churches on the feasts of the Virgin Mary (the Nativity, the Annunciation, the Purification, and the Assumption).

Throughout his tenure as pope, Sergius was active in restoring the churches of Rome, including Saint Peter's, Saint Paul's, and his own church of Santa Susanna. He is reported to have discovered a small silver box hidden in the sacristy of Saint Peter's which contains a portion of the "true cross," embedded on a jeweled cross. This relic is used in the feast of the Exaltation of the Cross, initiated by Sergius himself.

Summary

Sergius died in 701 and was buried in Saint Peter's. The cult of his sainthood began shortly after his death, and his life is celebrated by Catholics on September 8. During his lifetime, he developed a reputation for exceptional piety. Though Sergius was ineffective in bringing the Eastern and Western churches together, he was important in extending the influence of the Church in the West, especially in England. In addition, he was successful in helping to bring about an end to the schism that had split the church of Italy. Most important, however, was his successful resistance to the attempts of the Eastern emperors to achieve hegemonic control of the Church.

It has often been argued that the popes of this time acquired temporal power through the strength of their own vaulting ambitions. This claim is clearly false where Sergius is concerned. He could hardly have been ambitious to become pope in the first place; indeed, one almost gets the impression that he became pope against his will.

Bibliography

Mann, Horace K. *The Lives of the Popes in the Early Middle Ages.* Vol. 2. Reprint. Wilmington, N.C.: Consortium Books, 1980. Contains a chapter devoted to the life of Sergius. Very important for an understanding of the general era in which Sergius lived and of the lives of the popes who came immediately before and after him.

Richards, Jeffrey. *The Popes and the Papacy in the Early Middle Ages, 476-752.* London: Routledge and Kegan Paul, 1979. Innovative analysis of the social, economic, and political factors affecting the evolution of the Papacy in its early days.

Schnürer, Gustav. *Church and Culture in the Middle Ages.* Vol. 1, *350-814.* Translated by George J. Undreiner. Paterson, N.J.: St. Anthony Guild Press, 1956. Meticulous study of the influence of the Church on the secular pursuit of material happiness and intellectual mastery of the world. Written from a philosophical point of view.

Ullmann, Walter. *The Growth of Papal Government in the Middle Ages.* 3d ed. London: Methuen and Co., 1970. A study of the factors contributing to and hindering the evolution of papal government. Focuses especially upon the relation between church and state. Important discussion of Sergius' role in the Trullan Synod.

_____. *A Short History of the Papacy in the Middle Ages.* London: Methuen and Co., 1972. A more general study by the foremost authority in the field. Focuses primarily upon the Papacy, very little on individual popes. Good discussion of the influence of the Papacy throughout Europe. Enormous bibliography.

Mark Pestana

SESOSTRIS III

Born: Date unknown; place unknown
Died: 1843 B.C.; place unknown
Area of Achievement: Government
Contribution: Sesostris' egocentric nature inspired him to be the first king of ancient Egypt to pursue a truly imperialistic policy, conducting war in the Levant and extending Egypt's southern border. His lasting impact was on Egypt's social structure, where he eliminated the vestiges of the indigenous nobility.

Early Life

Sesostris III is commonly considered the son of Sesostris II, who ruled from 1897 to 1878 B.C., and Queen Nefertiti II, but his origins are not certain. The same uncertainty concerns a possible coregency with the latter, for which there is no indisputable evidence. It is assumed that he became King of Egypt in 1878 B.C. and ruled until 1843 B.C., although the latest attested year of his reign is the year 19. Sesostris adopted the official name Netjery-kheperu.

Life's Work

Nothing is known about Sesostris' life prior to his ascent, or about events during the early years of his reign. The earliest preserved inscription dates from his fifth year of rule. It was found in Ezbet el-Saghira, in Egypt's northeastern delta. This find is not isolated; other material relating to Sesostris has been discovered in the same region. A seated statue of the king was found at Tell Nebesheh, in addition to material at Qantir, Bubastis, and Tanis. These finds may indicate the concern of Sesostris with Egypt's northeastern border.

Yet Sesostris' interests did not end at this border. There is a report about a military campaign by a follower of Sesostris named Khu-Sobek, leading to the capture of a region called Sekemem. This region has been identified with Shekhem (biblical Sichem), but because a deep military penetration into Palestine lacks substantiation, this identification has been disputed.

That there was a concerted political interest in the Levant during the reign of Sesostris is suggested by the considerable number of Egyptian objects found in the Levant, namely at Megiddo and Gezer, which date to Sesostris' reign. These objects probably reflect diplomatic rather than military activity. Such an evaluation is supported by a group of Egyptian texts commonly labeled "Execration Texts." These texts consist of magical incantations pronounced to influence the chiefs in a wide range of city-states in Palestine and Syria. Although their political effectiveness could be questioned, they display an astounding familiarity with the political situation in the Levant at the time. The claim in a hymn to Sesostris that "his words control the Asiatics" also points to the influence of Sesostris on the affairs of Syria and Palestine by diplomatic means rather than by military interference.

Egypt's interests in the exploration of the mineral resources of the Sinai Peninsula seem to have been a major force in the political contacts to the East. During the reign of Sesostris, mining in Serabit el-khadim on Sinai's western side was limited. Further, no addition to the local sanctuary of the goddess Hathor was constructed during his reign. During the ensuing reign of Amenemhet III, the Sinai mines were extensively explored. This exploration was probably a result of Sesostris' influence on the Levant scene.

The chief military activity of Sesostris was directed southward against Nubia and was specifically intended to gain control over the area of the Nile's Second Cataract. Four campaigns by the king are attested by inscriptions, namely in the eighth, tenth, sixteenth, and nineteenth years of his reign. There is no indication that this military activity was in response to any prior aggression or danger. Instead, it seems that Sesostris embarked on the campaigning for imperialistic goals and personal vainglory. At that time, Egyptian authority extended as far south as the northern end of the Second Cataract, where the fortress of Buhen (opposite modern Wadi Halfa) guarded the border. The very inhospitable terrain of the cataract region appears to have been scarcely populated, but south of it was an important Nubian state with Kerma as its center. Apparently, Sesostris aspired to subdue it and to incorporate it into his realm, goals which he ultimately failed to achieve.

Major preparations preceded the first campaign in the eighth year of his reign. In order to move troops and equipment southward, a canal more than two hundred feet long, seventy-five feet wide, and twenty-two feet deep was cut through the rocks forming the First Cataract. Sesostris met with fierce resistance, and the advance proved much more difficult than anticipated. Although the king directed the campaign in person, the proclaimed goal "to overthrow the wretched Kush" turned out to be a more difficult task than the repelling of nomadic tribesmen. At least three more campaigns followed. As a result of these military efforts, Egypt's southern frontier was pushed some forty miles southward, but it did not advance into the fertile stretch beyond. At strategically dominating places, Sesostris had fortresses built on either side of the Nile River, specifically at Semna (Heh) and Kumna, to shield the dearly won frontier. An inscription there states the king's political principles:

> Southern boundary made in the Year 8 under the majesty of the King of Upper and Lower Egypt Sesostris, may he be given life forever, in order to prevent any Nubian from crossing it by water or by land, with a ship or any herd, except a Nubian who shall come to do trading at Yken or with a commission. Every good thing shall be done to them, but without allowing a ship of Nubians to pass by Heh going north—forever.

The conquest itself held hardly any advantages, except as a potential bridgehead for later operations. The resistance it encountered prevented those plans from succeeding, an indication that a state of considerable military power opposed Sesostris' expansionist efforts.

By his sixteenth year in power, Sesostris apparently realized the futility of his aspirations and decided to make the frontier permanent at Semna and Kumna. Despite his limited success, he announced it as a great personal achievement:

> Every successor of mine shall maintain this boundary which my majesty has made—he is my son born to my majesty. He who shall abandon it and shall not fight for it—he is not my son, he is not born to me.
>
> My majesty had a statue of my majesty set up at this boundary which my majesty made in order that one might stay with it and in order that one fight for it.

The egocentric attitude of Sesostris is clearly apparent in these lines. Indeed, Sesostris was the first king of ancient Egypt to receive worship as a god during his lifetime; this divinization, however, was limited to Nubia. Three hundred years later, Thutmose III erected a temple for him at Semna as the "god of Nubia." Sesostris' personality left its lasting mark on Egypt proper. Few monuments of him, however, are preserved; they are especially scarce in Middle Egypt. Sesostris favored the temple of Osiris at Abydos and was also active at Thebes.

During Sesostris' reign, all traces of the indigenous nobility of Egypt disappeared. There are no texts expounding a specific policy, but from the results there can be no question that Sesostris intended to be the sole Egyptian leader, eliminating any potential competition. His methods remain obscure, but the possibility of forced exile is likely. While Sesostris streamlined the social structure by enforcing one single center, the disappearance of the hereditary nobility had its dangers. As long as a strong personality occupied the throne, the affairs of Egypt prospered. When such a ruler was lacking, however, there was nobody in the society to provide the leadership necessary to keep the ship of state on course. It is fitting that fifty-seven years after Sesostris' death the political structures disintegrated rapidly.

Sesostris had a large mud-brick pyramid built at Dahshûr. Attached to it are the burial places for the members of the royal family. From these tombs come some stunning jewelry, a part of which is housed in the Metropolitan Museum of Art. Later traditions adopted Sesostris as a legendary hero, and stories about him were related by Herodotus and Diodorus. The stories conflate some of his exploits with those of other kings, especially Ramses II, to a romantic quasi history.

Summary

While Sesostris III was unquestionably an exceptionally strong personality on the throne of Egypt, his excessive ego brought not only blessings but also potential dangers. He demonstrated military determination unparalleled by any earlier king and opened the conquest of Upper Nubia. By concentrating the social structure exclusively on himself and eliminating the indigenous nobility, he initiated the transformation of Egypt from a conservative, traditional society into a politically motivated populace.

Bibliography

Adams, William Yewdale. *Nubia: Corridor to Africa*. Princeton, N.J.: Princeton University Press, 1977. Primarily concerns Egypt's advance into Nubia. Contains twelve pages of illustrations, bibliographic references, and an index.

Delia, Robert D. *A Study of the Reign of Senwosret III*. Ann Arbor, Mich.: University Microfilms International, 1980. This volume is the only comprehensive study of Sesostris' reign. It covers all of its aspects and discusses the available sources in detail.

Gardiner, Alan. *Egypt of the Pharaohs*. Oxford: Oxford University Press, 1961. A fine general account of the history of ancient Egypt. Includes a short bibliography, some illustrations, and an index.

Hayes, William C. "The Middle Kingdom in Egypt." In *The Cambridge Ancient History*, edited by I. E. Edwards, C. J. Gadd, and N. G. L. Hammond. Vol. 1, *Early History of the Middle East*. 3d ed. Cambridge: Cambridge University Press, 1971. A thorough discussion not only of one reign but also of the political tendencies of the time.

Lichtheim, Miriam. *Ancient Egyptian Literature: A Book of Readings*. Berkeley: University of California Press, 1973. Contains good translations of two major pieces of writing concerning Sesostris. Includes bibliographic references.

Hans Goedicke

SHAPUR II

Born: c. 309; Iran
Died: 379; Iran
Areas of Achievement: Government and warfare
Contribution: Shapur was one of the greatest rulers of the Sassanid Dynasty in pre-Islamic Iran. Succeeding to the throne after a period of internal confusion, he restored the fortunes of the Sassanid Empire and extended its frontiers in all directions.

Early Life
Shapur II was the eighth in the long line of rulers of the Sassanid Dynasty, which dominated much of the Middle East between 224 and 651. The first two Sassanid shahs (kings), Ardashir I and Shapur I, descendants of hereditary priests of the Zoroastrian fire temple at Istakhr in the southwestern Iranian province of Fars, replaced the disintegrating rule of the Parthians with an aggressive military monarchy based on domination of the Plateau of Iran and expansion outward in all directions. In the east, the Sassanids advanced deep into Afghanistan as far as the land near the upper Indus River. To the northeast, they crossed the Amu Darya River and the Hisar range in what is now the Soviet Union. In the northwest, they claimed overlordship in Armenia, Iberia, and Albania (areas corresponding to the modern Armenian, Georgian, and Azerbaijani Soviet Socialist Republics). In the west, they disputed hegemony with the Romans over upper Mesopotamia, between the Tigris and Euphrates rivers (the conjunction of modern Turkey, Iraq, and Syria). Shapur I enjoyed spectacular successes over three Roman emperors, celebrated in his bas-reliefs at Naqsh-i Rustam and Bishapur: Gordianus III, who was murdered by his troops in 244 while campaigning against the Sassanids; Philip the Arabian, who was compelled to negotiate a humiliating peace; and Valerian, who was taken prisoner by Shapur after a battle near Edessa in 260 and who died in captivity.

Ardashir and Shapur I ruled over an empire of diverse races, religions, and languages; from their Parthian predecessors they inherited a situation of regional fragmentation, a society Iranologists refer to as "feudal." The first two Sassanid shahs recognized the pluralistic composition of their empire, but they were determined to crush the independence of the feudal nobility. They wanted to establish a highly centralized autocracy in which the Shahanshah (King of Kings) shone with a refulgence derived from his being endowed with the unique qualities of *farr* (the divine favor reserved for monarchs) and *hvarna* (the charisma of kingship).

Following Shapur I's death in 272, his immediate successors failed to maintain the momentum: A series of short-lived, unimpressive rulers allowed the army to deteriorate, and the Romans counterattacked with vigor. In 283,

Emperor Carus advanced to within sight of the walls of Ctesiphon, the Sassanid metropolis near modern Baghdad. His successor, Diocletian (c. 245-316), then determined to stabilize Rome's eastern frontiers by constructing limes (a defensive line of forts and earthworks) from the great bend of the Euphrates northward into Armenia, the traditional bone of contention between Romans and Iranians. As a result, war broke out, and in the ensuing campaigns the Iranians fared badly. On one occasion, the family of Narses, the shah, fell into Roman hands, together with a large booty. By the Peace of Nisibis of 298, Narses was forced to relinquish not only upper Mesopotamia between the Tigris and Euphrates but also territory on the east bank of the Tigris; all trade between the two empires was to go through Nisibis, and Armenia passed definitively into the Roman sphere of influence, to which it tended to be drawn anyway, as a consequence of the Armenian king's adoption of Christianity around 303.

With the death of Hormizd II, a grandson of Shapur I, in 309 the imperial line appeared to have ended, but a ray of hope lay with a pregnant wife or concubine of the late ruler. Tradition has it that the future Shapur II was designated shah while still in his mother's womb by the crown being placed on her belly. In another version of the story, the high priest sat the woman upon the throne, a diadem was held over her head, and gold coins were poured into the crown. The events of Shapur's long reign are fairly well documented in Latin, Syriac, and Arabic sources, although there is a dearth of source material in Middle Persian. Moreover, later Arabic and Persian accounts, although quite detailed, have a tendency to confuse happenings in the reign of Shapur II with those in the reign of Shapur I.

Of Shapur II's early years nothing is known. The first third of his reign was probably spent learning the business of government, consolidating the royal authority, and taming the habitually turbulent nobility. Such campaigning as there was occurred on the exposed Arabian marches of the empire, where Bedouin raiders penetrated the prosperous agricultural settlements of lower Mesopotamia and perhaps even threatened Ctesiphon. One solution to the problem was to construct defensive lines similar to the Roman limes, with which the Iranians were already acquainted in upper Mesopotamia, but Shapur also resorted to a "forward policy" of punitive expeditions. There may be more than a grain of truth in late accounts of the shah leading his handpicked warriors, mounted on racing dromedaries, into the fastnesses of the Arabian Desert, but it is probable that he campaigned against the Ghassanid Arab clients of the Romans in the direction of Syria rather than, as much later traditions assert, crossing the central plateau to attack Yathrib (modern Medina) or to invade Yemen. More plausible are references to Arab piratical raids upon the coastline of Fars which prompted Shapur to send out a naval expedition to raid the island of Bahrain and the mainland behind it.

Life's Work

During the first thirty years of Shapur's life, roughly coinciding with the long reign of Constantine the Great (306-337), Rome was the dominant power on the frontier, but in 337 the accession of Constantius II, who controlled only the eastern provinces and whose future seemed uncertain, signified a change. At the same time, in Armenia, a party among the Armenian nobles opposed to the recent Christianization of the kingdom expelled their ruler and turned to Iran for assistance. Shapur took the field and, crossing the Tigris, besieged Nisibis in 338 (but without success), while the Romans forcibly reinstated the Armenian king. For the next decade or more, an undeclared peace settled on the western frontier, broken by sporadic border forays, while the shah campaigned in the East.

Since the time of Ardashir, the former Kushan territories of Bactria (north of the Hindu Kush Mountains, in Afghanistan), Sogdiana (beyond the Amu Darya River), and Gandhara (in eastern Afghanistan and the upper Indus country) had been ruled by Sassanid governors, probably a cadet line of the royal house, who used the title of Kushanshah (King of the Kushans). During the 340's, this arrangement seems to have broken down, perhaps as a result of a steady flow of nomads into these regions from the steppes to the north.

This nomadic influx diverted Shapur's attention from the West, and it may have been partly the fear of an attack from that quarter while he was preoccupied in the East that prompted him to order the systematic persecution of his Christian subjects, a campaign which had begun in 337 at the time of his first confrontation with Rome. The reason for this policy lay in Constantine's adoption of Christianity for the Roman Empire, some two decades after the Christianization of Armenia. Thus Shapur viewed the Christian communities in the Sassanid Empire as a fifth column which would rise up in support of their coreligionists in the event of the Romans' breaking into the Iranian homeland. He may also have undertaken this policy with the idea of endearing himself to the intolerant Zoroastrian priesthood. Certainly, the persecution, ferocious in the extreme, ended the notion that the Sassanid Empire was a kind of religious melting pot, for at this time, Manichaeans and Jews were also exposed to harassment (although less severe than that experienced by Christians). In the course of the persecutions, the ancient city of Susa in southwestern Iran, which sheltered a Christian see and a large Christian population, revolted. It was, therefore, razed, and several hundred war elephants were brought in to help with the demolition.

In 350, Shapur returned to the offensive in the West. Constantius was embroiled in civil wars, while in Armenia, Tigranes V had been pursuing a crooked policy of playing off Rome against Iran. Shapur, exasperated by his double-dealing, now had him seized and executed, replacing him with Tigranes' son, Arshak II. Meanwhile, the shah planned to besiege Nisibis.

Shapur II

Once more, the prize eluded him. This time, a looming crisis in the East demanded his immediate presence there. The former penetration of the eastern provinces by nomadic bands had given way to the threat of all-out invasion by a people who appear in the sources as "Chionites." This nomadic confederacy probably consisted of a majority of people of Iranian stock led by a ruling elite of Huns, who now make their appearance in Iranian history for the first time. Several years of hard campaigning against the Chionites resulted in their defeat in 356 and, in the following year, their submission as tributaries of the empire.

With the East now pacified, Shapur turned to the West again and in 359 undertook the siege of the great fortress of Amida (modern Diyarbakir, in Turkey) on the upper Tigris. The fighting went on for seventy-three days before the final, successful assault. The Roman historian Ammianus Marcellinus watched from the battlements as "the king himself, mounted upon a charger and overtopping the others, rode before the whole army, wearing in place of a diadem a golden image of a ram's head set with precious stones...." Yet a leading scholar has hypothesized recently that Ammianus Marcellinus was mistaken, since Shapur wore a different headdress, and that the wearer of the ram's head was another Kushanshah, who was serving as an auxiliary to his overlord. Early in the course of the siege, the son of Grumbates, the Chionite ruler, was killed, and after his body had been burned in accordance with Hunnish custom, his father demanded vengeance. The city was then closely besieged. The Iranian contingents were deployed on every side. Of the allies, the Chionites were on the east, the Gelani (tribesmen from Gilan and Mazandaran in northern Iran) were on the south, the Albanians (from modern Soviet Azerbaijan) were on the north, and the Sakas (from Seistan in eastern Iran) were on the west. Ammianus Marcellinus wrote: "With them, making a lofty show, slowly marched the lines of elephants, frightful with their wrinkled bodies and loaded with armed men, a hideous spectacle, dreadful beyond every form of horror...."

Eventually, Amida fell, after heavy casualties on both sides. It was to be Shapur's supreme triumph. In the following year, more cities in upper Mesopotamia were taken by the Iranians, but thereafter the fighting seems to have entered a desultory phase which continued until Emperor Julian (361-363) resolved to restore Rome's fortunes in the East. Julian moved swiftly. He traversed Mesopotamia virtually unopposed to within sight of the walls of Ctesiphon, the Iranians preferring not to give battle and adopting a "scorched earth" strategy. Julian was killed in a skirmish, and his successor, Jovian (363-364), was eager to extract his forces at minimal cost. Shapur obtained possession of Nisibis at last, together with all upper Mesopotamia, and Rome abandoned its protectorate over Armenia. Arshak II, who had initially demonstrated commitment to the Iranian connection, had long since proved himself duplicitous, openly aligning himself with the Romans at the time of Julian's campaign. Now, he was abandoned to the wrath of his erstwhile overlord, who had him seized and held captive until his death (c. 367).

By then, however, Shapur had systematically ravaged Armenia, deporting thousands of captives, who were redistributed throughout the empire during the course of a campaign which also took him into Iberia (that is, modern Georgia), where he expelled a Roman client ruler and installed his own candidate (c. 365). The emperor Valens reacted to this humiliation by sending troops into both Armenia and Iberia to restore the status quo. In Iberia, the country was now divided between two kings, both bearing the same name—one was a puppet of Rome, the other a puppet of Iran.

In Armenia, the Romans installed Pap, the son of Arshak II, as king. As with other Armenian kings, however, Pap could not resist the temptation of seeking to play one power off against the other. At various times between 370 and 374, he seems to have entered into negotiations with Shapur which probably included some kind of submission. Getting wind of Pap's treachery, Valens summoned him to Tarsus to answer charges of treason, but he escaped and made his way back to Armenia, where he was subsequently assassinated at a banquet given by local Roman commanders.

Pap was replaced by a kinsman, Varazdat, whom a considerable section of the Armenian nobility was unwilling to acknowledge, while Shapur refused to recognize his accession and sent troops to oust him. With the Goths in the Balkans threatening Adrianople, Valens needed a speedy settlement of the eastern frontier. Thus some kind of arrangement was negotiated between the two great powers around 377, although the sources do not specify the existence of a peace treaty at that time. Armenia was *de facto*, if not *de jure*, partitioned, the greater part of the country passing under Iranian control. Thus, Shapur had attained a major objective of Sassanid rulers: Armenia and Iberia were partitioned into spheres of influence, and with Albania tributary, Iran dominated almost the entire region between the Caspian Sea and the Black Sea. After Shapur's death, a formal treaty between Iran and Rome during the reign of Shapur III (383-388) regularized the previous partition arrangements regarding Armenia. Then, when the king of Iranian Armenia died in 392, Bahram IV installed his own brother, Vramshapuh, on the throne, while Roman Armenia was formally integrated into the Roman provincial administration.

Little is known regarding the internal conditions of Iran during the time of Shapur II, but the evidence suggests that he vigorously pursued his predecessors' goals of curbing the power of the nobility. The favors which he lavished upon the Zoroastrian priesthood (to which may be added his relentless persecution of the Christians) were probably intended to secure the support of this influential class. Yet in the course of helping to create an official Zoroastrian state church, well endowed, privileged, and powerful, he also ensured that it was firmly under the control of the Shahanshah.

Shapur II

Like his namesake, Shapur I, Shapur II played an active role in promoting new urban centers and in restoring older foundations which had been languishing. Thus, he enlarged the city of Gundeshapur in Khuzestan (southwestern Iran), originally built by Shapur I's Roman prisoners, where he founded the university, observatory, and medical school which were to become so famous in the early Islamic period. Having carried out the destruction of Susa around 350, he ordered an entirely new city to be constructed nearby, known as Iran-khwarra Shapur (Shapur's fortune of Iran), while another city, Iranshahr-Shapur, often referred to by its Aramaic name of Karkha de Ledan, was founded upstream from Susa. He also rebuilt Nishapur (or Niv-Shapur, meaning "the good deed of Shapur").

Summary

The reign of Shapur II marks one of the climactic phases of Sassanid rule. With the frontiers of his empire stretching from Diyarbakir in the west to Kabul in the east and from the Caucasus Mountains to the southern shores of the Persian Gulf, with his effective—if brutal—subjugation of all internal elements which seemed to challenge his autocratic exercise of power, and with his tight grip upon the Zoroastrian church, Shapur II must be rated as one of the most successful of all Sassanid monarchs. At his death, he was succeeded by Ardashir II, whose relationship to him is a matter of dispute but who was probably his son.

In the light of Shapur II's long reign, it is surprising that so few major monuments have survived from this period. One of the six bas-reliefs carved in the gorge at Bishapur in Fars known as "Bishapur VI," has been widely attributed to him, although some scholars have identified it with Shapur I. Those who believe that it dates from Shapur II's reign have variously interpreted it as commemorating a victory over Kushan, Roman, or even internal Iranian foes, while a recent study claims that it represents the submission of Pap.

The surviving sources do not allow for much speculation about the personality of Shapur II, although the known facts point to a ruler of great energy, ambition, and pride. Like those of most Sassanid rulers, his profile can be readily identified on coins, seals, and metal objects by virtue of a distinctive crown. Shapur's crown consists of the characteristic *korymbos* (a balloon-shaped bun of hair wrapped in a fine cloth and perhaps symbolizing the terrestrial or celestial globe) above a tiara of stepped crenellations with long ribbons billowing out behind. Several formal representations of him survive in the royal hunting scenes which decorate ceremonial silver dishes. One of the finest of these shows the shah in profile, mounted, turning about in his saddle to shoot a springing lion, while a second lion is being trampled beneath his horse's hooves. He wears a tunic and the baggy pantaloons favored by other Iranian peoples, his long, straight sword hangs loosely from his belt, and he draws the typical compound bow of the steppe peoples, the weapon so feared by the Romans and other adversaries of the Iranians. As with all Sassanid art, including a remarkable silver-overlay head attributed to Shapur II in the Metropolitan Museum of Art in New York, the expression is highly stylized but proclaims calm concentration, fearlessness, and regal dignity, attributes which fit well with what is known of Shapur II.

Bibliography
Ammianus Marcellinus. *Res gestae*. Translated by John C. Rolfe. 3 vols. Cambridge, Mass.: Harvard University Press, 1935-1939. Sometimes described as the last classical historian of the Roman Empire, Ammianus Marcellinus served in the Iranian campaigns of Constantius and Julian and was an eyewitness at the siege of Amida. His history includes a topographical description of the Sassanid Empire, as well as an account of contemporary Iranian manners and customs.
Azarpay, Guitty. "Bishapur VI: An Artistic Record of an Armeno-Persian Alliance in the Fourth Century." *Artibus Asiae* 43 (1981-1982): 171-189. An absorbing discussion of the Bishapur bas-relief attributed to Shapur II, identifying the scene as representing the submission of Pap to the Sassanid shah.
Bivar, Adrian David Hugh. *Catalogue of the Western Asiatic Seals in the British Museum*. London: British Museum Publications, 1962. For the student of the Sassanid period, this book is essential for understanding Sassanid iconography.
_____. "The History of Eastern Iran." In *The Cambridge History of Iran*, edited by Ehsan Yarshater, vol. 3. Cambridge: Cambridge University Press, 1983. This chapter, by one of the leading authorities on the eastern Iranian lands in pre-Islamic times, is essential for elucidating the still-obscure relations of the Sassanid shahs with their Kushan, Chionite, and Ephthalite neighbors.
Frye, Richard N. "The Political History of Iran Under the Sasanians." In *The Cambridge History of Iran*, edited by Ehsan Yarshater, vol. 3. Cambridge: Cambridge University Press, 1983. Recommended as the best account in English of the reign of Shapur II within the overall setting of Sassanid rule, by one of the leading scholars in the field. For an alternative, see the same author's *The History of Ancient Iran* (1984).
Ghirshman, Roman. *Iran, Parthians and Sassanians*. London: Thames and Hudson, 1962. The best general account of Sassanid art, magnificently illustrated. An additional strength of this book is that it relates artistic developments on the Iranian plateau to those in adjoining regions of Afghanistan and Central Asia.
Göbl, Robert. "Sasanian Coins." In *The Cambridge History of Iran*, edited by Ehsan Yarshater, vol. 3. Cambridge: Cambridge University Press, 1983.

In Göbl's own words, "this coinage is an invaluable source of information about the history, culture, and economic life of the Sasanian state." Easily the best introduction to the subject.

Harper, Prudence O. *The Royal Hunter: Art of the Sasanian Empire*. New York: Asia Society, 1978. This exhibition catalog illustrates well the range of Sassanid craftsmanship and includes a photograph of the silver-overlay head in the Metropolitan Museum of Art attributed to Shapur II.

Herrmann, Georgina. *The Making of the Past: The Iranian Revival*. Oxford: Elsevier-Phaidon, 1977. Beyond any doubt, the best general introduction to the Sassanid period, accompanied by fine illustrations. Written by an acknowledged authority on Sassanid bas-reliefs.

Whitehouse, David, and Andrew Williamson. "Sasanian Maritime Trade." *Iran: Journal of the British Institute of Persian Studies* 11 (1973): 29-49. An interesting discussion of a little known aspect of Sassanid history, prefaced by an account of Shapur II's activities in the Persian Gulf.

Gavin R. G. Hambly

SHŌTOKU TAISHI

Born: 573; Honshu, Japan
Died: 621; Kauga, Honshu, Japan
Areas of Achievement: Government and religion
Contribution: As regent for his aunt, Empress Suiko, Shōtoku is credited with strengthening the central government, solidifying the rule of the imperial family, and transforming Japan's civilization through adoption of Confucian and Buddhist institutions and values.

Early Life

Little is known about Shōtoku Taishi's life; what is recorded is more legend than fact. *Nihongi* (*Nihongi: Chronicles of Japan from the Earliest Times to* A.D. *697*, 1896), completed in 720, describes stages and events in Shōtoku's life, beginning with a wondrous birth. His mother, the Empress-consort, was walking near the imperial stables when she suddenly gave birth. Shōtoku was "able to speak at once and grew up so wise that he could listen to and understand ten men's petitions simultaneously and decide their cases without error."

Son of Emperor Yōmei, Shōtoku rose to eminence in a time of intense political rivalry among several clans. Among these, the Yamato clan, claiming divine descent, was accepted as the imperial line by the fifth century, while the Soga and the Mononobe contended for the position closest to the throne. Interwoven with their political strife were disagreements over a newly arrived faith, Buddhism.

In 582—some sources have it as early as 538—the King of Paekche in Korea sent the emperor an image of Buddha along with scriptures and a letter recommending the worship of Buddha to bring blessings and prosperity upon Japan. He had a twofold reason for his action: As a devoted Buddhist, he wanted to propagate Buddhist teachings and, as a ruler faced with powerful enemies, he hoped for an alliance with Japan. The Japanese court was favorable to the new religion, but it asked the other clans for advice regarding its final acceptance or rejection. (In his youth, Shōtoku studied under a Korean Buddhist monk as well as a Confucian scholar—indicative of the court's openness to foreign culture.) The Soga and Mononobe took opposite sides in the ensuing dispute. Under its chieftain, Soga Umako, the Soga and its allies defeated the Mononobe in battle and, by 587, Buddhism's status in Japan was secure. It would become a major vehicle for Soga Umako and Shōtoku in their joint efforts to strengthen Japan politically and culturally.

Life's Work

Soga Umako placed his niece Suiko on the throne in 595—some sources have it 592—and arranged that she appoint Shōtoku regent. Shōtoku married Umako's daughter, thus cementing an already close relationship. According to *Nihongi*, Shōtoku "had general control of the government, and was entrusted with all the details of the administration." For almost thirty years, the two men collaborated to establish a strong central government.

Nihongi, written at a time when the Soga were out of favor and power, credits Shōtoku with major achievements between 592 and 622. In book 22, two political moves by Shōtoku are listed: initiation of a twelve-cap system of court ranks and authorship of a seventeen-article constitution. The twelve-cap system was an innovation in that, at least theoretically, offices would be based on personal merit rather than on privileged class. In actuality, the new system, begun in 603, was primarily a means of distinguishing ranks by means of different cap patterns and colors. Shōtoku was concerned with creating a well-developed bureaucracy, dependent on the emperor's will. Lineage remained very important in obtaining office, however, as it would well into the twentieth century.

Historians disagree over authorship of the seventeen-article constitution. Nevertheless, *Nihongi* states that in 604 Shōtoku prepared the constitution as the fundamental law of the land. It was a set of moral and political principles, combining Buddhist and Confucian concepts and values. As did Buddhism, Confucianism came to Japan through Korea—long a channel of Chinese culture to Japan.

In the fourth century, around 368-369, Japanese troops had invaded Korea, establishing a colony, Mimana, on the southern tip of the peninsula. In addition to the colony, three Korean states vied for dominance from the fourth to the seventh century: Silla, Paekche, and Koguryo. Silla gradually overthrew her rivals—Mimana in 562, Paekche in 663, and Koguryo in 668, unifying Korea. The flow of refugees to Japan was at its height during the seventh century. Korean and Chinese immigrants brought with them continental culture, contributing many skills and much wealth to Japanese clans wherever they settled.

During its Sui Dynasty (581-616), China was seen by Japan's leaders as a powerful nation, highly developed politically and culturally. Even pre-Sui, Chinese histories record Japanese missions to China. Although there had been missions during the first and second centuries, these remained sporadic, unlike the more sustained ones of the seventh through the ninth centuries. Clan chiefs were eager to select Chinese ideas and institutions which would strengthen the imperial line and their own power within the socioeconomic hierarchy. Umako and Shōtoku further believed that adopting Chinese institutions would help unify Japan and raise its cultural level. During Shōtoku's regency, at least three embassies were sent to China—in 600, 607, and 608. The Sui emperor responded with an embassy in 608. Japan was aiming not only at emulating China but also at becoming her equal.

Chinese influence is readily apparent in the seventeen-article constitution.

Its first three articles give basic principles of government, while the remaining fourteen give practical guidelines for efficient functioning of the government: Value harmony; reverence the "Three Treasures" (Buddha, the law, the monks); obey imperial commands; behave decorously; deal impartially with all cases; chastise the evil and encourage the good; fit the right man to the office; attend court early, retire late; observe good faith with one another; cease from wrath and learn from others; deal out sure reward and punishment; the government alone levies taxes; officials attend to their functions; avoid envy; prefer public good to private; employ the people in [forced] labor at seasonable times; and consult with others on important matters.

Buddhism is specifically mentioned only in the second article. Shōtoku, although devoutly Buddhist, turned to Confucian models for guidance in reorganizing the government. Confucianism stressed cultivation of virtue and dedication to public service. These and other Confucian ideals are clearly evident in all the articles—especially articles 1, 2, 4, 9, 10, 14, 15, and 17. Some of the articles, however, are more revelatory than others about the conditions which faced Shōtoku as he began his reform. For example, articles 12, 14, and 16 address abuses prevalent at the time: arbitrary taxation by clan lords, jealousy among officials, and the corvee (forced labor). Overall, the constitution aimed at subduing the clans under the throne and unifying the nation.

Summary

Perhaps Shōtoku Taishi was, as some historians claim, a puppet of Soga Umako. Nevertheless, he is revered by the Japanese as a wise ruler who unified the nation, opened direct relations with China, and, by importing continental civilization, raised Japan's civilization to new heights. In particular, Shōtoku's promotion of Buddhism—through sponsorship of temples and temple schools, study of the scriptures, and advancement of the arts—gave Japan a rich spiritual as well as artistic foundation for future development. This borrowing from and imitation of Chinese civilization would continue into the late ninth century. Fifteen missions were sent to T'ang China (618-907) between 630 and 838.

Aided by Soga Umako, Shōtoku Taishi led Japan to a higher political and cultural plane than it had attained before his regency. A strong central government now curbed clan rivalries, and the expansion of Buddhist thought and art enriched all areas of life. The Taika Reforms, begun in 645, would continue Shōtoku's policy to bring all people directly under the power of the throne, united politically and spiritually.

Bibliography

Anesaki, Masaharu. *History of Japanese Religion*. Rutland, Vt.: Charles E.

Tuttle Co., 1963. This study begins with an explanation of Shinto and concludes with the effects of World War II on organized religion. The middle section deals with the introduction of Buddhism and its establishment in Japan. Includes a good bibliography.

_____. *Prince Shōtoku: The Sage Statesman*. Tokyo: Boonjudo Publishing House, 1948. This work is a brief biography containing legends about the prince. Includes a good analysis of Shōtoku's contributions to Japanese government and culture. Much space is given to his promotion of Buddhism and its effects on Japan.

Hane, Mikiso. *Japan: A Historical Survey*. New York: Charles Scribner's Sons, 1972. Specifically written for the nongeneralist, this work covers all areas well: political, social, cultural, intellectual, and economic. It begins with geography and the mythological beginnings of Japan. Excellent bibliography.

Hyoe, Murakami, and T. J. Harper, eds. *Great Historical Figures of Japan*. Tokyo: Japan Culture Institute, 1978. This is a collection of short essays on eminent figures from the sixth to the twentieth century. Includes an excellent analysis of Shōtoku as person and as myth.

Reischauer, Edwin O. *Japan: The Story of a Nation*. Rev. ed. New York: Alfred A. Knopf, 1974. A concise history of Japan from its beginnings to 1973. Chapter 2 is the most useful: "The Adoption of the Chinese Pattern." Includes an excellent bibliography, although quite brief.

Sansom, George. *A History of Japan*. Vol. 1, *To 1334*. Stanford, Calif.: Stanford University Press, 1958. This study begins with the origins of the Japanese and ends with the Mongol invasions. Chapter three is the most helpful: "The Yamato State." Includes a very good bibliography and helpful footnotes.

Tsunoda, Ryusaku, Wm. Theodore deBary, and Donald Keene, eds. *Sources of Japanese Tradition*. Vol. 1. New York: Columbia University Press, 1958. This collection of source readings provides the general reader with all areas of Japanese civilization from earliest history to the eighteenth century.

Varley, H. Paul. *Japanese Culture*. 3d ed. Honolulu: University of Hawaii Press, 1984. Intended for the general reader, this study covers religion, philosophy, and the arts, and connects cultural with political and institutional trends. Includes an excellent bibliography.

Carol Berg

SIGER OF BRABANT

Born: c. 1235; probably Brabant
Died: c. 1282; Orvieto
Area of Achievement: Philosophy
Contribution: By combining his mastery of Latin Averroistic philosophy with his intention to remain loyal to the institution and doctrines of the Roman Catholic church, Siger was able to help clarify the enduring questions concerning the relationship of philosophy to theology and of reason to revelation.

Early Life

Most of the details of Siger of Brabant's life, especially his early life, appear to be irretrievably lost. He was born about 1235, probably in or near the region of Brabant, in what is modern Belgium. Beyond these few sketchy facts, however, historians can only speculate.

Scholars suppose that his academic training was typical for his day. Siger's education began with the trivium, which consisted of introductory instruction in grammar, dialectic, and rhetoric. Such studies were designed not only to aid the student in speaking sense plainly and compellingly but also in speaking it beautifully. This course of study typically was followed by the quadrivium, which consisted of instruction in mathematics, music, geometry, and astronomy.

Sometime between 1255 and 1260, Siger seems to have come to the University of Paris to study in the Faculty of Arts. There he developed the philosophical prowess upon which his reputation chiefly rests. There also most of the important events in his turbulent academic career occurred. Significantly, Siger and the works of Aristotle made their way into the university at almost the same time. In those days, the university was agitated by the ancient Greek works of philosophy and science that, by means of Arab commentators and commentaries, were enjoying new prominence in the Latin-speaking world of Western intellect. Because these writings offered conclusions that were apparently well conceived and well reasoned, and because these conclusions occasionally stood at odds with Christian orthodoxy, conflict ensued.

Scholars had various responses to the problem of what relationship should exist between the newly emerging Greek thought and Christian theology. On the left were those called "the secular Aristotelians," who pursued their philosophical studies without regard to Christian doctrine. On the right were the orthodox Roman Catholic theologians such as Thomas Aquinas and his mentor, Albertus Magnus. They believed that, if properly understood, reason and revelation could not conflict. If ever they appeared to conflict, an error could be presumed either in one's philosophizing or in one's theologiz-

Siger of Brabant

ing, or both. To them, because all truth came from God, and because God could not lie, truth admitted no contradictions. With such reasonings the secularists were unconcerned. As will be seen, Siger would assume a position between the two sides and, from those two sides, would receive the severest forms of opposition, especially after the works of Aristotle were officially admitted to the university's course of study and curricular adjustment became necessary.

After approximately five years of university study, Siger received his degree. He studied at, was graduated from, and later taught at a university racked by internal dissent.

Life's Work

Siger joined the Faculty of Arts in the mid-1260's. Even though (unlike many of his colleagues) he never went on to join the theological faculty, he acted as a loyal son of the Church. Despite the fact that many of his philosophical propositions stood in opposition to received dogma, and despite the fact that he was condemned twice for erroneous teaching, Siger remained, at least in his own views, a faithful Roman Catholic.

Siger's doctrinal deviations are centered on four major ideas. First, unlike traditional views of God that pictured Him as Creator, Siger viewed God as the *primum Mobile* (or First Mover). That is, God's role in making the world was not to create it *ex nihilo* (out of nothing) but to shape it, or form it, out of a preexisting yet shapeless matter. This matter was independent of God, not created by God, and was eternal. God's role was to move upon the matter in such a way as to shape it, not to create it. Hence, He is the First Mover.

Second, as a correlative of the previous premise, Siger believed in an eternal cosmos. To him, not only was matter eternal, but so also was the world it constituted. By this Siger did not mean to say that the world is now like it always has been. The world changes; it always has changed and it always will change. Yet, of the various changes through which the world has passed, the change from nonexistence to existence, or the change from existence back to nonexistence, was not among them. To Siger, the world was eternal.

Third, Siger advocated monopsychism, or the belief that the intellect that all men share is the same and unitary. It is one and indivisible throughout the human race. It alone survives death. Thus, the phenomenon of individuality is a temporary epiphenomenon. It will prove a meaningless and unenduring contortion of personality upon the face of an underlying and undying world soul. Put differently, the world soul (or world mind), not men themselves, is immortal. The soul (or what appears to be the soul) is not one person's— much less does it constitute a human being. The individual intellect returns to the world intellect when a person dies.

Fourth, Siger advocated what is often, but mistakenly, termed "the double truth theory." Genuine "double-truthism" holds that two propositions, one philosophical and one theological, could be opposites and could both be true. This Siger did not believe. While he did affirm that what is true for reason may not necessarily be true for faith, he did not let the two ideas stand as equal opposites. When philosophical ideas and theological doctrines collided, Siger would give the palm to faith. Thus, while thinkers such as Thomas Aquinas believed that good theology and good philosophy could not conflict, Siger believed that they could. When they did, they were not considered to be both true and opposites. They were reconciled by sacrificing philosophy to theology.

For many churchmen, that sacrifice was not enough. They pressed Siger for further explanation. Siger's response was two-sided. First, Siger said that when he taught such ideas to his students he was not affirming that they were absolutely true, only that Aristotle and other philosophers affirmed them. Second, Siger professed to approach his work solely from the standpoint of reason. He said that human reason, while useful, was fallible, and that its conclusions, though perhaps philosophically unassailable, were provisional. Thus, Siger attributed these heretical ideas to past thinkers, on the one hand, and to the occasionally undependable workings of the human intellect, on the other. This defense, he believed, would exonerate him; it did not.

In 1270, Siger was condemned by Étienne Tempier, Bishop of Paris, for his unacceptable Averroistic doctrines. In spite of this condemnation, however, Siger and the other Averroists on the Faculty of Arts continued to teach their heterodox opinions in private. In 1272 they were prohibited from dealing with any theological matters. When this measure failed, all private teaching was banned.

In 1277 Siger was condemned again in an official denunciation of 219 heretical ideas, most of which were attributed to Siger and to Boethius of Dacia. As a result, Siger was summoned to appear before Simon du Val, the Inquisitor of France. He refused to appear and protested his innocence on all charges. He then appealed to the pope for protection and relief and fled to Rome. Siger never returned to Paris from his self-imposed exile in Italy. He died in about 1282, in Orvieto, where he is thought to have been assassinated by his insane secretary.

Summary

Some thinkers are important not for the conclusions they reach but for the questions they raise and the issues and conflicts that swirl around them. Siger is such a thinker. The history of Western thought has been punctuated by the persistent repetition of conflict between the advocates of faith and those of reason. Because such thinkers deal with ultimate concerns, and because opposing viewpoints on such questions are vigorously advanced and vigorously opposed, the conflict that surrounds them is varied and intense. In

Siger of Brabant

other words, Siger of Brabant's life is proof, if proof is needed, that ideas have consequences.

For Siger those consequences were often difficult and eventually tragic. Furthermore, not even at his death did the turmoil surrounding him come to a close. Both the philosophers and the theologians thought him a martyr. To the philosophers, he was a twice condemned and brutally murdered champion of philosophical and academic freedom. The theologians, by contrast, point to the tradition that late in life Siger recanted his unorthodox philosophical views and was converted to the beliefs of Thomas Aquinas. That, they argue, is the reason Dante was able not only to place Siger in Paradise but also to make him the recipient of Thomas' lavish praise. That also is the reason he died, they say. His secretary, a convinced Averroist, did not wish to see Siger exercise his considerable talents on behalf of Thomism, and he killed him to prevent it. That the two sides both claimed Siger for their own is eloquent testimony to his significance, at least to his contemporaries.

Bibliography

Copleston, Frederick. *A History of Philosophy.* Vol. 2, *Mediaeval Philosophy.* Garden City, N.Y.: Doubleday and Co., 1962. The chapter "Latin Averroism: Siger of Brabant," though brief and little concerned with the details of Siger's life, is a useful and erudite account of some of the salient aspects of his thought as seen against its historical background. Includes a selected bibliography, although none of the entries is in English.

Gilson, Étienne. *Dante and Philosophy.* Translated by David Moore. New York: Harper and Row, Publishers, 1963. Part of chapter 4, "The Symbolism of Siger of Brabant," along with the sections "Concerning the Averroism of Siger of Brabant" and "Concerning the Thomism of Siger of Brabant," constitutes one of the most complete and insightful delineations in English of Siger's thought. Gilson's treatment is well balanced, well informed, thoroughly documented, and readable.

Gonzalez, Justo L. *The History of Christian Thought.* Vol. 2, *From Augustine to the Eve of the Reformation.* Nashville: Abingdon Press, 1971. The chapter "Extreme Aristotelianism" is a lucid and useful account of Siger's ideas, especially with regard to their theological implications. Gonzalez, like Copleston, gives little attention to the details of Siger's life. His bibliography, though fairly extensive, comprises primarily non-English titles.

Hyman, Arthur, and James J. Walsh, eds. *Philosophy in the Middle Ages: The Christian, Islamic, and Jewish Traditions.* Indianapolis, Ind.: Hackett Publishing Co., 1973. In a twelve-page chapter entitled "Siger of Brabant," the editors provide a brief and informative account of Siger's life and thought and of the intellectual milieu in which he lived. They also reproduce an earlier translation of Siger's "Question on the Eternity of the

World." The chapter concludes with a brief bibliography, a substantial portion of which consists of non-English titles.

Michael E. Bauman

SAINT SIMEON STYLITES

Born: c. 390; Sis, near Nicopolis, Syria
Died: 459; Telneshae (Telanissos), Syria
Area of Achievement: Religion
Contribution: An ascetic who spent the greater part of his career perched in prayer atop a sixty-foot pillar, Simeon was one of the most controversial figures of the fifth century. Although he left behind no works of enduring value, he was the conscience and spiritual example for Syrian Christians in the patristic period.

Early Life
Simeon Stylites was born of Christian parents in the town of Sis (in northern Syria) around 390. He was baptized in his youth by his very pious parents, who provided a home life in which religious matters were a frequent topic of conversation. Until he was about thirteen years old, Simeon spent his time shepherding his father's flocks in the neighborhood of Sis; this was a task which, according to the Syriac biography of Simeon, he discharged with great diligence and sometimes to the point of exhaustion.

The occupation of shepherd improved Simeon's strength, gentleness, speed, and endurance but had little effect upon his slight build. A dreamy boy, he would often meditate while watching the campfire flame and burn storax as a tribute to the ubiquitous God of his parents. Because of his kindly disposition, he was a favorite with the other shepherds, and to show his generosity he would often forgo food until his friends had eaten.

The turning point in Simeon's life occurred shortly after his thirteenth birthday. One Sunday, while attending church, he was deeply moved by the Gospel reading for that day, which included the Beatitudes "Blessed are they that mourn" and "Blessed are the pure of heart." Simeon asked the congregation the meaning of these words and how one might attain the blessedness referred to in the Gospels. An old man who was present suggested that the monastic life was the surest but steepest path to holiness because it was characterized by prayer, fasting, and austerities designed to mortify the flesh and purify the soul.

Upon hearing this reply, it is said, Simeon withdrew to the pasture lands with his flocks to burn storax and meditate upon what the old man had said. One day, in the course of his meditations, Simeon had the first of the many visions described in his biographies. In it, Christ appeared to him under the disquieting visage of the apocalyptic Son of Man and commanded him to build a sound foundation upon which it would be possible to erect the superstructure of an edifice unparalleled in all human history.

Simeon took this vision to mean that it was his life which was to be the foundation of a great work which Christ would complete. The marvelous nature of this work, however, demanded a foundation of extraordinary strength and endurance. In Simeon's reckoning, that meant that special sacrifices would be required, and these would best be accomplished within the confines of a monastic community.

Life's Work

The various biographies differ about how Simeon spent his monastic period. Less reliable biographies mention an initial two-year sojourn, near Sis, at the monastery of the abbot Timothy, where Simon is said to have learned the psalter by heart. Theodoret's biography and the Syriac biography, on the other hand, indicate that Simeon first took the tonsure at the monastery of Eusebona at Tell 'Ada, between Antioch and Aleppo. Whichever is the accurate narrative, the sources agree that Simeon's stay at Eusebona was charged with many extraordinary occurrences.

To mortify his flesh, Simeon engaged in fasts lasting many days, exposed himself to extremes of inclement weather, and humbly but steadfastly endured the jeering of envious monastics and the onslaught of demonic forces (whether real or imagined). One peculiar austerity, which Theodoret identifies as the principal cause of Simeon's eviction from Eusebona, serves as an example of this ascetic's willpower (and fanaticism). Finding a well rope made of tightly twisted, razor-sharp palm leaves, Simeon wrapped it snugly around his midriff. So tight was the wrapping that the flesh swelled on either side of the coils as they cut progressively deeper into his flesh. Finally, after Simeon had begun to show some signs of discomfort, the Abbot of Eusebona had the bindings forcibly removed, despite Simeon's protestations. So deep had the rope cut into Simeon's body that the bloody wound had matted the bindings and robes together. For three days, the monks had to apply liquids to soften Simeon's clothes in order to remove them, the result being that when the rope was finally uncoiled it brought with it pieces of Simeon's flesh and a torrent of blood.

From this last austerity, Simeon's recovery was slow, nearly leaving him an invalid. Tired of the bickering and petty jealousies which Simeon's practices had aroused among his monastic brothers—and probably not a little horrified at Simeon's fanatical zeal—the Abbot of Eusebona discharged Simeon, giving him his blessing and forty dinars for food and clothing.

Simeon's expulsion from the monastery at Eusebona was significant because it was typical of the response of abbots to ascetic practices which went beyond the bounds of good sense. Simeon's own desire to perform acts of supererogation, even at the expense of disobedience to his superior, may seem to suggest that he deserves to be classed among the Sarabaitic monks—those who were described by Saint Jerome and John Cassian as thwarting all authority. The various biographies, however, are unanimous in proclaiming Simeon's freedom from the grasping, care-ridden personality of a Sarabaite.

After leaving the monastery, Simeon's life more closely resembled the lives of the anchorites, described by Cassian as hermits who were the most fruitful of the monastics and achieved greater heights of contemplation because they withdrew to the desert to face the assaults of demons directly. According to Cassian, John the Baptist was the forerunner of the anchorites. It is this group that most probably can claim Simeon as its own.

After his dismissal from the monastery at Eusebona, Simeon wandered to the foot of Mount Telneshae in northern Syria. Intent upon beginning a special set of austerities for the Lenten season, he approached an almost deserted hermitage and asked its keeper to provide a cell in which he might seclude himself. There, Simeon fasted for forty days. Not satisfied with this feat of extraordinary endurance, he determined to undertake a three-year fast. Frightened by the duration and severity of the proposed fast, the keeper of the hermitage, Bassus, convinced Simeon that such a work was imprudent and that he ought to divide the period in half, lest he kill himself. Simeon agreed.

It was the completion of the year-and-a-half fast that established a name for Simeon. News of his endurance and holiness was carried abroad. Everywhere people began to talk about the Syrian phenomenon: The backwater of Telneshae had been graced by God; a saint had come to dwell there. People began to flock to the hermitage to seek the wisdom of this holy man and his curative powers. When they returned home, they brought with them stories of his marvelous abilities, abilities which were the fruit of his extreme asceticism.

For about ten years, Simeon practiced his asceticism in an open cell on Mount Telneshae, each year repeating the particulars of his original Lenten fast.

One day, sometime around the year 422, Simeon had a vision which was to distinguish him forever as an ascetic of a special kind. Twenty-one days into his Lenten fast, Simeon beheld an apparition. He saw a man, noble in stature, dressed in a military girdle, face radiant as the sun, praying aloud. After finishing his prayer, the stranger climbed up on the pillar-shaped stone, three cubits (about four and a half feet) high, which stood near Simeon's cell and served as a makeshift altar. Standing on the stone, the stranger folded his hands behind his back, bowed toward Simeon, and looked heavenward with his hands outstretched. For three days and three nights the stranger thus prayed before vanishing.

Simeon regarded this experience as a decisive revelation. From that point onward, he was to practice his fasts standing on a column of stone, exposed to the extremes of weather. He had been called to be a stylite (from the Greek *stulos*, meaning "pillar").

At first Simeon's new practice aroused the ire of the Christian leaders in the region. It may have been the novelty of Simeon's practice which angered them or it may have been that Simeon's peculiar form of worship seemed a retrogression, a return to the adoration practiced in Syria in pre-Christian times—particularly in Hierapolis. Lucian of Antioch wrote that in Hierapolis, twice a year, a priest would ascend a tall column to commune with the goddess Attar'athae and the rest of the Syrian pantheon. It may have seemed to the local religious leaders that Simeon was reviving the form, if not the content, of this pagan worship.

Whatever the cause of the displeasure of the Christian leaders, its expression diminished as quickly as the public adulation of Simeon increased. One can imagine what a powerful sight the stylite must have been, a sight which awakened deep and elemental associations in the pilgrims (particularly the Syrians). He must have been a spectacle: an emaciated figure, arms raised in unceasing prayer, perched atop a narrow column whose diameter provided barely enough room for the saint to recline. Simeon's figure could be seen on his spindle 365 days a year, regardless of the weather, at all times of day. He could be seen silhouetted against the rising and setting sun, shining in the midday azure sky, and brilliantly illuminated against Stygian thunderclouds by stroboscopic flashes of lightning. Finally, add to the image a constant procession of pilgrims winding their way up Mount Telneshae (some nearly exhausted from the great distances traveled but still hopeful that they might be healed, find advice, or discover a holy truth) and one has some idea of the deep impression which Simeon Stylites made upon his age.

For thirty-seven years, Simeon stood atop pillars of various sizes under all conditions. Many pagans were converted by his miracles and example, and even those barbarians who remained unconverted held the saint in the highest esteem. If the biographers are to be trusted, three emperors (Theodosius, Leo I, and Marcian) sought his advice about difficult state matters. Also, two surviving, but possibly spurious, letters attributed to Simeon indicate that he intervened on the side of the Christians when Emperor Theodosius issued an edict to restore Jewish property unlawfully seized by Christians and that he wrote to Emperor Leo I to approve the opening of the Council of Chalcedon in 451.

Concerning the exact time of Simeon's death, his biographers give different accounts. They mark the date as Friday, July 24, Wednesday, September 2, or Friday, September 25, in the year 459. Whatever the precise date, the accounts agree that Simeon died in prayer surrounded by his disciples.

For four days the corpse of the saint was paraded throughout the region, and on the fifth day it was carried through the streets of the great city of Antioch to the accompaniment of chanting, the burning of incense and candles, a constant sprinkling of fine perfumes, and many miraculous cures and signs. The body of the blessed Simeon was laid to rest in the great cathedral of Constantine, an honor which had never before been awarded either saint or statesman. There it remained for a while, despite even the attempts of Emperor Leo to have it transported to his own court as a talisman against evil. Eventually, the cult of Simeon grew so significantly that a pilgrimage church, in the style of Constantine's cathedral, was built at Qal'at Saman to house Simeon's remains.

Summary

Unlike great philosophers, theologians, and statesmen, Simeon Stylites left no great works of intellect or polity behind. Of the surviving letters attributed to him, it is difficult to say which are spurious and which are original because of their contradictory doctrinal positions and obvious redactions. What, then, can be made of Simeon's life? What was its impact upon the world of the fifth century? It is possible to describe the impact of Simeon as twofold. First, he contributed a peculiar ascetic technique which was imitated and extended by other stylites, such as Daniel, Simeon Stylites the Younger, Alypius, Luke, and Lazarus. As an ascetic practice, Simeon's method was one of the most severe. Yet, if practiced in a pure spirit, it held great promise: It could transform its adherent into a channel of supernatural grace.

Second, Simeon contributed something symbolic to the world of the fifth century. Regardless of which accounts of his wisdom and his importance to the social and theological controversies are accurate, all of his biographers asserted that Simeon's chief significance was as a religious symbol. His was a life whose worth must be measured in terms of the possibilities of the human spirit, not in terms of practical results or durable goods. His actions—like the actions of many other saints in the various world religions—were a testimony to the existence of values which transcend those of the visible world. Because he demonstrated the power of these values through a concrete form of supererogatory practice, people could grasp them easily. That is the reason he was so respected: He enacted his belief.

Bibliography

Brown, Peter. *The Cult of the Saints: Its Rise in Latin Christianity*. Chicago: University of Chicago Press, 1981. Useful for its general analysis of the phenomena associated with saint devotion. Although Brown's work is about the cult of the saints in the patristic Latin West, some of his arguments can be extended by analogy to Eastern Christianity. Particularly pertinent are his discussions of saintly patronage, the gift of perseverance, and the power associated with saintly presence. The cult of devotion which developed after Simeon's death manifests these features as clearly as any Western cult.

Butler, Alban. "'St. Simeon the Stylite." In *Lives of the Saints*, edited by Herbert Thurston and Donald Attwater, vol. 1. New York: P. J. Kenedy and Sons, 1962. A classic work of Roman Catholic hagiography. Nevertheless, this work provides a brief and, for the most part, accurate synthesis of Simeon's biographies. A good, succinct summary of Simeon's life.

Downey, Glanville. *Ancient Antioch*. Princeton, N.J.: Princeton University Press, 1963. The most accessible book on the history of ancient Antioch from its origins to the decline of the Roman Empire, it is a condensation of another work by Downey, cited below. Since Simeon was at the center of many political and theological controversies of his day, this book helps situate his involvement within the social, cultural, and religious history of Syria's most important city. Contains some maps and illustrations.

——————. *A History of Antioch in Syria: From Seleucus to the Arab Conquest*. Princeton, N.J.: Princeton University Press, 1961. One of the most ambitious histories of Antioch from the time of the Seleucids until the Arab conquest, this work contains a wealth of historical information on ancient Christian and pre-Christian Antioch. Downey treats Simeon as one of the major forces to be reckoned with in any interpretation of fifth century Syrian history. Very useful for situating Simeon against the cultural history of his country. Contains maps and illustrations.

Lent, Frederick. "The Life of Simeon Stylites: A Translation of the Syriac Text in Bedjan's *Acta martyrum sanctorum*, Vol. IV." *Journal of the American Oriental Society* 35, no. 1 (1915): 104-198. The only translation of this Syriac life of Simeon into English. In comparison to Theodoret's biography, this work is much more episodic and contains more details which are historically questionable. It is, however, useful for capturing the spirit of the man.

Torrey, Charles C. "The Letters of Simeon the Stylite." *Journal of the American Oriental Society* 20 (1899): 251-276. This article is a translation of three Syriac letters attributed to Simeon. Because of their obvious partisan inventions, their authenticity is questionable. Yet they make an intriguing study of the way the authority of Simeon was marshaled to defend the Monophysite branch of the Syrian church.

Voobus, Arthur. *History of Asceticism in the Syrian Orient: A Contribution to the History of Culture in the Near East*. 2 vols. Stockholm: Louvain, 1965. The seminal work on Syrian asceticism and spirituality. Contains much material on the life of Simeon as well as his successors. The most useful work for anyone interested in studying the phenomenon of asceticism and the forms it assumed in the Syrian environment.

Thomas Ryba

SAINT SIRICIUS

Born: c. 335 or 340; probably in or near Rome
Died: November 26, 399; Rome
Area of Achievement: Religion
Contribution: Siricius was the first pope to exercise his authority throughout the Roman Empire. In the process, he set precedents which were to be used to great effect by his successors.

Early Life
Siricius, who was probably born circa 335 or 340, was Roman by birth. Little of his early life is known. He was ordained by Pope Liberius as a lector and later as a deacon. Siricius would have received the standard Roman clerical education, and he may well have been classically educated also. His entire career was spent in the church of Rome.

On December 11, 384, Liberius' successor, Damasus I, died. By this time, the papacy had become increasingly politicized, and there followed intense campaigning for his office. The candidates included Siricius, Ursinus, who had also been a candidate and responsible for rioting in the election of 366, and Jerome, who seems to have been Damasus' favorite. Later that month, or perhaps early in January of 385, Siricius was elected and consecrated the next pope; a congratulatory letter from the emperor still survives. Ursinus and his partisans were then officially expelled from Rome. Jerome, perhaps believing that he was no longer welcome, also departed, settling in Palestine with several of his own protégés.

Life's Work
Siricius' activities during his pontificate are known primarily from the letters which he sent or received and from the account given in the sixth or seventh century *Liber pontificalis* (*The Book of the Popes*, 1916).

Siricius became pope at a time when the bishops of Rome were just beginning to exercise their claimed large-scale ecclesiastical authority. Several of his letters, for example, contain the first of the papal decrees later collected as canon law.

Some of Siricius' letters document his desire to formalize ecclesiastical discipline and practices. He was concerned, for example, that the proper procedures be followed in the choice of bishops and in appointments to other ranks of the clergy. On February 10, 385, he replied to a letter which Bishop Himerius of Tarragona in Spain had written to Damasus. He discussed the proper way to deal with converted Arians and Novatians (they were not to be rebaptized); the proper times for baptism (Easter and Pentecost but not Christmas); and various classes of individuals, such as penitents, incontinent monks and nuns, and married priests. This epistle is the first of the papal decretals. Elsewhere, Siricius decreed that new bishops must have more than one consecrator, that bishops should not ordain clerics for another's church or receive those deposed by another bishop, and that a secular official, even if baptized, could not hold a clerical office.

Decrees such as these exemplify the papal role of overseer of ecclesiastical procedures throughout the Empire. Siricius and his successors portrayed themselves as the inheritors of the authority of Peter. Siricius even claimed to have something of Peter within himself: "We bear the burdens of all who are weighed down, or rather the blessed apostle Peter, who is within us, bears them for us...." Siricius also claimed that the Bishop of Rome was the head of the college of all the bishops, and that bishops who did not obey him should be excommunicated. He asserted that his decisions, the *statuta sedis apostolicae* (the statutes of the apostolic see), should have the same authority as church councils. Like other bishops, Siricius also appropriated some of the trappings and authority of the secular government. For example, he referred to his decrees with the technical word *rescripta*, the same word used by the emperors for their responses to official queries.

At this time, however, it appeared that the authority of the Roman see was on the wane. In the east, the Council of Constantinople in 381 had assigned the Bishop of Constantinople, the capital of the eastern part of the Empire, the same honorary status as the Bishop of Rome. Nor was Siricius even the most influential bishop in Italy: He was overshadowed by Ambrose in Milan. Ambrose not only was a man of greater abilities but also was the bishop of an imperial capital. Milan, not Rome, was where emperors now tended to reside. As a result, Ambrose had the ear of the emperors. Despite his claims, Siricius was able to impose his direct authority only upon some of the local, rural bishops, whose elections he oversaw. He is said to have ordained thirty-two bishops "in diverse locations" as well as thirty-one priests and sixty deacons for the city of Rome.

In spite of these limitations, Siricius energetically tried to assert the authority of his see. In the east, he attempted to assume some administrative responsibility in Illyria by instructing Archbishop Anysius of Thessalonica to see to it that episcopal ordinations were carried out properly. The pope wished to restrict the influence not only of the see of Constantinople, which also claimed authority over Thessalonica, but also of Ambrose in Milan. Ambrose, however, had anticipated Siricius and already exercised a supervisory role in Illyria. In 381, at the emperor's request, he had assembled a council at Aquileia to investigate irregularities in the Illyrian church. As a result, Siricius made little progress there.

Siricius also belatedly became involved in a schism which had occurred at Antioch, where there were rival claimants to the bishopric. Ambrose in 391 had been instrumental in the summoning of a church council in southern Italy, at Capua, to consider the matter, and the results were forwarded to the

East. Although Siricius must have been involved, the extent of his participation is uncertain. Subsequently, according to the Eastern writer Severus of Antioch, Siricius wrote to the Antiochenes on his own initiative. He recommended that there should be only one bishop, whose election conformed with the canons of the Council of Nicaea. Shortly thereafter, the Council of Caesarea did in fact recognize the claimant who met Siricius' criteria.

In the north, Siricius became involved in other ecclesiastical controversies. In 386, he wrote to the emperor Magnus Maximus, then resident in Trier, about a priest named Agroecius, whom Siricius accused of having been wrongfully ordained. Maximus' reply survives. Noting that the matter should be dealt with by the Gallic bishops themselves, the emperor answered:

> But as regards Agroecius, whom you claim had wrongly risen to the rank of presbyter, what can I decree more reverently on behalf of our catholic religion than that catholic bishops judge on this very matter? I shall summon a council of those who dwell either in Gaul or in the Five Provinces, so it may judge with them sitting and considering the matter.

Maximus also forwarded to Siricius the results of his investigations into the Priscillianists, whom he referred to as "Manichees." Priscillian and his followers already had appealed to Ambrose and to Siricius' predecessor Damasus and been rebuffed by both. In 386, they were condemned at a synod at Trier, and Priscillian and several of his supporters were executed; others were sent into exile. This heavy-handed secular interference in ecclesiastical affairs was considered a bad precedent, and Siricius, like Ambrose and Martin of Tours, seems to have denied Communion to those bishops, such as Felix of Trier, who had supported the executions. The resultant "Felician schism" lasted until circa 400. This incident may be behind the curious account in *The Book of the Popes* of Siricius' discovery of Manichaeans in Rome and his exiling of them.

Like many of his successors, Siricius attempted to impose his authority through church councils held in Rome, attended at this time primarily by local bishops. A synod assembled on January 6, 386, dealt with matters of ecclesiastical discipline. A council of 385-386 issued nine canons concerning ecclesiastical discipline, which were sent to the African church on January 6, 386. This council met in Saint Peter's Basilica and is the first known to have met at the Vatican.

Another local concern of Siricius was a problem caused by a certain Jovinian, who, after abandoning his life as a monk, began to teach that ascetic practices such as celibacy and fasting served no useful purpose. Jovinian even went so far as to claim that Mary, by having children, had ceased to be a virgin. He also asserted that those who had been properly baptized were incapable of sin. Jovinian was denounced to Siricius, who in 390 or 392 assembled a local synod which excommunicated the former monk and eight of his followers. This news was carried to Milan, where Jovinian had fled, but Ambrose assembled another synod and excommunicated him again.

Siricius' papacy also saw the final decline of pagan worship. The emperor Theodosius I in a series of decrees formalized Christianity as the only legal religion in the Empire. As a result, this period saw the construction and expansion of the churches and sacred buildings at Rome, often at the expense of pagan temples. The Basilica of Saint Paul on the Via Ostiensis (Ostian Way) was rebuilt during Siricius' papacy in the same general shape it now has and was dedicated in 390. Siricius also rebuilt the Church of Saint Pudentiana. On November 26, 399, Siricius died, and he was buried in the cemetery of Priscilla, at the Basilica of Sylvester, on the Via Salaria. By the seventh century, his tomb was venerated by pilgrims coming to Rome.

Summary

A man of only middling talents, Siricius was more of an administrator than an innovator. In the realm of ecclesiastical politics, he had to compete with others, such as the bishops of Milan and Constantinople, who were situated in imperial capitals and who had imperial support. Nevertheless, Siricius, who had a strong view of the rights and responsibilities of the Bishop of Rome, did what he could to strengthen the position of his see. During his tenure, the pope ceased to be merely another bishop and truly began to assume an empire-wide presence.

Siricius established a secure foundation for papal authority upon which several of his fifth century successors were to build. His Italian rival Ambrose had died in 397, and with the withdrawal of the imperial administration to Ravenna, Milanese authority rapidly declined. In the fifth century, Innocent I and Leo I were successful in establishing a papal vicariate in Illyria. Leo, later called "the Great," also was able to gain the support of the imperial government in his attempts to assert his ecclesiastical hegemony at least in the western part of the Empire.

The last years of the fourth century were a very critical period of history. Not only was the Roman Empire beginning to split into eastern and western halves, but also the "barbarian invasions" already had begun in the East, even though they had yet to affect the West. As the influence of the state weakened, the Church assumed greater authority. Even though Siricius could not foresee the fall of the Western Empire later in the fifth century, his attempts to establish the authority of the see of Rome set many precedents for the great power the popes soon were to exercise.

Bibliography

Duchesne, Louis. *Early History of the Christian Church from Its Foundation to the End of the Fifth Century*. Vol. 2. New York: Longmans, Green and Co., 1912. Still one of the best histories of the early Church, it places

Siricius' activities in their broader historical context. Based primarily upon the original sources.

Janini, José Cuesta. *S. Siricio y las cuatro temporas.* Valencia: Seminario Metropolitano de Valencia, 1958. The only detailed modern study of Siricius.

Loomis, Louise Ropes, trans. *The Book of the Popes.* Vol. 3. New York: Columbia University Press, 1916. This volume contains a translation of the biography of Siricius found in *Liber pontificalis*, a compilation which dates back to the sixth or seventh century. It is a mixture of tradition, myth, and solid historical fact.

MacDonald, J. "Who Instituted the Papal Vicariate of Thessalonica?" *Studia Patristica* 4 (1961): 478-482. A discussion of Siricius' role in the ecclesiastical politics of Illyria in the late fourth century, with references to other, similar studies.

Migne, Jacques Paul, ed. *Patrologiae Cursus Completus: Series Latina.* Vol. 13. Paris: J. P. Migne, 1855. A collection of Siricius' letters, written in Latin.

Pietri, Charles. *Roma christiana: Recherches sur l'Église de Rome, son organisation, sa politique, son idéologie, de Miltiade à Sixte III, 311-440.* 2 vols. Rome: École Français de Rome, 1976. The most complete modern study of the church of Rome during the times of Siricius and his contemporaries. Very extensively annotated with many references to other recent studies of the period.

Ralph W. Mathisen

CLAUS SLUTER

Born: c. 1340-1350; probably Haarlem, Netherlands
Died: c. 1405-1406; Dijon, France
Area of Achievement: Art
Contribution: Sluter's innovations in creating individually distinct and expressively sculptured figures brought to Western art a new realism. Credited with bridging the late Gothic and the early Renaissance in northern Europe, Sluter and his name are synonymous with the Burgundian school of sculpture.

Early Life

Many details of Claus Sluter's life have been lost, as have many of the sculptures he created. What is known of his early life is that he was born in Haarlem, Netherlands, and around 1379 or 1380 he moved to Brussels. Some historians believe that while in Brussels Sluter created the sculpture for the porch of the Brussels Town Hall. Dated around 1380, the Brussels sculpture, a set of seated prophets, resembles some of the sculpture Sluter created at Champmol, Dijon, later in the decade. The figures at Brussels reveal traces of individualization, the quality that would distinguish Sluter's art. Up to this time, figures depicted with individually distinct characteristics, although slightly detectable at the time, were unusual in Europe. Sculptural figures were generally solemnly posed and rigid, presenting abstract representations rather than individual characterizations. Personal details such as hair, beards, and clothing were stylized in formal patterns rather than depicted naturally.

Sculpture was also usually subordinated to the architecture it was intended to decorate, confined within the niches in which it was enclosed or barely distinguished from the columns on which it was mounted. After sculptors completed their work, statues were provided with personal details by painters. This polychromatic process was the common artistic practice through Sluter's time and continued well into the sixteenth century. As for the figures on the Brussels Town Hall, historians hesitate to attribute them to Sluter because of scanty evidence. In addition, although the sculptures reveal qualities of individual expression, Sluter did not single-handedly introduce sculptural realism. The work that he would complete in the next two decades, however, would more than any other sculpture contribute to its development. The Town Hall sculpture, therefore, regardless of attribution, provides early examples from which to study Sluter's development. The sculpture reveals the degree to which Sluter developed his own style in contrast to his early work and that of his contemporaries.

Life's Work

In 1385, Sluter went to Dijon, the center of the Duchy of Burgundy. Rich and prosperous, the Duchy of Burgundy was the source of one of the great ages of artistic patronage, promoting the most talented architects, sculptors, stained-glass designers, illuminators, and painters from all over Europe. Sluter worked for the court of Philip the Bold, the Duke of Burgundy. Philip was a brother to Jean de France, the Duke of Berry, and to Charles V, the King of France. The three projects that have established Sluter's reputation were commissioned by Philip the Bold for the monastery he founded, the Chartreuse of Champmol.

Arriving at Philip's court, Sluter worked as the head sculptor under another artist, Jean (Hennequin) de Marville. Marville had designed the architectural and iconographic scheme for the Champmol portal when he died in 1389. Sluter, now responsible for completing the project, created the six figures adorning the portal—the Virgin and Child, flanked by a kneeling duke and duchess (Philip and Margaret), and Saint John the Baptist and Saint Catherine. Canopies frame each figure except for those of the Virgin and Child, whose canopy, now missing, was decorated with angels bearing the instruments of the Passion. The corbels on which Saint John and Saint Catherine stand depict two prophets reading a manuscript. The corbels bearing Philip and Margaret are decorated with shield bearers (the same figures that are said to resemble the statues on the Brussels Town Hall).

The composition of the Virgin and Child in the center pillar, or *trumeau*, flanked by propitiating prophets and patrons, is traditional. Sluter's modeling of the figures is far from traditional, however, as the bodies suggest movement, and their faces evoke emotion. The canopies or niches no longer frame the figures, which are positioned so that they turn toward the Virgin holding Christ. Saint John and Saint Catherine, about to kneel, emphasize the inward movement; each knee points to and breaks the space occupied by Philip and Margaret.

The movement and unity of the scene are enhanced by Sluter's modeling of the drapery. The figures' clothes fall into heavy diagonal folds, and the natural breaks in the clothes suggest the movement of these robust figures. As the folds of the Virgin's garb emphasize her swayed pose, the diagonals of her robes meet just above her left hip, on which the Christ child rests, suggesting Mary's efforts to secure Him. The viewer's eye is now focused on the heavily draped figure of Christ, the thematic and visual center of the scene. The visual and iconographic play continue as Christ is visually distracted, looking up at the angels who carry the instruments of Passion, the symbols of His eventual suffering. Sluter provided these figures with individual gestures, depicting them with realistic facial features and expressions. This personalized treatment, particularly of Philip and Margaret, was exemplary of the new change in sculpture. The faces are not abstractions or idealized portraits but individual representations. Their solemn expressions are suitable for the emotions that the religious scene demands. Yet Sluter also provided the mundane details revealed in the faces—furrowed brows, wrinkled eyes, pursed mouths, and even double chins.

Sluter's next project was entirely his own, a Calvary scene built in the center of a well in the cloister of the Chartreuse. The sculpture is unquestionably the dominant interest in the structure, also known as the Well of Moses. A large hexagonal base provides the structure for the central and slightly larger-than-life sculptures of six Old Testament figures—Moses, Isaiah, Daniel, Zechariah, Jeremiah, and David. Each figure, broad-shouldered and heavily modeled, dwarfs the niches and columns and gives the impression that if it were not affixed, it could descend from the pedestal. Angels with varied expressions of grief fly above the Old Testament figures. Their spreading wings support the cornices on which once stood the Calvary scene—the Virgin, Saint John, and Saint Mary Magdalene surrounding Christ on the Cross. Only a fragment remains of this scene—the head and torso of Christ, which are now in the museum of Dijon.

As is the tradition for religious sculpture, the Old Testament figures are identified symbolically. Each carries a scroll with a text that relates the story of the death of Christ. Breaking with tradition, however, Sluter individualizes each figure, providing distinct physiognomies. Moses possesses a stern, fixed expression, suggesting his anger at the sight of the Jews worshipping the golden calf. Zechariah, with a despondent look suggesting his rejection by his people, bows his head and avoids the viewer's gaze. Jeremiah and David are sunk in meditation; each is modeled with deeply defined brows that encircle closed eyes. Daniel and Isaiah twist to see and hear each other from around one of the corners of the base, presumably to discuss the advent of Christ, who is traditionally portrayed. Thorns pierce His brow and the spear's wound scars His left side. His nearly emotionless face is outlined by finely detailed long hair and beard; His eyes and mouth are gently closed, portraying the divine man recently crucified.

The architectural plan of Sluter's final project, the tomb of Philip the Bold at Champmol, was established during Marville's time. The style was once again traditional. The recumbent figure of the duke is mounted on a black marble slab, and two angels kneel at his head. An open gallery runs along the base of the tomb, and within its niches, forty figures form a procession mourning the duke's death. Although some of the figures were completed following his design after his death, all the sculpture is attributed to Sluter. The duke's figure was badly damaged in 1791 and poorly restored in the nineteenth century. The figures in mourning, however, are well preserved and reveal the culmination of Sluter's development. Ten choirboys, clergy, and thirty mourners weave in and out of the niches, creating an undulating effect around the tomb. Unlike the larger-than-life stature of the sculpture from the Well of Moses, these figures are in miniature, no higher than two feet. Each figure maintains a strikingly fresh pose, and individual gestures rather than detailed facial expressions create the emotional and dramatic effect. Some figures hold their hands in silent prayer or clench them to their chests. With dramatic effect, the hands are highlighted against finely modeled flowing robes, which were perhaps shaped to hint at the position of the hands folded beneath them.

This dramatic and natural rendering of drapery, always Sluter's trademark, creates excitement in the play between the physical features the viewer sees and those covered by or partially glimpsed through the gowns and robes. Only a hand protrudes from beneath the flowing robes of one mourner; in another, the eyes are hidden and only the lower half of a solemn face appears. Some figures are completely covered, the grief expressed through the swayed or bent figure whose shape underneath can only be guessed.

Sluter died in late 1405 or early 1406, before he completed the tomb. His nephew, Claus de Werve, finished the project in 1410, and historians have no doubt that he closely followed Sluter's plans. Overall, the tomb reveals the high point of Sluter's technique. Its monumentality is achieved not by mere stature and size but by subtle and minimal suggestion of individual movement and expression.

Summary

In creating sculptures expressive of human qualities, whether personal emotions or bodily movements, Claus Sluter broke the stylized and static quality of sculpture that was common in the Middle Ages. His work influenced much of the sculpture of the first half of the fifteenth century throughout northern Europe, France, Germany, and the Low Countries, and extended as far as Spain and Switzerland (through the efforts of his assistants). Sluter is often compared to the great Italian masters Donatello and Jacopo della Quercia, who were also transitional figures whose work contributed or led to the high development of Renaissance sculpture.

Sluter's work helped to establish the independence of sculpture from architecture and painting. No longer would sculpture provide merely the ornament for buildings; it could well be the center of interest, as it would become in the Renaissance. Sculpture, too, could provide the dramatic unity and realism found in painting. Given the realism achieved by Sluter and later sculptors, polychroming would be unnecessary to provide realistic and naturalistic detail. Sluter demonstrated how sculptures attained their own beauty and interest.

Sluter also influenced the development of painting in northern Europe; in particular, his work opened the way for the development of realistic portraiture. While credited with directly or indirectly influencing the work of some of the most important painters—the Master of Flémalle, Rogier van der Weyden, and Konrad Witz—Sluter's most direct influence was on Jan van Eyck, who worked for the Burgundian Court in the generation following

Sluter's death. Sluter is noted as having inspired van Eyck's interest in painting lifelike compositions that created the three-dimensional effect of sculpture. Indeed, van Eyck and Sluter played similar roles in the development of a basic tenet of Western art: Each, through close attention to detail, created the illusion of reality through his art.

Bibliography
Cartellieri, Otto. *The Court of Burgundy*. New York: Alfred A. Knopf, 1929. Reprint. New York: Barnes and Noble Books, 1972. In a narrative style, this work re-creates the political and artistic flavor of the fourteenth and fifteenth century Burgundian court. Chapter 2 focuses on Sluter as Philip the Bold's favorite sculptor and vividly describes Sluter's life and work at the Champmol monastery. Includes photographs of sculpture.
David, Henri. *Claus Sluter*. Paris: P. Tisné, 1951. Though this examination of the artist has been published only in French, it is valuable even for readers unfamiliar with that language, for it provides very fine photographic plates of Sluter's sculptures.
Forsyth, William H. *The Entombment of Christ: French Sculptures of the Fifteenth and Sixteenth Centuries*. Cambridge, Mass.: Harvard University Press, 1970. Chapter 5, "Burgundy," explores the history of the Duchy of Burgundy and Sluter's lasting influence in French sculpture—well beyond his death and the demise of the political power and independence of Burgundy.
Gardner, Arthur. *Medieval Sculpture in France*. New York: Macmillan, 1931. Historical background of the Duke of Burgundy's artistic efforts at Champmol, featuring Sluter's work. Excellent description and photographs of individual sculptures.
Male, Emile. *Religious Art in France: The Late Middle Ages, a Study of Medieval Iconography and Its Sources*. Edited by Harry Bober. Translated by Marthiel Mathews. Princeton, N.J.: Princeton University Press, 1986. Written by one of the most eminent historians of medieval art. Provides an analysis of the iconography of the Well of Moses.
Marks, Richard. "Sculpture in the Duchy and County of Burgundy, c. 1300-1500." *Connoisseur* 194 (March, 1977): 154-163. Accounts for the rise of Burgundian sculpture to its primary place among French schools. Explains influence of Netherlandish carvers, notably Sluter. Provides very good photographs and descriptions of sculpture and discusses background to the rise of the Duchy of Burgundy's power and influence in Europe.

Steven P. Schultz

SNORRI STURLUSON

Born: 1178 or 1179; Hvamm, Iceland
Died: September 23, 1241; Reykjaholt, Iceland
Areas of Achievement: Historiography and literature
Contribution: Snorri preserved the myths, poetry, history, and culture of the early Germanic people; in doing so, he created an original literature of permanent significance and renown for himself as one of the foremost authors of the Middle Ages.

Early Life
Snorri Sturluson was the son of Sturla Thortharson, a shrewd and ambitious landholder who had acquired wealth and power through incessant legal feuds with neighboring farmers and other devious manipulations of the law. Snorri's mother, Guthńy, was the daughter of Bothvar Thortharson, who was descended from the famed warrior-poet Egill Skallagrímsson. When Snorri was three, he was taken (for reasons which are obscure) by Jón Loptsson, the most powerful chieftain in Iceland, to live at Oddi, Jón's family estate in southern Iceland, as a foster son. Oddi had been for several generations the center of Iceland's highest culture and functioned as an informal school for clerics as well as for the study of law, history, Latin, and skaldship (poetry). Snorri thus spent his formative years in an atmosphere which engendered a respect for learning and culture and which provided him with a thorough knowledge of law, history, and skaldship.

Snorri's father died in 1183, and his mother, a woman of extravagant tendencies, soon squandered Snorri's patrimony. Snorri thus lacked the means to establish himself in a society in which wealth was important. He remained at Oddi after the death of Jón Loptsson in 1197 and seems to have remained there for several years following his marriage in 1199 to Herdís, daughter of Bersi the Rich. The marriage appears to have been one arranged solely for money—a marriage typical of the chieftain class in medieval Iceland. Following the death of his father-in-law, Snorri inherited and moved to Bersi's estate at Borg, which was also the ancestral homestead of the saga-hero Egill Skallagrímsson, Snorri's distant relative. Thus, through marriage and inheritance of extensive properties, Snorri went from being penniless to being a very rich young man, but his desire for money, power, and fame was unsatisfied. In 1206 he left his wife and their son and daughter in Borg and moved to Reykjaholt, an estate more glamorous and famous. Within a few years, Snorri had greatly increased his fortune and stature. One evidence of his standing is the fact that he was twice elected to the influential post of "lawspeaker" for the Althing, the Icelandic high court. Because laws in Iceland were not originally written, the lawspeaker's duty was to preserve them by memory and to pronounce the letter of the law in doubtful cases. Given the litigious nature of Icelandic society, a lawspeaker had numerous opportunities for enriching himself through unscrupulous dealings and subtle manipulations of the law, opportunities of which Snorri fully availed himself.

It must be noted, however, that Snorri was in many ways merely a product of his times. The Sturlung Age (mid-twelfth century to the fall of the Commonwealth in 1262), so named because of the predominance of Snorri's family, was a time of great moral corruption, licentiousness, turbulence, and bloodshed. *Sturlunga saga* (*Sturlunga Saga*, 1970, 1974), written by Snorri's nephew Sturla Thortharson in the thirteenth century, gives a particularly unflattering portrait of Snorri in his willingness to exploit enmities for personal gain; his disregard for friendship, kinship, or alliance; and his seeming indifference to questions of right and wrong. Historians have wondered to what extent Snorri's early poverty and the influence of his foster father, Jón, contributed to Snorri's character. Certainly Snorri's avarice and thirst for power appear as serious character flaws, but the mystery is that they are so ironically inconsistent with the character and personality that readers sense in his writings. Beyond doubt, however, is that Snorri's avarice led to an increasing immersion in feuds and legal quarrels which did not always turn out to his financial advantage, which made him many enemies, and which led ultimately to his violent death. Before that grim ending, however, Snorri did achieve one of his life's goals. Through successful lawsuits, advantageous marriages for his children, and a liaison with the country's wealthiest woman (Hallveig Ormsdóttir), he became, like his foster father before him, the wealthiest, most powerful man in Iceland.

Life's Work

Nevertheless, Snorri had another goal in life, beyond wealth and power. He desired fame as a skald (poet), something which could best be achieved through recognition at royal courts. He had composed poems to the rulers of Norway even before he set sail for the Norwegian court in 1218, and on one occasion he was rewarded with the gift of a sword, a shield, armor, and an invitation to visit. Little is known of Snorri's first trip to Norway except that he attached himself to Earl Skúli, regent for King Haakon Haakonsson, who was then a boy of thirteen. Snorri was given lavish gifts and the title of baron, and he was charged with a major diplomatic mission: to settle disputes between Icelandic and Norwegian merchants and to persuade the Icelanders to become subjects of the Norwegian crown. Upon his return, Snorri did nothing to advance the royal cause, but he did write a poem, no longer extant, in honor of Earl Skúli and King Haakon (*Háttatal*, 1223). Presumably, it was during this period of his life, between 1220 and 1235, that Snorri wrote the major works for which he has been universally recognized and which secured his lasting fame: *Snorra Edda* (c. 1220-1230; partial translation as *The Prose Edda by Snorri Sturluson*, 1916, 1954), better known as *The*

Prose Edda, and *Heimskringla* (*The Heimskringla: Or, Chronicle of the Kings of Norway*, 1844).

Snorri's *The Prose Edda* is a handbook for the composition of skaldic poetry, which in the twelfth century was doubly jeopardized: by the Church, which frowned on the pagan mythology contained in the *kenningar* (that is, the unique system of paraphrasis and metaphor used by skaldic poets), and by the dancing ballads, or songs, which were becoming popular. Even the noblemen who were frequently honored in skaldic verse began expressing a preference for a simpler, less oblique poetry. *The Prose Edda* was Snorri's attempt to preserve an intellectual and poetic tradition that was vanishing. It demonstrates his love for and his thorough knowledge and mastery of this difficult, esoteric art. *The Prose Edda*, in addition to a prologue, has three parts. "Háttatal" (list of meters) consists of 102 stanzas in one hundred different "meters," composed in honor of Haakon Haakonsson and Earl Skúli (this poem is not, however, the one dedicated in 1223 to Haakon and Skúli). "Skáldskaparmál" ("Poetic Diction") records a number of old tales about gods, giants, dwarfs, and heroes to illustrate the two primary technical devices of skaldic poetry: *heiti* (poetic names) and *kenningar* (poetic circumscriptions). "Gylfaginning" ("The Beguiling of Gylfi") presents a comprehensive survey of Old Norse mythology; it is on this section that the reputation of *The Prose Edda* chiefly rests. Gylfi, King of Sweden, comes in disguise to the citadel of the gods to learn their secrets. Finding three of them—known as High, Equally High, and Third—sitting on the high seat, Gylfi proceeds to ask them questions concerning the origin of the world, the gods, and the end of the world. In response, the gods recite classic tales which present the complete cycle of Northern mythology, from the birth of the universe to the destruction of the cosmos (Ragnarok) and its rebirth. Besides being an indispensable compendium of Scandinavian mythology, "The Beguiling of Gylfi" reveals Snorri's mastery of the art of storytelling. The stories are told with a charm, sophistication, and satiric wit which is rare in any age and which only a natural storyteller can command. To placate the Church (Iceland had accepted Christianity around 999), Snorri included in his work a disclaimer about the veracity of his pagan stories ("Christians... must not believe in pagan gods or that these tales are true in any... way"), but he succeeds in bringing the stories and the gods to life. In the end, however, the myths are revealed as a delusion: Gylfi heard a loud crash; looking around, he saw that there was no citadel, nothing but a level plain. Thus, the myths were a heathen deception which temporarily beguiled Gylfi and which has continued to beguile readers.

The Heimskringla is indisputably Snorri's greatest achievement. It begins with the Swedish kings of legendary times and chronologically follows the dynasty across to Norway to the year 1177. Actual history begins with Halfdan the Black, who ruled in the first half of the ninth century, and with

Halfdan's son Harald I Hårfager (Fairhair), the first king of Norway, who ruled from 872 to 930. Each king is given a saga, but the saga of the royal saint of Norway, Olaf II Haraldsson, is Snorri's masterpiece, both in its extended consideration (some three hundred pages) and in its quality.

Snorri has been praised as being a more realistic and critical historian than his predecessors—with the exception of Ari the Learned, whose work Snorri knew and admired. (Ari is the only one of his sources that Snorri mentions by name in his foreword.) To appreciate Snorri as historian, something of his methods and assumptions must be taken into consideration. In part, he used written sources (only some of which survive), but he also made important use of oral literature—folktales, tales told by wise people, and particularly skaldic poems, which he regarded as his most trustworthy source. The idea of relying on poetry as a source for history appears ludicrous to a modern historian, but for a historian of a preliterary age, poetry may be the only source available. Some modern commentators have conceded that skaldic poetry's rigid form and meter render it less subject to corruption than other forms of oral literature. Snorri presents his own argument for skaldic veracity in his foreword:

> At the court of King Harald [Fairhair] there were skalds, and men still remember their poems and the poems about all the kings who have since his time ruled in Norway; and we gathered most of our information from what we are told in those poems which were recited before the chieftains themselves.... We regard all that to be true which is found in those poems about their expeditions and battles. It is [to be sure] the habit of poets to give highest praise to those princes in whose presence they are; but no one would have dared to tell them to their faces about deeds which all who listened, as well as the prince himself, knew were only falsehoods and fabrications. That would have been mockery, ... not praise.

In "Oláfs saga Helga" ("Saint Olaf's Saga"), which is part of *The Heimskringla*, Snorri reminds readers that one of the functions of the skald was to be a truthful recorder of events: Olaf called his skalds to be important witnesses at his final battle at Stiklestad.

It is Snorri's own concern with truth and realism which makes "Saint Olaf's Saga" a masterpiece. He rejects much of the tendentious, hagiographic tradition associated with Saint Olaf, ignoring some of the early miracles and rationalizing others. Snorri presents a man of complex psychological shadings, a man who was a ruthless Viking and an ambitious king, who nevertheless became a saint as he gradually faced the painful trials at the end of his life. Snorri's objectivity allows readers to understand and appreciate the motives of those who opposed Olaf as well as Olaf's own view. His superb dramatic gift brings a host of characters to life, while his narrative skillfully interweaves complicated stories of internal politics with the king's saga. It is s incorporation of epic tradition with high standards of historical truthfulness which has caused some scholars, such as Lee M. Hollander, to assert that Snorri bears favorable comparison with Thucydides, the great Greek historian:

> Considering the great disparity in general culture and intellectual advancement between his [Snorri's] times and Periclean Greece we may marvel all the more at Snorri's genius. His work is unique in European historiography in presenting us with a continuous account of a nation's history from its beginnings in the dim prehistoric past down into the High Middle Ages.

Summary

In many ways, Snorri Sturluson's own death seems as fateful and tragic as any about which he wrote. Like many of his subjects, Snorri came to grief partly because of bad political judgment and partly because of character flaws. During his second journey to Norway (1237-1239), he failed to seek out King Haakon and spent his time instead with Earl Skúli, who was now the king's enemy. Rumors circulated that Skúli had in a secret ceremony made Snorri an earl and that Skúli planned a revolt against the king. The king issued a ban on travel from Norway, but Snorri in open defiance sailed to Iceland, at least partly in hope of recovering some property which his own relatives had seized. Haakon then sent a letter to Snorri's estranged son-in-law, Gissur Thorvaldsson, ordering that Snorri be brought to Norway or that he be killed, because he had committed high treason. Because of Snorri's avarice and treatment of his relatives, Gissur and his followers chose to surprise Snorri the night of September 23, 1241, at Reykjaholt and kill him rather than deliver him to the king. Ironically, the king claimed Snorri's properties and thus gained the foothold in Iceland that he needed. Twenty-three years after Snorri's death, Iceland was subjugated to the Norwegian crown; the country remained under a foreign ruler until the Republic was proclaimed in 1944.

Snorri Sturluson's life seems in many ways a paradigm of the vices and virtues of the Sturlung Age. He was energetic, astute, imaginative, well learned, and a leader. Yet these qualities were vitiated by the controlling passion of greed, which according to Snorri's nephew Sturla in *Sturlunga Saga* led directly to his death. So great is the discrepancy between Sturla's depiction of Snorri and the Snorri that readers encounter in his writings, that some have doubted that Snorri could be the author of *The Prose Edda* or *The Heimskringla* or *Egils saga* (c. 1222-1230; *Egil's Saga*, 1893), which computer-aided scholarship has recently tended to ascribe to him. Given the remoteness of the times and the scant evidence which survives, such questions will inevitably continue to be the focus of scholarly debate, as will the question of whether Snorri should be revered chiefly as historian or as literary stylist. In the meantime, *The Heimskringla* has become a kind of national bible ɪ Norwegians, who found inspiration in it for their nineteenth and twentie century struggle for national emancipation, and *The Prose Edda* remains invaluable, delightfully readable sourcebook of northern mythology aɪ culture.

Bibliography
Ciklamini, Marlene. *Snorri Sturluson*. Boston: Twayne Publishers, 1978. complete discussion of Snorri's life and writings. Includes summaries and detailed literary analysis of all Snorri's works with a view to placing them ɪ the context of medieval European culture. A selected bibliography coɪ tains few entries in English.

Einarsson, Stefán. *A History of Icelandic Literature*. New York: Johns Hoɪ kins University Press, 1957. Provides a succinct summary of Snorri life and achievements as well as comprehensive background material o twelfth and thirteenth century literature and life. Extensive survey of sag literature.

Hallberg, Peter. *The Icelandic Saga*. Translated by Paul Schach. Lincoln University of Nebraska Press, 1962. An introductory work which provide a lucid overview of the Sturlung Age as portrayed in *Sturlunga Saga*. Con tains a summary and interpretation of *Egil's Saga*. Discusses theories o origin, composition, and significance of saga literature.

Snorri Sturluson. *Heimskringla: History of the Kings of Norway*. Translatec by Lee M. Hollander. Austin: University of Texas Press, 1964. In addition to the most readable translation of Snorri's major work, Hollander offers an introduction to Snorri's life and times filled with valuable insights and information and written in a way which seems to belie the immense scholarship it required. Probably the best introduction to Snorri's life and work.

Turville-Petre, G. *Origins of Icelandic Literature*. Oxford: Clarendon Press, 1953, reprint 1967. Examines the uses that Snorri made of some of his sources to illustrate the skald's imaginative and creative genius. Accepts the theory that Snorri was the author of *Egil's Saga*.

Karen A. Kildahl

WAKE TECHNICAL COMMUNITY COLLEGE

3 3063 00054 3297

For Reference
Do Not Take
From the Library